# Family Law for Paralegals

# The McGraw-Hill Paralegal List

## WHERE EDUCATIONAL SUPPORT GOES BEYOND EXPECTATIONS.

Introduction to Law & Paralegal Studies
Connie Farrell Scuderi
ISBN: 0073524638
© 2008

Introduction to Law for Paralegals
Deborah Benton
ISBN: 007351179X
© 2008

Basic Legal Research, Second Edition
Edward Nolfi
ISBN: 0073520519
© 2008

Basic Legal Writing, Second Edition
Pamela Tepper
ISBN: 0073403032
© 2008

Contract Law for Paralegals
Linda Spagnola
ISBN: 0073511765
© 2008

Civil Law and Litigation for Paralegals
Neal Bevans
ISBN: 0073524611
© 2008

Torts for Paralegals
ISBN: 0073376930
© 2009

Real Estate Law for Paralegals
ISBN: 0073376957
© 2009 Publishes 01/04/08

Legal Research and Writing for
Paralegals
Pamela Tepper and Neal Bevans
ISBN: 007352462X
© 2009

Wills, Trusts, and Estates for Paralegals
George Kent
ISBN: 0073403067
© 2008

The Law Office Reference Manual
Jo Ann Lee
ISBN: 0073511838
© 2008

The Paralegal Reference Manual
Charles Nemeth
ISBN: 0073403075
© 2008

The Professional Paralegal
Allan Tow
ISBN: 0073403091
© 2009

Ethics for Paralegals
Linda Spagnola and Vivian Batts
ISBN: 0073376981
© 2009

Family Law for Paralegals
George Kent
ISBN: 0073376973
© 2009

Criminal Law for Paralegals
ISBN: 0073376965
© 2009

Law Office Management for Paralegals
ISBN: 0073376949
© 2009

Legal Terminology Explained for Paralegals
Edward Nolfi
ISBN: 0073511846
© 2009

For more information or to receive desk copies, please contact your McGraw-Hill Sales Representative

# Family Law for Paralegals

**George W. Kent**

*Keiser University*

McGraw-Hill
Higher Education

Boston   Burr Ridge, IL   Dubuque, IA   New York   San Francisco   St. Louis
Bangkok   Bogotá   Caracas   Kuala Lumpur   Lisbon   London   Madrid   Mexico City
Milan   Montreal   New Delhi   Santiago   Seoul   Singapore   Sydney   Taipei   Toronto

# McGraw-Hill
# Higher Education

FAMILY LAW FOR PARALEGALS

Published by McGraw-Hill, a business unit of The McGraw-Hill Companies, Inc., 1221 Avenue of the Americas, New York, NY, 10020. Copyright © 2009 by The McGraw-Hill Companies, Inc. All rights reserved. No part of this publication may be reproduced or distributed in any form or by any means, or stored in a database or retrieval system, without the prior written consent of The McGraw-Hill Companies, Inc., including, but not limited to, in any network or other electronic storage or transmission, or broadcast for distance learning.

Some ancillaries, including electronic and print components, may not be available to customers outside the United States.

This book is printed on acid-free paper.

2 3 4 5 6 7 8 9 0 VNH/VNH 0 9

ISBN   978-0-07-337697-4
MHID 0-07-337697-3

Vice president/Editor in chief: *Elizabeth Haefele*
Vice president/Director of marketing: *John E. Biernat*
Sponsoring editor: *Natalie J. Ruffatto*
Developmental editor II: *Tammy Higham*
Marketing manager: *Keari Bedford*
Lead media producer: *Damian Moshak*
Media producer: *Marc Mattson*
Director, Editing/Design/Production: *Jess Ann Kosic*
Lead project manager: *Susan Trentacosti*
Senior production supervisor: *Janean A. Utley*
Designer: *Marianna Kinigakis*
Media project manager: *Mark A. S. Dierker*
Outside development: *Beth Baugh*
Cover and interior design: *Pam Verros, pv design*
Typeface: *10.5/13 Times New Roman*
Compositor: *Aptara, Inc.*
Printer: *Von Hoffmann*
Cover credit: © *Loretta Hostettler/iStockPhoto*

**Library of Congress Cataloging-in-Publication Data**

Kent, George W.
    Family law for paralegals / George W. Kent — 1st ed.
       p. cm. — (The McGraw-Hill paralegal list)
    Includes index.
    ISBN-13: 978-0-07-337697-4 (alk. paper)
    ISBN-10: 0-07-337697-3 (alk. paper)
    1. Domestic relations—United States. 2. Legal assistants—United States. I. Title.
KF505.Z9K46 2009
346.7301′5—dc22

                                                                      2008007220

The Internet addresses listed in the text were accurate at the time of publication. The inclusion of a Web site does not indicate an endorsement by the authors or McGraw-Hill, and McGraw-Hill does not guarantee the accuracy of the information presented at these sites.

www.mhhe.com

# Dedication

To my grandmother, who taught me the meaning of family and whose unconditional love supported me throughout my life

# About the Author

George W. Kent has been a paralegal instructor for Keiser College since 1997. In 2002, he received the Faculty Teaching Excellence Award, the highest faculty award given by the Keiser collegiate system. He practiced law for many years but later changed direction, concentrating on business endeavors, legal writing, and teaching at the college level. These endeavors include: the development of online paralegal courses; being a freelance editor for a national publishing company; and writing, editing, and publishing law books/materials on subjects such as municipal law, insurance law, and the proper service of legal process. *Family Law for Paralegals* is the second text-book authored by George Kent for the McGraw-Hill Paralegal Titles series, following his earlier textbook *Wills, Trusts, and Estates for Paralegals*.

# Preface

I have had the pleasure of teaching paralegal classes for more than a decade. Like many instructors who begin teaching with no formal education on how to teach, I taught the law the way I was taught the law. The results were disastrous! I quickly realized that the way the law is taught in law school is ill suited for the paralegal classroom. I started over, writing new lectures and developing new lesson plans. The objective was to present the material in a way that would be accessible to the paralegal student.

One major roadblock to reaching my objective was the textbooks themselves. They seemed to be written by lawyers for law students. They did not communicate the information in a way that was readily accessible by most paralegal students.

This textbook is a new approach to a textbook on family law. It is based on the lectures and learning tools that I developed over the years to help my students. I had two main goals for this textbook.

First, it must present the information in a way that is readily accessible to the paralegal student. To achieve this goal, I've presented the material in a manner that the student can easily digest, while also understanding its importance to his or her future career. It is written in a way that first shows the students why the subject is important and then introduces them to the skill sets they will need when they get into the field.

Second, the text must provide real-life practice for the students. To achieve this goal, students are presented with hands-on assignments throughout the textbook. The students are consistently asked to demonstrate their knowledge of the material covered in a chapter by completing tasks associated with that material.

## ORGANIZATION OF TEXT

The text contains 14 chapters that are divided into two parts. It starts with a nonconventional introductory chapter. Like most textbooks, Chapter 1 provides the student with an introduction to some of the key concepts and terms that will be covered throughout the remaining chapters. Unlike most textbooks on the subject, it also gives paralegals an introduction to what their duties would be in a family law firm and a warning of the possible ethical issues they may face.

The textbook is designed to take students through the steps needed to develop the required skills, without overwhelming them during the process. Part One of the textbook introduces students to the legal concepts associated with family law. It does so by using real-world examples and direct, clear language. Part Two provides students with the skills needed to do some common tasks that they will be asked to perform—including the drafting of key documents associated with divorce, dissolution of marriage, and adoption—as well as introduces students to the various legal proceedings associated with those matters.

## TEXT DESIGN

Chapters are laid out in a manner that ensures that students will have the opportunity to learn the appropriate legal concepts and the necessary vocabulary, to develop their legal reasoning skills, and to demonstrate their knowledge of the material. Each chapter contains the following:

- *Client Interview.* Students are given a simple fact pattern that will be referred to within the chapter.
- *Case in Point.* Students are provided with at least one full-length case opinion that they are asked to brief.
- *Research This.* Students are given an assignment designed to help develop their research and writing skills.
- *Ethics Alert.* Students are presented with ethics issues related to the topic covered by the chapter.
- *Cyber Trip.* Students are given the opportunity to take at least one Cyber Trip that allows them to explore the Web to learn more about the law relating to the chapter's topics.
- *Real World Discussion Topics.* Students are presented with a fact pattern taken from an actual court case to help them develop their analytical skills.
- *Portfolio Assignment.* Students are given assignments that require them to analyze a fact pattern and draft documents associated with material covered in the chapter.

This textbook provides students the opportunity to learn about family law and develop the skill sets they will need to succeed in the legal field. I hope they will agree that the goals of the book have been met.

## OTHER LEARNING AND TEACHING RESOURCES

Online Learning Center, **www.mhhe.com/kent09**

The **Online Learning Center (OLC)** is a Web site that follows the text chapter-by-chapter. OLC content is ancillary and supplementary germane to the textbook—as students read the book, they can go online to review material or link to relevant Web sites. Students and instructors can access the Web sites for each of the McGraw-Hill paralegal texts from the main page of the Paralegal Super Site. Each OLC has a similar organization. An Information Center features an overview of the text, background on the author, and the preface and table of contents from the book. Instructors can access the instructor's manual and PowerPoint presentations from the IRCD. Students see the Key Terms list from the text as flashcards, as well as additional quizzes and exercises.

# Acknowledgments

I want to thank Beth Baugh, Freelance Developmental Editor; Tammy L. Higham, Developmental Editor, Career Education, McGraw-Hill; and Natalie Ruffatto, Sponsoring Editor, Career Education, McGraw-Hill, for all of their hard work during the development of this textbook. Their support and encouragement were greatly appreciated.

I would like to especially thank my wife, Cathy, for the hours she spent proofreading the numerous drafts of this textbook and the uneasy task of putting up with my many moods during the writing process. This is the second textbook that she has helped me write and I am happy to say that we are still married despite it all!

Finally, special thanks needs to be given to the reviewers who provided invaluable feedback during the steps to completion of the final draft:

Sally Bisson
*College of Saint Mary*

Belinda Clifton
*International Institute of the Americas*

Claudia M. Doege
*Santa Barbara Business College*

Tyiesha Gainey
*Tidewater Tech*

Tameiko Allen Grant
*Florida Metropolitan University*

Tracy Kaiser
*Manor College*

Michael Kilkelly
*Middlesex Community College*

Ralph Porzio
*St. John's University*

Kathleen Reed
*University of Toledo*

Joanne Spillman
*Westwood College*

# A Guided Tour

*Family Law for Paralegals* explores the wide variety of civil wrongs that can harm an individual and the remedies available to that injured party. Utilizing many practical learning tools, the text is a step-by-step approach in understanding private harms and proving their prima facie elements. The text is written in a very concise and sequential manner, beginning with intentional torts, continuing through the steps of negligence, and finishing with the different liabilities and agency law. The many practical assignments allow students to enjoy the study of torts and apply it to their work as practicing paralegals. The pedagogy of the book applies three main goals:

- Learning outcomes (critical thinking, vocabulary building, skill development, issues analysis, writing practice).

- Relevance of topics without sacrificing theory (ethical challenges, current law practices, technology application).

- Practical application (real-world exercises, practical advice, portfolio creation).

## Chapter Objectives

Introduce the concepts students should understand after reading each chapter as well as provide brief summaries describing the material to be covered.

---

**CHAPTER OBJECTIVES**

**After reading this chapter and completing the assignments, you should be able to:**

- Discuss what prenuptial agreements are and the reasons they are used
- Describe who needs a prenuptial agreement.
- Understand how the law treats prenuptial agreements differently than other contracts.
- Understand what can and cannot be included in a prenuptial agreement.
- Discuss what cohabitation agreements are and the reasons they are used.
- Distinguish between premarital agreements and cohabitation agreements.
- Understand the drafting process to create prenuptial agreements and cohabitation agreements.

# Client Interview

Describes a simple fact pattern at the beginning of the chapter. The facts are referred to throughout the chapter to introduce and explain key legal issues to students.

# Cyber Trip

Provides students with the opportunity to explore the Web to learn more about the law relating to the chapter's topics.

# Case in Point

Exposes students to real-world examples and issues through a case chosen to expand on key topics discussed in chapter. To demonstrate their understanding of the case, students are then asked to prepare a brief of the case.

**RESEARCH THIS**

As demonstrated by Figure 3.5, a number of states still recognize common law marriages. Others have recognized them in the past.

Research the statutory and case law of your state relating to common law marriages and answer the following questions:

1. Does your state recognize common law marriages? If so, what is required to create a common law marriage? Does your state

recognize it for all purposes or is it limited to specific legal matters, such as inheritance?

2. Has your state ever recognized common law marriages? If so, when did it stop? How does it deal with common law marriages from before that date?

3. Does your state recognize common law marriages from other states that allow for them?

## Research This

Gives students the opportunity to investigate issues more thoroughly through hands-on assignments designed to develop critical research skills.

**ETHICS ALERT**

Chapter 1 contained a discussion of ethics and how it relates to the family law firm, including the topic of conflict of interest. The paralegal is faced with many ethical issues in the family law firm. Two topics discussed in this chapter may create a moral dilemma for some paralegals: cohabitation and same-sex marriages. Paralegals must always put the desires and needs of the client first and take all steps possible to keep their personal beliefs from interfering with this obligation.

If a paralegal finds that his or her own personal beliefs may be creating a barrier to doing the best job possible for the client, he or she should request to work on another case. Ultimately, if these issues create too much of a problem for the paralegal, the person may need to consider working for another law firm or in a different area of the law.

## Ethics Alert

Describes ethical issues and situations that paralegals often face when practicing family law.

**Summary**

The word marriage is one that laypeople often think they understand. However, review of the material covered in this chapter makes it clear that legal professiona including paralegals, must be aware of the many different ways that this term is us in the law.

Even more important, the whole concept of marriage is under extreme politic and social examination. State governments have been divided on their approach these changes, especially the issues relating to same-sex couples. Some states ha provided for civil unions and domestic partnerships as an alternative to marriage f same-sex couples. In two states, Massachusetts and New Jersey, state courts have he that the state statutes limiting marriage to a man and a woman violate the state co stitution.

To further complicate this area of family law, some marriages have defects th may impact their validity. Examples include putative marriage and sham marriage

## Chapter Summary

Provides a comprehensive review of the key concepts presented in the chapter.

## Key Terms

Key legal terms throughout the chapters are defined in the margin and provided as a list at the end of each chapter. A common set of definitions is used consistently across the McGraw-Hill paralegal titles.

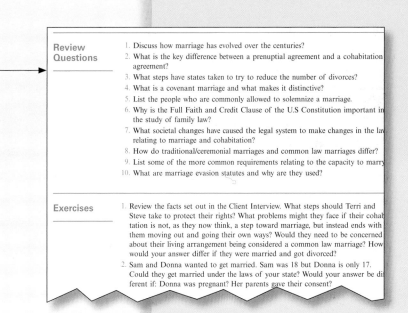

| Key Terms | Ceremonial marriage aka traditional marriage | Premarital preparation course |
| | Cohabitation agreement | Prenuptial agreement |
| | Common law marriage | Proxy marriage |
| | Covenant marriage | Putative marriage |
| | Marriage | Same-sex marriage |
| | No fault divorce | Sham marriage |
| | | Solemnization |

## Review Questions and Exercises

Emphasize critical thinking and problem-solving skills as they relate to tort law. The Review Questions focus on more specific legal concepts learned in each chapter. The Exercises introduce hypothetical situations and ask students to determine the correct answers using knowledge gained from studying topics in each chapter.

**Review Questions**

1. Discuss how marriage has evolved over the centuries?
2. What is the key difference between a prenuptial agreement and a cohabitation agreement?
3. What steps have states taken to try to reduce the number of divorces?
4. What is a covenant marriage and what makes it distinctive?
5. List the people who are commonly allowed to solemnize a marriage.
6. Why is the Full Faith and Credit Clause of the U.S Constitution important in the study of family law?
7. What societal changes have caused the legal system to make changes in the law relating to marriage and cohabitation?
8. How do traditional/ceremonial marriages and common law marriages differ?
9. List some of the more common requirements relating to the capacity to marry.
10. What are marriage evasion statutes and why are they used?

**Exercises**

1. Review the facts set out in the Client Interview. What steps should Terri and Steve take to protect their rights? What problems might they face if their cohabitation is not, as they now think, a step toward marriage, but instead ends with them moving out and going their own ways? Would they need to be concerned about their living arrangement being considered a common law marriage? How would your answer differ if they were married and got divorced?
2. Sam and Donna wanted to get married. Sam was 18 but Donna is only 17. Could they get married under the laws of your state? Would your answer be different if: Donna was pregnant? Her parents gave their consent?

## Real World Discussion Topics

Present students with a fact pattern taken from an actual court case to help them develop their analytical skills.

**REAL WORLD DISCUSSION TOPICS**

A husband and wife were married for two years and had two children of the marriage. When they decided to get divorced, they were able to agree to the terms of the property settlement, that the wife would have custody of the children, that the husband would pay $1,000 a month in child support, which was in excess of the state's child support guidelines, and provide medical and dental insurance coverage for the children. The agreement was drafted by the wife's attorney and signed by the husband, who did not seek out legal representation even though the wife's attorney told him he should do so if he felt he needed independent legal advice.

The wife filed for divorce and requested relief according to the terms of the agreement. The husband objected to this because the terms of the agreement were inequitable. The court rejected the husband's argument.

Did the court abuse its discretion by awarding the amount included in the parties' settlement agreement, even though it exceeded the amount that would have been awarded using the statutory crit... *See Matter of Marriage of ... en, 122 ... 190, 888 P2...*

# Portfolio Assignments

Ask students to use the skills mastered in each chapter to reflect on major legal issues and create documents that become part of the paralegal's portfolio of legal research. The Portfolio Assignments are useful as both reference tools and as samples of work product.

# Brief Contents

# Table of Contents

# Family Law for Paralegals

# Part One

# Legal Concepts Associated with Family Law

# Chapter One

# Introduction to the Family Law Office

## CHAPTER OBJECTIVES

**After reading this chapter and completing the assignments, you should be able to:**

- Understand how family law interrelates with other areas of the law.
- Understand the duties paralegals are often called upon to perform in a family law firm.
- Identify potential ethical issues that might be faced in the family law firm.
- Understand some of the complexities in working in a family law firm.

Paralegal students usually look forward to studying family law because it is perhaps one of the most familiar areas of law to the average person. Why? The main reason is because most people have been personally involved in a divorce or have had a friend or relative who has been divorced. Although estimates vary, some sources state that 40 percent to 50 percent of first marriages will end in divorce. Second marriages have an even lower success rate, especially if there are stepchildren. Some estimates are as high as 60 percent to 67 percent of second marriages ending in divorce.

It is important to remember, however, that family law includes far more than just divorces and dissolution of marriages. It also involves happier activities, such as adoptions.

Chapter 1 introduces students to some of the general concepts associated with family law and to the tasks that family law paralegals may be called upon to complete in the family law firm. These tasks are diverse, and it is important to understand the complexities of the family law office before beginning the actual study of family law itself.

Finally, paralegal students will be introduced to some of the unique ethical issues that they may face in a family law firm. After reviewing these topics, it should become apparent that the importance of keeping one's ethical responsibilities in mind at all times is nowhere more important than in the family law office.

Jim Johnson was somewhat depressed as he drove to his attorney's office. He never dreamed that his marriage would fall apart, even though he had read news stories that reported that as many as 50 percent of marriages end in divorce. He always thought his marriage would be in the 50 percent that would not end that way. Now he was driving to his attorney's office to begin the divorce process. His wife, Claudia, had already hired an attorney. He was upset about how the divorce would affect his two children, Jan and David, and he was dismayed that his world seemed out of control. He was concerned about what would happen in the upcoming months. Jim's life would be changing in many ways and this worried him very much.

## WHY THIS CHAPTER IS IMPORTANT TO THE PARALEGAL

The family law office is a complicated place. This chapter provides paralegal students with an introduction to the family law office, including a discussion of the duties they will be called upon to complete and also some of the ethical issues they will face. Just as important, students will be provided with some insight into the emotional aspects of working in a family law firm.

## INTRODUCTION TO FAMILY LAW

When you hear the phrase **family law**, the first thing that probably comes to mind is divorce. Although divorce is a major component of family law, the reality is that this area of the law is far more all-encompassing than most people imagine. It includes:

- Marriage
- Cohabitation
- Premarital agreements
- Cohabitation agreements
- Divorce
- Dissolution of marriage
- Annulment
- Alimony
- Child custody
- Visitation
- Child support
- Paternity
- Division of marital property and debts
- Adoption
- Civil litigation
- Civil procedure

A review of these topics reveals that the study of family law covers a wide array of information. It is also an area of law that is subject to tremendous change as our society changes.

Societal changes that have become increasingly important and that have resulted in changes in the law include the following:

- Domestic violence, including spouses, significant others, and children. The legal system is increasingly called upon to address these matters as more cases are

**family law**
Area of the law that involves family-related matters such as divorce, prenuptial agreements, postnuptial agreements, adoptions, child custody, wills, and probate.

**CYBER TRIP**

A wide variety of statistics are available on divorce, including interesting data on the number, timing, and duration of marriages and divorces in the United States. To learn more about marriage and divorce statistics in the United States, visit www.census. gov/prod/2005pubs/ p70-97.pdf.

reported. Although abuse of family members has undoubtedly occurred throughout history, society today has recognized the need to address these abuses and has attempted to offer relief to its victims. The very definition of what constitutes abuse, both psychological and physical, has changed over the years. For example, some forms of corporal discipline used with children during the 1950s, which were considered acceptable at the time, might be considered child abuse today.

- Child support, child custody, and payment of alimony. These issues have become increasingly more complicated as society becomes more mobile. The legal system also must deal increasingly with child custody and support issues arising from cases involving children born out of wedlock. Published reports indicate that as many as 37 percent of the children born in the United States in 2005 were to unmarried women.

- Stem cell research and in vitro fertilization. The advancement of science has created these new issues, which have required the legal system to answer questions it never had to previously address.

- Same-sex marriage. There is increasing political debate over the issue of same-sex marriages.

Family law is, therefore, not only broad and complicated but rapidly changing. This puts pressure on family law paralegals to stay up-to-date on the laws that impact their profession.

Traditionally, paralegals needed to stay apprised about changes in the laws of their state, since each state creates the laws regulating family law within its boundaries. Although some movement has occurred since the 1970s to make laws uniform between the states in such areas as divorce, dissolution of marriage, and child custody, state laws involving family law issues still vary significantly. Some states have enacted **uniform laws or statutes**, legislation proposed by the National Conference of Commissioners on Uniform State Laws, in an effort to deal with the fact that family law issues increasingly involve parties who reside in more than one state. It is essential, however, to keep in mind that the laws that impact family law can vary dramatically from state to state. Paralegals must, therefore, be aware of the specific laws that apply in their state and also of **case law** that has interpreted or applied the statutes to specific cases. Appendix A contains information on research sources that can help locate the laws of all 50 states and the District of Columbia.

The increased mobility of the American society has also resulted in the federal government becoming more active in the enacting legislation that has an effect on family law. Examples include the Parental Kidnapping Prevention Act of 1980, which requires every state to enforce the terms of any child custody determination entered by another state, and the Child Support Recovery Act of 1992, which made it a federal crime to willfully fail to pay child support for a child living in another state. This increased involvement of the federal government in matters that involve family law will be discussed many times throughout this text.

## THE EMOTIONAL ASPECT OF WORKING IN A FAMILY LAW FIRM

Many areas of the law present legal professionals with emotional challenges. For example, criminal law can be a problem for some paralegals because many of their firm's clients are, in fact, guilty. Paralegals who cannot in good conscience assist in the defense of someone they know is guilty, such as a child molester, may be better suited to work in another area of the law.

**uniform statute**
Model legislation drafted by the National Conference of Commissioners on Uniform State Laws, dealing with areas of the law such as sales transactions.

**case law**
Published court opinions of federal and state appellate courts; judge-created law in deciding cases, set forth in court opinions.

**CYBER TRIP**

To learn more about uniform laws, how they are created, and when they become law, visit the National Conference of Commissioners on Uniform State Laws Web site at www.nccusl.org.

Working in a family law firm can present similar challenges. To demonstrate this, take a moment and reread the Client Interview at the beginning of the chapter about one person's personal hardship.

Think about those facts. Here is Jim, a man who never dreamed he would get a divorce, having to face the reality of getting one. Like many people who have gone through the divorce process, he is emotionally shaken and probably more vulnerable than at any other time of his life. At few other times in the average person's life will he or she seek out legal help during such an emotional period. It is important for the paralegal student to understand this so as to avoid mistakes, even ones that are well intentioned.

Jim is faced not only with the obvious emotional issues, such as the breakup of his family, but also less obvious issues, such as the financial impact of the divorce. Will he and Claudia be able to afford and maintain two households plus meet their financial obligations to their children? Will their children be able to adjust to the changes in their lives that will result from the divorce?

Unfortunately, the divorce process requires clients to make life-changing decisions that will affect them for years to come just when they are emotionally unprepared to deal with them. As a result, it is important that paralegal students realize that they not only need to understand the law that applies to a client's case, but also that they will need to have a great degree of compassion and understanding of the client's personal situation. The paralegal and his or her supervising attorney must, of course, balance this with firmness to guide the client toward meeting deadlines and other requirements associated with the case.

In addition, family law paralegals must be aware of the emotional impact that some of the cases that they work on will have on them. Legal professionals are human, and working with people who are going through a dramatic change in their lives can be emotionally draining on them as they attempt to help their clients. Paralegals must be vigilant to keep their own mental well-being in mind to sustain both their professional and personal lives.

## INTERRELATIONSHIP BETWEEN FAMILY LAW AND OTHER AREAS OF THE LAW

Because each area of the law, such as family law, is so complex, it is essential that the paralegal student study one area at a time. This complexity has also caused attorneys to specialize their practices to certain areas of the law, similar to how doctors specialize.

Paralegal students must also understand that areas of the law do, in fact, interrelate. What follows is a discussion of how various areas of the law interrelate with family law. *This is not to say that the paralegal in a family law firm will deal with all of these other areas.* Instead it is intended to demonstrate the importance of understanding that no area of the law stands alone.

### Business Entities

When most people think of businesses, they think of large companies like General Motors or Sears, but many companies in the United States are still family-owned businesses. Family-owned businesses create special issues that must be dealt with both before marriage and during a divorce.

For example, Tonya Summers is the daughter of John Summers, president and majority stockholder of Summers Electronics, Inc., a family-owned company that makes circuit boards for some of the largest electronic companies in the country. Tonya, who is engaged to marry Jeff Jones, might consider a prenuptial agreement to protect her possible future interests in the family business in case of a divorce.

Partnerships also create unique problems that a family law firm may be called upon to deal with during a divorce or at the death of one of the partners.

## Civil Litigation

**civil litigation**
Lawsuits that do not involve criminal prosecution.

As mentioned earlier, most people think of divorce when they hear the phrase "family law." Divorce is a form of **civil litigation** because it is a legal action that requests that a court do a specific act, order the dissolution of marriage.

## Contract Law

Many of the documents prepared in a family law firm are contracts. Two examples are prenuptial agreements and postnuptial agreements. A prenuptial agreement is an agreement entered into by a couple in anticipation of their getting married. A post-nuptial agreement is an agreement entered into by a married couple after their marriage. An example of a postnuptial agreement is a settlement agreement, which is a contract that the husband and wife enter into in contemplation of divorce that sets out matters such as alimony, child custody, and the distribution of marital property.

## Criminal Law

Unfortunately, family law firms are increasingly dealing with domestic violence, including child abuse and spousal abuse. One of the first things a firm might be called upon to do when starting a divorce case is the filing of a motion for a restraining order to protect the client from the acts of his or her spouse.

## Ethics

Although all areas of the law present various ethical challenges, family law is particularly susceptible to these issues. The reason for this is simple: the clients are often in a very vulnerable and emotional state when they visit the family law firm, and they can become quite dependent on their attorneys and their staff. As noted previously, this is especially true of the paralegal who is handling the case because it is the paralegal with whom the client comes into contact the most. Paralegals must exercise care when starting a personal relationship with a client because it can cloud their professional judgment and create potential conflicts of interest.

Another potential ethical issue that can arise in family law is the unauthorized practice of law. An increasing number of states have adopted simplified divorce proceedings, many of which have standardized forms that people can use to handle their own divorce. This apparent simplicity has caused many paralegals to cross the line and actually engage in the unauthorized practice of law by completing forms for other people. The *Cleveland Bar Association v. Coats, d.b.a. Paramount Paralegal Services* set out in the following Case in Point demonstrates the consequences of crossing the line from being a paralegal to practicing law.

## Real Property

The most valuable asset that most Americans own is their house. A house is often more than just an asset in family law. It is also the family's home, the place where they live together as a family. It is where parents raise their children and plan for the future. Divorce changes all of that. It requires that a determination be made of what happens to the home. Does one spouse get to stay in the home until the minor children reach the age of 18? Is it sold at the time of the divorce? If so, how will the sums be distributed?

In addition to the family house, other real property issues may have to be dealt with in a divorce. Perhaps the family owns a vacation home or runs a business that owns real property. The division of this property may also be part of the final divorce and the division of the couple's property.

*Cleveland Bar Association v. Coats, D.B.A. Paramount Paralegal Services*
No. 2002-2118
Submitted Feb. 12, 2003
Decided April 9, 2003

Per Curiam.

**{¶1}** On two occasions since 1995, respondent, Andra Coats, d.b.a. Paramount Paralegal Services, assisted others in their claims before the Ohio Bureau of Employment Services and appeared as their representative. He has also drafted divorce complaints and judgment entries for filing on behalf of pro se litigants. Respondent has a college degree with a major in paralegal studies; however, he has never been licensed to practice law in Ohio, and he did not provide this representation under a licensed attorney's supervision.

**{¶2}** On July 9, 2001, relator, Cleveland Bar Association, filed a complaint charging respondent with having engaged in the unauthorized practice of law and sought to permanently enjoin this conduct. Respondent was served with the complaint but did not answer. He was also served notice of a December19, 2001, hearing to be held before the Board of Commissioners on the Unauthorized Practice of Law, but he did not appear.

**{¶3}** The board found, mainly on the basis of his testimony during an investigative deposition, that respondent's filings, appearances, and preparation of documents, all of which were completed without a licensed attorney's supervision, constituted the unauthorized practice of law. As the board explained, "The unauthorized practice of law consists of rendering legal services for another by any person not admitted to practice in Ohio," citing Gov.Bar R. VII(2)(A). Moreover, the practice of law includes conducting cases in court, preparing and filing legal pleadings and other papers, appearing in court cases, and managing actions and proceedings on behalf of clients before judges, whether before courts or administrative agencies. *Richland Cty. Bar Assn. v. Clapp* (1998), 84 Ohio St.3d 276, 278, 703 N.E.2d 771; *Cincinnati Bar Assn. v. Estep* (1995), 74 Ohio St.3d 172, 173, 657 N.E.2d 499. Accord *Cleveland Bar Assn. v. Picklo,* 96 Ohio St.3d 195, 2002-Ohio-3995, 772 N.E.2d 1187, at ¶ 5.

**{¶4}** The board recommended that we find that respondent engaged in the unauthorized practice of law, that we enjoin such conduct, and that we order the reimbursement of costs and expenses incurred by the board and relator. We adopt, in the main, the board's findings[1] and its recommendation. Accordingly, respondent is hereby enjoined from all further conduct on another's behalf, whether it involves preparing a legal document, filing, or appearing before a tribunal, that constitutes the unauthorized practice of law. All expenses and costs are taxed to respondent.

Judgment accordingly.

---

[1] The board also made a factual finding that respondent had represented clients in proceedings before the Social Security Administration. We do not adopt this finding because relator abandoned this aspect of its case during the board hearing.

January Term, 2003

MOYER, C.J., RESNICK, F.E. SWEENEY, PFEIFER, COOK, LUNDBERG

STRATTON and O'CONNOR, JJ., concur.

## Research and Writing

Although technically legal research and writing is not a separate area of the law, it is usually a separate course taken by all paralegal students. Legal research and writing is more appropriately referred to as a skill. It is a skill that paralegals will use no matter what area of the law they work in. The paralegal in the family law firm will need to be able to locate, read, and understand statues, rules of court, case law, forms, and other documents in order to fulfill his or her role in the law firm. Appendix A contains information that may be helpful in researching the law relating to family law.

## Tax Law

It is probably not surprising that tax law interacts with family law since it seems to increasingly permeate all areas of our lives! Tax law has traditionally had different rules that apply to families, such as the way they are treated for income tax purposes. It also affects many situations that occur after a divorce. For example, child support payments are not deductible by the person who pays them and are not treated as income to the person who receives them. On the other hand, alimony payments may be deducted from

**CASE BRIEF ASSIGNMENT**

Read and brief the *Cleveland Bar Assn. v. Coats,* 98 Ohio St.3d 413, 786 N.E.2d 449 (2003) case. (See Appendix A for information on how to brief cases.)

the income of the payor and included as income of the person receiving the payments. Tax law, therefore, is often a factor to be considered in the family law firm.

### Torts

**tort**
A civil wrongful act, committed against a person or property, either intentional or negligent.

**Torts** are civil wrongs that result in the injury to people or their property. Now you may wonder how in the world torts might be involved in family law! Some examples of torts may help in understanding how torts may come up in a family law firm. Battery is both a crime and a tort. This is true of other acts such as false imprisonment. Intentional infliction of emotional distress is another example of a tort that may be brought up in a family law firm. Traditionally, family members, such as a husband and wife or a parent and a child, were not allowed to sue one another. The reason for this was that the law assumed that such lawsuits would be disruptive of the family unit. Today, many states have abolished this restriction.

### Wills, Trusts, and Estates

**blended family**
Family made up of one or more parents having been previously married and having children of that previous marriage. Sometimes referred to as stepfamilies.

**intestate**
The state of having died without a will.

Planning for the future is a high priority for most families. One key tool for planning for the future is the use of wills and trusts. This is especially true today, as we have seen an increase in **blended families**. Since a family may include stepchildren who will not receive anything from a stepparent's estate if that person dies **intestate**, stepparents may need to have a will to ensure that their desires regarding their stepchildren are carried out. Although a family law firm might not draft wills or trusts as part of the services it provides to its clients, wills and trusts can be an issue in the family law firm.

Let's use the Griffith family as an example of how family law and the law of wills, trusts, and estates interrelate. Dave Griffith, who was previously married and had two children, and Mary Griffith, who has one child from a previous marriage, may be unaware of the fact that if they die intestate, their stepchildren will receive nothing from the stepparent's estate. This may be their desire, but it may not be. A will is one way to resolve this issue if Dave and Mary want to provide for their stepchildren.

Another will-related issue that commonly comes up in divorces is the need to write a new will when the parties are starting the divorce process. The wills of married couples often include provisions for the other spouse that more than likely are inconsistent with their desires when they are getting a divorce. Although state laws may address this issue, it is preferable for the law firm to help the client draft a new will reflecting the changes.

## THE ROLE OF THE PARALEGAL IN THE FAMILY LAW FIRM

Paralegals play an active role in almost every area of the family law firm. The following describes just some of the duties they may be called on to perform.

*Conduct client interview.* The paralegal is often the one who gathers the necessary information about the case from the client. One critical part of the information-gathering process is the client interview. The paralegal does this by asking a series of questions that are designed to obtain the relevant information about the case. A questionnaire or **checklist** is used to ensure that all the required questions are asked. Client interviews are conducted for many aspects of family law, such as adoptions, prenuptial agreements, and divorces. Figure 1.1 contains a sample Client Interview Questionnaire.

**checklist**
Tool used in law offices to ensure that adequate information is obtained from the client to properly complete the task.

*Maintain attorney's calendar.* Many of the activities of the family law firm are time sensitive, and meeting time deadlines is critical. Examples include dates for the filing of responsive pleadings, hearing dates, and trial dates. Keeping track of these important dates not only helps the office operate efficiently but also makes sure that the client's case is handled properly. This in turn helps protect the attorney from possible legal malpractice actions.

## I. Personal Information

**Client**
Name _____
Address _____
Phone Number _____
Occupation _____
Social Security Number _____
DOB _____
Member of the Military _____ (Y/N)

**Spouse**
Name _____
Address _____
Phone Number _____
Occupation _____
Social Security Number _____
DOB _____
Member of the Military _____ (Y/N)

**Children**
Name _____
Address _____
Phone Number _____
Occupation _____
Social Security Number _____
DOB _____

## II. Marriage

Date of Marriage _____
Place of Marriage _____
Prior Marriages _____
Date of Separation _____

## III. Reasons for Divorce

Grounds for Divorce _____
Grounds for Annulment (if any) _____

## IV. Jurisdiction and Venue

How long has client resided in state? _____
How long have the parties lived in the state as husband and wife? _____
Is one spouse residing in another state? If yes, where? _____

## V. Property of marriage

Nature, approximate value, and location of property: _____

## VI. Document Checklist

|  | Received on | In File |
| --- | --- | --- |
| Marriage license/certificate | _____ | _____ (Y/N) |
| Previous dissolution of marriage decrees | _____ | _____ (Y/N) |
| Children: |  |  |
|     Medical hospital records | _____ | _____ (Y/N) |
|     Letters from psychiatrist, psychologist, teachers, etc. | _____ | _____ (Y/N) |
| Prior agreements as to marital property, including prenuptial agreements, marriage settlement agreements or any agreement relating to the ownership of property | _____ | _____ (Y/N) |
| Tax records | _____ | _____ (Y/N) |
| Checking account records | _____ | _____ (Y/N) |
| Savings account records | _____ | _____ (Y/N) |
| Stocks/bonds records | _____ | _____ (Y/N) |
| Real property—title | _____ | _____ (Y/N) |
| Personal property (list) | _____ | _____ (Y/N) |
| Business interest documentation | _____ | _____ (Y/N) |
| Safe deposit box(es) information | _____ | _____ (Y/N) |
| Will/trusts | _____ | _____ (Y/N) |
| Other assets (list) | _____ | _____ (Y/N) |
| Debts (list) | _____ | _____ (Y/N) |

**FIGURE 1.1**
**Sample Client Interview Questionnaire**

**tickler file**
System of tracking dates and reminding what is due on any given day or in any given week, month, or year.

**CYBER TRIP**

As is the case in all businesses and professions, computers are increasingly used in carrying out all kinds of tasks. Law offices rely on computer software to help them maintain their calendars and tickler systems. Many different software systems are available.

Visit www.abacuslaw.com/forms/freedemo/freedemo.php to learn more about one of these software packages. The Abacus Law site not only provides information on the product but also allows you to take advantage of a free demonstration of the product.

A paralegal may also be required to maintain a **tickler file**, also referred to as a *tickler system,* to ensure that critical dates are remembered and the appropriate action is taken. Memory alone is not enough because so many things are going on in the family law office. The tickler system, combined with a filing checklist, helps the paralegals do their job well and also keeps them out of trouble!

*Maintain records.* A wide variety of documents are collected as part of the handling of family law cases. Examples of these include: reports from government agencies, reports from experts, wills and other legal documents required to complete the tasks associated with the client's case, and forms needed to prepare the required paperwork for completion of the client's case. The paralegal will often be called upon to maintain an orderly system of tracking and managing these files.

*Conduct legal research.* Paralegals may be asked to research statutory and case law needed to aid in the preparation of the client's case. The need for good research skills is complicated by the fact that the laws relating to many family law matters vary from state to state. The research may not be limited to the law of the state in which the paralegal works. It may also include the law of other states and federal laws.

*Act as notary public.* Many documents must be notarized and the paralegal is often tasked with this job. The process of becoming a notary usually requires making an application, paying a fee, and taking an oath. Some states also require the person to post a bond, take classes, and take a test. Information on the requirements for becoming a notary in all 50 states can be found at www.nationalnotary.org/howto/.

*Determine the client's assets.* The divorce process is a complicated one. The parties need to resolve many issues, including things like alimony, child support, and the division of marital property. The paralegal may be required to assist in the determination of the valuation of property, including arranging for the appraisal of real property and personal property.

*Draft legal documents.* Paralegals play a vital role in the area of drafting legal documents in many areas of the law, and this is of course true in the family law firm. Examples of the documents that are prepared in a family law firm include: petition for dissolution of marriage, summons, affidavits, temporary motion for child custody, temporary motion of child support, property settlement agreements, separation agreements, and orders of dissolution of marriage.

*File documents.* The paralegal will often be responsible for seeing that certain documents are filed with the court. Examples include: petitions for dissolution of marriage, answers to the petition for dissolution of marriage, motion for restraining orders, and filing of adoption petitions. The paralegal may be called upon to actually take the document to the appropriate court for filing. Other times the documents may be filed by mail or a runner/courier. Electronic filing is also increasingly being used. Whatever the means used to file the document, it is often the paralegal's responsibility to ensure that documents are filed in a timely manner.

*Serve documents.* The law requires that certain legal papers be served on certain people. The paralegal is often the one who takes the necessary steps to provide the documents to the necessary parties pursuant to state law or procedure.

*Schedule hearing and trial dates.* Numerous hearings may be required in scheduling during the divorce case. Examples include hearings on request for temporary child support and the final hearing on the dissolution of marriage petition. The paralegal may be the one responsible for scheduling and keeping track of these hearing dates.

*Assist client in preparing forms.* Many states have mandatory disclosure forms that must be completed as part of the divorce process. These forms include information on each party's monthly income, expenses, and other financial information. Although it is ultimately the client's responsibility to accurately complete the forms, the forms often intimidate clients and the paralegal may have to assist them in their completion.

*Assist in the discovery process.* A wide variety of information must be obtained to properly handle a client's case. This information may include locating assets or obtaining information on a spouse's infidelity. The paralegal's duties may include obtaining, analyzing, and organizing the information obtained in the **discovery** process.

*Locate expert witnesses.* Paralegals will often be responsible for locating **expert witnesses**, scheduling their interviews/depositions, and confirming their availability for trial. Expert witnesses are individuals who have a special knowledge of a particular field that can help the judge rule in a case. In family law, expert witnesses are often used to resolve issues such as child custody.

*Assist at hearings and trials.* Paralegals sometimes will attend hearings/trials with their attorney to aid in handling documents and information relating to the case.

*Assist with postjudgment matters.* Sometimes the needs of a client may require that his or her case be brought back to court to resolve issues such as enforcement of child support or to modify a court decree because there has been a change in circumstances. Other times a case may need to be appealed to a higher court to resolve an issue of law. Paralegals are actively involved in postjudgment matters and will be called upon to assist in a variety of functions, such as drafting documents.

**discovery**
The pretrial investigation process authorized and governed by the rules of civil procedure; the process of investigation and collection of evidence by litigants; process in which the opposing parties obtain information about the case from each other; the process of investigation and collection of evidence by litigants.

**expert witness**
A witness who has special knowledge of a subject based on education or experience in the field.

## ETHICAL PROBLEMS PRESENT IN THE FAMILY LAW FIRM

**Legal ethics** is often a misunderstood phrase. In fact, if you ask a member of the general public what legal ethics are, you will probably be told that there is no such thing! That is because most people equate ethics with morality. The reality is that professional ethics are not always morality based. Instead, the term relates to conduct that is expected of professionals in their dealings with clients, the courts, and society. These professional ethics may, in fact, seem contrary to morality-based ethics. An example of this is the duty of confidentiality that an attorney owes a client. In a criminal case, this can mean that an attorney may be asked to vigorously defend an individual the attorney knows is guilty of the crime that the person is being accused of committing. Legal ethics require that the attorney maintain this confidence even though it may result in a guilty person being set free. The reason for this is that the law recognizes the fact that a lawyer can only provide a proper defense of a client if all of the facts of the case are known, even facts the client would be reluctant to share if it were not for the duty of confidentiality.

**legal ethics**
A code of conduct set out to regulate the proper conduct and behavior of attorneys.

The family law office presents attorneys and their staff with many ethical issues. As a member of the staff, the paralegal is bound by the same ethical standards as his or her supervising attorney. In addition, many state bar associations have now set out specific rules governing paralegals. A brief discussion of some of the ethical issues that a paralegal may encounter while working in a family law firm follows.

## Unlicensed Practice of Law

The *Cleveland Bar Association v. Coats, d.b.a. Paramount Paralegal Services* case discussed earlier demonstrates the difficulties that can occur when paralegals are found to cross the line into the unauthorized practice of law. The modern trend of allowing individuals to prepare and file their own divorces papers has increased the likelihood that a paralegal may inadvertently cross that line. Estimates indicate that as many as 75 percent of the people getting divorced handle their own cases. The estimates are even higher in California, where it is said that 80 percent handle their own cases.

States have recognized that not only are an increasing number of couples seeking divorces but also that a need exists for a simple and inexpensive divorce procedure that individuals themselves can handle. Some states now provide simplified divorce forms for use in these cases. In addition, a number of states are using self-help clinics and providing assistance in the family law clerk's office for those couples who wish to complete their own divorce without the aid of an attorney.

Although simplified forms are provided by government agencies in many states, it does not mean that these forms are easy to fill out for many people. They are just modified versions of the forms attorneys have used in the past. It is all too tempting for the paralegal to try to help a friend or relative complete the forms, without an attorney's supervision, and begin the unauthorized practice of law. Paralegals can provide approved forms in many states, but explaining the forms or helping the client complete them may constitute the unauthorized practice of law.

## Breach of Confidentiality

Paralegals learn a lot of information about their clients while working in the family law firm. Much of it may be very embarrassing to the client if it is divulged to others outside the law firm or even to those inside the firm who do not have a need to know about the case. This information includes financial records, psychiatrist reports, psychologist reports, criminal records, and wills and trusts.

## Falsely Attesting to an Affidavit, Such as When a Paralegal Is a Notary

Paralegals who are often also notary publics may be asked to witness or attest to documents as part of their duties in a family law firm. These include affidavits to be filed with the court. There is nothing wrong with performing this function if it is done

### ETHICS ALERT

Paralegals must be on guard against purposely or inadvertently violating their duty of confidentiality to the client. No matter how innocent something seems, or the fact that the paralegal is telling a trusted friend or spouse, information about the case should stay at the office.

An example might demonstrate how easily this duty of confidentiality can be broken. Kay worked as a paralegal in a firm that handles mostly contested divorces. While working on one particularly nasty divorce, she ran across a medical report about the firm's client, a promi-

nent government official. She couldn't wait to get home to tell her husband about what she read. That night she told him that this prominent individual, whose name she did not mention, had been treated for impotency. Even though the name was not mentioned, it was obvious to the husband who the official was. Did she breach her duty of confidentiality to the client? Yes! What happens at the law office should stay at the law office. Kay's attempt to cleverly hide the client's name did not mean that the information should be made public.

properly. Problems can arise, however, because the law office is a very busy place. Sometimes this busy atmosphere will make it tempting to notarize a document that the person did not see signed. This can become an issue if the paralegal is called to testify as to what occurred when the affidavit was sworn to and notarized by the paralegal.

## Conflict of Interest

Attorneys must be careful to avoid possible conflict of interests, or even an appearance of a conflict of interest. So, what is a **conflict of interest**? A conflict of interest can occur when an attorney's own interest conflicts with the best interest of the client, such as possible competing business interests. It can also occur when there is a conflict between the best interests of two people who the attorney is simultaneously representing. Sometimes these conflicts can be overcome if a written, knowledgeable consent is obtained from the client. If a conflict exists or appears to exist, it is a matter that must be resolved by the attorney, not the paralegal.

> **conflict of interest**
> Clash between private and professional interests or competing professional interests that makes impartiality difficult and creates an unfair advantage.

The issue of simultaneous representation does occur occasionally in a family law firm. If a husband and wife feel that they have a truly amicable divorce and have worked out all issues relating to the divorce, they may want to have only one attorney handle the case. Why? They feel it will save them money. As a general rule, an attorney cannot represent both spouses in a divorce, even if the divorce is truly amicable. Even in the rare instances it is allowed, an attorney and his or her staff must be careful to watch for any signs that the parties have conflicting interests in the case. That is the time the attorney may have to withdraw as legal counsel to both parties. As with most ethical issues, it is better to avoid the problem by playing it safe from the beginning by representing only one party even if the ethical rules of the state allow simultaneous representation.

## Solicitation

As almost anyone who watches TV can attest to, attorneys can advertise. You see attorneys advertising their services in almost every imaginable place, including billboards, radio ads, and newspapers. In fact, one wonders what would happen to the phone companies' profits if attorneys could no longer advertise in the yellow pages of the phone book!

Since advertising is all right, why should the law firm be concerned about solicitation? Isn't advertising the same thing as solicitation? Not under the ethical rules that regulate attorneys. Advertising is general in nature. It is aimed at a broad group of people who might need the attorney's services. Solicitation, on the other hand, is directed to a specific person or a specific, limited group of people. Direct in-person solicitation is generally prohibited, as is solicitation by phone. However, a solicitation letter to a specific target group is usually allowable. For example, an attorney may send out a mailing to all people who have recently received a traffic violation. It is important to note that states vary on how solicitation by mail is regulated.

These are just some of the ethical issues that paralegals are faced with while working in the family law firm. Additional comments on ethics will be given in Ethics Alerts throughout the textbook.

 **RESEARCH THIS**

Research the applicable law of your state relating to solicitation and advertising. What are the distinctions between them? What limitations are there on how attorneys can advertise in your state?

## Summary

Family law is a fascinating and complex area of the law. Paralegals will work with clients during some of the best times of clients' lives, such as helping them through an adoption procedure, and the worst times of clients' lives, such as a bitterly contested divorce. As is the case in all areas of the law, the paralegal must be certain that his or her personality and background lend themselves to working under the conditions discussed in this chapter.

Paralegals must also develop the necessary skills to complete the many duties they will be asked to perform. High on the list of those skills is the ability to locate, read, and understand state laws relating to family law. It is always important to remember that the law is not stagnant. It changes constantly and paralegals must take reasonable steps to stay up-to-date as the law changes in order to perform their jobs properly.

## Key Terms

Blended family

Case law

Checklist

Civil litigation

Conflict of interest

Discovery

Expert witness

Family law

Intestate

Legal ethics

Tickler file

Tort

Uniform statute

## Review Questions

1. Chapter 1 introduces the paralegal student to the fact that family law is interrelated to many other areas of the law. Does this mean that the family law paralegal will deal with all of the areas of the law discussed in this chapter as part of his or her job functions?

2. List the areas of the law that interrelate with family law and give an example of each.

3. List five of the duties a paralegal may be called upon to perform in a family law firm.

4. What is a tickler file and why is it important in a family law firm?

5. What should the paralegal do to avoid the unauthorized practice of law?

6. What is a conflict of interest and why should it be avoided?

7. What are uniform statutes and how are they involved in the study of family law?

8. Chapter 1 includes a discussion of societal changes that have impacted the law. What are they and why is understanding such changes important to the paralegal student?

9. Why is it important that family law paralegals be aware of the fact that their clients are often under emotional stress, such as when they are getting a divorce?

10. Why is it important that paralegals develop good research and writing skills no matter what area of the law they may work in?

## Exercises

1. Review the facts set out in the Client Interview. What are some of the concerns that a paralegal might have in working on Jim Johnson's case? Include in your answer the possible emotional impact that the case will have on both the paralegal and Jim, the duties the paralegal may be called upon to complete in the case, and any possible ethical issues that might arise.

2. Mrs. Johnson brought a legal malpractice claim against Jimmy Johns claiming that he negligently represented her at the trial of her dissolution of marriage

case. Johns hired Fred Wolfgang to represent him in the legal malpractice action. Wolfgang had represented Mr. Johnson in the appellate case involving the final judgment entered in the Johnsons' dissolution of marriage. On appeal the court reversed the property, alimony, and attorney fee provisions of the final judgment and remanded the case to the trial court. Wolfgang entered a notice of appearance before the trial court in the case on behalf of Mr. Johnson. What ethical issues are presented in this case? Do the facts present the possible disclosure of confidential information? Should Wolfgang be allowed to represent Johns in the legal malpractice action?

3. Sharon Towers operates a business that sells a wide variety of business and legal forms. These forms include those that can be used in dissolution of marriage cases. They are available in printed "fill in the blank" forms and also on computer disk. Jill Alexander came to Sharon's business to purchase forms so that she could handle her own divorce without hiring an attorney. She told Sharon that she was not good with these kind of things and asked for her help in selecting the right forms as well as helping her complete the forms for filing. Sharon is not a lawyer. Based on the information provided in this chapter and research of the statutory and case law of your state, including rules regulating the practice of law, what can Sharon do for Jill without crossing the line into the unauthorized practice of law?

4. Research the laws of your state to determine what procedures and forms are available for simplified divorce cases that individuals can use without the aid of an attorney. How are the necessary forms provided to the public? Are they available online? Is there a charge and, if there is, what is the cost of the forms? Does your state allow court personnel to assist in completion of the simplified forms?

5. Visit the Abacus Law site at www.abacuslaw.com/forms/freedemo/freedemo.php or the site of any other company that provides a free trial of software that includes case management and calendaring. Using the facts set out in the Client Interview and supplementing them as needed, use the calendaring and case management features of the software to get an idea of how it works and how it may be useful in the law office.

 **REAL WORLD DISCUSSION TOPICS**

Paralegals are often tempted to go out to work on their own without the supervision of an attorney. Although states vary on what a paralegal can do without attorney supervision, paralegals must be very careful when attempting to do so.

A paralegal in South Carolina ran this ad in the yellow pages under "Paralegals: "IF YOUR CIVIL RIGHTS HAVE BEEN VIOLATED—CALL ME."

He also distributed a business card with the same message on it. His business card and letterhead refer to him as "Paralegal Consultant."

Do this ad and the paralegal's business card constitute solicitation? Has he crossed the line into the unauthorized practice of law? If so, why? See *State v. Robinson*, 321 S.C. 286, 468 S.E.2d 290 (1996).

 **PORTFOLIO ASSIGNMENT**

In light of the fact that an increasing number of states provide forms for individuals to handle their own divorces, there is the temptation for paralegals to complete theses forms for their friends or for other people for a fee. Research the case law of your state and find a case that defines what constitutes the unauthorized practice of law, preferably one involving a paralegal. Write a brief paper that sets out your findings.

# Chapter 2

# Premarital and Cohabitation Agreements

## CHAPTER OBJECTIVES

**After reading this chapter and completing the assignments, you should be able to:**

- Discuss what prenuptial agreements are and the reasons they are used.
- Describe who needs a prenuptial agreement.
- Understand how the law treats prenuptial agreements differently than other contracts.
- Understand what can and cannot be included in a prenuptial agreement.
- Discuss what cohabitation agreements are and the reasons they are used.
- Distinguish between premarital agreements and cohabitation agreements.
- Understand the drafting process to create prenuptial agreements and cohabitation agreements.

Chapter 2 introduces the paralegal student to one of the most important and fastest-growing areas of family law—prenuptial and cohabitation agreements. These agreements are increasingly being used by those who are entering into marriage, especially now that it may be the second or third attempts at marriage for many people, and by those who have decided to live together and not get married. The chapter also discusses the law that impacts these agreements and provides information on how to draft them.

## CLIENT INTERVIEW

Margaret was the daughter of a successful South Florida businessman, William McArthur, and enjoyed a comfortable life growing up. She married Joe Smith shortly after graduation from high school and had two children. Soon after her marriage, Joe went to work in her father's business. Joe and William worked well together, and William slowly turned over more and more of the duties associated with the business to his son-in-law.

## WHY THIS CHAPTER IS IMPORTANT TO THE PARALEGAL

Too often people go to an attorney only after a problem occurs in their lives. Like most endeavors, a little planning before entering into a marriage can avoid a lot of problems in the event of a divorce. More and more people are going to see an attorney to learn how to protect their rights and interest before they get married or move in together.

This is a key reason why this chapter is important to the paralegal student. Paralegals working in a family law firm will be asked to deal with clients who desire to have a prenuptial agreement or cohabitation agreement prepared. The paralegal needs to be familiar with the law relating to these documents and also with the basic concepts associated with their drafting.

## WHAT ARE PREMARITAL AGREEMENTS?

It is often said that there are two times in people's lives that they look at life through rose-colored glasses, and during those times the last thing most of them think about is getting legal advice, even though it may be needed. One is when they think about pursuing the American dream of starting their own business. The other is when they are preparing to get married. In both these situations the individuals' emotions cause them to think of only the good things that will happen and not the real-life problems that may occur. Add to this the fact that most people get married because they are in love, and it is easy to see why most cannot objectively view the consequences of their acts.

This explains why the vast majority of those who are anticipating marriage do not consult an attorney. If they did, many problems could be avoided. Attorneys are trained to raise questions as to what may go wrong in a given situation and take steps to protect their clients from those potential problems. Couples in love usually lack the objectivity to see the potential problems. Those rose-colored glasses blur their vision!

A **prenuptial agreement**, also referred to as a *premarital agreement,* is one tool an attorney may use to help protect his or her clients from the problems that come up when a couple divorces. State law regulates the creation and enforcement of premarital agreements. Like other areas of family law, there has been a movement toward uniformity between the laws of the states. Currently, 26 states have passed the Uniform Premarital Agreement Act (UPAA), and additional states are considering its adoption. See Figure 2.1 for a list of states that have adopted the UPAA and Figure 2.2 for an example of a statute from one of those states.

Most people think of prenuptial agreements as something only the wealthy need. Donald Trump has been in the news many times relating to his marriages and prenuptial agreements. In fact, in his book *Trump, The Art of the Comeback,* Mr. Trump states that you should always have a prenuptial agreement. He has even been quoted as saying that Paul McCartney was "idiotic" for not having a prenuptial agreement prior to his marriage to Heather Mills.

**prenuptial agreement**
An agreement made by parties before marriage that controls certain aspects of the relationship, such as management and ownership of property.

| | | |
|---|---|---|
| Arizona | Indiana | North Dakota |
| Arkansas | Iowa | Oregon |
| California | Kansas | Rhode Island |
| Connecticut | Maine | South Dakota |
| Delaware | Montana | Texas |
| District of Columbia | Nebraska | Utah |
| Hawaii | Nevada | Virginia |
| Idaho | New Mexico | Wisconsin |
| Illinois | North Carolina | |

Other states considering its adoption as of 2007:
Florida
Mississippi
Missouri
U.S. Virgin Islands
West Virginia

**FIGURE 2.1**
**States That Have Adopted the Uniform Premarital Agreement Act**

## NORTH DAKOTA CENTURY CODE
## TITLE 14. DOMESTIC RELATIONS AND PERSONS
## CHAPTER 14-03.1. UNIFORM PREMARITAL AGREEMENT ACT.

**14-03.1-01. Definitions.** As used in sections 14-03.1-01 through 14-03.1-08:

1. A person has "notice" of a fact if the person has knowledge of it, receives a notification of it, or has reason to know that it exists from the facts and circumstances known to the person.
2. "Premarital agreement" means an agreement between prospective spouses made in contemplation of marriage and to be effective upon marriage.
3. "Property" means an interest, present or future, legal or equitable, vested or contingent, in real or personal property, including income and earnings.

**14-03.1-02. Formalities.** A premarital agreement must be a document signed by both parties. It is enforceable without consideration.

**14-03.1-03. Content.**

1. Parties to a premarital agreement may contract with respect to:
   a. The rights and obligations of each of the parties in any of the property of either or both of them whenever and wherever acquired or located.
   b. The right to buy, sell, use, transfer, exchange, abandon, lease, consume, expend, assign, create a security interest in, mortgage, encumber, dispose of, or otherwise manage and control property.
   c. The disposition of property upon separation, marital dissolution, death, or the occurrence or non-occurrence of any other event.
   d. The modification or elimination of spousal support.
   e. The making of a will, trust, or other arrangement to carry out the provisions of the agreement.
   f. The ownership rights in and disposition of the death benefit from a life insurance policy.
   g. The choice of law governing the construction of the agreement.
   h. Any other matter, including their personal rights and obligations, not in violation of public policy or a statute imposing a criminal penalty.
2. The right of a child to support may not be adversely affected by a premarital agreement.

**14-03.1-04. Effect of marriage.** A premarital agreement becomes effective upon marriage.

**14-03.1-05. Amendment-Revocation.** After marriage, a premarital agreement may be amended or revoked only by a written agreement signed by the parties. The amended agreement or the revocation is enforceable without consideration.

**14-03.1-06. Enforcement.**

1. A premarital agreement is not enforceable if the party against whom enforcement is sought proves that:
   a. That party did not execute the agreement voluntarily; or
   b. The agreement was unconscionable when it was executed and, before execution of the agreement, that party:
      (1) Was not provided a fair and reasonable disclosure of the property or financial obligations of the other party;
      (2) Did not voluntarily sign a document expressly waiving any right to disclosure of the property or financial obligations of the other party beyond the disclosure provided; and
      (3) Did not have notice of the property or financial obligations of the other party.
2. If a provision of a premarital agreement modifies or eliminates spousal support and that modification or elimination causes one party to the agreement to be eligible for support under a program of public assistance at the time of separation or marital dissolution, a court, notwithstanding the terms of the agreement, may require the other party to provide support to the extent necessary to avoid that eligibility.
3. An issue of unconscionability of a premarital agreement is for decision by the court as a matter of law.

**14-03.1-07. Enforcement of unconscionable provisions.** Notwithstanding the other provisions of this chapter, if a court finds that the enforcement of a premarital agreement would be clearly unconscionable, the court may refuse to enforce the agreement, enforce the remainder of the agreement without the unconscionable provisions, or limit the application of an unconscionable provision to avoid an unconscionable result.

**14-03.1-08. Enforcement-Void marriage.** If a marriage is determined to be void, an agreement that would otherwise have been a premarital agreement is enforceable only to the extent necessary to avoid an inequitable result.

**14-03.1-09. Limitation of actions.** Any statute of limitations applicable to an action asserting a claim for relief under a premarital agreement is tolled during the marriage of the parties to the agreement. However, equitable defenses limiting the time for enforcement, including laches and estoppel, are available to either party.

**FIGURE 2.2**   **North Dakota Uniform Premarital Agreement Act**

Mr. McCartney may agree, since he is, as this book is being written, watching as the details of his divorce are being worked out between the attorneys without a prenuptial agreement.

Margaret from the preceding Client Interview is an example of someone who has a financial interest that may be jeopardized if she divorces Joe. She certainly would benefit from consulting an attorney to better understand what her rights are and how her interest can be protected.

Although the wealthy may recognize the need for legal counsel prior to marriage, even many people who have relatively little to protect are seeking out legal assistance in drafting a prenuptial agreement. The large number of divorces is one reason. The large number of second marriages is another.

Some common reasons why a person may need a prenuptial agreement include:

- One or both parties have children/grandchildren from a previous marriage.
- One person comes into the marriage with a larger financial net worth than the person he or she is marrying.
- A person wants to protect an inheritance, such as Margaret from the Client Interview.
- One person has an interest in an existing business.
- One person has a desire to alter the amount his or her spouse will receive in the case of his or her death.

Prenuptial agreements are contracts. They must meet all of the requirements of a valid contract to be enforceable. However, unlike a traditional contract, the law has additional special rules because the parties may be too romantically involved to protect their own interest. They cannot negotiate the contract "at arm's length" as is the case in most contracts.

## DRAFTING A PREMARITAL AGREEMENT

Since a prenuptial agreement is a type of contract, it must comply with the laws regulating contracts in the state in which the agreement is written. Many states have applied traditional contract law, subject to some modifications, to determine what is required to draft a valid prenuptial agreement.

Although this discussion is not intended to be a comprehensive discussion of the law relating to contracts, which is better suited for coverage in a contracts class, a brief review of the basic requirements for a valid contract may be helpful at this point. These requirements include the following:

1. **Offer.** The offer is the starting point for most contracts. It can be John offering to sell his used Corvette to Mike for $15,000.
2. **Acceptance.** The other party must accept the offer. Mike could accept the sale based on the purchase price of $15,000.

**offer**
A promise made by the offeror to do (or not to do) something provided that the offeree, by accepting, promises or does something in exchange.

**acceptance**
The offeree's clear manifestation of agreement to the exact terms of the offer in the manner specified in the offer.

**CYBER TRIP**

Visit www.law.upenn.edu/bll/archives/ulc/fnact99/1980s/upaa83.htm to review the entire text of the Uniform Premarital Agreement Act.

3. **Meeting of the minds.** The parties have the same understanding of the terms of the agreement. John and Mike agree to what is being sold, its price, when it will be delivered and when payment would be made.

4. **Capacity.** Both parties must have the legal and mental capacity to enter into a contract. Legal capacity means being 18 years or older, and mental capacity, being able to understand the consequences of one's acts.

5. **Consideration** (note that the UPAA eliminates the need for consideration in a premarital agreement in states that have adopted it). The simplest definition of consideration is the reason a person entered into the contract. In the Corvette example, John's reason to enter into the contract is the $15,000, and for Mike it is the car itself. In those states that still require consideration for premarital agreements, consideration can refer to the marriage itself, the mutual promise contained in the agreement, the act of one spouse agreeing to give up any claim to the other's premarital property in exchange for an agreed to amount of alimony in the event of a divorce, or just the waiver of right by each party.

6. **Legality.** The consideration of the contract must be legal. A contract to sell illegal drugs would be an example of an illegal contract. In the case of premarital and cohabitation agreements, they must be more than just an agreement for the exchange of sexual favors to avoid raising legality issues.

7. Form/writing (**Statute of Frauds**). Some contracts are required by law to be made in writing. Common examples of these kind of contracts are those for the sale of real property, the promises to pay the debts of another, contracts that cannot be performed in one year, *and premarital agreements*.

The law, however, does recognize that there is at least one key difference between most contracts and premarital agreements. In most contracts, the parties are looking out for their own best interest. In the law, this is often referred to as dealing "at arm's length." There is a degree of objectivity on the part of the parties during the negotiation and execution of the contract.

People entering into a marriage contract, however, lack this objectivity. The culprit? Love. For this reason, state statutory and/or case law requires that the parties do certain things to overcome this lack of objectivity. An example of this is the legal requirement that the parties both disclose their financial information prior to the signing of the contract. This requirement is intended to allow the total picture of the other person's financial estate. After all, how can you waive or limit your rights to the other person's estate if you do not fully understand what you are giving up?

Other factors that the courts may look at when examining the enforceability of a prenuptial agreement include the following:

- Did both parties have the opportunity to seek out independent legal counsel? Although there is not a requirement that both parties actually have their own independent legal counsel, many states require that they be given the opportunity to do so. That the parties had an opportunity to seek independent legal counsel should be stated in the premarital agreement itself.

- Are the terms of the agreement fair in light of the status of both parties? In many premarital agreement cases, there is a discrepancy in the financial situations of the two parties. After all, they are often used to protect the separately owned property of the more financially secure party. If the terms of the agreement are too one-sided, however, a court may rule that the terms of the agreement constituted an **unconscionable contract** and refuse to enforce it.

- Do the facts of the case show that the agreement was entered into voluntarily? Since a premarital agreement is a contract, it can be challenged in the same manner as any other contract can be, including challenges based on lack of voluntariness. This includes challenges based on **duress** or other factors that indicate that one party did not voluntarily enter into the contract, such as inadequate time for one party to fully appreciate the consequences of signing the premarital agreement.

- Did the agreement follow the requirements set out in the state's prenuptial agreement statute?

- Do the facts show that one party was induced to sign the agreement by some fraudulent act or statement?

See the *Lashkajani v. Lashkajani* Case in Point for a discussion of the history of how the State of Florida has dealt with prenuptial agreements. Florida is now considering the adoption of the UPAA.

States that have adopted the UPAA have specific requirements for a valid prenuptial agreement, including what can and cannot be included.

Whether a state has or has not adopted the UPAA, paralegals must keep in mind the importance of researching the case law of their state to ensure that they understand the totality of the law relating to premarital agreements. Court opinions often explain the meaning of statutory provisions. They also may be the basis for the legal requirements themselves, if there is no statue that regulates the creation of premarital agreements.

**duress**
Unreasonable and unscrupulous manipulation of a person to force him to agree to terms of an agreement that he would otherwise not agree to. Also, any unlawful threat or coercion used by a person to induce another to act (or to refrain from acting) in a manner that he or she otherwise would not do.

## DISCLOSURE

Disclosure of financial assets by both parties is a critical part of the process of creating a valid premarital agreement. This is true whether the parties have a comparable financial status or one is very wealthy and the other is not. The duty to disclose includes a requirement of disclosing the character, amount, and value of the property individually owned at the time the terms of the agreement are being negotiated. In addition, any other information that would have material relevance to the proposed premarital agreement should be disclosed. Sufficient time should be allowed between the time disclosure is made and the time the premarital agreement is executed to allow the parties to review the information and consult with their attorneys, CPAs, or other advisers to ensure they understand the information. When a client has a doubt about the truthfulness of the information provided, he or she may want to investigate the information in more detail.

The law generally imposes a fiduciary relationship between the parties who are anticipating entering into a premarital agreement because, as previously noted, they are not negotiating at arm's length as they would in other financial negotiations. Accordingly, full disclosure is advisable whether or not it is required by law. Although courts may allow constructive notice of a party's financial situation, such as when the one party has independent knowledge of the other's financial situation, it is better practice to make full disclosure and avoid the possibility of a successful challenge of the premarital agreements in the event of a divorce.

 **RESEARCH THIS**

The law relating to requirements of a valid premarital agreement is complicated and varies by state. Research the statutory and case law of your state to determine what the requirements of a valid premarital agreement are. Your research should include information on what courts consider in deciding if the agreement was entered into voluntarily, what constitutes full financial disclosure, whether or not constructive notice is recognized by the courts, and what constitutes an unconscionable provision in a premarital agreement.

# STEPS IN DRAFTING A PRENUPTIAL AGREEMENT

The first key step in preparing to draft any legal document is to gather all of the needed information. This is done by completion of a client questionnaire, which the paralegal is often required to ensure is completed with all relevant information. Figure 2.3 contains a sample questionnaire that can aid in the gathering of the key initial information.

The next step is to locate sample clauses that can be used in the preparation of the agreement. How this is done has changed dramatically over the years. Law firms have

---

### Client Information

Client's Full Name: _____
a/k/a: _____
Address: _____
Occupation: _____
Age: _____
Name, age, and other relevant information (e.g. disability) of children: _____
Personal Property Owned: _____
Real Property Owned: _____
Life insurance policies (include name of current beneficiary): _____

### Prospective Spouse Information

Full Name: _____
a/k/a: _____
Address: _____
Occupation: _____
Age: _____
Name, age, and other relevant information (e.g. disability) of children: _____
Personal Property Owned: _____
Real Property Owned: _____
Life insurance policies (include name of current beneficiary): _____
Has prospective spouse hired an attorney?
If yes, attorney's name, address and phone number: _____
If no, indicate reason: _____

### Agreement Information

Planned date of marriage: _____
Effective date of agreement: _____
State in which couple will reside: _____
Life insurance policies (that will be acquired as part of agreement or for which beneficiary will be changed): _____
Liability for debts (if yes, specify debts): _____
Property that will be considered marital/community: _____
Property that will be considered separate: _____
Property to be exchanged/transferred: _____
Ownership of marital home: _____
Specifics as to responsibilities for payment of cost of housing and other living expenses: _____
Responsibility for payment of other expenses (e.g. medical insurance): _____
Special provisions if either party dies during marriage: _____
Special provisions relating to children of prior marriage(s): _____
Other information: _____

### Exchange of Information

Medical information: _____ Yes _____ No _____ NA
Financial information: _____ Yes _____ No _____ NA
Disclosure of credit reports/information from law enforcement: _____ Yes _____ No _____ NA

---

FIGURE 2.3   Questionnaire: Prenuptial Agreement

traditionally used books containing sample clauses to help draft legal documents. These books provided clauses that could be selected for use to meet the needs of a particular client. They were often developed based on research of statutory and case law.

Fortunately, today's law offices rely less on traditional books for this purpose and more on clauses that are electronically stored on computers. The form databases might be maintained by the law firm itself or they may be accessed on Internet legal databases such as Westlaw and LexisNexis. These forms are easy to access, modify, and assemble than the older book method.

Keep in mind that documents such as premarital agreements usually contain a number of similar clauses, such as information like names, dates, and so on. Other clauses vary dramatically from client to client based on a person's individual needs. Figure 2.4 contains a relatively simple prenuptial agreement. Depending on the complexity of a couple's financial situations and the terms that are agreed to, prenuptial agreements can be very lengthy documents.

Finally, it is time to create the prenuptial agreement. Assembling the clauses that will be used into a single, comprehensive document does this. The goal is to create a

This prenuptial agreement is entered into on the _____ day of _____, 20____ between _____ (prospective wife) and _____ (prospective husband), collective referred to herein as the "Parties."

Whereas the Parties intend to marry under the laws of the State of _____ and wish to set out the rights, privileges and liabilities that each will have in the event of death, divorce or other termination of their marriage, they agree and acknowledge:

(1) This prenuptial agreement is made in consideration of the parties entering into marriage because of love and not because of possible changes in the financial condition of either party due to their marriage.

(2) The Parties enter into this prenuptial agreement voluntarily.

(3) The Parties have been represented by independent legal counsel to aid in the drafting of this prenuptial agreement and have been made aware of their legal rights and the consequences of entering into this prenuptial agreement.

(4) The Parties have exchanged full disclosure of their assets and liabilities and have had adequate time to review this information.

(5) All property owned respectively by each party prior to the marriage, as well as any property acquired during their marriage, is to be considered separate property, unless otherwise set out in this prenuptial agreement. Documents setting out the property owned by the prospective wife and prospective husband are set out in Scheduled A and B, respectively, which are attached hereto and made a part hereof.

(6) Each party will be responsible for the payment of debts he/she incurred prior to the marriage and/or during the marriage and the property of the other party will not be liable for payment of those debts unless otherwise agreed to in writing between the Parties.

(7) In the event of separation, divorce, or other termination of their marriage, the Parties waive any right to make claims for support, maintenance, alimony of any kind, to division of property.

(8) This prenuptial agreement is binding and will inure to the benefit of the Parties, successors, and personal representatives.

This agreement will be enforced under the laws of the State of _____.

Signed this _____ day of 20____.

_____
Prospective Wife

_____
Prospective Husband

_____
Witness

_____
Witness

**FIGURE 2.4**   **Sample Prenuptial Agreement**

finished product that expresses the desires of the client and meets the legal requirements of the state it is to be used in.

## OTHER CLAUSE THAT CAN BE INCLUDED IN A PREMARITAL AGREEMENT

The sample premarital agreement included in Figure 2.4, the sample contained in Appendix C, and the more detailed example included in the Cyber Trip demonstrate the wide variety of clauses that can be included in these contracts. As is the case with most legal documents, the amount of detail depends largely on the facts of the particular client for whom it is being prepared.

A few examples of the variety of clauses that may be employed to meet the needs of a client include:

*Waiver of rights to estate of other spouse*—This clause expressly waives any rights the surviving spouse may have to the estate of the other spouse in the event of his or her death. Modern inheritance law makes it difficult for a spouse to disinherit a spouse by will in most circumstances. This clause is one way this can be legally accomplished. It may be used in conjunction with a clause that provides the surviving spouse with a lump sum payment.

*Grant of life estate*—The prospective spouses may want to grant each other a life estate in real and personal property owned prior to getting married. This would allow a spouse to use and benefit from the property until the time of his or her death.

*Life insurance*—This clause sets out the specific agreement the parties have to life insurance policies. For example, it may provide that a new insurance policy for a specified dollar amount will be taken out by the husband with the wife as named beneficiary within so many days of the marriage.

*Support of children from a prior marriage*—With the growing number of children being raised in homes of their stepparents, the parties may use this clause to set out any specific agreement as to what obligations, if any, the stepparent will

**CYBER TRIP**

The prenuptial agreement set out in Figure 2.4 is a very short example of such an agreement. Prenuptial agreements can be very lengthy documents depending on the unique circumstances of the parties involved.

To view a 26-page prenuptial agreement visit: www.hodgsonruss.com/files/1_2_1/Prenuptial Agreement.pdf.

**ETHICS ALERT**

Paralegals should always remember a very important fact when they are performing work such as drafting a prenuptial agreement: paralegals are not licensed to practice law. Although it is acceptable for the paralegal to draft legal documents under attorney supervision, paralegals sometimes run into trouble in two areas.

First, since the completion of these forms can seem easy after working with them for a period of time, the paralegal may be tempted to help out a friend who is getting married by drafting a prenuptial agreement for the couple to use. After all, the paralegal may have helped draft dozens of them at his job in the law firm. What could be wrong with doing one for his friend? Plenty! By doing this one, the paralegal is no longer working under the supervision of a licensed attorney. The paralegal has crossed the line into the unauthorized practice of law.

Second, the paralegal must be sure to avoid situations where he or she is working in a law firm but the supervising lawyer is no longer really reviewing the paralegal's work. This problem often arises when a paralegal has worked for a particular lawyer for a long period of time. The attorney grows to respect and trust the abilities of the paralegal and no longer sees a need to review the paralegal's work. The attorney is even more likely to come to this conclusion since there are always time pressures in a law office. Unfortunately, this can create problems for both the paralegal and the attorney. The paralegal's acts may constitute the unauthorized practice of law since the work was not really done under the supervision of an attorney, and the attorney may have violated his or her ethical duty to the client.

Supreme Court of Florida
*Lashkajani v. Lashkajani*
No. SC03-1275
June 30, 2005

CANTERO, J.

\*\*\*

## I. FACTS

In 1989, after three months of negotiations (assisted by separate counsel), the Lashkajanis executed a prenuptial agreement. They were married shortly thereafter. Their marriage lasted about ten years and produced three children. In 2000, however, the wife filed for divorce. She argued that the agreement was unfair to her and that she was coerced into signing it. The circuit court found the husband's "financial disclosure to be full and frank," and the agreement "fair and [not] grossly disproportionate to the detriment of the Wife." The court concluded the agreement was valid and enforceable.

\*\*\*

Based on the agreement's attorney's fees provisions, the court awarded the husband "the reasonable attorney's fees and costs involved in his defense of the parties' prenuptial agreement," which it calculated at $63,022.92. The court also granted the wife's attorney's fees and costs under section 61.16, finding that her "pursuit of efforts to set aside the prenuptial agreement were taken in good faith and with a colorable legal and factual basis," and were therefore not frivolous. Considering the relative financial inequality of the parties, the court awarded the wife $117,022.42 in attorney's fees.

The wife appealed the award of fees to the husband.

\*\*\*

## II. ANALYSIS

The narrow issue before us, as the district court asked it, is whether a prenuptial agreement may contract away a future obligation to pay attorney's fees and costs during the marriage by providing for prevailing party attorney's fees in actions seeking to enforce the agreement. As explained below, we hold that it may.

### FLORIDA CASES ON NUPTIAL AGREEMENTS

Until about 1970, Florida law limited the ability of married couples to execute contracts defining their respective rights upon dissolution of the marriage. The majority rule was that "agreements to facilitate or promote divorce are illegal as contrary to public policy." *Allen v. Allen,* 150 So. 237, 238 (Fla. 1933); *see Gallemore v. Gallemore,* 114 So. 371, 372 (Fla. 1927); *see also Posner v. Posner,* 233 So. 2d 381, 382 (Fla. 1970) *("Posner I")* (citing *Allen* and

*Gallemore* as the long-held majority rule at the time); Developments in the Law—The Law of Marriage and Family: Marriage as Contract and Marriage as Partnership: The Future of Antenuptial Agreement Law, 116 *Harv. L. Rev.* 2075, 2078 (2003) (noting that nuptial agreements were traditionally invalid and citing Florida and California as early jurisdictions recognizing their validity).

In 1970, however, the law began to cautiously evolve towards enforcement of these agreements. In *Posner I,* we held that antenuptial agreements "should no longer be held to be void ab initio" on public policy grounds. 233 So. 2d at 385. We based our decision on the changing societal views towards marriage: "With divorce such a commonplace fact of life, it is fair to assume that many prospective marriage partners . . . might want to consider and discuss . . .—and agree upon, if possible—the disposition of their property and the alimony rights of the wife in the event their marriage, despite their best efforts, should fail." *Id.* at 384. Therefore, we allowed couples contractually to limit post-dissolution alimony payments. In the follow-up case of *Posner v. Posner,* 257 So. 2d 530 (Fla. 1972) *("Posner II"),* however, we limited this freedom by allowing a court to modify the agreement. *Id.* at 535; *see also* Belcher, 271 So. 2d at 13 (noting that *"Posner I* holds, upon the satisfaction of certain conditions, that antenuptial agreements limiting alimony to a certain amount are enforceable (and subject to modification as held in *Posner II*)").

Shortly after *Posner II,* we considered in Belcher "whether or not by express provision in an antenuptial agreement the husband can, by the payment of a present, fixed consideration, contract away his future obligation to pay alimony, suit money and attorney's fees during a separation prior to dissolution of the marriage." 271 So. 2d at 8. We held that "[u]ntil there is a decree of dissolution of the marriage, thus ending her role as wife, the wife's support remains within long-established guidelines of support by the husband which cannot be conclusively supplanted by his advance summary disposition by agreement." *Id.* at 11. Given the husband's long-established obligation of spousal support "under the historical line of cases since shortly after Florida became a state in 1845," *id.* at 9, tradition and the perceived need to protect women led the Court to conclude that prejudgment support obligations cannot be waived.

Finally, in *Casto v. Casto,* 508 So. 2d 330 (Fla. 1987), we confirmed that even unreasonable nuptial agreements regarding post-dissolution property and support, if freely executed, are enforceable. *Id.* at 334. In that case, we explained the circumstances that would justify invalidating a nuptial agreement. We stated that there were two ways an otherwise enforceable nuptial agreement may be held invalid. *Id.* at 333. First, the agreement may be set aside or modified by a court if it was "reached under fraud, deceit, duress, coercion, misrepresentation, or overreaching." *Id.* Second, if the agreement is "unfair or unreasonable . . . given the circumstances of the parties," and the trial court finds the agreement "disproportionate to the means of the defending spouse," then the rebuttable presumption is that "there was either concealment by the defending spouse or a . . . lack of knowledge by the challenging spouse of the defending spouse's finances at the time the agreement was reached." *Id.* Further, incompetence of counsel is not a ground to set aside a valid nuptial agreement. *Id.* at 334.

As the cited cases demonstrate, the evolution in Florida law approving prenuptial agreements concerning post-dissolution support has so far not extended to provisions waiving the right to recover pre-judgment support such as temporary alimony. In fact, in the more than thirty years since *Belcher,* Florida courts consistently have rejected attempts to waive prejudgment support. See *Fernandez v. Fernandez,* 710 So. 2d 223, 225 (Fla. 2d DCA 1998) (noting that "Belcher still requires one spouse, who has the ability, to support the other more needy spouse until a final judgment of dissolution is entered even in the face of an antenuptial agreement to the contrary"); *Appelbaum v. Appelbaum,* 620 So. 2d 1293 (Fla. 4th DCA 1993) (holding that a waiver cannot be conclusive for the period before dissolution); *Lawhon v. Lawhon,* 583 So. 2d 776, 777 (Fla. 2d DCA 1991) (noting that a husband's duty of spousal support during the marriage cannot be "waived or contracted away in an antenuptial agreement"); *Urbanek v. Urbanek,* 484 So. 2d 597, 601 (Fla. 4th DCA 1986) (holding that allowing a husband to offset attorney's fees from a lump sum award would "allow the husband to contract away his responsibility for his wife's prejudgment attorney's fees, which he may not do").

The evolution in our law, therefore, has been toward greater freedom of contract regarding post-dissolution spousal support, while recognizing the continuing obligations of support before the marriage is dissolved. The issue in this case falls in the interstices between these two principles. That is, we consider not a provision concerning spousal support, but one providing for prevailing party attorney's fees in litigation surrounding the enforcement of the prenuptial agreement itself. We now discuss that issue.

## PREVAILING PARTY PROVISIONS IN A VALID PRENUPTIAL AGREEMENT

We reiterate that the issue as presented in the certified question is narrow, and we decide it as such. Specifically, we need not, and do not, decide today whether provisions in a prenuptial agreement concerning pre-dissolution support may be enforced. We decide only whether prevailing party attorney's fees provisions in such agreements, concerning litigation over the validity of the agreements themselves, are enforceable. We hold that they are. Because prenuptial agreements regarding post-dissolution support are enforced "as a matter of contract," and prevailing party clauses have long been enforceable in ordinary contracts, we find no reason not to enforce them here. Moreover, while these clauses technically involve an expense incurred during marriage, they are more closely related to enforcing the prenuptial agreement, which distributes assets after marriage, than they are to ensuring that each spouse supports the other during the marriage.

Valid prenuptial agreements regarding post-dissolution support are contracts. While we still recognize "a vast difference between a contract made in the market place and one relating to the institution of marriage," *Posner I,* 233 So. 2d at 382, we enforce valid prenuptial agreements regarding post-dissolution support "as a matter of contract." *Belcher,* 271 So. 2d at 10. The

difference is in the standard we use to determine the contract's validity. When deciding whether to enforce a prenuptial agreement, trial courts must "carefully examine the circumstances" surrounding the agreement because parties to a prenuptial agreement are not "dealing at arm's length." *Casto,* 508 So. 2d at 334.

Provisions in ordinary contracts awarding attorney's fees and costs to the prevailing party are generally enforced. See *Price v. Tyler,* 890 So. 2d 246, 250 (Fla. 2004) (explaining that the only way to recover attorney's fees and costs is if a statute authorizes it or the contract so provides). Trial courts do not have the discretion to decline to enforce such provisions, even if the challenging party brings a meritorious claim in good faith. See *Brickell Bay Club Condo. Ass'n, Inc. v. Forte,* 397 So. 2d 959, 960 (Fla. 4th DCA), review denied, 408 So. 2d 1092 (Fla. 1981). Such provisions exist to "protect and indemnify" the interests of the parties, not to enrich the prevailing party. See *Blount Bros. Realty Co. v. Eilenberger,* 124 So. 41, 41 (Fla. 1929) (upholding a clause to pay attorney's fees because "a contract to pay attorney's fees is one, not to enrich the holder of the note, but to protect and indemnify him against expenditures necessarily made or incurred to protect his interests"); *see also Dunn v. Sentry Ins. Co.,* 462 So. 2d 107 (Fla. 5th DCA 1985) ("A contractual provision that the losing party will pay the prevailing party's attorney's fees is an agreement for indemnification. . . .").

Prevailing party clauses in prenuptial agreements can be distinguished from provisions regarding pre-dissolution support. Provisions waiving the right to temporary alimony or attorney's fees and costs incurred in the dissolution proceedings are included to enrich the parties entering the agreement. In contrast, prevailing party clauses protect the agreement itself. Their purpose is to indemnify the party who relied on the agreement and constitute a disincentive to one who may frivolously challenge it.

Furthermore, prevailing party clauses hardly implicate the state's interest in ensuring that each spouse supports the other during the marriage. *Belcher* articulated two reasons for prohibiting spouses from contracting out of their duty of support. 271 So. 2d at 9, 10. First, the state remains an "interested party" in the contract until the marriage is dissolved. *Id.* at 9. Because prenuptial agreements have been enforced only to the extent they address post-dissolution property and support arrangements, they take effect when the state is no longer an interested party. Therefore, the state is not an interested party in clauses to protect and enforce the agreement. Second, the state's interest in prenuptial agreements is limited to ensuring that each spouse "is adequately cared for by [his or] her own income and assets" during the dissolution proceeding. *Id.* at 10. If one spouse lacks support, and the other is able to provide it, the court must be able to intervene in equity. *Id.* Prevailing party clauses implicate neither of these concerns. They do not address either spouse's need for support. They merely solidify the party's agreement by providing a disincentive to spouses who may frivolously challenge it.

We repeat what we held in Casto: "Courts . . . must recognize that parties to a marriage are not dealing at arm's length, and, consequently, trial judges must carefully examine the circumstances to determine the validity of . . . [nuptial] agreements." 508 So. 2d at 334. The courts of this state play an important role in the smooth and equitable administration of dissolution proceedings. Our holding today does not undermine this important role, nor does it affect our holdings in *Casto* and other cases that courts may scrutinize nuptial agreements to ascertain that the parties acted without compulsion and based on full disclosure. Although contract principles play a role in dissolution proceedings, courts must remember that proceedings under chapter 61 are in equity and governed by basic rules of fairness as opposed to the strict rule of law. *See* § 61.011, Fla. Stat. (1995) ("Proceedings under this chapter are in chancery."). The legislature has given trial judges wide leeway to work equity in chapter 61 proceedings. *See, e.g.,* § 61.001, Fla. Stat. (1995). *Rosen v. Rosen,* 696 So. 2d 697, 700 (Fla. 1997). Therefore, we limit our holding in this case to answering the certified question in the affirmative. Subject to the limitations explained in *Casto,* prenuptial agreements providing for prevailing party attorney's fees in actions seeking to enforce or prevent the breach of a nuptial agreement are enforceable.

## III. CONCLUSION

For the reasons stated above, we hold that prenuptial agreement provisions awarding attorney's fees and costs to the prevailing party in litigation regarding the validity and enforceability of a prenuptial agreement are enforceable. We answer the certified question in the affirmative and quash the district court's decision.

It is so ordered.

PARIENTE, C.J., and WELLS, ANSTEAD, QUINCE, and BELL, JJ., concur.

LEWIS, J., concurs in result only.

**Source:** Retrieved from: www.law.fsu.edu/library/flsupct/sc03-1275/sc03-1275.html.

---

assume for the support and care of the child from the previous marriage. A similar clause may be used to assure that children of a previous marriage will be provided for in the surviving spouse's will.

*Religion of children*—This clause is used to specify any agreement the parties may have as to the religious faith any children of the marriage will be raised and educated in.

*Adoption of children of prospective spouse*—This clause allows the one prospective spouse to agree to adopt the children of the other.

## WHAT CANNOT BE INCLUDED IN A PRENUPTIAL AGREEMENT

Courts give the parties to a premarital agreement wide latitude on what they include in the agreement. There are, however, some limitations. Courts often state that a clause of a premarital agreement cannot violate an overriding public policy. The biggest limitation relates to terms of the agreement that affect the care or custody of a child. The court protects the child's best interests when looking at these terms. For example, courts do not allow a parent the right to agree to waive child support in a prenuptial agreement, and if one is included, it is not binding on the court.

The UPPA also recognizes some limitations on what can be contained in premarital agreements. These include anything that would be in violation of public policy or a statute imposing a criminal penalty and anything that would adversely affect the rights of a child to support.

## WHAT ARE COHABITATION AGREEMENTS?

A **cohabitation agreement** is a contract entered into by individuals who intend to live together other than as man and wife. Cohabitation agreements can set out the rights and responsibilities of each party during the time that they are married and set out the terms of what will occur when they separate. A sample cohabitation agreement is set out in Figure 2.5. It can be used by heterosexual couples or same-sex couples. The law traditionally treats nonmarried couples as strangers when they separate. Cohabitation agreements can avoid the problems associated when nonmarried couples separate, in a way that is similar to prenuptial agreements. This is demonstrated in the *Polisk v. Layton* case. It should be noted, however, that most states have established laws relating to the requirements of prenuptial agreements and how they will be enforced in the event of a divorce. This is not true of cohabitation agreements. Instead courts will apply traditional contract law when asked to interpret and enforce a cohabitation agreement.

**CASE BRIEF ASSIGNMENT**

Read and brief the *Lashkajani v. Lashkajani,* 911 So.2d 1154 (Fla. 2005) case. (See Appendix A for information on how to brief cases.)

**cohabitation agreement**
A contract setting forth the rights of two people who live together without the benefit of marriage.

**CYBER TRIP**

Visit www.divorcesource.com/tables/domestic agreements.shtml. Use the information provided at this Web site as a starting point to learn more about how your state deals with cohabitation agreements.

**FIGURE 2.5**

**Sample Cohabitation Agreement**

*Source:* Retrieved from http://family.findlaw.com/marriage/living-together/le18_6_1.html. © 2008 FindLaw, a Thomson business. Reprinted with permission.

## SAMPLE COHABITATION AGREEMENT

The following form is intended for illustrative purposes only. You and your attorney can use this sample as a guide in drafting a cohabitation agreement that best protects your interests and complies with the laws in effect where you live.

_____, Cohabitant No. 1, and _____, Cohabitant No. 2, hereinafter jointly referred to as the Cohabitants, who now live/will live together in the future (circle one) at _____, in the city of _____, county of _____, state of _____, hereby agree on this _____ day of _____, in the year _____, as follows:

1. The Cohabitants wish to establish their respective rights and responsibilities regarding each other's income and property and the income and property that may be acquired, either separately or together, during the period of cohabitation.
2. The Cohabitants have made a full and complete disclosure to each other of all of their financial assets and liabilities.
3. Except as otherwise provided below, the Cohabitants waive the following rights:
   a. To share in each other's estates upon their death.
   b. To "palimony" or other forms of support or maintenance, both temporary and permanent.
   c. To share in the increase in value during the period of cohabitation of the separate property of the parties.
   d. To share in the pension, profit sharing, or other retirement accounts of the other.
   e. To the division of the separate property of the parties, whether currently held or hereafter acquired.
   f. To any other claims based on the period of cohabitation of the parties.
   g. To claim the existence of a common-law marriage.
4. [SET FORTH RELEVANT EXCEPTIONS HERE. For instance, if both cohabitants are contributing to the debt repayment on the home owned by one party, they may agree that any increase in equity during the period of cohabitation will be fairly divided between them.]
5. The Cohabitants agree to divide the household expenses as follows:

| Monthly Expenses | Cohabitant No. 1 | Cohabitant No. 2 |
|---|---|---|
| Rent or Mortgage | $_____ | $_____ |
| Telephone | $_____ | $_____ |
| Gas | $_____ | $_____ |
| Electricity | $_____ | $_____ |
| Water & Sewer | $_____ | $_____ |
| Garbage Collection | $_____ | $_____ |
| Cable Television | $_____ | $_____ |
| Cellular Phone | $_____ | $_____ |
| Internet Service | $_____ | $_____ |
| Property Taxes | $_____ | $_____ |
| Insurance: | | |
| Homeowners/Renters | $_____ | $_____ |
| Auto(s) | $_____ | $_____ |
| Recreational Vehicle | $_____ | $_____ |
| Debt Payments: | | |
| Vehicle #1 | $_____ | $_____ |
| Vehicle #2 | $_____ | $_____ |
| Home Equity Loan | $_____ | $_____ |
| Other Loans | $_____ | $_____ |
| Credit Card #1 | $_____ | $_____ |
| Credit Card #2 | $_____ | $_____ |
| Credit Card #3 | $_____ | $_____ |
| Day Care | $_____ | $_____ |
| Transportation Expenses: | | |
| Gasoline | $_____ | $_____ |
| Parking/Commuting | $_____ | $_____ |

**FIGURE 2.5**
*(concluded)*

| | | |
|---|---|---|
| Vehicle Maintenance | $_____ | $_____ |
| Licenses | $_____ | $_____ |
| Food: | | |
|   Groceries | $_____ | $_____ |
|   Take-out Food | $_____ | $_____ |
|   Restaurants | $_____ | $_____ |
|   School Lunches | $_____ | $_____ |
| Household Expenses: | | |
|   Cleaning Supplies | $_____ | $_____ |
|   Cleaning Service | $_____ | $_____ |
|   Yard Maintenance | $_____ | $_____ |
|   Home Maintenance | $_____ | $_____ |
|   Home Security | $_____ | $_____ |
|   Home Improvements | $_____ | $_____ |
|   Home Furnishings | $_____ | $_____ |
|   Appliances | $_____ | $_____ |
| Personal Expenses: | | |
|   Entertainment | $_____ | $_____ |
|   Travel | $_____ | $_____ |
|   Gifts | $_____ | $_____ |
|   Hobbies | $_____ | $_____ |
|   Babysitting | $_____ | $_____ |
| Pet-care Costs | $_____ | $_____ |
| Donations | $_____ | $_____ |
| Other Expenses | $_____ | $_____ |
| | $_____ | $_____ |
| | $_____ | $_____ |
| | $_____ | $_____ |
| TOTAL EXPENSES: | $_____ | $_____ |

6. [ADDITIONAL PROVISIONS HERE. These can cover just about any issue, from custody of pets to allocating household chores. The legal obligation to pay child support to any children of the Cohabitants cannot, however, be modified by agreement of the parties.]

7. Each Cohabitant is represented by separate and independent legal counsel of his or her own choosing.

8. The Cohabitants have separate income and assets to independently provide for their own respective financial needs.

9. This agreement constitutes the entire agreement of the parties and may be modified only in a writing executed by both Cohabitants.

10. In the event it is determined that a provision of this agreement is invalid because it is contrary to applicable law, that provision is deemed separable from the rest of the agreement, such that the remainder of the agreement remains valid and enforceable.

11. This agreement is made in accordance with the laws of the state of _____, and any dispute regarding its enforcement will be resolved by reference to the laws of that state.

12. This agreement will become null and void upon the legal marriage of the Cohabitants.

I HAVE READ THE ABOVE AGREEMENT, I HAVE TAKEN TIME TO CONSIDER ITS IMPLICATIONS, I FULLY UNDERSTAND ITS CONTENTS, I AGREE TO ITS TERMS, AND I VOLUNTARILY SUBMIT TO ITS EXECUTION.

_____        _____
**Cohabitant No. 1**                 **Cohabitant No. 2**

Witnessed by:

_____        _____
(Witness or counsel signature)        (Witness or counsel signature)

[NOTARY PUBLIC MAY AFFIX STAMP HERE]

# CASE IN POINT

District Court of Appeal of Florida, Fifth District
*Emma POSIK, Appellant v. Nancy L.R. LAYTON, Appellee*
No. 96-2192
March 27, 1997
Rehearing Denied June 11, 1997

HARRIS, Judge.

Emma Posik and Nancy L. R. Layton were close friends and more. They entered into a support agreement much like a prenuptial agreement. The trial court found that the agreement was unenforceable because of waiver. We reverse.

Nancy Layton was a doctor practicing at the Halifax Hospital in Volusia County and Emma Posik was a nurse working at the same facility when Dr. Layton decided to remove her practice to Brevard County. In order to induce Ms. Posik to give up her job and sell her home in Volusia County, to accompany her to Brevard County, and to reside with her "for the remainder of Emma Posik's life to maintain and care for the home," Dr. Layton agreed that she would provide essentially all of the support for the two, would make a will leaving her entire estate to Ms. Posik, and would "maintain bank accounts and other investments which constitute non-probatable assets in Emma Posik's name to the extent of 100% of her entire non-probatable assets." Also, as part of the agreement, Ms. Posik agreed to loan Dr. Layton $20,000 which was evidenced by a note. The agreement provided that Ms. Posik could cease residing with Dr. Layton if Layton failed to provide adequate support, if she requested in writing that Ms. Posik leave for any reason, if she brought a third person into the home for a period greater than four weeks without Ms. Posik's consent, or if her abuse, harassment or abnormal behavior made Ms. Posik's continued residence intolerable. In any such event, Dr. Layton agreed to pay as liquidated damages the sum of $2,500 per month for the remainder of Ms. Posik's life.

It is apparent that Ms. Posik required this agreement as a condition of accompanying Dr. Layton to Brevard. The agreement was drawn by a lawyer and properly witnessed. Ms. Posik, fifty-five years old at the time of the agreement, testified that she required the agreement because she feared that Dr. Layton might become interested in a younger companion. Her fears were well founded. Some four years after the parties moved to Brevard County and without Ms. Posik's consent, Dr. Layton announced that she wished to move another woman into the house. When Ms. Posik expressed strong displeasure with this idea, Dr. Layton moved out and took up residence with the other woman.

Dr. Layton served a three-day eviction notice on Ms. Posik. Ms. Posik later moved from the home and sued to enforce the terms of the agreement and to collect on the note evidencing the loan made in conjunction with the agreement. Dr. Layton defended on the basis that Ms. Posik first breached the agreement. Dr. Layton counterclaimed for a declaratory judgment as to whether the liquidated damages portion of the agreement was enforceable.

The trial judge found that because Ms. Posik's economic losses were reasonably ascertainable as to her employment and relocation costs, the $2,500 a month payment upon breach amounted to a penalty and was therefore unenforceable. The court further found that although Dr. Layton had materially breached the contract within a year or so of its creation, Ms. Posik waived the breach by acquiescence. Finally, the court found that Ms. Posik breached the agreement by refusing to continue to perform the house work, yard work and cooking for the parties and by her hostile attitude which required Dr. Layton to move from the house. Although the trial court determined that Ms. Posik was entitled to quantum meruit, it also determined that those damages were off-set by the benefits Ms. Posik received by being permitted to live with Dr. Layton. The court did award Ms. Posik a judgment on the note executed by Dr. Layton.

Although neither party urged that this agreement was void as against public policy, Dr. Layton's counsel on more than one occasion reminded us that the parties had a sexual relationship. Certainly, even though the agreement was couched in terms of a personal services contract, it was intended to be much more. It was a nuptial agreement entered into by two parties that the state prohibits from marrying. But even though the state has prohibited same-sex marriages and same-sex adoptions, it has not prohibited this type of agreement. By prohibiting same-sex marriages, the state has merely denied homosexuals the rights granted to married partners that flow naturally from the marital relationship. In short, "the law of Florida creates no legal rights or duties between live-ins." *Lowry v. Lowry*, 512 So.2d 1142 (Fla. 5th DCA 1987) (Sharp, J., concurring specially). This lack of recognition of the rights which flow naturally from the break-up of a marital relationship applies to unmarried heterosexuals as well as homosexuals. But the State has not denied these individuals their right to either will their property as they see fit nor to privately commit by contract to spend their money as they choose. The State is not thusly condoning the lifestyles of homosexuals or unmarried live-ins; it is merely recognizing their constitutional private property and contract rights.

Even though no legal rights or obligations flow as a matter of law from a non-marital relationship, we see no impediment to the parties to such a relationship agreeing between themselves to provide certain rights and obligations. Other states have approved such individual agreements. In *Marvin v. Marvin*, 18 Cal.3d 660 (1976), the California Supreme Court held:

> [W]e base our opinion on the principle that adults who voluntarily live together and engage in sexual relations are nonetheless as competent as any other persons to contract respecting their earnings and property rights. . . . So long as the agreement does not rest upon illicit meretricious consideration, the parties may order their economic affairs as they choose. . . .

In *Whorton v. Dillingham*, 202 Cal.App.3d 447 (1988), the California Fourth District Court of Appeal extended this principle to same-sex partners. We also see no reason for a distinction.

The Ohio Court of Appeal also seemed to recognize this principle in *Seward v. Mentrup,* 87 Ohio App.3d 601 (1993):

> Appellant contends that she is entitled to a legal or equit- able division of the property accumulated by the parties' joint efforts during the time they lived together. It is ap- pellant's belief that her relationship with appellee was "more like a marriage," and that consequently, she is en- titled to reimbursement for money she contributed to- ward capital improvements to appellee's residence. . . .

The evidentiary materials clearly indicate that there were no written contracts or agreements governing the parties' [lesbian] relationship . . .

> Based upon *Lauper* [*v. Harold,* 23 Ohio App.3d 168 (1985)], a property division, per se, applies only to marriages. We see no reason to deviate from this po- sition. Accordingly, the trial court had no authority to divide property absent a marriage contract *or similar agreement,* and the court correctly granted summary judgment to appellee on appellant's breach of con- tract claim. (Emphasis added).

In a case involving unmarried heterosexuals, a Florida appel- late court has passed on the legality of a non-marital support agreement. In *Crossen v. Feldman,* 673 So.2d 903 (Fla. 2d DCA 1996), the court held:

> Without attempting to define what may or may not be "palimony," this case simply involves whether these parties entered into a contract for support, which is something that they are legally capable of doing.

Addressing the invited issue, we find that an agreement for sup- port between unmarried adults is valid unless the agreement is inseparably based upon illicit consideration of sexual services. Certainly prostitution, heterosexual or homosexual, cannot be condoned merely because it is performed within the confines of a written agreement. The parties, represented by counsel, were well aware of this prohibition and took pains to assure that sexual services were not even mentioned in the agreement. That factor would not be decisive, however, if it could be determined from the contract or from the conduct of the parties that the primary reason for the agreement was to deliver and be paid for sexual services. *See Bergen v. Wood,* 14 Cal.App.4th 854 (1993). This contract and the parties' testimony show that such was not the case here. Because of the potential abuse in marital-type rela- tionships, we find that such agreements must be in writing. The Statute of Frauds requires that contracts made upon consider- ation of marriage must be in writing. This same requirement should apply to non-marital, nuptial-like agreements. In this case, there is (and can be) no dispute that the agreement exists.

The obligations imposed on Ms. Posik by the agreement in- clude the obligation "to immediately commence residing with Nancy L.R. Layton at her said residence for the remainder of Emma Posik's life. . . ." This is very similar to a "until death do us part" com- mitment. And although the parties undoubtedly expected a sexual relationship, this record shows that they contemplated much more. They contracted for a permanent sharing of, and participat- ing in, one another's lives. We find the contract enforceable.

We disagree with the trial court that waiver was proved in this case. Ms. Posik consistently urged Dr. Layton to make the will as

required by the agreement and her failure to do so was sufficient grounds to declare default. And even more important to Ms. Posik was the implied agreement that her lifetime commitment would be reciprocated by a lifetime commitment by Dr. Layton—and that this mutual commitment would be monogamous. When Dr. Layton introduced a third person into the relationship, although it was not an express breach of the written agreement, it explains why Ms. Posik took that opportunity to hold Dr. Layton to her ex- press obligations and to consider the agreement in default.

We also disagree with the trial court that Ms. Posik breached the agreement by refusing to perform housework, yard work, provisioning the house, and cooking for the parties. This con- duct did not occur until after Dr. Layton had first breached the agreement. One need not continue to perform a contract when the other party has first breached. *City of Miami Beach v. Carner,* 579 So.2d 248 (Fla. 3d DCA 1991). Therefore, this conduct did not authorize Dr. Layton to send the three-day notice of eviction which constituted a separate default under the agreement.

We also disagree that the commitment to pay $2,500 per month upon termination of the agreement is unenforceable as a penalty. We agree with Ms. Posik that her damages, which would include more than mere lost wages and moving ex- penses, were not readily ascertainable at the time the contract was created. Further, the agreed sum is reasonable under the circumstances of this case. It is less than Ms. Posik was earning some four years earlier when she entered into this arrangement. It is also less than Ms. Posik would have received had the long- term provisions of the contract been performed. She is now in her sixties and her working opportunities are greatly reduced.

We recognize that this contract, insisted on by Ms. Posik before she would relocate with Dr. Layton, is extremely favor- able to her. But there is no allegation of fraud or overreaching on Ms. Posik's part. This court faced an extremely generous agreement in *Carnell v. Carnell,* 398 So.2d 503 (Fla. 5th DCA 1981). In *Carnell,* a lawyer, in order to induce a woman to be- come his wife, agreed that upon divorce the wife would receive his home owned by him prior to marriage, one-half of his dis- posable income and one-half of his retirement as alimony until she remarried. Two years after the marriage, she tested his commitment. We held:

> The husband also contends that the agreement is so unfair and unreasonable that it must be set aside . . . "The freedom to contract includes the right to make a bad bargain." The controlling question here is whether there was *overreaching* and not whether the bargain was good or bad.

Contracts can be dangerous to one's well-being. That is why they are kept away from children. Perhaps warning labels should be attached. In any event, contracts should be taken se- riously. Dr. Layton's comment that she considered the agree- ment a sham and never intended to be bound by it shows that she did not take it seriously. That is regrettable.

We affirm that portion of the judgment below which ad- dresses the promissory note and attorney's fees and costs as- sociated therewith. We reverse that portion of the judgment that fails to enforce the parties' agreement.

AFFIRMED in part; REVERSED in part and REMANDED for further action consistent with this opinion.

**Source:** From Westlaw. Used with permission from ThomsonWest.

**CASE BRIEF ASSIGNMENT**

Read and brief the *Posik v. Layton,* 695 So.2d 759 (Fla. 5th DCA 1997) case. (See Appendix A for information on how to brief cases.)

# DRAFTING A COHABITATION AGREEMENT

Drafting a cohabitation agreement is very similar to drafting a premarital agreement. Like a prenuptial agreement, a cohabitation agreement is a contract. Drafting one shares the following steps with drafting a premarital agreement:

1. Gather the necessary information.
2. Locate forms/clauses that can be used to "assemble" a finished agreement.
3. Create the finished agreement for review by the paralegal's supervising attorney.

There are, however, some significant differences between a premarital agreement and a cohabitation agreement.

First, unlike the case with premarital agreements, the courts generally assume that the parties are operating at arm's length. The courts view these agreements in much the same way as they do any other contract. They expect the parties to protect themselves during the negotiation of the agreement.

Second, cohabitation agreements can be created in a number of ways, including:

- *Express contracts* that set out the terms of the agreement in writing. This is similar to how a premarital agreement is created.

- *Implied in fact contracts,* which are contracts that are created by the acts of the parties. Put simply, if the parties acted as if there was a contract, then the courts will most likely say that there was a contract.

- *Implied in law contracts,* also called *quasi contracts,* are contracts that courts create to prevent some injustice. Although the term contract is used, these really are not contracts at all. They are missing the key element of intent normally required to form a contract. Instead, the court is creating what amounts to contractual obligations to avoid one person being the recipient of **unjust enrichment** under the circumstances of the case.

**unjust enrichment**
The retention by a party of unearned and undeserved benefits derived from his own wrongful actions regarding an agreement.

Obviously, the paralegal is involved with the drafting of express contracts. However, law firms are often the place people go when they feel they've been treated badly after splitting up with the person with whom they have been cohabitating. Then the paralegal may be called upon to assist the lawyer in developing a legal argument, such as an implied in fact contract, to protect the client who was not wise enough to consult an attorney to write a cohabitation agreement beforehand! The case of *Marvin v. Marvin,* 18 Cal. 3d 660, 134 Cal. Rptr. 815 (1976), is perhaps one of the most famous cases in this area of the law. It involved a couple, one of whom was a famous actor at the time, Lee Marvin, who had an oral agreement, which was never reduced to writing, about what would occur upon separation. This left it to a court to decide how it would determine if a contract existed and, if it did, what the terms of the agreement were. The court found that the couple had entered into an enforceable oral contact. *Marvin v. Marvin* led to the creation of the word **palimony**. Palimony and the *Marvin v. Marvin* case will be discussed in more detail in Chapter 6.

**palimony**
A division of property between two unmarried parties after they separate or the paying of support by one party to the other.

# WHAT CANNOT BE INCLUDED IN A COHABITATION AGREEMENT

As is the case with premarital agreements, cohabitation agreements may be held void if they violate some overriding public policy. For example, in the past, courts invalidated cohabitation because to do otherwise would be to condone unmarried sexual relations. In fact, this was one of the issues dealt with by the court in *Marvin.* That court set out the doctrine that reflects the modern view on this issue; that is, that a cohabitation agreement will only be invalidated on the basis of sex if sex is an express condition of the agreement.

## RESEARCH THIS

States vary on the enforceability of cohabitation agreements and what legal theories are used to protect the rights of the parties to such an agreement. Research the statutory and case law of your state to determine how your state deals with the creation of cohabitation agreements and their enforcement.

## Summary

Many legal problems can be avoided by advanced planning. This is especially true in the case of people planning to live together or those planning to get married. In either case, advanced planning can eliminate or at least reduce the number of legal issues that must be resolved under less pleasant circumstances, such as when the parties divorce or separate.

For the couples who plan to marry, a premarital agreement is often a good idea. Such agreements are no longer just for the rich. Many people have a prenuptial agreement for a variety of reasons, such as providing for a child from a previous marriage. While premarital agreements are contracts, the courts and the state statutes treat them somewhat differently than most contracts. These differences are based on the understanding that those entering into premarital agreements do so differently than if they were entering into any other contract, such as buying a car.

Increasingly, nonmarried couples are also seeking assistance from law firms to help them protect their rights. The cohabitation agreement is the most common tool used by the attorney to protect the client's best interests and desires.

Paralegals are often instrumental in the drafting of both premarital and cohabitation agreements. They use form databases to help them select the proper clauses to use in creating the agreement and do so under the supervision of an attorney.

Proper use of these two agreements can help make life easier for clients if their relationships do not work out. They provide a certain peace of mind if the relationships end in divorce or separation.

## Key Terms

Acceptance
Capacity
Cohabitation agreement
Consideration
Duress
Legality
Meeting of the minds
Offer
Palimony
Prenuptial agreement
Statute of Frauds
Unconscionable contract
Unjust enrichment

## Review Questions

1. What are some of the reasons prenuptial agreements are used?
2. How do the requirements for a prenuptial agreement differ from most contracts? Why does the law treat them differently?
3. What are the steps in drafting a prenuptial agreement?
4. What is an unconscionable contract and why is this legal concept important in the drafting of a prenuptial agreement?
5. What is financial disclosure and why is it important in the law relating to prenuptial agreements?
6. What are some of the reasons that cohabitation agreements are used?
7. Discuss the steps that should be taken in the preparation of a cohabitation agreement.

8. Why have cohabitation and prenuptial agreements grown in use in recent years?

9. What is a client questionnaire and why should one be used to help in the preparation of a prenuptial or cohabitation agreement?

10. What cannot be included in a prenuptial agreement?

---

**Exercises**

1. Using the information contained in the Client Interview as a starting point, draft a prenuptial agreement for Margaret that would be executed before she marries Joe Smith. Complete the Prenuptial Agreement Questionnaire, adding facts as needed to complete the form. You can use the sample prenuptial agreement set out in this chapter as a beginning point for your agreement, but you should supplement it with additional clauses that might be appropriate in this case. Appendix A contains information on finding legal information on the Internet.

2. George was in college when he met Lynn. She worked as a waitress at a local restaurant. They began dating and Lynn wanted to get married. George didn't want to end the relationship but knew that marriage did not fit into his plans. Once he received his degree in architecture, he planned to move to a big city and put his mark on the city's landscape. So, instead of marriage, he convinced Lynn to let him move into her apartment. He also allowed Lynn to support him until graduation, with the understanding that he would pay her back. They never put the agreement in writing nor did Lynn worry about it because she thought they would get married one day. Shortly after graduation, George moved to Miami and never saw Lynn again. He also never paid her back for the money she spent helping him complete college. What legal principles might provide Lynn relief?

3. Eric is engaged to marry Jill. Eric is a very wealthy person, having inherited millions of dollars when his father passed away. He is in love with Jill but had read many stories about what happened to wealthy people when they got a divorce and did not have a prenuptial agreement. He has come to your firm to have one prepared. He wants to exclude payments of any sort in the event of a divorce. He does not want Jill to receive anything from his personal assets, alimony or child support. His plan is to have her sign the agreement the night before the wedding, so he wants to make sure that the prenuptial agreement includes a statement that Jill knowingly waives her right to independent legal counsel. What legal issues are presented in this case? How should the firm proceed in drafting the agreement?

4. Jeremy is engaged to marry Sondra and has come to your firm to help in drafting a premarital agreement. Jeremy is 15 years older that Sondra and has no children. Sondra has one child from a previous marriage. Jeremy wants to provide for Sondra's child as if it were his own. He also wants to provide for Sondra if he should die while they are married but wants to limit what she would receive to $500,000. In the event that they ever divorced, he is willing to continue to provide for the child and pay Sondra $500,000 in exchange for her waiving any and all rights to his property and assets. You are asked by your supervising attorney to begin the drafting process of Jeremy's premarital agreement. What clauses might be used to take care of Jeremy's concerns and desires?

5. Suzanne is a successful businessperson. She became very wealthy after she started a chain of popular sport bars. She is engaged to marry Gregg, a local lawyer whom she had met when he had handled a few of her business transactions. They are both in their 50s and have been previously married. Suzanne has two children from her previous marriage and Gregg has one. All of the children are adults.

The couple has no plans for having any children after their marriage. While Gregg has made a good living as an attorney, Suzanne is far wealthier than he. Suzanne has retained your firm to give her advice on the need for a premarital agreement. Should she have a prenuptial agreement? If no, explain why. If yes, explain why and indicate what matters should be addressed in the agreement.

## REAL WORLD DISCUSSION TOPICS

1. Debra and David were planning to get married on August 26. On August 22, four days before the wedding, the parties signed a premarital agreement. David was represented by counsel at the time of the signing but Debra was not. Both parties declared that the other had "fully disclosed [his or her] present approximate net worth" and that each party "had full opportunity for review of [the] agreement and both parties acknowledge their understanding of the effect and content" of it. David listed six parcels of real estate, both developed and undeveloped, three vehicles, and a business checking account as his separate property. He did not, however, assign specific values to these assets. Debra had no assets. The agreement was signed by the parties and properly witnessed. Their son, Matthew, was born six months later. Approximately seven years after the marriage, Debra filed for divorce.

   If the parties were married and divorced in a state that has adopted the Uniform Premarital Agreement Act, would Debra be able to challenge the premarital agreement at the time of the divorce? Would the answer be different if it took place in a state that has not adopted the UPAA? See *Marsocci v. Marsocci,* 911 A.2d 690 (R.I. 2006).

2. Parties, both of whom had previous marriages, executed a prenuptial agreement in 1995. Both parties were represented by their own attorneys. Both parties included their financial disclosures to the agreement that showed a net worth of approximately $55 million for Denny and a net worth of approximately $127,500 for Colleen. The husband's statement was prepared in June 1995 using April 1995 valuations. The statement was not shared with the wife or her attorney until after the wedding invitations had been mailed and receptions had been planned and scheduled. The parties were married shortly thereafter.

   The prenuptial agreement included the provisions that stated that each party has had a full and satisfactory opportunity to inspect/appraise the property of the other and understood its nature and value. In the event of a divorce, the husband also agreed to pay the wife $144,000.00 in thirty-six equal installments of $4,000.00. In the event that the wife institutes an action for annulment or divorce and is awarded a decree of annulment or divorce from the husband, she agreed to receiving payments set forth above for a period not to exceed three years from the date of commencement of such action. These payments would cease in the event of the wife's death or remarriage or cohabitation with an adult male to whom she is not married. The parties expressly agreed that the wife would make no other claim against the husband.

   The prenuptial agreement also provided if the husband should institute action for divorce or annulment, he would be required to make the above payments to wife for no more than three years and provide her with a condominium. In the event the wife initiated such action, she would be entitled to remain in the marital residence following the grant of the annulment or dissolution for "a period of six (6) months plus one (1) year for each full year that the parties shall have been married prior to such action."

   How should the court rule as to the enforceability of the provisions relating to alimony? Would your answer change if the state in which this marriage/divorce took place had adopted the Uniform Premarital Agreement Act? See *Sanford v. Sanford,* 694 N.W.2d 283 (S.D., 2005).

## PORTFOLIO ASSIGNMENT

Research the case and statutory law of your state to determine the requirements to create a valid cohabitation agreement. Write a summary of the requirements, including any specific statutory or case law that relates to cohabitation agreements that are entered into between same-sex couples.

# Chapter 3

# Marriage and Cohabitation

## CHAPTER OBJECTIVES

**After reading this chapter and completing the assignments, you should be able to:**

- Describe how the word *marriage* is used in family law.

- Explain what legal concepts are associated with a traditional marriage.

- Explain what the legal requirements are to enter into a valid marriage.

- Explain what steps some states are taking to reduce the number of divorces.

- Discuss the societal changes that are impacting the law relating to marriage and cohabitation.

- Understand some of the reasons a couple might need a prenuptial agreement or a cohabitation agreement.

Every family law textbook has a chapter devoted to marriage. After all, it is fundamental to the understanding of family law. These chapters used to be relatively simple because most people readily understood the concepts of marriage, and the law relating to marriage became fairly settled throughout the country after the 1970s.

This is no longer the case. In fact, the very definition of marriage is currently the topic of discussion throughout the United States and in many countries around the world.

Chapter 3 introduces paralegal students to the basic concepts relating to marriage. In addition, students will be given information associated with the volatile topics relating to marriage and cohabitation.

### CLIENT INTERVIEW

Terri and Steve have known each other a number of years. As time went by, they became romantically involved. They have decided not to get married but instead just move in together. They have not discussed the details of things like who will pay what bills or other expenses. They both bring with them a number of personal items, such as a television and a stereo system. Terri and Steve think this may be the first step toward marriage but, for now, they know living together will work out because they are in love.

## WHY THIS CHAPTER IS IMPORTANT TO THE PARALEGAL

Chapter 1 presented the paralegal student the big picture of how complex family law is, how working in a family law firm involves far more than handling divorces cases, and how family law is interrelated to other areas of the law.

Chapter 3 takes a step back and introduces the paralegal student to what is perhaps the most fundamental area of the study of family law—marriage. It is the cornerstone to the understanding of this area of the law. For this reason alone, this chapter is very important to the paralegal student.

Chapter 3 is also important because it demonstrates how complicated even a seemingly simple topic can be. Understanding these complexities and the major societal changes that are taking place relating to marriage and cohabitation is critical to the paralegal student's understanding of family law.

## WHAT IS MARRIAGE?

Although it is difficult to identify the exact origins of marriage, it has been with us for a very long time. Marriage has changed dramatically as time has gone by and continues to evolve as society attempts to adapt to continued changes. Many of the rituals and requirements of today's marriage can trace their beginnings to England and the Anglo-Saxons. In fact, the manner in which marriage is entered into in the United States has it beginnings from those historical developments that were incorporated into the common law and ultimately into the state statutes that regulate marriage today. English common law has also had an effect on other issues, such as what factors can cause a marriage to be invalidated by the courts.

**Marriage** traditionally has meant the union of a man and a woman as husband and wife. The term has been used in a variety of ways over the years. There are **ceremonial marriages (also known as traditional marriages)**, **common law marriages**, **covenant marriages**, **putative marriages**, and **same-sex marriages**, to name just a few.

Marriage has evolved and changed over the centuries. It is an institution that has legal, societal, and religious implications. Many contend that its most basic function is to provide for a stable environment to have and raise children, thus perpetuating the human species. Whatever its origins, it is certainly an institution that is intertwined into many areas of the law. For example, it is a basis for determining property rights in probate and intestacy proceedings and provides tax advantages in some cases to married couples.

This evolution of marriage is ongoing. The very definition of marriage is currently under great debate, specifically whether it should include same-sex marriage, which will be dealt with later in this chapter.

## TRADITIONAL MARRIAGES

Traditional marriages are the kind of marriages that most people think of when they hear the word *marriage*. They are marriages that comply with the laws of the state in which the marriage was entered into. It is important to note that the regulation of marriage is a state function, and the validity of a marriage is determined by the laws in the state in which it was entered into. If a traditional marriage is valid in the state in which the marriage was entered into, the general rule is that the marriage will be recognized in other states. This will be discussed in more detail in the topics relating to same-sex marriages.

State laws vary on the specific requirements, but they are relatively simple to comply with. For example, in Florida a marriage must be between a man and a woman,

**marriage**
A union between a man and a woman.

**ceremonial marriage aka traditional marriage**
A marriage between a man and a woman that was entered into by a civil or religious ceremony.

**common law marriage**
A form of marriage that is legally recognized in certain states, if the two people have been living together for a long period of time, have represented themselves as being married, and have the intent to be married.

**covenant marriage**
The couples make an affirmative undertaking to get counseling prior to the marriage and to seek counseling if contemplating divorce.

**putative marriage**
The couple completes the requirements in good faith, but an unknown impediment prevents the marriage from being valid.

**same-sex marriage**
Marriage of two people of the same sex living together as a family.

**solemnization**
A formalization of a marriage, as in for example a marriage ceremony.

**premarital preparation course**
Course designed to strengthen marriages and reduce divorce.

**proxy marriage**
An agent for the parties arranges the marriage for the couple.

both parties must be 18 years of age (with some exceptions), the couple must have a marriage license issued by a county court judge or the clerk of the circuit court, the marriage must be **solemnized** by a person authorized to do so under state law, the couple cannot be closely related as defined by statute, and there is a 3-day waiting period unless one or both of the people have taken a **premarital preparation course**. Figure 3.1 contains the state statutes on the requirements for a valid marriage. Figure 3.2 contains a sample of an application for marriage license used in Nevada.

In the vast majority of marriages the parties attend the ceremony in person. There are occasions, however, where circumstances do not allow this to occur. In situations where either or both of the parties cannot attend the ceremony, many states allow a third party, who is granted authority to act in this capacity, to stand in for the missing person. This is referred to as a **proxy marriage**.

Many states have enacted ways to encourage adults to take a premarital preparation course prior to getting married. For example, in Florida, if one or both of the parties have taken such a course, the waiting period is reduced. It is important to note that Florida, like some other states, does not require that the course be taken. Instead these states offer incentives, such as the elimination of the waiting period and reducing the amount of the marriage license. Some states, such as Oklahoma and Maryland, have statutory provisions for the reduction of the license fees if the course is taken. Other states require minors to take a premarital course in some cases.

| | | | |
|---|---|---|---|
| Alabama | Ala. Code tit. 30 ch. 1 | Nevada | Nev. Rev. Stat. tit. 11, ch. 122 |
| Alaska | Alaska Stat. tit. 25 Ch. 5 | New Hampshire | N.H. Rev. Stat. Ann. tit. XLIII, ch. 457 |
| Arizona | Ariz. Rev. Stat. Ann. tit. 25 ch. 1 art. 1 | New Jersey | N.J. Rev. Stat. tit. 37 |
| Arkansas | Ark Code Ann. tit. 9, sub. 2, § 11 | New Mexico | N.M. Stat. Ann. art., ch. 40 |
| California | Cal. Family Law Code §§ 300-500 | New York | N.Y. Dom. Rel.i art. 1, 2 and 3 |
| Colorado | Colo. Rev. Stat. tit. 14 art. 2 §§ 14-2-101 et seq | North Carolina | N.C. Gen. Stat. ch. 51 |
| | | North Dakota | N.D. Cent. Code ch. 14-03 |
| Connecticut | Conn. Gen. Stat. title 46b, § 815e | Ohio | Ohio Rev. Code Ann. tit. 31, ch. 3101 |
| Delaware | Del. Code. Ann. tit.13, ch. 1 | | |
| Florida | Fla. Stat. ch. 741.01, et seq | Oklahoma | Okla. Stat.tit. 43 |
| Georgia | Ga. Code Ann. §§ 19-3-1–19-3-68 | Oregon | Or. Rev. Stat. ch. 106 |
| Hawaii | Haw. Rev. Stat. ch. 572 | Pennsylvania | Pa. Code tit. 23, pt. 1 |
| Idaho | Idaho Code tit. 32 ch. 2, 3, and 4 | Rhode Island | R.I. Gen laws tit.15, ch. 15-1, et seq |
| Illinois | Ill Rev. Stat. ch.750 CS 5 Parts II and III | South Carolina | S.C. Code Ann. tit. 20, ch. 1 |
| Indiana | Ind. Code tit. 31 art. 11 | South Dakota | D.D. Codified Laws Ann. tit. 5, ch. 1 |
| Iowa | Iowa Code ch. 595 | | |
| Kansas | Kan. Stat. Ann. ch. 23, art.1 | Tennessee | Tenn. Code Ann. tit. 36, Ch. 3 |
| Kentucky | Ky. Stat. Ann. ch. 402 | Texas | Tex. Family Code Ann. tit. 1, ch. 1 and 2 |
| Louisiana | La. Rev. Stat. tit. IV, ch. 1 | | |
| Maine | Me. Rev. Stat. Ann. tit. 9, ch. 23 | Utah | Utah Code Ann. tit.30, ch. 1 |
| Maryland | Md. Family Law Code Ann. §§ 2-201 et seq | Vermont | Vt. Stat. Ann, tit. 15, ch. 1 |
| | | Virginia | Va. Code Ann. tit. 20, ch. 2 |
| Massachusetts | Mass. Gen. L. tit. III ch. 207 | Washington | Wash. Rev. Code ch. 26.04 |
| Michigan | Mich. Comp. Laws ch. 551 | West Virginia | W. Va. Code ch. 48, art. 2 |
| Minnesota | Minn.Stat. ch. 517 | Wisconsin | Wis. Stat. ch. 765 |
| Mississippi | Miss.Code tit. 93, ch. 1 | Wyoming | Wyo. Stat. tit. 20, ch. 1 |
| Missouri | Mo. Rev. Stat. ch. 451 | District of Columbia | D.C. Code div. VIII, tit. 46, sub. 1, ch. 4 |
| Montana | Mont. Code ann. tit. 40, ch. 1 | | |
| Nebraska | Neb. Rev. Stat.ch. 42 | | |

**FIGURE 3.1**   **State Statutes Specifying Marriage Requirements**

CLARK COUNTY CLERK'S OFFICE
201 Clark Avenue, P.O. Box 551603
Las Vegas, NV 89155-1603

*Please Print Clearly*
**INFORMATION FOR MARRIAGE LICENSE**

(Groom and Bride - Please complete your own individual form.)

Male___   Female___   Today's Date_____

┌─────────────────────────────────┐
│ **Office Use Only** │
│ ID_____ │
└─────────────────────────────────┘

NAME (A)
First_____ Middle _____ Last_____

Resident City (B)                Resident State                Resident Country
_____   _____   _____

Date of Birth _____ Age_____ Birth State_____ Birth Country_____
    (C)        Month/Day/Year                    (D)

Social Security #              Marital Status (Check One)         Number of this Marriage
    (E)                            (F)                                  (G)
_____    Never Married___ Divorced___ Widowed___ Annulled___   _____

Date Divorce or Annulment Final (Month/Day/Year)_____ If Widowed, when? _____
          (H)                                                          (I)
Where divorced, annulled or widowed? (J)

City_____ State_____ Country_____

PARENTS' NAME(S)

Mother's First_____ Middle_____ Maiden_____
    (K)

Mother's                              Mother's
Birth State_____ Birth Country_____
    (L)

Father's First_____ Middle_____ Last_____
    (M)

Father's                              Father's
Birth State_____ Birth Country_____
    (N)

Mailing
Address:_____
    (O)
_____

**FIGURE 3.2**
**Nevada Application for Marriage License**
*Source:* Retrieved from www.co.clark.nv.us/clerk/pdf/Marriage_Application_Info/Marriage%20License%20Information.pdf.

**CYBER TRIP**

Visit www.flgov.com/pdfs/q_and_a.pdf to read the answers to a number of interesting questions relating to the requirements of getting married in the state of Florida. The site also includes interesting information on matters associated with marriages.

**CYBER TRIP**

To learn more about the legal requirements in the state of Florida, visit http://orangeclerk.onetgov.net/service/marriage.shtml, then search for similar sites in your state.

# CAPACITY TO ENTER INTO MARRIAGE

As has previously been mentioned, state law regulates how a valid marriage must be entered into. The laws of the states do vary but some requirements relating to capacity include the following:

1. Age. Historically the age to marry was very young, 12 years old for women and 14 years old for men. Today states have generally increased the age requirement, often to 18 years of age, for the issuance of a marriage license. Many states provide lower ages in some situations, such as pregnancy or with the consent of the minor's parents.

2. Mental capacity. The individuals consenting to marriage need to be of sound mind, which generally means they understand the consequences of entering into marriage, such as the nature of the relationship being entered into and the responsibilities that are associated with marriage.

3. Physical capacity. The ability to consummate the marriage.

4. Relationship. State law requires that the parties not be too closely related, as set out in the state statute. Common exclusions include: parent/child, uncle/niece, aunt/nephew, and first cousins.

## WHO CAN SOLEMNIZE A MARRIAGE

State statutes specify who can solemnize a marriage. These statutes commonly include: members of the clergy, notary publics, magistrates, justices of the peace, and judges.

## COVENANT MARRIAGES

As is evident from the preceding discussion of premarital preparation courses, there has been a growing concern over the increase of divorces in the United States. Many feel that the reason for this is that people enter into marriage too lightly, knowing how easy it is to get a divorce in **no fault divorce** states if things do not go as they planned in their marriage. An example of a no fault statute is included in Figure 3.3.

Some states are now allowing couples to elect to enter into a marriage that will be terminated under the no fault laws or one in which it is more difficult to terminate the marriage. The latter form of marriage is referred to as a covenant marriage. Married couples are required to undergo premarital education before marriage and go through counseling before they are granted a divorce. There may also be a separation period, such as 18 months. Arkansas, Arizona, and Louisiana have passed some version of a covenant marriage statute and others are considering covenant marriages. Figure 3.4 sets out the Louisiana Covenant Marriage Statute.

## COMMON LAW MARRIAGES

Common law marriages, also referred to as *consensual marriages* and *informal marriages,* have been the subject of much discussion and misunderstanding over the years. Put simply, a man and a woman create a common law marriage by living together and holding themselves out as husband and wife to the community. In states that recognize them, this type of marriage is as valid as ones that are formally solemnized. In states where they are not recognized, they are considered void, although they are recognized if validly entered into in another state. The following *Mott v. Duncan Petroleum Trans.* case is an example of how a court of one state may be called upon to determine the validity of a common law marriage entered into in another state.

One long-standing myth associated with common law marriages is that the couple must live together for a specific period of time, usually 7 years. This is not true. The key is that the couple hold themselves out as husband and wife and that they have

**no fault divorce**
A divorce in which one spouse does not need to allege wrongdoing by the other spouse as grounds for the divorce.

**CYBER TRIP**

To learn more about covenant marriages, visit www.supreme.state.az.us/dr/pdf/covenant.pdf.

**FIGURE 3.3**
**California Statute on No Fault Divorces**
*Source:* Retrieved from: www.leginfo.ca.gov/cgi-bin/waisgate?WAISdocID= 3723037800+0+0+0& WAISaction=retrieve.

CALIFORNIA CODES
FAMILY.CODE
SECTION 2310-2313

2310. Dissolution of the marriage or legal separation of the parties may be based on either of the following grounds, which shall be pleaded generally:
(a) Irreconcilable differences, which have caused the irremediable breakdown of the marriage.
(b) Incurable insanity.

2311. Irreconcilable differences are those grounds which are determined by the court to be substantial reasons for not continuing the marriage and which make it appear that the marriage should be dissolved.

**FIGURE 3.4**
**Louisiana Covenant Marriage Statute**

**RS 9:272**
**PART VII. COVENANT MARRIAGE**

§27§272. Covenant marriage; intent; conditions to create

A. A covenant marriage is a marriage entered into by one male and one female who understand and agree that the marriage between them is a lifelong relationship. Parties to a covenant marriage have received counseling emphasizing the nature and purposes of marriage and the responsibilities thereto. Only when there has been a complete and total breach of the marital covenant commitment may the non-breaching party seek a declaration that the marriage is no longer legally recognized.

B. A man and woman may contract a covenant marriage by declaring their intent to do so on their application for a marriage license, as provided in R.S. 9:224(C), and executing a declaration of intent to contract a covenant marriage, as provided in R.S. 9:273. The application for a marriage license and the declaration of intent shall be filed with the official who issues the marriage license.

C. A covenant marriage terminates only for one of the causes enumerated in Civil Code Article 101. A covenant marriage may be terminated by divorce only upon one of the exclusive grounds enumerated in R.S. 9:307. A covenant marriage agreement may not be dissolved, rescinded, or otherwise terminated by the mutual consent of the spouses.

Acts 1997, No. 1380, §3; Acts 2006, No. 249, §1.

agreed to live as husband and wife. This agreement can be established either expressly by the parties or implied by the facts surrounding their particular situation. Living together by itself is not enough to show such an agreement. In addition, unlike traditional marriages, there is no need for a marriage license to enter into a common law marriage and there is generally no public record of the marriage.

Common law marriages are currently recognized by 13 jurisdictions. Figure 3.5 contains a list of those states. In addition, some states have grandfathered in common law marriages entered into prior to a certain date. However, even states that do not allow common law marriages recognize valid common law marriage entered into in states that allow them.

Common criteria for the creation of a common law marriage often include that the parties:

1. Are a man and a woman.

2. Are of legal age and capable of giving consent and entering into a marriage.

3. Are legally capable of entering a solemnized marriage under the provisions of the laws of the state.

**CYBER TRIP**

Visit these sites to learn more about common law marriages: www.unmarried.org/common.html and www.ncsl.org/programs/cyf/commonlaw.htm.

**FIGURE 3.5**
**Common Law Marriage States**

The following states currently recognize common law marriages:

- Alabama
- Colorado
- Iowa
- Kansas
- Montana
- New Hampshire (for purposes of inheritance)
- Oklahoma
- Pennsylvania
- Rhode Island
- South Carolina
- Texas
- Utah
- Washington, D.C.

## Mott v. Duncan Petroleum Trans.
### 51 N.Y.2d 289, 414 N.E.2d 657(1980)

JASEN, Judge.

On this appeal claimant-appellant Mary Mott asserts that she is the widow of John Mott by virtue of a common-law marriage allegedly contracted in the State of Georgia and seeks to recover death benefits pursuant to the Workers' Compensation Law. (Workers' Compensation Law, s 16.) The Workers' Compensation Board, however, denied the benefits sought upon the ground that John and Mary Mott were never legally married. The issue on this appeal is whether the Workers' Compensation Board erred in failing to properly apply the law of the State of Georgia in determining the Motts' marital status.

In 1964, Mary and John Mott took up residence together in Islip, New York. From that time until the time of John's death in a work-related accident in 1973, the Motts constantly lived together, in claimant's words "as husband and wife." During the course of this relationship, the Motts conducted much of their legal and financial business as if they were in fact married. Bank loans were apparently applied for together, certain tax records adjusted, and the like. Indeed, upon John's death, Mary Mott was awarded limited letters of administration as John Mott's "widow." However, notwithstanding the above incidents of "marriage," it is undisputed that John and Mary Mott were never ceremonially married in New York or elsewhere. Claimant concedes as much.

Claimant instead predicates her claim for death benefits upon the existence of an alleged common-law marriage, contracted in the State of Georgia. She testified at the hearing of this matter that she and Mr. Mott traveled to Georgia on several occasions, staying there for weeks at a time with her daughter. She claims that the couple intended to take up permanent residence in Georgia, to start a business there, and to make Georgia their home, although it is undisputed that none of these intentions were ever fulfilled. Claimant also asserts that while in Georgia she and decedent lived together as husband and wife and represented themselves to the local community as such. On the basis of this evidence, claimant concludes that a valid common-law marriage was effected in Georgia.

The Workers' Compensation Board, however, concluded that John and Mary Mott were not legally married and, as a result, denied Mary's claim for death benefits. The board found that "the decedent and Mary Mott were residents of New York State" and held that "the parties marital status must be determined under New York State Law which does not recognize common law marriages, with the exception of a common law marriage previously declared valid in another State." The board then concluded that "(t)he parties' trip to the State of Georgia was merely a visit and the parties returned to New York State's jurisdiction without having effected a common law marriage in Georgia." The Appellate Division, finding that the board's determination was supported by substantial evidence, affirmed, one Justice dissenting. There should be a reversal.

While it is clearly within the province of the Workers' Compensation Board to decide, as a factual matter, whether claimant and John Mott were ever legally married, the board must weigh such facts as it finds against a proper legal standard. Thus, before the court can undertake a review of the administrative fact-finding process which resulted in a finding that the Motts were not married, we must first determine if a proper legal standard was used in arriving at this conclusion. If an improper legal standard was used, review of the fact-finding process is impossible.

It has long been settled law that although New York does not itself recognize common-law marriages (L.1933, ch. 606; Domestic Relations Law, s 11; see, e.g., Matter of Benjamin, 34 N.Y.2d 27, 30, 355 N.Y.S.2d 356, 311 N.E.2d 495), a common-law marriage contracted in a sister State will be recognized as valid here if it is valid where contracted (see e.g., Matter of Watts, 31 N.Y.2d 491, 495, 341 N.Y.S.2d 609, 294 N.E.2d 195; Shea v. Shea, 294 N.Y. 909, 63 N.E.2d 113; Matter of Pecorino, 64 A.D.2d 711, 407 N.Y.S.2d 550). The law to be applied in determining the validity of such an out-of-State marriage is the law of the State in which the marriage occurred. (Matter of Watts, 31 N.Y.2d 491, 341 N.Y.S.2d 609, 294 N.E.2d 195, supra; Matter of Farber v. U. S. Trucking Corp., 26 N.Y.2d 44, 47, 308 N.Y.S.2d 358, 256 N.E.2d 521.) Moreover, this rule has been specifically applied to cases involving entitlement to workers' compensation death benefits. (Matter of Lieblein v. Charles Chips, Inc., 32 A.D.2d 1016, 301 N.Y.S.2d 743, decision on remand affd. 28 N.Y.2d 869, 322 N.Y.S.2d 258, 271 N.E.2d 234.) Thus, in determining whether claimant is entitled to death benefits as the widow of John Mott, the Workers' Compensation Board must first determine whether the Motts were married under the law of the State of Georgia.

Common-law marriages are legal in Georgia and have been recognized in that State since at least 1860. (Brown v. Brown, 234 Ga. 300, 215 S.E.2d 671.) While the burden of proving the existence of such a marriage is on the party asserting its validity (id.; see also, Drawdy v. Hesters, 130 Ga. 161, 60 S.E. 451), all that need to be shown to establish a marriage is that the parties are able to contract, that a contract of marriage was made and that the marriage was consummated according to the law. (Ga.Code Ann., s 53-101.)

Proof of the existence of a contract of marriage must include proof of a "present intent to marry" in the State of Georgia. (Peacock v. Peacock, 196 Ga. 441, 26 S.E.2d 608.) However, such proof can consist of circumstantial evidence including "the act of living together as man and wife, holding themselves out to the world as such, and repute in the vicinity and among neighbors and visitors that they are such, and indeed all such facts as usually accompany the marriage relation and indicate the factum of the marriage." (Murray v. Clayton, 151 Ga.App. 720, 721, 261 S.E.2d 455, quoting Clark v. Cassidy, 62 Ga. 407, 411.) No public or private de facto ceremony is required (Alberson v. Alberson, 237 Ga. 622, 229 S.E.2d 409) and for all that appears, no minimum stay in Georgia is required (Ga.Code Ann., s 53-101). In sum, Georgia law appears to be quite liberal in allowing such unions, subject only to the difficulty which a litigant may have in convincing a fact finder of the existence of an actual contract.

Based upon the foregoing review of the law of Georgia and of this State, it appears that the determination of the Workers' Compensation Board was premised upon an erroneous view of applicable law. First, the board appeared to assume that New York recognizes only out-of-State marriages "previously declared valid in another state." As noted earlier, this view is too limited. (*See, e.g., Matter of Watts*, 31 N.Y.2d 491, 495, 341 N.Y.S.2d 609, 294 N.E.2d 195, *supra*.) Second, the board also assumed that a mere "visit" to Georgia could not result in a valid Georgia marriage. Given the apparent liberality of the Georgia rule with respect to common-law marriages, this too was error. Finally, the board failed even to consider the behavior of the parties in New York as evidence of their intent to marry. While such evidence is not alone determinative, and is of course secondary to evidence of the parties' conduct in Georgia, it is at the very least relevant to show whether the parties viewed themselves as man and wife upon their trip to Georgia. (*Cf. Matter of Farber v. U. S. Trucking Corp.*, 26 N.Y.2d 44, 308 N.Y.S.2d 358, 256 N.E.2d 521, *supra*.)

Having concluded that the board applied an improper standard of law on the issue of marital status, we deem it inappropriate to express our view as to whether the evidence in this case would support a finding of a common-law marriage had the proper legal standard been applied. This question must be decided by the administrative agency. The case must, therefore, be remanded to the Workers' Compensation Board for a redetermination of the factual question of whether claimant and John Mott effected a common-law marriage in the State of Georgia, based upon the legal standards enunciated herein. (*See Matter of Lieblein v. Charles Chips, Inc.*, 32 A.D.2d 1016, 301 N.Y.S.2d 743, decision on remand affd. 28 N.Y.2d 869, 322 N.Y.S.2d 258, 271 N.E.2d 234, supra.)

Accordingly, the order of the Appellate Division, 72 A.D.2d 654, 421 N.Y.S.2d 416, should be reversed, with costs, and the matter remitted to the Appellate Division, Third Department, with directions to remand for further proceedings in accordance with this opinion.

Retrieved from Westlaw on 7/24/07.

**Source:** From Westlaw. Reprinted with permission from Thomson West.

4. Have cohabited.
5. Have mutually assumed marital rights, duties, and obligations.
6. Have held themselves out as and are recognized as husband and wife.

**CASE BRIEF ASSIGNMENT**

Read and brief the *Mott v. Duncan Petroleum Trans.* case. (See Appendix A for information on how to brief cases.)

### RESEARCH THIS

As demonstrated by Figure 3.5, a number of states still recognize common law marriages. Others have recognized them in the past.

Research the statutory and case law of your state relating to common law marriages and answer the following questions:

1. Does your state recognize common law marriages? If so, what is required to create a common law marriage? Does your state recognize it for all purposes or is it limited to specific legal matters, such as inheritance?

2. Has your state ever recognized common law marriages? If so, when did it stop? How does it deal with common law marriages from before that date?

3. Does your state recognize common law marriages from other states that allow for them?

## SAME-SEX MARRIAGES

Perhaps one of the most controversial issues in Family Law since the 1990s is that of same-sex marriage. It was brought to national attention when the Hawaii Supreme Court ruled that the state needed to demonstrate a compelling reason to prohibit same-sex marriages. Although the court did not rule that people of the same sex could marry, it did raise constitutional issues that drew the public's attention.

The issue took on even greater attention when the Massachusetts Supreme Court ruled the statute limiting marriage to a man and a woman was "incompatible with the constitutional principles of respect for individual autonomy and equality under law." See *Goodridge v. Mass. Department of Public Health*, 440 Mass. 309, 798 NE2d 941 (2003). More recently, the New Jersey Supreme Court ruled in *Lewis v. Harris*, 188 N.J. 415, 908 A.2d 196 (2006) that its state's statute limiting marriage to a man and a woman was unconstitutional under the state's constitution.

These cases both held that the state statutes limiting who can marry were unconstitutional under the *state's constitution* because they did not identify a constitutionally adequate reason for the limitation. That does not mean that statutes limiting marriage to a man and a woman are not subject to challenges under the U.S. Constitution. In fact, in a case allowing a referendum to amend the Massachusetts Constitution to specify a marriage can only be between one man and one woman, Justice Greaney stated the amendment would be subject to such a challenge. See *Schulman v. Attorney General,* 447 Mass. 189, 850 NE2d 505 (July 10, 2006).

It is important to note that courts in other states have upheld their statutes that limit marriage to a man and a woman. Two noteworthy cases occurred in Washington and New York. In both cases the highest court in both states upheld the marriage statutes.

In *Hernandez v. Robles,* 7 N.Y.3d 338, 855 N.E.2d 1 (2006), the New York Court of Appeals rejected contentions that the Domestic Relations Law violated due process and equal protection clauses of the New York State Constitution. While the court recognized that there are many benefits of marriage, including tax advantages, rights in probate and intestacy proceedings, rights of support, and insurance coverage, it found that the legislature had a rational basis to limit marriage to heterosexual couples. Specifically the court stated that the limitation was rationally related to the legitimate government interest in protecting the welfare of children. The court did stress, however, that it was not ruling on whether the legislature should or should not allow for same-sex marriages. Instead it noted that it was a matter to be left to the state legislature to determine.

In a similar case, the Washington Supreme Court upheld the state's Defense of Marriage Act, which is discussed in more detail later, as it related to prohibit same-sex marriages. The court ruled that the act did not violate the state's constitution or the state's Equal Protection Amendment because the legislature had a relational basis to limit marriage to heterosexual couples to promote procreation and the well-being of children. See *Andersen v. King County,* 158 Wash.2d 1, 138 P.3d 963 (2006).

Ultimately it may not be a question of how state courts rule on the validity of state statutes that limits marriage to a man and a woman. The question will instead be whether states will be required to recognize same-sex marriages that were validly entered into in another state. Many legal scholars argue that all states must recognize these marriages under the rules applied to resolve conflict of laws, which require recognition absent a violation of public policy. Others argue that such marriages will have to be recognized by all states under the full faith and credit clause of the U.S. Constitution.

In 1996, Congress attempted to address this issue with the passage of the Defense of Marriage Act, often referred to as DOMA. DOMA defines marriage as a union between a man and a woman, provides that states do not have to recognize same-sex marriages from another state and that the federal government will not recognize same-sex marriages. Most states have adopted their own DOMA statutes.

The next question that must be addressed is whether the DOMA act is itself constitutional or whether it is in conflict with the full faith and credit clause. There is no clear answer to this question. Instead, the fate of DOMA will most likely have to be answered by the U.S. Supreme Court. There is even discussion of a need to adopt an amendment to the U.S. Constitution to resolve this issue.

The language of the full faith and credit clause of the Constitution is set out in Figure 3.6.

**FIGURE 3.6**
**Full Faith and Credit Clause of the U.S Constitution**

**Article. IV**
**Section. 1.**

Full Faith and Credit shall be given in each State to the public Acts, Records, and judicial Proceedings of every other State. And the Congress may by general Laws prescribe the Manner in which such Acts, Records and Proceedings shall be proved, and the Effect thereof.

# MARRIAGE EVASION ACTS

Some states have passed marriage evasion statutes that provide a marriage validly entered into in one state may not be recognized by the couple's home state if they left the state to avoid a prohibition that would have prevented them from marrying in their home state. This is aimed at stopping people who could not legally get married in their home state from getting married in another state where they meet the requirements of that state's marriage statute and then returning to live in their home state. These type of statutes have existed in the past, but there is a new interest in them in light of the changing legal landscape of same-sex marriages. The Uniform Marriage Evasion Act, which has been adopted in its entirety by Illinois, Louisiana, Massachusetts, Vermont, and Wisconsin, is set out in Figure 3.7; and the Massachusetts version of the act is set out in Figure 3.8.

---

## 🏛 ETHICS ALERT

Chapter 1 contained a discussion of ethics and how it relates to the family law firm, including the topic of conflict of interest. The paralegal is faced with many ethical issues in the family law firm. Two topics discussed in this chapter may create a moral dilemma for some paralegals: cohabitation and same-sex marriages. Paralegals must always put the desires and needs of the client first and take all steps possible to keep their personal beliefs from interfering with this obligation.

If a paralegal finds that his or her own personal beliefs may be creating a barrier to doing the best job possible for the client, he or she should request to work on another case. Ultimately, if these issues create too much of a problem for the paralegal, the person may need to consider working for another law firm or in a different area of the law.

---

## POLICY—THE UNIFORM MARRIAGE EVASION ACT

The Uniform Marriage Evasion Act, which has two main provisions, has been adopted by the following States:

- Illinois
- Louisiana
- Massachusetts
- Vermont
- Wisconsin

**The first provision:** If a resident prohibited from marrying under the law of the State goes to another State for the purpose of avoiding this prohibition and contracts a marriage which would be void within his/her home State, that marriage will be held to be void by the home State, just as if the marriage had been entered into there. (Several States which have not adopted the Uniform Marriage Evasion Act as a whole have adopted this first provision; see summary of State laws in GN 00305.165.)

**The second provision:** Prohibits the marriage within the State of persons residing and intending to continue residing in another State, if the marriage would be void if contracted in the individual's home State. A marriage in violation of this prohibition is void in the State of marriage, just as it would be void in the State of divorce or in the individual's home State. It is also void in all jurisdictions by the general rule that, in determining the validity of a marriage, the courts will look to the law of the jurisdiction where the marriage occurred.

**FIGURE 3.7**
**The Uniform Marriage Evasion Act**
*Source:* Retrieved from https://s044a90.ssa.gov/apps10/poms.nsf/lnx/0200305155!opendocument.

---

### CERTAIN MARRIAGES PROHIBITED

**Chapter 207: Section 11. Non-residents; marriages contrary to laws of domiciled state**
Section 11. No marriage shall be contracted in this commonwealth by a party residing and intending to continue to reside in another jurisdiction if such marriage would be void if contracted in such other jurisdiction, and every marriage contracted in this commonwealth in violation hereof shall be null and void.

**FIGURE 3.8**
**Massachusetts Marriage Evasion Statute**

Colorado Court of Appeals of Colorado
*Combs v. Tibbitts*
Case No. 05CA0937
October 5, 2006

Plaintiff, Michael Combs, appeals from the trial court's judgment finding that the written contract he entered into with defendant, Brenda Tibbitts, is an enforceable separation agreement. We vacate the judgment and remand for further proceedings.

The following facts were stipulated to by the parties. Plaintiff legally married a woman other than defendant in 1972, and remained married to her at all relevant times. From 1978 until 1999, he cohabited with defendant in a relationship the parties referred to as a "religious" or "celestial" marriage. Plaintiff and defendant had five children together, two of whom were still minors at the time of these proceedings.

In addition to their domestic relationship, the parties were also involved in a business that sold vitamins and herbal extracts. Plaintiff testified that he was sole proprietor of that business, and that defendant worked there as an employee.

When the parties terminated their domestic relationship, plaintiff drafted an agreement, entitled "Domestic Agreement and Writ of Divorce." It states that both parties agree to dissolve "their relationship as man and wife," and provides that plaintiff "will pay [defendant] the sum of $4,000.00 each month until [plaintiff] reaches the age of 65 years old or dies, or [until] a total of $868,000.00" has been paid, whichever occurs first. The agreement indicates that the sums to be paid "will be construed as alimony and child support." The agreement requires plaintiff to pay defendant a lump sum of $100,000, and to pay all expenses incurred for the couple's children for "emergencies and treatments encountered in accidents." Other provisions, not pertinent here, address the parties' agreement concerning plaintiff's contact with the children. The document states that it is the final agreement and that "[n]othing else is agreed to or implied."

After entering into the agreement, plaintiff paid defendant $100,000, which she applied toward the purchase of a residence for herself and the parties' children. Plaintiff also paid defendant $4,000 per month from November 1999 until February 2004, for an approximate total of $160,000.

Plaintiff commenced this action seeking a declaratory judgment regarding the rights and obligations of the parties under the agreement; return of the amounts he had paid to defendant; and partition and sale of the real property defendant purchased using the funds paid. He alleged in the complaint that he was induced to enter into the agreement based on his mistaken belief that he and defendant were married, and that defendant fraudulently concealed from him the fact that the parties were not legally married. (These allegations were directly contradicted by his trial testimony, which indicated he always knew that he was not legally married to defendant.) He further alleged that defendant induced him to enter into the agreement by fraudulently concealing from

him the fact that he had no legal obligation to pay her any amount.

In her answer, defendant stated that the parties' agreement was not based upon marriage. She claimed that both parties knew plaintiff had a legal wife and asserted that the payments contemplated under the agreement were intended as child support and severance pay related to the services she had contributed to plaintiff's business. Defendant asserted counterclaims for unjust enrichment based on plaintiff's alleged failure to pay the promised sums; entry of judgment for the delinquent payments, in the event the agreement were found valid; and entry of judgment for child support, in the event the agreement were found to be invalid. Plaintiff asserted numerous defenses to the counterclaims.

\* \* \*

Following a bench trial, the court ruled that the parties were putative spouses pursuant to § 14-2-111, C.R.S. 2006. It based its ruling on plaintiff's admission that he entered into the agreement because of his mistaken religious belief that he was married to defendant. The court further found that plaintiff's belief that he was married to defendant was evidenced by both the title of the agreement and his allegation in the complaint that he believed he was married to defendant. The court ordered that the agreement was enforceable as a separation agreement between the parties and concluded that plaintiff had failed to make the required payments to defendant beginning in March 2004 for a total arrearage of $48,000. The court entered judgment for defendant in that amount, and awarded prejudgment interest in the amount of $2,079.30 and costs of $620.

\* \* \*

## PUTATIVE MARRIAGE STATUTE

Plaintiff first contends that the trial court erred in determining that defendant was his putative spouse within the meaning of the putative marriage statute. We agree.

Section 14-2-1 10(1)(a), C.R.S. 2006, states that a marriage entered into prior to the dissolution of an earlier marriage of one of the parties is prohibited. However, § 14-2-111 provides that any person who has cohabited with another in the good faith belief that he was married to that person is a putative spouse until knowledge of the fact that he is not legally married terminates his status and prevents acquisition of further rights. A putative spouse acquires the rights conferred upon a legal spouse, including the right to maintenance, whether or not the marriage is prohibited under § 14-2-110, declared invalid, or otherwise terminated by court action. Section 14-2-111.

Here, it is undisputed that, at all times, both parties knew that plaintiff was legally married to another person throughout the period of his cohabitation with defendant. Plaintiff testified, "We've never ever . . . believed that we were legally married," and defendant testified to the same effect. Therefore, there is no record support for the trial court finding that there was a putative marriage under § 14-2-111. Neither plaintiff nor defendant had a good faith belief that the two were validly married, and neither qualifies as a putative spouse. *See People v. McGuire*, 751 P.2d 1011 (Colo. App. 1987) (knowledge that one is married to another person negates good faith belief required to obtain benefit of putative spouse statute).

We conclude that the court erred in ruling that the parties were putative spouses, and in relying on a belief held by plaintiff that he had entered into a "religious" or "celestial" marriage with defendant. As stated in *People v. McGuire, supra*, "[s]ection 14-2-111 was enacted to protect innocent participants in meretricious relationships and the children of those relationships," not for "the purpose of affording protection to the perpetrator of an invalid *marriage." People v. McGuire, supra*, 751 P.2d at 1012.

\*\*\*

Because the parties were not legally married and the putative spouse statute does not apply, the trial court erred when it characterized the parties' agreement as a separation agreement and awarded maintenance to defendant. *See* §§14-10-112, 14-10-114.

\*\*\*

## ENFORCEABILITY OF AGREEMENT UNDER BASIC CONTRACT PRINCIPLES

Plaintiff finally contends that the trial court erred in failing to consider whether the agreement is valid and enforceable on other grounds. He argues that the case must be remanded for further proceedings. We agree.

Courts will not intervene to enforce, revoke, or rescind agreements between cohabiting parties where the sole consideration is based on past, present, or future sexual relations. *Houlton v. Prosser*, 118 Colo. 304, 194 P.2d 911(1948); *Baker v. Couch*, 74 Colo. 380, 221 P. 1089 (1923). Our supreme court has held that nonmarried, cohabiting couples may legally contract with each other so long as sexual relations are merely incidental to the agreement, and enforcement of such agreements may be sought under either law or equity. *Salzman, supra*.

No appellate court of this state has construed an agreement governing the termination of a relationship such as the one presented here, and we have found no cases on point within the United States. *Cf. Whitney v. Whitney*, 194 Okla. 361, 151 P.2d 583 (1944) (unwitting party to bigamous marriage may maintain suit against other party for fraudulent inducement into marriage, notwithstanding written contract for property division previously entered into by parties, which plaintiff alleged was void).

We conclude that, aside from the sufficiency of the parties' agreement pertaining to child support, as discussed above, general contract principles govern the analysis of the remaining provisions of the agreement. *See In re Marriage of Lafaye, supra*, 89 P.3d at 459 (general contract principles apply to agreements that are not governed by the Uniform Dissolution of Marriage Act).

We have already concluded that, because the parties were not legally married, payments denominated for "alimony"(by which the parties apparently meant "maintenance") are unenforceable. Nevertheless, defendant testified at trial that, to the extent the payments made to her were for anything other than child support, they were intended as severance pay for her work in plaintiff's business. Furthermore, at oral argument, counsel for defendant suggested that the payments might be construed as compensation related to the dissolution of a business relationship.

On remand, the trial court must make findings as to whether, under general contract law principles, the parties' contract is enforceable for any lawful purpose. Included within that review, the court must determine whether the prerequisites for formation of a contract have been met, and must specifically rule on the issues of consideration and meeting of the minds, which have been raised by plaintiff.

If the trial court determines that the agreement constitutes a valid contract, it must then determine whether there has been a breach of the contract, and if so, whether such breach was material.

The judgment is vacated, and the case is remanded for further proceedings as directed.

JUDGE MÁRQUEZ and JUDGE GRAHAM concur.

**Source:** Retrieved from www.courts.state.co.us/coa/opinion/2006/2006q4/05CA0937.pdf.

**CASE BRIEF ASSIGNMENT**

Read and brief the *Combs v. Tibbitts*, 148 P.3d 430 (Colo. App. 2006) case. (See Appendix A for information on how to brief cases.)

# PUTATIVE MARRIAGES

A putative marriage is one that appears valid, was entered into in good faith by at least one of the parties, but has a legal impediment, of which the parties were unaware, that made it invalid. Note that one of the requirements for establishing a putative marriage is that the parties were unaware of the defect that prevents the marriage from being valid. If one of the parties is aware, and the other is not, only the party who is unaware can claim to be a putative spouse. This is important because a putative spouse may be able to make a claim to a portion of the marital property and spousal support. Some states have specific statutes dealing with putative spouses such as the one discussed in the *Combs v. Tibbitts* case.

## SHAM MARRIAGE

A **sham marriage** is a marriage that is entered into for some personal reason, other than love. The key question that must be answered to determine if a marriage is a sham marriage is whether the parties intended to live as husband and wife and create a life together. Historically marriages were sometimes not based on love. For example, royal marriages were often arranged to accomplish a political advantage. Today, sham marriages are often associated with attempting to avoid immigration laws or attempts to gain social security benefits.

While sham marriages may meet all of the legal qualifications of being married, the law will usually declare them void. Ones designed to evade immigration laws may also constitute criminal acts.

**sham marriage**
Marriage in which the parties never intended to live as a married couple.

## CIVIL UNION

A civil union is similar to a traditional marriage but is entered into by same-sex couples. Civil unions are intended to extend the same rights under state law as those allowed to traditional married couples.

Vermont has led the way in the area of civil unions. Figure 3.9 sets out the Vermont civil union statute. To date, Vermont, California, New Jersey, and Connecticut allow civil unions or similar domestic partnerships.

**FIGURE 3.9**
**Vermont Civil Union Statutes**

*Source:* Retrieved October 26, 2006, from www.leg. state.vt.us/statutes/sections. cfm?Title=18&Chapter=106.

---

**Title: Health**
**Chapter 106: CIVIL UNION; RECORDS AND LICENSES**

**§ 5160. Issuance of civil union license; certification; return of civil union certificate**

(a) Upon application in a form prescribed by the department, a town clerk shall issue a civil union license in the form prescribed by the department, and shall enter thereon the names of the parties to the proposed civil union, fill out the form as far as practicable and retain a copy in the clerk's office. At least one party to the proposed civil union shall sign the application attesting to the accuracy of the facts stated. The license shall be issued by the clerk of the town where either party resides or, if neither is a resident of the state, by any town clerk in the state.

(b) A civil union license shall be delivered by one of the parties to a proposed civil union, within 60 days from the date of issue, to a person authorized to certify civil unions by section 5164 of this title. If the proposed civil union is not certified within 60 days from the date of issue, the license shall become void. After a person has certified the civil union, he or she shall fill out that part of the form on the license provided for such use, sign and certify the civil union. Thereafter, the document shall be known as a civil union certificate.

(c) Within ten days of the certification, the person performing the certification shall return the civil union certificate to the office of the town clerk from which the license was issued. The town clerk shall retain and file the original according to sections 5007 and 5008 of this title.

(d) A town clerk who knowingly issues a civil union license upon application of a person residing in another town in the state, or a county clerk who knowingly issues a civil union license upon application of a person other than as provided in section 5005 of this title, or a clerk who issues such a license without first requiring the applicant to fill out, sign and make oath to the declaration contained therein as provided in section 5160 of this title, shall be fined not more than $50.00 nor less than $20.00.

(e) A person making application to a clerk for a civil union license who makes a material misrepresentation in the declaration of intention shall be deemed guilty of perjury.

(f) A town clerk shall provide a person who applies for a civil union license with information prepared by the secretary of state that advises such person of the benefits, protections and responsibilities of a civil union and that Vermont residency may be required for dissolution of a civil union in Vermont. (Added 1999, No. 91 (Adj. Sess.), § 5.)

### § 5161. Issuance of license

(a) A town clerk shall issue a civil union license to all applicants who have complied with the provisions of section 5160 of this title, and who are otherwise qualified under the laws of the state to apply for a civil union license.

(b) An assistant town clerk may perform the duties of a town clerk under this chapter. (Added 1999, No. 91 (Adj. Sess.), § 5.)

### § 5162. Proof of legal qualifications of parties to a civil union; penalty

(a) Before issuing a civil union license to an applicant, the town clerk shall be confident, through presentation of affidavits or other proof, that each party to the intended civil union meets the criteria set forth to enter into a civil union.

(b) Affidavits shall be in a form prescribed by the board, and shall be attached to and filed with the civil union certificate in the office of the clerk of the town wherein the license was issued.

(c) A clerk who fails to comply with the provisions of this section, or who issues a civil union license with knowledge that either or both of the parties to a civil union have failed to comply with the requirements of the laws of this state, or a person who, having authority and having such knowledge, certifies such a civil union, shall be fined not more than $100.00. (Added 1999, No. 91 (Adj. Sess.), § 5.)

### § 5163. Restrictions as to minors and incompetent persons

(a) A clerk shall not issue a civil union license when either party to the intended civil union is:
1. under 18 years of age;
2. non compos mentis;
3. under guardianship, without the written consent of such guardian.

(b) A clerk who knowingly violates subsection (a) of this section shall be fined not more than $20.00. A person who aids in procuring a civil union license by falsely pretending to be the guardian having authority to give consent to the civil union shall be fined not more than $500.00. (Added 1999, No. 91 (Adj. Sess.), § 5.)

### § 5164. Persons authorized to certify civil unions

Civil unions may be certified by a supreme court justice, a superior court judge, a district judge, a judge of probate, an assistant judge, a justice of the peace or by a member of the clergy residing in this state and ordained or licensed, or otherwise regularly authorized by the published laws or discipline of the general conference, convention or other authority of his or her faith or denomination or by such a clergy person residing in an adjoining state or country, whose parish, church, temple, mosque or other religious organization lies wholly or in part in

*(cont.)*

**FIGURE 3.9**
*(continued)*

**CYBER TRIP**

To learn more about Vermont's civil unions, visit www. sec.state.vt.us/ otherprg/civilunions/ civilunions. html#What% 20are%20the% 20legal% 20consequences% 20of%20a%20civil% 20union.

**FIGURE 3.9**
*(concluded)*

> this state, or by a member of the clergy residing in some other state of the United States or in the Dominion of Canada, provided he or she has first secured from the probate court of the district within which the civil union is to be certified, a special authorization, authorizing him or her to certify the civil union if such probate judge determines that the circumstances make the special authorization desirable. Civil unions among the Friends or Quakers, the Christadelphian Ecclesia and the Baha'i Faith may be certified in the manner used in such societies. (Added 1999, No. 91 (Adj. Sess.), § 5.)

**CYBER TRIP**

To learn more about domestic partnerships in California, visit www.sos.ca.gov/dpregistry/dp_faqs.htm.

## DOMESTIC PARTNERSHIPS

A domestic partnership is a means for same-sex couples, and heterosexual couples in some states, to live together without entering into marriage or a civil union. Some states have passed laws that grant domestic partners certain rights normally associated with married couples, including inheritance rights to the partner's estate, rights to file jointly on insurance forms, hospital visitation rights, and rights relating to the deceased partner if there is no will. California, Hawaii, Maine, Oregon, Washington, and the District of Columbia have passed legislation relating to domestic partnerships, although the statutes vary as to what rights are granted and who can enter into domestic partnerships. States allow for the couples to file a declaration of domestic partnership and are provided a copy of a certificate of registration. For example, in California the parties may file the Declaration of Domestic Partnership with the secretary of state. As is the case with other areas of family law, the specifics of what rights are granted vary by jurisdiction. Figure 3.10 contains California's Declaration of Domestic Partnership form.

## COHABITATION

The word *cohabitation* in its most literal meaning is the act of living together, but here it will be used specifically to describe couples living together instead of getting married. Cohabitation is now a commonly used alternative to traditional marriage that many people are considering. In fact, its popularity is one of the reasons that, for the first time in history, married couples are now a minority of households in the United States according to census figures. Published reports indicate that 4.9 million unmarried men and women cohabitate, as compared to 500,000 in 1970. This change reflects not only a shift in the makeup of households; it also puts pressure on the legal system to adjust to these changes.

Traditionally the law has addressed issues relating to married couples. Statutes set out the legal requirements to create and dissolve a marriage. Statutes set out rights and liabilities of each spouse when the couple divorced, such as property distribution and payment of alimony. They also set out procedures to decide child custody and child support issues.

Initially these statutes did not apply to unmarried couples. The law has been changing to reflect the increased number of unmarried couples, especially as they relate to child custody and child support. Often this is accomplished by applying things like contract law to determine the rights of nonmarried parties when they decide to separate.

**Cohabitation agreements** are one way that couples can resolve separation issues ahead of time. Much like a **prenuptial agreement**, a cohabitation agreement is a contract entered into by the couple that sets out the specifics of their living arrangement and what will happen in the event they separate. Cohabitation and prenuptial agreements are discussed in detail in Chapter 2.

**cohabitation agreements**
A contract setting forth the rights of two people who live together without the benefit of marriage.

**prenuptial agreement**
An agreement made by parties before marriage that controls certain aspects of the relationship, such as management and ownership of property.

## State of California
### Secretary of State

**FILE NO:** _____

This Space For Filing Use Only

## DECLARATION OF DOMESTIC PARTNERSHIP
(Please read instructions on reverse side before completing form.)

We the undersigned, do declare that we meet the requirements of
Family Code section 297, as follows:

- Both persons have a common residence.
- Neither person is married to someone else or is a member of another domestic partnership with someone else that has not been terminated, dissolved, or adjudged a nullity.
- Both persons are not related by blood in a way that would prevent them from being married to each other in this state.
- Both persons are at least 18 years of age.
- Both persons are members of the same sex, **OR**
  One or both of the persons of opposite sex are over the age of 62 and meet the eligibility criteria under Title II of the Social Security Act as defined in 42 U.S.C. section 402(a) for old-age insurance benefits or Title XVI of the Social Security Act as defined in 42 U.S.C. section 1381 for aged individuals.
- Both persons are capable of consenting to the domestic partnership.
- Both persons consent to the jurisdiction of the Superior Courts of California for the purpose of a proceeding to obtain a judgment of dissolution or nullity of the domestic partnership or for legal separation of partners in the domestic partnership, or for any other proceeding related to the partners' rights and obligations, even if one or both partners ceases to be a resident of, or to maintain a domicile in, this state.

The representations are true and correct, and contain no material omissions of fact to the best of our knowledge and belief.

| | | | |
|---|---|---|---|
| Signature | (Last) | (First) | (Middle) |
| Signature | (Last) | (First) | (Middle) |
| Mailing Address | City | State | Zip Code |

E-Mail Address(es) (optional)

**NOTARIZATION IS REQUIRED**
State of California
County of _____

On _____, before me, _____ Notary Public, personally
appeared _____
personally known to me (or proved to me on the basis of satisfactory evidence) to be the person(s) whose name(s) is/are subscribed to the within instrument and acknowledged to me that he/she/they executed the same in his/her/their authorized capacity(ies), and that by his/her/their signature(s) on the instrument the person(s), or the entity upon behalf of which the person(s) acted, executed the instrument.
WITNESS my hand and official seal.

Signature of Notary Public

[PLACE NOTARY PUBLIC SEAL HERE]

SEC/STATE NP/SF DP-1 (REV 01/2007)

**FIGURE 3.10** **California Declaration of Domestic Partnership**

*Source:* Retrieved from www.sos.ca.gov/dpregistry/forms/sf-dp1.pdf.

## Summary

The word marriage is one that laypeople often think they understand. However, a review of the material covered in this chapter makes it clear that legal professionals, including paralegals, must be aware of the many different ways that this term is used in the law.

Even more important, the whole concept of marriage is under extreme political and social examination. State governments have been divided on their approach to these changes, especially the issues relating to same-sex couples. Some states have provided for civil unions and domestic partnerships as an alternative to marriage for same-sex couples. In two states, Massachusetts and New Jersey, state courts have held that the state statutes limiting marriage to a man and a woman violate the state constitution.

To further complicate this area of family law, some marriages have defects that may impact their validity. Examples include putative marriage and sham marriages.

## Key Terms

Ceremonial marriage aka traditional
  marriage
Cohabitation agreement
Common law marriage
Covenant marriage
Marriage
No fault divorce

Premarital preparation course
Prenuptial agreement
Proxy marriage
Putative marriage
Same-sex marriage
Sham marriage
Solemnization

## Review Questions

1. Discuss how marriage has evolved over the centuries?
2. What is the key difference between a prenuptial agreement and a cohabitation agreement?
3. What steps have states taken to try to reduce the number of divorces?
4. What is a covenant marriage and what makes it distinctive?
5. List the people who are commonly allowed to solemnize a marriage.
6. Why is the Full Faith and Credit Clause of the U.S Constitution important in the study of family law?
7. What societal changes have caused the legal system to make changes in the laws relating to marriage and cohabitation?
8. How do traditional/ceremonial marriages and common law marriages differ?
9. List some of the more common requirements relating to the capacity to marry.
10. What are marriage evasion statutes and why are they used?

## Exercises

1. Review the facts set out in the Client Interview. What steps should Terri and Steve take to protect their rights? What problems might they face if their cohabitation is not, as they now think, a step toward marriage, but instead ends with them moving out and going their own ways? Would they need to be concerned about their living arrangement being considered a common law marriage? How would your answer differ if they were married and got divorced?
2. Sam and Donna wanted to get married. Sam was 18 but Donna is only 17. Could they get married under the laws of your state? Would your answer be different if: Donna was pregnant? Her parents gave their consent?

3. Catherine and Don, realizing they could not get married in their home state because they were both too young, decided to go to a nearby state that allowed people their age to marry. Would Catherine and Don's home state have to recognize their marriage?

4. Jack and Steven live in Missouri, a state that does not allow same-sex marriage. They decide to go to Massachusetts to get married. Research the laws of your state and of Massachusetts. Based on your findings, would Jack and Steven be able to get legally married in Massachusetts? Assuming that they were able to do so, would Missouri be required to recognize the marriage?

5. Wendy and Larry lived together for many years. They opened a joint checking account and owned their home in both their names. While many people assumed they were married, neither Wendy nor Larry thought of themselves as being married. They viewed themselves as just two people in love who lived together. If you live in a state that recognizes common law marriage, research your state's statutory and case law to determine if they would meet the requirements for creating a common law marriage. If your state does not recognize common law marriages, select a state that does, research the statutory and case law of that state and determine if Wendy and Larry's relationship would meet the requirements to create a common law marriage.

## REAL WORLD DISCUSSION TOPICS

Owen and Peggy were first cousins and were married on August 30 in Colorado, in accordance with the laws of that state. At the time of the marriage, Owen was a resident of Kansas and Peggy was a resident of Oklahoma. They lived as a couple in Kansas after the marriage. They later experienced marital difficulties and in contemplation of divorce, they entered into a separation and property settlement agreement. Owen subsequently executed a will that omitted any mention of Peggy, and in April 1979, he filed a petition for divorce from her. Owen died before the completion of the divorce process. Peggy filled a petition to take one-half of his estate as his surviving spouse.

Would the marriage entered into in Colorado be valid in Kansas, even though a marriage between first cousins would be invalid if entered into in Kansas? Would your answer change if Kansas had a marriage evasion statute and it could be shown that Owen and Peggy went to Colorado to avoid the limitation to their marriage imposed by the laws of Kansas? How would the courts of your state deal with a situation like that of Owen and Peggy?

## PORTFOLIO ASSIGNMENT

Locate the statute of your state that sets out the requirements to enter into a valid marriage and make a list of them. Write a summary of how they compare to the requirements of a valid marriage in the state of Florida as set out in this chapter.

# Chapter 4

# Divorce, Dissolution, and Annulment

## CHAPTER OBJECTIVES

**After reading this chapter and completing the assignments, you should be able to:**

- Distinguish between annulment, dissolution, and divorce.

- Understand the reasons a marriage may be annulled.

- Understand the consequences of an annulment.

- Be able to describe the differences between a no fault divorce and a fault divorce.

- Be able to discuss the most common grounds required to get a fault divorce and some of the defenses that can be raised.

- Understand the requirements to obtain a no fault divorce.

- Understand the distinction between a divorce and dissolution of marriage.

The reality of today's society is that married couples are seeking to terminate marriages by divorce or dissolution in large numbers. This chapter introduces the paralegal student to some of the basic concepts associated with divorce, dissolution, and the less common annulment proceeding.

## CLIENT INTERVIEW

Lisa Bailey was a little confused over her situation and decided it would be best to visit her attorney to help her understand her options at this point. Although the laws of her state require that a person be 18 to get married, she was only 16 when she married Paul. Her relationship with him had deteriorated during their one year of marriage. She wondered what her options were to end the marriage at this point, if she decided to do so.

## WHY THIS CHAPTER IS IMPORTANT TO THE PARALEGAL

The paralegal is a key player in the family law firm team when it comes to divorces, which comprises a large amount of the family law firm's caseload. The paralegal is often called upon to handle duties that include interviewing the client, gathering information about the case, doing legal research, and helping prepare the necessary documents associated with the divorce process.

Chapter 4 provides paralegal students with a basic understanding of the most fundamental concepts associated with the family law practice—divorce as well as dissolution of marriage and annulment. Understanding these legal concepts is critical to paralegals performing their duties in the family law firm.

## WHAT ARE THE DIFFERENCES BETWEEN A DIVORCE AND AN ANNULMENT?

If you asked most people the difference between divorce and annulment, you would probably get a blank stare. Everyone knows a lot about divorces, but few really understand the distinction between the divorce and annulment. The distinction is, however, an important one in the study of family law.

The key difference between the two is simple. Divorce is the legal dissolution of a valid marriage. It returns the couple to the status of single persons. Annulment is the declaration that no valid marriage was entered into by the parties.

The impact each has on the people involved is more complicated, as will be demonstrated in this chapter.

## VOID VERSUS VOIDABLE

As was discussed in Chapter 3, it is relatively simple to comply with the statutory requirements for entering into a valid marriage. Despite this fact, not all marriages are properly entered into. As a result, a marriage that does not conform to the laws of the state where it was entered into or that was not voluntarily entered into may be **void** or **voidable**. In those cases, couples may have the option of seeking an annulment rather than divorce if they wish to end their marriage.

The distinction between void and voidable is important in other areas of the law, such as contract law, but it is critical in the discussion of annulment.

The law treats a void marriage as if it never existed. The reasons a marriage may be void vary by state, but examples include incestuous marriages, same-sex marriages, and bigamous marriages. Since the law treats void marriages as if they had never existed, theoretically no legal proceeding is required to end the marriage. Couples may still go through the annulment process to resolve issues associated with their relationship, such as property distribution.

A voidable marriage is one that can be nullified if one or both of the parties decide to end the marriage. Unlike a void marriage, a voidable marriage is presumed to be valid until such time as the parties decide to end it by seeking an annulment. Reasons a marriage may be voidable include age, duress, **fraud**, mental capacity, and **coercion**.

## ANNULMENTS

As noted previously, an annulment is a legal process that declares that no valid marriage ever existed. This should not be confused with a church annulment, sometimes referred to as a declaration of nullity, which is a separate procedure performed

**void**
A transaction that is impossible to be enforced because it is invalid.

**voidable**
Having the possibility of avoidance of performance at the option of the incapacitated party.

**fraud**
A knowing and intentional misstatement of the truth in order to induce a desired action from another person.

**coercion**
Compelling someone to do an act through physical force or threat of physical force.

pursuant to the rules of the church and has no bearing on the legal status of the married couple.

Annulments are sought to have a marriage nullified. It is a procedure that is sought based on the marriage being void or voidable. This is true even though, as previously noted, in cases involving a void marriage it is not technically required since a void marriage never existed.

Annulments are dealt with in the same manner as dissolution of marriage cases and are handled by the courts that have jurisdiction over dissolution of marriage cases.

Family law textbooks have usually included extensive discussions of annulments and the grounds for getting an annulment. This is probably true for a number of reasons. Annulments present a number of interesting legal concepts, such as the difference between void and voidable. These concepts are used in other areas of the law and their discussion reinforces the point that all areas of the law are interrelated.

Another reason that family law textbooks devote a lot of space to annulments is that they were often used by married couples who might not be able to get a divorce under older, stricter fault divorce laws. The number and frequency of annulments has undoubtedly decreased as states have enacted no fault divorce laws that make a divorce easier and cheaper to obtain, although in some states they are still commonly used.

In any case, the legal concept of annulments is an important one for the paralegal student to understand.

## Grounds for an Annulment

As noted in the earlier discussion of the distinction between void and voidable, the law recognizes a number of factors to be considered by a court when dealing with a request to have a marriage annulled. These include age, fraud, duress, coercion, relationship/**incest**, capacity, impotence, and **bigamy**.

**incest**
Marriage/sexual relations between closely related relatives or family members.

**bigamy**
One spouse knowingly enters a second marriage while the first remains valid.

Void marriages violate some overriding public policy as set out in the applicable state statute. These include relationship/incest and bigamy. Voidable marriages are those a spouse can void if he or she decides to do so upon learning of the deficiency in the marriage. Reasons for a marriage to be considered voidable include being under the age as set out by statute at the time of the marriage, a spouse was induced to marriage by fraud or duress on the part of the other spouse, the parties lacked mental capacity due to things like intoxication, or it is discovered that one of the parties is impotent.

The reasons that a marriage may be declared voidable share one common element. They each involve a defect in the marriage that may be injurious to one of the people involved. That person has the right to decide if it is something he or she can accept and live with or if it is something that is a deal breaker and a basis to end the marriage.

Let's use incompetence as an example. Suppose a man and a woman meet each other in a bar in Las Vegas. They have a good time, but drink a little too much that evening. They decided that it would be a great idea to get married. What happens when they sober up and realize what has happened the night before? In this case, they could agree to stay married or, assuming that both of them lacked the mental capacity to know what the consequences of their actions were, either party could decide to end the marriage by annulment.

That is not to say that either party gets to decide to void a voidable marriage. In some cases it is only the innocent person who can seek an annulment. An example of this is a marriage obtained by use of fraud. Perhaps the husband lied about wanting to have children and the wife wanted children. In fact, it was one of the main reasons she married him. In that case, only the wife would be able to seek an annulment. She was the person who was injured by the deception, and the law would not allow the husband to annul the marriage because he created the situation.

It is important to note that the wife would not have an unlimited time to seek an annulment because of the husband's fraud. Courts generally allow deceived parties a reasonable amount of time to seek legal remedies such as an annulment. So the wife in our example would only have a reasonable period of time to protect her rights once she becomes aware of the fact the husband does not want to have children.

The *Meagher v. Maleki* case, which is set out in the Case in Point, presents an interesting discussion of the law relating to fraud and marriage.

Figure 4.1 provides an example of some of the more common reasons why an annulment might be sought. Figure 4.2 sets out the North Dakota annulment statute that contains the state's grounds for annulment.

## Consequences of an Annulment

Having a marriage annulled often creates more questions than answers. For example, what if there are children of the marriage? What happens to the property acquired during the marriage? Can either person get alimony? What about child support?

These questions grow out of the very reason people seek annulment; that is, the legal concept that the marriage is declared to have never existed. That declaration must be reconciled with the reality of things such as the parties having children. The modern trend is to recognize the children of a marriage that is annulled as being legitimate and the court handling the annulment will also deal with questions such as child custody, visitation, and support. The procedure used to accomplish these things does vary by state.

**FIGURE 4.1**
**Examples of Grounds for Annulment**

| Reason for Annulment | Void or Voidable | Example |
|---|---|---|
| Age | Voidable | One or both parties of the marriage were not of legal age to enter into a valid marriage. |
| Fraud | Voidable | One party deceived the other *about* something critical to that party's deciding to marry. An example is one party stating he/she wants children but does not. |
| Duress | Voidable | One party uses actual threats of harm to induce the other to marry. |
| Relationship/incest | Void | States set out limitations on how closely a person can be married to the other party. For example, a parent cannot marry his/her child. |
| Capacity | Voidable | One or both parties are too intoxicated at the time of their marriage to have the legal capacity to consent to the marriage. |
| Impotence | Voidable | One party to the marriage was permanently impotent at the time of the marriage. |
| Bigamy | Void | One party is already legally married at the time of entering into a new marriage. |

**FIGURE 4.2**

2005 North Dakota
Annulment of
Marriage Statute

**CHAPTER 14-04**

**ANNULMENT OF MARRIAGE**

**14-04-01. Grounds for annulling marriage.** A marriage may be annulled by an action in the district court to obtain a decree of nullity for any of the following causes existing at the time of the marriage:

1. That the party in whose behalf it is sought to have the marriage annulled was under the age of legal consent, as defined in section 14-03-02, or that such party was of such age as to require the consent of the party's parents or guardian and such marriage was contracted without such consent, unless, after attaining legal age, such party freely cohabited with the other as husband or wife.
2. That the former husband or wife of either party was living, and the marriage with such former husband or wife was then in force.
3. That either party was of unsound mind, unless such party, after coming to reason, freely cohabited with the other as husband or wife.
4. That the consent of either party was obtained by fraud, unless such party afterwards, with full knowledge of the facts constituting the fraud, freely cohabited with the other as husband or wife.
5. That the consent of either party was obtained by force, unless such party afterwards freely cohabited with the other as husband or wife.
6. That either party was at the time of the marriage physically incapable of entering into the marriage state, and such incapacity continues and appears to be incurable.
7. That the marriage was incestuous.

Some state statutes also allow for property settlement and, in some instances, alimony. Others may take a more equitable approach in deciding the distribution of the property of the annulled marriage.

Annulments may also have an impact on the inheritance rights of the spouses once the annulment is granted. For example, it is not uncommon for a person to have a will that leaves everything to his or her spouse. A client would need to be advised to change his or her will when getting an annulment if there was such a will.

## Defenses to Annulment

**defense**
Legally sufficient reason to excuse the complained-of behavior.

In some cases an annulment may not be granted by a court because of a **defense** raised by one of the parties. One of the most common examples is when the innocent party is aware of the problem but continues to stay in the marriage. This is true of impediments such as fraud, duress, age (once the person has reached legal age to marry), refusal to have sex/have children, impotence, and competency (if the party continues to stay in marriage after regaining competency).

### RESEARCH THIS

The laws relating to annulment vary greatly from state to state. Research the case and statutory laws of your state relating to annulment. Your search should include the grounds on which an annulment may be granted, the differences between void and voidable marriages, the consequences of annulment, and what defenses are available to an annulment action. Write a summary of your findings.

In the Court of Appeal of the State of California
First Appellate District
Division Two
*Meagher v. Maleki*
A106079
Filed 7/18/05

\*\*\*

## FACTS AND PROCEDURAL BACKGROUND

Appellant Ann Marie Meagher is a physician licensed as a psychiatrist. Respondent Malekpour Maleki is a real estate broker and investor, and has also been an importer and wholesaler of jewelry and Persian rugs. Meagher and Maleki first met socially in October 1997. At the time, Meagher was partially disabled and nearing retirement age, but was still working part time for the City and County of San Francisco. Maleki was in his late sixties and was living on the income from some real property he owned. Meagher believed Maleki to be a well-educated millionaire with expertise in real estate and finance.

Meagher and Maleki developed a romantic relationship, and became engaged in February 1998. They also entered into a business relationship, in the course of which Meagher bought three residential properties as an investment. Meagher bought the first property (in San Francisco) through Maleki as broker, and the other two (in Daly City and Concord) directly from him. With respect to the properties that Meagher bought directly from Maleki, he promised her that when they were sold, he would reimburse her for their purchase price. Meagher thought that he had done so, but realized later that the reimbursement had not been complete.

\*\*\*

On August 28, 1999, after entering into the agreements for the business venture, Meagher and Maleki married. At the time of the marriage, the parties were already living together in Meagher's home in Tiburon. Meagher had between $1 million and $1.5 million in assets in addition to the substantial equity in her expensive home. For some time after the marriage, Meagher continued to work part time, and Maleki managed the parties' business venture. During this period, Meagher drew money out of her retirement savings in order to fund additional real estate investments made by the business venture.

Meagher continued to believe that Maleki was wealthy until sometime in February 2002, when Maleki told Meagher that the couple did not have enough money to cover either their living expenses or their business expenses, which included a large tax bill. At that point, Meagher began to doubt what Maleki had been telling her about his financial situation and about how he was running their business venture. She revoked a power of attorney she had given him, and demanded more information about the business venture. At that point, Maleki became hostile and began talking about getting a divorce. Meagher still wanted to make the marriage work, however, because she did not want a divorce for religious reasons.

In mid-April 2002, however, Maleki told Meagher that he would divorce her if she did not put all her assets, including her home and pension, into joint tenancy and give him total control. At that point, Meagher began to suspect that Maleki had married her just for her money. She asked Maleki to buy out her share of the business venture, as he had always represented to her he had the means to do, but he told her that he could not and did not want to do so.

The parties separated in April or May 2002, and on May 6, 2002, Meagher filed a petition for dissolution of the marriage.

\*\*\*

## DISCUSSION

On this appeal, Maleki does not challenge the trial court's factual findings that he fraudulently misrepresented his financial circumstances to Meagher prior to the marriage, and that he deceived her in connection with the business venture. He argues, however, that, as a matter of law, a prospective spouse's fraud regarding financial matters is not a proper basis upon which to order an annulment.

The longstanding general rule in California is that "a marriage may only be annulled for fraud if the fraud relates to a matter which the state deems vital to the marriage relationship. [Citations.]" (*Bruce v. Bruce* (1945) 71 Cal.App.2d 641, 643.) As one court explained, "because of its peculiar position as a silent but active party in annulment proceedings[,] the state is particularly interested in seeing that no marriage is declared void as the result of fraud unless the evidence in support thereof is both clear and convincing. Thus[,] . . . [because] '[t]he state has a rightful and legitimate concern with the marital status of the parties[,] . . . the fraud relied upon to secure a termination of the existing status must be such fraud as directly affects the marriage relationship and *not merely such fraud as would be sufficient to rescind an ordinary civil contract.*' [Citations.]" (*Williams v. Williams* (1960) 178 Cal.App.2d 522, 525, italics added [affirming denial of annulment based on trial court's factual findings either that wife did not misrepresent that she was widowed rather than divorced, or that husband did not rely on her representation in deciding to marry her].)

The most recent published opinion upholding an annulment on the basis of fraud dates from 1987, and involves the paradigm example of a spouse who "harbors a secret intention at the time of the marriage not to engage in sexual relations with [the other spouse]. [Citations.]" (*In re Marriage of Liu* (1987) 197 Cal. App.3d 143, 156; accord, e.g., *Handley v. Handley* (1960) 179 Cal.App.2d 742, 746; *Millar v. Millar* (1917) 175 Cal. 797.) Similarly, "the secret intention of a woman concealed from her husband at the time of marriage never to live with him in any home provided by him would be a fraud going to the very essence of the marriage relation and of such a vital character as to constitute a ground for annulment." (*Bruce v. Bruce, supra,* 71 Cal.App.2d at p. 643.) Annulment has also been held justified based on a wife's concealment that at the time of marriage she was pregnant by a man other than her husband (*Hardesty v. Hardesty* (1924) 193 Cal. 330; *Baker v. Baker* (1859) 13 Cal. 87), or on a party's concealment of his or her sterility (*Vileta v. Vileta* (1942) 53 Cal. App.2d 794) or intent to continue in an intimate relationship with a third person (*Schaub v. Schaub* (1945) 71 Cal.App.2d 467).

As these cases illustrate, annulments on the basis of fraud are generally granted only in cases where the fraud related in some way to the sexual or procreative aspects of marriage. The only California case of which we are aware that granted an annulment on a factual basis not directly involving sex or procreation is *Douglass v. Douglass* (1957) 148 Cal.App.2d 867 (*Douglass*). In *Douglass,* the Court of Appeal reversed a judgment denying an annulment to a woman whose husband, prior to their marriage, had "falsely and fraudulently represented to her that he was an honest, law abiding, respectable and honorable man" (*id.* at p. 868), and that he had only one child from a prior marriage, who was " 'well provided for.' " (*Ibid.*) In fact, the husband had been convicted of grand theft only a few years earlier and was still on parole, and three months after the marriage he was arrested for parole violation due to his failure to support his two children from his prior marriage.

The *Douglass* court acknowledged that the test for annulment based on fraud is "whether the false representations or concealment were such as to defeat the essential purpose of the injured spouse inherent in the contracting of a marriage." (*Douglass, supra,* 148 Cal.App.2d at pp. 868–869.) The opinion in *Douglass* went on to state in rather general terms that because "the fraud of the [husband] in concealing his criminal record and true character was a deceit so gross and cruel as to prove him to [the wife] to be a man unworthy of trust," refusing her request for an annulment would be "unjust and intolerable." (*Id.* at p. 870.) The facts of *Douglass* make clear, however, that the court did not grant an annulment based merely on the husband's general untrustworthiness. In holding the wife entitled to an annulment, the court relied in part on the fact that she already had two children from a former marriage, and that because of this, the "essentials of the marital relationship," from the wife's perspective, necessarily included having "husband of honorable character whom she could respect and trust, . . . and who would be a suitable stepfather for her children." (*Id.* at pp. 869–870.) When the wife learned the truth about the husband's failure to provide for his own children, her "hopes were shattered and her purposes defeated." (*Id.* at p. 870.) Thus, even in *Douglass,* the fraud that the court found to be sufficient grounds for annulment had some nexus with the child-rearing aspect of marriage.

In the absence of fraud involving the party's intentions or abilities with respect to the sexual or procreative aspect of marriage, the longstanding rule is that neither party "may question the validity of the marriage upon the ground of reliance upon the express or implied representations of the other with respect to such matters as character, habits, chastity, *business or social standing, financial worth or prospects,* or matters of similar nature." (*Schaub v. Schaub, supra,* 71 Cal.App.2d at p. 476, italics added.) In *Marshall v. Marshall, supra,* 212 Cal. 736,

740, for example, the court expressly held that the trial court properly denied relief to a wife who sought an annulment on the basis of her husband's "fraudulent representation as to his wealth and ability to support and maintain" her, when in fact he was "impecunious" and subject to "harassment by creditors." (*Id.* at pp. 737–738; accord, *Mayer v. Mayer* (1929) 207 Cal. 685, 694–695 [shoe salesman's misrepresentation that he owned shoe store not sufficient grounds for annulment].)

More recent case law has not changed this longstanding rule. In 1993, for example, the Fourth District reversed a judgment granting an annulment to a wife who discovered after the marriage that her husband had concealed the facts that he had a severe drinking problem for which he declined to seek help, and that he did not intend to work for a living. Even though the wife also alleged that the couple's "sex life after marriage was unsatisfactory," the court still found that the fraud did not "go to the *very essence* of the marital relation" and therefore was not sufficient as a basis for an annulment. (*In re Marriage of Johnston* (1993) 18 Cal.App.4th 499, 500–502, italics in original.)

In the present case, Meagher does not contend that there is any evidence that Maleki lied to her about his marital history, or that he concealed an intention not to have sexual relations with her, not to live with her after the marriage, or not to discontinue an intimate relationship with a third party. On the contrary, the parties began living together even before their marriage and continued to do so for well over two years thereafter, and Meagher cites to no evidence in the record that she ever expressed any dissatisfaction with the intimate aspects of their relationship. Instead, she argues that the financial fraud at issue in this case is "at least as contrary to the essence of marriage" as the types of fraud that have been held sufficient to justify annulment. She cites no authority, however, either in California or elsewhere, for the proposition that annulment can be granted based on fraud or misrepresentation of a purely financial nature. As already noted, the cases are entirely to the contrary. Accordingly, we agree with Maleki that the fraud established in this case, as a matter of law, was not of the type that constitutes an adequate basis for granting an annulment.

Because we reverse the trial court's decision on this basis, we need not and do not address Maleki's alternative arguments that Meagher failed to establish the elements of her fraud claim. We leave it to possible future trial court proceedings to determine whether Meagher is entitled to rescission of the agreements underlying the business venture on the ground of fraud, and if so, what remedies are appropriate (*see generally, e.g., Runyan v. Pacific Air Industries, Inc.* (1970) 2 Cal.3d 304, 316 [purpose of rescission is to restore both parties to their former position as far as possible and to bring about substantial justice by adjusting equities between parties]), including what effect rescission may have on the characterization of the assets of the business venture as separate or community property for dissolution purposes.

## DISPOSITION

The judgment is reversed, and the case is remanded to the trial court for further proceedings. In the interests of justice, the parties shall each bear their own costs on appeal.
RUVOLO, J.

**Source:** Retrieved from www.courtinfo.ca.gov/opinions/archive/ A106079.DOC

# DIVORCE

Any discussion of divorce must examine the types of divorce that may be used to end a marriage. Two types of divorce that are essential to an understanding of this topic are Fault Divorce and No Fault Divorce.

### Divorce: Fault

Historically, states required a spouse to show grounds, in other words a legally recognized reason, to allow the marriage to be ended by divorce. Although states have moved away from the need to show fault, as noted in the upcoming discussion of no fault divorces, some still require such a showing in certain circumstances.

The most common statutory grounds for establishing fault include:

- Abandonment/desertion. Abandonment/desertion occurs when one spouse voluntarily, without justification, and without consent, or wrongful act of the other spouse, leaves that spouse for the period specified by state law. In situations where one spouse must leave because of the misconduct of the other, states apply the legal concept of constructive desertion. Constructive desertion allows the spouse who left to file for divorce based on desertion.

- Adultery. Adultery occurs when a married person has voluntary sexual activity with someone other than his or her spouse. To constitute a ground for divorce, the act must occur before the filing for divorce. Note the use of the word *activity*. Acts other than actual sexual intercourse, such as oral sex, may constitute the sufficient act to constitute adultery, unless otherwise provided by statute.

- Cruelty/abuse. Treatment by one spouse of the other that makes living together intolerable can constitute a ground for divorce. The mistreatment can be by physical violence or conduct that is mentally or physically injurious. The difficulty is that there is no simple judicial or statutory rule that states what is and is not cruelty or abuse. Instead courts use a case-by-case method to determine if the facts and circumstances surrounding a particular case constitute cruelty/abuse. Courts have great leeway in determining if an act or a combination of acts crosses the line and satisfies the statutory requirements for granting a divorce based on this ground. Statutes themselves vary on the terminology used to describe cruelty/abuse, including extreme cruelty, cruel and inhuman treatment, and cruel and repeated cruelty.

- Drug/alcohol abuse. Habitual illegal drug or alcohol abuse is a ground for divorce in some states, while other statutes require that the use of drugs/alcohol contributed to the failure of the marriage.

- Duress. Statutes vary on whether duress is a ground for divorce. Some allow it if physical force or threats of physical force caused the person to enter into a marriage he or she would not otherwise have entered into.

- Fraud. Fraud can be a basis for divorce if one party fraudulently induced the other to enter into marriage if the fact in question related to the validity of the marriage. Examples include undisclosed sexual impotence and that the woman was pregnant by another man at the time of marriage.

- Imprisonment. If specified by statute, imprisonment of one spouse for the time period specified by statute can be a ground for divorce.

- Insanity. Insanity is a ground for divorce in a number of states. Many require that the spouse who has been adjudicated insane must be institutionalized for a specific period of time before filing for divorce.

- Nonsupport. The voluntary failure to provide for the support of a spouse can be a basis for a divorce in some states if the failure continues for the statutorily prescribed time.

**CASE BRIEF ASSIGNMENT**

Read and brief the *Meagher v. Maleki,* 131 Cal.App.4th 1, 31 Cal.Rptr.3d 663 (Cal. App. 2005) case. (See Appendix A for information on how to brief cases.)

**RESEARCH THIS**

If your state allows for fault divorces, research the statutory and case law relating to the grounds for divorce and write a brief summary of your findings.

If your state does not allow for fault divorces, select a state that does and research the statutory and case law relating to the grounds for divorce and write a brief summary of your findings.

## Divorce: No Fault

Divorce laws underwent major changes in the 1970s. The reasons were many, but as a general statement, society began to feel that husbands and wives should have an easier way to divorce if they both agreed that the marriage was irretrievably broken.

As a result of the recognized problems associated with fault divorces, many states began to change their laws. This eliminated a couple's need to falsely allege one of the recognized grounds for divorce or, in some cases, to actually commit the required act in order to get a divorce. States replaced the more traditional statutes with ones that provided a simple and relatively inexpensive process to end a marriage. This has continued to the point that all states allow some form of a no fault divorce.

As the name implies, no fault laws only require an allegation that the marriage is irretrievably broken or that irreconcilable differences exist. There is no need to allege fault on the part of the other spouse. In some states, such as Florida, only one of the spouses needs to live in the state for a period of six months before filing for divorce and then must merely allege that the marriage is irretrievably broken. If the other spouse does not contest this allegation, the only proof that is required is that the spouse who filed the divorce has lived in the state for the preceding six months.

Other states still require that the spouse go through a waiting or separation period before the final divorce can be granted. These periods vary by state and may be months, a year, or more.

Figure 4.3 provides the state statutes that deal with grounds for divorce, including no fault divorces.

## Defenses to Divorce

The issue of defenses to a divorce also relates to whether the divorce is a fault or no fault divorce.

A number of defenses may be allowed in fault divorce cases. These include:

- **Condonation**, which is based on the same legal theory as discussed in defenses to annulment, can be used as a defense to divorce when a spouse has been aware of the ground for divorce but forgives those acts and continues in the marriage despite them.

- **Recrimination** is the defense that the person seeking the divorce was, in fact, himself or herself guilty of an act that would be grounds for divorce.

- **Connivance** occurs when one spouse allows or consents to the other committing the acts that are alleged as grounds for the divorce.

- **Collusion** is a defense based on the spouses agreeing that the act necessary to be a ground for divorce was committed, or at least appear that the act was committed.

**condonation**
Defense in divorce based on spouse's awareness of a ground for divorce but who expressly or impliedly forgives those acts.

**recrimination**
Defense in divorce based on the fact the person seeking the divorce was, in fact, him- or herself guilty of an act that would be grounds for divorce.

**connivance**
Defense in divorce action that is based on the fact that one spouse allowed or consented to the other committing the acts that are alleged as grounds for the divorce.

**collusion**
Illegally created agreement of the parties.

| | | | |
|---|---|---|---|
| Alabama | Ala. Code tit. 30 ch. 2.1, et seq. | Nevada | Nev. Rev. Stat. § 125.010 |
| Alaska | Alaska Stat. §§ 25.24.200, 25-24-050 | New Hampshire | N.H. Rev. Stat. Ann. ch. 458 |
| | | New Jersey | N.J. Rev. Stat. tit. 2A ch. 34-2 |
| Arizona | Ariz. Rev. Stat. Ann. tit. 25 ch. 312, 901, 903 | New Mexico | N.M. Stat. Ann. art. 4, §§ 40-4-1 et seq. |
| Arkansas | Ark Code Ann. tit. 9, ch. 12-301 | New York | N.e Y. Dom. Rel. *art. 10* |
| California | Cal. Family Law Code §2310 | North Carolina | N.C. Gen. Stat. §§ 50-5.1, 50.6 |
| Colorado | Colo. Rev. Stat. art. 10 § 14-10-106 | North Dakota | N.D. Cent. Code ch. 14-05-03 |
| Connecticut | Conn. Gen. Stat. tit. 46b, ch. 40 | Ohio | Ohio Rev. Code Ann. § 3105.01 |
| Delaware | Del. Code. Ann. tit.13, ch. 1505 | Oklahoma | Okla. Stat.tit. 43 § 101 |
| Florida | Fla. Stat. ch. 61.052 | Oregon | Or. Rev. Stat. §§ 107.025, 107.036, 107.015 |
| Georgia | Ga. Code Ann. §§ 19-5-3 | | |
| Hawaii | Haw. Rev. Stat. tit. Ch. 41 | Pennsylvania | Pa. Code tit. 23, § 3301 |
| Idaho | Idaho Code tit. 32 ch. 603, 610 | Rhode Island | R.I. Gen laws tit.15, ch. 15-5-2, et seq |
| Illinois | Ill Rev. Stat. ch.750 ch. 5, para. 401 | South Carolina | S.C. Code Ann. ch. 3, § 20-3-10 |
| Indiana | Ind. Code tit. 31 art. 15 ch. 2-3 | South Dakota | D.D. Codified Laws Ann. tit. 5, ch. 25-4-2, 25-4-17, 25-4-18 |
| Iowa | Iowa Code §§ 598.5, 598.17 | Tennessee | Tenn. Code Ann. §§ 36-4-101, 36-4-103 |
| Kansas | Kan. Stat. Ann. ch. 60, art.16 | | |
| Kentucky | Ky. Stat. Ann. ch. 403.140 | Texas | Tex. *Family* Code Ann. §§ 6.001-6.007 |
| Louisiana | La. Code Civ. Proc. Art. 103 | | |
| Maine | Me. Rev. Stat. Ann. tit. 19A, § 902 | Utah | Utah Code Ann. § 30-3-1 |
| Maryland | Md. *Family Law* Code Ann. §7-103 | Vermont | Vt. Stat. Ann, tit. 15, §§ 551, 555 |
| Massachusetts | Mass. Gen. L. tit. III ch. 208 | Virginia | Va. Code Ann. § 20-91 |
| Michigan | Mich. Comp. Laws ch. 552.6 | Washington | Wash. Rev. Code § 26.09.030 |
| Minnesota | Minn.Stat. §§518.06, 158.13 | | |
| Mississippi | Miss. Code Ann. § 93.5.1, et seq. | West Virginia | W. Va. Code §§ 48-5-202 and 48-5-209 |
| Missouri | Mo. Rev. Stat. §452.305 | Wisconsin | Wis. Stat. § 767.07 |
| Montana | Mont. Code Ann. tit. 40, ch. 4 | Wyoming | Wyo. Stat. §§ 20-2-104, 20-2-105 |
| Nebraska | Neb. Rev. Stat.ch. 42 §§ 361, 362 | District of Columbia | D.C. Code Ann. §§ 904, 905, 906 |

**FIGURE 4.3**  **State Statutes: Grounds for Divorce**

## ETHICS ALERT

The discussion relating to the defenses to a fault divorce brings up an important ethical issue a paralegal might face. Whether a paralegal is working on a fault divorce or a no fault divorce, certain things must be alleged and sometimes proven in court. It is important that the paralegal does not participate in any way to produce false evidence, including knowingly using false information as part of a defense in a divorce action. The law firm has a duty to zealously represent its clients, but the rules do not allow for the firm or its employees to be a party to such activities.

**CYBER TRIP**

Although the legal consequences of a divorce are easily established, the emotional impact of divorce is more complicated and has become a major discussion point in the law and society. There is a growing question about these consequences of divorce as they have become more common, especially as a divorce's effect on the children of the marriage becomes more visible. Use the Web sites set out in Appendix A to learn more about the social impact of divorces and how states are trying to address the social problems associated with divorce.

As the law has moved toward no fault divorces, these defenses, like the need to allege grounds for divorce such as adultery, cruelty/abuse, abandonment, imprisonment/insanity, and undisclosed sexual impotence in order to get a divorce, are not as frequently used.

Obviously, few defenses are available in no fault divorces. The reason for this is that one spouse merely need allege that the marriage is irretrievably broken or that irreconcilable differences exist between the spouses. States generally do not require that this allegation be proven, only stated as true by one of the spouses. Some states do allow the other spouse to contest the allegation that the marriage is irretrievably broken. If this allegation is contested, then the state statutes often grant the judge the power to require additional things to be accomplished before determining whether the marriage is irretrievably broken. For example, a statute may allow a judge to order that the parties undergo marital counseling.

In fact, the defenses just discussed have been specifically abolished in many no fault states. See Figure 4.4. This is because when the states eliminated the need to state grounds for divorce, the associated defenses were no longer needed. Since all that is required is for one party to state that the marriage is irretrievably broken, the only issue that can be raised is that the nonfiling party denies that the marriage is irretrievably broken. The judge in the proceeding may require additional proceedings when a minor child is involved if such an allegation is made.

### Consequences of a Divorce

The law has developed a set of standards on how to deal with issues relating to most aspects of a divorce. These include the resolution of matters such as child support, child custody, visitation, alimony, and distribution of property and debts.

The biggest legal problems relate not so much from the divorce procedure itself but instead involve the enforcement of the final order of dissolution of marriage. Key areas of concern are child support payments, alimony payments, and child visitation rights. These issues are discussed in more detail in later chapters.

Societal impacts of divorces are not so clear-cut. The one thing that is certain is that divorce is common in the United States. While divorce rates do vary somewhat by state, as is demonstrated by the figures contained in Figure 4.5, every state has had to face the reality of the large numbers of divorces that are granted every year. Increasingly states have been trying to slow down the rise in divorces to protect the institution of marriage and the children of the marriage. As mentioned in Chapter 3, one method has been to offer the option of covenant marriages, which make it more difficult to get a divorce.

## DISSOLUTION

The terms *divorce* and *dissolution of marriage* are often used interchangeably. Although this is acceptable in general conversation, there can be a critical difference between them depending on the state in which the proceeding is taking place. For example, many states have eliminated the use of the word *divorce* and instead use *dissolution of marriage.* In those states, the legally correct term is *dissolution,* but it is essentially the same as divorce.

Other states have created by statute a separate means of terminating a marriage that is specifically referred to as dissolution. It is a form of no fault termination of marriage in which the parties agree to the terms of their separation. These include spousal support, child support, division of marital assets, parental rights, and so on. The judge is asked to grant the termination of the marriage and approve

FIGURE 4.4
**Florida Dissolution of Marriage Statute**

61.052 Dissolution of marriage. —

(1) No judgment of dissolution of marriage shall be granted unless one of the following facts appears, which shall be pleaded generally:

(a) The marriage is irretrievably broken.

(b) Mental incapacity of one of the parties. However, no dissolution shall be allowed unless the party alleged to be incapacitated shall have been adjudged incapacitated according to the provisions of s. 744.331 for a preceding period of at least 3 years. Notice of the proceeding for dissolution shall be served upon one of the nearest blood relatives or guardian of the incapacitated person, and the relative or guardian shall be entitled to appear and to be heard upon the issues. If the incapacitated party has a general guardian other than the party bringing the proceeding, the petition and summons shall be served upon the incapacitated party and the guardian; and the guardian shall defend and protect the interests of the incapacitated party. If the incapacitated party has no guardian other than the party bringing the proceeding, the court shall appoint a guardian ad litem to defend and protect the interests of the incapacitated party. However, in all dissolutions of marriage granted on the basis of incapacity, the court may require the petitioner to pay alimony pursuant to the provisions of s. 61.08.

(2) Based on the evidence at the hearing, which evidence need not be corroborated except to establish that the residence requirements of s. 61.021 are met which may be corroborated by a valid Florida driver's license, a Florida voter's registration card, a valid Florida identification card issued under s. 322.051, or the testimony or affidavit of a third party, the court shall dispose of the petition for dissolution of marriage when the petition is based on the allegation that the marriage is irretrievably broken as follows:

(a) If there is no minor child of the marriage and if the responding party does not, by answer to the petition for dissolution, deny that the marriage is irretrievably broken, the court shall enter a judgment of dissolution of the marriage if the court finds that the marriage is irretrievably broken.

(b) When there is a minor child of the marriage, or when the responding party denies by answer to the petition for dissolution that the marriage is irretrievably broken, the court may:

1. Order either or both parties to consult with a marriage counselor, psychologist, psychiatrist, minister, priest, rabbi, or any other person deemed qualified by the court and acceptable to the party or parties ordered to seek consultation; or

2. Continue the proceedings for a reasonable length of time not to exceed 3 months, to enable the parties themselves to effect a reconciliation; or

3. Take such other action as may be in the best interest of the parties and the minor child of the marriage.

If, at any time, the court finds that the marriage is irretrievably broken, the court shall enter a judgment of dissolution of the marriage. If the court finds that the marriage is not irretrievably broken, it shall deny the petition for dissolution of marriage.

(3) During any period of continuance, the court may make appropriate orders for the support and alimony of the parties; the primary residence, custody, rotating custody, visitation, support, maintenance, and education of the minor child of the marriage; attorney's fees; and the preservation of the property of the parties.

(4) A judgment of dissolution of marriage shall result in each spouse having the status of being single and unmarried. No judgment of dissolution of marriage renders the child of the marriage a child born out of wedlock.

(5) The court may enforce an antenuptial agreement to arbitrate a dispute in accordance with the law and tradition chosen by the parties.

(6) Any injunction for protection against domestic violence arising out of the dissolution of marriage proceeding shall be issued as a separate order in compliance with chapter 741 and shall not be included in the judgment of dissolution of marriage.

(7) In the initial pleading for a dissolution of marriage as a separate attachment to the pleading, each party is required to provide his or her social security number and the full names and social security numbers of each of the minor children of the marriage.

(8) Pursuant to the federal Personal Responsibility and Work Opportunity Reconciliation Act of 1996, each party is required to provide his or her social security number in accordance with this section. Each party is also required to provide the full name, date of birth, and social security number for each minor child of the marriage. Disclosure of social security numbers obtained through this requirement shall be limited to the purpose of administration of the Title IV-D program for child support enforcement.

**FIGURE 4.5**
**Ranking of Divorces by State**

| State | 2004 Rank | Divorce Rate per 1,000 in 2004 | State | 2004 Rank | Divorce Rate per 1,000 in 2004 |
|---|---|---|---|---|---|
| District of Columbia | 1 | 1.7 | Montana | 23 | 3.8 |
| Massachusetts | 2 | 2.2 | New Hampshire | 25 | 3.9 |
| Pennsylvania | 3 | 2.5 | Utah | 25 | 3.9 |
| Illinois | 4 | 2.6 | Vermont | 25 | 3.9 |
| Minnesota | 5 | 2.8 | Virginia | 28 | 4.0 |
| Iowa | 5 | 2.8 | Oregon | 29 | 4.1 |
| North Dakota | 5 | 2.8 | Washington | 29 | 4.1 |
| Connecticut | 8 | 2.9 | Arizona | 31 | 4.2 |
| New Jersey | 9 | 3.0 | Colorado | 32 | 4.4 |
| Rhode Island | 9 | 3.0 | North Carolina | 32 | 4.4 |
| New York | 9 | 3.0 | Mississippi | 34 | 4.5 |
| Wisconsin | 12 | 3.1 | New Mexico | 35 | 4.6 |
| Maryland | 12 | 3.1 | Alabama | 36 | 4.7 |
| South Carolina | 14 | 3.2 | West Virginia | 36 | 4.7 |
| South Dakota | 14 | 3.2 | Florida | 38 | 4.8 |
| Kansas | 16 | 3.3 | Alaska | 38 | 4.8 |
| Michigan | 17 | 3.5 | Kentucky | 40 | 4.9 |
| Texas | 18 | 3.6 | Tennessee | 41 | 5.0 |
| Maine | 18 | 3.6 | Idaho | 42 | 5.1 |
| Nebraska | 18 | 3.6 | Wyoming | 43 | 5.3 |
| Delaware | 21 | 3.7 | Arkansas | 44 | 6.3 |
| Ohio | 21 | 3.7 | Nevada | 45 | 6.4 |
| Missouri | 23 | 3.8 | United States | mean | 3.7 |

*Note:* Data not available for: California, Georgia, Indiana, Louisiana, Hawaii, Oklahoma.

the agreement that the parties have entered into. In these states, divorce refers to a court finding that grounds exist for termination of the marriage. Figure 4.6 contains some of the key Ohio statutory provisions relating to dissolution of marriage in that state.

## SEPARATION

In some situations, married couples decide that they want to live separately but not get divorced. The reasons for this vary. Examples of why it is sometimes desired include one spouse wanting to remain on the spouse's health insurance policy, or the couple wants a trial separation. Many states do provide for this in some cases, referring to it as *legal separation* or *separate maintenance*.

States that recognize this right of action allow a spouse to seek spousal and child support payments from the other spouse in much the same manner in which he or she would if the couple were actually getting a divorce, which is discussed in detail in subsequent chapters. The amount of the support award is based on the need of the requesting spouse and the other spouse's ability to pay. One important difference from the matters that can be resolved in an action seeking separate maintenance and a divorce is that only support can be sought in a separate maintenance action and not matters involving the resolution of property. Payment of separate maintenance normally ceases when the parties resume cohabitation, or there is dissolution of the marriage or the death of a spouse.

## 3105.08 Converting divorce action into dissolution action.

At any time before a final judgment is entered in a divorce action, the spouses may convert the action for divorce into an action for dissolution of marriage by filing a motion with the court in which the divorce action is pending for conversion of the divorce action. The motion shall contain a petition for dissolution of marriage that satisfies the requirements of section 3105.63 of the Revised Code. The action for dissolution of marriage then shall proceed in accordance with sections 3105.61 to 3105.65 of the Revised Code with both spouses designated as petitioners. No court fees or costs normally charged upon the filing of an action shall be charged upon the conversion of the action for divorce into an action for dissolution of marriage under this section.

## 3105.63 Separation agreement provisions.

(A)(1) A petition for dissolution of marriage shall be signed by both spouses and shall have attached and incorporated a separation agreement agreed to by both spouses. The separation agreement shall provide for a division of all property; spousal support; if there are minor children of the marriage, the allocation of parental rights and responsibilities for the care of the minor children, the designation of a residential parent and legal custodian of the minor children, child support, and parenting time rights; and, if the spouses so desire, an authorization for the court to modify the amount or terms of spousal support provided in the separation agreement. If there are minor children of the marriage, the spouses may address the allocation of the parental rights and responsibilities for the care of the minor children by including in the separation agreement a plan under which both parents will have shared rights and responsibilities for the care of the minor children. The spouses shall file the plan with the petition for dissolution of marriage and shall include in the plan the provisions described in division (G) of section 3109.04 of the Revised Code.

(2) The division of property in the separation agreement shall include any participant account, as defined in section 148.01 of the Revised Code, of either of the spouses, to the extent of the following:

(a) The moneys that have been deferred by a continuing member or participating employee, as defined in that section, and that have been transmitted to the Ohio public employees deferred compensation board during the marriage and any income that is derived from the investment of those moneys during the marriage;

(b) The moneys that have been deferred by an officer or employee of a municipal corporation and that have been transmitted to the governing board, administrator, depository, or trustee of the deferred compensation program of the municipal corporation during the marriage and any income that is derived from the investment of those moneys during the marriage;

(c) The moneys that have been deferred by an officer or employee of a government unit, as defined in section 148.06 of the Revised Code, and that have been transmitted to the governing board, as defined in that section, during the marriage and any income that is derived from the investment of those moneys during the marriage.

(3) The separation agreement shall not require or permit the division or disbursement of the moneys and income described in division (A)(2) of this section to occur in a manner that is inconsistent with the law, rules, or plan governing the deferred compensation program involved or prior to the time that the spouse in whose name the participant account is maintained commences receipt of the moneys and income credited to the account in accordance with that law, rules, and plan.

(B) An amended separation agreement may be filed at any time prior to or during the hearing on the petition for dissolution of marriage. Upon receipt of a petition for dissolution of marriage, the court may cause an investigation to be made pursuant to the Rules of Civil Procedure.

(C) If a petition for dissolution of marriage contains an authorization for the court to modify the amount or terms of spousal support provided in the separation agreement, the modification shall be in accordance with section 3105.18 of the Revised Code.

**FIGURE 4.6**
**Key Ohio Statutory Provisions Relating to Dissolution of Marriage**

## Summary

The law has long tried to deal with the reality that some married couples no longer want to be married. We have moved from a time when it was very difficult to get a divorce and when all divorces had to be based on fault, to a time when all 50 states have some form of no fault divorce.

Annulments, once a common way for couples to end their marriage, allow a judge to declare that the marriage has never existed. The annulment can be granted because the marriage is void, such as a case involving bigamy, or voidable at the request of one or both of the parties, such as cases involving the lack of capacity. State laws have adjusted to provide for the legitimacy of the children born in a marriage that was subsequently ended and for the resolution of financial issues resulting from the annulment.

The law has also had to deal with societal changes that put pressure on the states to make it easier to get a divorce.

Starting in the 1970s and growing in popularity since then, no fault divorces have become the norm. The divorce can be obtained with one spouse merely alleging that there are irreconcilable differences between the parties or a similar statement in order to obtain a divorce.

The law is still playing catch-up on issues that are related to divorce, such as collection of child support, collection of alimony, child visitation, and abuse.

## Key Terms

Bigamy
Coercion
Collusion
Condonation
Connivance
Defense

Fraud
Incest
Recrimination
Void
Voidable

## Review Questions

1. What is the difference between a divorce and an annulment?
2. What is the difference between void and avoidable? Why is it important in understanding annulments?
3. List the reasons why a marriage may be voidable?
4. What are some of the consequences of a divorce?
5. What are some of the consequences of an annulment?
6. What are the most common grounds for a fault divorce? How do they differ from the grounds that need to be alleged in a no fault divorce?
7. What defenses are available in a fault divorce? In a no fault divorce?
8. What defenses are available in an annulment action?
9. What are the differences between divorce and dissolution of marriage?
10. What is separation and why is it used by some married couples?

## Exercises

1. Review the facts contained in the Client Interview. What legal issues are presented in those facts? Explain both what they are and the possible ways in which they could be resolved.
2. Jacob and Janice have been married for 10 years. Jacob has been incarcerated in the state penitentiary for a period of 3 years. He still has 2 years remaining to serve on his sentence. Janice wants a divorce but Jacob does not. Based on the

laws of your state, would Janice be able to get a divorce? Would it be a no fault or a fault divorce? If it would need to be a fault divorce, what would be the grounds for the divorce?

3. Ken has been married to Alicia for 2 years. One year after their marriage, Alicia was admitted to a state mental hospital after attempting to commit suicide. Ken wants a divorce. Alicia doesn't object, but her doctor feels that she is not capable of consenting to the divorce. Based on the laws of your state, would Ken be able to get a divorce? Would it be a no fault or a fault divorce? If it would need to be a fault divorce, what would be the grounds for the divorce?

4. Jan and Dorothy decide to live together. They each have assets, such as savings accounts and cars, and Jan owns the home in which the couple plans to live. Under the laws of your state, would they need a written cohabitation agreement to protect their rights if they separate or have the courts of your state protected the rights of couples who have cohabitated once they separate? If the courts of your state have protected the rights of cohabitants upon separation, what facts have they considered to determine if there were an informal agreement between the parties as to what would occur at separation?

5. Scott and Bernice have been married for 7 years. Scott is very unhappy in his marriage. He wants a divorce, feeling that the marriage is irretrievably broken. Would he be able to get a no fault divorce in your state? Would your answer be different if Bernice does not agree that the marriage is irretrievably broken? If yes, what would Scott have to do to get a divorce?

## REAL WORLD DISCUSSION TOPICS

The parties divorced and, pursuant to an agreement between them, the husband began paying alimony to the wife. Payments were to continue until such time as either party died, or the wife remarried. The wife remarried, but that marriage was subsequently annulled.

Should the husband's obligation to pay alimony revive when the wife's later marriage was annulled? See *Fredo v. Fredo,* 49 Conn.Supp. 489, 894 A.2d 399 (2005); *Watts v. Watts,* 250 Neb. 38, 547 N.W.2d 466 (1996).

## PORTFOLIO ASSIGNMENT

1. Review section 61.052, Florida Statutes, which is shown in Figure 4.4. Make a list of the requirements set out in that statute to get a divorce. Include what proof must be submitted, what defenses can be raised, what latitude the court has to grant the divorce, and any other item you feel is relevant. Next, locate your state's statute on this topic and make a similar list. Compare the similarities between the two statutes.

2. Review the facts from the Client Interview at the beginning of the chapter. Research the relevant statutory and case law of your state to determine what options are available to Lisa. Write a summary of your findings.

# Chapter 5

# Division of Property and Debts

## CHAPTER OBJECTIVES

**After reading this chapter and completing the assignments, you should be able to:**

- Distinguish between real and personal property.
- Discuss the various ways property can be owned jointly.
- Understand what marital property and separate property are and why they are important to the distribution of property in a divorce.
- Discuss property that may be considered marital property.
- Describe the concept of equitable distribution.
- Distinguish between distribution in a common law state and a community property state.
- Understand how actions of one spouse may cause separate property to be subject to a claim by the other spouse in a divorce.

---

Like alimony and child custody, the division of property and the division of debts are often difficult matters to resolve. This can be true when the attorneys for the husband and wife are trying to negotiate a property settlement agreement or when the matter is being left to a judge to decide.

Chapter 5 introduces the paralegal student to how property is classified and how this classification impacts the ultimate distribution of the couple's property when they get divorced. Students will also learn about some of the approaches that judges take

**CLIENT INTERVIEW**

Judy and John Harley were married for 10 years. It was the second marriage for them both. Judy owned her home at the time of her marriage. During the course of their marriage, Judy made mortgage payments out of the couple's joint checking account. While Judy deposited almost all of the money into the joint account, John had full access to it and could write checks from it as he pleased. John, who liked to think of himself as a real mister-fix-it, spent a lot of time improving the home by doing things like adding a new deck and a new patio. The funds for these projects came from the joint checking account. John did all of the labor associated with the completion of the projects. The couple had few other assets. Judy has come to your firm to handle her divorce case.

when trying to resolve issues relating to the distribution of property when the parties themselves cannot reach an amicable agreement.

## WHY THIS CHAPTER IS IMPORTANT TO THE PARALEGAL

The division of property and partitioning of debts are critical parts of the divorce process. Whether an attorney is negotiating a settlement of how the property and debts will be divided or he or she is preparing for a hearing before a judge who will resolve the issue, the paralegal will be called upon to assist in completing these tasks.

This means that the paralegal must be familiar with the legal concepts associated with this area of the law and the state statutes that apply. This chapter provides the paralegal student with essential information on these matters and gives them the necessary background to understand how and why things are being done in the law office.

## PROPERTY

Since a key part of the material covered in this chapter deals with property, a basic introduction to some of the legal principles relating to property is a good starting point to begin the chapter.

### Real versus Personal Property

There are two main categories of property—**real property** and **personal property**.

Real property is the land and all property permanently attached to it, such as buildings. In divorce cases, the marital home is often the real property that must be dealt with when dividing property.

Personal property can be best described as anything that is not real property. There are two classifications of personal property—tangible and intangible. **Tangible property** is readily recognized by most people. Examples include cars, iPods, furniture, clothes, and jewelry. **Intangible property** is personal property where the true value of the item cannot be touched. Examples include stocks, bonds, trademarks, and goodwill.

### How Property Is Owned

The next concept that needs to be addressed is the matter of how property is owned. That may seem simple enough, but the law can make even simple concepts, like ownership, complicated. This is especially true when a person owns property jointly with another person.

A person can own property jointly or concurrently with other people in a number of ways. They include:

**Tenancy in Common.** This is one of the most frequently used forms of co-ownership of property. It allows two or more people to own an undivided share of the whole property. The parties do not need to own an equal share of the property. For example, three people could own a lot in Sunrise Estates as tenants in common. One could own a 50 percent interest in the property, one could own a 30 percent interest in the property and one could own a 20 percent interest in the property.

**Joint Tenancy with Right of Survivorship (JTWROS).** This form of ownership is used by people who want to own property jointly and want it to pass to the co-owners when one of the tenants dies. Unlike tenants in common, each person must own an equal part of the property. In many states this is often how husbands and wives own property, although JTWROS is not limited to married couples nor is it limited to ownership by only two people.

---

**real property**
Land and all property permanently attached to it, such as buildings.

**personal property**
Movable or intangible thing not attached to real property.

**tangible property**
Personal property that can be held or touched, such as furniture or jewelry.

**intangible property**
Personal property that has no physical presence but is represented by a certificate or some other instrument, such as stocks or trademarks.

**tenancy in common**
A form of ownership between two or more people where each owner's interest upon death goes to his or her heirs.

**joint tenancy with right of survivorship (JTWROS)**
Form of tenancy that requires four unities: (1) possession, (2) interest, (3) title, and (4) time.

**FIGURE 5.1**
**States That Allow Some Form of Tenancy by the Entirety**

| | | |
|---|---|---|
| Alaska | Kentucky (real property only) | North Carolina (real property only) |
| Arkansas | Maryland | Oklahoma |
| Delaware | Massachusetts | Oregon (real property only) |
| District of Columbia | Michigan (real property only) | Pennsylvania |
| Florida | Mississippi | Rhode Island |
| Hawaii | Missouri | Tennessee |
| Illinois (real property only) | New Jersey | Vermont |
| Indiana (real property only) | New York (real property only) | Virginia |
| | | Wyoming |

**FIGURE 5.2**
**Community Property State Statutes**

Arizona—Ariz. Rev. Stat. Ann § 25-211
California—Cal. Family Code §§ 760-761
Idaho—Idaho Code § 32-906
Louisiana—La. Civ. Code Ann. art. 2335
Nevada—Nev. Rev. Stat.§ 123.220, et seq,
New Mexico—N.M. Stat. Ann. § 40-3-1 et seq,
Texas—Tex. Code Ann. § 3.003
Washington—Wash. Rev. Code § 26.16.030
Wisconsin—Wis. Stat. §766.001(2)

**tenancy by the entirety**
A form of ownership for married couples, similar to joint tenancy, where the spouse has right of survivorship.

**Tenancy by the Entirety**. This form of ownership is very similar to JTWROS with one major difference—only married couples can own property as tenants by the entirety. This form of ownership developed from the idea that a man and a woman become a separate entity when they marry. The married couple own property as one entity, so when one dies, the surviving spouse still owns the entire property. Tenancy by the entirety is not recognized in all states. Married couples who live in states that do not recognize tenancy by the entirety usually own the property as JTWROS or as community property, if their home state recognizes this form of ownership. Figure 5.1 lists the states that recognize tenancy by the entirety in some form.

**community property**
All property acquired during marriage in a community property state, owned in equal shares.

**Community Property**. This form of co-ownership was created by statute in the states of Arizona, California, Idaho, Louisiana, Nevada, New Mexico, Texas, Washington, and Wisconsin. Community property includes property that is acquired during the time a couple is married, with limited exceptions, and is owned equally by each spouse. This is true even if the property is titled in one spouse's name. Figure 5.2 provides the statute numbers relating to community property for those states that recognize this form of ownership.

## GENERAL CONCEPTS RELATING TO THE DIVISION OF PROPERTY

Division of property is often one of the sticking points in achieving an agreement between the parties in a divorce. Big things, such as the marital home, and smaller things, like the family pet, can be a source of conflict during the divorce process.

The first thing that must be understood is what particular items of property are really in dispute and, absent a separation agreement between the parties, subject to the control of the judge handling the case. Remember, it is always a good idea for the parties to make these decisions rather than leaving them to a judge to decide. Any divorce attorney who has practiced in the field for at least a few years has *many* stories of how his or her client lost out because she or he insisted on letting the judge decide how the property would be distributed.

Two specific concepts must be understood in the discussion of the division of property: what is marital property and what is nonmarital property. In general, only **marital property** is subject to distribution as part of a divorce. Marital property is referred to as community property in community property states. Marital property is that property that the couple accumulated during the course of the marriage, with some exceptions, such as if the property was a gift to only one spouse or inherited by only one spouse. All other property is classified as **separate property**. Identification of marital property is a critical part of the property distribution process in both common law and non-common-law states.

A quick review of the definition of community property and of the general principles associated with it may leave the impression that division of community property should be fairly straightforward, but it must be emphasized that, since it is created by state statute, the laws do vary from one community property state to another.

Some community property states take a direct approach to the division of community property in the event of a divorce or dissolution of marriage. For example, California provides that the community property should be divided equally because marriage is a joint undertaking and each spouse has contributed equally, in one manner or another, to the accumulation and preservation of the property. Other community property states, such as Texas and Wisconsin, provide that the judge should distribute the community property equitably.

Things are a little more complicated in non-community-property states. These states start with the concept that the marital property will be divided equally but may make adjustments to obtain an **equitable distribution** of the property. The criteria that a judge may use in making decisions relating to property distribution are set out

**marital estates (marital property)**
The property accumulated by a couple during marriage, called community property in some states.

**separate property**
One spouse is the exclusive owner.

**equitable distribution**
Divides the assets acquired during the marriage between the parties.

---

## RESEARCH THIS

Understanding the concepts associated with community property is important to paralegal students who live in either a community property state or a non-community-property state. As has been demonstrated by the discussion of how different community property states deal with the distribution of community property in the case of a divorce, it is essential that paralegals students who live in those states understand the specific laws of their state.

It is also important that students in non-community-property states be aware of the difference because, even though a married couple may be seeking a divorce or dissolution of marriage in a non-community-property state, they may have acquired property while living in a community property state. The question then becomes how a judge will deal with that property in the divorce or dissolution of marriage case.

If you live in a community property state, research the laws of your state and at least one other community property state relating to how property is classified as community property and how that property is distributed in the event of a divorce or dissolution. Write a one-page paper discussing the differences and similarities between the statutes of both states.

If you live in a non-community-property state, research the laws of your state relating to the division of property that is owned as community property in a divorce or dissolution that takes place in your state. Next, research the laws of a community property state relating to how property is classified as community property and how that property is distributed in the event of a divorce or dissolution. Write a one-page paper discussing the treatment of community property in a divorce or dissolution in your state and of your findings of the statutes in the community property state.

---

**40-4-202. Division of property.**

(1) In a proceeding for dissolution of a marriage, legal separation, or division of property following a decree of dissolution of marriage or legal separation by a court which lacked personal jurisdiction over the absent spouse or lacked jurisdiction to divide the property, the court, without regard to marital misconduct, shall, and in a proceeding for legal separation may, finally equitably apportion between the parties the property and assets belonging to either or both, however and whenever acquired and whether the title thereto is in the name of the husband or wife or both. In making apportionment, the court shall consider the duration of the marriage and prior marriage of either party; the age, health, station, occupation, amount and sources of income, vocational skills, employability, estate, liabilities, and needs of each of the parties; custodial provisions; whether the apportionment is in lieu of or in addition to maintenance; and the opportunity of each for future acquisition of capital assets and income. The court shall also consider the contribution or dissipation of value of the respective estates and the contribution of a spouse as a homemaker or to the family unit. In dividing property acquired prior to the marriage; property acquired by gift, bequest, devise, or descent; property acquired in exchange for property acquired before the marriage or in exchange for property acquired by gift, bequest, devise, or descent; the increased value of property acquired prior to marriage; and property acquired by a spouse after a decree of legal separation, the court shall consider those contributions of the other spouse to the marriage, including:

   (a) the nonmonetary contribution of a homemaker;

   (b) the extent to which such contributions have facilitated the maintenance of this property; and

   (c) whether or not the property division serves as an alternative to maintenance arrangements.

(2) In a proceeding, the court may protect and promote the best interests of the children by setting aside a portion of the jointly and separately held estates of the parties in a separate fund or trust for the support, maintenance, education, and general welfare of any minor, dependent, or incompetent children of the parties.

(3) Each spouse is considered to have a common ownership in marital property that vests immediately preceding the entry of the decree of dissolution or declaration of invalidity. The extent of the vested interest must be determined and made final by the court pursuant to this section.

(4) The division and apportionment of marital property caused by or incident to a decree of dissolution, a decree of legal separation, or a declaration of invalidity is not a sale, exchange, transfer, or disposition of or dealing in property but is a division of the common ownership of the parties for purposes of:

   (a) the property laws of this state;

   (b) the income tax laws of this state; and

   (c) the federal income tax laws.

(5) Premarital agreements must be enforced as provided in Title 40, chapter 2, part 6.

---

**FIGURE 5.3**   **Montana Statute on Distribution of Property**

by statute, and insight into the statute's application can be gained from case law, although it is important to keep in mind that the courts are given great latitude when deciding what constitutes an equitable distribution in a given case. This is because it is trial judges who have all of the facts of cases before them, and they are in the best position to make these important decisions. In addition, a judge's final order represents an effort to equitably divide the property based on the individual facts of a case. As a result, appellate courts are very reluctant to overturn the judge's final order. Figure 5.3 contains the Montana statute dealing with the distribution of property.

As noted in Chapter 3, the parties can agree to the details of property distribution and other matters in a prenuptial agreement. However, a poorly drafted prenuptial agreement can result in situations where a judge may still be asked to determine how to distribute certain items in a divorce proceeding. The *Valdes v. Valdes* case, set out next, is an excellent example of how a lack of consideration of key points when drafting the prenuptial agreement resulted in the need for judicial determination regarding the distribution of property.

In the District Court of Appeal of Florida
Third District
Case Nos. 3d02-2364, 3d02-1388
*Valdes v. Valdes*
Opinion filed June 9, 2004

PER CURIAM.

Pablo J. Valdes, the former husband, appeals from the Final Judgment of Dissolution of Marriage, awarding equitable distribution of the enhancement value of non-marital property, and from an Attorney Fees Order requiring that the former husband pay a portion of Ibis Morejon Valdes', the former wife's, attorney fees. Mrs. Valdes cross-appeals from the Final Judgment to the extent that the trial court made an unequal distribution of the enhancement valuation. We reverse in part and affirm in part.

Mr. and Mrs. Valdes were married in 1991. Mr. Valdes came into the marriage with a net worth of $8,000,000, consisting primarily of real estate holdings. Mrs. Valdes came into the marriage with approximately $180,000, consisting primarily of personal property. Three children were born out of the marriage, all of them are minors. Prior to the marriage, the parties entered into a Prenuptial Agreement, which the parties stipulated was valid. The parties waived any entitlement to alimony in the prenuptial agreement, and Mr. Valdes agreed to pay $100,000 to Mrs. Valdes upon the dissolution of their marriage. Additionally, the prenuptial agreement specifically provided that each party would retain his or her respective premarital property, and any property or assets acquired during the marriage wherein title was held individually. Specifically, the prenuptial agreement provided in pertinent part:

> Whereas, it is the intention of [the Wife] to waive, relinquish and bar her statutory rights and interests, including alimony and support as the Wife or Widow of [the Husband], and to the real, personal and mixed property owned by [the Husband] at the present time, or to be acquired by him in the future, unless otherwise specified in this Agreement.

\* \* \*

5. PROPERTY ACQUIRED PRIOR TO MARRIAGE: Each of the Parties represent to the other that he or she owns the real and personal property listed on Exhibits "C" and "D" disclosed at the time of executing this Agreement. Each Party represents to the other that they shall have no interest in or to said property nor make any claim against said property in the future should their marriage be dissolved by a Court of Competent Jurisdiction, unless title to the property listed in said Schedules should change subsequent to marriage into joint ownership, or as otherwise provided in this Agreement.

6. PROPERTY ACQUIRED AFTER MARRIAGE: The Parties acknowledge to each other that subsequent to their marriage they may purchase for their own individual interest either real, personal or mixed property. Each Party acknowledges and agrees that the other Party may purchase any real, personal or mixed property subsequent to their marriage and if said property is taken or titled in the individual name of said Party purchasing same, the other Party shall have no interest in said after acquired property, nor make any claim to said property should this marriage be dissolved by a Court of Competent Jurisdiction, or should said property remain in the Estate of said Party, at the time of the Party's demise.

7. PROPERTY ACQUIRED AFTER MARRIAGE, NOT TO BE CONSIDERED MARITAL ASSETS: The Parties agree that any and all assets acquired by them, wherein ownership or title is not taken jointly or as tenants by the entireties, shall be presumed to be non-marital assets, and shall be considered the separate property of the person acquiring same.

The prenuptial agreement was silent on the issue of enhancement or appreciation of the parties' non-marital property.

The parties separated in March of 2000. During the dissolution proceedings, Mrs. Valdes asserted six separate claims against Mr. Valdes. After several days of trial, the court entered an Order of Involuntary Dismissal against Mrs. Valdes as to five of the six claims. Specifically, the trial court found that, consistent with the prenuptial agreement, the parties maintained separate finances during the marriage, including separate bank accounts, and filed separate tax returns. Additionally, the trial court found that Mr. Valdes paid Mrs. Valdes' taxes. During the marriage, Mrs. Valdes worked on behalf of Mr. Valdes' business projects and received a salary to that end, even when she did not work, which she retained in her separate bank account. The court also found that Mr. Valdes paid all of the household expenses and that the parties did not acquire any joint assets or property during the course of the marriage. Thus, only Mrs. Valdes' claim for equitable distribution remained.

As part of her equitable distribution claim, Mrs. Valdes asserted that certain properties were owned by her, and that she was entitled to the enhanced value of Mr. Valdes' non-marital property. The court found that the two properties were Mr. Valdes' non-marital property. However, the court found that absent a specific waiver of the enhanced value to non-marital property in the prenuptial agreement, the enhancement value of the non-marital assets resulting from marital efforts were subject to equitable distribution. Mrs. Valdes presented evidence that Mr. Valdes' net worth increased by $8,000,000 during the marriage. The court found it difficult to separate Mr. Valdes' premarital assets from his non-marital assets obtained during the marriage, finding that Mr. Valdes' non-marital assets are "regularly in play and interrelated to all other properties." As a result, the court calculated the enhancement value as suggested by Mrs. Valdes and found that the properties are so intermingled that the increase in Mr. Valdes' net worth should be classified as a marital asset. Consequently, the court set the marital assets value at $8,000,000—Mr. Valdes' increased net worth.

Nevertheless, the court found that an unequal distribution was warranted because Mr. Valdes' net worth was grounded upon his business acumen and the development of assets which belonged to him prior to the marriage. Additionally, the court found that Mr. Valdes paid all of the expenses during the marriage, which allowed Mrs. Valdes to increase her personal financial status, and retain an enhanced home free and clear, plus the $100,000 she received under the prenuptial agreement. Thus, the court set the marital assets amount at $8,000,000 and awarded Mrs. Valdes, among other things, including the marital home which husband waived any interest to, $800,000. The court also entered an Order on attorney fees, awarding partial fees to Mrs. Valdes.

Mr. Valdes appeals from the portion of the Final Judgment which determines that the entirety of the increase in his net worth was a marital asset, and from the trial court's Order on attorney fees which finds that Mrs. Valdes was the "prevailing party" in the litigation below. Mrs. Valdes cross-appeals from the Final Judgment to the extent the trial court found that an unequal distribution of the only "marital asset" was warranted, resulting in Mrs. Valdes recovering less than ten percent of the value of the asset. Additionally, Mrs. Valdes challenges the trial court's rounding down of the enhancement value of the marital asset from $8,506,399.75 to $8,000,000.

## EQUITABLE DISTRIBUTION OF ENHANCEMENT VALUE

In *Doig v. Doig*, 787 So. 2d 100, 103 (Fla. 2d DCA 2001), the Court held that a prenuptial agreement providing that: "neither party shall make any claim or acquire any interest in the other party's separate property if it increases in value during the marriage" addressed only passive appreciation of property and did not preclude application of section 61.075, Florida Statutes which provides that increases in value of a non-marital asset that are attributable to marital labor or funds are subject to equitable distribution. *Doig*, 787 So. 2d at 103; *see also* § 61.075, Fla. Stat. Similarly, in *Irwin v. Irwin*, 857 So. 2d 247 (Fla. 2d DCA 2003), the Second District reversed a Final Judgment of Dissolution, finding that "[t]he agreement did not specifically reserve Mr. Irwin's marital earnings as his separate property, and thus did not exclude Mrs. Irwin's claim to share in the value of assets purchased with those earnings. Nor did the agreement waive Mrs. Irwin's claim to her rightful share of the marital asset consisting of the enhanced value of Mr. Irwin's separate property that resulted from the contribution of marital

funds or labor." *Irwin*, 857 So. 2d at 248 (citations omitted); *Witowski v. Witowski*, 758 So. 2d 1181 (Fla. 2d DCA 2000).

In the instant case, the prenuptial agreement does not address enhancement value. *See Worley v. Worley*, 855 So. 2d 632, 634 (Fla. 2d DCA 2003) (A prenuptial agreement does not waive the right to enhancement in value of "non-marital" property unless the waiver is unambiguously expressed in the agreement); *Witowski v. Witowski*, 758 So. 2d 1181 (Fla. 2d DCA 2000); *see also White v. White*, 617 So. 2d 732 (Fla. 2d DCA 1993) (where the parties did not specify alimony in the agreement, the court found that wife did not expressly waive right to alimony); *cf. Cameron v. Cameron*, 591 So. 2d 275 (Fla. 5th DCA 1991) (where the Fifth District affirmed trial court's interpretation of prenuptial agreement as waiving all rights to non-marital property assets where the agreement specifically provided that: "[I]t is the intention of [wife] to waive and relinquish her rights of dower and other statutory rights and interests, as wife or widow of [husband], in and to real, personal, and mixed property owned by [husband] . . .". Specifically, the prenuptial agreement in the instant case provides: the parties "shall have no interest in or to said property nor make any claim against said property;" and "assets acquired by [the parties], wherein ownership or title is not taken jointly or as tenants by the entireties, shall be presumed to be non-marital assets, and shall be considered the separate property of the person acquiring same." Accordingly, we conclude that the trial court properly found that Mrs. Valdes did not waive her right to seek equitable distribution of the enhanced value of non-marital properties, despite the prenuptial agreement. Additionally, the enhancement value of the non-marital properties was the result of marital labor from both parties. *See Cameron v. Cameron*, 591 So. 2d 275 (Fla. 5th DCA 1991).

However, we reverse the valuation of the enhancement on the ground that there is no Record evidence to support the trial court's valuation of the enhancement value of the non-marital property/assets. Section 61.075(3), Florida Statutes, require that any distribution of assets or liabilities be supported by factual findings in the judgment based on competent substantial evidence. § 61.075(3), Fla. Stat. In the instant case, the court's valuation was based strictly on Mr. Valdes' net worth, which presumably also includes other assets not subject to the valuation. Where the Final Judgment does not identify the property, nor its value, we cannot affirm the court's rationale for the distribution. Accordingly, we reverse the calculation of the enhancement value and remand for further proceedings consistent with section 61.075, Florida Statutes.

\* \* \*

Reversed in part, affirmed in part and remanded.

**Source:** Retrieved from www.3dca.flcourts.org/Opinions/3d02-2364.pdf.

## MARITAL HOME

The marital home presents some unique problems in deciding who, if either party, will get it in the divorce. One reality that makes the marital home important is that it is most Americans' major financial asset. The value of the family cars, furniture, clothing, and so on may not amount to much when compared with the family home.

And, with fewer employers offering traditional pensions or retirement plans, the family home is also a key part of the financial planning for retirement.

So the marital home is a financial asset, just like all the others being distributed in the divorce. Or is it? The reality is that it is much more, especially if there are children of the marriage. To them it is the home they are growing up in, it may determine the school they will go to after the divorce, and it determines who their neighborhood friends are.

A court may be asked, therefore, to delicately balance the financial needs of the parties with the emotional needs of the children. For example, the court may allow the custodial parent to remain in the marital home until all of the children reach majority. Then it may be sold and the proceeds split between the parties.

The judge also may award the home as lump sum alimony to the custodial parent, using his or her judicial powers to make an equitable distribution of the property in light of all the factors in the case. Or the judge may require the home to be sold and the proceeds to be divided to take care of the unique needs of the parties.

Like many areas of dissolution of marriage law, the judge is asked to make difficult decisions on a case-by-case basis.

> **CASE BRIEF ASSIGNMENT**
>
> Read and brief the *Valdes v. Valdes*, 894 So.2d 264 (Fla. Dist. Ct. App. 2004) case. (See Appendix A for information on how to brief cases.)

## PENSIONS AND RETIREMENT PLANS

Couples often plan for their retirement during the course of their marriage and may have participated in some type of retirement plan and/pension. In fact, these assets may constitute one of the largest that a couple may have, second only to the marital home in many cases.

For most Americans, this asset is often accrued as part of their employment. It can be a traditional pension, in which the employee has a right to receive a pension when he or she retires. It may provide for monthly payments or in one lump sum payment.

Another type of retirement plan, which is growing in popularity, is referred to as a 401(k) plan. In this plan, an employee may designate a certain percentage of his or her income to be deducted from each paycheck. The employer may also match all or a portion of the employee's contribution.

Key to the discussion of pension plans is the concept of vesting. A pension or 401(k) is said to be fully **vested** when the employee can leave and take the full value of the pension, including the employer's contribution in the employee's 401(k) account. It is common for 401(k) plans to provide partial vesting of the amount contributed by the employer based on the number of years that the employee remains on the job. For example, the plan may provide that 25 percent of the employer's portion will vest for each year the employee remains employed by the employer until being fully vested after the completion of four years of employment. The amount invested by the employee is, however, 100 percent at all times.

**vested**
Having a present right to receive the benefit of the performance when it becomes due.

Some people also start their own retirement funds. One popular method of doing this is through individual retirement accounts (IRAs). These can be purchased through banks and other financial institutions.

Traditional retirement finds, 401(k) retirement funds, and IRAs have one thing in common—they take advantage of tax deferral provisions in the IRS code. This means that the taxes on the income, such as interest on the investment, are not paid until they are withdrawn.

Members of the United States Armed Forces also are eligible for retirement benefits after honorably serving for 20 years. Unlike other retirements and pensions, the military retirement plan does not vest; instead it is a question of whether the 20-year time requirement was met or not.

So, can these retirement funds be part of the division of property in a divorce case? Yes, they can. Just as they do for their other property, married couples could decide to divide an interest in the retirement fund as part of their settlement agreement, or, if they cannot agree to terms relating to the pension fund, the court may be called upon to resolve the issue. In those cases, the court can look at the retirement plans and/or pensions as an asset to be part of the marital property to be distributed. It may also issue a **qualified domestic relations order** (QDRO) that requires that the retirement benefits, or a percentage thereof, be paid to the nonemployee spouse.

The United States recognized the power of state courts to award the nonmilitary spouse a portion of military retirement benefits with the passage of the Uniformed Services Former Spouse's Protection Act (USFSPA) in a divorce, dissolution, or legal separation. The amount the nonmilitary spouse can claim of the retirement payments is determined by the time the military spouse served while the couple was married.

Military retirement pay is also subject to a QDRO, if the spouses have been married for a minimum of 10 years.

The Waln case, set out in the next Case in Point, provides an informative example of how a court is called upon to resolve issues relating to pensions, such as when the employer, in this case a governmental body, includes a spendthrift clause in the terms of the pension.

**qualified domestic relations order (QDRO)**
Retirement account distributions' legal documentation requirement for ultimate distribution.

**CYBER TRIP**

To learn more about the Uniformed Services Former Spouse's Protection Plan, visit www.military.com/benefits/retiree/uniformed-services-former-spouses-protection-act.

---

**RESEARCH THIS**

Research the statutory and case law of your state to determine if a court in your jurisdiction would have ruled in the same manner as the Wisconsin Appellate Court did in *Waln v. Waln.*

---

## OTHER ASSETS

Although some assets are readily identifiable and valued, the value of others is a little less obvious.

Let's use an example. Suppose Katrina drops out of college so that she can work full-time to support her husband, Richard, while he completes medical school. The couple had decided that this would be the wisest thing to do because he would be able to finish his education quicker and start his career in a high-paying profession. They also agreed that Katrina would go back to school and complete her education. The couple divorced a number of years after Richard began to practice medicine.

Would Richard's medical degree and his professional license be considered a marital asset or at least be subject to a claim by Katrina?

States differ on how to deal with this issue. Some do allow the spouse to make claims against the degree/license under circumstances similar to those of Richard and Katrina. Others do not. The trend is to treat them as a marital asset. The following case of *In re Marriage of Lee* demonstrates how one court addressed this issue.

But it is not just professional degrees and licenses that have a value. What about a celebrity's goodwill that grows from his or her celebrity status—is that a marital asset? In New Jersey, a judge ruled that the husband's celebrity status was a marital asset and subject to equitable distribution. The ruling was upheld on appeal. See *Piscopo v. Piscopo,* 232 N.J.Super. 559, 557 A.2d 1040 (N.J.Super.A.D., 1989).

Pets can also present some unique issues in a divorce. The law treats pets as property, but most people do not view them as such. In fact, published reports indicate that 63

Court of Appeals
Decision
Dated and Filed
February 23, 2005
Cornelia G. Clark
Clerk of Court of Appeals
NOTICE
This opinion is subject to further editing. If published, the official version will appear in the bound volume of the Official Reports.
A party may file with the Supreme Court a petition to review an adverse decision by the Court of Appeals. *See* WIS. STAT. § 808.10 and RULE 809.62.
Appeal No.
04-1271-FT
Cir. Ct. No. 03-FA-14
State of Wisconsin
In Court of Appeals

*In re the Marriage of:*

*Larry M. Waln, Petitioner-Respondent v. Barbara J. Waln, Respondent-Appellant*

¶1 PETERSON, J. Barbara Waln appeals from a divorce judgment. She argues the circuit court erred by concluding the spendthrift provision of WIS. STAT. § 62.63(4) barred it from considering Larry Waln's pension from the City of Milwaukee as part of the marital estate. We agree, reverse the judgment and remand with directions to consider the pension.

## BACKGROUND

¶2 Barbara and Larry Waln were married in 1977. At the time of their divorce, they had been married for twenty-six years. Larry worked for the City of Milwaukee Police Department from 1976 until 1995, when he filed for duty disability. In 1996, he began duty disability, which provides him a monthly payment and continues accrual of service time on his pension. In 2007, when Larry turns sixty-three, his duty disability will end and his pension payments will begin.

¶3 When Larry turns sixty-three, he may designate a pension beneficiary and select a payout option from the following: (1) single life annuity, providing no payments after his death; (2) fifty percent joint survivor annuity, providing his beneficiary with half the pension after his death; or (3) percentage payable after death, providing his beneficiary with any elected percentage of the pension after his death. His choice of payout option affects the amount of the monthly pension payment he receives.

¶4 On September 9, 2003, the date of the final divorce hearing, the value of Larry's pension was $363,260.70. The value of the rest of the divisible marital estate was approximately $132,000. At the hearing, Barbara sought half of Larry's monthly pension payment, when and if it is paid; an order directing Larry to elect the fifty percent joint survivor annuity pension payout option and name Barbara beneficiary; and an order directing Larry to assist her in obtaining life insurance on his life, at her expense, for the time period between the divorce and the commencement of pension payments.

¶5 The circuit court found, due to the spendthrift provision of WIS. STAT. § 62.63(4), Larry's pension was "not subject to property division." The court declined to order a specific beneficiary or payout election because it concluded it was barred from doing so by the statute or, alternatively, would decline to do so due to the uncertainty of the future "health and financial situation" of the parties. The court ordered Larry to assist Barbara in obtaining life insurance on his life at her expense.

¶6 Barbara moved for reconsideration. She argued that even if the pension was not subject to division through a domestic relations order by virtue of WIS. STAT. § 62.63(4), the pension was a marital asset that must be considered when dividing the property. The motion was denied.

\* \* \*

## DISCUSSION

¶8 The division of property at divorce is governed by WIS. STAT. § 767.255.[1][4] Generally, all property, other than property acquired by a spouse through gift or inheritance, is presumed to be divided equally between the spouses. WIS. STAT. § 767.255. The presumption of equal property division may be altered after considering the factors enumerated in WIS. STAT. § 767.255(3).

¶9 Wisconsin courts usually consider a pension as property, rather than income, and "either divide it or divide other marital assets to effect a *de facto* pension division." *Steinke v. Steinke*, 126 Wis. 2d 372, 379-80, 376 N.W.2d 839 (1985) (citing *Schafer v. Schafer*, 3 Wis. 2d 166, 171, 87 N.W.2d 803 (1958) (postal service pension was "incapable of division by the court" but should have been considered when dividing the marital estate)). As the *Steinke* court explained:

> A spouse's interest in a pension plan is in the nature of property of the marital estate to be divided. The marital

estate represents the total of the wealth of property brought into the marriage by either party, as well as wealth accumulated during the marriage, pursuant to the parameters of sec. 767.255, Stats. The division of the estate, presumed to be equal, effectuates the policy that each spouse makes a valuable contribution to the marriage and that each spouse should be compensated for his or her respective contributions. An interest in a pension plan is part of the wealth brought to, or accumulated during, the marriage. As with other property constituting the marital estate, the value of the pension interest must be included in the property division.

*Id.* at 380–81 (footnote omitted).

¶10 Larry argues, however, that because his pension is governed by a statutory spendthrift provision, his pension cannot be considered by the court when dividing the parties' property at divorce. The spendthrift provision, contained in WIS. STAT. § 62.63(4), provides:

Except as provided in s. 49.852 and subject to s. 767.265, all moneys and assets of a retirement system of a 1st class city and all benefits and allowances, both before and after payment to any beneficiary, granted under the retirement system are exempt from any state, county or municipal tax or from attachment or garnishment process. The benefits and allowances may not be seized, taken, detained or levied upon by virtue of any executions, or any process or proceeding issued out of or by any court of this state, for the payment and ratification in whole or in part of any debt, claim, damage, demand or judgment against any member of or beneficiary under the retirement system. No member of or beneficiary under the retirement system may assign any benefit or allowance either by way of mortgage or otherwise. The prohibition against assigning a benefit or allowance does not apply to assignments made for the payment of insurance premiums. The exemption from taxation under this section does not apply with respect to any tax on income.

Larry claims that this language bars the circuit court from dividing his pension, either directly or indirectly.

¶11 There is little case law interpreting how the statutory spendthrift provision governing government pensions affects the court's power to equitably divide marital assets at divorce. In *Courtney v. Courtney*, 251 Wis. 443, 29 N.W.2d 759 (1947), the plaintiff sought to garnish her former husband's City of Milwaukee pension payments to satisfy unpaid alimony. The pension was governed by a statutory spendthrift provision. *Id.* at 445. The court concluded that the wife could not use garnishment to reach the funds because alimony judgments are subject to revision and thus are not final judgments. *Id.* at 450. However, it also held the divorce court retained the authority, even in the face of the spendthrift provision, to enforce its decree and could reach the pension funds through quasi-garnishment. *Id.* at 451.

¶12 While *Courtney* involved alimony, not property division, its reasoning for allowing the pension funds to be reached, even in the face of a broad spendthrift provision, is instructive. The court stated that the pension funds "are created for the protection, not only of the employee or insured, but for the protection of his family. Similarly, the purpose of exemptions is to relieve the person exempted from the pressure of claims that are hostile to his and his dependents' essential needs." *Id.* at 449. In light of those purposes, the pension was reachable for alimony payments. *Id.*

¶13 *Lindsey* also involved a City of Milwaukee pension, this time in the context of property division. *Lindsey,* 140 Wis. 2d at 686. The issues in *Lindsey* were whether, in light of the spendthrift provision, a pension was subject to a domestic relations order and whether the court had the discretion to order the employee spouse to make a specific payout selection. *Id.* at 686-87. We concluded the spendthrift provision barred direct division of the pension. *Id.* at 694. However, we also concluded that the circuit court retained broad discretion to order the employee spouse to make a specific payout election or enter other orders to protect the non-employee spouse's interest in the pension funds. *Id.* at 696–97. We remanded to the circuit court "to consider whether it should exercise its discretionary authority to direct [the employee spouse] to select a specific retirement payout option and to consider what other orders, if any, are appropriate in the event a selection is made which runs counter to [the non-employee spouse's] interests." *Id.* at 698.

¶14 Larry argues that *Lindsey* cannot be read to hold that pensions must be considered in the marital estate. In *Lindsey,* we declined to address the employee spouse's arguments regarding alleged error in the property division of the pension because of his failure to file a cross-appeal. *See id.* at 698 n.10. Thus, we did not directly address the issue raised in this case, whether a spendthrift provision prevents a pension from being considered in the marital estate.

¶15 Nonetheless, our reasoning in *Lindsey* is relevant here. We examined a spendthrift provision and determined that the circuit court had the discretion to order a specific payout selection or enter other orders to protect the non-employee spouse's interest in the pension. Implicit in the holding is that the non-employee spouse does, in fact, have an interest in those funds. That conclusion is consistent with the policies embraced in the legislative scheme of WIS. STAT. chs. 766 and 767—shared ownership of assets during marriage and presumptive equal division of assets at divorce—and does no violence to the language of the spendthrift provision of WIS. STAT. § 62.63(4), which bars direct division of those funds.

¶16 Larry also argues that because the legislature has amended other spendthrift provisions to allow direct division but has not amended WIS. STAT. § 62.63(4) to do the same, the legislature intended to exempt his pension from any type of consideration at divorce. *See* WIS. STAT. § 40.08(1m) (permitting division of state retirement by qualified domestic relations order), and WIS. STAT. § 40.80(2r) (permitting division of state deferred compensation by domestic relations order). However, "[n]umerous variables, unrelated to conscious endorsement of a statutory interpretation, may explain or cause legislative inaction." *Wenke v. Gehl Co.,* 2004 WI 103, ¶33, 274 Wis. 2d 220, 682 N.W.2d 405. Additionally, Larry's interpretation of the legislature's intent regarding the spendthrift provision contradicts the policies contained in WIS. STAT. chs. 766 and 767. *See* WIS. STAT. § 766.62 (classifying deferred employee benefits as marital property) and WIS. STAT. § 767.255 (presumption of equal division of marital estate).

¶17 The spendthrift provision for Larry's pension, WIS. STAT. § 62.63(4), bars a court from directly dividing the pension. However, the pension is still a marital asset accumulated during the course of the marriage. Even when a court cannot divide a pension through a domestic relations order, the court "retains broad discretion in dividing a pension plan between the parties." *Lindsey,* 140 Wis. 2d at 696. The court has the discretionary authority to order the employee spouse to make a specific payout election or enter other orders "in the event a selection is made which runs counter to [the non-employee spouse's] interests." *Id.* at 698. Therefore, the spendthrift provision, while barring a direct order dividing the pension, does not usurp the court's ability to effectuate an equitable division of the parties' assets, including the pension.

¶18 Because the circuit court erroneously concluded the spendthrift provision left it no discretion to consider the pension when dividing the marital estate, we reverse and remand with directions to consider the pension.

*By the Court.*—Judgment reversed and cause remanded with directions.

**Source:** Retrieved from www.wicourts.gov/ca/opinion/DisplayDocument. html?content=html&seqNo=7508 on July 11, 2007.

percent of cat owners purchase their pets gifts and 75 percent of dog owners consider their dog a member of the family. It should, therefore, not be a surprise that couples often disagree on who should get the family pet when getting a divorce. In fact, in 2007, a Wisconsin state legislator, who reportedly went through a contentious divorce that involved the family dog, proposed legislation that would govern how couples handle custody disputes involving their pets. The bill would have prohibited judges from ordering couples to share custody of the pet, absent agreements between the parties. Instead the judge could award the pet to one party or send it to the Humane Society.

## VALUATION OF MARITAL ASSETS

To determine what a fair and equitable distribution of property is, a value needs to be assigned to the marital property. That may sound simple and with some assets it *is* a simple process. For example, the value of a bank account is easily determined by verifying the amount in the account on a specific day. Other assets may not be as easy to assign a value.

Let's use John and Judy as an example, but with a few additional facts. One of John's aunts had left a large collection of Royal Doulton figurines to the couple when she died. John and Judy had no idea of why she left these collectible items to them or if they had any value. To the casual observer, these figurines looked no different from cheap ones that could be bought at the local Wal-Mart. The reality is that they were very valuable collectibles. John and Judy could not put an accurate value on them, nor could the paralegal who may be asked to help determine the value of the Harleys' marital property. Instead an appraiser will probably have to be hired to determine the fair market value of the figurines.

Property that is sometimes difficult to value includes:

- Antiques
- Collectible items
- Classic automobiles
- Coin and stamp collections
- Stocks and bonds
- Furniture
- Real estate—both residential and commercial
- Copyrights, patents, and other intellectual property

Experts and appraisers are often called upon to assist the law firm in the valuation of assets that are not easily determined. Paralegals should develop a list of these professionals who can be called upon when the valuation of property is difficult to establish. Examples of the experts who could be included on such a list are antique appraisers, real estate agents, stockbrokers, and accountants.

**CASE BRIEF ASSIGNMENT**

Read and brief the *Waln v. Waln,* 280 Wis.2d 253, 694 N. W.2d 452 (App., 2005) case. (See Appendix A for information on how to brief cases.)

*In re Marriage of Lee*
282 Mont. 410, 938 P.2d 650
(1997)

## BACKGROUND

Shawn and Lisa were married in 1985. At the time of their marriage, neither party owned any significant assets. No children were born of the marriage.

Lisa obtained a Bachelor of Arts degree in radio/television advertising management in 1983 and worked full-time until 1987, when she quit due to job-related stress. Lisa suffers from health problems but maintains an active lifestyle and full-time employment. Following the parties' separation, Lisa was employed by a veterinary clinic earning $1,600 per month. She applied to law school in 1995 but was not admitted.

Shawn obtained a Bachelor of Science degree in 1986 and his doctorate in veterinary medicine in 1990 from Washington State University. He financed his education with loans, in his name only, that totaled $61,500. From 1983 to 1996, he also obtained a total of $50,000 from his parents. No promissory notes were executed for these funds, and no interest or specific repayment plan was discussed.

Between 1986 and 1988, Lisa received $45,000 from her grandmother's estate, which was deposited in a joint account in the names of Lisa, her mother, and her brother. The inheritance was apparently spent for the joint living expenses of Shawn and Lisa. From 1984 to 1993, Shawn and Lisa reported total taxable incomes of $103,462 and $101,111 to the IRS.

In 1993, the parties moved to Hamilton, Montana, to establish the Montana Large Animal Veterinary Clinic, obtaining a $108,000 SBA loan and a $30,000 unsecured loan to open the clinic. The SBA loan is a joint loan between Shawn and Lisa and is guaranteed by Shawn's parents. The other loan is personal to Shawn. Eighty-four thousand dollars is still owed on the SBA loan.

Shawn and Lisa opened the clinic in 1993. They projected their first-year income at $120,000, which was exceeded by $10,000, but they underestimated their expenses. Although their business plan projected a break-even first year after a $30,000 salary, the Lees suffered a loss of over $18,000 with no salary. The parties offered conflicting evidence regarding Lisa's involvement with the clinic. Shawn acknowledged that Lisa attempted to promote the clinic among horse owners and performed bookkeeping and office functions, but denied that she played a significant role as a veterinary assistant as originally planned.

In 1994, Shawn petitioned for dissolution of marriage. Lisa requested temporary maintenance of $4,800 per month, based on her ordinary living expenses established during the marriage. The court awarded her $1,500 per month in temporary maintenance and $175 per month for the care of the parties' horses. On March 28, 1995, the District Court issued a writ of execution in favor of Lisa for unpaid maintenance, but then the court ordered the writ returned. Shawn moved to modify temporary maintenance due to insufficient income.

After Shawn failed to make any substantial maintenance payments, a contempt hearing was held. The court ordered Shawn incarcerated for one day and allowed him twenty days to bring temporary maintenance into compliance. On July 11, 1995, the District Court heard Shawn's motion to modify temporary maintenance. The court found that the clinic had a "negative value." In 1994, Shawn reported $101,700 in gross receipts, leaving the clinic with a net loss of $2,600, with no salary paid. In 1995, the clinic grossed $75,000. The court determined that Shawn had proven unable to support himself and to pay maintenance and ordered cessation of temporary maintenance. It also reserved jurisdiction to reconsider modification of temporary maintenance retroactively and ordered Shawn to provide Lisa with health insurance until the parties' marriage was dissolved.

At trial, Shawn testified that the parties' breakup caused a decline in patronage, and he lost accounts due to ownership changes. He relied on a friend for a place to live and basic living expenses, supplemented by loans from his parents. Dr. Brown, a veterinarian with a large animal practice in Missoula, Montana, testified that in 1995 his gross income was $95,000. Dr. Kelly, a veterinarian with a large animal practice in Corvallis, Montana, testified that during the first year of her clinic in 1995, she earned over $10,000 per month in gross receipts.

The District Court calculated the parties' assets as $64,775 and the debts incurred during the marriage as $228,455. It then divided the marital estate as follows:

|  | Shawn | Lisa |
|---|---|---|
| Assets | $ 38,500 | $26,275 |
| Debts | −$190,204 | −$38,251 |
| Net Distribution | −$151,704 | −$11,976 |

The court concluded that Shawn should be liable for the debt owed to his parents, and Lisa should be liable for her contract for deed obligations associated with property acquired after the parties' separation. The court dissolved the marriage, retroactively modified its 1994 order requiring temporary maintenance, ordered Shawn to pay maintenance of $100 a year for five years and $686 in back-due temporary maintenance, and ordered Shawn and Lisa to bear their own legal fees. Lisa appeals from the findings, conclusions, final decree, and other rulings issued during the action.

## DISCUSSION

\*\*\*

¶ 2. Did the District Court err when it awarded maintenance of $100 a year to Lisa?

Lisa requested $3,333 monthly in maintenance for sixty months to fund a law school education, pay bills, and provide for living expenses. The court awarded her $100 in annual maintenance for five years based on its determination that Shawn had insufficient income to meet the needs of himself and Lisa. Lisa argues the court erred because: (1) it did not consider all of the requirements of § 40-4-203, MCA; (2) it did not impute income to Shawn; and (3) it did not provide Lisa with rehabilitative maintenance.

We review a district court's award of maintenance to determine if the court's findings are clearly erroneous. *In re Marriage of Eschenbacher* (1992), 253 Mont. 139, 142, 831 P.2d 1353, 1355. The District Court made the following findings of fact concerning maintenance:

> 54. Lisa lack[s] sufficient property to provide for her reasonable needs. She will emerge from this action with a negative net worth and in debt. She [owns] an adequate home but has insufficient resources to finish the remodeling and . . . no equity in the property.
>
> 55. Lisa is able to support herself at a spartan level while making payments on the debt allocated to her through appropriate employment. . . . She has a college education and a varied work history at responsible jobs. She is currently a business manager of a prospering veterinary clinic . . . receiving . . . net pay of $603.85 biweekly. . . . Lisa lacks sufficient disposable income to monthly retire her current debts in full, obtain health insurance, or the medical care she requires, much less the upper middle class lifestyle the couple originally aspired to. Nevertheless she has continued to retain custody of the horses the [c]ourt concluded should be sold to pay expenses. . . .
>
> 56. Shawn is leaving the marriage under a staggering debt load and with a far worse negative net worth than Lisa. After three years in Montana . . . his professional practice is in a downward spiral with three successive years of losses. His **655 business is worth less now than three years ago. His professional income is enough to make payments on the marital debt sufficient to prevent collection suits and foreclosure as well as immediate business accounts payable, but is insufficient to provide any draw or salary. His personal needs are being met by his parents and . . . this situation is [not] likely to change without his bankruptcy or closure of the practice and acceptance of an employment position which would likely carry a monthly salary . . . insufficient to service the debt load and provide any other income for his individual needs or individual acquisition of capital assets.

Based on these facts, and the other factors required by § 40-4-203, MCA, the District Court concluded that no significant award of maintenance was warranted or possible. However, because it was concerned that a near-term reversal of Shawn's fortunes following the final decree could cause an inequitable long-term result, it ordered Shawn to pay Lisa maintenance of $100 per year for five years, subject to modification by Lisa upon a showing of changed circumstances *418 so substantial and continuing as to make the terms of the decree unconscionable under § 40-4-208(2)(b), MCA.

The District Court found that Lisa lacked sufficient property to provide for her reasonable needs but also found that she was able to support herself through appropriate employment. These findings do not appear to meet the statutory criteria necessary for maintenance under § 40-4-203, MCA, which require as a condition precedent to an award of maintenance, that the court must find the spouse seeking maintenance "lacks sufficient property to provide for [her] reasonable needs; and is unable to support [her]self through appropriate employment." Section 40-4-203(1), MCA; *See also In re Marriage of Luisi* (1988), 232 Mont. 243, 247-48, 756 P.2d 456, 459. However, this Court has held the term "appropriate employment," as used in § 40-4-203, MCA, "must be determined with relation to the standard of living achieved by the parties during the marriage." *Luisi,* 756 P.2d at 459.

The District Court qualified its findings by explaining that Lisa was able to support herself at a spartan level through appropriate employment. The court considered Lisa's need for health insurance, her continuing medical problems, her income and debt, and lowered standard of living. The court also considered Shawn's financial situation and ability to meet his needs when it awarded Lisa $100 in annual maintenance. We conclude that the District Court's findings are not clearly erroneous, and that in its sixty findings the court adequately considered the factors contained in § 40-4-203, MCA, when it awarded maintenance.

Lisa argues that the District Court should have imputed income to Shawn to reflect his earning capacity and his ability to pay maintenance. The findings do not support such a result. The evidence showed that Shawn's clinic suffered from a decline in gross receipts due to a loss of clients and increased competition from other veterinarians, not from his lack of willingness to work. We hold that the District Court did not err when it did not impute income to Shawn.

Lisa also claims that she is entitled to an award of rehabilitative maintenance because her full-time employment from 1984 to 1987 made it possible for Shawn to attend school and obtain his degree, that she contributed her inheritance to support Shawn, and that her earnings between 1990 and 1993 supplemented Shawn's employment before he established his practice in Hamilton. Shawn argues that through extensive loans he financed his own education and part of the parties' living expenses. He notes that over the first decade of the parties' relationship they had nearly equal earnings. He maintains *419 that his education and license have no intrinsic value, are not marketable or transferrable, and have no value apart from his professional practice. We agree.

In a majority of jurisdictions that have ruled on the question, it has been held that an educational degree or a professional license does not constitute marital property subject to division by the court in a marriage dissolution proceeding. *See* 24 Am.Jur.2d Divorce and Separation § 898 (1983). Such items have no exchange or transferrable value. *In re Marriage of Graham* (1978), 194 Colo. 429, 574 P.2d 75, 77. They are personal to the holder, terminate upon death, and are not subject to inheritance, assignment, sale, conveyance, or pledge. *Graham,* 574 P.2d at 77. They are intellectual achievements which may potentially assist in the future acquisition of property but possess none of the usual attributes of property. *Graham,* 574 P.2d at 77. *See also* 4 A.L.R.4th 1294 (1981).

The District Court recognized that a spouse may have an equitable claim to repayment for any investment she may have made in the license holder's education or career enhancement to allow that license holder to attain his education and training. The record demonstrates that Shawn financed his own education with student loans included as liabilities in his distribution of the marital estate. Lisa did not put her career on hold or place her own advanced educational plans, if any, on hold for the sake of Shawn's advancement. According to the record, she was voluntarily unemployed during three of the four years that Shawn attended veterinary school. After Shawn's graduation, the parties lived primarily on Shawn's professional income for three years before moving to Hamilton. Between the years of 1984 and 1993, the parties reported nearly the same amount of income to the IRS. It does not appear that Lisa had difficulty finding appropriate self-sustaining employment since the parties' separation by using her premarital education and the work skills acquired during marriage. Under the facts of this case, the District Court did not abuse its discretion when it did not consider Shawn's veterinary degree as part of the marital estate.

Lisa suggests she should have been awarded rehabilitative maintenance pursuant to § 40-4-203, MCA, so that she could establish herself at a professional level similar to Shawn's. This Court and other jurisdictions have considered the concept of rehabilitative maintenance. In *Marriage of Williams,* this Court affirmed a ten-year $162,597 maintenance award to an attorney's wife based on the value of her lost career. *420 In re Marriage of Williams* (1986), 220 Mont. 232, 714 P.2d 548. Likewise, in *Downs v. Downs* (1990), 154 Vt. 161, 574 A.2d 156, the Vermont Supreme Court considered the case of a spouse who had contributed to the education and training of her husband, a physician, when there was insufficient property for distribution. The court held "when one spouse obtains a professional degree during the marriage, but the marriage ends before the benefits of the degree can be realized, the future value of the professional degree is a relevant factor to be considered in reaching a just and equitable maintenance award." *Downs,* 574 A.2d at 159. *See also Washburn v. Washburn* (1984), 101 Wash.2d 168, 677 P.2d 152; *Reiss v. Reiss* (A.D.1985), 205 N. J.Super. 41, 500 A.2d 24.

We need not decide whether rehabilitative maintenance is receivable in situations where one spouse sacrifices an education or career to enable the other spouse to obtain a professional degree, education, or license. Even if this Court adopted that concept, the facts of this case would not justify such an award. We hold that the District Court did not abuse its discretion when it did not provide Lisa with rehabilitative maintenance.

Lisa argues that she is entitled to maintenance and a property settlement because she was instrumental in preparing a business plan for the SBA loan. The District Court correctly determined that there was insufficient evidence to conclude that the business plan was instrumental in securing the parties' SBA loan. As the court found, it is more likely that, because the parties possessed no collateral and no net worth, the willingness of Shawn's parents to guarantee the loan carried more weight in the bank's decision than the business plan.

The District Court's findings in support of its maintenance award are not clearly erroneous. We hold that the District Court did not err when it awarded Lisa $100 in annual maintenance for five years.

5. Did the District Court err when it valued Shawn's veterinary practice?

Following a maintenance modification hearing held on July 11, 1995, the District Court found that Shawn's practice had a negative value. Lisa argues that there is insufficient evidence in the record to support the court's finding. Lisa did not file a complete transcript of the hearing as required by Rule 9(b), M.R.App.P. As a result, we cannot review the sufficiency of the evidence on that issue.

The distribution of marital property in a dissolution proceeding is governed by § 40-4-202, MCA. Under this statute, a district court is vested with broad discretion to distribute the marital estate in a manner which is equitable to each party according to the circumstances of the case. *In re Marriage of Smith* (1995), 270 Mont. 263, 267, 891 P.2d 522, 525. The standard of review of a district court's division of marital property is whether the court's findings are clearly erroneous. *In re Marriage of Hogstad* (1996), 275 Mont. 489, 496, 914 P.2d 584, 588. If substantial credible evidence supports the district court's judgment, it will not be disturbed absent an abuse of discretion. *Hogstad,* 914 P.2d at 588.

Lisa claims that when the District Court divided the marital estate, it did not consider the value of the clinic's good will. The findings and conclusions indicate otherwise. The District Court found that Shawn's professional practice is a marital asset eligible for equitable distribution. It determined that the only recognizable value of a professional practice over and above the net value of its tangible physical assets is the present value of its good will, i.e. the extent to which the practitioner's net profits exceed that of the average practitioner in the region of the practice. *In re Marriage of Hull* (1986), 219 Mont. 480, 712 P.2d 1317. The value of the tangible assets of Shawn's practice is far more than fully secured by his SBA loan.

The court also found that through competition Shawn's potential market share has been eroded and that his practice has no good will to be distributed. There is substantial credible evidence from Shawn's testimony and financial records to support the court's finding that the clinic has a "negative value." Therefore, the court's finding is not clearly erroneous. We conclude that the District Court did not abuse its discretion when it valued Shawn's veterinary practice.

¶ 6. Did the District Court err when it did not consider Lisa's contribution of premarital property and inherited funds?

Lisa argues that the court did not consider her premarital property when it divided the marital estate. The District Court found that neither party owned any significant assets at the time of their marriage. We conclude that the District Court did not abuse its discretion.

Lisa also argues that the court did not consider her inheritance in its division of the marital estate. Whether inherited property is a marital asset remains a question to be treated on a case-by-case basis. *In re Marriage of Kimm* (1993), 260 Mont. 479, 485, 861 P.2d 165, 169. The District Court found that, "No proof was presented to document Lisa's representations and the [c]ourt is unable to verify her claims as to the disposition of her inheritance." At trial, Lisa testified that she used her inheritance for living expenses when she was not working after 1987. The remainder was spent for a pickup truck and other personal property still in Lisa's possession. Lisa is not entitled to a credit in the division of the marital estate based on her inheritance. We hold that the District Court did not abuse its discretion when it did not include Lisa's inherited funds in the marital estate.

7. Did the District Court err when it refused to hear Lisa's testimony as an expert witness concerning the value of the clinic?

Lisa argues that the court abused its discretion when, at trial, it refused to hear her opinion concerning the value of the clinic because she was not qualified under Rule 702, M.R.Evid. The determination of the qualification of an expert witness is a matter of discretion for the trial court. Absent a showing of abuse of that discretion, the decision will not be disturbed. *In re Marriage of Arrotta* (1990), 244 Mont. 508, 511, 797 P.2d 940, 942.

After sustaining Shawn's objection regarding Lisa's proposed expert testimony, the District Court allowed Lisa to make an offer of proof. Lisa testified that the average annual gross income for veterinary practices in western Montana similar to Shawn's is $263,000. The issue of Lisa's proposed expert testimony is not determinative in this case. We conclude that the District Court did not abuse its discretion when it determined that Lisa was not qualified to testify as an expert witness.

\* \* \*

We affirm the District Court's findings of fact, conclusions of law, final decree of dissolution, and other rulings issued during the action.

**Source:** From Westlaw. Reprinted with permission from Thomson-West.

## RESEARCH THIS

Locate the laws that set out how marital assets are valued in your state. Does your state specify that assets be valued at their fair market value? Does the statute specify which date should be used for valuation of the assets or does it leave it to the judge's discretion?

### CASE BRIEF ASSIGNMENT

Read and brief the *In re Marriage of Lee,* 282 Mont. 410, 938 P.2d 650 (1997) case. (See Appendix A for information on how to brief cases.)

### CYBER TRIP

To learn more about how property is valued in a divorce, visit www.divorcesource.com/archives/valuation.shtml.

Issues relating to the distribution of property and debts are often resolved through negotiations between the parties or other forms of alternate dispute resolution. Negotiations and other forms of alternate dispute resolution will be dealt with in more detail in Chapter 12.

Unless the parties agree to the division of marital property, a judge will make a final determination of the value of the property. Judges are generally given a great degree of discretion when determining the equitable distribution of property, but some evidence as to the valuation of the property is required on which the judge will base his or her decision in order to ensure that the property distribution plan is, in fact, equitable. This evidence is provided by the parties and can include testimony of experts, such as those mentioned above, other testimony, and documentary evidence, such as receipts. The assets are usually valued at their fair market value at the date specified by statute, less the amount of any encumbrances, liens, or mortgages. This may be the date the complaint was filed, the date of the hearing on valuation, the date of the divorce, or the date of distribution of the assets.

## ALLOCATION OF DEBTS

The typical American family has many debts. They may have a mortgage on the house, a loan for the car, and unsecured credit card debt. The court has the power to order either the husband or wife to pay a particular bill. It is just another example of how a judge must create an overall dissolution of assets and obligations to reach a fair and just decision.

As in the case of assets, judges are called upon to distribute marital debt in a fair and equitable manner. The judge is also granted broad discretion in determining what

**CYBER TRIP**

Although divorce certainly has an impact on the credit of both men and women, women do face some distinct issues relating to their credit after a divorce. To learn more about the issues relating to women and divorce, and specifically the effect that divorce has on a person's credit, visit www.in.gov/dfi/education/MiniLessons/wdiv.htm. This site is maintained by the Indiana Department of Financial Institutions and presents a "minicourse" on this topic.

constitutes a fair and equitable distribution of the debts and liabilities of the marriage, just as in the distribution of assets.

One important note—just because a judge orders one party to pay a particular debt does not mean the creditor is bound by the order. If the husband is ordered to pay the Visa bill, which was a joint account in both the husband's and wife's names, but fails to do so, Visa can go after either or both parties.

It is important that couples who have decided that divorce is in their future start planning on how to minimize the negative impact the divorce may have on their individual credit. Steps that can be taken include the following:

- Close joint accounts and open individual accounts.
- Remove the other spouse's name from any individual credit or bank account on which he or she is listed as an authorized user.
- Stay in contact with creditors and stay current on the payment of bills during the course of the divorce proceedings. Creditors can be asked to transfer the debt to the name of the person who will be responsible, but they are not required to.

## OTHER MATTERS ASSOCIATED WITH DIVISION OF PROPERTY

As was demonstrated by the discussion of professional degrees being an asset to be dealt with in a divorce, many things affect the distribution of assets. This is also true when dealing with what would otherwise be separate assets of either the husband or the wife.

Sometimes a spouse may do something to change how the court views an asset. Two common examples are sweat equity and commingling of funds.

*Sweat equity* occurs when a spouse performs some act, such as improvements on a home that is the other spouse's separate property, that increases the value of that property. For example, Dan and Opal get married. Opal owns her own home. They agree that they will live in that house but that Opal will retain the house as her own, separate property. However, Dan completes an extensive remodeling of the house and even puts in a swimming pool with his own money. If Dan and Opal ever get divorced, Dan may not be able to claim the house as marital property but could make a claim for the increase in value his contributions made to the value of the house. The *Ory v. Ory* case set out in the next Case in Point is an example of such an argument made by a husband.

*Commingling of funds* is another act that may have unexpected consequences. Let's use Dan and Opal as an example again, except this time Dan does not make improvements on the house. Instead Opal makes the mortgage payments, insurance payments, and payments on the cost of repairs from a joint checking account that she has with Dan. Dan has his paycheck automatically deposited to that checking account, and the couple makes no effort to identify whose money is paying what bills. These acts, as was true with Dan's home improvements, may give him a claim to an interest in Opal's house.

**dissipating**
Wasting the marital estate.

**Dissipating** may also have an effect on a court's distribution of marital property. Dissipation occurs when a spouse intentionally depletes the marital assets in anticipation of a divorce. Courts that are tasked with the job of making an equitable distribution of the marital property may examine the circumstances surrounding the reduction of marital assets and offset the amount from the wrongdoing spouse's distribution of the remaining marital assets.

Although numerous factors can be considered in the equitable distribution of property, some common ones include:

- Spouses' age
- Spouses' physical and mental condition
- Earning potential of each spouse
- Monetary and nonmonetary contributions of the parties during the marriage
- Length of the marriage
- Value of the marital property
- Marital debts
- Need of custodial parent to retain marital home while raising children of the marriage
- Tax consequences
- Contribution of one spouse toward the education/career of the other spouse
- Impact on the need for alimony

**FIGURE 5.4**
**Factors Used to Determine the Equitable Distribution of Property**

Dissipation is an example of economic fault, an act of a spouse that had a negative impact on the assets of the marriage and/or affected the economic needs of the other spouse. Drug addiction of one spouse who sold marital assets to pay for his or her addiction is another example of economic fault, as is spousal abuse that resulted in increased long-term medical care or loss of earning capacity.

Although economic fault is recognized as a factor in determining equitable distribution of marital property, fault, such as adultery, is no longer considered in most jurisdictions. This is another aspect of the no fault divorce movement. A number of states do, however, allow noneconomic fault as a factor to be considered in the equitable division of property. Figure 5.4 sets out some of the other factors courts can look at to determine the equitable distribution of property.

**ETHICS ALERT**

Divorces can become very bitter, which can cause people to behave in uncharacteristic ways. They can rationalize their behavior but, in the end, some of it crosses legal and ethical lines. This can occur when a spouse decides that he or she wants a divorce and starts to plan for when it occurs. The spouse may begin to hide marital property. Or a spouse may begin overspending with the intent of reducing the assets of the marriage.

It is important that the paralegal does not become party to such acts or ignore that they are occurring. Instead, the paralegal should report his or her suspicions to the supervising attorney immediately.

## SEPARATION AGREEMENTS

Although the parties of a marriage may both agree to a divorce, they may still have disputes over things like child custody and visitation and who gets the marital property.

These issues can be resolved in one of several ways, including the application of a premarital agreement, the negotiation of a separation agreement, or the use of a mediator to help the parties reach an agreement; when all else fails, a judge may be called upon to resolve the issues.

In the Court of Appeals of the State of Mississippi
*Ory v. Ory*
No. 2004-Ca-00545-Coa
May 2, 2006
Modified Opinion on Motion for Rehearing
En Banc

BARNES, J., for the Court.

\*\*\*

## SUMMARY OF FACTS AND PROCEDURAL HISTORY

¶3. Alan and Sharon Ory were married on November 4, 1995, in Lamar County, Mississippi, and lived together until on or about October 20, 2001. During their marriage, Alan was an employee and part-owner of SpeeDee Oil Change in Hattiesburg, and Sharon worked as a respiratory therapist at Forrest General Hospital, also in Hattiesburg. On October 24, 2001, Alan filed for divorce on the grounds of habitual cruel and inhuman treatment and adultery, or in the alternative, irreconcilable differences. Sharon answered and counterclaimed that she also was entitled to a divorce on the ground of habitual cruel and inhuman treatment, or in the alternative, irreconcilable differences. On January 24, 2003, the Chancery Court of Lamar County issued an order granting Alan the divorce on the ground of habitual cruel and inhuman treatment. The order granting the divorce ("judgment of divorce") stated that the chancery court reserved for a later date other issues such as the distribution of the marital assets. After hearings held in September and October 2003, the chancellor issued a final judgment which ordered the distribution of the marital assets ("distribution judgment"); this judgment was issued on January 23, 2004.1

¶4. In arriving at the distribution, the chancellor evaluated the following assets:

a. An eighty-acre parcel of land deeded to Sharon prior to the marriage;
b. The Orys' marital home and a five-acre section of the larger parcel, upon which the home was constructed;
c. The appreciation during the marriage of Alan's share of the SpeeDee Oil Change franchise;
d. Sharon's retirement fund of $36,520, accumulated during the marriage;
e. A motorcycle, tractor, pick-up truck, desk, and tools.

¶5. In the distribution judgment, the chancellor valued the marital assets at $280,077 and awarded each party fifty percent of the marital estate, or $140,038.50 apiece. Sharon was awarded the marital home, fee simple title to the entire eighty-acre parcel of land, the contents of her retirement account, and the furnishings in the home. Alan was awarded the appreciation in value of the SpeeDee Oil Change franchise as well as the motorcycle, tractor, truck, desk, and tools. Because the value of the assets distributed to Sharon slightly outweighed those awarded to Alan, the chancellor required that Sharon pay Alan a total of $13,034.50 to make up for the imbalance. Additionally, the chancellor ordered Sharon to reimburse Alan $49,000 for payments he made prior to the marriage to pay off a lien on Sharon's parcel of land. Taking into account the effect of the $49,000 payment, Sharon's award was effectively reduced to $91,038.50, and Alan's award increased to $189,038.50.

¶6. Dissatisfied with the chancellor's distribution, Alan filed a motion for new trial asserting that the chancellor's decision was against the overwhelming weight of the evidence. Upon the chancery court's denial of his motion, Alan, represented by new counsel, appealed to this Court, asserting the following: (1) that the chancellor erred in awarding the divorce on the ground of habitual cruel and inhuman treatment; (2) that the chancellor erred in characterizing the seventy-five-acre parcel of land and certain funds as non-marital assets; (3) that the chancellor erroneously calculated the mathematics of the equitable distribution; and (4) that the chancellor erred in distributing the marital assets. We affirm in part and reverse and remand in part.

\*\*\*

## ISSUES AND ANALYSIS

\*\*\*

## II. WHETHER THE CHANCERY COURT ERRED IN CHARACTERIZING THE SEVENTY-FIVE-ACRE PARCEL OF LAND AND CERTAIN FUNDS AS NON-MARITAL ASSETS.

¶12. In the distribution judgment, the chancellor found that while the marital home and five-acre parcel of land upon which the home was situated were marital assets, the remaining seventy-five-acre parcel was not a marital asset subject to equitable distribution. Alan challenges this finding, and claims that the land became a marital asset because of his efforts to improve the land and because of his contribution of funds in removing a lien from the property. Furthermore, Alan contests the chancellor's finding that $35,000 that Sharon put into the home was not a marital asset.

¶13. "For purposes of divorce proceedings, the marital estate consists of property acquired or accumulated by the parties during the course of the marriage." *Hankins v. Hankins,*

866 So. 2d 508, 511 (¶13) (Miss. Ct. App. 2004) (citing *Hemsley v. Hemsley,* 639 So. 2d 909, 915 (Miss. 1994)). The marital estate is subject to equitable distribution upon the divorce of the parties. *Id.* However, not all property acquired during the course of a marriage is "marital"; those assets attributable to a party's separate estate prior to marriage are considered non-marital property not subject to equitable distribution. *Id.* While this is the general rule, non-marital assets may lose their status as such if the party commingles the asset with marital property or uses them for familial benefit. *Johnson v. Johnson,* 650 So. 2d 1281, 1286 (Miss. 1994).

¶14. In the present case, there is no serious dispute that Sharon owned the property prior to her marriage to Alan. Though Alan argued at trial and again in his briefs that he "bought" the land from Sharon's parents, the record does not support his contentions. The record shows that the land in question, in Sharon's family for over 100 years, was encumbered by a mortgage of $49,000. Before the marriage, Alan paid off this lien with his personal funds, but title in the property remained solely in Sharon's name. While Alan's contribution removed a cloud from the property, the record is absent of any evidence showing that Alan purchased the land. Sharon testified that prior to Alan's offer to remove the lien, she had secured a loan to refinance the property. Therefore, Alan's argument that Sharon would have "lost" the property without him, and that therefore he "bought" the property, is not supported by the record. The chancellor's distribution judgment, however, recognized the value of Alan's contribution, and reimbursed him the $49,000.

¶15. Because there is no question that the seventy-five-acre parcel belonged to Sharon's separate estate prior to the marriage, if Alan is to have any interest in the property, it can only come about through the commingling doctrine. *See Hankins,* 866 So. 2d at 511 (¶16). Alan contends that the parcel was converted to a marital asset due to his efforts to improve the land. The record shows that Alan made some efforts to improve the land; the testimony is unclear as to what extent his efforts improved the seventy-five-acre tract versus the five-acre parcel upon which the marital home was built. Nevertheless, the record reflects that Alan cleared a portion of the land, hauled dirt onto the property, and had a large number of seedlings planted on the property. Alan did not, however, put forth sufficient evidence to prove that his activity was so pervasive as to convert the entire seventy-five-acre parcel into a marital asset, or show how the land increased in value during his marriage to Sharon. Thus, we cannot find that the chancellor was manifestly wrong in characterizing the parcel as a non-marital asset.

¶16. Alan also asserts that the chancery court erred in characterizing certain funds as non-marital assets. At the distribution hearing, Sharon testified that at the beginning of her marriage to Alan, she owned a 1991 Cavalier mobile home. She testified that Alan paid $30,000 to pay off a lien on the home, and that when the home was subsequently sold for $19,000, the proceeds were put back into the house the couple was constructing. Additionally, Sharon testified that during the marriage she received $16,000 in personal injury proceeds as a result of an automobile accident. Sharon stated at the distribution hearing that these funds "went back into knobs and door handles and window blinds and the wallpaper and furniture and appliances for the house." In the distribution

judgment, the chancellor assigned to the marital home and five-acre tract a total value of $180,000, which represented the value suggested in an appraisal report on the property. The chancellor subtracted from this figure $28,443, representing the balance of the mortgage on the property. From the resulting figure of $151,557, the chancellor subtracted $35,000 that Sharon had contributed to the purchase of the home. This $35,000 figure represented the total of the proceeds from the personal injury settlement and the sale of the mobile home.

¶17. It is clear from the record that the entire $19,000 in proceeds from the sale of the mobile home should not have been characterized as a non-marital asset. Sharon testified that prior to the marriage, she had paid a down payment of $4,500 on the home and had made monthly payments of $418.84 for "six or seven years." However, it is undisputed that Alan paid approximately $30,000 to clear the lien from the home, and that the mobile home later sold for $19,000. We reverse the chancellor's characterization of the entire $19,000 as a non-marital asset, and remand for a recalculation of the award that takes into account the contributions of both parties.

¶18. Alan also challenges the chancellor's characterization of Sharon's $16,000 personal injury award as a non-marital asset. While proceeds from personal injury actions are not generally deemed marital assets, they can lose their non-marital status through commingling with marital assets. *Myrick v. Myrick,* 739 So. 2d 432, 434 (¶7) (Miss. Ct. App. 1999). The record shows that Sharon invested the entire $16,000 in furnishings for the marital home; this is a clear example of commingling. Exacerbating the error is the fact that Sharon was awarded the marital home and its furnishings. The $16,000 injury award was used to furnish the home; thus, the chancellor's award gave Sharon double credit for her contribution. Finding error, we reverse the chancellor's characterization of the personal injury proceeds as non-marital assets.

¶19. In sum, we uphold the chancellor's finding that the seventy-five-acre parcel of land was a non-marital asset. However, because we find error in the chancellor's calculation of the portion of the proceeds from the sale of the mobile home to which Sharon is entitled, and in the chancellor's determination that Sharon's $16,000 personal injury settlement was a non-marital asset, we remand to the chancery court for a distribution of these assets in a manner consistent with this opinion.

## III. WHETHER THE CHANCERY COURT ERRED IN THE MATHEMATICS OF THE PROPERTY DIVISION.

¶20. Alan testified at the distribution hearing that when he sold his share of the SpeeDee Oil Change franchise for $500,000, he "paid out" $296,000 in expenses related to the sale. Included in the $296,000 figure were payments to business partners, a payment to the franchise's parent company, capital gains taxes, and a payment to pay off a business loan. The chancellor's distribution judgment mistakenly quoted a figure of $296,000[6] as the amount Alan netted in the sale, rather than the amount he *paid out* pursuant to the sale. The chancellor used the $296,000 figure in calculating the appreciation in value of the SpeeDee Oil Change franchise during the Orys' marriage. The miscalculation was significant; using the $296,000 figure, the chancellor arrived at an appreciation value of $127,000. Had the chancellor used $204,000 as the net profit (resulting from sale price of $500,000 minus expenses of $296,000), he would have arrived at an appreciation of only $35,000.

¶21. Though the chancellor clearly erred in his calculation, this does not end the inquiry. Alan testified that he "ha[d] $250,000 left" after the sale of the franchise. It is mathematically impossible that Alan could be left with this sum after paying $296,000 in expenses related to the sale. In order for Alan to have $250,000 after the sale, the sale price must have been over $500,000, or the value of the business at the time of sale must have been the sale price plus the value of certain bank accounts Alan retained after the sale. Annette Turner, Sharon's expert witness, testified that both the sale price and the amount remaining in the bank accounts at the time of the sale had to be considered. She concluded that Alan actually received $314,932 for his interest when the SpeeDee Oil Change franchise was sold. Thus, it appears that the value Alan retained after the sale of the business was between $250,000 and $314,392.

¶22. We remand this issue to the chancery court so that it might revisit the issue of the valuation of the SpeeDee Oil Change franchise, and the corresponding appreciation in value of the franchise during the Orys' marriage.

## IV. WHETHER THE CHANCELLOR ERRED IN DISTRIBUTING THE MARITAL ASSETS.

¶23. Though we have found that the chancellor erred in calculating the value of certain assets, we do not find that the chancellor erred in attempting to distribute the marital assets equally. The chancellor took into consideration the equitable distribution principles embodied in *Ferguson v. Ferguson*, 639 So. 2d 921, 927 (Miss. 1994), and did not commit manifest error. However, Alan claims that the chancellor erred in distributing the marital assets because he did not take into account Sharon's adultery. We note that in the distribution judgment, the chancellor made no mention of the relative fault of the parties. Marital misconduct is a factor entitled to be given weight by the chancellor when the misconduct places a burden on the stability and harmony of the marital and family relationship. *Singley v. Singley*, 846 So. 2d 1004, 1007 (¶8) (Miss. 2002) (citing *Ferguson*, 639 So. 2d at 927). While Sharon did admit that she had engaged in adulterous activity, Alan put forth no evidence to show that Sharon's conduct affected the stability of the marriage. Had Alan put forth some evidence of how Sharon's conduct affected the marriage, it is possible that the chancellor might have erred in ignoring that proof. However, because Alan did not put forth such evidence, we cannot find the lower court in error. This issue is without merit.

**Source:** Retrieved from www.mssc.state.ms.us/Images/Opinions/CO31358.pdf on April 12, 2007.

**CASE BRIEF ASSIGNMENT**

Read and brief the *Ory v. Ory*, 936 So.2d 405 (Miss. Ct.App. 2006) case. (See Appendix A for information on how to brief cases.)

## Summary

The distribution of property and the assignment of debt are important parts of the divorce procedure. They can be accomplished by the parties through a separation agreement or by the court applying the relevant statutory and case law.

Marital property, that is, the property acquired by the parties during the course of the marriage, is normally the only property that a court will be responsible for distributing. Today, many courts are including professional degrees, licenses, and goodwill as marital assets in certain circumstances.

Some community property states divide the marital property 50/50, while other community property states and non-community-property states start with a 50/50 split of the marital assets between the parties but will make adjustments to achieve an equitable distribution.

The acts of the spouses themselves may also influence what property is distributed in the divorce. Sweat equity, commingling of funds, and dissipation may allow a spouse to make a claim against property that would otherwise be considered separate property of the other spouse.

| | | |
|---|---|---|
| Community property | Qualified domestic relations order | **Key Terms** |
| Dissipating | (QDRO) | |
| Equitable distribution | Real property | |
| Intangible property | Separate property | |
| Joint tenancy with right of survivorship | Tangible property | |
| (JTROS) | Tenancy by the entirety | |
| Marital estates (marital property) | Tenancy in common | |
| Personal property | Vested | |

**Review Questions**

1. What is the difference between tangible personal property and intangible personal property?
2. What is the difference between joint tenancy with right of survivorship and tenancy by the entirety?
3. What is the difference between marital property and separate property?
4. Why is the term equitable distribution important in the distribution of property?
5. Discuss the factors a judge in a common law state may consider in deciding what constitutes an equitable distribution of marital property.
6. What makes the decision on what will happen to the marital home a difficult one for a judge to decide?
7. Are retirement funds subject to distribution as marital property?
8. How do courts deal with professional degrees/licenses when deciding an equitable distribution of property in a divorce?
9. If a judge orders a husband to pay the Visa bill, which was a joint account with his wife, can Visa sue the wife if the husband fails to pay?
10. What is dissipation and why is it important in family law?

**Exercises**

1. Review the facts of the Client Interview. Does John Harley have a basis to claim an interest in Judy's home as part of the property distribution, if the couple got divorced? Explain your answer. What could Judy have done to protect her rights in the home?
2. Steve and Barbara Belinoff were married for 25 years and had two children, both of whom are now adults. Steve owns a variety of classic automobiles. Barbara has a large collection of art. They own their marital home as tenants by the entirety and also own a number of rental properties. All of their property was acquired during the marriage. Barbara has retained your firm to represent her in her divorce. Your supervising attorney has asked that you assist in the valuation of the marital property. What other professionals/appraisers might you need to help you

in this task and why will they be needed? What additional information will you need to move forward on this assignment from your supervising attorney?

3. Don and Kelly were married for 15 years. During most of that time, they had a good marriage. Don was a professional and made a very good living. Kelly was a stay-at-home mom. They have one child, Liz, who has Down syndrome. She is 8 years old and has lived her entire life in her parents' marital home. In the past 2 years, Don has begun to drink heavily. Kelly is convinced that he is an alcoholic. He has been spending money without regard to the impact it has had on the family's financial situation. Kelly also suspects that he has been taking money from their savings account. What legal issues are presented in this factual setting that relate to the material discussed in this chapter?

4. Chris Bunnell married Stephanie just after they graduated from college 30 years ago. She worked as a nurse to put Chris through medical school. Once he graduated, they moved back to their hometown. Chris opened his medical office, and Stephanie was the nurse/office manager. The practice prospered, and Chris opened a small hospital in town, which grew over the years. Last year he began having an affair with another woman who works at the hospital. Stephanie has come to your office to find out what may be involved in the event she divorces Chris. What rights might she have to the property acquired during their marriage? What factors might the courts look at in trying to distribute the couple's marital property?

5. José and Carmelita Sanchez were married for many years. Carmelita is worried that if she tries to get a divorce, José will try to ruin her financially. She has not discussed the matter of the divorce with him because she feels he will begin spending their money and hiding assets. Carmelita has come to your office. What are some of the steps that she can take to protect herself financially and protect her credit rating?

## REAL WORLD DISCUSSION TOPICS

A husband and wife were married for 36 years and had no minor children at the time the husband sought an absolute divorce, which was granted in 1990. The court subsequently entered an order of equitable distribution that required equal distribution of the marital property. The court included income earned from rental property, which was owned as tenancy by the entirety, during the time between the couple's separation and the order of equitable distribution.

Should the court have classified the property as marital property? If not, could the court have considered the income from the rental property as part of an equitable distribution of the property? See *Chandler v. Chandler*, 108 N.C.App. 66, 422 S.E.2d 587 (N.C.App. 1992).

## PORTFOLIO ASSIGNMENT

Research the statutory and case law of your state relating to the topics discussed in this chapter. Write a paper setting out what property may be distributed in a divorce, what factors a judge can consider in ordering the division of property and debts, and how much discretion a judge has in this process.

# Chapter 6

# Alimony

## CHAPTER OBJECTIVES

**After reading this chapter and completing the assignments, you should be able to:**

- State the primary criteria for the award of alimony.

- Explain the other factors a court may consider when determining what type of alimony should be awarded.

- List and distinguish between the types of alimony a court may award.

- Explain how long alimony must be paid and what factors cause payment to stop.

- Explain the tax consequences of alimony payments.

- Describe why the use of a separation agreement is sometimes advisable in resolving issues relating to alimony.

Chapter 6 introduces the paralegal student to a topic that often causes some of the most heated discussions when people are trying to negotiate a separation agreement, even more so if the decision is left to the judge. That topic is alimony.

This chapter discusses what alimony is; the types of alimony a court may award; the factors that can be considered in determining whether to award alimony and, if awarded, how much; the tax consequences of alimony; and the value of a settlement agreement to resolve issues surrounding alimony.

## CLIENT INTERVIEW

Juan and Carmen Martinez were married for almost 20 years. They have two children, a boy, 13, and a girl, 6. Carmen, an RN, worked as a nurse to help put her husband through medical school. After he began practicing medicine, Carmen stopped work as a nurse so that the couple could start a family. She has devoted her time since then to caring for her children, taking care of the family home, and doing volunteer work at their church.

Juan became involved with Janet, a nurse he works with at the local hospital. He has decided he wants to get a divorce and start a new life with Janet.

Carmen has come to your firm to represent her in the divorce. She indicates that, among other things, she is interested in receiving alimony from Juan. She provides information that shows that he makes $250,000 a year. She does not want to go back to work because she wants to be there for the children when they return from school and on the weekends.

Chapter 6 also discusses a concept that is often associated with alimony, even though it involves unmarried couples, called *palimony*. Palimony is the division of property between two unmarried parties after they separate or the paying of support by one party to the other.

## WHY THIS CHAPTER IS IMPORTANT TO THE PARALEGAL

Alimony is a somewhat complicated area of the law and one that is often confusing to the general public. To adequately perform their duties in a law office, paralegals must be familiar with alimony and how it may be used in a divorce proceeding. The paralegal will often be required to gather information that relates to the issue of alimony and perform legal research to better determine a client's position when it comes to the award of alimony.

A basic understanding of the concepts discussed in this chapter will provide the paralegal student with the ability to communicate in an intelligent way on the subject and also understand why certain information is important.

## WHAT IS ALIMONY?

When divorce proceedings are started, perhaps no other word strikes greater fear in a person's heart than the word *alimony*!

**divorce *a mensa et thoro***
Divorce from bed and board.

Alimony traces its origins back to the English ecclesiastical courts and a time when the husband was the owner of the property of the marriage. A type of limited divorce referred to as **divorce *a mensa et thoro***, which means a divorce from bed and board, was used when the couple decided to separate. Alimony was a method to ensure that the wife would not become destitute after the separation and that the husband remained responsible for her maintenance for the rest of her life. The divorces granted by the courts of that time did not end the marriage, but instead provided for the separation of the husband and wife. Today divorces, also referred to as **divorce *a vinculo matrimonii***, and dissolutions of marriage are absolute, yet the legal concept created by the ecclesiastical courts still is contained in state law in the form of alimony.

**divorce *a vinculo matrimonii***
Total divorce.

Alimony, often referred to as *spousal support,* is the periodic payment by one spouse to the other by order of a court. It is, however, more complicated than this, as will be seen in the detailed discussion in this chapter.

Historically, it was the husband who was most apprehensive about the possibility of having to pay alimony. But as divorce laws have been changed to be gender neutral, both men and women may be required to pay alimony. State statutes usually set out broad statements relating to alimony and when it may be ordered. See Figure 6.1 for an example of such a statute.

The fact that alimony laws are now gender neutral was dramatically brought to the nation's attention in 1992 when Joan Lunden, a famous news broadcaster and television personality, was ordered to pay support to her ex-husband. And it is not just women celebrities and stars who have had to deal with paying alimony. Successful businesswomen, including Kim Shamsk, president of a large temporary staffing company, have also been ordered to pay their ex-husbands' alimony. Shamsk was 47 at the time of her divorce and was required to pay alimony to her 65-year-old retired baseball player ex-spouse. And with the increasing number of stay-at-home dads, many average working women have been required to pay alimony when the couple divorces.

**458:19 Alimony. –**

I. Upon motion of either party for alimony payments, the court shall make orders for the payment of alimony to the party in need of alimony, either temporary or permanent, for a definite or indefinite period of time, if the motion for alimony payments is made within 5 years of the decree of nullity or divorce and the court finds that:

   (a) The party in need lacks sufficient income, property, or both, including property apportioned in accordance with RSA 458:16-a, to provide for such party's reasonable needs, taking into account the style of living to which the parties have become accustomed during the marriage; and

   (b) The party from whom alimony is sought is able to meet reasonable needs while meeting those of the party seeking alimony, taking into account the style of living to which the parties have become accustomed during the marriage; and

   (c) The party in need is unable to be self-supporting through appropriate employment at a standard of living that meets reasonable needs or is allocated parental rights and responsibilities under RSA 461-A for a child of the parties whose condition or circumstances make it appropriate that the parent not seek employment outside the home.

II. Upon motion of either party, the court may make orders for the payment of an alimony allowance when such orders would be just and equitable.

III. Upon a decree of nullity or divorce, or upon the renewal, modification, or extension of a prior order for alimony, the court may order alimony to be paid for such length of time as the parties may agree or the court orders.

IV. (a) The court may make orders for alimony in a lump sum, periodic payments, or both.

   (b) In determining the amount of alimony, the court shall consider the length of the marriage; the age, health, social or economic status, occupation, amount and sources of income, the property awarded under RSA 458:16-a, vocational skills, employability, estate, liabilities, and needs of each of the parties; the opportunity of each for future acquisition of capital assets and income; the fault of either party as defined in RSA 458:16-a, II(l); and the federal tax consequences of the order.

   (c) In determining amount and sources of income, the court shall not consider a minor child's social security benefit payments or a second or subsequent spouse's income. The court may consider veterans' disability benefits collected by either or both parties to the extent permitted by federal law.

   (d) The court may also consider the contribution of each of the parties in the acquisition, preservation, or appreciation in value of their respective estates and the noneconomic contribution of each of the parties to the family unit.

   (e) In any proceeding for modification of an existing alimony order, the earned or unearned income and social security disability payments of a spouse of the obligor party shall not be considered a source of income to that obligor party for the purpose of modification, unless the obligor party resigns from or refuses employment or is voluntarily unemployed or underemployed, in which case the income of a subsequent spouse may be imputed to the obligor party only to the extent that such obligor party could have earned income in his or her usual employment. In such actions, the court may consider the veteran's disability benefits of a spouse of the obligor party to the extent permitted by federal law.

V. The unanticipated consequences of changes in federal tax legislation or regulations may be grounds to modify any alimony order or agreement.

VI. The court shall specify written reasons for the granting or denial of any motion for an alimony allowance.

VII. In cases where the court issues an order for permanent alimony for a definite period of time, such order may be renewed, upon the petition of either party, provided that such petition is made within 5 years of the termination date of the permanent alimony order. Nothing in this paragraph shall be construed to change or alter in any way the terms of the original alimony order.

**FIGURE 6.1**

**New Hampshire Alimony Statute**

*Source:* Retrieved on 4/6/08 from www.gencourt.state.nh.us/rsa/html/XLIII/458/458-19.htm.

Paralegal students must keep in mind that alimony is a separate and distinct concept from child support. It is just one more tool a judge has to create a fair and equitable dissolution of marriage. Alimony can be used in conjunction with property distribution and child support to reach that goal.

 **RESEARCH THIS**

Although all states have statutory and case law dealing with the criteria courts should follow when determining if alimony should be awarded and, if so, how much, the law does vary, sometimes dramatically, from state to state. It is critical that paralegals know and understand the specific laws of their state in order to perform their duties in a family law firm.

Research the statutory and case laws of your state and compare them to the New Hampshire statute set out in Figure 6.1. Are the criteria similar, or do they vary from the New Hampshire statute? If you live in New Hampshire, research the statutory and case law of a neighboring state and compare them to the New Hampshire statute.

## FACTORS TO BE CONSIDERED IN AWARD OF ALIMONY

As will be seen later in this chapter, there are many types of alimony. Judges are given a certain degree of flexibility in determining which, if any, of these types of alimony is appropriate to use in a specific case. Unlike child support, which is discussed in Chapter 8, most states do not have a set formula that a court must follow when determining how much or which type of alimony should be awarded.

Instead courts are called upon to determine the amount and type of alimony that should be used in the event that the parties have not already addressed the matter of alimony in a premarital or settlement agreement. To do this a judge may consider a variety of factors. No one factor is necessarily controlling on the judge's decision. Rather, the judge will look at all relevant factors to determine what is best in a particular case.

The two fundamental factors that a judge must first consider are the ability of one spouse to pay alimony and the need of the other to receive alimony. To determine the paying spouse's ability to pay, the judge will consider the person's income from employment, income from investments, pension income, and other forms of income that may be available. Allowable deductions will be reduced from the total income to determine the paying spouse's net income. To determine the need of the receiving spouse, the judge will look at whether the receiving spouse will have the financial ability to maintain the lifestyle that he or she enjoyed during the course of the marriage.

To assist in determining need, courts will look at a variety of other factors:

- *The length of the marriage.* The length of the marriage is often a factor a judge uses to determine if an award of alimony is appropriate. Generally, the longer the marriage, the greater the chance for an award of alimony. Some states, such as Utah, specify that alimony cannot be ordered for longer than the number of years the couple was married. See Utah Code 1953 § 30-3-5 (8)(h).

- *The age of the spouses.* An older spouse may have difficulty in finding employment, especially if he or she has been out of the workplace for an extended period of time. This factor may increase the likelihood of an award of alimony.

- *The earning capacity of each spouse.* If there is a significant difference in the earning capacity of the two parties, the likelihood of an award of alimony is increased.

- *The education level of the spouses and any special training either spouse may have.* Since education and training can be factors in the ability of a person to get a job, they likewise are factors that can be considered in determining both one spouse's ability to pay alimony and the other's need to receive it.

- *The need for additional education on the part of one spouse to be self-supporting in the future.* This factor is often important in the award of temporary alimony, since it provides the receiving spouse financial support while he or she gets the necessary education/training to become self-supporting.

- *The mental and physical condition of the spouses.* Poor mental or physical health of one spouse may increase the need for an award of alimony, since that spouse is less likely to be able to support him- or herself.

- *The financial resources of each spouse.* These can include both marital assets and nonassets of each spouse.

- *The presence of minor children in the home.* If minor children are still at home, it may limit the ability of the spouse awarded primary custodial parent from working outside the home.

- *The standard of living enjoyed by the spouses while married.*

- *The contribution each party has made to the marriage.* This can be things like the money earned by a spouse or the homemaker's contribution to the household and raising the children.

- *Contribution of one spouse to aid in the education or training of the other that increased that spouse's earning capacity.*

- *Fault.* Although states may allow for no fault divorces, many states allow for the consideration of fault, that is, whose actions may have been a contributing factor in causing the divorce, to be considered when determining whether alimony should be awarded. In seeking an equitable award of alimony, some states allow the court to consider whether the spouse seeking alimony also may have been guilty of misconduct. Courts should not, however, use alimony as a means of punishing the errant spouse. Nor should adultery alone be the basis for an award of alimony.

After reviewing this list it should be very clear that a court must look at a wide range of factors in order to reach an appropriate award of alimony. Figure 6.2 provides a summary of some of the factors a court may consider. It should also be obvious that judges are granted a great degree of latitude in deciding the issues relating to the award

**CYBER TRIP**

To learn more about the history of alimony and how one state, Nevada, has dealt with the award of alimony, visit www.divorcenet.com/states/nevada/alimony_weakest_link. The site also includes the results of an interesting survey of judges who were presented with a spousal support fact setting and asked to determine how much alimony should be awarded.

---

As is true with the determination of what constitutes an equitable distribution of marital property, judges are given leeway in deciding if alimony should be granted and, if so, how much.  Some factors that can be considered include:

- Financial ability to pay by the paying spouse
- Need for alimony by receiving spouse
- Length of marriage
- Age of the spouses
- Earning capacity of each spouse
- Education level of each spouse
- Need of additional education of a spouse to rejoin the workforce
- Mental and physical condition of each spouse
- Financial resources available to each spouse
- Whether minor children of the marriage are living at home
- Financial and nonfinancial contribution made by each spouse to the marriage
- Contribution of one spouse to aid in the education/training of the other spouse
- Fault

**FIGURE 6.2**
**Factors Considered by Courts to Determine If Alimony Will Be Awarded and, If So, How Much**

of alimony. This fact has come under increasing discussion in the legal community. Many feel that more specific alimony guidelines need to be established. One judge, Judge Farmer, felt strongly enough about the need for a change to write a concurring opinion in *Bacon v. Bacon,* which is set out in the following Case in Point, in which he presented a number of thoughtful points on the matter. Other states, such as Pennsylvania, have taken steps toward resolving this issue or have recognized the need for change.

## TYPES OF ALIMONY

As with most things with the law, the subject of alimony is not as simple as it may first appear. How could this be? After all, everyone know what alimony is, don't they?

Yes, most people have an idea of what alimony is. But most people mistakenly believe that there is only one type of alimony. A number of different types of alimony can be used to reach the best results based on the facts of a particular case. The following discussion describes the different types.

**permanent alimony**
Alimony paid for an indefinite period of time.

**Permanent alimony**, also referred to as *periodic alimony,* is what most people think of when they hear the word *alimony.* It is intended to continue for an indefinite period of time. The payments normally end when either party dies or the recipient remarries.

Courts will look at several factors when they are required to rule on the award of permanent alimony. The starting point is the determination of whether one spouse has the ability to pay alimony and the other has a need to receive alimony. But the judge may consider other factors to decide whether an award of alimony is appropriate and, if so, the amount that should be awarded. Factors such as the length of the marriage, the age of the parties, the earning abilities of the parties, the health of the parties, the value of each party's estate, and the standard of living enjoyed by the parties during their marriage can all be considered in selecting the appropriateness of an award of alimony and determining what amount should be awarded.

**alimony pendente lite (APL)**
Temporary order for payments of a set amount monthly while the litigation continues.

**Alimony pendente lite** (APL), which is also referred to as *temporary alimony,* is the term that usually refers to alimony that is paid between the time of the separation of the husband and wife and the entry of the final judgment of divorce.

**rehabilitative alimony**
Alimony, usually granted to a specific time, which is intended to allow the receiving party time to gain needed education or training to enter the workforce.

**Rehabilitative alimony** is alimony that is to be paid for a specific time. This is often used to allow a spouse time to get additional education or job skills that will allow him or her to be self-sufficient. It is also used to provide for the spouse who may stay at home to care for a minor child.

**reimbursement alimony**
Alimony used to reimburse the receiving spouse for working or providing financial assistance that enhanced the spouse's future.

**Reimbursement alimony** is used to reimburse the receiving spouse for working or providing financial assistance that enhanced the spouse's future. An example would be a woman who works to put her husband through medical school.

**bridge-the-gap alimony**
Alimony intended to aid the receiving spouse's move from being married to being single.

**Bridge-the-gap alimony**, as its name implies, is a way to help a spouse move from being married to being single. It is paid for a specific time. This form of alimony is recognized in some jurisdictions. Bridge-the-gap alimony is often confused with rehabilitative alimony, even by judges trying to decide which type of alimony to award. The key difference is what the alimony is intended to do. Rehabilitative alimony is intended to rehabilitate the person who will receive it, such as providing him or her with the necessary skills to be self-supporting. Bridge-the-gap alimony is intended for short-term, unique situations where another form of alimony, including rehabilitative alimony, would not be appropriate.

**lump sum alimony**
Alimony paid in a specific amount that is not subject to modification.

**Lump sum alimony**, also referred to as *alimony in gross,* is often used as part of a property settlement. Its purpose is to ensure that the distribution of the marital property is equitable. Judges often award one spouse's interest in the marital home to the other as lump sum alimony. Unlike permanent alimony, once lump sum alimony has been awarded, it does not terminate upon the receiver's remarriage or death. It is also not subject to modification if it involves assets such as the marital home, but lump

*Bacon v. Bacon*
819 So.2d 950
(Fla.4th DCA 2002)

STONE, J.

The wife appeals from a final judgment of dissolution of marriage on grounds that the trial court's award of permanent periodic alimony was an abuse of discretion. We agree and reverse. The record reflects that not all of the wife's needs were considered in arriving at the court's award of alimony and that the trial court erred in construing the limits of its discretion in awarding alimony under section 61.08, Florida Statutes.

The parties were married for twenty-seven years. The husband has a successful career as a bond trader with an annual income of $288,000. There were two children born to the couple, both of whom have attained the age of majority. The wife, a high school graduate, worked only part-time as a secretary until the birth of the couple's second child. When the husband's father came to live with the family after being diagnosed with Parkinson's disease, the couple agreed that the wife would quit her job and become a full-time homemaker and caretaker of her father-in-law.

The wife sought an after-tax permanent alimony award of $8,515 per month based upon her existing expenses and the parties' standard of living. The court awarded $3,275 per month, approximately 13 1/2% of the husband's present income. This award was based on the testimony of the husband's accountant, who claimed the wife could sustain herself on much less than she was requesting and the testimony of a vocational expert who stated she was employable. The husband's accountant/witness calculated the wife's "reasonable" future expenses to be only $6,000 per month. The vocational witness testified that the wife could earn between $17,000 and $23,000 per year if she were to commence full-time employment.

In considering the wife's needs, the court recognized that the couple had maintained a comfortable lifestyle, but accepted the deductions made by the husband's expert on the wife's estimated needs. The expert reduced the requested amount by arbitrarily deducting from the wife's current charitable contributions and her personal and household expenses based on his belief that those expenses would be less if she were living alone. In reaching his conclusion, the expert, and ultimately the trial court, assumed the wife would find a smaller home for $200,000. He predicted that once she moved in, she would have lower utilities and home care expense and would spend less time and money for travel, entertainment, civic activities, and hobbies, i.e., caring for her horses and stables. The expert then allocated $20,000 for moving expenses which he assumed would be sufficient.

Neither the expert nor the trial court took into consideration any increase in the wife's expenses attributable to her working a full-time job while still trying to retain her existing standard of living.

The court accepted the testimony of the husband's accountant, that by completely altering the wife's existing investment portfolio, consisting of her equitable distribution and retirement accounts, and after subtracting 20%, the amount the wife would need for a down payment on a $200,000 home, and after deducting $20,000 for incidental expenses arbitrarily allotted for move-in costs, the wife could realize an almost $2,000 per month return if she invested at 6%. In order to earn this amount, however, the wife would have to change the existing investment scheme and, in the process, suffer a substantial loss in principal. The reinvestment scheme also assumes the wife would have proceeds available from the sale of the marital home which is not yet on the market.

In summary, the court assessed the wife's needs, pre-tax, as $6,000 per month ($72,000 per year). The court concluded that the wife's needs could be satisfied by adding $23,164 in assumed interest income on investments, plus $16,000 in imputed full-time employment income, and an alimony award of $39,300 annually ($3,275 per month). In arriving at his decision, the trial judge announced that he was "required" to impute full-time employment income to the wife, notwithstanding that such was against his better judgment in this case.

We recognize that as long as the award is "within the parameters of reasonableness," the trial court's alimony award should not be disturbed on appeal. *Canakaris v. Canakaris*, 382 So.2d 1197, 1204 (Fla.1980). However, in this case, we conclude that the court's imputation of income was an abuse of discretion, requiring reversal.

Section 61.08, Florida Statutes, provides:

> In determining a proper award of alimony or maintenance, the court shall consider all relevant economic factors, including but not limited to:
>
> ***
>
> (g) All sources of income available to either party.
> The court may consider any other factor necessary to do equity and justice between the parties.

In *Mallard v. Mallard*, 771 So.2d 1138 (Fla.2000), the Florida Supreme Court delineated the following criteria to be examined in awarding alimony: (a) the parties' earning ability, (b) age, (c) health, (d) education, (e) duration of marriage, (f) standard of living, and (g) the value of the parties' estate.

Although, certainly, the trial court should consider prospective employment as a potential source of income to the wife, it is also required to consider the other factors, including those "necessary to do equity and justice." *See Kreisler v. Kreisler*, 752 So.2d 1288 (Fla. 5th DCA 2000); *Brock v. Brock*, 690 So.2d 737 (Fla. 5th DCA 1997). Nothing in the statute mandates that minimum wage income must be immediately imputed for the purpose of reducing alimony that would otherwise be ordered. *See Shrove v. Shrove*, 724 So.2d 679 (Fla. 4th DCA 1999) (noting that imputation of income is only one factor that should be considered in determining alimony award but is not mandatory where child support is not at issue).

Furthermore, given the wife's lack of present employment, her acknowledged entitlement to permanent alimony, the length of this marriage, the standard of living enjoyed by the parties, and the husband's undisputed ability to pay, there is no statutory or other mandate that the trial court impute income requiring that she obtain a full-time job immediately. *See Laz v. Laz,* 727 So.2d 966, 967 (Fla. 2d DCA 1998); *Atkins v. Atkins,* 611 So.2d 570, 573 (Fla. 1st DCA 1992); *see also* § 61.08, Fla. Stat. (2000). Even if under the facts of this case it were found necessary for the wife to be employed, some consideration must be given to her need for rehabilitative or bridge-the-gap alimony to that end. *See Canakaris,* 382 So.2d at 1202; *Winn v. Winn,* 669 So.2d 1155 (Fla. 5th DCA 1996).

Here, the record makes it evident that the trial court misinterpreted the mandatory aspect of its obligation to consider the enumerated factors when the judge said:

> I am to, in a sense, under the case law to put her [the Wife] in the same situation as she would be in if she had never met her husband, but they had maybe an arms-length transaction, gone into a joint venture, distributed their assets that they were able to marshal over twenty-seven years and leave her at the same place she would have otherwise been.
>
> * * *
>
> The law says and requires her to go back to work. I have to follow that law and I will. I have problems with it. I think her contribution is undervalued and I hope some day that will be rectified. . . .

The statute, as interpreted, albeit reluctantly, by the trial court, would not allow the court to consider, for example, the fact that one spouse stays home by mutual agreement and raises the children, while the other spouse is able to accumulate twenty or more years of business or professional experience and earning ability. This interpretation would also leave the court with no discretion to remedy the glaring inequality that exists where, post-dissolution, one spouse continues to earn an income in an atmosphere of his choice, while the former homemaker, who developed no income-earning skills during the marriage, is forced to work under far more unpleasant conditions.

We do note that in *Crowley v. Crowley,* 672 So.2d 597 (Fla. 1st DCA 1996), the trial court awarded an amount of alimony "sufficient to place her in a position substantially similar to that she would be had the marriage not occurred." *Id.* at 599. The First District reversed, stating: "The husband has not cited, and we have not found, any authority that would support the trial court's effort to use the alimony award to place the wife in the financial position she would have occupied had the 19 year marriage not occurred. To the extent the award reflects this effort, it is erroneous." *Id.*

Further, in imputing income to the wife, the court assumed that she must and could become employed immediately. At a minimum, the court should have awarded sufficient alimony to cover the wife's total present need until such time as the wife is able to find reasonable employment, at which time modification might be in order.

Although the husband correctly asserts that the wife would have a lower electric bill and mortgage payment upon purchasing a smaller home, it is also true that other expenses would necessarily increase if she were working full time. Patently, if the wife must obtain employment, then many of her current expenses will change. For example, she will need to purchase work-related clothing; she may need to have those clothes drycleaned; she may need to buy lunch every day; she would need to use gasoline to drive to and from work; she may need to purchase prepared meals; and she may need to pay others to handle responsibilities that she might otherwise perform in maintaining her home and lifestyle. No mention was made of this inevitable fact, apparently because of the husband's concession of ability to pay and the wife's reliance on receiving her present expenses.

All other things being equal, "periodic alimony is used to provide the needs and the necessities of life to a former spouse *as they have been established by the marriage of the parties.*" *Canakaris,* 382 So.2d at 1201 (emphasis added); *Gove v. Gove,* 579 So.2d 756, 757 (Fla. 4th DCA 1991); *see also Knoff v. Knoff,* 751 So.2d 167, 167 (Fla. 2d DCA 2000). Here, maintaining that standard of living for both parties did not mandate paring the wife's expenses and maximizing her income while, at the same time, disregarding the ability of the husband to more fully participate in her support without sacrificing his own standard of living. The goal is to afford her the style of living that the parties, together, established over a period of twenty-seven years.

As the record reflects that the wife was short-changed by the totality of the foregoing, we reverse the judgment and remand for the trial court to reconsider the amount of alimony.

HAZOURI, J., concurs.

FARMER, J., concurring specially.

I agree with the reversal because a party entitled to alimony was "shortchanged." *See Canakaris v. Canakaris,* 382 So.2d 1197, 1204 (Fla.1980) ("in viewing the totality of the circumstances, one spouse should not be 'shortchanged.'"). I write, however, to express my view that broad discretion in the award of alimony is no longer justifiable and should be discarded in favor of guidelines, if not an outright rule.

This case admirably illustrates the need for reform. The parties may quibble over other details, but the essential facts in outline are these: (1) long term marriage (27 years) with no children still in their minority; (2) a party with annual income of $288,000; (3) the other party, who hasn't worked outside the home since early in the marriage, has imputable wages no better than minimum. *Canakaris* establishes a policy of discretion rather than rules in the determination of alimony, which the Legislature has been loathe [*sic*] to contradict. This policy favoring discretion-and under the reasonableness test of *Canakaris* the broadest and most deferential one, at that—in determining claims of *955 alimony is now under serious challenge in the literature. I think entitlements to alimony ought to be standardized—i.e., set by guidelines which the trial judge can vary within fixed limits only upon reasons supported by the record.

In this case, the party seeking alimony asked for $8,500 monthly, or little more than 35% of the payor's $288,000 annual income. The amount actually awarded by the trial judge comes to about 14% of the payor's income. In *Canakaris,* the payor's annual income was almost $150,000, and the annual alimony awarded was $26,000—or about 17% of the payor's income. The supreme court found that amount "neither unreasonable nor arbitrary," explaining:

> "We acknowledge that reasonable persons might differ as to what is an appropriate sum for permanent periodic alimony in this cause, but we find it is within the parameters of reasonableness; therefore, there can be no finding of an abuse of discretion."

382 So.2d at 1204. If 17% for the functionally equivalent range of income was "neither unreasonable nor arbitrary," then 14% is probably within the range of discretion as well.

Without guidelines or standards the amount awarded in this case could well appear to some judges to be within the general ambit of "reasonableness," especially if the trial judge could properly consider, as the majority acknowledges, imputing minimum wage income to a party who has not worked in 28 years but seems otherwise able to do so. Thus, under *Canakaris* it can be plausibly argued that this award is not an abuse of discretion.

The *Canakaris* insistence on discretion makes the amount of alimony almost always a subject of litigation. When a critical issue may be resolved only in litigation, outcomes are not predictable and a strong incentive for settling is removed. Because chapter 61 contains a provision providing for an adverse party to pay the attorney's fees of the other party, incentives to litigate are even intensified, and family assets are placed in peril of being lost to fees and costs that would otherwise be avoided if outcomes were predictable. Assets given to fees and costs are not available to provide income and support to families; nor are they available for descent and distribution to children.

If I were the Legislature setting guidelines for alimony for cases within the essential *956 facts of this category, 35% of a payor's income could be within a reasonable range. Under the partnership theory of marriage and alimony, 35% of payor's income is not unjustifiable for incomes ranging above $200,000. A statute setting such guidelines would add a world of predictability to dissolution of marriage litigation, thereby operating to promote settlements and reduce attorney's fees and thus avoid costly and time-consuming appeals like this one.

**Source:** From Westlaw. Reprinted with permission from ThomsonWest.

sum alimony in the form of installment payments may be subject to modification in a future judicial proceeding.

Each different type of alimony is like a tool in the judge's toolbox. The judge can use one or more of these tools to draft an equitable final judgment, or the parties can use them to draft a separation agreement that is agreeable to both parties. For an example of how one state court described some of the types of alimony mentioned in this chapter, as well as the discretion a court has in deciding such issues, see *Canakaris v. Canakaris*, 382 So.2d 1197 (Fla. 1980).

**CASE BRIEF ASSIGNMENT**

Read and brief the *Bacon v. Bacon*, 819 So.2d 950 (Fla. Dist. Ct. App. 2002) case. (See Appendix A for information on how to brief cases.)

## HOW LONG MUST ALIMONY BE PAID?

The answer to this question depends on a variety of circumstances, including what type of alimony is awarded.

Permanent alimony is potentially the longest-lasting form of alimony. Payment of permanent alimony can continue until it is modified or vacated by the court or there is a change in the condition of one of the parties. Two common changes that will terminate the payment of permanent alimony are the death of the paying or receiving party or the remarriage of the receiving spouse, unless otherwise agreed to in the separation agreement. The first time limit, death, is an easy one to understand and apply. The second, remarriage, is the one that creates most of the problems. Since more and more people are living together outside of marriage, many people get very upset that they are still paying alimony even though their ex is living with someone else just as if he or she were married, but without the license.

Although states are gradually changing their statutes relating to the impact cohabitation has on the continued payment of alimony, one approach that can be used to limit problems with permanent alimony is to make provisions for it in the separation agreement entered into by the parties. This too can be tricky. How do you establish what living together is? Does the ex have to live with another person for a specific period of time? Does the ex have to maintain a separate residence from the person he or she is seeing in order to continue to receive the alimony payments? Careful wording of such a clause is critical to protect the interests of both spouses after the divorce.

In the Court of Appeals of Tennessee at Nashville
*Booker v. Booker*
No. M2005-01455-COA-R3-CV
Filed on October 26, 2006

## OPINION

\*\*\*

## II.

Husband appeals and raises the following issues:

1. Does the evidence preponderate against the trial court's award of alimony *in solido* and its award of alimony *in futuro*.
2. Does the evidence preponderate against the trial court's division of the marital property.

## III.

\*\*\*

## B.

A trial court has broad discretion in fashioning a division of marital property. *Fisher v. Fisher*, 648 S.W.2d 244, 246 (Tenn. 1983); *Barnhill v. Barnhill*, 826 S.W.2d 443, 449-50 (Tenn. Ct. App. 1991). It has the same broad discretion with respect to an award of alimony. *Aaron v. Aaron*, 909 S.W.2d 408, 410 (Tenn. 1995); *Anderton v. Anderton*, 988 S.W.2d 675, 682 (Tenn. Ct. App. 1998).

In evaluating whether a trial court has abused its discretion, we are bound by the principle that the trial court "will be upheld so long as reasonable minds can disagree as to propriety of the decision made." *Eldridge v. Eldridge*, 42 S.W.3d 82, 85 (Tenn. 2001) (quoting *State v. Scott*, 33 S.W.3d 746, 752 (Tenn. 2000) and *State v. Gilliland*, 22 S.W.3d 266, 273 (Tenn. 2000)). A trial court abuses its discretion when it "applie[s] an incorrect legal standard, or reache[s] a decision which is against logic or reasoning that cause[s] an injustice to the party complaining." *State v. Shirley*, 6 S.W.3d 243, 247 (Tenn. 1999) (citation omitted). An appellate court cannot substitute its judgment for that of the trial court. *Myint v. Allstate Ins. Co.*, 970 S.W.2d 920, 927 (Tenn. 1998).

## IV.

Husband's primary contention with respect to the trial court's alimony decrees is that Wife failed to demonstrate any need for either type of alimony. He argues that the parties' respective financial and other circumstances are virtually the same. As to the award of alimony *in futuro,* Husband asserts that Wife is not economically disadvantaged and does not need to be rehabilitated. Husband also contends that the trial court's alimony decrees were designed to punish him for his conduct during the marriage.

There are no hard and fast rules governing spousal support decisions. *Anderton,* 988 S.W.2d at 682. Generally, trial courts "have the prerogative to determine the type of spousal support that best fits the circumstances of the case and may award several different types of support in the same case when the facts warrant it." *Id.* Tennessee law provides four different types of alimony that may be appropriate in combination or alone: "rehabilitative alimony, alimony in futuro, also known as periodic alimony, transitional alimony, or alimony in solido, also known as lump sum alimony." T.C.A. § 36-5-121(d)(1) (2005).

Decisions regarding spousal support require a careful balancing of the statutory factors and depend upon the unique facts of each case. *Anderton,* 988 S.W.2d at 683. T.C.A. § 36-5-121(i) sets forth a list of relevant factors for a trial court to consider in determining whether alimony is appropriate, and if so, the nature, amount, length of term, and manner of payment:

(1) The relative earning capacity, obligations, needs, and financial resources of each party, including income from pension, profit sharing or retirement plans and all other sources;

(2) The relative education and training of each party, the ability and opportunity of each party to secure such education and training, and the necessity of a party to secure further education and training to improve such party's earnings capacity to a reasonable level;

(3) The duration of the marriage;

(4) The age and mental condition of each party;

(5) The physical condition of each party, including, but not limited to, physical disability or incapacity due to a chronic debilitating disease;

(6) The extent to which it would be undesirable for a party to seek employment outside the home, because such party will be custodian of a minor child of the marriage;

(7) The separate assets of each party, both real and personal, tangible and intangible;

(8) The provisions made with regard to the marital property, as defined in § 36-4-121;

(9) The standard of living of the parties established during the marriage;

(10) The extent to which each party has made such tangible and intangible contributions to the marriage as monetary and homemaker contributions, and tangible

and intangible contributions by a party to the education, training or increased earning power of the other party;

(11) The relative fault of the parties, in cases where the court, in its discretion, deems it appropriate to do so; and

(12) Such other factors, including the tax consequences to each party, as are necessary to consider the equities between the parties.

The "real need of the [disadvantaged] spouse seeking the support is the single most important factor . . . [and next] the courts most often consider the ability of the obligor spouse to provide support." *Aaron*, 909 S.W.2d at 410 (citation omitted).

In this case, the trial court determined that decrees of alimony *in solido* and alimony *in futuro* were appropriate. Specifically, the trial court set aside to Wife $23,000 of the value of the marital residence as alimony *in solido*. It also awarded her $500 per month as alimony *in futuro*. The trial court's judgment states that the following factors support such an award: "the duration of the marriage, the education of the parties, the earning capabilities of the parties, the age of the parties, physical and mental health, the contribution to the assets, and the relative fault of the parties." The statement of the evidence reflects the trial court's decision from the bench in slightly more detail:

> I find that [Husband] has a higher earning capacity than [Wife], Tenn. Code Ann. § 36-5-121(i)(1); that he has greater education and training than she does, § 36-5-121(i)(2); that the marriage is of long duration, § 36-5-121(i)(3); that both parties made tangible and intangible contributions to the marriage, § 36-5-121(i)(10); and that [Husband's] fault was greater than [Wife's], § 36-5-121(i)(11).

The record reveals that the parties were married on October 16, 1979. At the time of the divorce hearing, Husband was 47 and Wife was 45. The couple have two children, both of whom have reached the age of majority. Wife testified that she was primarily responsible for raising the children throughout the marriage. She had a 20-year work history with the United States Corps of Engineers. Her salary was $41,000 per year. She has an associate's degree, and is presently pursuing a bachelor's degree. Wife testified that she suffers from some physical and mental health issues.

Husband has a bachelor's degree and a master's degree in Public Management. At the time of the hearing below, he was earning $45,239 per year at the Department of Defense in Washington, D.C. In addition, he was receiving a disability payment of $1,147 per month as a result of his military service. Hence, Husband's total annual gross income was $59,003. Husband admitted to having one extramarital affair, and a divorce was granted to Wife on the basis of Husband's inappropriate marital conduct. However, Husband testified that Wife contributed to the demise of their marriage by complaining constantly and exhibiting violent behavior on several occasions.

\*\*\*

Wife testified that her house and automobile both needed repairs. Her statement of income and expense includes an allowance for these expenses. Wife's take-home pay is $2,372.33 per month. Her house is paid for and she has no debt.

We disagree with Husband's contention that Wife is not economically disadvantaged vis-a-vis him. Husband's gross income is approximately $18,000 per year more than Wife's annual salary of $41,000. Under the circumstances of this case, we agree with the trial court's implicit finding of Wife's economic disadvantage.

There is a statutory bias in favor of rehabilitative alimony. T.C.A. § 36-5-121(d)(2); *see also Crabtree v. Crabtree*, 16 S. W.3d 356, 358 (Tenn. 2000). According to the statutory definition, "[t]o be rehabilitated means to achieve, with reasonable effort, an earning capacity that will permit the economically disadvantaged spouse's standard of living after the divorce to be reasonably comparable to the standard of living enjoyed during the marriage, or to the post-divorce standard of living expected to be available to the other spouse, considering the relevant statutory factors and the equities between the parties." T.C.A. §§ 36-5-121(d)(2), (e)(1).

Wife's statement of income and expenses shows that Wife's current income is sufficient to meet her general obligations. However, the record as a whole militates in favor of a finding of need over and above Wife's general expenses. Wife testified that she is pursuing a bachelor's degree on a part-time basis and has secured a school loan. Her statement of expenses does not reflect any school expenses. By the same token, it does not provide for the establishment of a fund to cover the repayment of her loan. We hold that the record preponderates in favor of a factual finding that Wife has a need for spousal support. However, we disagree with the trial court's implicit finding that Wife cannot be rehabilitated. We believe she can be. Wife stated that she anticipates that she will complete her additional education in five years. Certainly, this additional education can be expected to enhance her capacity to earn more income than she is currently earning.

Considering the two most critical factors in making an award of alimony, the "real need" of the spouse and the ability of the obligor spouse to pay, as well as the remaining statutory factors set forth in T.C.A. § 36-5-121(i), this Court holds that an award of rehabilitative alimony of $500 per month for 60 months is appropriate. This period coincides with Wife's five-year education plan. The evidence preponderates against the trial court's decision to award Wife alimony *in futuro* of $500 per month. The record simply does not support an award of alimony "on a long-term basis or until death or remarriage." *See* T.C.A. § 36-5-121(d)(3).

The evidence does not preponderate against the trial court's decision to award Wife $23,000 alimony *in solido* in the form of a portion of her interest in the value of the marital residence. When this award is measured against the factors set forth in T.C.A. § 36-5-121(i), we cannot say that this award was an abuse of the trial court's broad discretion.

We find no evidence that the trial court's decrees regarding alimony were *improperly* prompted by Husband's misconduct. Under T.C. A. § 36-5-121(i), the "relative fault of the parties" is something a trial court is authorized to consider in the alimony question. The trial court in the instant case found that "[Husband's] fault was greater than [Wife's]." The evidence does not preponderate against this finding. There is no evidence suggesting that either of the alimony decrees was punitive in nature.

## V.

Husband contends that the trial court's division of marital property is not equitable. In addition, Husband maintains that the trial court improperly relied upon his misconduct in dividing the marital property.

T.C.A. § 36-4-121(a)(1) (2005) directs the trial court to "equitably divide . . . the marital property between the parties . . . in proportions as the court deems just." As explained by this Court in *Batson v. Batson,* 769 S.W.2d 849, 859 (Tenn. Ct. App. 1988),

> an equitable property division is not necessarily an equal one. It is not achieved by a mechanical application of the statutory factors, but rather by considering and weighing the most relevant factors in light of the unique facts of the case.

T.C.A. 36-4-121(c) sets forth the factors to be considered in dividing marital property***Fault of a party is not to be considered in dividing marital property. T.C.A. § 36-4-121(a)(1).

As demonstrated above, the trial court divided that portion of the marital estate, upon which the parties could not agree, such that Wife received assets valued at $84,200 and Husband received assets valued at $46,375. Wife also received several assets to which there was no value assigned in the statement of evidence or the final judgment, and the parties divided other undescribed personal property prior to the hearing without specifying the value of same. In addition, the trial court stated that each spouse was entitled to half of the other spouse's retirement. The record reveals that Wife will receive $441 per month as her half of Husband's retirement, which did not include his monthly disability payment at that time. Husband will receive his half of Wife's retirement when she becomes eligible to receive it. Neither the statement of the evidence nor the final judgment provides any explanation for the trial court's decision with regard to dividing the martial property between the parties.

\* \* \*

Finally, addressing Husband's contention that the trial court improperly considered his misconduct in making a division, it does not appear in the record that the trial court's decision was based upon a consideration of the fault of either party.

\* \* \*

CHARLES D. SUSANO, JR., JUDGE

**Source:** Retrieved from www.tsc.state.tn.us/OPINIONS/Tca/PDF/064/BookertjOPN.pdf.

## CASE BRIEF ASSIGNMENT

Read and brief the *Booker v. Booker,* 2006 WL 3044154 (Tenn. Ct. App. 2006) case. (See Appendix A for information on how to brief cases.)

The same problem must be resolved by the court in the event the parties cannot settle the matter themselves. The attorneys for each spouse will need to encourage the court to include sufficiently detailed conditions for the continuation of alimony in the final order of dissolution of marriage.

Temporary alimony, rehabilitative alimony, reimbursement alimony, and bridge-the-gap alimony are not as open-ended as permanent alimony. Settlement agreements and divorce decrees tend to be specific for how long the payments should last. For example, if rehabilitative alimony is awarded to allow a spouse to get a college degree, then the court may specify that the alimony be paid for 4 years.

Lump sum alimony, as its name implies, is a fixed payment amount that is made independent of whether the ex-spouse dies or remarries. It is often used as part of an overall property settlement between the parties. It can also be used as a type of reimbursement alimony.

## LIFE INSURANCE

Although many people have life insurance with the spouse as the named beneficiary during the marriage, life insurance may also be a tool in protecting a client in a divorce or dissolution. Since alimony is part of an equitable resolution of issues in a divorce or dissolution, its loss due to the death of the paying spouse may have an unfair result. One way to protect a client who will be receiving alimony is to have the paying spouse obtain a life insurance policy to secure the obligation. This can be accomplished in a number of ways, such as including the requirement as part of the separation agreement or including it as part of the judge's final order of dissolution of marriage. It is also important that safeguards are taken to ensure that the policy will be kept in force and not canceled at some future date by the paying spouse. This can be accomplished by including such a provision in the separation agreement or the judge's final order. Figure 6.3 sets out South Carolina's statute relating to a court's ability to make such an order.

**20-3-130(D)**—In making an award of alimony or separate maintenance and support, the court may make provision for security for the payment of the support including, but not limited to, requiring the posting of money, property, and bonds and may require a spouse, with due consideration of the cost of premiums, insurance plans carried by the parties during marriage, insurability of the payor spouse, the probable economic condition of the supported spouse upon the death of the payor spouse, and any other factors the court may deem relevant, to carry and maintain life insurance so as to assure support of a spouse beyond the death of the payor spouse.

**FIGURE 6.3**
**South Carolina Code of Laws 20-3-130(D)**

## TAX CONSEQUENCES

Many things must be considered when an attorney is assisting a client in drafting a separation agreement. One key consideration is how a particular provision in the agreement will affect the client's taxes. As a general rule, the spouse paying alimony is allowed to deduct the payments from his or her income for tax purposes. However, the receiving spouse has to include it as part of his or her taxable income.

In the past, attorneys have used this feature of the tax code to maximize what one spouse will receive overall under a separation agreement. For example, John and Sondra are getting a divorce. The couple has two children. Their attorneys are attempting to compromise on the terms of their settlement agreement. They may agree to a higher amount of alimony, as compared to payment of child support. Why? John has a higher income then Sondra, so he will benefit more from the tax deduction. Sondra will pay more taxes because she has to declare it as income but, since she is in a lower tax bracket, the amount will be lower than what John would have paid if the payment was not deducted from his income. The end result will be that the same amount paid by John would have the net affect of giving Sondra more money than she would have received if the payments were made as child support. See Figure 6.4 for additional information on tax implications of alimony and child support.

**IRS TAX TIP 2007-31**

If you were recently divorced and are paying or receiving alimony under a divorce decree or agreement, you need to consider the tax implication for your 2006 federal income tax return.
Here are the general guidelines:

- Alimony payments received from your spouse or former spouse are taxable to you in the year you receive them. Because no taxes are withheld from alimony payments, you may need to make estimated tax payments or increase the amount withheld from your paycheck.
- Alimony payments you make under a divorce or separation instrument are deductible if certain requirements are met. Any payments not required by such a decree or agreement do not qualify as deductible alimony payments.
- Child support is never deductible. If your divorce decree or other written instrument or agreement calls for alimony and child support, and you pay less than the total required, the payments apply first to child support. Any remaining amount is then considered alimony.
- If you paid or received alimony you must use Form 1040. You cannot use Form 1040A or Form 1040EZ. If you received alimony, you must give the person who paid the alimony your social security number or you may have to pay a $50 penalty.

For more information, including rules for divorces and separations before 1985, get Publication 504, Divorced or Separated Individuals, available on the IRS Web site at IRS.gov or by calling 800-TAX-FORM (800-829-3676).

**FIGURE 6.4**
**Paying or Receiving Alimony?**
*Source:* Retrieved from: www.irs.gov/newsroom/article/0,,id=106171,00.html on 2/22/07

**CYBER TRIP**

Visit www.irs.gov and look at Publication 504 to learn more about the tax consequences of alimony after a divorce. Pay particular attention to the information relating to settlement agreements entered into after 1984. List the rules relating to the deduction of alimony by the payor and when the deduction will not be allowed because the IRS deems the payment to be child support.

The IRS figured this out and, for agreements entered into in 1985 and after, it has made it more difficult to use this procedure. It is no longer just enough to name the payment as being alimony, it has to meet certain requirements or the IRS will consider it child support. An example of a provision in the separation agreement that would indicate the payment was not alimony, but instead child support, is one that stated the alimony would end when the child reaches the age of 18.

Tax consequence of alimony and child support can still be a consideration in drafting a settlement agreement, but the parties must be more careful when trying to take advantage of the deductibility of alimony.

## MODIFICATION

The initial decree awarding alimony is presumed to be correct as to the facts existing at the time of its award. Appellant courts are reluctant to overturn a lower court's award of alimony for this very reason. As such, unless fraud or mistake of fact can be shown, modification of the amount or type of alimony awarded is usually restricted to a change of conditions of the parties since the divorce and the initial award of alimony. Figure 6.5 contains a list of some of the reasons that alimony may be modified under the appropriate circumstances.

In addition, a foreseeable change in circumstances that was known at the time of the award of alimony is generally not a basis to seek modification, unless other factors are present. It is important, therefore, that attorneys make every effort to protect the interest of their clients when drafting an agreement or in giving input to the judge as to the contents of the final order awarding alimony. Let's use inflation as an example. A recent news report indicated that there are a record number of millionaires in the United States today. That same news report also went on to explain that it takes in the neighborhood of $7 million today to be in the same financial position as a person who was a millionaire in 1968. The principal reason is inflation. Although most clients may not be millionaires, the end result on the person who is receiving permanent periodic alimony is that inflation eats away at the buying power of the alimony payment. One way this can be addressed is the inclusion of a cost of living clause in the agreement or court order.

Examples of changes that may warrant a modification in the amount of permanent periodic alimony include:

- *Cohabitation with the opposite sex by the receiving spouse.* This basis can be used when it is included in the initial decree, in the separation agreement, or by statute. It must be shown that the new relationship improves the receiving spouse's economic situation. Not all states recognize cohabitation as a basis for modification absent its inclusion in the original decree, the separation agreement, or by statute.

**FIGURE 6.5**
**Reasons for Modification of Alimony**

The following are some examples of reasons that may, under certain circumstances, warrant a modification of permanent alimony:

- Cohabitation with the opposite sex by the receiving spouse
- Remarriage of paying spouse
- Fraud or mistake
- Substantial change in the financial situation
- Inflation

- *Remarriage of paying spouse.* In the past, courts were reluctant to modify alimony based on the remarriage of the paying spouse because the change in circumstances was something he or she did voluntarily. Some jurisdictions still follow this approach. Others take this change in condition into consideration to determine if the amount of alimony should be modified.

- *Fraud or mistake.* Modification of the original decree may be allowed if it can be shown that fraud or material mistake at the time of its award can be proven. Lump sum alimony can also be modified for this reason.

- *Substantial change in the financial situation.* The substantial or significant change of the financial situation of either the paying spouse or the receiving spouse can be a basis for modification of the amount of alimony. Temporary changes are not enough to justify a modification of alimony. Instead, factors such as the loss of employment, long-term illness, or disability of the paying spouse may be the basis to reduce the amount of alimony being paid. Likewise substantial change in the receiving spouse's financial condition may be considered as a basis for modification of the amount of alimony being paid.

---

### ETHICS ALERT

This textbook often mentions the client's mental state during the divorce process. What about the emotions evoked in the paralegal while working with clients who are going through the divorces?

Attorneys and paralegals are people, just like their clients. They may have gone through a divorce in the past. Infidelity may have been the reason for the divorce. They may have been upset on how the judge decided some of the issues in the divorce.

Put simply, just like their clients, attorneys and paralegals may have their own hot point buttons when it comes to certain divorce issues. The difference between them and their clients is that they are professionals who owe a duty to do the best job possible for their clients.

Let's see how this point can be tied to the topic of alimony. One of the factors that can be considered by a court in deciding if alimony should be awarded in some states is fault. In other words, the actions of one of the spouses, such as infidelity, was the reason the marriage ended. This is a highly emotional issue for people for a number of reasons, including their own moral and religious views.

A paralegal may be faced with an ethical dilemma when his or her firm has as its client the spouse who committed the infidelity. Although a judge may be able to consider fault in a divorce case, the client's attorney and paralegal should not let their own views of the client's actions stop them from negotiating the best possible deal when reaching a settlement.

---

## PALIMONY

The case of *Marvin v. Marvin*, 18 Cal. 3d 660, 134 Cal. Rptr. 815 (1976) created a lot of commotion in the legal field and got a lot of news attention at the time. The term **palimony** became part of the legal jargon, even though it is not technically a legal term and is not associated with alimony in any way. Instead it is the recognition of the fact that two consenting adults who decide to live together can enter into an agreement that will affect who gets what when they separate. In the *Marvin* case, the issue was whether the parties had an oral agreement that would provide Lee Marvin's female companion with certain rights upon separation. The California Supreme Court held that a court could look not only at an express contract between the parties but also at what their lawful expectations were. To establish what the expectations were,

**palimony**
A division of property between two unmarried parties after they separate or the paying of support by one party to the other.

**CYBER TRIP**

Learn more about the *Marvin* case by reading the court's opinion at www. victorslawpage. com/v/marvin/ Marvin1.htm. To learn more about palimony and other issues involved with unmarried couples living together, visit www. palimony.com.

the court could look at the conduct of the parties to determine if there was some other indication of an agreement between them.

More recently Johnnie L. Cochran Jr., now deceased, who was perhaps best known for being the lead attorney in the O.J. Simpson trial, was involved in a case that addressed questions that were left unanswered in the *Marvin* case. See *Cochran v. Cochran,* 89 Cal.App.4th 283, 106 Cal.Rptr.2d 899, Cal.App. (Cal 2 Dist. 2001). Mr. Cochran was in a long-term relationship with Patricia Cochran. They were never married, but Patricia began to use Cochran as her last name after the birth of their son. In fact, Mr. Cochran was married to other women during the time of his relationship with Patricia.

At one point during the course of their relationship, Mr. Cochran stated that he wanted to take care of Patricia for the rest of her life. In exchange, Patricia agreed to maintain a home for Mr. Cochran and their son and to continue their relationship.

One key issue resolved in *Cochran* was that of how long a couple must cohabitate for the principles set out in *Marvin* to be applied to their case. Mr. Cochran argued that, regardless of the fact that the two had a long-term relationship, the "living together" requirement of *Marvin* was not met because he only stayed at Patricia's house one or two days a week. The court rejected that argument. It stated that the parties shared a long-term, stable, and significant relationship and that was sufficient to raise an issue of fact as to cohabitation, even though the evidence indicated that they only lived together two to four days a week.

## Summary

Alimony is a payment that one spouse makes to the other based on a dissolution of marriage order entered by a court. It may be paid all at once, over a specific period of time, or until the receiving spouse dies or remarries, depending on the type of alimony awarded by the court.

Types of alimony include permanent alimony, temporary alimony, rehabilitative alimony, reimbursement alimony, bridge-the-gap alimony, and lump sum alimony. Each is a tool that a judge can use as a way to provide for one of the spouses. Courts give judges leeway in deciding which, if any, of these types of alimony is used to reach a fair settlement of the dissolution of marriage case, if the parties have not reached a separation agreement settling the issue of alimony.

Modification of alimony can be made under certain circumstances. These circumstances include the following: cohabitation with the opposite sex by the receiving spouse (normally only allowed if included in the settlement agreement or in the court's final order awarding alimony), remarriage of paying spouse, fraud or mistake, substantial change in the financial situation, and inflation (normally only allowed if included in the settlement agreement or in the court's final order awarding alimony). However, as a general rule, the change in circumstance cannot have been foreseeable at the time the award of permanent alimony was made.

Parties are generally well advised to try to reach a reasonably fair settlement agreement that expresses the desires of the parties rather than leaving the ultimate decision up to a court.

Palimony, while often associated with alimony, is not truly a form of alimony since it does not involve married couples. Instead it is one way that a court, or the parties themselves in an express agreement, can provide for the division of property between two unmarried parties after they separate or the paying of support by one party to the other.

Alimony pendente lite (APL)
Bridge-the-gap alimony
Divorce a mensa et thoro
Divorce a vinculo matrimonii
Lump sum alimony

Palimony
Permanent alimony
Rehabilitative alimony
Reimbursement alimony

1. What is alimony and why is it important in the divorce process?
2. What are some of the types of alimony that can be ordered by a court to be paid after a couple is divorced?
3. What is the purpose of each of the types of alimony listed in response to Question 2?
4. What is the starting point for a judge when considering whether alimony should be awarded?
5. List the other factors that a judge can consider when deciding if alimony should be awarded?
6. How long do permanent alimony payments continue? Why is the fact that many couples are now living together without getting married a problem when trying to reach an agreement on when permanent alimony payments should end?
7. Why is it usually advantageous for spouses to enter into a settlement agreement rather than leaving the details of the divorce order to the discretion of the court?
8. What are some of the tax consequences associated with the award of alimony?
9. Why are the tax consequences of alimony used in the negotiation between spouses' attorneys?
10. What has the IRS done to try to make taking advantage of these tax consequences more difficult?

1. Research the statutory and case law of your state dealing with the type of alimony that a court may award and the criteria that the court should consider when making its decision on which should be awarded. Based on the information contained in this chapter, and that obtained from researching the statutory and case law of your state, what might be the appropriate form or forms of alimony to use in the Martinezes' divorce based on the facts set out in the Client Interview? Would it make a difference if your firm represented Juan or Carmen? If yes, why?
2. Matt and Brittney met while in high school. They married shortly after graduation. Matt worked for a construction company, and Brittney went to work as a cashier at a local grocery store. Five years later, Matt injured his back and was unable to return to work as a construction worker. Brittney, while trying to be sympathetic, grew tired of Matt not working. She felt he should be able to find some type of employment even if it was not in the construction field. Her resentment increased once she was promoted to assistant manager and Matt was still unemployed. After 7 years of marriage, she wanted a divorce. What factors would the court look at to determine whether some form of alimony should be awarded in this case? Would Matt be able to obtain alimony? If so, what type of alimony would be appropriate?

3. Sam and Margaret decided to move in together. They did not want to get married, but felt that they would be living together for a long time. Margaret had been admitted to law school. They agreed that Sam would work to support them so that Margaret could devote herself to doing well in law school. Sam did, in fact, work to support her and Margaret did very well in law school. She did well enough to be offered a great job with a large law firm in Atlanta. Sam was very excited about the move until Margaret informed him that she would be going to Atlanta alone to start her new life. She wished Sam well. Sam decided to go to a lawyer to find out what his legal rights were in this situation. Based on the information provided in this chapter and on the laws of your state, would Sam have a right to palimony or under a similar concept recognized by your state?

4. Chuck and Susan had been married for almost 20 years before they got divorced. Chuck was a successful office equipment salesman. Susan was a stay-at-home mom. Susan was awarded permanent alimony in the amount of $1,500 per month. In the 5 years since the divorce the company Chuck worked for went out of business. Chuck was unemployed briefly but was lucky enough to find a job at a local office supplies company as a sales clerk. He was now making $20,000 a year, compared with the $80,000 he was making in his former job. Would Chuck be able to have the amount of alimony reduced? Would you need additional information to answer this question? Is so, what would you need to know?

5. Roger owned a local business that installed flooring in new homes. Vicki was a schoolteacher for many years. They had been married for 5 years when they had a child, Nicholas. They decided it would be best for their new baby if Vicki stayed home to care for the child. Three years later, Roger asked for a divorce. Vicki was agreeable but did not want to go back to work until Nicholas was ready to enter first grade. She also knew she would need to take some continuing education classes before she could begin teaching again. What forms of alimony might be appropriate in this case? Explain.

## REAL WORLD DISCUSSION TOPICS

Andy and Lynda were separated after 8 years of marriage and had two children. One child, a boy, was 7 and the other, a girl, 3.

Andy was a career military officer. Lynda was a draftsperson. He earned $4,817 per month net. She earned $1,445 per month net. Lynda's job was seasonal and she rarely worked during January and February.

The family traveled due to the requirements of Andy's military service. Lynda was primarily responsible for the care of the children. Lynda was unable to complete her engineering degree because, at one point, the family lived in Berlin.

She submitted a plan to the court that would allow her to get her degree in 6 years. She indicated that getting the degree would enable her to improve her employment position and become a registered engineer.

Should Lynda be awarded rehabilitative alimony? If yes, why? See *Ulsher v. Ulsher*, 867 P.2d 819 (Ak 1994).

## PORTFOLIO ASSIGNMENT

Research the statutory and case law of your state regarding the modification of alimony. Write a paper setting out the reasons that alimony may be modified.

# Chapter 7

# Child Custody and Visitation

## CHAPTER OBJECTIVES

**After reading this chapter and completing the assignments, you should be able to:**

- Discuss the changes that have occurred in the laws relating to child custody.

- Describe issues relating to visitation rights of grandparents.

- Distinguish between the different types of child custody and explain the use of each.

- Explain the reasons a child custody order may be modified.

- Explain how courts determine visitation rights.

Chapter 7 introduces the key legal concepts and issues associated with one of the most emotional areas of family law and the dissolution of marriage process—child custody. Although topics such as alimony certainly cause clients to get upset, child custody can cause parents to do some very dramatic things to accomplish what they think is best for their child. This chapter sets out some of the ways the legal system has developed to accomplish the critical goal of doing what is in the best interest of the child.

This chapter also introduces the paralegal student to the key concepts intertwined with the issue of custody, including visitation.

### CLIENT INTERVIEW

Ann Brewster is considering divorcing Todd, her husband of 15 years. They have only one child, Brenda, who is 6. Ann was a devote Catholic prior to her marriage. Todd, while having his own spiritual beliefs, is uncomfortable with organized religion. Ann moved out and lived with her parents while trying to decide on what would be best for the couple's future.

Ann and Todd live about 60 miles apart. She is intending to enroll Brenda in Catholic school starting the next school year. Todd opposes this move and wants the child to attend public school. Todd also wants to have equal custody with Ann. Ann has decided to proceed with the divorce and has made an appointment with your law firm to discuss her case.

## WHY THIS CHAPTER IS IMPORTANT TO THE PARALEGAL

Paralegals must be familiar with the many aspects of child custody and visitation to effectively perform their job in a family law firm. Issues relating to child custody come up in a large percentage of divorce cases and are often ones that the parties cannot resolve on their own. In addition, issues of visitation and sometimes custody can come up in situations where children are born out of wedlock. A review of the Client Interview will demonstrate how such a problem may arise in real-life situations. These difficulties, combined with the fact that paralegals are often responsible for gathering key information relating to child custody matters and in preparing the necessary documents, demonstrate the importance of this chapter to the paralegal student.

## CHILD CUSTODY

**child custody**
Arrangement between the parties for residential and custodial care of the minor children.

Like many of the terms that have been discussed so far, the phrase **child custody** is more complicated than it may first appear. As was the case in the discussion of alimony, the law has developed several ways to deal with child custody. One reason for this change is the increased recognition of the importance of having active participation by both parents in the raising of the child.

**tender years doctrine**
Legal presumption that states the mother should be awarded custody of a young child, unless she was deemed unfit.

Laws relating to child custody have also been changed to be gender neutral. A good example of this is the **tender years doctrine**. The tender years doctrine provided that the mother of young children be awarded child custody in most cases. States varied on what constituted a young child for the purpose of this doctrine, but 5 years old was often used. An exception to the tender years doctrine provided that custody might be denied a mother if she were deemed unfit.

Today states have abandoned the tender years doctrine and courts are increasingly leery of using age alone as a factor in deciding custody. That change is one of many that have occurred to treat men and women equally in matters associated with divorces, such as discussed with alimony in Chapter 6. If both parents are fit and there is no special reason to grant the mother custody, both parties should be given equal consideration for the award of custody.

### ETHICS ALERT

Divorce is often difficult for all involved, but it is the impact that it has on the children that is the most worrisome. They are the innocent bystanders in the divorce process, yet their lives are forever affected by it and the ultimate resolution of the issues of child custody and child support.

Unfortunately, some parents lose sight of the effect the divorce will have on their children. Worse still are those parents who use the children as a tool to try to intimidate the other spouse to agree to terms of dissolution that he or she would not otherwise agree to. For example, a man might threaten to seek custody of the children or remove them to another state if the wife does not agree to waive her right to alimony.

The paralegal should be on the lookout for signs of this kind of behavior and warn the supervising attorney if it occurs. This will allow the attorney to better represent the client and protect the client's interest.

The paralegal must also be on guard against letting his or her own personal history from intruding into the negotiation process between the parties. It may be that the paralegal has gone through a bitter divorce in which child custody was involved. The paralegal should not let his or her past history interfere with carrying out the client's desires when it comes to matters such as what agreements should be entered into on child custody and visitation.

# FACTORS CONSIDERED IN AWARD OF CUSTODY

The move away from the use of factors such as the tender years doctrine, and the granting of the right to parents to be considered equally in the award of custody of their child, represents just part of the changes that have occurred in the law with regard to child custody. The states now start with the presumption that some form of joint or shared custody is in the best interest of the child. The idea is that the child benefits from the active involvement of both parents.

This desire to have both parents actively involved in the raising of the child can create certain problems for the parents. The facts contained in the Client Interview are a good example of how complicated apparently simple things, like where a child should go to school, can become. Ann and Todd have differing opinions on what would be best for their child—a private Catholic school or a public school.

Considering the child's best interest is just the beginning of the analysis a court must make in determining custody. State statutes set out the factors that a judge can take into account in resolving issues of custody. See Figure 7.1 for an example of such a statute. Figure 7.2 contains a chart setting out the factors that Connecticut courts can use in determining matters relating to child custody.

Factors that may be used in reaching a decision on custody include:

- *Age and sex of child.* The modern trend is to downplay the age and sex of the child when deciding which parent should be the primary custodial parent. As noted in the discussion of the tender years doctrine, age is no longer a major consideration in the award of child custody in most cases. Some courts do, however, consider whether there is an emotional bond between the child and one of the parents that may exist partially because of the child's age and/or sex.

- *Preference of child.* The preference of the child is a proper consideration in the determination of issues relating to custody in some cases, but it is not controlling on the court. The maturity of the child is central to how much weight a court will give to the child's expressed desire as to custody. Courts vary on how old a child must be to possess the necessary maturity to express an informed opinion. Some courts have found that children 10 years and younger lack such maturity. The older the child is, however, the more likely the court will give his

---

**3011.** In making a determination of the best interest of the child in a proceeding described in Section 3021, the court shall, among any other factors it finds relevant, consider all of the following:

(a) The health, safety, and welfare of the child.

(b) Any history of abuse by one parent or any other person seeking custody against any of the following:

    (1) Any child to whom he or she is related by blood or affinity or with whom he or she has had a caretaking relationship, no matter how temporary.

    (2) The other parent.

    (3) A parent, current spouse, or cohabitant, of the parent or person seeking custody, or a person with whom the parent or person seeking custody has a dating or engagement relationship.

As a prerequisite to the consideration of allegations of abuse, the court may require substantial independent corroboration, including, but not limited to, written reports by law enforcement agencies, child protective services or other social welfare agencies, courts, medical facilities, or other public agencies or private nonprofit organizations providing services to victims of sexual assault or domestic violence. As used in this subdivision, "abuse against a child" means "child abuse" as defined in Section 11165.6 of the Penal Code and abuse against any of the other persons described in paragraph (2) or (3) means "abuse" as defined in Section 6203 of this code.

**FIGURE 7.1**
**California Family Code Section 3011**

*Source:* Retrieved from www.leginfo.ca.gov/cgi-bin/ displaycode?section= fam&group=03001- 04000&file=3010-3011 on 8/7/07.

**FIGURE 7.2**

**Factors a Court May Consider When Awarding Custody**

*Source:* 2005 Conn. Acts 258 § 3(c)—*Effective October 1, 2005,* Conn. Stats. § 46b-56(c) (2007). Retrieved from www.jud. state.ct.us/lawlib/ Notebooks/Pathfinders/ ChildCustody/childcustody. htm on 10/10/07.

In making or modifying any order as provided in subsections (a) and (b) of this section, the court shall consider the best interests of the child, and in doing so may consider, but shall not be limited to, one or more of the following factors:

1. The temperament and developmental needs of the child;
2. The capacity and the disposition of the parents to understand and meet the needs of the child;
3. Any relevant and material information obtained from the child, including the informed preferences of the child;
4. The wishes of the child's parents as to custody;
5. The past and current interaction and relationship of the child with each parent, the child's siblings and any other person who may significantly affect the best interests of the child;
6. The willingness and ability of each parent to facilitate and encourage such continuing parent-child relationship between the child and the other parent as is appropriate, including compliance with any court orders;
7. Any manipulation by or coercive behavior of the parents in an effort to involve the child in the parents' dispute;
8. The ability of each parent to be actively involved in the life of the child;
9. The child's adjustment to his or her home, school and community environments;
10. The length of time that the child has lived in a stable and satisfactory environment and the desirability of maintaining continuity in such environment, provided the court may consider favorably a parent who voluntarily leaves the child's family home pendent lite in order to alleviate stress in the household;
11. The stability of the child's existing or proposed residences, or both;
12. The mental and physical health of all individuals involved, except that a disability of a proposed custodial parent or other party, in and of itself, shall not be determinative of custody unless the proposed custodial arrangement is not in the best interests of the child;
13. The child's cultural background;
14. The effect on the child of the actions of an abuser, if any domestic violence has occurred between the parents or between a parent and another individual or the child;
15. Whether the child or a sibling of the child has been abused or neglected, as defined repectively in section 46b-120;
16. Whether the party satisfactorily complete participation in a parenting education program established pursuant to section 46b–69b.

or her opinion greater weight. For example, courts will generally give the opinion of a 16-year-old great weight when determining custody.

- *Primary caregiver.* The custody of very young children does present the court with some unique issues. The tender years doctrine was one approach that the law developed to deal with those issues. As the states moved away from the legal presumption that the mother would be the better parent for the care of very young children, other factors had to be considered to determine what is best for the child. One factor that may be considered is which parent is the primary caregiver of the child. Some states have established a presumption that the primary caregiver should be awarded custody. Others merely include it as a factor that the judge can consider to determine what is in the best interest of the child. The *In re Decker* case set out next is an example of how a court may apply the primary caregiver factor in custody matters.

- *Morality of parent.* The moral fitness of both parents may be considered by a judge when determining what is in the best interest of the child. This factor is generally limited to how it has or may directly or indirectly affect the well-being of the child and his or her physical, mental, and emotional development. Adultery is

In the Court of Appeals of Iowa
No. 3-258 / 02-1846
Filed May 29, 2003
*In Re the Marriage of Marcy Kay Decker and Vincent Drew Decker*

SACKETT, C.J.

Vincent Drew Decker appeals from the custodial and financial provisions of the decree dissolving his marriage to Marcy Kay Decker. Vincent contends (1) he, not Marcy, should have been awarded primary physical care of the parties' two children, Torrent, born November 11, 1996, and Canyon, born November 24, 1999, and (2) the financial provisions made in the decree were not equitable. We affirm.

Vincent and Marcy were married on August 5, 1995. In August of 2001 Marcy took the two children and left the home where the couple was residing. She moved in with her mother and her mother's boyfriend. Two days later she filed a petition for dissolution of marriage. Marcy kept the children from Vincent for a short period, but then temporary custody was awarded to Marcy. Vincent was awarded visitation and ordered to pay child support. Vincent paid all ordered child support and exercised the scheduled visitation.

Upon hearing the evidence, the district court found both parties were good parents and that the children were bonded to both of them. The court named Marcy the primary physical custodian, finding that she was a good, dependable, and experienced custodian and would see that the children maintained their relationship with Vincent. Vincent was named joint custodian, given visitation, and was ordered to pay child support in the amount of $993 a month and to provide medical insurance and pay certain uncovered medical expenses.

Vincent first contends he should have been named the physical custodian, as his life is more stable than Marcy's.

The controlling consideration in determining custody is the best interest of the child. Iowa R. App. P. 6.14(6)(o). In deciding this question, we review the record de novo. Iowa R. App. P. 6.4. We give weight to the findings of the trial court, but are not bound by them. *See In re Marriage of Novak*, 220 N.W.2d 592, 597 (Iowa 1974). There is no inference favoring one parent as opposed to the other in deciding which one should have custody. *See In re Marriage of Bowen*, 219 N.W.2d 683, 688 (Iowa 1974). We determine each case on its own facts to decide which parent can administer more effectively to the long-range interest of the child. *In re Marriage of Winter*, 223 N.W.2d 165, 166 (Iowa 1974). The critical issue is determining which parent will do a better job raising the child; gender is irrelevant, and neither parent should have a greater burden than the other in attempting to gain custody in an original custody proceeding. *See In re Marriage of Ullerich*, 367 N.W.2d 297, 299 (Iowa Ct. App. 1985).

To support his position on the custody issue Vincent points to his long-term employment at Rockwell Collins and the fact that he continues to reside in what the children knew as their family home. He advances that excellent child care is available at his worksite, which would provide him the opportunity to participate in the children's activities, and that he would be able

to spend more hours with the children than Marcy. He notes that the child care facility has first-aid certified staff and is more reliable than the many child care providers Marcy uses. Vincent further contends Marcy does not adequately supervise the children. He has concern about Marcy's boyfriend, who lives in her home, and about the other men with whom Marcy connected on the Internet during the time the parties lived in the same home. He notes that the man she is now living with had some twenty-five convictions, the majority of which are related to alcohol abuse or driving or driver's license questions. He acknowledges he did not want his marriage dissolved and is of the opinion that fact has been held against him.

Vincent contends the district court was not correct in finding that he was controlling and rigid, and he contends Marcy and the district court were incorrect about some of the requirements of the Baptist church to which he belongs. He contends while his church is important to him, it does not interfere with his ability to raise his children.

Marcy's response to Vincent's arguments for reversal is that we must give deference to the district court's determination, and we should not disturb it on appeal. Marcy contends the district court found her more credible and focuses on several issues where she and Vincent disagreed on certain issues. We agree with Marcy that we give deference to the district court's assessment of the credibility of witnesses. Iowa R. App. P. 6.14(6)(g); *In re Marriage of Callahan*, 214 N.W.2d 133, 136 (Iowa 1974); *Melchiori v. Kooi*, 644 N.W.2d 365, 369 (Iowa Ct. App. 2002). Despite the deference we have given the district court, we must still review the record de novo on the issues raised, and Marcy's failure to specifically respond to Vincent's arguments makes that review more difficult.

Marcy and Vincent were both employed outside the home at the time of their marriage. By agreement of the parties, upon the older child's birth Marcy became the child's primary caretaker, as it was Vincent who had the full-time, well-paying job with health insurance and other benefits. Their life revolved in large part around their children and the Baptist church. They purchased a home and acreage, and other than a mortgage on it, were debt free. Vincent apparently had ideas about maintaining a traditional-type family arrangement with which Marcy did not agree. Obviously feeling somewhat isolated with the care of two young children, she began exploring the outside world through the Internet and was corresponding with several men which understandably caused Vincent distress. With the marriage not going well, Marcy packed up the two children in August of 2001 and moved in with her mother and her mother's boyfriend. Two days later she filed a petition for dissolution of marriage. She let Vincent see the boys several times and then denied him visitation until a temporary custody order was entered, placing the children in her custody and providing Vincent have visitation, which he exercised. From Vincent's personal notes of the visitation, it is apparent that he engaged the children in age-appropriate activities and spent quality time with them. In addition to exercising scheduled visitation, Vincent promptly paid all court-ordered temporary support.

Marcy has been the primary-care parent, and we give this weight. The fact a parent was the primary caretaker prior to separation does not assure he or she will be the custodial parent. *In re Marriage of Kunkel,* 546 N.W.2d 634, 635 (Iowa Ct. App. 1996); *see also In re Marriage of Toedter,* 473 N.W.2d 233, 234 (Iowa Ct. App. 1991) (affirming physical care with father despite mother's role as primary caretaker); *Neubauer v. Newcomb,* 423 N.W.2d 26, 27–28 (Iowa Ct. App. 1988) (awarding custody of a child who had been in mother's primary care for most of life to father).

At the time of the dissolution hearing Marcy was seeking a nursing degree and had about another year of education. She was doing well in her studies, and besides attending school on a full-time basis, was employed for about nine hours a week. Vincent also was seeking additional education on a part-time basis, as it would provide him with an enhanced position at his current employer. Either parent, if granted primary physical care, will be required to have outside child care providers. Marcy's hours are not regular, but she has been able to use various extended family members for child care. She currently uses various extended family members to provide the children with care from her family, but this is inconsistent care.

Vincent has more regular hours. He also has available to him as an employee of Rockwell access to child care from the Rockwell Child Development Center. This center, available only to Rockwell employees, is on the Rockwell campus. It follows the Rockwell calendar and allows for employed parents' participation in class activities, field trip meetings, and lunches with the children. The staff is employed through the Cedar Rapids School District, and there are specific requirements for staff education and staff-to-child ratios. The planned curriculum incorporates play in a weekly learning theme. Rockwell deserves praise for providing such a facility for its employees' children, and the environment would provide the children with more consistency than the child care arrangement Marcy now uses.

Regarding other adults in the household, Marcy has not sought to address the relationship with her live-in companion. The record shows neither of them yet considers it to be a long-term commitment. While we understand Marcy's need for adult companionship, if a parent seeks to establish a home with another adult, that adult's background and his or her relationship with the children becomes a significant factor in a custody dispute. There are two reasons for this: (1) because of the place the companion will have in the child or children's lives, and (2) not less significantly, because the type of relationship the parent has sought to establish and the manner he or she has established it is an indication of where that parent's priority for his or her children is in his or her life.

The district court was concerned with Marcy's current relationship. The district court found, and we find no reason to disagree with her conclusions, that no sexual activity with the new companion took place in the children's presence. The inquiry does not stop here. Other than the numerous charges Marcy's companion has had, most of which are three to five years old, and the fact he contributes one half of the expenses

of the household, there is little in the record that establishes him either as a good or bad influence on the children.

We agree with the district court's stated concern about this relationship's effect on the children but accept the district court's determination that this should not preclude Marcy from receiving primary care.

Vincent argues the district court sought to believe Marcy's version of his religion, and he contends the district court held his religious beliefs against him. We do not believe the district court considered Vincent's religious beliefs and practices as a factor in determining primary physical care. We do not consider them a factor weighing against Vincent's claim for primary physical care on our de novo review. We recognize Vincent has the constitutional right to practice the religion of his choosing. *In re Marriage of Anderson,* 509 N.W.2d 138, 141 (Iowa Ct. App. 1993); *see also Loney v. Scurr,* 474 F. Supp. 1186, 1196 (S.D. Iowa 1979). It would be unconstitutional for us to put any restraint on the exercise of either of these parties' religious freedom. *Anderson,* 509 N.W.2d at 141. We do not favor one religion over another in a custody determination. *Id.; see also In re Marriage of Rodgers,* 470 N.W.2d 43, 45 (Iowa Ct. App. 1991); *Gould v. Gould,* 342 N.W.2d 426, 432–33 (Wis. 1984). However, we do consider in Vincent's favor values that he subscribes to as a part of his religion such as honesty, kindness, and responsibility to family. *Anderson,* 509 N.W.2d at 142; *see also McNamara v. McNamara,* 181 N.W.2d 206, 209–10 (Iowa 1970).

The court found Marcy has shown the ability to see that the children keep in contact with Vincent and has the insight to shelter the children from conflict between their parents. She found Vincent to have controlling behaviors. Marcy contends Vincent should have sought more visitation than was specified in the temporary custody order. Vincent testified that Marcy was so difficult in letting him have telephone contact with the children that he did not feel it was in their interest for him to seek additional visits. Our review of the record convinces us that neither Marcy nor Vincent has made the efforts that should and could have been made to support the position of the other parent in their children's lives. They both took a Children in the Middle class, and we can only trust they will each take the lessons taught there to heart. Their failure to cooperate is not in their children's interest. They further need to be aware that the Iowa courts do not tolerate hostility exhibited by one parent to the other. In *In re Marriage of Rosenfeld,* 524 N.W.2d 212, 215 (Iowa Ct. App. 1994), we addressed a situation where each parent sought to put the other parent in an unfavorable light and considered it a factor in modifying a custody award. *See also In re Marriage of Udelhofen,* 444 N.W.2d 473, 474–76 (Iowa 1989); *In re Marriage of Leyda,* 355 N.W.2d 862, 865–67 (Iowa 1984); *In re Marriage of Wedemeyer,* 475 N.W.2d 657, 659–60 (Iowa Ct. App. 1991). Vincent's wish that there not be a divorce and that there should be strong commitments to marriage are factors in his favor. However, it takes two to want to be married, and Marcy clearly does not want to be married to Vincent. She is seeking a different life. Vincent's inability to accept her position and his dwelling on the factors that contributed to the breakup of his marriage have gotten in the way of a relationship with Marcy that is in the children's interest.

The question is always which parent will do the better job of raising the children. *In re Marriage of Rodgers,* 470 N.W.2d 43, 44 (Iowa Ct. App. 1991). Marcy's position as the children's primary care parent, a position she accepted by agreement with

Vincent, weighs heavily in her favor. The child care available to Vincent through his employer is a strong point in his favor. The fact Marcy has brought a man with less than stellar credentials to live in her home does not weigh in her favor, nor does Vincent's tendency to focus on factors that are detrimental to their children's relationship with their mother weigh in his favor. Considering these and other factors in the record, we affirm the district court on this issue.

Vincent also challenges the equity of the financial provision made by the district court. The district court divided the assets and liabilities so that based on the district court's valuations, Marcy received $11,391 and Vincent received $20,400. To reach these figures Vincent was ordered to pay Marcy $19,000 in cash. In addition, Vincent was ordered to pay $5,230 towards Marcy's attorney fees. Vincent first contends the district court should have valued the personal residence of the parties at $94,400 rather than $115,000. The home was valued at the higher figure when the parties refinanced it in 2001. The lower figure represents an appraisal that Vincent secured from a Certified General Real Property Appraiser on March 13, 2002. The first appraisal had been completed eighteen months before trial, which was on September 11, 2001. The property was assessed for tax purposes by the county assessor at $79,000. Vincent contends the house should have been valued by the district court at $94,500.

We defer to the trial court when valuations are accompanied with supporting credibility findings or corroborating evidence. *In re Marriage of Vieth*, 591 N.W.2d 639, 640 (Iowa Ct. App. 1999). We find the valuations assigned by the trial court to the personal residence to be within the permissible range of evidence. *See In re Marriage of Brainard*, 523 N.W.2d 611, 616 (Iowa Ct. App. 1994).

Vincent next contends the district court should have determined the equity the parties had in their home by subtracting the mortgage balance at the time the parties separated from the home's value rather than by using the mortgage balance at the date of trial. Vincent contends he kept the payment current from the time of separation to the date of trial, so it is only fair that he benefit from the equity acquired as a result of these payments.

The date of the dissolution is the only reasonable time when an assessment of the parties' net worth should be undertaken. *Locke v. Locke*, 246 N.W.2d 246, 252 (Iowa 1976); *Schantz v. Schantz*, 163 N.W.2d 398, 405 (Iowa 1968). We value property for division purposes at its value at the time of the dissolution. *See Locke*, 246 N.W.2d at 252. It is the net worth of the parties at the time of trial which is relevant in adjusting property rights. *In re Marriage of Muelhaupt*, 439 N.W.2d 656, 661 (Iowa 1989); *In re Marriage of Moffatt*, 279 N.W.2d 15, 20 (Iowa 1979). Expenditures made during a separation should, in some cases, be considered in making an equitable distribution. *In re Marriage of Fall*, 593 N.W.2d 164, 168 (Iowa Ct. App. 1999). However, we find nothing here that justifies doing so, and we find no reason to disagree with the district court's refusal to do so.

Vincent also contends the district court abused its discretion in ordering Vincent to pay $5,230 to Marcy's attorney fees. We review for an abuse of discretion. *Muelhaupt*, 439 N.W.2d at 663. We affirm on this issue.

AFFIRMED.

**Source:** Retrieved from www.judicial.state.ia.us/court_of_appeals/recent_opinions/20030529/02-1846.doc.

---

an example of an act that may be considered by a judge in cases in which it can be shown that the parent's continued adulterous acts may negatively affect the well-being of the child in the future. However, courts have stated that the ruling on custody should not be used as a means to punish a parent for past adulterous acts that do not negatively influence the child. Sexual preference of one parent is not generally a consideration in the award of custody. However, some states allow it to be used as factor if the homosexual parent is living with his or her same-sex partner and it can be shown that it would not be in the best interest of the child.

- *Mental and physical health of parent.* As is the case with other factors that a court may consider in the award of custody, a parent's mental and physical health can be considered if it can be shown that the disability could have a negative impact on the child. As a general statement, a disability alone, without a showing that it could pose a risk to the child, should not be a factor in determination of custody.

- *Economic factors.* The financial and economic situation of the parents is not usually a factor in the determination of child custody. Instead, any economic disparity between the parents should be addressed in the award of child support.

- *Home environment.* The court may consider which parent is best able to provide a healthy and stable home environment in deciding custody issues.

- *Domestic violence, physical abuse, mental abuse or sexual abuse.* Although the law encourages the continued participation of both parents in the raising of their child, there are times that joint custody, or even visitation, presents issues that

**CASE BRIEF ASSIGNMENT**

Read and brief *In re The Marriage of Decker,* 666 N.W.2d 175 (Iowa Ct. App. 2003). (See Appendix A for information on how to brief cases.)

affect the welfare of the child. One area of increasing concern is abuse. Courts may refuse to award joint custody in these cases if it is determined that the child's safety and welfare is at risk.

- *Criminal conduct and use of drugs.* A conviction of a criminal act alone is not always determinative in the award of custody, unless the crime involves the abuse of the spouse or of the child. A pattern of continuing criminal activity or the fact that the parent is incarcerated at the time of the award of child custody is a factor to be considered by the court. Drug use or habitual alcohol use, especially in front of the child, may be a factor in the determination of what is in the child's best interest.

- *Religious beliefs.* Religion is a difficult factor for the courts to deal with because a parent's religious beliefs are inherently very personal. Courts must be careful not to favor, or appear to favor, one religion over another. Generally speaking, courts cannot base an award of custody on a parent's religious beliefs. Courts may consider which of the parents is more likely to continue to raise the child in the religious faith they had previously agreed to and in which the child had been previously raised. This is not a controlling factor, but it is one that can be a consideration. Religious practices that may be potentially injurious to the child may also be considered by the court.

- *Parent more likely to encourage visitation.* Since continued involvement of both parents in the child's life is to be encouraged, a court may consider which parent is more likely to be willing to comply with any visitation order that the court may enter. This may include a determination of whether a parent may be likely to remove the child from the court's jurisdiction.

- *Home study and or social investigation.* Courts often order a home study to determine where it would be better for the child to reside. The parents may also request such a study or an examination, testing, or interview by a mental health professional.

- *Abandonment.* A parent may forfeit his or her right to custody by abandonment of the child. The abandonment must be intentional on the part of the parent.

- *Relinquishment.* A party may relinquish his or her rights to custody of his or her child. Relinquishment generally must be in writing.

**CYBER TRIP**

To read one court's discussion of the issues of relocation of a child, read *Dupre v. Dupre*, 857 A.2d 242 (R.I., 2004) at www.courts. state.ri.us/supreme/ pdf-files/02-300.pdf.

---

 **RESEARCH THIS**

Research the statutory and case law of your state to determine how a child's age is used to determine which parent should be awarded primary physical custody. Has your state abolished the tender years doctrine? Is so, when, and was it done by statute or case law? How does your state use the primary caregiver factor in determining questions of custody? Are the results similar to what would occur if the tender years doctrine were applied?

---

## TYPES OF CUSTODY

The word *custody* is a simple one but one that has become more complicated as states have attempted to ensure that the courts put the child's best interests first. As noted, this usually involves the award of some kind of joint legal custody of the child that allows both parents the opportunity to be actively involved child rearing and physical custody that allows liberal contact with the child.

Paralegals must be familiar with the types of child custody that may be used by a court to meet the needs of a particular situation and to provide for the best interests of the child. A discussion of some of the types of custody is set out next.

- *Physical versus legal custody.* Although laypeople often use the term *custody* to cover virtually all aspects relating to the care and raising of a child, the legal professional must be familiar with two fundamental classifications of child custody. The first is **physical custody**, which is often what people are referring to when they use the word *custody*. Physical custody is where the child physically resides. **Legal custody** is a form of custody that grants the right to make legal decisions about the child's rearing and related matters, such as what school the child will attend and medical treatment that may be required. Today both parents usually share legal custody unless there is some other factor that makes this inadvisable, such as a parent being unfit or unable for some reason to make legal decisions. Each parent has an equal right to make the important decisions on how the child will be raised and cared for. The various forms of custody discussed in the following paragraphs refer to physical custody arrangements.

- *Temporary custody.* As the name implies, parties seek a temporary custody order, also referred to as a **pendente lite order**, to establish custody until the court enters an order of final dissolution of marriage. One or both of the parties may seek a temporary custody order for a variety of reasons. Perhaps the most common is that the spouses cannot agree on how custody should be set up until the divorce is final. There are also other reasons, such as the fact they have not decided if they will actually get a divorce, their state has a waiting period before the divorce will be final, or one of the spouses is not living up to the informal agreement the parties entered into in anticipation of the divorce. Whatever the reason, attorneys must often seek a temporary custody order to provide for custody of the child until the court can enter a final order.

- *Split custody.* **Split custody** separates siblings when determining child custody. For example, a couple may agree that the mother has custody of the couple's young daughter and the husband has custody of the teenage son. Courts are reluctant to use split custody because of the negative impact it may have on the children.

- *Sole custody.* **Sole custody** is where one person is awarded custody of the child. One parent can be granted sole physical custody, where the child lives most of the time with that parent, and the other parent has visitation rights. Often sole physical custody is combined with joint legal custody, where both parties have input on decisions relating to the child. There are also circumstances in which one parent may be awarded both sole physical and legal custody of a child. Courts may award sole physical and legal custody of a child to one parent in situations where one parent is deemed to be unfit, such as being a drug addict or having previous charges of child abuse.

- *Joint custody.* As mentioned previously, the courts often order some form of joint custody because it is deemed to be in the best interest of the child to have both parents' active involvement in his or her life. **Joint custodial arrangements** allow the child to live with each parent a significant amount of time.

  Joint legal custody allows both parents the right to participate in making decisions relating to the child. It may be where the child spends a substantial amount of time living with each parent. Or it may be that both parents may have both joint physical and legal custody of the child. Many legal scholars see joint legal and physical custody as being the trend as the legal system moves away from historical presumptions such as the tender years doctrine and moves more to gender-neutral laws.

**physical custody**
Child living with one parent or visiting with the noncustodial parent.

**legal custody**
The right and obligation to make major decisions regarding the child, including, but not limited to, educational and religious issues.

**pendente lite order**
Order entered while litigation is pending.

**split custody**
A custody arrangement in which siblings are separated.

**sole custody**
Only one of the divorcing spouses has both legal and physical custody, but the noncustodial parent may have visitation rights.

**joint custodial arrangements**
Detail the scope of the shared parental responsibility, whether legal, physical, or both.

**rotating custody**
A custody arrangement in which the child resides with each parent on a rotating basis.

**CYBER TRIP**

To learn more about rotating custody and why one state has created a legal presumption that it should not be used, visit www.law.fsu.edu/journals/lawreview/downloads/303/perrow.pdf.

- *Rotating custody.* In this form of custody the child resides with each parent on a rotating basis, with the child staying with each parent 50 percent of the time. Many states, such as Florida, discourage the use of **rotating custody**, unless the court finds that it is in the child's best interest. See, for example, *Hosein v. Hosein,* 785 So.2d 703 (Fla. Dist. Ct. App. 2001). Some courts have taken an innovative approach to rotating custody; they require that the parents rotate where they live, not the child. The child stays in the marital home and each parent moves into the home during the spouse's six months of custody. The idea is that this creates less of an impact on the child because it allows him or her to stay in the same home, attend the same school, be around his or her friends, and so on.

## PARENTING PLAN

Many states require couples who are getting divorced to file a parenting plan. Each parent can file a plan, in the event the parties cannot agree, or plans can be filed jointly. These plans are intended to allow the parents to help create the structure of custody and related matters that will be in force after the divorce. A sample of the Missouri Parenting Plan form is contained in Appendix B.

## MODIFICATION OF CHILD CUSTODY AND CHILD SUPPORT

Although the standard that courts use in determining whether a change in custody is warranted is the same as that used in the original custody proceeding (i.e., the best interest of the child), there is a different starting point. Custody of the child has already been determined and the court is now being asked to change the original order. Courts presume that it is in the child's best interest that the current custody arrangement stay in place because it protects the stability that the child has grown used to since the original custody decree was entered. A material change in circumstances must occur after the entry of the decree to allow a court to modify it. Otherwise, a court may be asked to repeatedly change custody, thereby causing instability in the child's life.

Courts use a two-step process to determine whether modification will be allowed. First, the court determines whether a substantial or material change has occurred since the entry of the final decree awarding custody, which warrants consideration of a possible change. Second, the court must consider evidence that supports the change and evidence that indicates the change should not be granted. Based on this consideration the court will determine what is in the child's best interest. This two-step process has been used and/or adopted in many states via statutes or case law. Some courts also use this process when asked to consider changes in visitation.

### Factors to Be Considered in Modification of Custody

The following are various factors that the courts may consider in custody modifications:

- *Custodial parent's relocation.* A custodial parent's relocation alone is not enough to warrant a change in custody, even if it may affect the visitation of the noncustodial parent. However, courts may use relocation as a basis to modify custody where relocation makes visitation very difficult or impossible. Another factor that can work against the application of the general rule that relocation of the custodial parent alone is not enough to change custody is when it can be shown that the move is intended to interfere with the noncustodial parent's visitation.

State of Michigan Court of Appeals
*Shelley Marie Medrano,Plaintiff-Appellee v. Kurt Bradley Medrano, Defendant-Appellant*
UNPUBLISHED October 28, 2004
No. 254842 Lapeer Circuit Court
LC No. 03-032557-DM
Before: Kelly, P.J., and Gage and Zahra, JJ

PER CURIAM.

Defendant appeals as of right the judgment of divorce challenging the trial court's award of custody, parenting time, and spousal support. We affirm.

Defendant first argues that the trial court erred in not granting him joint physical custody or greater parenting time than specified in the friend of the court guidelines. We disagree. "To expedite the resolution of a child custody dispute by prompt and final adjudication, all orders and judgments of the circuit court shall be affirmed on appeal unless the trial judge made findings of fact against the great weight of evidence or committed a palpable abuse of discretion or a clear legal error on a major issue." MCL 722.28. "When reviewing the trial court's findings of fact, this Court defers to the trial court on issues of credibility." *Mogle v. Scriver*, 241 Mich. App. 192, 201; 614 N.W.2d 696 (2000). "To whom custody is granted is a discretionary dispositional ruling. Therefore, a custody award should be affirmed unless it represents an abuse of discretion." *Fletcher v. Fletcher*, 447 Mich. 871, 880; 526 N.W.2d 889 (1994) (citations omitted).

Before turning to the best interest factors, a court must determine whether an established custodial environment exists. Whether a custodial environment is established is a question of fact. *Thompson v. Thompson*, 261 Mich. App. 353, 363 n 3; 683 N.W.2d 250 (2004). Whether there is an existing custodial environment determines the burden of persuasion on a party arguing for a custody change:

> While clear and convincing evidence must be presented to change custody if an established custodial environment exists, if no custodial environment exists, the trial court may modify a custody order if the petitioning party can convince the court by a preponderance of evidence that it should grant a custody change.[*Hayes v Hayes*, 209 Mich. App. 385, 387; 532 N.W.2d 190 (1995) (citations omitted).]

The court found that "there is an established custodial environment over a significant period of time (the children's entire lives) with the Plaintiff." The evidence supports this finding. The court heard testimony that plaintiff was the children's primary caregiver and most responsible for their upbringing. Plaintiff testified that the parties agreed that plaintiff would postpone advanced education so she could stay home with the child. After the parties' son was born, plaintiff worked only part time so she could be home with the children.

Although defendant, his brother, and mother testified that defendant was fully involved in the children's upbringing, this does not preclude a finding that the children looked to plaintiff

for guidance, discipline, and comfort. MCL 722.27(1)(c) See also *Mogle, supra* at 197–198 (observing that an established custodial environment can exist with both parents). Deferring to the trial court's superior position to assess witness credibility, *id.* at 201, we conclude that the evidence does not clearly preponderate against the court's finding an established custodial environment with plaintiff. Therefore, defendant must present clear and convincing evidence that the children's best interest would be served by changing custody. *Hayes, supra* at 387.

"[A] trial court determines the best interests of the child by weighing the twelve statutory factors outlined in MCL 722.23." *Eldred v. Ziny*, 246 Mich. App. 142, 150; 631 N.W.2d 748 (2001). "The trial court need not necessarily engage in elaborate or ornate discussion because brief, definite, and pertinent findings and conclusions regarding the contested matters are sufficient. MCR 2.517(A)(2)." *Foskett v. Foskett*, 247 Mich. App. 1, 12; 634 N.W.2d 363 (2001). A parent may request joint custody, and the court is required to consider, though not necessarily grant, a parent's request and document the reasons for its decision. MCL 722.26a.

Contrary to defendant's assertion, the trial court elaborated its findings on each best interest factor. The court assessed best interest factors (a), (b), and (c) equally for both parties "when settlement assets, and child support are factored in." The court assessed factors (d) and (e) in favor of plaintiff, affirming its previous determination that an established custodial environment existed with plaintiff. The court scored factor (f) against defendant, "given Defendant's admitted extramarital affair and his less than credible testimony regarding the time of the affair, a wedding spat, and his commitment to spending time with the children." The court found that factor (g) was equal, and that factors (h) and (i) were inapplicable because the children were too young to go to school or express a custodial preference. Finally, the court found that factors (j) and (k) weighed in plaintiff's favor, "given the Defendant's deceptive and manipulative testimony" and "Defendant's controlling and verbally aggressive attitude." The court did not weigh any additional considerations under factor (l).

Defendant argues that the court erred in determining that factors (a), (b), and (c) weighed equally between the parties. Defendant does not specifically assert that he outweighs plaintiff with respect to the "love, affection, and other emotional ties" that exist between the children and the parties. MCL 722.23(a). Rather, he focuses on the parties' relative abilities to provide for the material needs of the children, factor (c), and to actively promote their education factor (b). But as noted in the discussion above regarding an established custodial environment, the evidence demonstrates that plaintiff took the lead in nurturing and caring for the children before the divorce. Further, the court recognized the disparity in earning capacity and assets between the parties, and indicated that it was equalizing this consideration through its handling of the property settlement. Therefore, defendant has not shown that the evidence clearly weighs against the court's assessment of factors (a), (b), and (c).

Defendant also argues that the court erred in scoring factors (d) and (e) in plaintiff's favor. The court found that plaintiff "had custody of the children throughout the divorce and was the primary caregiver prior to the divorce" and "[t]he children naturally look to the mother for care and nurturing." Defendant argues this was error because he had established a permanent residence and was committed to working toward a joint physical custody compromise.

Our Supreme Court has noted that factors (d) and (e) "are phrased somewhat awkwardly and there is clearly a degree of overlap between them. However, we are satisfied that the focus of factor e is the child's prospects for a stable family environment." *Ireland v. Smith,* 451 Mich. 457, 465; 547 N.W.2d 686 (1996). The court's findings on these factors were based on its prior finding of an established custodial environment with plaintiff, which we have already concluded was supported by the record evidence. Defendant fails to demonstrate how his new home or desire for joint custody make erroneous the court's finding that factors (d) and (e) favor plaintiff. Therefore, defendant has not shown that the evidence clearly weighs against the court's assessment of these factors.

Defendant also argues that the court erred in scoring factor (k) in plaintiff's favor.

Defendant appears to believe that the court's evaluation of the factor was based solely on a reported incident of domestic violence. But the court indicated that its assessment of factor (k) was based on defendant's general controlling and verbally aggressive attitude throughout the course of the hearings. Therefore, defendant has not shown that the evidence clearly weighs against the court's assessment of this factor.

Having found no error in the court's evaluation of the challenged best interest factors, we conclude that the court did not abuse its discretion in denying defendant's request for joint custody. As for increased parenting time, there is no evidence suggesting that the court abused its discretion by awarding parenting time under the friend of the court guidelines.[1]

1 We also note that the trial court awarded defendant significantly *more* parenting time than the child psychologist—whom defendant retained—would have recommended.

Defendant next argues that the court's financial settlement was unfair and inequitable, and that the court abused its discretion in ordering defendant to pay $9,000 of plaintiff's attorney fees. We disagree. The trial court's factual findings are reviewed for clear error, and the court's rulings on property division and financial support are reviewed to ensure they are fair and equitable in light of those facts. *Olson v. Olson,* 256 Mich. App. 619, 629; 671 N.W.2d 64 (2003). A trial court may order one party to pay the other party's reasonable attorney fees and litigation costs "if the record supports a finding that financial assistance is necessary because the other party is unable to bear the expense of the action." *Id.* at 635.

The court considers a variety of factors in awarding spousal support:

> The award of alimony is in the trial court's discretion. The main objective of alimony is to balance the incomes and needs of the parties in a way that will not impoverish either party, and alimony is to be based on what is just and reasonable under the circumstances of the case. Among the factors that should be considered are: (1) the past relations and conduct of the parties, (2) the length of the marriage, (3) the abilities of the parties to work, (4) the source and amount of property awarded to the parties, (5) the parties' ages, (6) the abilities of the parties to pay alimony, (7) the present situation of the parties, (8) the needs of the parties, (9) the parties' health, (10) the prior standard of living of the parties and whether either is responsible for the support of others, (11) contributions of the parties to the joint estate, (12) a party's fault in causing the divorce, (13) the effect of cohabitation on a party's financial status, and (14) general principles of equity. [*Olson, supra* at 631 (citations omitted).]

Defendant has not shown that the court clearly erred in its findings or awarded spousal support unfairly or inequitably. "[D]ue to the disparity in incomes and education," the court awarded plaintiff $250 per week support ($13,000 annually) for two years, with her share of her monthly health insurance premiums to be deducted from that amount. The court also ordered defendant to pay plaintiff $9,000 toward her attorney fees out of his share of the home equity proceeds. Given defendant's superior financial position and the fact that he has already purchased another home, the court did not abuse its discretion by allowing plaintiff to conserve more of her assets from the settlement. There is no indication that court's award was punitive.

Affirmed.

/s/ Kirsten Frank Kelly
/s/ Hilda R. Gage
/s/ Brian K. Zahra

**Source:** Retrieved from www.michbar.org/opinions/appeals/2004/102804/25051.pdf.

- *Acts by custodial parent that are intended to frustrate visitation.* Courts may consider the custodial parent's efforts to frustrate the noncustodial parent's exercise of his or her visitation rights continuous in nature and contrary to the best interest of the child.

- *Child's preference.* As in the initial award of child custody, the child's preference can be a factor in considering a change in custody. For modification, however, courts will apply a stricter standard than in the initial determination of custody because the change will modify an existing, presumably stable custody arrangement. Courts are often more willing to consider the child's preference as the child gets older and there are supporting reasons for the child to desire a change.

- *Economic change of circumstance.* As in the case of the initial award of custody, economic issues should not be a basis for a modification of child custody in and of itself. Change in child support is the proper remedy.

- *Neglect.* Neglect can be a basis for modification of child custody if it can be shown that there is a pattern of neglect or acts that demonstrate that the custodial parent cannot provide for the child. Examples include failure to provide medical care, a young child being left home alone, mental and physical abuse, failure to provide the child with a proper diet, or making sure the child attends school. Some jurisdictions do allow modification based on a single act if it is serious enough.

**CASE BRIEF ASSIGNMENT**

Read and brief the *Medrano v. Medrano,* 2004 WL 2413884 (Mich. Ct. App. 2004) case. (See Appendix A for information on how to brief cases.)

## DEATH OF A PARENT

One issue that may arise after a child custody order has been entered is the death of the custodial parent. The noncustodial parent normally becomes the custodial parent absent a contrary order being entered by the court. This can be contrary to the custodial parent's desires. Custodial parents will sometimes state in their wills that the noncustodial parent should not take custody of the child at their death, but such a declaration is not binding on the courts. Instead the court will look at what is best for the child if a third party, such as a grandparent, seeks custody of the child, but it is an uphill battle for a third party to be granted custody rather than the surviving biological parent.

## VISITATION

Visitation, like custody, is an area in which courts attempt to do what is in the child's best interests. This generally means the more visitations, the better. That is not to say visitation is unlimited or that it can be disruptive to the child's well-being, such as interfering with his or her education. Instead it means that the courts encourage liberal visitation that is consistent with the child's best interests.

One common issue that comes up in the family law firm, and in the lives of many divorced people, is the relationship between visitation and payment of child support. The typical way this arises is when the custodial parent refuses to allow the court-ordered visitation of the child because the noncustodial parent is not making his or her child support payments. Any attorney handling divorces as part of his or her practice has had many a phone call relating to this problem!

It seems to make perfect sense to the custodial parent that if the child support payments are not being made, then the visitation should be stopped until they are. The reality is that visitation is not connected with the payment of child support. The law promotes the interaction of each parent with the child. The law does provide a variety of ways to collect unpaid child support, which is dealt with in detail in Chapter 13. Withholding visitation is not one of them.

The desire for continued contact by both parents with the child is also reflected in other statutory provisions. For example, some states include repeated refusal to allow visitation as a basis for modification of the initial court-ordered custody arrangement. Even in cases where safety is an issue, states provide for supervised visitation so that some contact between parent and child can be maintained. Figure 7.3 explains the factors that are considered in resolving visitation cases in Virginia.

**FIGURE 7.3**
**Factors to Be Considered in Determining Child Visitation Schedules**

*Source:* Retrieved from: www.courts.state.va.us/ mediate/cover.htm.

---

**Visitation: Factors to Consider**

This checklist is to let you know what kinds of things judges may be considering when they set up child visitation schedules.

These schedules are meant to recognize that every family is different, but that unless there is a concern about abuse or neglect, all children need to have a schedule that is consistent and predictable for seeing each parent.

The judge will consider a lot of factors in making these decisions, but when you are thinking about a schedule for visitation that you will propose to the Other parent or to the judge, keep in mind that it should:
- Be child-focused;
- Encourage frequent and continuing contact with each parent;
- Preserve the dignity of all parties;
- Help families spend their time, money, and emotional resources in the best possible ways; and,
- Make it clear that children deserve a healthy, non-abusive family environment at all times.

---

In all cases, a visitation schedule is to be child-focused, recognizing that all loving parents want only the best for their child(ren) and knowing that they may have to give up some things that they would like to have, so that each child has a chance for a healthy, loving relationship with fit parents. Where the parties can't agree on a schedule of visitation for their child(ren), the court may consider the following things in making its decision:
- The age and developmental needs of each child, including:
  - Any special physical needs and the ability of each parent to address them (i.e., is the child being breast-fed and is there a way to address this need while with the father);
  - Any special psychological needs and the ability of each parent to address them;
  - Any input by therapists, school counselors, or other professionals seen by the child;
- The primacy of the parent/child relationship:  the ability of each parent to provide a healthy, non-abusive environment for each child, including:
  - Any indication of abuse or neglect by either parent, or by a current spouse or person sharing the home of either parent;
  - Any indication of a substance abuse problem by either parent, and the status of treatment, if any, that is being, or has been, received for this problem;
  - Any indication of domestic violence by either parent against the other, or by or against a current spouse or person sharing the home of either parent;
  - The availability of a "safe site" if the home of either parent is determined to be unsafe for visitation, or the possibility of supervised visitation where some contact is appropriate,
- The promotion of frequent and continuing contact with each parent, including:
  - Appropriateness of contact when the factors listed above are considered;
  - The willingness of each parent to encourage each child's relationship with the other parent;
  - The ability of each parent to foster the relationship of each child with siblings in either household;
  - The willingness of each parent to encourage the relationship between each child and significant third parties, in the child's life (grandparents, cousins, friends);
  - The ability of each parent to set appropriate limits and discipline effectively;
  - The willingness and ability of each parent to shield each child from "adult" conflicts with the other parent;
- The willingness and ability of each parent to abide by existing court orders; the practical impact of the visitation, including:
  - The day care and/or school schedules of each child;

**FIGURE 7.3**
*(concluded)*

- The extracurricular activities of each child, and/or medical, psychological, or dental appointments requiring scheduling and transportation;
- The distance each child would travel for visitation;
- The availability of transportation to each parent and the willingness and ability of each parent to share in the obligation of transportation for the purpose of visitation;
- The work schedules of each parent;
- The impact of 'special days' in scheduling visitation, including:
  - Balance of school days and weekend or holidays, where geographically feasible;
  - Recognition of days that are special for a child or a parent that are not traditional "holidays;" and,
- The impact of the visitation schedule on the dignity of parents and child(ren) and on the family's ability to preserve resources by maximizing appropriate time spent with each parent and by making the schedule sufficiently concrete that areas of uncertainty and disagreement are less likely to arise.

## GRANDPARENT RIGHTS

The law is constantly attempting to keep up with the changes that are taking place in society. This is certainly true of the changes brought about by the increased number of children being raised by grandparents. The 2000 U.S. Census estimated that 4.5 million children are being raised in grandparent-headed families! The U.S. Census is just one of a long string of estimates that indicate a dramatic increase in the number of grandparents or other relatives raising children.

This has raised many issues relating to two key areas discussed in this chapter: visitation and divorce. State laws have been trying to adapt to this new reality. Some, such as Florida, have attempted to grant grandparents substantial rights in visitation matters. Some setbacks have occurred, however, as the courts have attempted to balance the rights of parents with those of grandparents.

The difficulty arises from the fact that grandparents had no rights to visit their grandchildren if the parents did not want them to. State legislatures have struggled to balance the desirability of allowing grandparents visitation rights with the fundamental right of parents to be left alone from government interference with parents raising their child. See, for example, *Von Eiff v. Azicri*, 720 So.2d 510 (Fla. 1998).

Visitation issues arise under a variety of instances. These include problems that arise when there is an embittered divorce, death of one of the child's parents, and difficulty in scheduling visitation with the grandchild. In situations such as these, a grandparent may seek establishment of visitation by order of the court. State law sets out what rights a grandparent has to seek visitation rights. All 50 states provide for some form of grandparent visitation rights. Figure 7.4 presents the Alabama statute dealing with grandparent visitation rights.

Grandparents have great difficulty in being granted custody of their grandchildren. States' statutory and case law support the concept that the natural parents of a child have preference in the granting of custody. Reasons why a grandparent may seek to gain custody include neglect, abuse, abandonment, and unstable parents. Other situations that may allow a grandparent to gain custody include the following: the child's parents are deceased, the natural parents consent to the grandparent having custody, and the child has resided with the grandparent for an extended period of time.

The procedures for grandparents gaining visitation rights or custody are similar to those in the legal proceedings set out in Part Two of this textbook.

**FIGURE 7.4**
**Alabama Statute Dealing with Grandparent Visitation**

*Source:* Retrieved from www.legislature.state.al.us/ CodeofAlabama/1975/ coatoc.htm.

**Alabama §30-3-4.1** (a) For the purposes of this section, the term "grandparent" means the parent of a parent of a minor child, the parent of a minor child's parent who has died, or the parent of a minor child's parent whose parental rights have been terminated when the child has been adopted pursuant to Section 26-10A-27, 26-10A-28, or 26-10A-30, dealing with stepparent and relative adoption.

(b) Except as otherwise provided in this section, any grandparent may file an original action for visitation rights to a minor child if it is in the best interest of the minor child and one of the following conditions exist:

(1) When one or both parents of the child are deceased.

(2) When the marriage of the parents of the child has been dissolved.

(3) When a parent of the child has abandoned the minor.

(4) When the child was born out of wedlock.

(5) When the child is living with both biological parents, who are still married to each other, whether or not there is a broken relationship between either or both parents of the minor and the grandparent and either or both parents have used their parental authority to prohibit a relationship between the child and the grandparent.

(c) Any grandparent may intervene in and seek to obtain visitation rights in any action when any court in this state has before it any question concerning the custody of a minor child, a divorce proceeding of the parents or a parent of the minor child, or a termination of the parental rights proceeding of either parent of the minor child, provided the termination of parental rights is for the purpose of adoption pursuant to Sections 26-10A-27, 26-10A-28, or 26-10A-30, dealing with stepparent or relative adoption.

(d) Upon the filing of an original action or upon intervention in an existing proceeding pursuant to subsections (b) and (c), the court shall determine if visitation by the grandparent is in the best interests of the child. Visitation shall not be granted if the visitation would endanger the physical health of the child or impair the emotional development of the child. In determining the best interests of the child, the court shall consider the following:

(1) The willingness of the grandparent or grandparents to encourage a close relationship between the child and the parent or parents.

(2) The preference of the child, if the child is determined to be of sufficient maturity to express a preference.

(3) The mental and physical health of the child.

(4) The mental and physical health of the grandparent or grandparents.

(5) Evidence of domestic violence inflicted by one parent upon the other parent or the child. If the court determines that evidence of domestic violence exists, visitation provisions shall be made in a manner protecting the child or children, parents, or grandparents from further abuse.

(6) Other relevant factors in the particular circumstances, including the wishes of any parent who is living.

(e) The court shall make specific written findings of fact in support of its rulings. An original action requesting visitation rights shall not be filed by any grandparent more than once during any two-year period and shall not be filed during any year in which another custody action has been filed concerning the child. After visitation rights have been granted to any grandparent, the legal custodian, guardian, or parent of the child may petition the court for revocation or amendment of the visitation rights, for good cause shown, which the court, in its discretion, may grant or deny. Unless evidence of abuse is alleged or other exceptional circumstances, a petition shall not be filed more than once in any two-year period.

(f) If the court finds that the grandparent or grandparents can bear the cost without unreasonable financial hardship, the court, at the sole expense of the petitioning grandparent or grandparents, may appoint a guardian ad litem for the minor child.

(g) Notwithstanding the foregoing, a grandparent may not be granted visitation with a grandchild where the parent related to the grandparent has either given up legal custody voluntarily or by court order or has abandoned the child financially unless the grandparent has an established relationship with the child and the court finds that visitation with the grandparent is in the best interests of the child.

## RESEARCH THIS

Research the statutory and case law of your state to determine the rights grandparents have to seek visitation rights to their grandchildren and under what circumstances they may seek custody of their grandchildren.

What rights have been granted to grandparents with regard to visitation? How has the law relating to grandparents' rights changed since they were initially granted by the state?

## Summary

Although the basic legal principle associated with child custody—that the foremost consideration that a judge should use in determining issues relating to custody is what is in the best interests of the child—seems simple, its application is not.

There are two fundamental classifications of custody—physical custody and legal custody. Physical custody refers to where the child physically resides. Legal custody is a form of custody that grants the right to make legal decisions about the child's rearing and related matters. Today parents generally share legal custody. Courts are then left with determining what type of physical custody will be used in a particular case. They have a wide variety of custody arrangements to choose from, including split custody, sole custody, joint custody, and rotating custody. Temporary custody may also need to be used by the court to provide for the child while the issues of the case are resolved.

Courts are reluctant to modify custody once it is ordered. They presume that it is in the child's best interest that the current custody arrangement stay in place because it protects the stability that the child has grown used to since the original custody decree was entered. Although the guiding principle is the same (i.e., the best interests of the child), there must be a showing of a material change in circumstances that occurred after the entry of the decree to allow a court to modify it.

A two-step process is used to determine whether modification will be allowed. First, the court determines whether a substantial or material change has occurred since the entry of the final decree awarding custody, which warrants consideration of a possible change. Second, the court must consider evidence, both that which supports the change and that which indicates the change should not be granted. Factors that can be considered include the custodial parent's relocation, acts by the custodial parent that are intended to frustrate visitation, the child's preference, and neglect.

Increasingly, states have attempted to recognize the rights of grandparents, including the right to visitation. State legislatures have struggled to balance the desirability of allowing grandparents visitation rights with the fundamental right of parents to be left alone from government interference with parents raising their child. It is difficult for grandparents to gain custody of a child when there is a natural parent who desires custody. However, grandparents are raising their grandchildren in increasing numbers.

## Key Terms

Child custody
Joint custodial arrangements
Legal custody
Pendente lite order
Physical custody

Rotating custody
Sole custody
Split custody
Tender years doctrine

**Review Questions**

1. What is the tender years doctrine and why is it no longer used in determining child custody?
2. What is temporary custody and when is it used?
3. What is the difference between physical child custody and legal child custody?
4. What is split custody and why are courts reluctant to use it?
5. What is the difference between physical custody and legal custody? Why is the distinction important?
6. What is rotating custody and why are courts reluctant to use it?
7. List five of the factors that a court can consider when deciding child custody matters and discuss the importance of each.
8. Why do courts generally encourage liberal child visitation?
9. Why are courts reluctant to use the economic differences between parents as a factor in determining child custody issues?
10. When can adultery be used as a factor in the award of child custody?
11. How are states attempting to protect grandparents' rights as they relate to issues such as visitation?
12. What legal difficulties arise when a state attempts to grant grandparents rights to visitation?
13. What is a parenting plan?
14. What are some of the advantages of using separation agreements to settle matters relating to child custody and visitation?
15. Why is it difficult for a custodial parent to prevent custody being granted to the other parent when the custodial parent dies?

**Exercises**

1. Al and Roberta have been married for 9 years. They have one child, Maggie, who is 4 years old. Roberta has been a stay-at-home mother and been the child's primary caregiver. Al is a factory worker. He often works the late shift from midnight to 8 A.M., which means he sleeps most of the day. What custody arrangement would be appropriate in this situation? Research the law of your state to see if you can find case law to support your conclusion.

2. Jacob and Emily were married for 15 years. Emily is seeking a divorce because she found out that Jacob was having a long-term affair with another woman. Jacob is a very successful architect and Emily has been a stay-at-home mom, but worked as a nurse prior to her marriage. Jacob does not want to pay alimony and has threatened to seek physical custody of their 13-year-old. Jacob has been very close to his son and participated in many of his activities growing up. Based on the laws of your state, what is the likelihood that Jacob could be awarded primary physical custody of his son?

3. Andrew and Olivia have been married for over 20 years. They have two children Dorothy, age 4, and Andy, age 16. Olivia has been the primary caregiver for both children. Andrew has been very involved with Andy's activities since he became a teenager and they have grown very close. Andy has expressed a desire to live with his father. What factors should the court consider in making its decision on child custody?

4. Madison has been married to Michael for 12 years. They have a 4-year-old son. Madison has known that Michael has been having affairs with other women over

the years. She has finally had enough and has come to your firm to seek a divorce. She wants sole physical custody of their son and would prefer that some restriction on visitation be made to prohibit the boy from being exposed to Michael's many girlfriends. Are Madison's desires likely to be achieved under the laws of your state? What additional facts would be required to better determine Madison's rights as to custody?

5. Ethan and Abigail have one child, Hannah, who is 10 years old. Ethan is a wealthy businessman and can provide for all of Hannah's needs. Because of this, Ethan feels that he should have primary physical custody of the child. Abigail feels that Ethan had spoiled their daughter, perhaps in hopes of getting custody if the couple divorces. Whatever the reason, Hannah has said that she would prefer to live with her father when the couple ends their marriage. What factors would be considered by the court? How much weight will the court give to Hannah's desires? Why?

## REAL WORLD DISCUSSION TOPICS

1. Diane and George were married and had three children, Melissa, 10 years of age, and twins, Nicholas and Natalie, age 6. The parties separated and the mother initiated divorce proceedings on the ground of adultery. The parties reached an agreement settling all property and financial matters but could not agree as to custody of the children. The family court awarded custody of the children to the father, who lived with his parents, even though the children expressed a desire to live with their mother. Was the court correct in is decision? Would your answer change if it was shown that Diane often got the children to school late on numerous occasions? That Diane had a poor temperament and sometimes cursed the children? That George stated that the affair was over? See Brown v. Brown, 362 S.C. 85, 606 S.E.2d 785 (S.C.App. 2004).

2. Carmen and Keith McAdams were married in Italy. Carmen was an Italian citizen and Keith was in Italy coaching hockey. The couple have two children, Kenneth and Bryan. The couple moved often because of Keith's hockey coaching. They later moved to Bismarck, North Dakota, but shortly thereafter, Carmen was secretly moved to New York and lived in a safe shelter. Keith was unaware of the move.

   Keith began a divorce action in North Dakota after learning Carmen had taken the children to New York. The custody investigator assigned in the case recommended that Carmen receive custody of both children, concluding that Keith had a personality disorder and likely abused Carmen.

   The court awarded split custody, giving custody of Kenneth to Keith and Bryan to Carmen, basing its decision on Kenneth's alienation from his mother, which the court specifically found was caused by the father.

   Did the court err by awarding custody of Kenneth to his father and custody of Bryan to Carmen? What additional facts would you need to fully answer this question? See McAdams v. McAdams, 530 N.W.2d 647 (N.D. 1995).

## PORTFOLIO ASSIGNMENT

Review the facts from the Client Interview and identify the issues that Ann will face during and after the divorce as related to raising Brenda. Research the law of your state relating to these issues. Write a summary of your findings to help your supervising attorney prepare for Ann's initial consultation.

# Chapter 8

# Child Support and Paternity

## CHAPTER OBJECTIVES

**After reading this chapter and completing the assignments, you should be able to:**

- Demonstrate an understanding of what child support guidelines are and why they are important in the award of child support.

- Describe how the determination of child support to be paid has changed.

- Discuss the factors that a judge can use to deviate from the child support guidelines

- Discuss the reasons that child support can be modified.

- Understand why the establishment of paternity is required in some child support cases.

- Describe when child support ends.

Determining child support, like child custody, is one of the most important tasks a court may be asked to perform in a divorce case. To make matters a little more complicated for the court, child support is also one of the areas that the judge must examine even if the parties have entered into an agreement to the amount of child support to be paid.

States have reduced the uncertainty of how much child support will be paid by adopting child support guidelines. These guidelines are a starting point for judges, but the law does allow them to deviate from the guidelines in certain circumstances.

### CLIENT INTERVIEW

Shelby and Rodger Southworth were married for 12 years before they filed for dissolution of marriage. They had two children, Erin, age 10, and Joan, age 6. Rodger was a CPA and a successful businessman. His reported income for most of his career was in excess of $150,000, and he owned a controlling interest in a retail store in the local mall. Six months before filing the dissolution of marriage papers, he stopped working as a CPA, gave away his interest in the retail store, and became a self-described "beach bum." Shelby had helped her husband in his businesses over the years but had only earned a little more than minimum wage and no special skills that would allow her to get a good paying job. She is very concerned about her future and the future of her children. She has hired your firm to handle the dissolution case.

Chapter 8 introduces the paralegal student to many of the issues relating to child support. They include not just how the amount of child support is initially determined but also the factors the judge can consider in addition to the child support guidelines, the question of paternity, and how child support can be modified.

## WHY THIS CHAPTER IS IMPORTANT TO THE PARALEGAL

Child custody and child support go hand in hand in the family law office. These two issues will have to be resolved whenever there are children of a marriage and the parents are getting divorced, whether the issues are resolved by the parties or by the court.

Paralegals must understand the basic legal concepts associated with how the amount of child support is determined. They must also understand the state child support guidelines and how they are used in determining the amount of child support that will be awarded. The need for understanding these things should be obvious. Paralegals are often those who are responsible for gathering the necessary information to complete the requisite forms and complete those forms.

Paralegals must also make sure that they are aware of the state laws and court decisions that apply to their cases because the laws relating to child support do vary by state. This chapter provides a number of Research This assignments to help acquire this critical knowledge.

## CHILD SUPPORT

**Child support** has long been an issue dealt with almost exclusively by the states. In the past, judges had great latitude in deciding how much child support the noncustodial parent should pay. The judge balanced two basic considerations—the noncustodial parent's ability to pay and the needs of the child. To help in this decision-making process, the judge would also look at things like any disabilities or health issues a child might have, the child's educational needs, and the standard of living that a child was accustomed to while the parents were married.

These vague standards produced an amazing range of child support payment amounts ordered by the courts. They often did not have a real relation to the true cost of raising a child nor did they allow the parents to have any idea ahead of time of what kind of child support payments they would have to pay or would be receiving. Worse still, in a large number of cases, no child support was ordered at all to otherwise eligible custodial parents.

These inequities led to federal involvement to try to remove the uncertainties of the traditional way of determining the amount of child support. This was accomplished with the passing of the Family Support Act of 1988. It mandated that states create specific criteria to be applied in the award and modification of child support. The criteria would take into account the earnings and income of the noncustodial parent, be based on a numeric computation of the child support amount, and provide for health care for the children.

The amount of child support would be determined by the application of these criteria, and a **rebuttable presumption** would be created that the amount so determined was the proper amount of child support based on the facts of a particular case. Although a judge could deviate from this amount, he or she would have to include specific written findings of fact that would justify the deviation.

States have taken a variety of approaches to meet the dictates of the Family Support Act of 1988. Most states now have specific child support guidelines that judges must

**child support**
The right of a child to financial support and the obligation of a parent to provide it.

**rebuttable presumption**
In the law, an assumption that a fact is true unless proved otherwise.

follow when determining the amount of child support. They also have created child support worksheets to allow parents to calculate the amount of child support that will probably be required in their particular case. Figure 8.1 sets out Indiana's child support worksheet and a portion of its guideline schedule for weekly support payments.

Note that the federal mandate only requires the creation of a more standardized approach to determine the amount of child support. The law does not state specifically how this is to be accomplished. States have, therefore, taken different paths to meet the mandate.

Some use the percentage of income method, which is based on a percentage of the noncustodial parent's income and the number of children. Others use the combined income of the parents and apply a formula of how much each parent is required to pay toward the support of the child. The end result is similar, no matter which formula is used; the more one parent makes, the greater percentage of the support he or she will have to pay.

To add to the lack of uniformity of how states determine the amount of child support, some apply other methods on how to get to that final dollar amount of child support. Plus, even within states that use the same method, there are variances on how some things, such as income, are computed.

This is another reminder to the paralegal student of how important it is to be familiar with the laws of his or her state!

**🔍 RESEARCH THIS**

Locate the law of your state relating to child custody. How is income calculated for use in computing the amount of child support each parent will pay?

## ADJUSTMENTS TO CHILD SUPPORT GUIDELINES

**child support guidelines**
State statutory guidelines that are used to establish how much child support should be paid.

As noted earlier, a rebuttable presumption is created when **child support guidelines** are used to establish an amount of child support. Sometimes additional factors exist that might require a modification of that payment.

Reasons that may be considered for deviation from the amount indicated by the child support guidelines include:

- *Age of the child.* The child's age can be an important factor in determining the amount of child support. For example, as any parent of teenagers will tell you, the cost of raising a teenager can be far greater than raising a 4-year-old. Clothes, transportation, special events, and food can all be more expensive, which a court may consider in determining the amount of child support to award.

- *Health-care expenses.* Courts often order payment of health-care expenses as part of their final decree. In addition, courts will order health insurance to be maintained whenever possible. Extraordinary health-care needs of a child can be a basis for the court to increase the amount of child support to be paid by the noncustodial parent. The Employee Retirement Income Security Act (ERISA) requires that the group health plan of a parent provide coverage of the child under the plan.

- *Child-care costs.*

- *The amount of time the child will spend with each parent.* Courts may consider how much time the child will be with each parent when determining the appropriate amount of child support. If a child will be living 50 percent of the time with each parent, such as in split custody cases, the court may adjust the amount of child support accordingly.

- *Total financial assets available to each parent.* Although state child support guidelines are based on income of the parents, income is not the only factor a judge can consider when determining the appropriate amount of child support. The court can consider other factors, such as the earning capacity of the parent and overall financial situation of the parent. See Figure 8.1 for an example of a child support obligation worksheet from Indiana.

  Courts may also impute income to one parent when it appears that the income amount claimed appears to be unrealistic. Some parents go to great lengths to avoid meeting their child support obligations. The case from the Client Interview about Shelby and Rodger is an example of how far one person would go to avoid his financial obligations to his children.

- *Special needs of a child/Extraordinary medical, physiological, or dental expenses.* Children with special needs present the courts with another situation where judges may feel compelled to vary from the child support guideline. Special health-care or educational needs may be sufficient to justify a higher child support award.

- *The standard of living of the parents and the child prior to the divorce.* This is an interesting factor that recognizes the fact that children should be allowed to have the same advantages that they had while their parents were still married. This means that a child of a millionaire will receive more in the way of child support than a child whose parents are average working people. It does not mean that the wealthier parent will have to pay for unreasonable or extravagant expenses.

- *Seasonal variations of income of either spouse.* A parent may be employed in a business in which his or her income varies dramatically during different times of the year. For example, in Daytona Beach, Florida, concessionaires set up stands on the beach and make a very good living from May until September, but that income drops off when the weather gets colder and the beach crowds dwindle to almost nothing. A judge may need to consider this fact when determining the appropriate amount of child support payments to be paid throughout the year.

- *Whether children of a previous marriage are receiving child support from noncustodial parent.* Courts vary on whether or not and how this factor should affect the amount of child support payments in the dissolution of a second marriage. Some states allow consideration of this factor in determining the noncustodial parent's ability to pay child support in subsequent dissolution actions involving children.

- *Alimony/Financial needs of noncustodial parent.*

- *Cost of education.* States vary on whether the cost of education in a private institution is a factor to be considered in the award of alimony. Some state statutes do allow it to be considered. States also vary on whether the cost of college should be an awardable amount in child custody. Traditionally, most states have held that the obligation to pay child support included only maintenance until the child reached the **age of majority**. Some states, however, have moved away from this and now allow for the obligation for support to continue through college.

**CYBER TRIP**

Make up an imaginary couple who are planning to get divorced. Include each of the parties' names, the number of children, and other details needed to complete the calculations for determining the amount of child support.

Visit the Indiana Child Support Calculator at https://secure.in.gov/judiciary/childsupport/calculator/support.pl and complete the online step-by-step calculator using the facts of your imaginary couple.

**age of majority**
Age at which person attains full legal rights.

---

**RESEARCH THIS**

Research the case and statutory law of your state and determine whether it allows judges to award the costs of higher education as part of child support. If yes, are there any limits as to age and type of schools that the child must attend?

## Worksheet – Child Support Obligation

Each party shall complete that portion of the worksheet that applies to him or her, sign the form and file it with the court.  This worksheet is required in all proceedings establishing or modifying child support.

**IN RE:**                                    **CASE NO:**
                                              FATHER:
                                              MOTHER:

### CHILD SUPPORT OBLIGATION WORKSHEET (CSOW)

| Children | DOB | Children | DOB |
|---|---|---|---|
|  |  |  |  |
|  |  |  |  |
|  |  |  |  |

| | | **FATHER** | **MOTHER** | |
|---|---|---|---|---|
| 1. | **WEEKLY GROSS INCOME**<br>Subsequent Children Multipliers (Circle    .935 .903 .878 .863 .854) |  |  | |
| | A.    Child Support (Court Order for Prior Born Child(ren) |  |  | |
| | B.    Child Support (Legal Duty for Prior Born Child(ren) |  |  | |
| | C.    Maintenance Paid |  |  | |
| | D.    WEEKLY ADJUSTED INCOME (WAI)<br>Line 1 minus 1A, 1B, and 1C |  |  | |
| 2. | **PERCENTAGE SHARE OF TOTAL WAI** | % | % | |
| 3. | **COMBINED WEEKLY ADJUSTED INCOME**  (Line 1D) |  |  | |
| 4. | **BASIC CHILD SUPPORT OBLIGATION**<br>Apply CWAI to Guideline Schedules |  |  | |
| | A.    Weekly Work-Related Child Care Expense of each parent |  |  | |
| | B.    Weekly Premium – Children's Portion of Health Insurance Only |  |  | |
| 5. | **TOTAL CHILD SUPPORT OBLIGATION**   (Line 4 plus 4A and 4B) |  |  | |
| 6. | **PARENT'S CHILD SUPPORT OBLIGATION**  (Line 2 times Line 5) |  |  | |
| 7. | **ADJUSTMENTS** | | | |
| | (    ) Obligation from Post-Secondary Education Worksheet Line J. | + _____ | + _____ | |
| | (    ) Payment of work-related child care by each parent.<br>(Same amount as Line 4A ) | - _____ | - _____ | |
| | (    ) Child(ren)'s Portion of Weekly Health Insurance Premium $ _____.<br>(This will be a credit to the payor) | - _____ | - _____ | |
| | (    ) Parenting Time Credit $ _____. | - _____ | - _____ | |
| 8. | **RECOMMENDED CHILD SUPPORT OBLIGATION** | | | |

**EXPLAIN ANY DEVIATION FROM GUIDELINE SCHEDULES IN ORDER/DECREE.**

**I affirm under penalties for perjury that the foregoing representations are true.**

Father: _____

Dated: _____     Mother: _____

**UNINSURED HEALTH CARE EXPENSE CALCULATION**

A.    Custodial Parent Annual Obligation: (CSOW Line 4) $_____ + (PSEW § Two, Line I) $_____ = $_____  x 52 weeks x .06 = $ _____.

B.    Balance of Annual Expenses to be Paid:  (Line 2) _____ % by Father; _____ % by Mother.

**FIGURE 8.1**    State of Indiana Child Support Obligation Worksheet

*Source:* Retrieved from www.in.gov/judiciary/rules/child_support/docs/csow.doc on 3/09/07.

| IN RE: | | CASE NO: | | |
|---|---|---|---|---|
| | | FATHER: | | |
| | | MOTHER: | | |

### PARENTING TIME CREDIT WORKSHEET

| Children | DOB | Children | DOB |
|---|---|---|---|
| | | | |
| | | | |
| | | | |

| Line: | | |
|---|---|---|
| 1PT | Enter Annual Number of Overnights | |
| 2PT | Enter Weekly Basic Child Support Obligation – BCSO<br>(Enter Line 4 from Child Support Worksheet) | _____.\_ |
| 3PT | Enter Total Parenting Time Expenses as a Percentage of the BCSO (Enter Appropriate TOTAL Entry from Table PT) | ._____ |
| 4PT | Enter Duplicated Expenses as a Percentage of the BCSO<br>(Enter Appropriate DUPLICATED Entry from Table PT) | ._____ |
| 5PT | Parent's Share of Combined Weekly Income<br>(Enter Line 2 from Child Support Worksheet) | ._____ |
| | | |
| 6PT | Average Weekly Total Expenses during Parenting Time (Multiply Line 2PT times Line 3PT) | _____.\_ |
| 7PT | Average Weekly Duplicated Expenses<br>(Multiply Line 2PT times Line 4PT) | _____.\_ |
| 8PT | Parent's Share of Duplicated Expenses<br>(Multiply Line 5PT times Line 7PT) | _____.\_ |
| 9PT | Allowable Expenses during Parenting Time<br>(Line 6PT – Line 8PT) | _____.\_ |
| | Enter Line 9PT on Line 7 of the Child Support Worksheet as the Parenting Time Credit | |

**FIGURE 8.1**   *(continued)*

*(cont.)*

**FIGURE 8.1**
*(concluded)*

## STATE OF INDIANA
## GUIDELINE SCHEDULES FOR WEEKLY SUPPORT PAYMENTS

| Combined Weekly Adjusted Income | One Child | Two Children | Three Children | Four Children | Five Children | Maximum Spouse and Children 50% |
|---|---|---|---|---|---|---|
| $100 | $ 25 | $ 50 | $ 50 | $ 50 | $ 50 | $ 50 |
| 110 | 26 | 50 | 55 | 55 | 55 | 55 |
| 120 | 29 | 50 | 60 | 60 | 60 | 60 |
| 130 | 31 | 50 | 65 | 65 | 65 | 65 |
| 140 | 34 | 51 | 70 | 70 | 70 | 70 |
| 150 | 36 | 54 | 75 | 75 | 75 | 75 |
| 160 | 38 | 57 | 77 | 80 | 80 | 80 |
| 170 | 41 | 62 | 78 | 85 | 85 | 85 |
| 180 | 43 | 65 | 81 | 90 | 90 | 90 |
| 190 | 46 | 69 | 86 | 95 | 95 | 95 |
| 200 | 48 | 72 | 90 | 100 | 100 | 100 |
| 210 | 50 | 75 | 94 | 105 | 105 | 105 |
| 220 | 51 | 77 | 96 | 108 | 110 | 110 |
| 230 | 53 | 80 | 100 | 113 | 115 | 115 |
| 240 | 55 | 83 | 104 | 117 | 120 | 120 |
| 250 | 56 | 84 | 105 | 118 | 125 | 125 |
| 260 | 58 | 87 | 109 | 123 | 130 | 130 |
| 270 | 60 | 90 | 113 | 127 | 135 | 135 |
| 280 | 62 | 93 | 116 | 131 | 139 | 140 |
| 290 | 63 | 95 | 119 | 134 | 142 | 145 |
| 300 | 64 | 96 | 120 | 135 | 143 | 150 |
| 310 | 66 | 99 | 124 | 140 | 149 | 155 |
| 320 | 68 | 102 | 128 | 144 | 153 | 160 |
| 330 | 69 | 104 | 130 | 146 | 155 | 165 |
| 340 | 71 | 107 | 134 | 151 | 160 | 170 |
| 350 | 73 | 110 | 138 | 155 | 165 | 175 |
| 360 | 74 | 111 | 139 | 156 | 166 | 180 |
| 370 | 75 | 113 | 141 | 159 | 169 | 185 |
| 380 | 77 | 116 | 145 | 163 | 173 | 190 |
| 390 | 78 | 117 | 146 | 164 | 174 | 195 |
| 400 | 79 | 119 | 149 | 168 | 179 | 200 |
| 410 | 81 | 122 | 153 | 172 | 183 | 205 |
| 420 | 82 | 123 | 154 | 173 | 184 | 210 |
| 430 | 83 | 125 | 156 | 176 | 187 | 215 |
| 440 | 84 | 126 | 158 | 178 | 189 | 220 |
| 450 | 86 | 129 | 161 | 181 | 192 | 225 |
| 460 | 87 | 131 | 164 | 185 | 197 | 230 |
| 470 | 88 | 132 | 165 | 186 | 198 | 235 |
| 480 | 89 | 134 | 168 | 189 | 201 | 240 |
| 490 | 91 | 137 | 171 | 192 | 204 | 245 |
| 500 | 92 | 138 | 173 | 195 | 207 | 250 |
| 510 | 93 | 140 | 175 | 197 | 209 | 255 |
| 520 | 94 | 141 | 176 | 198 | 210 | 260 |
| 530 | 96 | 144 | 180 | 203 | 216 | 265 |

- *Travel costs for visitation.* Courts are allowed to consider the costs associated with travel for visitation as a deviation factor when applying the child support guidelines. Some legal scholars maintain that parents should share the cost since the goal is to encourage frequent visitation and as such travel should be considered as an ordinary and necessary expense.
- *Independent means of child.*

The following discussion of *Beck v. Beck* is an example of a case in which a trial court improperly deviated from the child support guidelines.

### RESEARCH THIS

Research the statutory and case law of your state to determine what factors may be considered by a judge in determining whether deviation from the child support guidelines is appropriate and what findings the judge must make to justify the deviation.

## DOES ONLY ONE PARENT PAY CHILD SUPPORT?

We normally think of only the noncustodial parent paying child support. Although that is generally what happens, that does not mean that the custodial parent doesn't contribute to the support of his or her child.

Let's use an example to demonstrate this fact. Joan and Dave are divorced. They have one child, Don, who is 8. The parties agree that Don will live with his mother. Dave also agrees to make monthly child support payments. Does this mean that Joan is not going to pay for the support of her child? Of course not! Child support guidelines have been established that set out what the total cost of raising a particular child will be based on his or her age, the financial situation of the parents, and other factors. Each parent will be required to pay part of that cost. In our example, Dave would pay Joan in a monthly payment for his share of the support. Joan would contribute her share when she pays for the normal household expenses, groceries, and so on. Why? Because both parents owe a duty to support their child.

### ETHICS ALERT

Although some people find it difficult to believe, there are many parents who go out of their way to avoid meeting their child support obligations after a divorce. It is often based on bitterness one parent has toward the other. Or it may have no rational reason, such as the desire by Rodger Southworth in the Client Interview to become a beach bum.

In the end, the reason or lack thereof really doesn't matter. What matters is that a child, an innocent party to the divorce, may suffer because he or she may not receive enough support to meet his or her needs.

Clients like Rodger can present an ethical dilemma for the paralegal working in the firm who is handling his case. He may be actively attempting to hide assets from the court in order to try to reduce the amount of child support

that he will have to pay. At the least, his actions indicate an apparent attempt to walk away from his obligations to his child.

This is a problem for the paralegal in a number of ways. The paralegal cannot ethically participate in hiding information from or distorting information given to the court. It may also be a problem because the paralegal may not feel he or she can work on Rodger's case in good faith since he apparently is trying to avoid supporting his child.

If the paralegal has concerns about his or her ability to zealously represent Rodger's best interest in the case, it is important that this information is communicated to the paralegal's supervising attorney as soon as possible so that someone else can be assigned to complete it.

In the Court of Special Appeals of Maryland
No. 2140
September Term, 2004
Nov. 3, 2005
*Beck v. Beck*

This appeal is from an award of child support that was less than the amount that would have been required by application of the child support guidelines, Maryland Code (1984, 2004 Repl. Vol.), Family Law Article ("F.L."), §§ 12-201 through 12-204. The Circuit Court for Kent County entered an order that required appellee, Richard H. Beck, Jr. ("the father"), to pay appellant, Kimberly Ann Beck ("the mother"), $700 per month in child support, rather than the guideline amount of $816.17 per month. The circuit court's explanation for the downward deviation from the guideline amount was: "[the father] has the half-sibling of [the Becks'] children he is raising and I think it's in [the Becks' children's] best interest that that child [*i.e.*, their half-sibling] should be supported in a reasonable manner."

The mother contends the circuit court erred in reducing the child support below the guideline amount solely on the basis of the presence in the father's household of the father's child from a previous relationship. We agree with her contention that F.L. § 12-202(a)(2)(iv) prohibits a departure based solely upon the presence of such a child in either parent's household, and that the finding made by the circuit court identified no other basis for the decreased amount. Accordingly, we hold that the reason given by the circuit court for the downward departure from the guideline amount is, as a matter of law, insufficient to justify the departure, and we shall remand the case to the circuit court for further proceedings not inconsistent with this opinion.

## BACKGROUND

The father and the mother were married on May 29, 1992. During the course of their marriage, two children were born. The father and the mother were granted a judgment of absolute divorce on April 18, 2001. At the time of the divorce, the mother was awarded legal custody and primary physical custody of the two children, and the circuit court ordered the father to pay child support of $608.45 per month.

In addition to the two marital children, the mother has a 13-year-old minor from a previous relationship living in her household, and the father has a 16-year-old minor from a previous relationship living in his household. The father has a fourth child, born after the divorce, for whom he is paying $300 per month in child support.

On April 7, 2004, the father, acting *pro se*, filed a "Petition/Motion to Modify Child Support." The father asserted a number of reasons why his child support obligation should be reduced, none of which are at issue here. The mother answered the father's petition and filed her own motion to increase the father's child support obligation.

The circuit court referred the case to a master. After two hearings, the master recommended that the father's child

support obligation remain unchanged because: (1) each party had a child from another relationship living with that party; and (2) the father was paying child support for his post-marriage child. The mother excepted to the master's findings. She argued that the child support obligation for the post-marriage child was not relevant, and she requested that the father's child support obligation be increased and set at the guideline amount.

During a hearing on November 1, 2004, the circuit court found that the father's child support obligation for his post-marriage child was not relevant because the child support guidelines allow a deduction only for pre-existing child support obligations. The circuit court entered an order dated November 4, 2004, in which the court, after finding that the guideline amount was $816.17 per month, departed downward from the guideline amount and ordered the father to pay child support in the amount of $700 per month. The circuit court justified its downward departure from the guideline amount with a conclusory finding that it was "because of the presence in the [father's] house of an older half-sibling whom he supports [that it is] in the best interests of [the Becks' marital children] that the [father] be able to adequately support the older half-sibling."

## ANALYSIS

F.L. § 12-202(a)(1) requires a court to use the child support guidelines "in any proceeding to establish or modify child support, whether pendente lite or permanent."

\* \* \*

There is a rebuttable presumption that the amount of child support which would result from the application of the guidelines . . . is the correct amount of child support to be awarded," F.L. § 12-202(a)(2)(i), but that "presumption [of correctness] may be rebutted by evidence that the application of the guidelines would be unjust or inappropriate in a particular case." F.L. § 12-202(a)(2)(ii); *Knott v. Knott*, 146 Md. App. 232, 251 (2002).

F.L. § 12-202(a)(2)(iii) sets forth a non-exhaustive list of factors that may be brought to the circuit court's attention by the parent seeking to rebut the presumption of correctness of the guidelines, and provides:

(iii) In determining whether the application of the guidelines would be unjust or inappropriate in a particular case, the court may consider:

1. the terms of any existing separation or property settlement agreement or court order . . . ; and

2. the presence in the household of either parent of other children to whom that parent owes a duty of

support and the expenses for whom that parent is directly contributing.

Although the statute specifies that the circuit court may consider "the presence in the household of either parent of other children to whom that parent owes a duty of support," F.L. § 12-202(a)(2)(iii)(2), the child support statute was amended in 2000 to further specify that this factor may not provide the *sole* basis for rebutting the presumption that the child support guideline is correct. F.L. § 12-202(a)(2)(iv); *Gladis v. Gladisova,* 382 Md. 654, 673 (2004); *Lacy v. Arvin,* 140 Md. App. 412, 420, 431 (2001).

The statute also provides that if "the court determines that the application of the guidelines would be unjust or inappropriate in a particular case, the court shall make a . . . finding on the record stating the reasons for departing from the guidelines," F.L. § 12-202(a)(2)(v), including, among other points, a statement that explains "how the finding serves the best interests of the child." F.L. § 12-202(a)(2)(v)(C).

\* \* \*

More specifically, F.L. § 12-202(a)(2)(v) provides:

(v) 1. If the court determines that the application of the guidelines would be unjust or inappropriate in a particular case, the court shall make a written finding or specific finding on the record stating the reasons for departing from the guidelines.

2. The court's finding shall state:

A. the amount of child support that would have been required under the guidelines;

B. how the order varies from the guidelines;

C. how the finding serves the best interests of the child; and

D. in cases in which items of value are conveyed instead of a portion of the support presumed under the guidelines, the estimated value of the items conveyed.

\* \* \*

In short, a downward departure is justified only when the circuit court finds that the guideline amount is unjust or inappropriate in a particular case. F.L. § 12-202(a)(2)(ii). And even when the guideline amount is found by the circuit court to be unjust or inappropriate, the circuit court must also find, in writing or on the record, that the downward departure is in the best interests of the child receiving the child support. F.L. § 12-202(a)(2)(v)(C).

As noted at the outset, the circuit court's findings in the Becks' case relative to the downward departure from the guideline amount were sparse, consisting of a comment on the record that "[the father] has the half-sibling of [the Becks'] children he is raising and I think it's in [the Becks' children's] best interest that that child [*i.e.,* their half-sibling] should be supported in a reasonable manner." This finding satisfies neither the requirement of F.L. § 12-202(a)(2)(iv) that there be a reason *other than* the presence of another child in the household, nor the requirement of F.L. § 12-202(a)(2)(v) that the departure serve the best interests of the child who is receiving the support. The similar finding that was incorporated into the written order of November 4, 2004, suffers from the same deficiencies.

\* \* \*

Prior to the 2000 amendment that added § 12-202(a)(2)(iv) to the child support statutory scheme, in *Dunlap v. Fiorenza,* 128 Md. App. 357, 368, *cert. denied,* 357 Md. 191 (1999), this Court affirmed a circuit court award that had granted a non-custodial father a downward departure from the guideline amount of child support on the basis that he had in his household two children from a subsequent relationship. Under the law then in effect, we held that the addition of two half-siblings in the non-custodial parent's household was a sufficient basis for the court to decrease the child support obligation. The circuit court judge in *Dunlap,* using language similar to that used by the circuit court judge in the case at bar, found that the downward departure benefitted the child receiving the support payment by ensuring that "his half-siblings do not have to do without (anymore than necessary)."

In a dissenting opinion in *Dunlap,* Judge Hollander argued that the majority was in error when it accepted the circuit court's finding that the mere presence of children from a subsequent marriage was, standing alone, a legally sufficient reason for departing from the guidelines.

\* \* \*

The General Assembly quickly reacted to *Dunlap* by adopting Acts of 2000, Chapter 121, now codified as F.L. § 12-202(a)(2)(iv), which provides:

(iv) The presumption [of correctness] may not be rebutted solely on the basis of evidence of the presence in the household of either parent of other children to whom that parent owes a duty of support and the expenses for whom that parent is directly contributing.

\* \* \*

In this case, there is no ambiguity in § 12-202(a)(2)(iv). The existence of children in the household of the parent paying child support, standing alone, cannot justify a departure from guideline amount.

\* \* \*

Because F.L. § 12-202(a)(2)(iv) precludes departing from the guidelines solely because of the presence of another child in the household of the non-custodial parent, it also precludes the court from granting a reduction, as the circuit court did in this case, solely to benefit a half-sibling living with the non-custodial parent. If the court's sole basis for reducing the support owed for the marital children under the guidelines is that it would be in the best interests of the marital children for their father to have more money available to spend on their half-sibling, that is an insufficient justification to satisfy the requirement of F.L. § 12- 13 202(a)(2)(v)(C) that the departure from the guideline amount be in the best interests of the marital children.

There may be other circumstances, however, that justify a downward departure as being in the interests of a couple's children. *See, e.g., Walsh v. Walsh,* 333 Md. 492, 505 (1994), in which the Court suggested that, if the non-custodial parent were paying the mortgage on the house occupied by the custodial parent, the combined burden of the mortgage payment and the full guideline amount might be unjust, such that it might be in the interests of the children to have the non-custodial parent pay the mortgage payment and a reduced level of child support in order to keep the house. For other hypothetical situations in which a downward departure might be in a child's best interests, *see Anderson v. Anderson,* 117 Md. App. 474, 486 (1997) ("child's needs [are] met by the lower award and the lower award permit[s] the noncustodial parent to maintain a better household for extended visitation"), *judgment vacated,* 394 Md. 294 (1998); and *In re Joshua W, supra,* 94 Md. App. at 504 (downward departure enables noncustodial parent of a child in foster care to "obtain the economic stability necessary to regain custody"). In this case, the circuit court made no finding that any such circumstances support a departure from the guidelines.

In deference to the circuit court's superior position to make such a factual finding, we remand the case for the circuit court to determine whether there are factors—other than improving the financial well-being of the marital children's half-sibling—that would cause a reduction in the child support payments for the marital children to be in their best interests. In the absence of such a finding, the circuit court must revise its order and award child support for the marital children in the guideline amount.

**Source:** Retrieved from www.courts.state.md.us/opinions/cosa/2005/2140s04.pdf.

**CASE BRIEF ASSIGNMENT**

Read and brief *Beck v. Beck,* 165 Md. App. 445, 885 A.2d 887 (Md. Ct. Spec. App. 2005). (See Appendix A for information on how to brief cases.)

**CYBER TRIP**

The U.S. Census Bureau has published a very interesting report on child support payments entitled *Custodial Mothers and Fathers and Their Child Support: 2005* by Timothy S. Grall. This article provides a wide range of information and statistics on child support income that custodial parents reported receiving from noncustodial parents. To view this report, go to www.census.gov/prod/2007pubs/p60-234.pdf.

## TO WHOM DOES THE RIGHT TO CHILD SUPPORT BELONG?

Does the right to child support belong to the custodial parent or the child? Some courts recognize that the child support is the right of the child. The custodial parent holds the payments in trust for the child. In those states, when the child reaches the age of 18, he or she might be able to bring a legal action against a parent who has not paid child support.

Others have held that the right to unpaid child support belongs to the custodial parent who had to pay the entire amount of child support until the child reached majority.

## PAYMENT OF CHILD SUPPORT

Pursuant to federal law, child support payments should be made by wage deduction. This allows the custodial parent to receive the payments in a timely manner. It also makes it easier on the paying parent since it is deducted from his or her paycheck in the same manner as taxes. Self-employed parents present a more difficult situation for the court, requiring it to make a specific order directing how the child support payments should be made. Figure 8.2 contains statistics from the U.S. Census Bureau on child support payments agreed to or awarded custodial parents for 2005.

## PATERNITY AND CHILD SUPPORT

Paternity is another area that the law has attempted to keep up with due to societal changes. In the past, the legal rights of a child were often determined by whether the child was born of a married couple or whether the child was born out of wedlock. Children born out of wedlock were considered illegitimate and had difficulty in establishing their rights to things like child support and inheritance.

Examples of how the law has changed as to paternity include the Uniform Paternity Act of 1973 and the Uniform Paternity Act of 2002. One goal of these laws was to have all children treated equally. The marital status of the child's parents was not the key. Instead the acts attempted to establish means for paternity to: (a) be voluntarily established, (b) be determined by genetic testing, and (c) allow for establishment of paternity by adjudication.

The states do vary on how paternity is actually established. For example, the man may voluntarily acknowledge that the child is his, often by signing an admission of paternity or a consent agreement.

Genetic testing is the key tool in establishing paternity in cases where the man does not admit being the father. Before DNA testing, few scientific tests were available to a court to aid in deciding paternity. A simple test to determine blood type of the man

| | **Received Payments** | | | | | | | |
| **CUSTODIAL MOTHERS** | **Total** | **Total** | **Total** | **Total** | **Full pay** | **Part pay** | **Did not receive payments** | **Child Support Not Awarded** |
|---|---|---|---|---|---|---|---|---|
| **Total** | **11,406** | **7,002** | **6,131** | **4,754** | **2,900** | **1,855** | **1,317** | **4,404** |
| Standard error | 262 | 207 | 194 | 171 | 134 | 107 | 93 | 165 |
| **Marital Status** | | | | | | | | |
| Married | 2,480 | 1,692 | 1,529 | 1,195 | 721 | 474 | 333 | 788 |
| First marriage | 660 | 394 | 364 | 281 | 150 | 131 | 83 | 266 |
| Divorced remarried | 1,698 | 1,228 | 1,102 | 872 | 558 | 314 | 230 | 471 |
| Divorced | 3,762 | 2,716 | 2,417 | 1,928 | 1,302 | 627 | 489 | 1,045 |
| Separated | 1,280 | 679 | 575 | 426 | 224 | 202 | 149 | 601 |
| Widowed 1/ | 145 | 74 | 69 | 50 | 21 | 28 | 19 | 71 |
| Never married | 3,739 | 1,840 | 1,541 | 1,155 | 631 | 524 | 386 | 1,899 |
| **Race and Ethnicity** | | | | | | | | |
| White alone | 7,644 | 5,045 | 4,447 | 3,568 | 2,221 | 1,347 | 879 | 2,599 |
| White alone, non-Hisp. | 6,009 | 4,197 | 3,688 | 2,993 | 1,885 | 1,107 | 695 | 1,811 |
| Black alone | 3,174 | 1,622 | 1,411 | 975 | 552 | 423 | 436 | 1,553 |
| Hispanic {any race) | 1,854 | 943 | 836 | 633 | 377 | 255 | 203 | 911 |
| **Age** | | | | | | | | |
| 15 to 17 years | 53 | 13 | 13 | 13 | 9 | 4 | 0 | 39 |
| 18 to 29 years | 2,894 | 1,518 | 1,263 | 937 | 500 | 437 | 326 | 1,376 |
| 30 to 39 years | 4,154 | 2,710 | 2,421 | 1,811 | 1,079 | 732 | 610 | 1,445 |
| 40 years and over | 4,305 | 2,761 | 2,434 | 1,993 | 1,312 | 681 | 441 | 1,544 |
| **Educational Attainment** | | | | | | | | |
| Less than H.S. grad | 1,718 | 821 | 674 | 490 | 271 | 219 | 164 | 896 |
| H.S. grad (or GED) | 4,101 | 2,478 | 2,193 | 1,647 | 953 | 694 | 545 | 1,623 |
| Same college—no degree | 2,667 | 1,773 | 1,557 | 1,176 | 728 | 447 | 382 | 894 |
| Associate degree | 1,263 | 815 | 729 | 611 | 381 | 230 | 119 | 449 |
| Bachelor or more | 1,657 | 1,114 | 978 | 831 | 567 | 264 | 147 | 543 |
| **Number Own Children Present from Absent Parent** | | | | | | | | |
| One | 6,362 | 3,570 | 3,114 | 2,469 | 1,527 | 942 | 645 | 2,792 |
| Two | 3,318 | 2,211 | 1,930 | 1,496 | 923 | 573 | 434 | 1,107 |
| Three | 1,253 | 920 | 818 | 610 | 364 | 246 | 208 | 332 |
| Four or more | 474 | 301 | 268 | 179 | 85 | 94 | 89 | 173 |

**FIGURE 8.2**   Child Support Payments Agreed to or Awarded Custodial Parents for 2005 (numbers in thousands)

*Source:* Retrieved from: www.census.gov/hhes/www/childsupport/chldsu05.pdf.

and comparing it with the blood type of the child was often used. Unlike DNA, all this test could show was whether the man was *not* the child's father.

With the advent of DNA testing, judges have a very useful tool to aid in establishing paternity in **paternity actions**. One judge who served many years in a circuit court in Florida had an interesting approach to the final hearing to adjudicate paternity. He would ask for the results of the DNA test. If they showed the man was indeed the father, the judge would reach into his pocket and pull out a cigar. He would then slide it across the table while saying "Congratulations, you are a father!"

Although the states do vary on the paternity procedure, they all have the right to use DNA testing to establish paternity and, if needed, can require the man to take the test. Figure 8.3 contains a sample complaint to establish paternity.

**paternity action**
A lawsuit to identify the father of a child born outside of marriage.

**Commonwealth of Massachusetts**
**The Trial Court**

_____Division      **Probate and Family Court Department**      **Docket No.** _____

**Complaint To Establish Paternity**

_____ , Plaintiff

v.

_____ , Defendant

1. Plaintiff, who resides at_____
   _____(Street and No.)_____(City or Town)_____

   _____ is
   _____(County)_____(State)_____(Zip)

   ☐  a child born out of wedlock.
   ☐  the mother/father of a child born out of wedlock.
   ☐  the guardian/custodian of a child born out of wedlock.
   ☐  the parent/personal representative of the mother/father of a child born out of wedlock.
   ☐  the Department of Social Services/agency licensed under G.L.M. c. 28A.
   ☐  the Department of Public Welfare/the Department of Revenue.

2. The child who is the subject of this complaint is:

   Name _____ Date of Birth _____

   _____
   _____(Street and No.)_____(City or Town)_____(County)_____(State)____(Zip)

3. Defendant, who resides at _____
   _____(Street and No.)_____(City or Town)_____(County)_____(State)____(Zip)

   is the father/mother of the above-named child who was born out of wedlock.

4. The plaintiff and defendant are not married.

5. The mother of the child was not married at the time of the child's birth and was not married within three hundred days before the birth of the child.

6. Wherefore, the plaintiff requests that the Court:

   ☐  adjudicate the plaintiff/defendant to be the father of the child.
   ☐  order a suitable amount of support for the child.
   ☐  order the plaintiff/defendant to maintain/provide health insurance for the benefit of the child.
   ☐  prohibit the defendant from imposing any restraint on the personal liberty of the plaintiff and/or child.
   ☐  grant the plaintiff/defendant custody of the child.
   ☐  grant the plaintiff/defendant visitation rights with the child.
   ☐  _____

   _____

Date _____      _____
                                            Signature of Attorney or Plaintiff, if pro se.

                                            Address _____

                                            _____

                                            Tel. No. (      ) _____

CJ-D 106 (4/94)                             B.B.O. # _____

**FIGURE 8.3   Sample Complaint to Establish Paternity**

*Source:* Retrieved from www.masslegalhelp.org/uploads/WL/ne/WLne5QHzTLeSp8rAxLpBNw/Complaint-to-Establish-Paternity.pdf.

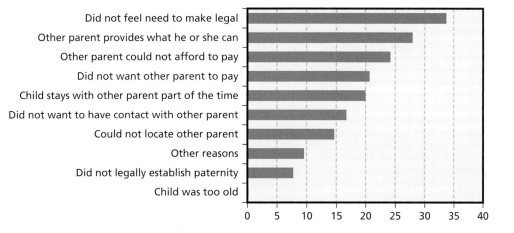

**FIGURE 8.4**
**Reasons Given by Custodial Parents for Why a Formal Legal Agreement Was Not Established**
*Note:* The results reported are for custodial parents who did not have any custodial agreements and those who had informal agreements with noncustodial parents.
*Source:* Obtained from: www.census.gov/prod/ 2007pubs/p60-234.pdf.

## SEPARATION AGREEMENTS

The issues of child custody, visitation, and child support are to a large degree ones that the parties can agree to in a separation agreement. As previously discussed, courts are not bound by these agreements if it appears they are not in the best interest of the child. Separation agreements are nonetheless a way for the parties to negotiate a custody plan that will work in light of their situations. This is especially true in setting out terms for visitation. While people often want to use terms such as liberal visitation, being specific in the separation is usually a good idea. Things like the child should be with the mother on Mother's Day, the father on Father's Day, with the spouses alternating Christmases and other holidays should be part of the agreement. Often divorces that begin amicably end up with one or both of the parties becoming bitter after the final judgment of dissolution of marriage is entered, such as when one of the parents starts to date. Specific terms in the separation agreement will be useful if the relationship between the parents deteriorate.

According to the U.S. Census Bureau, in 2005 57.3 percent of custodial parents had some type of agreement, whether informal or legally enforceable. or court award to receive financial support from the noncustodial parent for their children. Figure 8.4 sets out the reasons given by custodial parents for not having a legally enforceable agreement.

## TAX CONSEQUENCES

Child support payments are not considered income for the receiving custodial parent, and the paying noncustodial parent does not get to deduct the payment from his or her income tax. The parent who is paying the majority of the child's support, however, may claim the child as a dependent on his or her income tax. Either parent may be able to deduct payments for the medical care of the child that the parent makes during the year.

## TERMINATION OF CHILD SUPPORT

As has been seen in discussing college expenses and child support, the laws of individual states do vary with regard to many issues relating to child support. This also is true as to when child support ends.

Child support usually ends when the child reaches majority, although as noted in the discussion of payment of college expenses, some states allow child support to continue after that time. Other examples of when child support might continue after the child reaches the age of majority include when the child has a mental or physical condition that necessitates that child support payments continue, when the child has not completed high school, and when the parties have specifically agreed to the continued payment of child support after the child reaches the age of majority. Child support also ends upon the emancipation of the child.

Life insurance covering the life of the parent who is paying child support is often used to ensure that the parent's obligation will be satisfied in the event he or she dies before the child support would otherwise end. It is advisable to include a requirement to maintain such a policy in either the separation agreement or the final order of the court.

## CHILD SUPPORT INDEPENDENT OF MARRIAGE

Up to this point, the discussion has focused on child support as it relates to the divorce of a married couple. However, the obligation to pay child support is independent of marriage. The establishment of maternity and paternity creates the obligation. The procedures for establishing paternity and enforcement of child support will be covered in Chapter 13.

## SEPARATION AGREEMENTS AND CHILD SUPPORT

It is normally advantageous for parties to negotiate all of the issues involving their divorce/dissolution and put their agreements in writing in a separation agreement. Although child support is a topic that the parties can address in their separation agreement, state statutes limit its binding effect on the judge when considering the proper amount of child support to be awarded in a particular case. Judges will generally accept the child support terms of the separation agreement if the agreed to amount is greater than that required by using the state child support guidelines. However, if the amount is less than would be required using the guidelines, the judge is usually free to ignore the terms of the settlement agreement.

## MODIFICATION OF CHILD SUPPORT

Child support may be modified under certain circumstances. The initial factors the court considers when deciding if child support should be modified is whether a substantial change in circumstances has occurred since the entry of the dissolution/divorce decree and whether the change was foreseeable. The *Lozner v. Lozner* case in the following Case in Point provides an example of a case involving modification of child support.

Examples of factors that have been considered as grounds for a change, assuming the initial requirements set out above, include:

- Physical or mental impairment that occurred after the entry of the dissolution/ divorce decree.
- Changes in the cost of living (although there is a conflict of whether this is a grounds for modification in some jurisdictions).
- Retirement.
- Misconduct of the receiving spouse.
- Significant change in the financial worth of receiving spouse.
- Significant reduction in paying spouse's income.
- Change in the needs of the child.

The manner in which child support can be modified will be covered in Chapter 13.

Superior Court of New Jersey
Appellate Division
*Lozner v. Lozner*
Decided Oct. 30 2006

LEFELT, P.J.A.D.

## I

Plaintiff Lisa Lozner and defendant were married on August 15, 1992. Their son Michael was born on January 11, 1995. The parties separated in April of 1998 and, on March 7, 2000, they finalized their divorce. In accordance with a marital settlement agreement, the parties share joint legal custody of Michael and have designated plaintiff as "the Parent of Primary Responsibility," and defendant as "the Parent of Alternate Responsibility." Pursuant to the divorce judgment, defendant, who was in law school at the time, was to "pay child support in the amount of $98 per week [or $421 per month]."

As defendant progressed through college and law school, prior to and during his marriage, he acquired substantial student loans of approximately $240,000. Defendant also acquired approximately $50,000 of credit card debt, which he claims was incurred for educational purposes and to satisfy his child support obligations. Defendant graduated from law school in 2002, and was fortunate to obtain employment at the prestigious law firm of Cadwalader Wickersham & Taft in New York, where his financial prospects brightened considerably.

Defendant's "annual base salary" in 2004 was $135,000. In addition, the law firm periodically awards bonuses. In January 2003, for example, the firm awarded defendant a $4,509.65 bonus and in January 2004, it awarded him a $17,500 bonus. Defendant admitted earning $144,601 in 2004. According to defendant, his "Net Average Earned Income," during the period of January 1, 2004, to June 25, 2004, amounted to $8,664.74 per month. As contrasted with defendant's rising economic prospects, plaintiff works at a travel agency for limited hours, earning an annual gross income of approximately $30,000.

The parties' present dispute began in 2004 when plaintiff attempted to obtain an increase of defendant's support obligation based upon his substantially enhanced earnings. In opposition, defendant argued that plaintiff was underemployed and his large loan debt, which required monthly payments of approximately $2,500, precluded a substantial increase in child support over the $116 per week ($500 per month) he had been voluntarily paying since he became employed as a lawyer. In fact, during the hotly contested proceeding, defendant submitted, as noted by the trial court, "a shared parenting worksheet demonstrating he is owed a support obligation of $7.00 weekly."

The court granted defendant's motion and reduced his weekly child support from $231 ($993 monthly) to $173.68 ($746.82 monthly).

## II

While both parties agree that a remand is in order, they differ sharply on the content of any instructions that should be provided to the remand judge. Plaintiff argues, for example, that the child support award was too low because the judge should not have considered all of defendant's educationally related debt in reducing the guidelines-based award. In response, defendant argues that the judge should have reduced the support figure even further by properly considering defendant's almost $580 weekly student loan payments. This sharp dispute thus presents the issue of whether a large student loan debt constitutes a factor that may require alteration of a guidelines-based child support award. Resolution of this issue necessitates that we reconcile several knotty conflicting policies regarding student loans and child support. For example, further education often increases earning capacity over time that would be expected to inure eventually to a child's benefit. When further education is funded through student loans, however, a legally unavoidable regular repayment obligation is created. When determining child support, if a court were to disregard a large student loan debt, parents may be discouraged from financing further education, which may prove detrimental to their children. However, any benefit to the child would be elusive if the debt is so large that a dollar for dollar or substantial deduction would reduce current support to an alarmingly low level. This is compounded by the fact that student loan repayment often takes place over an extended period of time. If the child support is substantially reduced to ameliorate a parent's significant student loan repayment, a child may be deprived of any benefit that may have resulted from the parent's education-derived increased earning power because he or she may be emancipated by the time the student debt is retired.

## A.

The Child Support Guidelines are used to calculate fair and adequate child support awards, and approximate the percentage of parental net income spent on children in intact families. When determined pursuant to the guidelines, a child support order is rebuttably presumed to be correct.

A court may deviate from the guidelines only when good cause demonstrates that application of the guidelines would be inappropriate. When a court "finds that the guidelines are inappropriate in a specific case, it may either disregard the guidelines or adjust the guidelines-based award to accommodate the needs of the children or the parents' circumstances."

Among the several factors a court may consider in determining whether an adjustment of the guidelines is warranted is the "educational expenses for either parent to improve earning capacity." Although this factor does not specifically refer to student loans, educational expenses can be paid with funds obtained through such loans, which creates a repayment obligation that we cannot disregard.

We note further that the specific factors listed in P 21 of Appendix IX-A, which may require adjustment to guidelines-based child support awards, are not exclusive. Courts are specifically permitted to consider "other factors that could, in a particular case, cause the child support guidelines to be inapplicable or require an adjustment to the child support award."

Moreover, in instances where the guidelines do not apply, N.J.S.A. 2A:34-23(a) requires the court in establishing "the amount to be paid by a parent for support of the child," to consider among several other items the "[r]easonable debts and liabilities of each child and parent." Therefore, we hold that substantial loan debt can constitute a factor to be considered in determining whether alteration of a guidelines-based support award is warranted, provided the parent reasonably and necessarily acquired the loan for educational purposes with the goal of improving his or her earning capacity.

### B.

Obviously, not all debt liability can be considered the substantial equivalent of a student loan. For example, defendant's case information statement lists credit card debt as student loans, and without conducting any evidentiary hearing the trial court treated the two types of debt similarly. If a credit card were used to purchase books or pay tuition, this would constitute an educational expense and could be, for our purposes, substantially similar to debt incurred through student loans. But credit card debt acquired by a parent to maintain a comfortable life style while attending school is not the substantial equivalent of student loan debt. On the remand, therefore, the court must exclude debt that defendant acquired, but was not reasonably and necessarily incurred to further his education and eventually enhance his income or earning capacity.

A debt allegedly incurred to further education is necessary when the parent believes in good faith that the loan will eventually result in increasing his or her income. The debt is reasonable when it is not extreme in relation to the parent's expected economic benefit. *Ibid.* In this case, for example, the trial court should consider whether defendant's goals could have been achieved without incurring such overwhelming debt. Was there a reason defendant worked toward his undergraduate and graduate degrees for eleven consecutive years without obtaining a job in between? Or, could defendant have gone part time to law school, or attended a less expensive school? It should also not be forgotten that there are a variety of repayment plans for student loans and that consolidated student loans "equal to or greater than $60,000 [may] be repaid in not more than 30 years." 20 U.S.C.A. s 1078(c)(2)(vi).

It is defendant's burden to provide the court with "the amount of the loans, the terms of the loans, the amount attributable to principal and interest, and the amount of the loans that were used for education, child support, or other expenditures." Defendant must also reveal whether the loan terms allow defendant to reduce the size of monthly payments or consolidate the loans in some fashion.

### C.

After isolating only the reasonable and necessary school debt that was acquired to enhance defendant's earning capacity, the question the court must then confront is whether the best interests of the child require an adjustment of the support award. *Pressler, supra,* Appendix IX-A at 2237. The guidelines should not be altered unless defendant has rebutted the presumption "that an award based on the guidelines [is] the correct amount of child support [, or has established] that injustice would result" from their strict application. Thus, if good cause mandates an alteration, then the court must proceed to determine by how much and for what duration.

We do not have a statute as in *Svenningsen v. Svenningsen,* 641 N.W.2d 614, 615-16 (Minn.Ct.App.2002), that limits the consideration of debt to "18 months in duration, after which the support shall increase automatically to the level ordered by the court." Nevertheless, in reaching an equitable balance of the various policies involved, a court need not accord the student-loan-debtor parent a reduction of child support for the entire duration of the loan payback period. Rather, some lesser period may be crafted by the court to better balance the competing policies in the best interests of the child.

Most courts that have considered appropriate treatment of student loans have made adjustments to the supporting parent's net income. For example, in *State ex rel. Elsasser v. Fox,* 7 Neb.App. 667, 674, 584 N.W.2d 832 (1998) (father's total student loan was $17,000), the court deducted the parent's entire monthly payment of $178.09. Although it seems logical, when dealing with extraordinary student loan debt, to make an adjustment to the parent's net income, we do not wish to preclude any other reasonable method a judge may select to ameliorate any inequities and properly balance the competing interests.

In any event, we conclude that a dollar for dollar deduction of a student loan from net income that significantly and substantially reduces the child support award for many years would often not be in the best interests of the child. Such a reduction would usually fail to balance properly the competing concerns, especially those which seek to ensure that the child share in the supporting parent's economic good fortune. Defendant himself, in this case, inadvertently confirms this concern by arguing that after taking his enormous debt into account, his true earning capacity is so diminished that it is at the same level of a law student earning approximately $30,000 per year. Accordingly, we do not subscribe to a dollar for dollar deduction in all instances.

### D.

Regarding the amount of the reduction, we do not approve any percentage of net income to which the debtor's student loan repayment and child support must equal. Nevertheless, it is possible to accord the debtor parent a reduction based only upon a percentage of the monthly loan payment. In *Wilkins v. Wilkins,* 269 Neb. 937, 697 N.W.2d 280, 288 (2005), for example, the court affirmed "a deduction of 25 percent of [the debtor parent's] monthly student loan payment . . . from his monthly income."

Instead of beginning with a percentage in mind, however, the trial court should consider the effect on the family of any particular deduction that is being advanced. The relevant factors mentioned in N.J.S.A. 2A:34-23(a) can be utilized to make this assessment. For example, the court should evaluate what impact any deduction might have upon the needs of the child and the standard of living and economic circumstances of both parents. The court should also consider any other relevant factors including other sources of income and assets of each parent, the earning abilities of both parents, and the age and health of the child and each parent.

By considering these factors on remand, the court should attempt to balance fairly the needs of the parents and yet ensure that children remain adequately supported in accordance with their parents' financial wherewithal. The overall goal of every child support determination must not be forgotten: the best interests of the child remain paramount.

## III.

Besides contending that the child support order was too high because of defendant's extraordinary debt obligation, defendant also cross-appealed, challenging the motion judge's rulings on (1) plaintiff's housing costs; (2) defendant's partial responsibility for summer camp expenses for Michael; (3) defendant's responsibility for a portion of unreimbursed medical expenses incurred by plaintiff; (4) defendant's purported transportation costs incurred when visiting his son; and (5) plaintiff's voluntary underemployment. We find all of these contentions to be without merit and undeserving of any discussion in a written decision.

Reversed and remanded in part, affirmed in part.

**Note:** Citations to authority have been deleted and the opinion edited for brevity.

**Source:** From Westlaw. Reprinted with permission from Thomson West.

**CASE BRIEF ASSIGNMENT**

Read and brief *Lozner v. Lozner,* 388 N.J.Super. 471, 909 A.2d 728 (N.J.Super. A.D., 2006). (See Appendix A for information on how to brief cases.)

## Summary

The issues surrounding child support have been simplified in many ways since the adoption and use of child support guidelines. That is not to say that the question of how much child support should be paid is always simple to determine. The court can look at many factors to determine whether it should deviate from the guidelines.

Although it is usually good advice that the couple seeking the dissolution/divorce settle as many of the matters relating to the divorce as possible and to reduce these agreed-to terms into a written separation agreement, an exception to this general rule is the matter of child support and custody. The law allows the judge to look a little deeper to see whether the terms are in the best interest of the child.

When the parties cannot agree, the court must resolve issues relating to child support, child custody, and visitation. Courts are usually given great discretion in certain areas, such as child custody and visitation, but less when it comes to the award of child support. States have increasingly adopted child support guidelines that set out a specific formula that a judge must follow unless certain circumstances exist.

The judge must consider the child support guidelines when trying to decide the issue of child support, but that is often just the starting point. The judge may also consider numerous other factors such as: age of the child; health-care expenses; child-care costs; the amount of time the child will spend with each parent; the total financial assets available to each parent; special needs of a child; extraordinary medical, physiological, or dental expenses; the standard of living of the parents and the child prior to the divorce; seasonal variations of income of either spouse; whether there are children of a previous marriage who are receiving child support from the noncustodial parent; alimony/financial needs of noncustodial parent; and the cost of education.

Child support usually terminates when the child reaches majority or is emancipated. It can be modified if the court finds that a substantial, unforeseeable change in circumstances has occurred since the entry of the dissolution/divorce decree.

Paternity is another issue that a court may be asked to resolve. Most people think of child support when they hear of paternity tests, but fathers sometime seek the establishment of paternity so that they can have parental rights to the child or to establish visitation. No matter what the reason, the most common means of resolving the question of paternity is DNA testing.

## Key Terms

Age of majority
Child support guidelines
Child support

Paternity action
Rebuttable presumption

## Review Questions

1. Historically, what were the two basic considerations a judge used to determine what amount of child support should be awarded?
2. What is a rebuttable presumption?
3. What are child support guidelines and why are they important in establishing child support?
4. List and discuss five factors a judge may consider in deviating from the child support guidelines?
5. Can a judge require a parent to pay for his/her child's college education even if the child is over the age of majority?
6. Does only one parent pay child support?
7. Who does the right to child support belong to?
8. Why are child support payments normally paid by paycheck deduction?
9. What are the three means of establishing paternity under the Uniform Paternity Act?
10. Is an agreement as to the amount of child support that will be paid included in a separation agreement binding on the judge? Why?
11. What are the tax consequences of child support?
12. When does child support end?
13. Can child support be awarded independent of a dissolution of marriage action?
14. When can child support be modified?
15. When was the Family Support Act and what changes did it bring about?

## Exercises

1. Research the laws of your state relating to the issue of child support and learn how the amount of child support is determined. Using the facts you used to complete the first Cyber Trip assignment in the chapter, calculate the monthly amount of child support that would be due under the laws of your state.
2. Ryan and Grace were divorced three years ago. Since the divorce Ryan has had a significant increase in his yearly income. At the time of the divorce, he made $50,000 but now, after a big promotion, he is making $125,000. Grace also

works, earning $33,000, which is roughly the same as she made at the time of the divorce. Grace has custody of the couple's only child. She has retained your firm to seek an increase in the amount she was receiving in child support. Would an increase in child support be a possibility in this case? Explain why.

3. Before Tyler and Briana were married, Tyler had his future wife sign a premarital agreement in which she not only waived her right to alimony if the couple divorced but also the right to receive child support if they had any children. Briana is now considering divorcing Tyler. The couple has two children. She has set up an appointment with your firm to see what will be involved and the impact the terms of the premarital agreement will have on the award of child support. Research the laws of your state relating to the award of child custody and the right of a couple to waive it in a premarital agreement. Based on the results of your research, what are Briana's rights regarding child support? Would it make any difference if Briana was the primary wage earner and Tyler was a stay-at-home dad? Explain.

4. You are currently employed as a family law paralegal and have worked for the same firm for six years. Your firm is about to hire a new paralegal to be your assistant. Your boss has directed you to draft a paper explaining how your state determines the amount of child support. Research and write the document, which will be part of the training material used for the new paralegal.

5. Logan and Hailey have three children—John, Mike, and Connie. All three children are teenagers. John is 17, Mike is 15, and Connie is 13. Connie suffers from Down syndrome. Will the standard child support guidelines of your state be applicable in this case? If no, why? If yes, why?

 **REAL WORLD DISCUSSION TOPICS**

A husband and wife were married for two years and had two children of the marriage. When they decided to get divorced, they were able to agree to the terms of the property settlement, that the wife would have custody of the children, that the husband would pay $1,000 a month in child support, which was in excess of the state's child support guidelines, and provide medical and dental insurance coverage for the children. The agreement was drafted by the wife's attorney and signed by the husband, who did not seek out legal representation even though the wife's attorney told him he should do so if he felt he needed independent legal advice.

The wife filed for divorce and requested relief according to the terms of the agreement. The husband objected to this because the terms of the agreement were inequitable. The court rejected the husband's argument.

Did the court abuse its discretion by awarding the amount included in the parties' settlement agreement, even though it exceeded the amount that would have been awarded using the statutory criteria? See *Matter of Marriage of Petersen*, 132 Or.App. 190, 888 P.2d 23 (Or. App. 1994).

 **PORTFOLIO ASSIGNMENT**

Review the facts of the case set out in this chapter's Client Interview. Research the statutory and case law of your state to determine what methods a judge could use to establish the appropriate amount of child support to order Rodger to pay in light of his actions to avoid payment of child support. Write a summary of your findings.

# Part Two

## Legal Procedures Associated with Family Law

# Chapter 9

## Preparation for and Filing of Dissolution of Marriage Papers

### CHAPTER OBJECTIVES

**After reading this chapter and completing the assignments, you should be able to:**

- Distinguish the various types of divorces and identify forms associated with each type.

- Describe what information is required in the handling of both contested and uncontested divorces.

- Describe the steps in a divorce proceeding.

- Prepare a basic petition for dissolution.

- Prepare a basic answer to a petition for dissolution.

In previous chapters the many legal principles associated with things like child custody, child support, alimony, and property distribution have been discussed. Chapter 9 moves the paralegal student from theory to practice.

In this chapter, paralegal students are introduced to the specifics of the initial stages of the divorce process, including the sample forms used in the family law firm during this step of the divorce process.

### CLIENT INTERVIEW

Brenda and Sebastian Acres were married for 8 years. They have one child, Jacob, who is 7 years old. Brenda is a nurse at a local hospital and earns $52,000. Sebastian is a trial attorney, who earns $250,000. Their marital difficulties began about a year ago, during which time Sebastian had become the model father. He became coach of Jacob's T-ball team, active in his son's Boy Scout troop, and even started taking him to church, even though Sebastian had never attended church in the past. Sebastian filed for divorce and requested, among other things, that the court order rotating custody of the child. Brenda has hired your firm to represent her in the divorce.

## WHY THIS CHAPTER IS IMPORTANT TO THE PARALEGAL

Paralegals must know more than just the legal theories associated with family law. They must also know the nuts and bolts of how a divorce case is handled because they will be responsible for completing many of these tasks. This chapter provides paralegal students with an introduction to the divorce procedure and some of the key forms and duties they will be called upon to complete. These duties include obtaining information related to the divorce from the client, obtaining information through discovery, and completing various forms associated with the divorce process.

## OVERVIEW OF THE DIVORCE PROCESS

Divorce is a form of civil litigation. Like all forms of litigation, state laws and rules of court delineate the process that must be followed for a couple to obtain a divorce decree. The process requires knowledge of the law and the forms used to obtain the final judgment of dissolution of marriage.

The documents and information that will be required in the handling of a divorce largely depend on what type of divorce is involved. It varies, depending on whether it is a no fault divorce, a fault divorce, a contested divorce, a consent divorce, or a divorce of a covenant marriage.

A no fault divorce refers to the fact that the party seeking the divorce does not need to prove fault. A simple declaration that the marriage is irretrievably broken is enough in many states. That does not mean, however, that one or both of the parties will not contest other areas. Although they may be able to agree they want to end their marriage, they may not be able to agree on child custody, alimony, division of property, or who gets the family's pet dog!

A consent divorce is one in which the parties agree to all terms of the divorce. In many states this type of divorce can be handled without the aid of an attorney. These states provide simplified forms that allow the couple to set out the terms they have agreed to for their divorce. The **consent decree** is a document that includes all of the terms agreed to by the couple seeking the divorce. It may include agreements on child custody, child support, child visitation, alimony, division of personal property, division of real property, payments of debts, **qualified domestic relations order (QDRO)**, tax deductions for children of the marriage, and any other matters that the parties have agreed to relating to the divorce. This form of divorce is the quickest and most economical way for a couple to end their marriage if they can come to an agreement on the terms of the divorce.

A contested divorce is one of the most complicated forms of divorce. How complicated it is depends on what, if anything, the parties agree on. In cases where the parties can agree on little or nothing, the divorce procedure is similar to any civil law case. A petition is filed and served on the other party, the party served with the petition must respond within a specific period of time, a period of time is allowed for discovery, temporary motions may be filed and ruled on by the court, the case may be required to be heard by a mediator, and ultimately the case is heard by a judge. There is no jury in most divorce cases, unless specifically provided for by state constitution or statute. Instead the judge sits as the determiner of the facts of the case and makes a ruling based on them. In effect, he or she acts as both the judge and jury. If a jury is allowed, it will sit as the trier of fact.

**consent decree**
A decree that all parties to the case agree to.

**qualified domestic relations order (QDRO)**
Retirement account distributions' legal documentation requirement for ultimate distribution.

**CYBER TRIP**

To view forms used in a consent divorce provided by the Superior Court of Arizona, Maricopa County, visit www.superiorcourt. maricopa.gov/ssc/ forms/fc_dr7.asp.

## ETHICS ALERT

Consent divorces can be handled by the parties without the aid of an attorney, but many people are not comfortable with the idea of completing even simplified legal forms. These people will often seek out an attorney to do this for them. Attorneys who work in this field usually handle these divorces for a comparatively small fee.

As mentioned in Chapter 1, states vary on whether an attorney can simultaneously represent a husband and wife in a divorce proceeding, even if the parties have resolved all issues relating to the divorce. This is because there is a strong possibility that duel representation may be adverse to the interest of either the husband or the wife and that the attorney's independent professional judgment will be limited. Even if he or she is not allowed to represent both parties, an attorney may accept a consent divorce case with the express understanding that he or she only represents one party and that the other should seek independent legal counsel if the person does not agree with any matters relating to the divorce.

So how does this present an ethical issue for the paralegal?

Paralegals are often the eyes and ears of the attorney in his or her relations with the client. The paralegal will have far more contacts and conversations with the client than does the attorney. That means the paralegal is the person who is in the best position to see when a possible problem exists with a divorce case. One problem that can arise in a consent divorce case is that one party is not voluntarily consenting to the terms of the divorce. This can be due to **coercion** or **duress** by the other spouse.

It is important that a paralegal report any indications that one spouse may not be entering into the consent decree voluntarily. Ultimately it is the paralegal's supervising attorney who will make the decision on what action to take, such as withdrawing from the case, but he or she must have the information relating to the possible problem as soon as it is observed or sensed by the paralegal.

**coercion**
Act obtained by physical force or threat of physical force.

**duress**
Unreasonable and unscrupulous manipulation of a person to force him to agree to terms of an agreement that he would otherwise not agree to. Also, any unlawful threat or coercion used by a person to induce another to act (or to refrain from acting) in a manner that he or she otherwise would not do.

## Information Needed

Information gathering seems simple enough. However, whereas things like names of the parties, the date of their marriage, and similar matters certainly are easy to obtain, other information is not. Figure 9.1 contains a sample of a client interview checklist similar to ones often used in the law office to aid in information collection. See Appendix C for an additional example of a client interview checklist.

Although it is important to use a form such as the one set out in Figure 9.1 to ensure that the needed information is gathered, it is essential to keep in mind that this is not a cold, detached process like when a customer is opening a bank account or applying for a loan. The client is going through a very difficult time when he or she comes into the law office seeking help. This is true even in uncontested divorce cases. The paralegal must be careful to remember that fact, to avoid conducting a cold and clinical client interview.

Brenda Acres from the Client Interview is a good example of someone who may be depressed or distracted by the events occurring in her life. When Brenda comes into the law office, the last thing she needs is to be treated as if she were just a number and not as a client who needs help. As is true with most clients, Brenda will be dealing with the paralegal most of the time during the course of her divorce. It is part of the paralegal's duties to make the client feel comfortable and supported during this difficult period. Putting the client at ease not only makes it easier for the client but also helps the paralegal develop a good working relationship with the client. Building this relationship starts in the initial client interview and continues throughout the divorce process.

A good way to put clients at ease from the beginning is to not only listen to their concerns but also to provide the information they need to understand what will happen

**FIGURE 9.1**
**Sample Client
Interview
Questionnaire**

**I. Personal Information**

**Client**
Name _____
Address _____
Phone Number _____
Occupation _____
Social Security Number _____
DOB _____
Member of the Military ____ (Y/N)

**Spouse**
Name _____
Address _____
Phone Number _____
Occupation _____
Social Security Number _____
DOB _____
Member of the Military ____ (Y/N)

**Children**
Name _____
Address _____
Phone Number _____
Occupation _____
Social Security Number _____
DOB _____

**II. Marriage**

Date of Marriage _____
Place of Marriage _____
Prior Marriages _____
Date of Separation _____

**III. Reasons for Divorce**

Grounds for Divorce _____
Grounds for Annulment (if any) _____

**IV. Jurisdiction and Venue**

How long has client resided in state? _____
How long have the parties lived in the state as husband and wife? _____
Is one spouse residing in another state?  If yes, where? _____

**V. Property of Marriage**

Nature, approximate value, and location of property _____

**VI. Document Checklist**

|  | Received On | In File |
|---|---|---|
| Marriage license/certificate | _____ | ____ (Y/N) |
| Previous dissolution of marriage decrees | _____ | ____ (Y/N) |
| Children: |  |  |
|    Medical hospital records | _____ | ____ (Y/N) |
|    Letters from psychiatrist, psychologist, teachers, etc. | _____ | ____ (Y/N) |
| Prior agreements as to marital property, including prenuptial agreements, marriage settlement agreements or any agreement relating to the ownership of property | _____ | ____ (Y/N) |
| Tax records | _____ | ____ (Y/N) |
| Checking account records | _____ | ____ (Y/N) |
| Savings account records | _____ | ____ (Y/N) |
| Stocks/ bonds records | _____ | ____ (Y/N) |

| | | |
|---|---|---|
| Real property—title | _____ | _____ (Y/N) |
| Personal property (list) | _____ | _____ (Y/N) |
| Business interest documentation | _____ | _____ (Y/N) |
| Safe deposit box(es) information | _____ | _____ (Y/N) |
| Will/trusts | _____ | _____ (Y/N) |
| Other assets (list) | _____ | _____ (Y/N) |
| Debts (list) | _____ | _____ (Y/N) |

**FIGURE 9.1**
*(concluded)*

in the upcoming months. For example, a discussion of the steps that are involved in the divorce process can be very reassuring to the client. After all, although the paralegal may have handled hundreds of divorces, it is most likely the first time the client has ever been to an attorney. Therefore, the client needs to know what will happen, when things will happen, and what to do if he or she has a question or concern. Included in this conversation should be the roles the members of the legal team will play. For example, since the client may expect to speak to the attorney every time he or she calls, the paralegal should explain that the client's calls may be answered by the paralegal rather than the attorney. The paralegal can answer many of the client's questions more quickly and efficiently than waiting for the attorney to return a call. In the event it is a matter that requires the attorney's attention, the paralegal can make sure that the information is communicated to the client in a timely fashion.

The time spent reassuring the client and letting him or her know what to expect will make both client and paralegal more contented.

Gathering information is not always easy. One problem is that clients sometimes do not want the paralegal and attorney to know the complete story of what caused the divorce and matters relating to things like child custody. Although this may seem contrary to the client's best interests, the client will often trust the advice received from family members and friends. These people give their advice as to what the client should tell the lawyer about what is going on. These advice givers may have good intentions, but the creation of a story that seems to help the client get what he or she wants may actually end up causing problems because the attorney does not have a true understanding of the facts of the case. This can be particularly troubling in matters relating to delicate issues such as child custody and child visitation.

Difficult or not, information is critical in the completion of a divorce/dissolution case. Figure 9.2 sets out the steps that are involved in completing a divorce/dissolution case.

## Drafting Initial Pleadings

As has been noted, dissolution of marriage is a form of civil litigation. Because of this, the forms used are similar in format to other forms prepared in a civil litigation firm. It is important to note that although states use similar forms for each part of pleadings, they do vary from state to state. Paralegals should check with the rules of court of their state to learn more about the proper form and terminology of their state.

As is the case when most people make cakes, **pleadings** are seldom drafted from scratch. Instead they are drafted by using sample forms that are available from a variety of sources. Most law firms maintain a database of forms that can be used when drafting pleadings. In addition, forms are available in books, CDs, and online resources such as Westlaw and Lexis/Nexis.

When paralegal students first hear the word *form,* they usually think a complete form is available for their use, similar to a fill-in-the-blank form. This is certainly true, as some forms are available for laypeople to complete, such as the petition provided in Figure 9.4 later in this chapter. However, in the law offices, pleadings are usually

**CYBER TRIP**

Since drafting pleadings can be a little intimidating at first, a paralegal student can experiment with creating his or her own pleadings, keeping in mind that the format of pleadings does vary state by state, by using Microsoft Word. It provides a pleadings wizard that helps you create these documents. To learn more on how to use Microsoft Word in this manner, visit http://library.lls.edu/crc/pleadingpaper word2002.pdf or http://library.lls.edu/crc/pleading paperword97. pdf. But remember that the *exact format* of pleadings is dictated by the court rules of your state.

**pleadings**
Formal documents filed with the court that establish the claims and defenses of the parties to the lawsuit; the complaint, answer to complaint, and reply.

**FIGURE 9.2**
**The Divorce/**
**Dissolution Procedure**

### Steps in the Divorce Procedure

- Initial Consultation with Attorney—Client is interviewed by the attorney, often with the aid of the paralegal. Information is obtained from the client and the client is given an overview of the divorce process. What needs to be completed may vary depending on factors such as: whether the divorce is contested or not, whether there are minor children of the marriage, and whether there are issues relating to the distribution of marital property.
- Document Preparation—The initial documents are prepared. If the law firm is representing the person filing for divorce, this would include the Petition for Dissolution of Marriage. The first document normally drafted by the responding party is the Answer.
- Filing of Petition—The Petition for Dissolution of Marriage is filed with the clerk of the appropriate court.
- Summons and Service of Process—The petition is served on the other spouse along with a summons notifying the spouse on the number of days he or she has to respond to the petition.
- Answer/Default—A response, often referred to as an Answer, must be filed with the court by the person on whom the summons was served. A copy of the Answer must also be served on the opposing party or his or her attorney as provided for by the applicable laws or rules of procedure. Failure to file an answer may result in entry of a default judgment by the court.
- Temporary Orders/Emergency Orders (Custody, Alimony, Restraining Orders)—Divorce cases can take an extended period of time before a final judgment is entered. Often certain matters must be taken care of during the interim period. This includes seeking an award of temporary alimony and child support. There are also instances where there is a fear of possible physical abuse, one parent taking the child from the jurisdiction of the court and/or one spouse removing/destroying/dissipating marital assets. In those cases, a party may seek an order from the court to prevent such harm from occurring. A hearing will be held to resolve requests for temporary/emergency orders. Temporary motions and orders will be discussed in more detail in Chapter 10.
- Mediation/Negotiation—Many states now require that the parties attempt to resolve as many of the issues as possible that exist between them prior to trial. This is often accomplished by use of a mediator who attempts to aid the parties in resolving those issues. In addition, the parties themselves, through their attorneys, may also try to negotiate the resolution of these issues to avoid the costs and uncertainties of taking the case all the way through trial.
- Parenting Class (in some states)—Some states now require parents to take parenting classes as part of the divorce process. This is an effort to make the parents aware of the impact the divorce will have on the minor children of the marriage and reduce the stress on the children.
- Disclosure/Discovery—The parties in a divorce are required in many states to exchange certain financial information. In addition, other forms of discovery may be required to ensure that the information needed to properly protect the client's interest is obtained.
- Experts/Evaluation—Experts may be needed to assist in many areas of the divorce case. This includes experts to help determine the value of marital property and evaluate the emotional needs of the minor children of the marriage to aid in the determination of child custody matters. Some states require a psychological evaluation of the minor children of the marriage be performed.
- Case Assignment—Cases are assigned to a particular judge or magistrate for hearing.
- Settlement—At any time before the final judgment is ordered the parties can reach a settlement of the unresolved issues relating to the divorce action. Agreements as to child custody and child support are generally not binding on the court. Instead the court will attempt to ensure that the best interests of the child are being met.
- Trial—A trial will be held to resolve the remaining issues of the case. It may be held by the judge alone, a magistrate, or, in some states, a judge and jury.
- Ruling/Final Judgment—Based on the findings at trial, an order of final judgment of dissolution of marriage will be entered by the court.
- Appeal—In the event that either party feels that the court has made a mistake of law in its ruling, the party can file an appeal.

drafted using clauses from a variety of sources and, when necessary, specifically drafted for a unique need of the client.

Let's use a cake as a way to explain the difference between a fill-in-the-blank form and a customized pleading that uses clauses from form books. If you wanted a chocolate cake, you could just go to the bakery department of your local grocery store and buy one. It is easy and ready to eat. But it may not taste very good or be the type of chocolate cake that you really enjoy eating. Buying a cake from the store is kind of like using a fill-in-the-blank form. The form may be usable, but does it really fit the client's needs?

If the store-bought cake does not meet your needs, then you might want to bake your own cake. That is a little more work. You have to add milk, eggs, and so on, and bake it yourself to get the desired result. This process is similar to assembling a pleading using sample clauses available in form books to create a customized document that meets the specific needs of the client.

The initial pleading that is filed in civil actions, including a divorce, is referred to as a *petition* or a *complaint* depending on the state. Although the exact clauses that are used to draft a petition vary, they do share some common elements:

*Caption.* The **caption**, also referred to as the *case style,* contains critical information relating to the case itself. It sets out the name of the court, the case number, the names of the parties, and the title of the action. In most civil actions, the caption identifies the filing party as the plaintiff and the responding party as the defendant. Some states do not use these terms in dissolution of marriage cases. Instead they refer to the parties as husband and wife or as petitioner and respondent. Figure 9.3 gives examples of how captions vary by state.

> **caption**
> The full name of the case, together with the docket number, court, and date of the decision.

## RESEARCH THIS

Locate the statute or rule of court that specifies how the caption should be formatted and what information is included. Also, determine if a different caption must be used in a dissolution/ divorce action depending on whether it is a divorce or dissolution of marriage action, there is a settlement agreement, or the action is a fault/ no fault action.

*Title.* The **title** of a pleading is its name/designation. States vary on how a petition for dissolution/divorce is referred to. Examples include: Petition for Dissolution of Marriage, Petition for Divorce, Complaint for Divorce, Complaint in Divorce, Bill for Divorce, and Bill of Complaint for Divorce.

*Body.* The **body** of a pleading is where the key critical statements and **allegations** relating to the case are made. These include statements relating to jurisdiction, the parties, and the nature of the action.

*Prayer for relief.* The **prayer for relief** states what the court is being asked to do. In a divorce proceeding, this includes a request to grant the dissolution of marriage and approval of the parties' separation agreement.

*Subscription/verification.* **Verification** includes the signature of the person filing the document and verifying the truthfulness of the allegations made in the pleading. In divorce and dissolution of marriage actions, this is normally signed by the client, although other jurisdictions allow the attorney to sign and swear that he or she is unaware of any false allegation of facts. Failure to sign and verify the petition may result in the court lacking jurisdiction to grant the divorce/dissolution or

> **title**
> The name/designation of a pleading.
>
> **body**
> Main text of the argument section of the appellate brief.
>
> **allegations**
> Facts forming the basis of a party's complaint.
>
> **prayer for relief**
> A summation at the end of a pleading, which sets forth the demands by a party in the lawsuit.
>
> **verification**
> Acknowledgment by a party of the truthfulness of the information contained within a document.

**FIGURE 9.3**
**Examples of How Captions/Case Styles Vary by State**

| State | Caption/Case Style |
|---|---|
| Alabama: | IN THE CIRCUIT COURT FOR _____ County, Alabama<br>In re the marriage of _____, Plaintiff and _____, Defendant. |
| Alaska:<br>(Simplified<br>Procedure) | SUPERIOR COURT OF THE STATE OF ALASKA<br># _____ JUDICIAL DISTRICT<br>In the Matter of the Dissolution of marriage of<br>_____, Petitioner, and _____ Respondent |
| California: | SUPERIOR COURT OF CALIFORNIA, COUNTY OF _____<br>In re the marriage of _____, Petitioner, and _____,<br>Respondent |
| Connecticut: | IN THE SUPERIOR COURT OF THE STATE OF CONNECTICUT<br>_____, Plaintiff, vs. _____, Defendant |
| Delaware: | IN THE FAMILY COURT OF THE STATE OF DELAWARE<br>IN AND FOR _____ COUNTY<br>In re the Marriage of _____, Petitioner, and _____,<br>Respondent |
| Illinois: | IN THE CIRCUIT COURT OF THE _____ JUDICIAL DISTRICT,<br>_____COUNTY, ILLINOIS<br>In re the Marriage of _____, Petitioner, and _____, Respondent |
| Iowa: | IN THE DISTRICT COURT OF THE STATE OF IOWA<br>IN AND FOR _____ COUNTY<br>In Re the Marriage of _____ and _____<br>Upon the Petition of     )<br>_____          )     Petition for Dissolution of Marriage<br>(Petitioner)            )     Equity No. _____<br>And Concerning          )<br>_____          )<br>(Respondent)            ) |
| Massachusetts: | COMMONWEALTH OF MASSACHUSETTS, PROBATE COURT<br>_____, Co-Petitioner and _____ Co-Petitioner<br>(Used in no-fault divorce actions with settlement agreement.<br>Other captions used for actions that do not have a settlement<br>agreement or in fault divorce action.) |
| Mississippi: | CHANCERY COURT OF _____ COUNTY, STATE OF MISSISSIPPI<br>_____, Complainant, vs. _____, Defendant. |
| North<br>Carolina: | IN THE GENERAL COURT OF JUSTICE, ___ DIVISION,<br>NORTH CAROLINA, _____ COUNTY<br>_____, Plaintiff, vs. _____, Defendant. |
| Ohio: | IN THE COURT OF COMMON PLEAS OF _____ COUNTY, OHIO<br>_____, Plaintiff, vs. _____, Defendant (used in divorce<br>procedure) |

subject the petition to a motion to dismiss. The subscription/verification must comply with the requirements set out in the relevant state statute or court rule. See *Morrison v. Morison* set out in the following Case in Point.

Figure 9.4 contains a sample petition for simplified dissolution of marriage. See Appendix C for an additional example of a petition for dissolution of marriage.

**RESEARCH THIS**

Locate the family law forms that are provided to the citizens of your state who desire to handle their own dissolution of marriage. If your state does not provide such forms or if you live in Florida, locate forms provided by a state near your own.

IN THE CIRCUIT COURT OF THE JUDICIAL CIRCUIT,
IN AND FOR DUVAL COUNTY, FLORIDA

Case No.:XXXXX

Division: Family Law

_____,
Husband,
and

_____,
Wife.
Petition

### PETITION FOR SIMPLIFIED DISSOLUTION OF MARRIAGE

We, _____, Husband, and _____, Wife, being sworn, certify that the following information is true:

1. We are both asking the Court for a dissolution of our marriage.
2. Husband lives in *{name}* County, *{state}*, and has lived there since *{date}*. Wife lives in *{name}* County, *{state}*, and has lived there since *{date}*.
3. We were married to each other on *{date}* in the city of *{city}* in state of *{state}*, or country of *{country}*.
4. Our marriage is irretrievably broken.
5. Together, we have no minor (under 18) or dependent children **and** the wife is not pregnant.
6. We have made a marital settlement agreement dividing our assets (what we own) and our liabilities (what we owe). We are satisfied with this agreement. Our marital settlement agreement, Florida Family Law Rules of Procedure Form 12.902(f)(3), is attached. This agreement was signed freely and voluntarily by each of us and we intend to be bound by it.
7. We have each completed and signed financial affidavits, Florida Family Law Rules of Procedure Forms 12.902(b) or (c), which are attached to this petition.
8. Completed Notice of Social Security Number forms, Florida Supreme Court Approved Family Law Form12.902(j), are filed with this petition.
9. [ / **one** only] ( ) yes ( ) no Wife wants to be known by her former name, which was *{full legal name}*.
10. We each certify that we have not been threatened or pressured into signing this petition. We each understand that the result of signing this petition may be a final judgment ending our marriage and allowing no further relief.
11. We each understand that **we both must come to the hearing** to testify about the things we are asking for in this petition.
12. We understand that we each may have legal rights as a result of our marriage and that by signing this petition we may be giving up those rights.
13. We ask the Court to end our marriage and approve our marital settlement agreement.

**I understand that I am swearing or affirming under oath to the truthfulness of the claims made in this petition and that the punishment for knowingly making a false statement includes fines and/or imprisonment.**

Dated: _____

_____
Signature of HUSBAND
Printed Name: _____
Address: _____
City, State, Zip: _____
Telephone Number: _____
Fax Number: _____

STATE OF FLORIDA
COUNTY OF_____
Sworn to or affirmed and signed before me on _____ by _____ .

_____
NOTARY PUBLIC or DEPUTY CLERK
[Print, type, or stamp commissioned name of notary or deputy clerk.]

*(cont.)*

FIGURE 9.4
**Sample Petition for Simplified Dissolution of Marriage**
*Source:* Retrieved from www.flcourts.org/gen_public/family/forms_rules/index.shtml 2/28/07.

**FIGURE 9.4**
*(concluded)*

_____ Personally known
_____ Produced identification
_____ Type of identification produced

**I understand that I am swearing or affirming under oath to the truthfulness of the claims made in this petition and that the punishment for knowingly making a false statement includes fines and/or imprisonment.**
Dated: _____

_____
Signature of WIFE
Printed Name: _____
Address: _____
City, State, Zip: _____
Telephone Number: _____
Fax Number: _____

STATE OF FLORIDA
COUNTY OF
Sworn to or affirmed and signed before me on _____ by _____ .

_____
NOTARY PUBLIC or DEPUTY CLERK
[Print, type, or stamp commissioned name of notary or deputy clerk.]

_____ Personally known
_____ Produced identification
_____ Type of identification produced

## Domicile, Venue, and Jurisdiction

**subject matter jurisdiction**
A court's authority over the res, the subject of the case.

The next step in the divorce proceeding is the filing of the initial pleading in a court with **subject matter jurisdiction** over divorce cases. Subject matter jurisdiction is the power of the court to hear a lawsuit, in this case, a divorce. It is often tied to a specific time period that one or both parties have been **domiciled** in the state. For example, in Florida, one of the parties must reside in the state for at least six months before he or she files the petition for divorce.

**domicile**
The place where a person maintains a physical residence with the intent to permanently remain in that place; citizenship; the permanent home of the party.

**Venue** is a legal concept that is often confused with subject matter jurisdiction. The distinction is that venue refers to a specific geographical area of the state in which an action should be filed. For example, in Florida, the circuit courts of the state have subject matter jurisdiction over divorces. The proper venue, that is, which circuit court to file a divorce case in, is usually determined by where the parties live at the time of filing.

**venue**
County in which the facts are alleged to have occurred and in which the trial will take place.

The petition is then filed with the clerk of the court. A filing fee is required in almost all circumstances, although a waiver of the fee is available to indigent people in some states. Paralegals must be familiar with the filing fees required by their local courts, which usually can be obtained by visiting the clerk's office or the clerk's Web site.

**in personam jurisdiction**
A court's authority over a party personally.

The act of filing the petition with the court constitutes recognition of **in personam jurisdiction**, sometimes referred to as *personal jurisdiction,* by the party filing it. This does not, however, give the court power over the other party. This is acquired by notifying the other party that the petition has been filed in one of the following ways:

- Waiver of service—A person can waive the requirement of personal service by signing a written waiver of service. This form may be referred to as an *entry of appearance and waiver of service* in some states.
- Filing of a joint petition, if allowed by state law.
- Service by law enforcement officer—This is often the sheriff or other person allowed to serve process under the laws of the state. Figure 9.5 contains a sample summons.

# CASE IN POINT

*Morrison v. Morrison*
**716 S.W.2d 846**
**(Mo. Ct. App. 1986)**

KELLY, Judge.

This is an appeal from the St. Louis County Circuit Court's Order, Judgment and Decree of Dissolution of the Marriage of Ardell J. Morrison and Arthur L. Morrison. The appellant-husband argues that the trial court did not have jurisdiction because wife's pleading failed to comply with § 452.310.2 RSMo 1978. The judgment is set aside.

Respondent-wife filed her petition for dissolution of marriage in the St. Louis County Circuit Court on October 14, 1982. Wife's petition included a certificate of acknowledgement, in which she stated that she executed the petition as her own free, voluntary act. Wife signed the petition in the presence of a notary, but failed to have the petition verified.

Section 452.310.2 RSMo 1978 of the Marriage and Dissolution of Marriage Act provides in part: "The petition in a proceeding for dissolution of marriage or legal separation shall be *verified* and shall allege the marriage is irretrievably broken and shall set forth . . ." (emphasis added).

The requirement for a verified petition in a dissolution proceeding is jurisdictional. *In re: Marriage of Dunn*, 650 S. W.2d 638, 639 (Mo.App.1983). Absent a dissolution petition properly verified in accordance with the statutes, a trial court lacks authority to render a decree of dissolution. *American Industrial Resources, Inc., v. T.S.E. Supply Company,* 708 S.W.2d 806, 808 (Mo.App.1986).

Wife contends that jurisdiction in a dissolution proceeding is determined by § 452.320.1 RSMo 1978, which only requires that both parties state under oath by petition or otherwise that the marriage is irretrievably broken and does not include the verification requirements of § 452.310.2 RSMo 1978. We disagree.

It is clear that § 452.320 RSMo 1978 presumes the existence of a verified petition filed under § 452.310 RSMo 1978. In the case at bar, such a petition was not filed, and thus § 452.320 RSMo 1978 is not applicable.

We hold that the trial court was without jurisdiction. The judgment of the trial court entered August 12, 1985, is hereby set aside and held for naught.

CRANDALL, P.J., and PUDLOWSKI, J., concur.

**Source:** From Westlaw. Reprinted with permission from ThomsonWest.

---

- Service by mail—Service by mail is common after the initial pleading is filed but some states also allow initial service by certified mail with return receipt requested.

- Service by publication—Some states allow service to be made by publication if the missing spouse is known to still live in the state. If not, the requirements of the state's long-arm statute will need to be complied with. In either case, the filing spouse will need to show that he or she has made a diligent search to try to locate the other spouse.

- Filing a responsive pleading that recognizes the court's in personam jurisdiction— For example, the spouse files an answer to the petition for dissolution of marriage. This filing acknowledges the court's jurisdiction.

**In rem jurisdiction** is a court's power to resolve claims affecting property or status. In a divorce case, the marriage itself is the status that a court is being asked to make a ruling on. A court has in rem jurisdiction, and thereby the power to grant the divorce, if one or both of the spouses live in the state for the prescribed time. It should be noted that personal jurisdiction over the nonfiling spouse is not required to grant the divorce and dissolve the status of marriage. Personal jurisdiction is needed, however, to rule on matters such as property distribution and alimony.

**in rem jurisdiction**
A court's authority over claims affecting property.

The importance of personal jurisdiction in a divorce case involving children cannot be overstated. In America's highly mobile society, it is not uncommon for the non-custodial parent to live in a different state from the one where the child resides. The

---

**FL-110**

# SUMMONS (Family Law)

**CITACIÓN (Derecho familiar)**

**NOTICE TO RESPONDENT** *(Name):*

*AVISO AL DEMANDADO (Nombre):*

> **You are being sued.** *Lo están demandando.*

**Petitioner's name is:**

*Nombre del demandante:*

CASE NUMBER *(NÚMERO DE CASO):*

| | |
|---|---|
| You have **30 calendar days** after this *Summons* and *Petition* are served on you to file a *Response* (form FL-120 or FL-123) at the court and have a copy served on the petitioner. A letter or phone call will not protect you. | *Tiene **30 días corridos** después de haber recibido la entrega legal de esta Citación y Petición para presentar una Respuesta (formulario FL-120 ó FL-123) ante la corte y efectuar la entrega legal de una copia al demandante. Una carta o llamada telefónica no basta para protegerlo.* |
| If you do not file your *Response* on time, the court may make orders affecting your marriage or domestic partnership, your property, and custody of your children. You may be ordered to pay support and attorney fees and costs. If you cannot pay the filing fee, ask the clerk for a fee waiver form. | *Si no presenta su Respuesta a tiempo, la corte puede dar órdenes que afecten su matrimonio o pareja de hecho, sus bienes y la custodia de sus hijos. La corte también le puede ordenar que pague manutención, y honorarios y costos legales. Si no puede pagar la cuota de presentación, pida al secretario un formulario de exención de cuotas.* |
| If you want legal advice, contact a lawyer immediately. You can get information about finding lawyers at the California Courts Online Self-Help Center *(www.courtinfo.ca.gov/selfhelp)*, at the California Legal Services Web site *(www.lawhelpcalifornia.org)*, or by contacting your local county bar association. | *Si desea obtener asesoramiento legal, póngase en contacto de inmediato con un abogado. Puede obtener información para encontrar a un abogado en el Centro de Ayuda de las Cortes de California (www.sucorte.ca.gov), en el sitio Web de los Servicios Legales de California (www.lawhelpcalifornia.org) o poniéndose en contacto con el colegio de abogados de su condado.* |

**NOTICE:** The restraining orders on page 2 are effective against both spouses or domestic partners until the petition is dismissed, a judgment is entered, or the court makes further orders. These orders are enforceable anywhere in California by any law enforcement officer who has received or seen a copy of them.

*AVISO: Las órdenes de restricción que figuran en la página 2 valen para ambos cónyuges o pareja de hecho hasta que se despida la petición, se emita un fallo o la corte dé otras órdenes. Cualquier autoridad de la ley que haya recibido o visto una copia de estas órdenes puede hacerlas acatar en cualquier lugar de California.*

1. The name and address of the court are *(El nombre y dirección de la corte son):*

2. The name, address, and telephone number of the petitioner's attorney, or the petitioner without an attorney, are:
   *(El nombre, dirección y número de teléfono del abogado del demandante, o del demandante si no tiene abogado, son):*

Date *(Fecha):*                    Clerk, by *(Secretario, por)*_____, Deputy *(Asistente)*

| [SEAL] | **NOTICE TO THE PERSON SERVED:** You are served |
|---|---|
| | *AVISO A LA PERSONA QUE RECIBIÓ LA ENTREGA: Esta entrega se realiza* |
| | a. ☐   as an individual. *(a usted como individuo.)* |
| | b. ☐   on behalf of respondent who is a *(en nombre de un demandado que es):* |
| |     (1) ☐   minor *(menor de edad)* |
| |     (2) ☐   ward or conservatee *(dependiente de la corte o pupilo)* |
| |     (3) ☐   other *(specify) (otro – especifique):* |
| | **(Read the reverse for important information.)** |
| | *(Lea importante información al dorso.)* |

Page 1 of 2

Form Adopted for Mandatory Use
Judicial Council of California
FL-110 [Rev. January 1, 2006]

**SUMMONS**
**(Family Law)**

Family Code §§ 232, 233, 2040, 7700;
Code of Civil Procedure, §§ 412.20, 416.60–416.90
*www.courtinfo.ca.gov*

American LegalNet, Inc.
www.USCourtForms.com

---

**FIGURE 9.5**   **Sample Summons**

*Source:* Retrieved from www.courtinfo.ca.gov/forms/fillable/fl110.pdf on 8/28/07.

**California Courts Self-Help Center**
**Instructions for *Summons (Family Law)*, Form FL-110**
http://www.courtinfo.ca.gov/selfhelp/

**Top Part of Form**
*The respondent's name goes first at the top of the summons.*
*The petitioner's name goes underneath where indicated on the form.*

*Number 1.*
*You should set out the name and address of the court. It would read as follows:*
*Superior Court of California, County of _____ [put in your county]*
*[address of the court as it appears on the petition]*

*Number 2.*
*You need to put in your own name, address, and telephone number.*

*Bottom of Page—Notice to Person Served*
*Check Box 1—"As an individual".*

**Back of Form**
*Read all of the information on the back of this form, including restraining orders against:*
* *Removing the minor child or children of the parties, if any, from the state without the prior written consent of the other party or an order of the court;*
* *Canceling insurance or changing beneficiaries;*
* *Getting rid of property without the other spouse's written permission or a court order unless you must sell the property to pay for the necessities of life.*

These orders start for the petitioner as soon as the petition is filed. These orders start for the respondent as soon as he or she is served with the summons and petition. Unless the court decides to extend them, these restrictions end when your judgment is filed with the court.

**FIGURE 9.5**    *(concluded)*

complexities of dealing with differing laws in all 50 states caused many problems in the past. Similar issues are involved with spousal support (alimony).

To help reduce these issues, all 50 states have now enacted the **Uniform Interstate Family Support Act** (UIFSA). The act sets out how jurisdiction is established in cases involving the establishment, enforcement, or modification of child or spousal support. Figure 9.6 contains the Montana version of the portion of the UIFSA that sets out the bases for establishing jurisdiction over a nonresident. The act also requires that the laws of the state that had original jurisdiction over the case be applied in modification hearings taking place in another state.

**Uniform Interstate Family Support Act**
State law used in cases involving the establishment and enforcement of child or spousal support obligations when the obligor lives in one state and the obligee/children live in another.

## FILING AND SERVICE OF INITIAL PLEADING

As has been discussed, a court can acquire personal jurisdiction in several ways; one of the more common methods in all types of civil litigation is service by a law enforcement officer or other person allowed by law to serve initial pleadings. This is often the sheriff of the county in which the person being served resides. Sometimes sheriffs appoint private process servers to handle the actual service of process. In either case, a fee will be required to be paid in addition to the filing fee paid when the case is initially filed.

Proper service of process is important for a number of reasons. First, and perhaps most important, it gives the court personal jurisdiction over the person being served. Second, it also starts the clock ticking on when the defendant in the case must file his or her responsive pleading.

It is important that paralegals learn how service of process is completed in their state and who can properly serve process. This process is relatively simple and

**FIGURE 9.6**
Montana Code
Annotated 2005

**40-5-145. Bases for jurisdiction over nonresident.** In a proceeding to establish, enforce, or modify a support order or to determine parentage, a tribunal of this state may exercise personal jurisdiction over a nonresident individual or the individual's guardian or conservator if:

(1) the individual is personally served with notice within this state;
(2) the individual submits to the jurisdiction of this state by consent, by entering a general appearance, or by filing a responsive document having the effect of waiving any contest to personal jurisdiction;
(3) the individual resided with the child in this state;
(4) the individual resided in this state and provided prenatal expenses or support for the child;
(5) the child resides in this state as a result of the acts or directives of the individual;
(6) the individual engaged in sexual intercourse in this state and the child may have been conceived by that act of intercourse; or
(7) there is any other basis consistent with the constitutions of this state and the United States for the exercise of personal jurisdiction.

**CYBER TRIP**

Many states now provide detailed information on how to file a dissolution/ divorce action. Although this information is aimed at the general public, it can also be beneficial to the paralegal student to better understand the basics of the process.

Visit the Center for Arkansas Legal Services, Legal Aid of Arkansas & Arkansas Volunteer Lawyers for the Elderly to view an example of such information at http:// m47080.kaivo.com/ Home/PublicWeb/ DocDisclaimer/fact sheets/FSdivorce_ packet.pdf.

becomes very routine in the law office. Paralegals must not let the routine lull them into thinking it is not an important process. Failure to gain personal jurisdiction over a party because of improper service of process results in a court lacking jurisdiction to resolve the case, something that may be challenged at any time.

The *In re Marriage of Tsarbopoulos* that follows is an example of how complicated the issues relating to jurisdiction can become.

## AFFIDAVIT OF NONMILITARY SERVICE

The Soldiers' and Sailors' Civil Relief Act 1940, subsequently updated by the Servicemembers Civil Relief Act 2003, provides special rights and protection in legal matters to active members of the military. Included in these rights are the ability to delay judicial proceedings and the entry of default judgments against members of the armed forces. This may be a factor in bringing the divorce/dissolution case to a conclusion. For example, even if neither spouse is an active member of the military, an affidavit of nonmilitary-military service may be needed in cases where one spouse will not sign either a marital settlement agreement or an answer and waiver before a default judgment can be entered. The affidavit of nonmilitary service states that the person swearing to or affirming the truthfulness of the information contained in the form has personal knowledge that the spouse is not a member of the armed forces or that they have inquired of the armed forces of the United States and the U.S. Public Health Service and determined that the spouse is not a member of the armed forces. Figure 9.7 contains an example of a affidavit of nonmilitary service.

**CYBER TRIP**

To learn more about the Servicemembers Civil Relief Act 2003 and the Soldiers' and Sailors' Relief Act of 1940, visit http://usmilitary. about.com/od/ sscra/l/blsscra.htm.

**RESEARCH THIS**

Research the laws of your state to determine when an affidavit of nonmilitary service is needed and the procedures that need to be followed in filing it in a dissolution of marriage action.

STATE OF WISCONSIN, CIRCUIT COURT, _____ COUNTY  | *For Official Use*

Plaintiff: _____

-vs-

Defendant: _____     Case No. _____

**Affidavit of Nonmilitary Service**

_____ , being first duly sworn on oath, says that:
Plaintiff or Plaintiff's Attorney

1. I am the ☐ plaintiff or ☐ plaintiff's attorney in this case.

2. This affidavit is made for the purpose of obtaining a default judgment against the above named defendant.

3. I believe the defendant is not on active military duty at this time because (choose one):

   ☐ I know the defendant personally and s/he has never given any indication that s/he is in service with the United States military or National Guard.

   ☐ I contacted the defendant, who informed me on _____ (date) that s/he is not on active duty at this time.

   ☐ I see the defendant regularly and therefore believe s/he is not on active duty at this time.

   ☐ Other personal knowledge: _____

☐ 4. I checked the United States Department of Defense website and obtained a certificate showing that the defendant ☐ **is** ☐ **is not** on active duty status. This certificate is attached.

☐ 5. I have attempted to determine military status but do not have sufficient information. I have no reason to believe s/he is on active duty at this time.

Subscribed and sworn to before me

on _____

_____
Notary Public, State of Wisconsin

My commission expires: _____

_____
Signature of Plaintiff (Do not sign until you are under oath)

_____
Name Printed or Typed of Plaintiff

_____
Signature of Plaintiff's Attorney

_____
Name Printed or Typed of Plaintiff's Attorney

_____
Date

GF-175, 04/06  Affidavit of Nonmilitary Service                        50 USC App. §§ 521, §806.19, Wisconsin Statutes
**This form shall not be modified. It may be supplemented with additional material.**

**FIGURE 9.7**    **Wisconsin Court System Affidavit of Nonmilitary Service**

*Source:* Retrieved from www.wicourts.gov/circuit/ccform.jsp?FormNumber= GF-175 on 8/29/07.

*In re Marriage of Tsarbopoulos*
125 Wn. App. 273
(Division Three 2004.]

KURTZ, J .

## FACTS

Kristi Lee Tsarbopoulos and Anthony Tsarbopoulos were married in Ohio on December 12, 1986. They separated approximately 13 years later, on December 29, 1999. In the interim, they had three children: Harilaos (born October 21, 1992), Ioanna (born November 24, 1995), and Iason (born July 28, 1997).

Dr. Tsarbopoulos was born and raised in Greece. He attended graduate school at Michigan State University. From 1985 to 1987, Dr. Tsarbopoulos was employed at the Mayo Clinic in Rochester, Minnesota. In 1987, the family relocated to New Jersey where Dr. Tsarbopoulos was employed at the Schering-Plough Research Institute.

In 1997, the family moved to Athens, Greece, where Dr. Tsarbopoulos currently resides. In late December 1999, Ms. Tsarbopoulos and the children left Greece and moved to Colbert, Washington, to live with Ms. Tsarbopoulos's parents. Ms. Tsarbopoulos alleged that Dr. Tsarbopoulos was emotionally and physically abusive to her and the children, and she left to escape the abuse.

On January 6, 2000, a dissolution of marriage proceeding was instituted in Spokane County. On April 17, 2000, the court entered an order finding that Dr. Tsarbopoulos did not have sufficient contact with the state of Washington to impose personal jurisdiction over him. As a result, the dissolution action was dismissed in March 2002.

A second dissolution of marriage action was commenced on April 22, 2002. Ms. Tsarbopoulos retained a Greek attorney who employed a process server to effectuate service upon Dr. Tsarbopoulos. The process server attempted to serve Dr. Tsarbopoulos at his place of employment, an underground chemical laboratory in the Goulandris National History Museum, but Dr. Tsarbopoulos was not present. Consequently, the process server left the documents with Evangelos Gikas, whom the process server stated was Dr. Tsarbopoulos's "working assistant" at the museum. Clerk's Papers (CP) at 23.

Dr. Tsarbopoulos failed to respond or appear in the matter, and an order of default was entered on August 12, 2002. A decree of dissolution, parenting plan, and order of child support were entered on September 11, 2002. The decree of dissolution awarded property to Ms. Tsarbopoulos in the amount of a payment of $63,500, reflecting Ms. Tsarbopoulos's one-half interest in a joint investment account. The decree also ordered Dr. Tsarbopoulos to pay to Ms. Tsarbopoulos $10,000 for her attorney fees and ordered him to pay child support.

The order of child support obligated Dr. Tsarbopoulos to pay $10,397.40 in back child support and $2,599.35 per month from that date forward. The parenting plan provided that the children would reside with Ms. Tsarbopoulos and imposed restrictions upon Dr. Tsarbopoulos's contact with the children and Ms. Tsarbopoulos.

Several months later, Dr. Tsarbopoulos appeared and moved to vacate the decree of dissolution and the other orders that had been entered. After a hearing, the court ordered the decree of dissolution vacated. The court held that the service was ineffective under RCW 26.27.081. Also, the court found that the long-arm jurisdiction under RCW 4.28.185 did not apply factually to this case.

The court allowed the parties to brief the issue of statutory interpretation through a motion for reconsideration. On July 30, 2003, the court issued a memorandum opinion and order denying Ms. Tsarbopoulos's request for reconsideration. The order states that Ms. Tsarbopoulos contends that the service was perfected under Greek law, and Dr. Tsarbopoulos disputes that assertion. The court finds that both parties provide declarations supporting their positions, and therefore "[t]he court is without sufficient undisputed information and evidence to determine who is correct. The burden is on the party who is asserting jurisdiction." CP at 281.

The court next states that under Washington law, the service would not have been sufficient. The court stated, "[t]here are ways that notice could have been clearly given as required by the statute including personal service or service by mail. Service by either of these methods would have resolved the problem for petitioner and would have assured that the respondent had notice. Given the fact that such was not done and that the legality of service under Greek law is disputed, the court finds that notice and service requirements were not met." CP at 281-82.

Ms. Tsarbopoulos appeals.

## ANALYSIS

***Child Custody.*** Jurisdiction over custody matters must be determined consistent with the subject matter requirements of chapter 26.27 RCW, the UCCJA. The UCCJA bases its jurisdiction on the child's connection with the state. RCW 26.27.201. Accordingly, custody proceedings are proceedings in rem or proceedings affecting status. Personal jurisdiction over an affected parent is not a requirement. RCW 26.27.201(3). Due process, however, requires that Dr. Tsarbopoulos be given notice and the opportunity to be heard in accordance with the UCCJA. RCW 26.27.241(1). Under the UCCJA, Washington courts are to treat the resident of a foreign country as if he or she were a resident of a sister state for purposes of applying articles 1 and 2. RCW 26.27.051(1). Article 1 contains the notice provisions at issue here in RCW 26.27.081.

***RCW 26.27.081.*** RCW 26.27.081 provides:

(1) Notice required for the exercise of jurisdiction when a person is outside this state may be given in a manner prescribed for service of process by the law

of the state in which the service is made or given in a manner reasonably calculated to give actual notice, and may be made in any of the following ways:

(a) Personal delivery outside this state in the manner prescribed for service of process within this state;

(b) By any form of mail addressed to the person to be served and requesting a receipt; or

(c) As directed by the court, including publication if other means of notification are ineffective.

The term used throughout the statute is "may." As a result, we interpret the phrase "and may be made in any of the following ways" as providing permissive or discretionary methods rather than mandatory ones. In other words, if the foreign state where service is effectuated provides for a method of service that is not one of the enumerated methods, as in this case, the statute authorizes service by the alternate method approved by the foreign state.

**Service under Greek Law.** Next, the court must consider whether the service of Dr. Tsarbopoulos was effective under Greek law. The trial court observed that it had received contradictory declarations; therefore, the court was "without sufficient undisputed information and evidence to determine who is correct." The court decided the issue for Dr. Tsarbopoulos because the burden to prove jurisdiction fell upon Ms. Tsarbopoulos, and she failed to do so.

In support of their respective positions, the parties retained Greek attorneys who provided the court with declarations regarding proper service under Greek law. Ms. Tsarbopoulos's attorney, Titika Nikea-Mouratoglou, declared that the code of civil procedure provides for service of judicial documents at a person's residence, store, office, or laboratory. She also stated that the law provides if the person is not present at these places, the documents may be left with a director of the store, office, or laboratory, or to one of the partners, colleagues, employees, or servants.

Dr. Tsarbopoulos's Greek attorney, D. Boubouris, does not dispute Ms. Nikea-Mouratoglou's interpretation of the code.

\* \* \*

Mr. Boubouris asserts that service was not proper because Mr. Gikas, who accepted delivery of the documents, was not a director, partner, associate, or permanent employee, but "a person . . . who works at the said Museum under neither of the said capabilities."

\* \* \*

We conclude that service was given in a manner reasonably calculated to give actual notice to Dr. Tsarbopoulos and was effectuated in a manner sufficient under Greek law. Consequently, notice was sufficient under Greek law, RCW 26.27.081, and applicable due process standards.

**Other Relief.** In addition to granting custody of the Tsarbopoulos's children to Ms. Tsarbopoulos, the dissolution decree granted other relief, including the dissolution of the parties' marriage, calculation of child support obligations, and division of property. A proceeding dissolving marital bonds is a proceeding in rem. Where one party is domiciled in the state, the court has jurisdiction over the marriage and may dissolve it, even though the court is unable to obtain in personam jurisdiction over the nonresident spouse. By contrast, child support and property dispositions both require in personam jurisdiction over the affected person.

**Method of Service.** To satisfy due process, service of process must be performed with sufficient diligence to provide notice and opportunity to be heard. The constitutional requirement is that notice must be "reasonably calculated, under all the circumstances " to reach the intended person. The due process requirements of notice and opportunity to be heard apply regardless of whether the asserted jurisdiction is classified as in personam or in rem. Additionally, notice must be given in the manner prescribed by Washington's court rules and statutes.

CR 4.1(a) provides that "[a]ctions authorized by RCW 26.09 shall be commenced by filing a petition or by service of a copy of a summons together with a copy of the petition on respondent as provided in rule 4." When personal service is made outside the state of Washington and long-arm jurisdiction is asserted, there are additional statutory requirements. Under the long-arm statute, a respondent may be served outside the state of Washington if service cannot be made within the state. The long-arm statute, nevertheless, requires that the respondent be personally served. Typically, the statute provides service of process may be made upon any person who is subject to the jurisdiction of a court of this state by personally serving that person outside the state, as provided in RCW 4.28.180. RCW 4.28.185(2).

The statutory requirements for effective service of an out-of-state resident are impacted by CR 4(i), which provides for a number of alternative methods for service in a foreign country. In part, CR 4(i) provides that service of the summons and complaint may be effectuated in the manner prescribed by the laws of the foreign country, provided that the service is reasonably calculated, under all the circumstances, to give actual notice. In other words, the manner in which Dr. Tsarbopoulos was served satisfied Washington's service requirements, provided service was sufficient under Greek law and further provided it met the constitutional requirements of notice and opportunity to be heard.

We have already concluded that the method by which Dr. Tsarbopoulos was served was sufficient under Greek law and satisfied constitutional due process. Accordingly, notice was given in a manner prescribed by Washington court rules and statutes. For that reason, we reverse the order of the trial court vacating the order granting a dissolution of the parties' marriage. Because Ms. Tsarbopoulos was domiciled in Washington State and because Dr. Tsarbopoulos was provided notice and the opportunity to be heard, the court had jurisdiction over the marriage and the power to dissolve it.

**Personal Jurisdiction.** Even if the method by which Dr. Tsarbopoulos was served complied with Washington court rules and statutes, a Washington court may not assert personal jurisdiction over him unless he has at least minimal contacts with the state of Washington. RCW 4.28.185; *Kulko*, 436 U.S. at 92. In order to provide for child support and divide the parties' property, the trial court requires personal jurisdiction over Dr. Tsarbopoulos.

RCW 4.28.185 states that a person submits to the jurisdiction of a Washington court when living in a marital relationship within the state notwithstanding subsequent departure from the state. The statute also provides that a person submits to the jurisdiction of the court by engaging in the act of sexual intercourse within the state with respect to which a child may have been conceived. As the trial court observed, these provisions in the long-arm statute are not factually applicable to this case.

Ms. Tsarbopoulos nevertheless argues that her husband should be deemed to have submitted to the personal jurisdiction of Washington by his conduct. Specifically, she emphasizes his failure to support their children, the borrowing of money from her parents for family obligations, and Dr. Tsarbopoulos's use of her parents' address upon a British Airways account. In response, Dr. Tsarbopoulos argues that these actions were insufficient to allow the court to exercise personal jurisdiction over him.

In *Kulko,* the United States Supreme Court examined the very same question that is being presented to us—the adequacy of the contacts to warrant an exercise of long-arm jurisdiction over a noncustodial parent who is not supporting his children. *Kulko* holds that in order to sustain the foreign state's exercise of jurisdiction in a support action, the noncustodial parent's contacts with that state must be based on contacts by which the parent purposefully avails himself or herself of the privilege of conducting activities there, and of the benefits and protection of its laws. *Kulko,* 436 U.S. at 94. Conversely, the contacts will not suffice if the noncustodial connections with the foreign state are "too attenuated." *Id.* at 91.

\* \* \*

Here, the contacts with Washington are even less substantial than the contacts with California in *Kulko*. Dr. Tsarbopoulos did not consent to the relocation of his children from Greece to Washington. While Dr. Tsarbopoulos's failure to support his children is reprehensible, *Kulko* holds a parent's failure to pay child support to a child residing in Washington does not, by itself, give Washington courts jurisdiction over the nonpaying parent. Although Dr. Tsarbopoulos's failure to support his children benefits him financially, the benefit does not result from his contacts or relationship with Washington State, which is the test adopted by *Kulko*.

The additional facts urged by Ms. Tsarbopoulos—financial support provided by her family and Dr. Tsarbopoulos's use of the Washington address to qualify for airline mileage benefits—are insufficient to allow the court to exercise jurisdiction within due process standards. The acts are too attenuated and do not evidence the required intent to obtain an economic benefit as a result of a contact with Washington State. In short, we conclude that Dr. Tsarbopoulos's failure to support his children and his other contacts with Washington State are insufficient to permit the court to assert personal jurisdiction over him consistent with due process standards.

\* \* \*

In this case, Dr. Tsarbopoulos appeared for the first time by filing a motion for relief from judgment on February 20, 2003. In that motion, he argued that the judgment was void for lack of jurisdiction based upon insufficiency of process. While Dr. Tsarbopoulos appeared rather late, approximately five months after the decree of dissolution and the related orders were entered, this delay alone will not support a finding of waiver. Dr. Tsarbopoulos did not otherwise appear in the case, nor did he engage in discovery, file responsive pleadings, or behave in any manner inconsistent with an intent to assert this defense. As a result, insufficient facts exist to support a finding of waiver. The trial court did not err by declining to find that Dr. Tsarbopoulos waived his right to assert the defense of lack of jurisdiction based upon insufficient service of process.

In summary, we reverse the order of the superior court vacating the child custody order and the order granting a dissolution of marriage. In all other respects, we affirm the order of the superior court.

Note: Citations to authority have been deleted and the opinion edited for brevity.

**Source:** Retrieved from www.mrsc.org/nxt/gateway.dll?f=templates&fn= courts.htm$vid=courts:court.

**CASE BRIEF ASSIGNMENT**

Read and brief the *In re Marriage of Tsarbopoulos,* 125 Wash.App. 273, 104 P.3d 692 (Wash. Ct App. 2004) case. (See Appendix A for information on how to brief cases.)

## RESPONSE TO INITIAL PLEADINGS

Once the initial pleading has been served on the other party, he or she will need to file an answer to the allegations contained in the petition. Absent an agreement between the parties to the contrary, this must be done with the time specified by state law. For example, in Florida a defendant has 20 days to file a response to the initial pleading in most cases. States generally allow that responsive pleadings be served on the opposing party by mail or, if the person is represented by an attorney, by mailing a copy to the attorney. Figure 9.8 contains an example of an answer.

### RESEARCH THIS

Research the laws of your state relating to when a response must be filed to an initial pleading in a divorce or dissolution of marriage case. What are the ramifications if the responsive pleading is not made in a timely manner?

## ANSWER TO PETITION FOR DISSOLUTION OF MARRIAGE

**FIGURE 9.8**
**Sample Answer**
*Source:* Retrieved from
www.flcourts.org/gen_
public/family/forms_rules/
index.shtml 2/28/07.

I, *{full legal name}* _____, Respondent, being sworn, certify that the following information is true:

I. **I agree** with Petitioner as to the allegations raised in the following numbered paragraphs in the Petition and, therefore, **admit** those allegations: *{indicate section and paragraph number}* _____
_____.

2. **I disagree** with Petitioner as to the allegations raised in the following numbered paragraphs in the Petition and, therefore, **deny** those allegations: *{indicate section and paragraph number}* _____
_____.

3. I currently am unable to admit or deny the allegations raised in the following paragraphs due to lack of information: *{indicate section and paragraph number}*
_____
_____.

4. If this case involves a dependent or minor child(ren), a completed Uniform Child Custody Jurisdiction and Enforcement Act (UCCJEA) Affidavit, ❑ Florida Supreme Court Approved Family Law Form 12.902(d), is filed with this answer.

5. If this case involves a dependent or minor child(ren), a completed Child Support Guidelines Worksheet, ❑ Florida Family Law Rules of Procedure Form 12.902(e), is [ √ **one** only] ( ) filed with this answer or ( ) will be filed after the other party serves his or her financial affidavit.

6. A completed Notice of Social Security Number, ❑ Florida Supreme Court Approved Family Law Form 12.902(j), is filed with this answer.

7. A completed Family Law Financial Affidavit, ❑ Florida Family Law Rules of Procedure Form 12.902(b) or (c), [ √ **one** only] ( ) is filed with this answer or ( ) will be timely filed.

I certify that a copy of this document was [ √ **one** only] ( ) mailed ( ) faxed and mailed ( ) hand delivered to the person(s) listed below on *{date}* _____.

**Petitioner or his/her attorney:**
Name: _____
Address: _____
City, State, Zip: _____
Fax Number: _____

**I understand that I am swearing or affirming under oath to the truthfulness of the claims made in this answer and that the punishment for knowingly making a false statement includes fines and/or imprisonment.**

Dated: _____     _____
                              Signature of Respondent
                              Printed Name: _____
                              Address: _____
                              City, State, Zip: _____
                              Telephone Number: _____
                              Fax Number: _____

STATE OF FLORIDA
COUNTY OF
Sworn to or affirmed and signed before me on_____ by_____.

_____
NOTARY PUBLIC or DEPUTY CLERK

_____
[Print, type, or stamp commissioned name of notary or deputy clerk.]

_____ Personally known
_____ Produced identification
Type of identification produced

**Summary**

Unlike the legal principles relating to matters such as divorce, child support, alimony, and division of marital property, the procedures associated with the drafting of petitions and motions are relatively straightforward. Paralegals must be aware of the laws and rules of their state relating to the format of pleadings and how they are served on the opposing party.

That is not to say that all of the concepts discussed in this chapter are simple. Issues relating to jurisdiction can be confusing at times, even for people who are fairly familiar with civil litigation. Topics such as domicile, venue, subject matter jurisdiction, in personam jurisdiction, and in rem jurisdiction, though seemingly simple when a paralegal reads a definition, become more complex when he or she tries to apply it in a particular case. When in doubt a paralegal should research the laws and rules that apply to the case to clarify his or her understanding of a matter and, when in doubt, ask the supervising attorney.

The divorce process is very similar in many ways to other forms of civil procedure. States have started to realize that in many cases couples need to have a simplified means of obtaining a divorce, especially where there is little in dispute between the parties. These states offer divorce forms that are designed for the layperson to understand. Some examples of these have been included in this chapter.

Paralegals may seldom use the simplified forms in the family law office. Instead they may be called upon to create a pleading that is customized for the client's needs.

Paralegals often will be called upon to draft documents associated with a temporary order to provide for clients' needs until the court issues a final order. Examples of temporary orders include: restraining orders, injunctions, child custody, child support, and alimony.

Not all issues related to child support are handled in a divorce case. A parent can seek child support independent of marriage. The procedure to do so often involves establishment of paternity and proceeds in a similar manner with other petitions associated with family law.

**Key Terms**

| | |
|---|---|
| Allegations | Pleadings |
| Body | Prayer for relief |
| Caption | Qualified domestic relations order |
| Coercion | (QDRO) |
| Consent decree | Subject matter jurisdiction |
| Domicile | Title |
| Duress | Uniform Interstate Family Support Act |
| In personam jurisdiction | Venue |
| In rem jurisdiction | Verification |

**Review Questions**

1. What are the four common elements of a petition?
2. Identify the elements in the petition for simplified divorce contained in Figure 9.4.
3. What are some of the common pretrial motions used in divorce cases?
4. What is the difference between a no fault divorce and a consent divorce?
5. Describe the procedure that is followed in a typical divorce case.
6. What is the difference between domicile and venue?
7. What is the Uniform Interstate Family Support Act and why is it important in the study of family law?

8. Explain each of the following: in rem jurisdiction, in personam jurisdiction, and subject matter jurisdiction.

9. Why is obtaining in personam jurisdiction, also known as personal jurisdiction, important in civil litigation?

10. Why is proper service of process important?

11. What is an affidavit of nonmilitary service and why is it used?

---

### Exercises

1. Using the facts of the case set out in the Client Interview, draft an answer to the petition for dissolution of marriage filed by Sebastian. Supplement the facts provided as needed to draft the document.

2. Research the laws of your state relating to the initial service of process in a divorce case and write a summary of your findings.

3. Research the laws of your state to determine whether a parenting class is required in divorce cases in which there is a child of the marriage. If your state does not require such a class, research the laws of neighboring states and locate one that does require such a class. Write a paper describing what the stated purposes of the classes are and what the classes include.

4. Create a fact pattern of a couple who have been married for a number of years and have at least one child of the marriage. Draft a petition for dissolution of marriage based on this fact pattern.

5. Visit your local courthouse and go to the clerk of court's office or the appropriate office that deals with dissolution/divorce actions. Find out what services are provided by the office and see if you can get a sample of a summons used in your jurisdiction for use in dissolution of marriage case. If you are unable to personally visit a courthouse, go to the court's Web site and obtain this information.

## REAL WORLD DISCUSSION TOPICS

A husband and wife were married in New York State. They have one child of the marriage, a daughter, age 12. The husband and wife lived as a couple in New York and Pennsylvania. The husband later moved to Maine to take a position as a corporate executive. His wife did not move with him and she had no contacts with Maine. The husband filed for divorce in Maine because he could not meet the residency requirements of New York or Pennsylvania. The wife moved to dismiss the case alleging that the Maine court lacked personal jurisdiction over her and lacked in rem jurisdiction over the marital property.

Can the Maine court properly grant the husband a divorce? Can the Maine court issue an order awarding child support? Property distribution? See *Von Schack v. Von Schack*, 893 A.2d 1004 (Me. 2006).

## PORTFOLIO ASSIGNMENT

1. Research the laws of your state to determine: (a) the residency requirements for filing a divorce; (b) the court that has subject matter jurisdiction to hear a divorce case; and (c) the proper venue to file a divorce action for a person living in your city/county. Write a summary of your findings.

2. Prepare a petition for dissolution of marriage to be used by Sebastian Acres and an answer for use by Brenda. Supplement the facts provided in the Client Interview as needed to complete the two forms.

# Chapter 10

## Pretrial/Pendente Lite Motions and Orders

### CHAPTER OBJECTIVES

**After reading this chapter and completing the assignments, you should be able to:**

- Understand why pretrial motions are needed.
- Identify the most commonly used pretrial motions.
- Describe which temporary motions may be appropriate in different factual settings.
- Be able to draft basic motions for temporary relief.
- Understand the procedure that is used to obtain temporary orders.
- Discuss domestic violence statutes and why they have been enacted.

Chapter 10 discusses one area of the dissolution of marriage process that is often overlooked by the general public. Although most people are aware of many of the aspects involved in the process, such as the filing of a petition for dissolution of marriage and the final hearing on the petition, many may not consider the wide variety of matters that must be resolved between the filing and the entry of the final order. This is especially true in contested cases in which a great deal of time may pass before the case is completed.

Pretrial motions, also referred to as pendente lite motions, are used to help the client during this period. These motions can provide for temporary child support, temporary child custody and visitation, and temporary alimony. They can also be used to protect the assets of the client from being taken or destroyed by the other spouse.

Unfortunately, this time before the final hearing can also be a time when the client him- or herself may need to be protected from the other spouse. Domestic violence is a problem that has been increasingly recognized by the public. As a result, the legal system is attempting to be more responsive to the needs of those who are in possible danger. Temporary injunctions, restraining orders, and orders of protection are among the tools available for the family law firm to help protect the client in these situations.

## WHY THIS CHAPTER IS IMPORTANT TO THE PARALEGAL

Pretrial motions are an important step in the dissolution of marriage process in many cases. These motions can be used to allow family members to have sufficient means to live until a final order is entered in the case. They can also be used to protect clients from bodily harm and to protect their assets from being lost. The paralegal is often actively involved in gathering the necessary information needed to handle the case and in the preparation of the forms needed to meet the needs of the client. Chapter 10 provides the information needed to gain a basic understanding of the pretrial procedure and the forms associated with temporary motions.

## PRETRIAL MOTIONS

As with many legal proceedings, dissolution/divorce proceedings can take some time to complete. This is especially true if the parties cannot agree to all or some of the key decisions relating to the terms of the dissolution/divorce. The more the parties cannot agree, the longer the procedure may take. As previously mentioned, if the parties agree to the terms of a settlement agreement, the divorce procedure is a simple one. When they cannot do so, more steps are required to complete the process. Dissolutions/divorces that require the judge to ultimately decide what the parties will receive and other matters relating to the divorce can drag on for months, or longer. It is often said that the only people who always win in long, drawn-out cases are the attorneys, since their fees increase with every complication!

As if the dissolution/divorce is not emotional enough, the time between filing the necessary paperwork and the entry of the final decree can be even worse if the parties are fighting over legal matters. The reality is that both practical and critical matters must be dealt with before the final judgment of dissolution. A long delay in the finalization of the dissolution/divorce process presents many of the same issues that will have to be ultimately decided for inclusion in the final judgment. These issues include who the child will reside with during the time prior to final resolution of the action, what visitation will be required, the need for alimony and child support that will be required, and temporary injunctions to prevent abuse or the destruction of marital property. The different types of pretrial motions are described in the following sections.

### Motion for Temporary Child Custody and Visitation

It may be necessary to ask the court to make initial provisions for the care of the minor children of the marriage. As will be the case when the court is asked to decide on the permanent custody plan for the child, when an attorney files a **motion for temporary child custody and visitation** for his or her client, the court will try to determine what is in the child's best interest.

**motion for temporary child custody and visitation**
Motion filed by a party to provide for child custody and/or child visitation during the pendency of the dissolution action.

Courts will usually try to provide for equal access to the child during the divorce process since a final factual determination of what is best for the child has not yet been made. This can sometimes be accomplished by an order granting shared parental responsibility, unless the court determines that such a plan would be detrimental to the child. Both parents retain full parental responsibilities under this order, and they need to attempt to jointly make decisions affecting the child.

Some states allow courts to award temporary residential custody to one parent in cases where additional information is needed to decide about the custody of the child. Other states take the view that temporary physical custody should not be awarded, especially if the court had adequate information at the time to make a final custody order.

Figure 10.1 contains a sample motion for temporary relief. This sample is a simple form that MassLegalHelp.org provides in an effort to improve access to the legal system for low-income people. While paralegals will often use more sophisticated forms for their pleadings, the form contained in Figure 10.1 is an example of how simple legal forms can be, especially now that states have recognized the reality that many people in need of assistance from the legal system cannot afford to hire an attorney.

---

### ETHICS ALERT

Every chapter of this textbook has an Ethics Alert to remind paralegals that they must always remember the importance of their ethical responsibilities to their clients. Ethical behavior is expected of paralegals as members of the legal community.

Previous Ethics Alerts have focused on many of the situations that may create ethical problems in the family law firm. There are, however, obligations that paralegals owe to the legal profession itself. The American Bar Association and state bar associations have encouraged attorneys to volunteer their time to help those who otherwise could not afford to get legal advice. Attorneys throughout the country volunteer countless hours in this effort.

Paralegals also have skills that can help. Although they cannot give legal advice directly to individuals, they can help the attorneys who volunteer to help those who need legal advice. One way to do this is to volunteer time at a local legal aid society such as MassLegalHelp.org, which was mentioned earlier.

---

### RESEARCH THIS

Locate the organization that provides legal aid to low-income people in your area. This can usually be done by checking the phone book or checking the state bar association's Web site. Contact the legal aid organization by phone or e-mail or in person to learn more about the services it provides and whether paralegals are needed to volunteer to help provide those services.

---

### Motion for Temporary Child Support

**motion for temporary child support**
Motion filed by a party to obtain child support to provide for the care of the child during the pendency of the dissolution action.

Courts may also be called upon, when an attorney files a **motion for temporary child support**, to make initial decisions relating to child support to provide for a child's care during the pendency of the dissolution action. The power of the court to enter such an order is granted by state statute, and the courts enjoy a certain degree of latitude in its award. Temporary child support is used to ensure that the parent who has custody of the child during the divorce process has sufficient funds to support the child.

The starting point in determining whether temporary child support should be awarded, and if so, how much, is similar to that the court uses to make a final decision about the

**Commonwealth of Massachusetts**
The Trial Court
Probate and Family Court Department

Berkshire _____ **Division**

Docket No. 02W____

JANE DOE
**Plaintiff/Petitioner**

v.

JOHN DOE
**Defendant/Respondent**

**MOTION FOR**

Temporary Support

Now comes _JANE DOE_____ , the plaintiff/defendant/petitioner/respondent,
(name of moving party)

in this action who moves this Honorable Court as follows: _to order an increase in child support effective immediately, while her case is waiting to be decided._

---

**NOTICE OF HEARING**

This Motion will be heard at the Probate & Family

Court in _Pittsfield_
(city)

on _May 14th, 2003_
(month/day/year)

at _9:00 am_
(time of hearing)

_Jane Doe_
(signature)

_Jane Doe_
(PRINT name)

_100 main Street_
(street address)

_anywhere, Ma_          _0101_
(city or town)      (state)      (zip code)

Date: _March 22, 2003_

Tel. No. (800) _555 · 5555_

---

The within motion is hereby **ALLOWED — DENIED.**

_____          _____
Date                                    Justice of the Probate and Family Court

**INSTRUCTIONS**

1. Generally, refer to Mass.R.Civ.P./Mass.R.Dom.Rel.P. 5, 6 and 7; Probate Court Rules 6, 29, and 29B.
2. If the opposing party is represented by an attorney who has filed an appearance, service of this motion MUST be made on the attorney.
3. Certificate of Service on Reverse side must be completed.
4. All motions shall be accompanied by a proposed order which shall be served with the motion.

CJ-D 400 (08/02)

**FIGURE 10.1    Sample Motion for Temporary Relief**

(cont.)

*Source:* Retrieved from www.masslegalhelp.org/uploads/pa/8o/pa8oQjpO-Cynzv0nQqFFpA/Motion-for-Temporary-Support—sample.pdf.

COMMONWEALTH OF MASSACHUSETTS
THE TRIAL COURT
PROBATE AND FAMILY COURT

BERKSHIRE, ss.                                                Docket No. _02W___

*Jane Doe*_____, PLAINTIFF          **Plaintiff's - Defendant's**
                                                          **PROPOSED ORDER**
                    VS.

*John Doe*_____, DEFENDANT

Upon the MOTION FOR *Temporary support*_____
dated: *March 22nd*_____, *2003* and filed with this Court on *March 22,*_____, *2003*;

After hearing, and pending further order or judgment of this Court, IT IS ORDERED THAT:
[Describe in detail the relief/order you seek.]

☐ 1) plaintiff - and - defendant shall have the - shared - legal custody of: _____
_____, the minor child____ of the parties; plaintiff -
defendant shall have the physical custody of said child____ .

☐ 2) plaintiff - defendant shall have the following visitation rights:_____
_____ .

☑ 3) ~~plaintiff~~ - defendant shall pay, as child support, the sum of $ *130* *.00* each and every *week*
hereafter, beginning *3 / 22 /2003* to the ~~plaintiff~~ - ~~defendant~~ - Mass. DOR/CSE, by way of
income assignment effective, now-suspended.

☐ 4) plaintiff - defendant shall obtain - maintain medical - dental - optical insurance coverage of said
child ____ and of the plaintiff-defendant _____ .

☐ 5) plaintiff - defendant shall pay to plaintiff-defendant _____ % of the uninsured medical, dental,
hospital and optical expenses of the child____ .

☐ 6) [OTHER - PLEASE SPECIFY]_____
_____
_____

+-----------------------------------------------+
| **TEMPORARY ORDER**                           |
| The Court hereby adopts this proposed order; the parties |
| shall comply with the terms and provisions thereof. |
|                                               |
| _____   _____             |
|   Date        Justice of the Probate Court    |
+-----------------------------------------------+

*Jane Doe*_____
                    (signature)
*JANE   DOE*_____
                    (PRINT Name)
*100 Main street*_____
                    (street)
*Anywhere    MA*____  *0101*
(city or town)    (state)        (zip)
*800 · 555 · 5555*_____
                    (telephone No.)

DATE:___ *3/22/03*_____

emplate.io (rev. 1/02)

**FIGURE 10.1** *(concluded)*

amount of child support to be paid. Courts will look at the needs of the child, the ability of each parent to pay child support, and the standard of living enjoyed by the child during the marriage. Note the phrase "standard of living enjoyed by the child during the course of the marriage." This phrase is an important one, even if it is somewhat obscure. It also demonstrates the difficult job a judge has in determining what is an appropriate amount of temporary child support because no two cases are ever truly alike. To make that decision the judge must look at the lifestyle the child now enjoys. Clearly, more child support will be appropriate for the child being raised by a millionaire than one who is being raised in a family with an annual income of $50,000.

One interesting case involved the dissolution of a marriage between a husband, who was a billionaire, and a wife, who was a millionaire. They had one child, a daughter, who they agreed would live with the mother. The critical question to be resolved was how much child support should be paid. The husband maintained that the wife's lifestyle, that of a millionaire, should be the standard used by the court. The wife contended that this would not be fair to the daughter. Instead, it should be the life enjoyed while a daughter of a billionaire. She noted that while she owned a nice condo in the city, her husband owned numerous houses all over the world.

Although few cases are as extreme as the billionaire versus the millionaire dissolution/divorce, it does demonstrate the general concept behind the standard-of-living standard that a court will try to apply in all cases involving child support payments, whether temporary or permanent in nature. It also shows that the standard is not to provide an amount that will cover the "bare necessities" of life. Instead, it is to be an amount that will enable the child to continue life as he or she had before the dissolution began. No two cases are, therefore, exactly the same, which means a judge is given wide latitude in determining what the appropriate amount to award should be.

Parties will be required to provide a financial affidavit and a completed child support guidelines worksheet prior to the hearing, which may have already been completed at the initiation of the dissolution action. This worksheet will enable the court to determine what amount should be awarded based on the state's child support guidelines. Although the court must consider these guidelines in reaching its decision, they are minimum amounts and subject to change based on the overall facts of a particular case.

## Motion for Temporary Alimony

Just as a spouse may need temporary child support, at times a spouse may need support for him- or herself during the pendency of the dissolution process. In these cases, the spouse's attorney may file a **motion for temporary alimony**, to ask the court for an award of temporary alimony; the court has discretion over whether it is granted and if it is, its amount. Some states will also allow the court to consider marital misconduct, such as adultery, when deciding if an award of temporary alimony should be made.

To make this determination, the court will look at the same factors that will be used in ruling on permanent alimony. The starting point is one spouse's needs and the other's ability to pay.

Factors that can be considered include:

- The lifestyle the spouses enjoyed during the course of the marriage.
- Each spouse's property holdings.
- Each spouse's income and earning capacity.
- Health of the requesting spouse.
- The spouses' ages.
- Any special needs of the requesting spouse.
- The need of the receiving spouse during the pendency of the dissolution action.

**motion for temporary alimony** Motion filed by a party to obtain alimony/spousal support during the pendency of the dissolution action.

In the Court of Appeals of Tennessee at Knoxville
*Rowe v. Rowe*
No. E2005-01023-Coa-R3-Cv
Filed February 22, 2007
Opinion

## BACKGROUND

Husband and Wife were married in December of 1996. Approximately nineteen months later, Husband filed a complaint for divorce claiming Wife was guilty of inappropriate marital conduct or, in the alternative, that irreconcilable differences had arisen between the parties. An Order of Reconciliation was entered two months later. Sadly, the reconciliation did not last and the divorce proceedings were reinstated less than two years after they were suspended. Wife then answered the complaint, generally denying the pertinent allegations. Wife did, however, admit that irreconcilable differences had arisen between the parties. Wife also filed a counterclaim asserting, alternatively, that Husband was guilty of inappropriate marital conduct.

In January of 2001, the Trial Court entered an order awarding Wife temporary alimony of $1,200 per month pending the final hearing in the divorce proceedings. The Trial Court also ordered as temporary alimony that Husband make the lease payments and insurance payments on Wife's vehicle. In its order, the Trial Court specifically stated that the order was premised on "testimony of the parties, the parties' prior year's tax returns which were received as exhibits, the arguments of counsel, and the record as a whole." There is no transcript from this hearing or a statement of the evidence in the record on appeal.

Following a hearing in December of 2002, the Trial Court entered an order declaring the parties divorced pursuant to Tenn. Code Ann. § 36-4-129. The Trial Court ordered the parties to mediate all issues pertaining to "alimony in futuro," the property distribution, and attorney fees.

The Trial Court also ordered Husband to continue paying temporary alimony of $1,200 per month plus Wife's lease and insurance payments on her vehicle through May 31, 2003, by which time Wife was to have completed a Master's Degree program at the University of Tennessee.

The parties were unable to reach a mediated settlement agreement regarding the property distribution or alimony. Accordingly, a trial was held. As with the hearing on temporary alimony, there is no transcript from the trial or a statement of the evidence in the record on appeal. Following the trial, the Trial Court entered an order resolving the remaining issues, in pertinent part, as follows:

> At the time of the parties' marriage, [Husband] owned a home in Union County, Tennessee. The home was purchased for $86,500.00 in 1993. During the marriage . . . the parties made improvements to said home and in 2003 it was sold for $119,000.00. The Court finds

that the parties' residence did increase in value during the brief period of the marriage due in part to improvements made by the parties in that time period.

> The Husband had an extensive and valuable gun collection prior to the parties' marriage. The Husband's business required him to travel and appear at gun shows where he traded and appraised antique guns and collections. He also bought, sold, and traded in antique guns and gun accessories. The Wife testified that she traveled with him during the marriage and helped Husband in this business and helped him author and produce several books on antique guns that he sold; this testimony was disputed by the Husband. . . .

> The Wife claims an interest in the 1999 Ford van, several small bank accounts, Rowe Publications, Tom Rowe Books, and the parties' 2000 federal income tax refund. . . .

> A 1978 Valiant 40-foot sailboat was purchased in the fall of 1999 and extensive repairs were made to and on the boat. The source of funds to purchase the boat are at issue. The Husband contended that he sold two guns from his collection which he used to purchase the boat and do repairs on the boat. The Wife contended that the funds came from the sale of the gun books she helped him prepare and sell. She further testified that she assisted Husband in getting the boat in usable condition, this testimony was disputed by the Husband.

> The Court FINDS and ORDERS the following:

> That the value of Wife's interest in the marital home sale is $14,500.00. . . .

> That the Wife's equity in the 1999 Ford van is set at $3,500.00. . . .

> That the Husband is awarded sole title and possession of the 1992 Oldsmobile 88 and Husband's new 2002 vehicle, and Wife is entitled to no equity from them.

> That as to the 1978 sailboat bought in the fall of 1999, the Court accepts Husband's position that this purchase was made with funds from guns sold that were owned prior to the parties' marriage. Extensive repairs were made to the boat after the purchase and most of this was paid with a draw on [the] marital residence's equity loan. The Wife assisted in helping with the cleaning of the boat and assisted with the repairs, but gave no monetary assistance. The Court sets the value of her interest in the sailboat at $5,000.00. . . .

That the Wife's interest in the cash, Golden Medical Savings and the parties' IRS 2000 tax return is set at $1,874.00. . . .

That as to Wife's interest in Rowe Publications and Tom Rowe Books, the Court is of the opinion that this was an on-going business that the Husband had prior to the marriage and through his expertise in the field he was in. The Court sets the Wife's marital interest in this venture at $5,000. . . .

That during the early part of this litigation, the Wife incurred legal expenses in court appearances and contempt hearings in order to get temporary alimony and enforcement of the same. The Court orders that $15,000.00 in attorney fees be paid to Wife's attorney. Other than this, each party shall be responsible for their own attorney fees. . . .

That each party is vested with the marital personal property that is in their possession as their sole and separate property except as otherwise set forth herein. . . .

That as to the Wife's contention regarding the value of the guns bought during the terms of the marriage, the Court has to take into consideration that some guns were sold that were owned prior to the parties' marriage. The Court sets the value of the Wife's interest in the guns, powder cans, antique shooting medals, etc. at . . . $8,500.00. . . .

That the Husband is awarded the antique shooting range picture, the King Chains, Cartridge boards and the Steins. Wife is awarded her family silver in the Husband's possession. The parties shall arrange to simultaneously exchange these items. That the Husband's unpaid temporary alimony is found to be $1,900.00 unless the Husband immediately provides proof of payment of this judgment after [entry of] the November 28, 2001 [order]. . . .

That no permanent alimony is appropriate to be granted to either party.

After the Trial Court's judgment was entered, Husband filed a motion for new trial or to make additional findings of fact. In this motion, Husband requested, among other things, for the Trial Court to "treat all temporary alimony paid to [Wife] as a transfer of marital asset[s] due to the amount of alimony paid in relation to the value of the estate granted to [Wife]. . . ."

The Trial Court resolved Husband's motion for new trial or to make additional findings of fact stating:

That there is no current Tennessee case law to support [Husband's] position to treat his temporary alimony payments . . . as property settlement. The Court notes that there is even a dispute as to whether the issue of temporary alimony was properly raised at the final hearing as the issue of temporary or rehabilitative alimony was dealt with at the parties' December 12, 2002 hearing and no appeal was filed. As the December 12, 2002 Order reserved only the issue of alimony in futuro, the Court did not believe that any issues regarding temporary support were before him at the September 25, 2003 hearing. Therefore, [Husband's] Motion For a New

Trial or To Make Additional Findings of Fact is denied.

Husband appeals raising five issues, which we quote verbatim from his brief:

A. Whether the Trial Court abused its discretion in denying [Husband's] Motion For a New Trial or To Make Additional Findings of Fact on the matter of Temporary Alimony as Property Settlement.

B. Whether the Trial Court abused its discretion by failing to find the temporary alimony paid by [Husband] to [Wife] to be excessive in both amount and duration sufficient to affect the final division of property.

C. Whether the Trial Court abused its discretion by failing to consider the temporary alimony in its determination of the division of marital property.

D. Whether the Trial Court abused its discretion in the division of property.

E. Whether the Trial Court abused its discretion as to the determination of Marital and Premarital property.

## DISCUSSION

The factual findings of the Trial Court are accorded a presumption of correctness, and we will not overturn those factual findings unless the evidence preponderates against them. *See* Tenn. R. App. P. 13(d); *Bogan v. Bogan,* 60 S.W.3d 721, 727 (Tenn. 2001). With respect to legal issues, our review is conducted "under a pure *de novo* standard of review, according no deference to the conclusions of law made by the lower courts." *Southern Constructors, Inc. v. Loudon County Bd. Of Educ.,* 58 S.W.3d 706, 710 (Tenn. 2001).

Regarding an award of alimony, Tennessee courts have stated on numerous occasions that a trial court has broad discretion in determining the type, amount and duration of alimony, depending on the particular facts of each case. *See, e. g., Wood v. Wood,* No. M2003-00193-COA-R3-CV, 2004 WL 3008875 at *4, (Tenn. Ct. App. Dec. 28, 2004), *app. Denied June 27, 2005* (citing, *inter alia, Burlew v. Burlew,* 40 S.W.3d 465, 470 (Tenn. 2001) and *Sullivan v. Sullivan,* 107 S.W.3d 507, 511 (Tenn. Ct. App. 2002)). Appellate courts are disinclined to second guess a trial court's decision regarding alimony unless it is not supported by the evidence or is contrary to public policies reflected in the applicable statutes. *Nelson v. Nelson,* 106 S.W.3d 20, 23 (Tenn. Ct. App. 2002).

Tenn. Code Ann. § 36-5-121(b) authorizes a trial court to make an award of temporary alimony, also known as alimony *pendente lite*. This statute provides as follows:

The court may, in its discretion, at any time pending the final hearing, upon motion and after notice and hearing, make any order that may be proper to compel a spouse to pay any sums necessary for the support and maintenance of the other spouse, to enable such spouse to prosecute or defend the suit of the parties and to make other orders as it deems appropriate. Further, the court may award such sum as may be necessary to enable a spouse to pay the expenses of job training and education. In making any order under this subsection (b), the court shall consider the financial needs of each spouse and the financial ability of each spouse to meet those needs and to prosecute or defend the suit.

Tenn. Code Ann. § 36-5-121(b) (2005) (previously codified at Tenn. Code Ann. § 36-5-101(l)).

Husband attacks the award of temporary alimony on several fronts. In summary, Husband claims the amount and duration of the temporary alimony was excessive and, that being the case, he should get a credit against the property distribution for the amount of temporary alimony that was excessive. What Husband is asking us to do, however, is to back-track with the award of temporary alimony and compare and contrast its reasonableness with events that happened after the temporary alimony ended. In other words, Husband is arguing that based on the way the Trial Court distributed the marital property etc., following the trial on September 25, 2003, the award of temporary alimony which initially was made on January of 2001 and which continued through May of 2003 was improper. We must look to Tenn. Code Ann. § 36-5-121(b) (2005) to determine if the award of temporary alimony was proper.

An award of alimony is factually driven. Our ability to address Husband's challenges to the Trial Court's factual findings as to the propriety of the temporary alimony award is severely hampered if not eliminated by the absence of transcripts of the hearing or the trial, or any statement of the evidence prepared in accordance with Tenn. R. App. P. 24 (c). "This court cannot review the facts de novo without an appellate record containing the facts, and therefore, we must assume that the record, had it been preserved, would have contained sufficient evidence to support the trial court's factual findings." *Sherrod v. Wix*, 849 S.W.2d 780, 783 (Tenn. Ct. pp. 1992). Accordingly, the amount and duration of the temporary alimony awarded is affirmed.

Husband's remaining arguments all center around the division of marital property following the trial. Much of Husband's argument surrounding the division of marital property is tied into his previous argument surrounding the award of temporary alimony. Husband also argues that the marital property distribution was inequitable and the Trial Court erred when it awarded Wife any interest at all in his various businesses.

A division of marital property or a determination of what is marital versus separate property, or whether there had been an increase in value to separate property based on the contributions of the other spouse are all factually driven. Without a transcript of the trial or statement of the evidence, we cannot review the facts *de novo* relevant to the division of marital property. The Trial Court's order contains numerous findings relevant to the division of the marital property. At oral argument, Husband's counsel stated that there was a court reporter present at the trial, but the tape recording of the trial was destroyed while in the possession of the court reporter, albeit through no fault of the court reporter. We acknowledge that the lack of a transcript is through no fault of Husband or his counsel. However, this is no way alters the need for the transcript or a statement of the evidence in order for this Court to undertake an appropriate review of the Trial Court's factual findings.

Husband argues that we can rely on the facts that are present in the record when conducting our appellate review. We would agree with Husband if there was some way for us to determine that the facts that are contained in the record are all of the evidence that was presented to the Trial Court at trial. Unfortunately, there is nothing in the record that enables us to make that determination. This being so, we "assume that the record, had it been preserved, would have contained sufficient evidence to support the trial court's factual findings." *Id.* Therefore, we have no alternative but to affirm the Trial Court's classification of certain property as marital or separate property as well as its distribution of the marital property.

## CONCLUSION

The judgment of the Trial Court is affirmed, and this cause is remanded to the Trial Court for collection of the costs below. Costs on appeal are taxed to the Appellant, Thomas Walter Rowe, and his surety.

**Source:** Retrieved from www.tsc.state.tn.us/opinions/tca/PDF/071/RoweTOPN.pdf.

**CASE BRIEF ASSIGNMENT**

Read and brief the *Rowe v. Rowe,* 2007 WL 541813 (Tenn.Ct. App. 2007) case. (See Appendix A for information on how to brief cases.)

### RESEARCH THIS

Research the laws of your state, including statutes, cases, and rules of court, to determine where your state courts get their authority to grant temporary relief and the process used for obtaining that relief. Write a brief summary of your findings.

## Motion for Award of Temporary Attorney Fees, Suit Money, and Costs

When a **motion for award of temporary attorney fees, suit money, and costs** is filed, a spouse is requesting an award of temporary attorney fees and costs during the pendency of the dissolution action. In these situations the court will be called upon to determine what an appropriate fee would be by looking at factors such as the complexity of the case, the time needed to complete the work associated with the motions, and what would be a comparable fee in the locality for similar work. Fees are limited to those the court determines to be reasonably necessary. Other costs associated with the legal action may also be awarded.

## Motion for Temporary Injunction

An **injunction** is a court order that requires that a party refrain from acting a certain way to prevent harm. In granting an injunction, the court is attempting to prevent irreparable harm that it cannot otherwise prevent by using another legal remedy. A **temporary injunction**, or preliminary injunction, is an injunction that is used to protect a person or property for a particular period of time, often until the court can resolve other matters before the court. Temporary injunctions may be used in a number of ways in the family law firm. They can be used to protect both property and persons. For example, a temporary injunction may be sought to prevent the harassment of one spouse by the other while the dissolution of marriage action is working its way toward final judgment. Temporary injunctions can also be used to allow one spouse sole use of the marital home during the pendency of the dissolution action by enjoining the other spouse from living in the home.

Violation of temporary injunctions can result in civil contempt proceedings that result in fines or imprisonment. Often one spouse may be concerned over the possibility that the other spouse will attempt to remove their child from the state. The spouse may ask the court to issue a temporary injunction to prevent such an act. See Figure 10.2 for a sample of such a motion.

Temporary injunctions can also be used to prevent a spouse from transferring or selling marital assets. See *In re Marriage of Hartney* for a case dealing with the issue of transferring assets of the marriage.

## Temporary Injunction to Preserve Marital Property

As has been discussed previously, dissolution of marriages actions can bring out the worst in people. Although most will not be involved in physical or mental abuse, many people can rationalize the dissipation of assets or their removal from the state in order to prevent the other spouse from getting them. In these cases, the party who fears such acts may seek an injunction to be ordered by the court to prevent removal, dissipation, fraudulent transfer, or concealment of property, to prevent such acts. Some states require the spouse seeking this temporary injunction to furnish an injunction bond before it will be granted.

A more extreme tool is also available to a court that fears that a person will flee or remove marital assets from the jurisdiction of the court—the writ of *ne exeat*. This writ can be used to order a person not to leave the state, to remove a child from the state, or to remove marital property from the state. This is a very powerful writ and one that actually gives a sheriff the power to detain a person from leaving the state until he or she posts a bond to assure his or her appearance at court.

## Temporary Restraining Order and Orders of Protection

**Temporary restraining orders** are ones that prohibit a spouse or others who fall under the state's domestic abuse statutes from harming or harassing the other spouse. Domestic abuse statutes provide a means to offer protection when it can be shown that there is a threat of imminent harm or danger of domestic abuse. If the order is to be issued under a domestic violence statute, the parties must come within the statutory requirements. Figure 10.3 contains the Illinois Domestic Violence Statute. This usually includes spouses, persons living as spouses, former spouses, and, in some states, persons who regularly reside in the household. Violations of temporary restraining orders or orders of protection can be prosecuted as a crime, as criminal contempt, or as civil contempt. Figure 10.4 contains a sample request for a temporary restraining order.

INSTRUCTIONS FOR FLORIDA SUPREME COURT APPROVED FAMILY LAW FORM 12.941(a),
VERIFIED MOTION FOR TEMPORARY INJUNCTION TO PREVENT REMOVAL OF
MINOR CHILD(REN) AND/OR DENIAL OF PASSPORT SERVICES

**When should this form be used?**

You should use this form if you want the court to enter an **order** that your minor child(ren) is (are) not to be removed from the State of Florida while a case involving the child(ren)'s custody is pending, that passport services for the minor child(ren) be prohibited, and/or that existing passports be turned over to you.

This form should be typed or printed in black ink. If you want the court to enter an **ex parte** order, without giving the other side advance notice of the hearing, you should explain your reasons in paragraph 5 of this form. After completing this form, you should sign the form before a **notary public**. You should **file** the original with the **clerk of the circuit court** in the county where your case is pending and keep a copy for your records. You should also ask the clerk to process your **motion** though their emergency procedures.

**What should I do next?**

If the court enters an order without advance notice to the other party, you should take a **certified copy** of the order to the sheriff's office for further assistance. You must have this form and the court's order, served by **personal service** on the other party. You should read the court's order carefully. Look for directions in the order that apply to you and note the time and place of the **hearing** scheduled in the order. You should go to the hearing with whatever evidence you have regarding your motion.

If the court will not enter an order without advance notice to the other side, you should check with the clerk of court, **family law intake staff**, or **judicial assistant** for information on the local procedure for scheduling a hearing on your motion, unless the court sets a hearing in its order denying your request for an ex parte hearing. When you know the date and time of your hearing, you should file **Notice of Hearing (General)**, ❑ Florida Supreme Court Approved Family Law Form 12.923 or other appropriate notice of hearing form, and use personal service to notify the other party of your motion, the court's order, if any, and the hearing.

**Where can I look for more information?**

**Before proceeding, you should read "General Information for Self-Represented Litigants" found at the beginning of these forms.** For further information, see chapter 61, Florida Statutes, and rule 1.610, Florida Rules of Civil Procedure.

**Special notes...**

If you have an attorney, your attorney must certify in writing the efforts that have been made to give the other party notice, if no notice is given.

The court may require you to post a **bond** as a condition of the injunction.

With this form you must also file the following, if you have not already done so, and provide a copy to the other party:

• **Uniform Child Custody Jurisdiction and Enforcement Act (UCCJEA) Affidavit**, ❑ Florida Supreme Court Approved Family Law Form 12.902(d).

**Temporary Injunctions...** These family law forms contain a **Temporary Injunction to Prevent Removal of Minor Child(ren) and/or Denial of Passport Services (Ex Parte)**, ❑ Florida Supreme Court Approved Family Law Form 12.941(b), which the **judge** may use if he or she enters an order without a hearing, and a **Temporary Injunction to Prevent Removal of Minor Child(ren) and/or Denial of Passport Services (After Notice)**, ❑ Florida Supreme Court Approved Family Law Form 12.941(c), which the judge may use if he or she enters an order after a hearing. You should check with the clerk, family law intake staff, or judicial assistant to see if you need to bring a blank order form with you to the hearing. If so, you should type or print the heading, including the circuit, county, case number, division, and the parties' names, and leave the rest blank for the judge to complete at your hearing.

Remember, a person who is NOT an attorney is called a nonlawyer. If a nonlawyer helps you fill out these forms, that person must give you a copy of **Disclosure from Nonlawyer**, ❑ Florida Family Law Rules of Procedure Form 12.900 (a), before he or she helps you. A nonlawyer helping you fill out these forms also **must** put his or her name, address, and telephone number on the bottom of the last page of every form he or she helps you complete.

**FIGURE 10.2**   State of Florida Motion for Temporary Injunction to Prevent Removal of Minor Child(ren)

IN THE CIRCUIT COURT OF THE _____ JUDICIAL CIRCUIT,
IN AND FOR _____ COUNTY, FLORIDA

Case No.: _____
Division: _____

_____,
         Petitioner,
   and

_____,
         Respondent.

### VERIFIED MOTION FOR TEMPORARY INJUNCTION TO PREVENT REMOVAL OF MINOR CHILD(REN) AND/OR DENIAL OF PASSPORT SERVICES

( ) Petitioner ( ) Respondent requests the Court to enter a temporary injunction to prevent removal of the following listed minor child(ren) from the jurisdiction of this Court and deny passport services for the child(ren) and says:

1.  The minor child(ren) subject to this request is (are):

**Name**                              **Birth date**

_____

_____

_____

_____

_____

_____

2.  The child(ren) has (have) been a resident(s) of_____County, Florida since {date}_____.

3.  A completed Uniform Child Custody Jurisdiction and Enforcement Act(UCCJEA) Affidavit, ❑ Florida Supreme Court Approved Family Law Form 12.902(d), is filed with this motion.

4.  It is in the best interests of the minor child(ren) that the Court order the following:
[√ **all** that apply]

___ a. The child(ren) not be removed from the jurisdiction of this Court while litigation is pending because: _____

_____

_____.

___ b. Passport services for the minor child(ren) be prohibited because: _____

_____

_____.

___ c. Existing passports for the minor child(ren) be immediately turned over to ( ) Petitioner ( ) Respondent because: _____

_____

_____

_____.

5.  This motion should be granted ( ) with ( ) without notice to the other party. {If without notice, explain why there would be immediate and irreparable harm if the other party is given notice.}

_____

_____

_____

_____

_____

_____.

WHEREFORE, ( ) Petitioner ( ) Respondent requests the following from the Court:
[√ **all** that apply]

___ a. enter a temporary injunction to prevent removal of the child(ren) named above from the jurisdiction of this Court while this action is pending;

___ b. enter an order denying passport services for the minor child(ren);

*(cont.)*

**FIGURE 10.2**  *(continued)*

___ c. enter an order requiring that any existing passports for the minor child(ren) be immediately delivered to ( ) Petitioner ( ) Respondent;

___ d. enter a temporary injunction without notice to the other party.

I certify that a copy of this document was [ √ one only] ( ) mailed ( ) faxed and mailed ( ) hand delivered to the person(s) listed below on {date} _____ or ( ) was not delivered to the person(s) listed below because

_____

_____

_____ .

**Other party or his/her attorney:**
Name: _____
Address: _____
City, State, Zip: _____
Fax Number: _____

I understand that I am swearing or affirming under oath to the truthfulness of the claims made in this verified motion and that the punishment for knowingly making a false statement includes fines and/or imprisonment.

Dated: _____  _____

Signature of Party
Printed Name: _____
Address: _____
City, State, Zip: _____
Telephone Number: _____
Fax Number: _____

STATE OF FLORIDA
COUNTY OF

Sworn to or affirmed and signed before me on _____ by _____.

_____
NOTARY PUBLIC or DEPUTY CLERK

_____
[Print, type, or stamp commissioned name of notary or clerk.]

___ Personally known
___ Produced identification
Type of identification produced

**If the party filing this motion is represented by an attorney, the attorney must complete the following:**

I, the undersigned attorney for the movant, hereby certify in that the following efforts have been made to give notice. {if no efforts have been made, why} _____

_____

_____

_____

_____

_____

_____
Signature

_____
Florida Bar Number

_____
Printed Name

**IF A NONLAWYER HELPED YOU FILL OUT THIS FORM, HE/SHE MUST FILL IN THE BLANKS BELOW:**
[✎ fill in **all** blanks]
I, {full legal name and trade name of nonlawyer} _____,
a nonlawyer, located at {street} _____, {city} _____,
{state} _____, {phone} _____, helped {name} _____,
who is the [√ **one** only] ___ petitioner **or** ___ respondent, fill out this form.

**FIGURE 10.2**  *(concluded)*

Appellate Court of Illinois
Second District
*In re Marriage of Karen L. Hartney, Petitioner-Appellant, and Jeff Hartney, Respondent-Appellee*
No. 2-05-0039
March 22, 2005

JUSTICE McLAREN delivered the opinion of the court:

Petitioner, Karen Hartney, appeals the trial court's dismissal of her amended petition for a preliminary injunction enjoining respondent, Jeff Hartney, from transferring alleged marital assets. We reverse and remand.

Initially, we address Jeff's argument that we do not have jurisdiction of this case because the order dismissing Karen's petition for a preliminary injunction is not final and appealable. This court has jurisdiction to review nonfinal interlocutory orders pursuant to Supreme Court Rule 307(a)(1). 166 Ill. 2d R. 307(a)(1). Rule 307(a)(1) allows an appeal from an order "disallowing" an injunction. Further, we disagree with Jeff that Rule 307(a)(1) does not apply here because the order at issue granted a motion to dismiss. The fact that Karen's petition for an injunction was disallowed by an order dismissing the petition rather than an order denying the petition does not divest this court of jurisdiction. See *In re Marriage of Centioli*, 335 Ill. App. 3d 650, 653 (2002) (the court stated that it had jurisdiction to review an order granting a motion to dismiss a petition seeking a preliminary injunction). We also note that although Karen's amended petition was for a temporary restraining order and a preliminary injunction, she appeals only the trial court's order dismissing her petition for a preliminary injunction.

On appeal, Karen argues that the trial court erred by dismissing her amended petition for a preliminary injunction. Section 501(a)(2)(i) of the Illinois Marriage and Dissolution of Marriage Act (750 ILCS 5/501(a)(2)(i) (West 2002)) states that a party may seek a preliminary injunction to preserve the status quo of the marital estate during the pendency of the proceedings. To grant preliminary relief, the trial court must find that (1) the plaintiff possesses a certain and clearly ascertainable right that needs protection; (2) the plaintiff will suffer irreparable harm without the protection of the injunction; (3) there is no adequate remedy at law; and (4) there is a substantial likelihood that the plaintiff will succeed on the merits of the case. *In re Marriage of Schmitt*, 321 Ill. App. 3d 360, 371 (2001). A complaint for a preliminary injunction must plead facts that clearly establish a right to injunctive relief. *Schmitt*, 321 Ill. App. 3d at 371.

First, we consider whether Karen has shown a clearly ascertainable right in need of protection. Karen's petition alleged that Jeff sold $165,000 of marital assets, namely bonds, and transferred the proceeds out of a marital account for his personal use. Karen further alleged that Jeff threatened to remove more of the marital assets from the marital accounts. Karen has a right to claim assets from the marital estate as part of her marital property settlement. *Schmitt*, 321 Ill. App. 3d at 371. Thus, Karen has sufficiently pleaded a clearly ascertainable right in need of protection.

Karen has also alleged that she will suffer irreparable harm without the protection of the injunction. Karen stated in her affidavit that Jeff had already sold bonds and transferred the proceeds out of a marital account to an unknown location. Jeff also told Karen that he would transfer more marital assets out of the martial accounts. Karen sufficiently alleged that Jeff's actions posed a threat of dissipation, with Jeff having directed the liquidation of investments in the parties' accounts and the withdrawal of those funds. Thus, Karen sufficiently alleged irreparable harm. See *In re Marriage of Petersen*, 319 Ill. App. 3d 325, 336–37 (2001).

Karen has also adequately alleged that there is no adequate remedy at law. Jeff insists that Karen could obtain money damages and, thus, there is a legal remedy available. However, for a legal remedy to preclude injunctive relief, the remedy must be "clear, complete, and as practical and efficient to the ends of justice and its prompt administration as the equitable remedy." *In re Marriage of Joerger*, 221 Ill. App. 3d 400, 407 (1991). Allowing Jeff to sell marital assets and remove them from marital accounts, thus requiring Karen to seek money damages after the marital estate's value plummets, is not the most practical and efficient remedy here. Karen has sufficiently pleaded that there is no adequate remedy at law, and the alleged potential loss of value in the marital estate makes injunctive relief proper.

Jeff argues that Karen's petition for a preliminary injunction seeks to alter the status quo. We disagree. Courts have recognized the need to protect the status quo of financial assets in marital estates during the pendency of divorce proceedings. In *Petersen*, the Appellate Court, First District, affirmed a preliminary injunction enjoining a husband from withdrawing funds from the parties' retirement accounts. See *Petersen*, 319 Ill. App. 3d at 337. The *Petersen* court reasoned that the status quo needed to be maintained to prevent the "dissipation or destruction of the property in question." *Petersen*, 319 Ill. App. 3d at 337. A legal remedy is inadequate where damages are difficult to calculate at the time of hearing. *Joerger*, 221 Ill. App. 3d at 406. At this stage in the proceedings, how Jeff's actions would affect the marital estate is unknown. The status quo to be maintained by a preliminary injunction here is the prevention of dissipation or destruction of the property in question. Thus, the trial court erred by dismissing the petition without an evidentiary hearing. See *Petersen*, 319 Ill. App. 3d at 336–37.

The judgment of the circuit court of Du Page County is reversed, and the cause is remanded for further proceedings.

Reversed and remanded.

BOWMAN and BYRNE, JJ., concur.

**Sec. 112A–3.** Definitions. For the purposes of this Article, the following terms shall have the following meanings:

(1)   "Abuse" means physical abuse, harassment, intimidation of a dependent, interference with personal liberty or willful deprivation but does not include reasonable direction of a minor child by a parent or person in loco parentis.

(2)   "Domestic violence" means abuse as described in paragraph (1).

(3)   "Family or household members" include spouses, former spouses, parents, children, stepchildren and other persons related by blood or by present or prior marriage, persons who share or formerly shared a common dwelling, persons who have or allegedly have a child in common, persons who share or allegedly share a blood relationship through a child, persons who have or have had a dating or engagement relationship, persons with disabilities and their personal assistants, and caregivers as defined in paragraph (3) of subsection (b) of Section 12-21 of the Criminal Code of 1961. For purposes of this paragraph, neither a casual acquaintanceship nor ordinary fraternization between 2 individuals in business or social contexts shall be deemed to constitute a dating relationship.

(4)   "Harassment" means knowing conduct which is not necessary to accomplish a purpose which is reasonable under the circumstances; would cause a reasonable person emotional distress; and does cause emotional distress to the petitioner. Unless the presumption is rebutted by a preponderance of the evidence, the following types of conduct shall be presumed to cause emotional distress:

   (i)   creating a disturbance at petitioner's place of employment or school;

   (ii)   repeatedly telephoning petitioner's place of employment, home or residence;

   (iii)   repeatedly following petitioner about in a public place or places;

   (iv)   repeatedly keeping petitioner under surveillance by remaining present outside his or her home, school, place of employment, vehicle or other place occupied by petitioner or by peering in petitioner's windows;

   (v)   improperly concealing a minor child from petitioner, repeatedly threatening to improperly remove a minor child of petitioner's from the jurisdiction or from the physical care of petitioner, repeatedly threatening to conceal a minor child from petitioner, or making a single such threat following an actual or attempted improper removal or concealment, unless respondent was fleeing from an incident or pattern of domestic violence; or

   (vi)   threatening physical force, confinement or restraint on one or more occasions.

(5)   "Interference with personal liberty" means committing or threatening physical abuse, harassment, intimidation or willful deprivation so as to compel another to engage in conduct from which she or he has a right to abstain or to refrain from conduct in which she or he has a right to engage.

(6)   "Intimidation of a dependent" means subjecting a person who is dependent because of age, health or disability to participation in or the witnessing of: physical force against another or physical confinement or restraint of another which constitutes physical abuse as defined in this Article, regardless of whether the abused person is a family or household member.

(7)   "Order of protection" means an emergency order, interim order or plenary order, granted pursuant to this Article, which includes any or all of the remedies authorized by Section 112A-14 of this Code.

(8)   "Petitioner" may mean not only any named petitioner for the order of protection and any named victim of abuse on whose behalf the petition is brought, but also any other person protected by this Article.

(9)   "Physical abuse" includes sexual abuse and means any of the following:

   (i)   knowing or reckless use of physical force, confinement or restraint;

   (ii)   knowing, repeated and unnecessary sleep deprivation; or

   (iii)   knowing or reckless conduct which creates an immediate risk of physical harm.

(9.5)   "Stay away" means for the respondent to refrain from both physical presence and nonphysical contact with the petitioner whether direct, indirect (including, but not limited to, telephone calls, mail, email, faxes, and written notes), or through third parties who may or may not know about the order of protection.

(10)   "Willful deprivation" means wilfully denying a person who because of age, health or disability requires medication, medical care, shelter, accessible shelter or services, food, therapeutic device, or other physical assistance, and thereby exposing that person to the risk of physical, mental or emotional harm, except with regard to medical care and treatment when such dependent person has expressed the intent to forgo such medical care or treatment. This paragraph does not create any new affirmative duty to provide support to dependent persons.

**FIGURE 10.3   Illinois Domestic Abuse Statute**

*Source:* Retrieved from www.ilga.gov/legislation/ilcs/ilcs4.asp?DocName=072500050HArt%2E+112A&ActID=1966&ChapAct=725%26nbsp%3BILCS%26nbsp%3B5%2F&ChapterID=54&ChapterName=CRIMINAL+PROCEDURE&SectionID=61301&SeqStart=33800&SeqEnd=37290&ActName=Code+of+Criminal+Procedure+of+1963%2E.8/13/07.

(Source: P.A. 92–253, eff. 1–1–02; 93-811, eff. 1–1–05.)
(725 ILCS 5/112A–4) (from Ch. 38, par. 112A–4)

**Sec. 112A–4.** Persons protected by this article.
(a)   The following persons are protected by this Article:
    (i)   any person abused by a family or household member;
    (ii)   any minor child or dependent adult in the care of such person; and
    (iii)   any person residing or employed at a private home or public shelter which is housing an abused family or household member.
(b)   A petition for an order of protection may be filed only by a person who has been abused by a family or household member or by any person on behalf of a minor child or an adult who has been abused by a family or household member and who, because of age, health, disability, or inaccessibility, cannot file the petition. However, any petition properly filed under this Article may seek protection for any additional persons protected by this Article.

**FIGURE 10.3**   *(concluded)*

# PROCEDURE FOR OBTAINING A TEMPORARY ORDER

The following describes the steps involved in obtaining a temporary order.

*Pleading*—The motion seeking a temporary order must include a specific request for relief. For example, if the motion seeks a temporary restraining order, it must include allegations of fact that show that harm has been threatened or that harm may occur. In a motion that requests an injunction be issued, it must also allege that there is no adequate remedy at law.

*Disclosure*—When seeking orders for temporary child support or temporary alimony, financial disclosure is necessary to provide the judge with adequate information on which to base his or her order. This may be done by the financial statements or other financial disclosure documents filed with the initial petition for dissolution, or it may need to be completed at the time the spouse seeking financial assistance files the motion.

*Notice*—Notice of the hearing must be served on the other party pursuant to the rules of court.

*Hearing*—The party seeking relief has the burden to present sufficient evidence to support his or her motion. The other spouse will also be given the opportunity to submit evidence that rebuts the need for the relief sought.

*Ex parte proceeding*—An **ex parte** proceeding may be used if there is a threat of immediate injury to the party or if there is a possibility one parent will remove a child from the jurisdiction of the court. In these instances, an expedited proceeding, which does not require notice to the other party, may be used by the court in which the court will base its decision on a review of the verified motion or an affidavit to determine whether the party seeking relief sufficiently supports the motion. If an order is granted without notice to the other party, the order will be served on that party, who will be given the opportunity to have the temporary order modified or dissolved.

*Order*—The court will enter an order either granting the relief sought or denying such relief. Although judges or their clerks will sometimes write such orders, some judges will ask the attorney for the prevailing party to draft an order for review and use by the judge. Figure 10.5 contains a sample temporary restraining order.

**CYBER TRIP**

To learn more about restraining orders and issues relating to domestic violence visit:www. masslegalhelp.org/ domestic-violence

**ex parte**
A communication between one party in a lawsuit and the judge.

---

| **DV-100** | **Request for Order** | *Clerk stamps date here when form is filed.* |
| --- | --- | --- |

**(1)** Your name (person asking for protection):

_____

Your address *(skip this if you have a lawyer): (If you want your address to be private, give a mailing address instead):*

_____

City: _____ State: _____ Zip: _____

Your telephone number *(optional):* _____

*Fill in court name and street address:*

**Superior Court of California, County of**

Your lawyer *(if you have one): (Name, address, telephone number, and State Bar number):*

_____

_____

_____

**(2)** Name of person you want protection from:

_____

Description of that person: Sex: ☐ M ☐ F  Height: _____
Weight: _____ Race: _____ Hair Color: _____
Eye Color: _____ Age: _____ Date of Birth: _____

*Clerk fills in case number when form is filed.*

**Case Number:**

**(3)** Besides you, who needs protection? *(Family or household members):*

| Full Name | Age | Lives with you? | How are they related to you? |
| --- | --- | --- | --- |
| _____ | _____ | ☐ Yes ☐ No | _____ |
| _____ | _____ | ☐ Yes ☐ No | _____ |
| _____ | _____ | ☐ Yes ☐ No | _____ |
| _____ | _____ | ☐ Yes ☐ No | _____ |

☐ *Check here if you need more space. Attach Form MC-020 and write "DV-100, Item 3—Protected People" by your statement. NOTE: In any item that asks for Form MC-020, you can use an 8 1/2 x 11-inch sheet of paper instead.*

**(4)** What is your relationship to the person in **(2)**? *(Check all that apply):*

a. ☐ We are now married or registered domestic partners.
b. ☐ We used to be married or registered domestic partners.
c. ☐ We live together.
d. ☐ We used to live together.
e. ☐ We are relatives, in-laws, or related by adoption *(specify relationship):* _____
f. ☐ We are dating or used to date.
g. ☐ We are engaged to be married or were engaged to be married.
h. ☐ We are the parents together of a child or children under 18:

  Child's Name: _____ Date of Birth: _____
  Child's Name: _____ Date of Birth: _____
  Child's Name: _____ Date of Birth: _____

  ☐ *Check here if you need more space. Attach Form MC-020 and write "DV-100, Item 4h" by your statement.*

i. ☐ We have signed a Voluntary Declaration of Paternity for our child or children. *(Attach a copy if you have one.)*

**This is not a Court Order.**

| Judicial Council of California, *www.courtinfo.ca.gov*<br>Revised July 1, 2007, Mandatory Form<br>Family Code, § 6200 et seq. | **Request for Order**<br>**(Domestic Violence Prevention)** | **DV-100,** Page 1 of 4<br>→<br>American LegalNet, Inc.<br>www.FormsWorkflow.com |
| --- | --- | --- |

**FIGURE 10.4** **California Request for Temporary Restraining Order**

*Source:* Retrieved from www.courtinfo.ca.gov/forms/fillable/dv100.pdf.

Case Number: _____

Your name: _____

**(5)** Other Court Cases

    a.  Have you and the person in **(2)** been involved in another court case?  ☐ No  ☐ Yes

       If yes, where?  County: _____  State: _____

       What are the case numbers? *(If you know):* _____

       What kind of case? *(Check all that apply):*

         ☐ Registered Domestic Partnership  ☐ Divorce/Dissolution  ☐ Parentage/Paternity  ☐ Legal Separation
         ☐ Domestic Violence  ☐ Criminal  ☐ Juvenile  ☐ Child Support  ☐ Nullity  ☐ Civil Harassment
         ☐ Other *(specify):* _____

    b.  Are there any domestic violence restraining/protective orders now (criminal, juvenile, family)?

       ☐ No  ☐ Yes  *If yes, attach a copy if you have one.*

## What orders do you want? Check the boxes that apply to your case. ☑

**(6)** ☐ **Personal Conduct Orders**

    I ask the court to order the person in **(2)** not to do the following things to me or any of the people listed in **(3)** :

    a.  ☐ Harass, attack, strike, threaten, assault (sexually or otherwise), hit, follow, stalk, molest, destroy
        personal property, disturb the peace, keep under surveillance, or block movements

    b.  ☐ Contact (either directly or indirectly), or telephone, or send messages or mail or e-mail

    *The person in **(2)** will be ordered not to take any action to get the addresses or locations of any protected
    person, their family members, caretakers, or guardians unless the court finds good cause not to make the order.*

**(7)** ☐ **Stay-Away Order**

    I ask the court to order the person in **(2)** to stay at least _____ yards away from *(check all that apply):*

    a.  ☐ Me              e.  ☐ The children's school or child care
    b.  ☐ The people listed in **(3)**    f.  ☐ My vehicle
    c.  ☐ My home         g.  ☐ Other *(specify):* _____
    d.  ☐ My job or workplace                 _____

    If the person listed in **(2)** is ordered to stay away from all the places listed above, will he or she still be able
    to get to his or her home, school, job, or place of worship?  ☐ Yes  ☐ No  *(If no, explain):* _____

    _____

**(8)** ☐ **Move-Out Order**

    I ask the court to order the person in **(2)** to move out from and not return to *(address):*

    _____

    I have the right to live at the above address because *(explain):* _____

    _____

**(9)** ☐ **Child Custody, Visitation, and Child Support**

    I ask the court to order child custody, visitation, and/or child support. *You must fill out and attach
    Form DV-105.*

**(10)** ☐ **Spousal Support**

    *You can make this request only if you are married to, or are a registered domestic partner of, the person in **(2)**
    and no spousal support order exists. To ask for spousal support, you must fill out, file, and serve Form FL-150
    before your hearing.*

**This is not a Court Order.**

| Revised July 1, 2007 | **Request for Order**<br>**(Domestic Violence Prevention)** | **DV-100**, Page 2 of 4<br>→ |

**FIGURE 10.4**  *(continued)*

*(cont.)*

Case Number: _____

Your name: _____

## What orders do you want? Check the boxes that apply to your case. ☑

(11) ☐ **Record Unlawful Communications**

I ask for the right to record communications made to me by the person in (2) that violate the judge's orders.

(12) ☐ **Property Control**

I ask the court to give ***only*** me temporary use, possession, and control of the property listed here:

_____

(13) ☐ **Debt Payment**

I ask the court to order the person in (2) to make these payments while the order is in effect:

☐ *Check here if you need more space. Attach Form MC-020 and write "DV-100, Item 13—Debt Payment" by your statement.*

Pay to: _____ For: _____ Amount: $ _____ Due date: _____

Pay to: _____ For: _____ Amount: $ _____ Due date: _____

Pay to: _____ For: _____ Amount: $ _____ Due date: _____

(14) ☐ **Property Restraint**

I am married to or have a registered domestic partnership with the person in (2). I ask the judge to order that the person in (2) not borrow against, sell, hide, or get rid of or destroy any possessions or property, except in the usual course of business or for necessities of life. I also ask the judge to order the person in (2) to notify me of any new or big expenses and to explain them to the court.

(15) ☐ **Attorney Fees and Costs**

I ask that the person in (2) pay some or all of my attorney fees and costs.
*You must complete and file Form FL-150,* Income and Expense Declaration.

(16) ☐ **Payments for Costs and Services**

I ask that the person in (2) pay the following:
*You can ask for lost earnings or your costs for services caused directly by the person in (2) (damaged property, medical care, counseling, temporary housing, etc.). You must bring proof of these expenses to your hearing.*

Pay to: _____ For: _____ Amount: $ _____

Pay to: _____ For: _____ Amount: $ _____

Pay to: _____ For: _____ Amount: $ _____

(17) ☐ **Batterer Intervention Program**

I ask the court to order the person listed in (2) to go to a 52-week batterer intervention program and show proof of completion to the court.

(18) **No Fee to Serve (Notify) Restrained Person**

*If you want the sheriff or marshal to serve (notify) the restrained person about the orders for free, ask the court clerk what you need to do.*

**This is not a Court Order.**

**FIGURE 10.4** *(continued)*

Case Number:

Your name: _____

## What orders do you want? Check the boxes that apply to your case. ☑

(19) ☐ **More Time for Notice**

I need extra time to notify the person in ② about these papers. Because of the facts explained on this form, I want the papers served up to _____ days before the date of the hearing. *For help, read Form DV-210-INFO.*

*If necessary, add additional facts:* _____

_____

(20) ☐ **Other Orders**

What other orders are you asking for? _____

_____

☐ *Check here if you need more space. Attach Form MC-020 and write "DV-100, Item 20—Other Orders" by your statement.*

(21) **Guns or Other Firearms**

I believe the person in ② owns or possesses guns or firearms.   ☐ Yes   ☐ No   ☐ I don't know

*If the judge approves the order, the person in ② will be required to sell to a gun dealer or turn in to police any guns or firearms that he or she owns or possesses.*

(22) Describe the most recent abuse.

a. Date of most recent abuse: _____

b. Who was there? _____

c. What did the person in ② do or say that made you afraid?

_____

_____

_____

_____

_____

d. Describe any use or threatened use of guns or other weapons: _____

_____

e. Describe any injuries: _____

_____

f. Did the police come?   ☐ No   ☐ Yes

If yes, did they give you an Emergency Protective Order?   ☐ Yes   ☐ No   ☐ I don't know

*Attach a copy if you have one.*

☐ *Check here if you need more space. Use Form MC-020 and write "DV-100, Item 22—Recent Abuse" by your statement.*

☐ *Check here if the person in ② has abused you (or your children) other times. Use Form DV-101 or Form MC-020 to describe any previous abuse.*

I declare under penalty of perjury under the laws of the State of California that the information above is true and correct.

Date: _____

_____          _____
*Type or print your name*                          *Sign your name*

**This is not a Court Order.**

Revised July 1, 2007          **Request for Order**          DV-100, Page 4 of 4
                              **(Domestic Violence Prevention)**

**FIGURE 10.4**   *(concluded)*

| **DV-110** | **Temporary Restraining Order and Notice of Hearing** | *Clerk stamps date here when form is filed.* |

**(1)** Name of person asking for protection (protected person):
_____

Protected person's address *(skip this if you have a lawyer): (If you want your address to be private, give a mailing address instead):*
_____

City: _____ State: _____ Zip: _____
Telephone number: _____
Protected person's lawyer *(if any): (Name, address, telephone number, and State Bar number):*
_____
_____
_____

*Fill in court name and street address:*

**Superior Court of California, County of**

**(2)** Restrained person's name:
_____
Description of that person: Sex: ☐ M ☐ F Height: _____
Weight: _____ Race: _____ Hair Color: _____
Eye Color: _____ Age: ____ Date of Birth: _____

*Fill in case number:*

**Case Number:**

**(3)** List the full names of all family or household members protected by this order: _____
_____

**(4)** **Court Hearing Date** *(Fecha de la Audiencia)*
*Clerk will fill out section below.*

Name and address of court if different from above:

| **Hearing Date** | Date: _____ Time: _____ _____ |
| | Dept.: _____ Rm.: _____ _____ |

To the person in **(2)** : At the hearing, the judge can make restraining orders that last for up to 5 years. The judge can also make other orders about your children, child support, spousal support, money, and property. File an answer on Form DV-120 before the hearing. At the hearing, you can tell the judge that you do not want the orders against you. Even if you do not attend the hearing, you *must* obey the orders.

*Para la persona nombrada en* **(2)** : *En esta audiencia el juez puede hacer que la orden de restricción sea válida hasta un máximo de 5 años. El juez puede también hacer otras órdenes acerca de niños, manutención, dinero y propiedad. Presente una respuesta en el formulario DV-120 antes de la audiencia. Si Usted se opone a estas órdenes, vaya a la audiencia y dígaselo al juez. Aunque no vaya a la audiencia, tiene que obedecer estas órdenes.*

To the person in **(1)** : At the hearing, the judge will consider whether denial of any orders will jeopardize your safety and the safety of children for whom you are requesting custody, visitation, and child support. Safety concerns related to the financial needs of you and your children will also be considered.

**(5)** **Temporary Orders (Ordenes Temporales)**
Any orders made in this form end at the time of the court hearing in **(4)**, unless a judge extends them.
Read this form carefully. All checked boxes ☑ and items 10 and 11 are court orders.

*Todas las órdenes hechas en esta formulario terminarán en la fecha y hora de la audiencia en* **(4)** *, al menos que un juez las extienda. Lea este formulario con cuidado. Todas las casillas marcadas ☑ y los artículos 10 y 11 son órdenes de la corte.*

**This is a Court Order.**

Judicial Council of California, *www.courtinfo.ca.gov*
Revised July 1, 2007, Mandatory Form
Family Code, § 6200 et seq. Approved by DOJ

**Temporary Restraining Order and Notice of Hearing (CLETS—TRO)**
**(Domestic Violence Prevention)**

DV-110, Page 1 of 5
→

American LegalNet, Inc.
www.FormsWorkflow.com

**FIGURE 10.5** Temporary Restraining Order and Notice of Hearing

Case Number:

Your name: _____

**6** ☐ **Personal Conduct Orders**

The person in ② must ***not*** do the following things to the protected people listed in ① and ③:

a. ☐ Harass, attack, strike, threaten, assault (sexually or otherwise), hit, follow, stalk, molest, destroy personal property, disturb the peace, keep under surveillance, or block movements

b. ☐ Contact (either directly or indirectly), or telephone, or send messages or mail or e-mail

☐ Except for brief and peaceful contact as required for court-ordered visitation of children unless a criminal protective order says otherwise

c. ☐ Take any action, directly or through others, to get the addresses or locations of any protected persons or of their family members, caretakers, or guardians. *(If item c is not checked, the court has found good cause not to make this order.)*

Peaceful written contact through a lawyer or through a process server or another person in order to serve legal papers is allowed and does not violate this order.

☐ A criminal protective order on Form CR-160 is in effect. Case Number: _____

County *(if known):* _____ Expiration Date: _____ *(If more orders, list them in item* **16***)*

**7** ☐ **Stay-Away Order**

The person in ② must stay at least_____ yards away from:

a. ☐ The person listed in ①

b. ☐ The people listed in ③

c. ☐ Home ☐ Job ☐ Vehicle of person in ①

d. ☐ The children's school or child care

e. ☐ Other *(specify):* _____

_____

**8** ☐ **Move-Out Order**

The person in ② must take only personal clothing and belongings needed until the hearing and move out immediately from *(address):* _____

**9** ☐ **Child Custody and Visitation Order**

a. ☐ You and the other parent must make an appointment for court mediation *(address and phone number):*

_____

b. ☐ Follow the orders listed in Form DV-140, which is attached.

**10** **No Guns or Other Firearms or Ammunition**

The person in ② cannot own, possess, have, buy or try to buy, receive or try to receive, or in any other way get guns, firearms, or ammunition.

**11** **Turn in or sell guns or firearms.**

The person in ②:

• Must sell to a licensed gun dealer or turn in to police any guns or firearms that he or she has or controls. This must be done within 24 hours of being served with this order.

• Must bring a receipt to the court within 48 hours of being served with this order, to prove that guns and firearms have been turned in or sold.

**12** ☐ **Property Control**

Until the hearing, *only* the person in ① can use, control, and possess the following property and things:

_____

_____

**This is a Court Order.**

**Temporary Restraining Order
and Notice of Hearing (CLETS—TRO)**
(Domestic Violence Prevention)

**FIGURE 10.5** *(continued)*

*(cont.)*

**Your name:** _____

**Case Number:** _____

**(13) ☐ Property Restraint**

If the people in ① and ② are married to each other or are registered domestic partners, they must not transfer, borrow against, sell, hide, or get rid of or destroy any property, except in the usual course of business or for necessities of life. In addition, each person must notify the other of any new or big expenses and explain them to the court. *(The person in ② cannot contact the person in ① if the court has made a "no contact" order.)*

**(14) ☐ Unlawful communications may be recorded.**

The person in ① can record communications made by the person in ② that violate the judge's orders.

**(15) No Fee to Notify (Serve) Restrained Person**

If the sheriff serves this order, he or she will do it for free.

**(16) ☐ Other Orders** *(specify):* _____
_____
_____

**(17)** If the judge makes a restraining order at the hearing, which has the same orders as in this form, the person in ② will get a copy of that order by mail at his or her last known address. *(Write restrained person's address here):*

_____

If this address is not correct, or to know if the orders were made permanent, contact the court.

**(18) ☐ Time for Service**

| **Ⓐ    To:  Person Asking for Order** | **Ⓑ    To:  Person Served With Order** |
|---|---|
| Someone 18 or over—**not you or the other protected people**—must personally "serve" a copy of this order to the restrained person at least _____ days before the hearing. | If you want to respond in writing, someone 18 or over—**not you**—must "serve" Form DV-120 on the person in ①, then file it with the court at least _____ days before the hearing. |

*For help with Service or answering, read Form DV-210-INFO or DV-540-INFO.*

Date: _____

▶ _____
*Judge (or Judicial Officer)*

---

**Certificate of Compliance With VAWA**

This temporary protective order meets all Full Faith and Credit requirements of the Violence Against Women Act, 18 U.S.C. § 2265 (1994) (VAWA) upon notice of the restrained person. This court has jurisdiction over the parties and the subject matter; the restrained person has been or will be afforded notice and a timely opportunity to be heard as provided by the laws of this jurisdiction. **This order is valid and entitled to enforcement in each jurisdiction throughout the 50 United States, the District of Columbia, all tribal lands, and all U.S. territories, commonwealths, and possessions and shall be enforced as if it were an order of that jurisdiction.**

---

**This is a Court Order.**

**FIGURE 10.5**   *(continued)*

Case Number: _____

Your name: _____

## Warnings and Notices to the Restrained Person in ②

**(19) If you do not obey this order, you can be arrested and charged with a crime.**
- It is a felony to take or hide a child in violation of this order. You can go to prison and/or pay a fine.
- If you travel to another state or to tribal lands or make the protected person do so, with the intention of disobeying this order, you can be charged with a federal crime.
- If you do not obey this order, you can go to prison and/or pay a fine.

**(20) You cannot have guns, firearms, and/or ammunition.**

You cannot own, have, possess, buy or try to buy, receive or try to receive, or otherwise get guns, firearms, and/or ammunition while the order is in effect. If you do, you can go to jail and pay a $1,000 fine. You must sell to a gun dealer or turn in to police any guns or firearms that you have or control. The judge will ask you for proof that you did so. If you do not obey this order, you can be charged with a crime. Federal law says you cannot have guns or ammunition if you are subject to a restraining order made after a noticed hearing.

**(21) After You Have Been Served With a Restraining Order**
- Obey all the orders.
- If you want to respond, fill out Form DV-120. Take it to the court clerk with the forms listed in item ㉒.
- File DV-120 and have all papers served on the protected person by the date listed in item ⑱ of this form.
- At the hearing, tell the judge if you agree or disagree with the orders requested.
- Even if you do not attend the hearing, the judge can make the restraining orders last for 5 years.

**(22) Child Custody, Visitation, and Support**
- Child Custody and Visitation: If you do not go to the hearing, the judge can make custody and visitation orders for your children without hearing your side.
- Child Support: The judge can order child support based on the income of both parents. The judge can also have that support taken directly from your paycheck. Child support can be a lot of money, and usually you have to pay until the child is 18. File and serve a *Financial Statement* (Form FL-155) or an *Income and Expense Declaration* (Form FL-150) so the judge will have information about your finances. Otherwise, the court may make support orders without hearing your side.
- Spousal Support: File and serve a *Financial Statement* (Form FL-155) or an *Income and Expense Declaration* (Form FL-150) so the judge will have information about your finances. Otherwise, the court may make support orders without hearing your side.

**(23)** **Requests for Accommodations**
Assistive listening systems, computer-assisted real-time captioning, or sign language interpreter services are available if you ask at least five days before the proceeding. Contact the clerk's office or go to *www.courtinfo.ca.gov/forms* for *Request for Accommodations by Persons With Disabilities and Order* (Form MC-410). (Civil Code, § 54.8.)

## This is a Court Order.

**FIGURE 10.5**   *(continued)*                                                            *(cont.)*

Your name: _____

Case Number: _____

## Instructions for Law Enforcement

**(24) Start Date and End Date of Orders**

The start date is the date next to the judge's signature on page 3. The orders end on the hearing date on page 1 or the hearing date on Form DV-125, if attached.

**(25) Arrest Required If Order Is Violated**

If an officer has probable cause to believe that the restrained person had notice of the order and has disobeyed the order, the officer must arrest the restrained person. (Penal Code, §§ 836(c)(1), 13701(b).) A violation of the order may be a violation of Penal Code section 166 or 273.6.

**(26) Notice/Proof of Service**

Law enforcement must first determine if the restrained person had notice of the orders. If notice cannot be verified, the restrained person must be advised of the terms of the orders. If the restrained person then fails to obey the orders, the officer must enforce them. (Family Code, § 6383.)

Consider the restrained person "served" (noticed) if:

- The officer sees a copy of the *Proof of Service* or confirms that the *Proof of Service* is on file; *or*
- The restrained person was at the restraining order hearing or was informed of the order by an officer. (Fam. Code, § 6383; Pen. Code, § 836(c)(2).) An officer can obtain information about the contents of the order in the Domestic Violence Restraining Orders System (DVROS). (Fam. Code, § 6381(b)(c).)

**(27) If the Protected Person Contacts the Restrained Person**

Even if the protected person invites or consents to contact with the restrained person, the orders remain in effect and must be enforced. The protected person cannot be arrested for inviting or consenting to contact with the restrained person. The orders can be changed only by another court order. (Pen. Code, § 13710(b).)

**(28) Child Custody and Visitation**

- Custody and visitation orders are on Form DV-140, items (3) and (4). They are sometimes also written on additional pages or referenced in DV-140 or other orders that are not part of the restraining order.
- **Forms DV-100 and DV-105 are not orders. Do not enforce them.**

**(29) Enforcing the Restraining Order in California**

Any law enforcement officer in California who receives, sees, or verifies the orders on a paper copy, or on the California Law Enforcement Telecommunications System (CLETS), or in an NCIC Protection Order File must enforce the orders.

**(30) Conflicting Orders**

A protective order issued in a criminal case on Form CR-160 takes precedence in enforcement over any conflicting civil court order. (Pen. Code, § 136.2(e)(2).) Any nonconflicting terms of the civil restraining order remain in full force. An emergency protective order (Form EPO-001) that is in effect between the same parties and is more restrictive than other restraining orders takes precedence over all other restraining orders.

---

*Clerk's Certificate*

*[seal]*

I certify that this Temporary Restraining Order is a true and correct copy of the original on file in the court.

Date: _____ Clerk, by_____ , Deputy

## This is a Court Order.

**Temporary Restraining Order
and Notice of Hearing (CLETS—TRO)**
(Domestic Violence Prevention)

**FIGURE 10.5** *(continued)*

# DRAFTING PRETRIAL MOTIONS

The drafting of a pretrial motion is very similar to that of the initial pleading. Like the petition for dissolution of marriage, **pretrial motions** contain a caption, body, prayer for relief, and subscription verification. The caption is generally the same as the petition, while the title of the pleading differs. For example, instead of titling the pleading Petition for Dissolution of Marriage, the pleading will be Motion for Temporary Support. As is the case with the drafting of the initial petition for dissolution of marriage, the paralegal will use one of a variety of forms available to produce a finished product that will meet the needs of the client's case.

**pretrial motions**
Used to challenge the sufficiency of evidence or the suppression of allegedly tainted evidence or other matters that could impact the focus, the length, and even the need for trial.

**Summary**

Pretrial motions are fairly common in dissolution cases, especially when there are many areas of contention between the parties that delay the ultimate resolution of the case. Common motions that may be used include: motion for temporary child custody and visitation, motion for temporary child support, motion for temporary alimony, motion for award of temporary attorney fees, suit money, and costs, and motions for temporary injunction, temporary injunction to preserve marital property, and temporary restraining order and orders of protection. Each of these motions is a tool in the attorney's toolbox that can be used to help meet the specific needs of his or her client. Some are critical in helping protect the physical and mental well-being of the client. Others are used to allow the client to have as normal a life as possible until his or her case is resolved.

States are increasingly recognizing the need for low-income people to have access to the legal system, especially to provide protection and support during the dissolution of marriage process. Many now offer free forms that are relatively simple to complete to those who need them. A number of these forms have been included in this chapter to familiarize the paralegal student with what resources are available to the public and the general format of these forms. Some states also have legal aid organizations that help low-income people work their way through the dissolution/divorce process.

Ultimately paralegals become familiar with the many temporary motions that are available to meet the needs of their clients and are able to develop the necessary drafting skills for use in their clients' cases.

**Key Terms**

Ex parte
Injunction
Motion for award of temporary
  attorney fees, suit money, and costs
Motion for temporary alimony
Motion for temporary child custody
  and visitation

Motion for temporary child support
Pretrial motions
Temporary injunction
Temporary restraining order

**Review Questions**

1. What are pretrial motions and why are they used in the family law firm?
2. What is the purpose of a motion for temporary custody and visitation?
3. Why should a paralegal be concerned about low-income people having access to the legal system?
4. Where do courts get the power to enter an order granting temporary child support?

5. What is the initial step a court takes to determine whether temporary child support should be granted?

6. When should a motion for temporary alimony be used?

7. What factors can a court consider to decide whether a motion for temporary alimony should be granted?

8. What is a motion for award of temporary attorney fees, suit money, and costs and why is it used?

9. What is an injunction? How does it differ from a temporary injunction?

10. What temporary motion is used to prevent a spouse from transferring or selling marital assets?

11. What are domestic abuse statutes and why are they important in a family law firm?

12. What punishment can be imposed for violation of a temporary restraining order?

13. What is the procedure that is followed to obtain pretrial orders?

14. What motion(s) require the submission of financial disclosure forms?

15. What is an ex parte hearing and when is it used?

---

**Exercises**

1. Based on the facts contained in the Client Interview, determine what temporary motions might be required to protect and provide for Sue and John while the dissolution of marriage action proceeds through the legal system. Draft the necessary motions. Create additional facts as needed.

2. Kevin has come to your firm to assist him in getting a divorce from his wife, Julia. Kevin has informed you that he has been a victim of spousal abuse. He has not called the police because he is embarrassed. Research the statutory and case law of your state to find out what statutes provide protection of a spouse in Kevin's situation and what steps must be taken. Would an ex parte hearing be appropriate in his case? Explain.

3. Research the case and statutory laws of your state relating to the award of temporary custody. Does your state allow the award of temporary custody? If yes, when are these temporary orders allowed?

4. Research the laws of your state relating to the award of temporary alimony. What factors can be considered by a court when it is determining if such award should be made? Locate a case that explains these criteria and how they should be applied.

5. Write a description of the process used in your state to determine if temporary child support should be awarded and, if it is, how much should be awarded.

## REAL WORLD DISCUSSION TOPICS

1. A husband, a 53-year-old licensed physician specializing in neurology, worked a full 5-day week for about 8 hours a day. His 1999 Federal Income Tax Form 1120 showed that gross receipts for his group practice were reported to be $3,434,356. His financial affidavit reported a net weekly income of $2,339 per week, and total weekly living expenses of $2,123 per week. His total cash assets shown on his financial affidavit are $1,831,360, and the plaintiff lists total cash assets of $388,292.73 on her affidavit.

   The wife is also a licensed physician and is 53 years old. Her gross monthly salary for the past 11 months was $4,000, and her net weekly salary is $670 per week. Her weekly household and living expenses as listed on her financial affidavit amount to $12,981 per month, or $3,000 per week. Her salary was, however, suspended by her employer, a nonprofit agency for children, because of lack of funding for her position. The couple has one minor child, who is 17. What temporary relief might be appropriate in this case? Explain why. See *Kremenitzer v. Kremenitzer,* 2001 WL 58086 (Conn.Super., 2001).

2. Julian and Susan were married in 1981. They separated in early 2000 and thereafter maintained separate residences. Two years later Julian filed a petition seeking dissolution of the marriage and equitable distribution of the marital assets. Susan filed an answer and a counter petition for dissolution of marriage seeking equitable distribution of the marital assets, including exclusive use of the marital home, temporary and permanent alimony, and attorney's fees. Julian subsequently filed a verified motion for a temporary injunction to prevent dissipation of marital assets, alleging that Susan had, without his knowledge or consent, withdrawn $500,000 from his IRA account, sold real property owned by the parties, and dissipated other marital assets. He requested the court to issue a temporary injunction enjoining Susan from further dissipating the marital assets in order to preserve the status quo. Should the motion for a temporary injunction be granted? See *Kanter v. Kanter,* 850 So.2d 682 (Fla.App. 4 Dist., 2003).

## PORTFOLIO ASSIGNMENT

Review the facts contained in the Client Interview. Your firm will be handling Sue's dissolution of marriage case. Based on the facts given, determine which motions for temporary relief might be appropriate in her case. Research the laws and rules of your state that relate to those motions. You should also locate forms that might be used to draft the motions. Write a summary of what your research has revealed about the law of your state. You should also draft the motions that you feel are appropriate in Sue's case. Create additional facts as needed to complete the motions.

# Chapter 11

# Discovery

## CHAPTER OBJECTIVES

**After reading this chapter and completing the assignments, you should be able to:**

- Identify some of the more common discovery devices that can be used to obtain facts in dissolution of marriage cases.

- Explain how discovery differs in a dissolution of marriage case from discovery in other civil litigation.

- Explain why the discovery process is used.

- Discuss what sanctions can be imposed when a party does not comply with a discovery request.

Since a divorce is a form of civil litigation, divorce cases often involve conflicting interests that ultimately may have to be resolved by a court. This is especially true in a contested divorce where the parties may be in disagreement about child custody, alimony, and/or the distribution of marital property. The more disagreement, the more work that is involved in completing the case. Discovery is one process that an attorney can use to do the best possible job for his or her client. Information is key to fairly resolving issues involved in a divorce. For example, how can an attorney be sure that a proposed distribution of property is equitable if he or she is not certain that all the facts about the finances of each party are known?

Discovery provides the parties a method of learning all of the facts relating to the case so as to better prepare their cases and is an important part of all civil litigation. This chapter provides an overview of the discovery process and some of the specific aspects that are important in the family law firm.

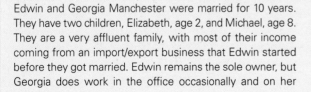

## CLIENT INTERVIEW

Edwin and Georgia Manchester were married for 10 years. They have two children, Elizabeth, age 2, and Michael, age 8. They are a very affluent family, with most of their income coming from an import/export business that Edwin started before they got married. Edwin remains the sole owner, but Georgia does work in the office occasionally and on her computer at home processing orders for the products bought and sold by the company. Edwin has hired an attorney and filed for divorce. He has made it clear to Georgia that he wants sole custody of Michael and doesn't want Georgia to get alimony. Georgia has hired your firm to represent her in the divorce.

# WHY THIS CHAPTER IS IMPORTANT TO THE PARALEGAL

This chapter gives the paralegal student some insight into how the **discovery** process is used in civil litigation. It does not give a detailed presentation of all aspects of the discovery process, which is something best left for a civil litigation class. However, it is important to consider how discovery may be used in the family law firm, specifically in a dissolution of marriage action. A basic understanding of this process is important to paralegal students and will help them to complete the tasks that are assigned to them in the family law office. It also will give paralegal students an awareness of how the discovery process is used to meet the needs of their clients.

## WHAT IS DISCOVERY?

Discovery is the method of gathering information necessary to properly prepare a case. It is used in virtually all lawsuits and many other legal proceedings. The goal is to allow a party to obtain information that will enable the person to have the information needed to persuade a judge to rule in the party's favor.

What can be discovered? Almost anything that is relevant to the case and not protected by some privilege is discoverable. Examples include: documents, photographs, financial information, computer files, e-mails, and bank statements. Parties are given broad leeway in what information can be obtained in the discovery process.

## DISCOVERY AND FAMILY LAW

Although discovery is used in many legal proceedings, it is not used as extensively in dissolution of marriage cases, for a number of reasons. One reason may be to save time and money. Another may be because attorneys feel they know enough to proceed with the case from the information the client provided or from information the other party provided. In the end, however, discovery should be used whenever it is needed to do the best job possible for the client.

As noted, discovery is a process that allows a party to obtain information that may be important to the case. Some information is obtained informally, such as by the client interview and the completion of the client questionnaire. In addition, attorneys will often be willing to exchange information to facilitate the completion of a settlement agreement, if it is agreeable to the client. Other information may have to be obtained by the formal discovery process, which is the focus of this chapter.

It is now common for states to require mandatory disclosure of certain information in dissolution of marriage cases, such as an exchange of information about income, expenses, assets, and liabilities. For example, in Florida, parties in a dissolution action that seeks financial relief, such as child support, alimony, and/or distribution of assets, must provide the other party with items such as a financial affidavit and a completed child support guidelines worksheet. This information is to be provided without notice from the other party. Instead, this is intended to be an automatic procedure under which each party provides the required information as soon as possible. In addition, the parties are required to provide updated information if any of it proves incorrect or changes have occurred that make the information no longer materially true, even if there is no requirement to do so in other civil litigation discovery under the rules of a particular state.

Some states' court rules relating to family law merely encourage the parties to voluntarily exchange information and documents. Formal discovery and depositions can only be conducted by stipulation between the parties or by court order. See, for example, Rule 25 of the South Carolina Family Court Rules.

**discovery**
The pretrial investigation process authorized and governed by the rules of civil procedure; the process of investigation and collection of evidence by litigants; process in which the opposing parties obtain information about the case from each other; the process of investigation and collection of evidence by litigants.

**CYBER TRIP**

To see an example of how courts have adopted rules that set out how to use discovery in dissolution of marriage actions, see the Florida Family Law Rules of Procedure, specifically §§ 12.285–12.407, at www.floridabar. org/TFB/ TFBResources.nsf/ Attachments/ 416879C4A88CBF04 85256B29004BFAF8/ $FILE/311FamLaw. pdf?OpenElement.

The family law attorney will need to review the facts and information specific to his or her case before deciding how extensive the discovery process will be in a particular case. Factors that are considered include how much the parties have already agreed on, whether there are any usual issues presented in the case, and the amount, type, and value of the assets involved. The personalities of the parties may also be a factor. An uncooperative party makes it more likely that a formal discovery process will be needed.

## INFORMAL DISCOVERY

Discovery can take many forms. In fact, some form of discovery occurs almost all dissolution of marriage cases. It may take the form of the mandatory financial disclosure previously discussed. Or it may be a more formal form of discovery that will subsequently be discussed in more detail.

In many situations, the best approach is informal discovery, which is the voluntary exchange of information between the parties. The information is exchanged directly between the attorneys for each spouse without any formal request filed pursuant to the court rules of discovery. This is particularly helpful in cases where the parties both want the case to be resolved as quickly as possible and there is no reason to believe that either spouse is not being forthcoming and truthful about the information being disclosed.

There are many benefits to using informal discovery. The two most important are that it saves both time and money. The procedure can move as quickly as the parties want it to and it eliminates the need and expense of taking depositions, and so on. It also results in a money savings to the client because the gathering of this information takes far less time and is often accomplished by the paralegal, thus reducing the number of hours the attorney will bill for his or her hours. Although an attorney may bill the client for the hours his or her paralegal works on the client's case, the hourly rate is normally significantly less than that of the attorney.

However, while informal discovery has its benefits, the attorney and paralegal must be vigilant in looking for any signs that the other side is not being completely forthcoming about the information being requested or might be hiding information. This is an example of why it is important to understand not just the law affecting the client's case, but also the personalities of the participants in the case. For example, have the attorneys on both sides of the case worked together on previous dissolution cases? If yes, were there any problems during the exchange of information or any discovered after the conclusion of the case? The attorney must also attempt to appraise the forthrightness of his or her own client, since the client may have an agenda that is inconsistent with the use of informal discovery. The client is also a source of information about the reliability of his or her spouse in the informal discovery process.

Examples of information that can be exchanged between the parties in informal discovery include:

- Tax returns
- Bank account statements
- Stock brokerage records
- Financial statements
- Expense records
- Relevant business records
- Deeds
- Insurance policies
- School records
- Health records

Information may also be obtained from third parties in some situations. In these cases, written consent of the other spouse is usually required. Examples of third parties who may have relevant information include accountants, financial advisers, and health-care providers.

## THE DISCOVERY PROCESS

To a large extent, the discovery process is conducted pursuant to the rules of discovery for the jurisdiction in which the case is being tried. This means that the allowed acts are taken without judicial action or involvement, unless something goes wrong such as one party refusing to provide the requested information. The rules tend to be flexible to allow the parties to find out the needed information and recognize the fact that a party may have to change the direction of his or her search based on what is learned during the discovery process. The rules regulating discovery vary by state, which is yet another reminder of why a paralegal student must be aware of the state laws and rules of procedure in his or her state.

The party seeking information notifies the other party, using one of the discovery devices discussed next, that certain information or testimony is requested. The receiving party must respond in a timely manner as set out in the rules of procedure. In the event that the party does not do so, an order to compel may be sought from the court to compel the individual to provide the information or **sanctions** may be sought to punish the party for not providing the information as required by law.

**sanctions**
Penalty against a party in the form of an order to compel, a monetary fine, a contempt-of-court citation, or a court order with specific description of the individualized remedy.

## DISCOVERY DEVICES

As previously mentioned, informal discovery is often used in dissolution of marriage cases and, in some states, the parties are required to provide certain information to the other party under mandatory discovery/disclosure. This does not mean that the other discovery devices provided for under the rules of court are not available.

When needed, all available discovery devices can be used. These include the following.

- **Request for admissions** are written requests for admission of truth about matters that are relevant to the case. If the party does in fact admit that the specific statement is correct, there is no need to prove it at trial. The party also may be deemed to have admitted the truth of a statement by inaction; that is, by failing to file a written response or objection to the questions in the time allowed for by the rules of court. Requests for admissions can only be used with the other party in the divorce action. Unlike the other discovery devices, requests for admission are not intended to obtain information or documents. Instead they are intended to limit the number of things that must be proved at trial. Figure 11.1 contains an example of a sample request for admissions form from North Dakota.

**request for admission (request to admit)**
A document that provides the drafter with the opportunity to conclusively establish selected facts prior to trial.

- **Interrogatories** are a list of written questions that are served on a party that must be answered in writing within the time prescribed by law. Unlike requests for admissions, interrogatories are not asking for an admission as to a fact, but instead are intended to gather specific information in response to the questions presented. They are similar to requests for admission in that interrogatories can only be used with the other party in the divorce action.

  One of the advantages of interrogatories is that they are a relatively inexpensive means of discovery compared with others, such as depositions. The disadvantages

**interrogatory**
A discovery tool in the form of a series of written questions that are answered by the party in writing, to be answered under oath.

**FIGURE 11.1**
**North Dakota Request for Admission Form**

**North Dakota Rules of Civil Procedure**
**FORM 21. REQUEST FOR ADMISSION UNDER RULE 36**

Plaintiff A.B. requests defendant C.D. within _____ days after service of this request to make the following admissions for the purpose of this action only and subject to all pertinent objections to admissibility which may be interposed at the trial:

1. That each of the following documents, exhibited with this request, is genuine.

[Here list the documents and describe each document.]

2. That each of the following statements is true.

[Here list the statements.]

Signed: _____
                    Attorney for Plaintiff

Address: _____

are that they are usually limited in number, you must often use standardized interrogatories, and there is no spontaneity in the questions that are being asked. Figure 11.2 sets out Florida's Standard family law interrogatories.

**RESEARCH THIS**

Research the statutes and rules of court of your state relating to the use of interrogatories in dissolution of marriage cases. Does your state require use of standard interrogatories? If it does, how many questions are included? Can a party add additional questions to those included in the standard interrogatories? If so, how many additional questions can be added?

**ETHICS ALERT**

The discovery process is an important part of civil litigation, including matters relating to family law. Spouses involved in a contested divorce often feel that they are being treated badly by the other spouse in the divorce proceeding or are angry because of the other spouse's actions that led to the divorce. A spouse sometimes uses this feeling to rationalize actions that may be improper, such as withholding information that he or she feels may be detrimental to his or her case. It is important that the paralegal does not get caught up in this deception, such as knowingly including inaccurate information in the documents prepared as part of the discovery process. A paralegal who feels that the client is not being completely honest in his or her disclosures in the discovery process should inform the supervising attorney immediately.

**deposition**
A discovery tool in a question-and-answer format in which the attorney verbally questions a party or a witness under oath.

• **Depositions** are a discovery device that allows the attorney to ask questions of the person being deposed, who in turn must respond under oath. Depositions are usually taken before a court reporter. Some states allow depositions to be taken based on written questions. Although this option may be useful in limited circumstances, oral depositions are more effective. This is because a large part of communication is nonverbal, which is lost when read on a printed page. The expression on a person's face or the tone of his or her voice can be cues to the attorney asking the questions to take a different approach to the questions being asked. This is one of the main advantages of depositions, as is the fact that you can use depositions for gathering information from individuals who are not parties to the action. The disadvantages of depositions are that they are expensive and sometimes difficult to orchestrate.

IN THE CIRCUIT COURT OF THE_____JUDICIAL CIRCUIT,
IN AND FOR_____COUNTY, FLORIDA

Case No.:

Division:

_____,

Petitioner,

and

_____,

Respondent.

**STANDARD FAMILY LAW INTERROGATORIES
FOR ORIGINAL OR ENFORCEMENT PROCEEDINGS**

---

**TO BE COMPLETED BY THE PARTY SERVING THESE INTERROGATORIES**

I am requesting that the following standard questions be answered: [ √ **all** that apply]

| _____1 | _____2 | _____3 | _____4 | _____5 | _____6 | _____7 |
|---|---|---|---|---|---|---|
| Background Information | Education | Employment | Assets | Liabilities | Miscellaneous | Long Form Affidavit |

In addition, I am requesting that the attached {#}_____questions be answered.

---

The answers to the following questions are intended to supplement the information provided in the Financial Affidavits, ❏ Florida Family Law Rules of Procedure Form 12.902(b) or (c). You should answer the group of questions indicated in the above shaded box. The questions should be answered in the blank space provided below each separately numbered question. If sufficient space is not provided, you may attach additional papers with the answers and refer to them in the space provided in the interrogatories. You should be sure to make a copy for yourself. Each question must be answered separately and as completely as the available information permits. All answers are to be made under oath or affirmation as to their truthfulness.

I, {name of person answering interrogatories}_____,
being sworn, certify that the following information is true:

1. **BACKGROUND INFORMATION:**
   a. State your full legal name and any other name by which you have been known.
   b. State your present residence and telephone numbers.
   c. State your place and date of birth.

2. **EDUCATION:**
   a. List all business, commercial, and professional licenses that you have obtained.
   b. List all of your education including, but not limited to, vocational or specialized training, including the following:
      (1) name and address of each educational institution.
      (2) dates of attendance.
      (3) degrees or certificates obtained or anticipated dates of same.

3. **EMPLOYMENT:**
   a. For each place of your employment or self-employment during the last 3 years, state the following:
      (1) name, address, and telephone number of your employer.
      (2) dates of employment.
      (3) job title and brief description of job duties.
      (4) starting and ending salaries.
      (5) name of your direct supervisor.
      (6) all benefits received, including, for example, health, life, and disability insurance; expense account; use of automobile or automobile expense reimbursement; reimbursement for travel, food, or lodging expenses; payment of dues in any clubs or associations; and pension or profit sharing plans.
   b. Other than as an employee, if you have been engaged in or associated with any business, commercial, or professional activity within the last 3 years that was not detailed above, state for each such activity the following:
      (1) name, address, and telephone number of each activity.
      (2) dates you were connected with such activity.
      (3) position title and brief description of activities.
      (4) starting and ending compensation.

*(cont.)*

**FIGURE 11.2**    Florida's Standard Family Law Interrogatories

(5) name of all persons involved in the business, commercial, or professional activity with you.

(6) all benefits and compensation received, including, for example, health, life, and disability insurance; expense account; use of automobile or automobile expense reimbursement; reimbursement for travel, food, or lodging expenses; payment of dues in any clubs or associations; and pension or profit sharing plans.

c. If you have been unemployed at any time during the last 3 years, state the dates of unemployment. If you have not been employed at any time in the last 3 years, give the information requested above in question 3.a for your last period of employment.

4. **ASSETS:**

a. **Real Estate.** State the street address, if any, and if not, the legal description of all real property that you own or owned during the last 3 years.  For each property, state the following:

(1) the names and addresses of any other persons or entities holding any interest and their percentage of interest.

(2) the purchase price, the cost of any improvements made since it was purchased, and the amount of any depreciation taken.

(3) the fair market value on the date of your separation from your spouse.

(4) the fair market value on the date of the filing of the petition for dissolution of marriage.

b. **Tangible Personal Property.** List all items of tangible personal property that are owned by you or in which you have had any interest during the last 3 years including, but not limited to, motor vehicles, tools, furniture, boats, jewelry, art objects or other collections, and collectibles whose fair market value exceeds $100. For each item, state the following:

(1) the percentage and type interest you hold.

(2) the names and addresses of any other persons or entities holding any interest.

(3) the date you acquired your interest.

(4) the purchase price.

(5) the present fair market value.

(6) the fair market value on the date of your separation from your spouse.

(7) the fair market value on the date of the filing of the petition for dissolution of marriage.

c. **Intangible Personal Property.** Other than the financial accounts (checking, savings, money market, credit union accounts, retirement accounts, or other such cash management accounts) listed in the answers to interrogatories 4.d and 4.e below, list all items of intangible personal property that are owned by you or in which you have had any ownership interest (including closed accounts) within the last 3 years, including but not limited to, partnership and business interests (including good will), deferred compensation accounts unconnected with retirement, including but not limited to stock options, sick leave, and vacation pay, stocks, stock funds, mutual funds, bonds, bond funds, real estate investment trust, receivables, certificates of deposit, notes, mortgages, and debts owed to you by another entity or person. For each item, state the following:

(1) the percentage and type interest you hold.

(2) the names and addresses of any other persons or entities holding any interest and the names and addresses of the persons and entities who are indebted to you.

(3) the date you acquired your interest.

(4) the purchase price, acquisition cost, or loaned amount.

(5) the fair market value or the amounts you claim are owned by or owed to you:

(a) presently, at the time of answering these interrogatories.

(b) on the date of your separation from your spouse.

(c) on the date of the filing of the petition for dissolution of marriage.

**You may comply with this interrogatory (4.c) by providing copies of all periodic (monthly, quarterly, semiannual, or annual) account statements for each such account for the preceding 3 years.  However, if the date of acquisition, the purchase price and the market valuations are not clearly reflected in the periodic statements which are furnished then these questions must be answered separately. You do not have to resubmit any periodic statements previously furnished under rule 12.285 (Mandatory Disclosure).**

d. **Retirement Accounts:** List all information regarding each retirement account/plan, including but not limited to defined benefit plans, 401k, 403B, IRA accounts, pension plans, Florida Retirement System plans (FRS), Federal Government plans, money purchase plans, HR10 (Keogh) plans, profit sharing plans, annuities, employee savings plans, etc. that you have established and/or that have been established for you by you, your employer, or any previous employer.  For each account, state the following:

**FIGURE 11.2**   *(continued)*

(1) the name and account number of each account/plan and where it is located.

(2) the type of account/plan.

(3) the name and address of the fiduciary plan administrator/service representative.

(4) the fair market value of your interest in each account/plan.

    (a) present value

    (b) value on the date of separation

    (c) value on the date of filing of the petition for dissolution of marriage

(5) whether you are vested or not vested; and if vested, in what amount, as of a certain date and the schedule of future vesting.

(6) the date at which you became/become eligible to receive some funds in this account/plan.

(7) monthly benefits of the account/plan if no fair market value is ascertained.

(8) beneficiary(ies) and/or alternate payee(s).

e. **Financial Accounts.** For all financial accounts (checking, savings, money market, credit union accounts, or other such cash management accounts) listed in your Financial Affidavit, in which you have had any legal or equitable interest, regardless of whether the interest is or was held in your own name individually, in your name with another person, or in any other name, give the following:

(1) name and address of each institution.

(2) name in which the account is or was maintained.

(3) account numbers.

(4) name of each person authorized to make withdrawals from the accounts.

(5) highest balance within each of the preceding 3 years.

(6) lowest balance within each of the preceding 3 years.

**You may comply with this interrogatory (4.e) by providing copies of all periodic (monthly, quarterly, semi-annual, or annual) account statements for each such account for the preceding 3 years. You do not have to resubmit account statements previously furnished pursuant to rule 12.285 (Mandatory Disclosure).**

f. **Closed Financial Accounts.** For all financial accounts (checking, savings, money market, credit union accounts, or other such cash management accounts) closed within the last 3 years, in which you have had any legal or equitable interest, regardless of whether the interest is or was held in your own name individually, in your name with another person, or in any other name, give the following:

(1) name and address of each institution.

(2) name in which the account is or was maintained.

(3) account numbers.

(4) name of each person authorized to make withdrawals from the accounts.

(5) date account was closed.

g. **Trust.** For any interest in an estate, trust, insurance policy, or annuity, state the following:

(1) If you are the beneficiary of any estate, trust, insurance policy, or annuity, give for each one the following:

    (a) identification of the estate, trust, insurance policy, or annuity.

    (b) the nature, amount, and frequency of any distributions of benefits.

    (c) the total value of the beneficiaries' interest in the benefit.

    (d) whether the benefit is vested or contingent.

(2) If you have established any trust or are the trustee of a trust, state the following:

    (a) the date the trust was established.

    (b) the names and addresses of the trustees.

    (c) the names and addresses of the beneficiaries.

    (d) the names and addresses of the persons or entities who possess the trust documents.

    (e) each asset that is held in each trust, with its fair market value.

h. **Canceled Life Insurance Policies.** For all policies of life insurance within the preceding 3 years that you no longer hold, own, or have any interest in, state the following:

(1) name of company that issued the policy and policy number.

(2) name, address, and telephone number of agent who issued the policy.

(3) amount of coverage.

(4) name of insured.

(5) name of owner of policy.

(6) name of beneficiaries.

(7) premium amount.

(8) date the policy was surrendered.

(9) amount, if any, of monies distributed to the owner.

(*cont.*)

**FIGURE 11.2** (*continued*)

i. **Name of Accountant, Bookkeeper, or Records Keeper.** State the names, addresses, and telephone numbers of your accountant, bookkeeper, and any other persons who possess your financial records, and state which records each possesses.

j. **Safe Deposit Boxes, Lock Boxes, Vaults, Etc.** For all safe deposit boxes, lock boxes, vaults, or similar types of depositories, state the following:

(1) The names and addresses of all banks, depositories, or other places where, at any time during the period beginning 3 years before the initiation of the action, until the date of your answering this interrogatory, you did any of the following:

(a) had a safe deposit box, lock box, or vault.

(b) were a signatory or co-signatory on a safe deposit box, lock box, or vault.

(c) had access to a safe deposit box, lock box, or vault.

(d) maintained property.

(2) The box or identification numbers and the name and address of each person who has had access to any such depository during the same time period.

(3) All persons who have possession of the keys or combination to the safe deposit box, lock box, or vault.

(4) Any items removed from any safe deposit boxes, lock boxes, vaults, or similar types of depositories by you or your agent during that time, together with the present location and fair market value of each item.

(5) All items in any safe deposit boxes, lock boxes, vaults, or similar types of depositories and fair market value of each item.

5. **LIABILITIES:**

a. **Loans, Liabilities, Debts, and Other Obligations.** For all loans, liabilities, debts, and other obligations (other than credit cards and charge accounts) listed in your Financial Affidavit, indicate for each the following:

(1) name and address of the creditor.

(2) name in which the obligation is or was incurred.

(3) loan or account number, if any.

(4) nature of the security, if any.

(5) payment schedule.

(6) present balance and current status of your payments.

(7) total amount of arrearage, if any.

(8) balance on the date of your separation from your spouse.

(9) balance on the date of the filing of the petition for dissolution of marriage.

**You may comply with this interrogatory (5.a) by providing copies of all periodic (monthly, quarterly, semi-annual, or annual) account statements for each such account for the preceding 3 years. You do not have to resubmit account statements previously furnished under rule 12.285 (Mandatory Disclosure).**

b. **Credit Cards and Charge Accounts.** For all financial accounts (credit cards, charge accounts, or other such accounts) listed in your Financial Affidavit, in which you have had any legal or equitable interest, regardless of whether the interest is or was held in your own name individually, in your name with another person, or in any other name, give the following:

(1) name and address of the creditor.

(2) name in which the account is or was maintained.

(3) names of each person authorized to sign on the accounts.

(4) account numbers.

(5) present balance and current status of your payments.

(6) total amount of arrearage, if any.

(7) balance on the date of your separation from your spouse.

(8) balance on the date of the filing of the petition for dissolution of marriage.

(9) highest and lowest balance within each of the preceding 3 years.

**You may comply with this interrogatory (5.b) by providing copies of all periodic (monthly quarterly, semi-annual, or annual) account statements for each such account for the preceding 3 years. You do not have to resubmit account statements previously furnished under rule 12.285 (Mandatory Disclosure).**

c. **Closed Credit Cards and Charge Accounts.** For all financial accounts (credit cards, charge accounts, or other such accounts) closed with no remaining balance, within the last 3 years, in which you have

**FIGURE 11.2**  *(continued)*

had any legal or equitable interest, regardless of whether the interest is or was held in your own name individually, in your name with another person, or in any other name, give the following:
(1) name and address of each creditor.
(2) name in which the account is or was maintained.
(3) account numbers.
(4) names of each person authorized to sign on the accounts.
(5) date the balance was paid off.
(6) amount of final balance paid off.

**You may comply with this interrogatory (5.c) by providing copies of all periodic (monthly, quarterly, semi-annual, or annual) account statements for each such account for the preceding 3 years. You do not have to resubmit account statements previously furnished under rule 12.285 (Mandatory Disclosure).**

6. **MISCELLANEOUS:**
   a. If you are claiming a special equity in any assets, list the asset, the amount claimed as special equity, and all facts upon which you rely in your claim.
   b. If you are claiming an asset or liability is nonmarital, list the asset or liability and all facts upon which you rely in your claim.
   c. If the mental or physical condition of a spouse or child is an issue, identify the person and state the name and address of all health care providers involved in the treatment of that person for said mental or physical condition.
   d. If custody of minor children is an issue, state why, and the facts that support your contention that you should be the primary residential parent or have sole parental responsibility of the child(ren).

7. **LONG FORM AFFIDAVIT:** If you filed the short form affidavit, Florida Family Law Rules of Procedure Form 12.902(b), and you were specifically requested in the Notice of Service of Standard Family Law Interrogatories to file the Long Form Affidavit, Form12.902(c), you must do so within the time to serve the answers to these interrogatories.

I certify that a copy of this document was [√ **one** only] ( ) mailed ( ) faxed and mailed ( ) hand delivered to the person(s) listed below on {date}.

**Other party or his/her attorney:**
Name:
Address:
City, State, Zip:
Fax Number:

**I understand that I am swearing or affirming under oath to the truthfulness of the answers to these interrogatories and that the punishment for knowingly making a false statement includes fines and/or imprisonment.**

Dated:

           Signature of Party
           Printed Name:
           Address:
           City, State, Zip:
           Telephone Number:
           Fax Number:

STATE OF FLORIDA
COUNTY OF

Sworn to or affirmed and signed before me on_____by_____.

        NOTARY PUBLIC or DEPUTY CLERK

        [Print, type, or stamp commissioned name of notary or clerk.]

_____ Personally known
_____ Produced identification
Type of identification produced

**IF A NONLAWYER HELPED YOU FILL OUT THIS FORM, HE/SHE MUST FILL IN THE BLANKS BELOW:** [✍ fill in **all** blanks]
I, {full legal name and trade name of nonlawyer}_____, a nonlawyer, located at {street}_____, {city}_____, {state}_____, {phone}_____, helped {name}_____,
who is the [ √ **one** only] ____ petitioner **or** ____ respondent, fill out this form.

**FIGURE 11.2** (concluded)

In the Court of Appeals of Iowa
No. 4-082 / 03-1285
Filed June 23, 2004
*In Re The Marriage of Marilyn Claire Wofford and Peter Stanley Vonderheide*
Upon the Petition of Marilyn Claire Wofford, Petitioner-Appellant, and Concerning Peter Stanley
Vonderheide, Respondent-Appellee
Appeal from the Iowa District Court for Jefferson County, Daniel P. Wilson, Judge

A wife appeals from an order that allowed the husband to discover information the wife asserts is protected by privilege. **AFFIRMED**.

ZIMMER, J.

Claire Wofford[1] seeks interlocutory review and reversal of a district court discovery order. She contends the order permitted her husband, Peter Vonderheide, to inquire into matters protected by statutory privilege. We affirm the district court.

## I. BACKGROUND FACTS AND PROCEEDINGS

Claire Wofford and Peter Vonderheide married in 1999. Although the couple had no children, Claire has two daughters, A. W. and E. W., from a prior marriage. The girls' father died in January 2002 leaving Claire as the surviving parent with sole legal custody.

In November 2002 Claire asked Peter to leave the family residence, and filed a petition for dissolution of the parties' marriage. The petition alleged Peter had been "sexually abusive with respect to" A. W., then nearly sixteen years old, and E. W., then twelve years old.[2] The petition sought an order requiring Peter to vacate the family residence, as well as a temporary and permanent injunction preventing him from having any contact with Claire, A. W., or E. W. Based on the allegations in her petition, Claire obtained an ex parte order and injunction from the district court barring Peter from the marital home and prohibiting contact with Claire and her daughters.

At the time Claire filed her petition, Peter was working as a teacher at the Maharishi School of the Age of Enlightenment (MSAE). Claire's daughters attend the same school. Soon after the ex parte order and injunction were entered, Claire informed Peter's employer of the allegations of sexual abuse. The school placed Peter on administrative leave.

Claire also contacted the Department of Human Services (DHS) shortly before she filed her petition. A DHS investigation concluded the alleged sexual abuse of Emily was not confirmed. It reached the same conclusion regarding allegations Peter had indecently exposed himself to either girl. However, with regard to A. W., DHS made a founded report of mental injury.

During the course of discovery in the dissolution proceedings, the parties have had several disputes over the extent of the information to which Peter was entitled. Many of the disputes arose over Peter's requests to discover information relating to the sexual abuse allegations. The dispute that gave rise to this appeal concerned whether questions Claire was asked during her deposition inquired into privileged matters. In particular, Claire's attorney and E. W. and A. W.'s guardian ad litem lodged privilege objections to questions regarding communications occurring during counseling sessions with counselor Mike Davis and involving either Claire and Peter, or Claire, E. W. and A. W.; communications during counseling sessions with psychologist Michelle Greene that involved Claire, E. W. and A. W.; a journal A. W. composed in conjunction with counseling; and a meeting at the children's school, MSAE, that involved Claire, Dr. Greene, and school employees.

Peter filed a motion with the court that requested an order compelling testimony in these areas from not only Claire, but also from Davis and Dr. Greene. The district court entered an order that allowed Peter to inquire into the various disputed areas, but provided that information to be elicited from E. W. and A. W. should come from the guardian ad litem. Peter was prohibited from contacting A. W. or E. W. directly. The court appeared to conclude that, to the extent Claire could establish any of the communications were protected by the spousal privilege of Iowa Code section 622.9 (2001), or the physician-patient privilege of section 622.10, the privilege had been abrogated by Iowa Code section 232.74.[3]

After her motion to reconsider the court's order was denied, Claire filed an application for interlocutory appeal. The supreme court granted her application, and the matter comes before us for review. Claire asserts the district court erred in determining that section 232.74 abrogated the privileges of sections 622.9

---

[1] Both parties refer to Marilyn Claire Wofford as "Claire Wofford." For the purpose of this opinion we too will refer to the appellant by her middle, rather than first, name.

[2] Claire alleges that Peter is a sexual addict. She contends that during the course of the marriage on nights when she, Peter and the girls all slept in a "family bedroom," to enable Claire to engage in "nighttime parenting," Peter would masturbate in the couple's raised bed, while the girls were in their own beds nearby. She also contends Peter masturbated over his clothes while in front of the girls, and used pictures of the girls to masturbate at a fertility clinic. She further asserts Peter talked to A. W. while A. W. was wearing only a towel, and would enter the bathroom while A. W. was in the bathtub in order to hand her the phone. Peter disputes these allegations.

[3] The district court's ruling does not contain any definitive findings or conclusions that the matters sought to be discovered by Peter were in fact privileged, under sections 622.9 and 622.10 or any provision of law, or that any such privilege was abrogated by section 232.74. However, reviewing the totality of the court's ruling, it appears the court did conclude that, to the extent any privileges existed, they were abrogated by section 232.74. The court recognized that section 232.74 abrogated any privilege under sections 622.9 and 622.10, and noted that section 232.74 "may result in a waiver" of the privileges asserted by Claire.

and 622.10, and that Peter should accordingly be precluded from inquiring into or otherwise discovering information surrounding the school meeting, A. W.'s journal, and the communications during counseling sessions. Peter contends section 232.74 did abrogate any existing privilege and, alternatively, that privilege was waived.

## II. SCOPE OF REVIEW

We review a district court's statutory interpretation for the correction of errors at law. *In re Marriage of Hutchinson*, 588 N.W.2d 442, 446 (Iowa 1999). We reverse a district court's discovery ruling if it is based on legal error, or the court abused its discretion. *Squealer Feeds v. Pickering*, 530 N.W.2d 678, 681 (Iowa 1995). Abuse occurs if the ruling is based on grounds or reasons clearly untenable or unreasonable. *Id.*

## III. DISCUSSION

Section 232.74 provides:

> Sections 622.9 and 622.10 and any other statute or rule of evidence which excludes or makes privileged the testimony of a husband or wife against the other or the testimony of a health practitioner or mental health professional as to confidential communications, do not apply to evidence regarding a child's injuries or the cause of the injuries in any judicial proceeding, civil or criminal, resulting from a report pursuant to this chapter or relating to the subject matter of such a report.

This section, which seeks to abrogate privilege, must be narrowly construed. *See State v. Anderson*, 636 N.W.2d 26, 35–36 (Iowa 2001).

Upon review of the record we agree with Peter that his requested discovery is pertinent to allegations that he sexually abused his stepdaughters, and thus seeks "evidence regarding a child's injuries or the cause." *See id.* at 36–37. In addition, our supreme court has concluded that "most reports of child abuse will constitute a report under" chapter 232. *Id.* As a report was made in this case that related to the alleged sexual abuse of E. W. and A. W., there has been a qualifying report under chapter 232. *See State v. Spaulding*, 313 N.W.2d 878, 880 (Iowa 1981). The only remaining question is whether this particular dissolution proceeding is one "relating to" the alleged sexual abuse.

Previous cases applying section 232.74 have involved criminal prosecutions for the same allegedly abusive actions that were at the heart of the DHS report. Our supreme court has concluded that such criminal proceedings are ones relating to the alleged child abuse. *See Anderson*, 636 N.W.2d. at 32; *State v. Johnson*, 318 N.W.2d 417, 439 (Iowa 1982). We presume the court would reach the same result regarding a juvenile court action, such as a child in need of assistance proceeding, where the adjudication was dependent upon the alleged abuse reported to DHS. Our supreme court has also indicated that a criminal proceeding may "result from" a DHS report if such a report prompts the filing of criminal charges. *See State v. Jackson*, 383 N.W.2d 578, 581 (Iowa 1986). The common theme, whether the judicial proceeding results from or relates to the subject matter of the report, is that the issues to be resolved by the proceeding hinge on the veracity of the alleged actions giving rise to the report.

It is fair to say that in most instances, section 232.74 will have no application to dissolution proceedings that do not involve issues relating to child custody. As we have already mentioned, E. W. and A. W. are not Peter's children. Accordingly, he has no right to custody, care, or visitation. Moreover, the allegations of sexual abuse in Claire's petition do not have obvious relevance to issues such as division of marital property and alimony, which the district court may need to resolve when dissolving the parties' marriage. Nevertheless, the allegations of sexual abuse have become the focus of these dissolution proceedings because of the allegations in Claire's petition and her request for permanent injunctive relief. The petition for dissolution states,

> [T]he Department of Human Services has instructed the petitioner to seek a no contact order and an order requiring the Respondent to vacate the homestead in lieu of a juvenile action, which they say will be filed if these applications are not made and granted.

The purpose behind chapter 232 is the protection of children, and ensuring their welfare. *See* Iowa Code § 232.1; *State v. Cahill*, 186 N.W.2d 587, 589 (Iowa 1971). We believe section 232.74 seeks to promote that purpose, in cases of alleged abuse, by elevating a full and fair hearing of the issue over statutorily created privileges. *See Miller v. Marshall County*, 641 N.W.2d 742, 748 (Iowa 2002) (citing *Anderson*, 636 N.W.2d at 35) ("In determining the particular meaning of a statutory term, we seek to find a reasonable construction that serves the statute's purpose."). In this case, the district court will be presumably be asked to evaluate disputed claims of sexual abuse, and then determine whether Claire's request for a permanent injunction should be granted. Accordingly, we conclude the district court properly determined that this proceeding is one "relating to" the subject matter of the DHS report, and thus section 232.74 should be applied to abrogate any privileges that might be asserted and proved under sections 622.9 and 622.10.[4] Seeing no legal error by the court, or any demonstrated abuse of discretion, we affirm the district court's discovery order.

AFFIRMED

---

4  Because we conclude the district court properly decided the abrogation issue, we need not address Peter's additional contention that Claire waived any existing privilege. We do note, however, that even the limited record before us reveals evidence Claire consented to the disclosure of at least some of the communications that she now asserts are subject to privilege.

**Source:** Retrieved from www.judicial.state.ia.us/court_of_appeals/recent_opinions/20040623/03-1285.asp.

**FIGURE 11.3**

**Examples of Documents That May Be Included in a Request for Production**

**request for production of documents (request to produce)**
A discovery device that requests the production of certain items, such as photographs, papers, reports, and physical evidence; must specify the document sought.

- Financial statements
- Bank statements, net worth statements, stockbroker statements, dividend statements and statements from similar accounts
- Copies of federal and state tax returns (including attachments)
- Copies of insurance policies
- Copies of deeds and tax appraisal of property
- Copies of trust documents
- Copies of promissory notes
- Inventory of special value, such as fine art, jewelry and stocks/bonds
- Relevant business documents
- Copies of documents relating to retirement plan(s)

- **Request for production of documents** is a discovery device that allows an attorney to obtain documents, even those in the possession of individuals or entities who are not a party to the action. This procedure can be very helpful in obtaining documents such as business records, financial information in possession of nonparties, and income tax filings. Figure 11.3 contains a list of examples of what documents might be requested. Figure 11.4 contains the North Dakota request for admission form.

---

**North Dakota Rules of Civil Procedure**
**FORM 20. MOTION FOR PRODUCTION OF DOCUMENTS, ETC. UNDER RULE 34**

Plaintiff A.B. moves the court for an order requiring defendant C.D.

(1) To produce and to permit plaintiff to inspect and to copy each of the following documents:

[Here list the documents and describe each of them.]

(2) To produce and permit plaintiff to inspect and to photograph each of the following objects:

[Here list the objects and describe each of them]

(3) To permit plaintiff to enter [here describe property to be entered ] and to inspect and to photograph [here describe the portion of the real property and the objects to be inspected and photographed ].

(4) To file a verified list of (a) any designated documents, papers, accounts, books, letters, photographs, objects, or tangible things not privileged which are or have been in his possession, custody, or control, relevant to the subject matter of the pending action, whether it relates to the claim or defense of the plaintiff or to the claim or defense of any other party, and (b) the identity and location of persons having knowledge of relevant facts.

Defendant C.D. has the possession, custody, or control of each of the foregoing specified documents and objects and of the above mentioned real estate. Each of them constitutes or contains evidence relevant and material to a matter involved in this action, as is more fully shown in Exhibit 1 hereto attached.

Defendant C.D. possesses information pertaining to the matters set forth in paragraph (4) above.

Signed: _____
Attorney for Plaintiff

Address: _____
NOTICE OF MOTION

[Contents the same as in Form 14]

EXHIBIT 1

STATE OF NORTH DAKOTA,   )
                            )
County of _____           )

A.B., being duly sworn says:

(1) [Here set forth all that plaintiff knows which shows that defendant has the papers or objects in his possession or control.]

(2) Here set forth all that plaintiff knows which shows that each of the above mentioned items is relevant to some issue in the action.]

[Jurat]

Signed: A.B.

---

**FIGURE 11.4** North Dakota Motion for Production of Documents

*Source:* Retrieved from www.court.state.nd.us/court/rules/civil/form20.htm

**FIGURE 11.5**
**North Dakota Rule of Civil Procedure on Physical and Mental Exams of Persons**

### RULE 35. PHYSICAL AND MENTAL EXAMINATION OF PERSONS

**(a) Order for Examination.** If the mental or physical condition (including the blood group) of a party, or a person in the custody or under the legal control of a party, is in controversy, the court in which the action is pending may order the party to submit to a physical or mental examination by a suitably licensed or certified examiner or to produce for examination the person in the party's custody or legal control. The order may be made only on motion for good cause shown and upon notice to the person to be examined and to all parties and must specify the time, place, manner, conditions, and scope of the examination and the person or persons by whom it is to be made.

**(b) Report of Examiner.**

(1) If requested by the party against whom an order is made under Rule 35(a) or the person examined, the party causing the examination to be made shall deliver to the requestor a copy of a detailed written report of the examiner setting out the examiner's findings, including results of all tests made, diagnoses and conclusions, together with like reports of all earlier examinations of the same condition. After delivery the party causing the examination is entitled upon request to receive from the party against whom the order is made a like report of any examination, previously or thereafter made, of the same condition, unless, in the case of a report of examination of a person not a party, the party shows inability to obtain it. The court on motion may make an order against a party requiring delivery of a report on such terms as are just, and if an examiner fails or refuses to make a report the court may exclude the examiner's testimony if offered at the trial.

(2) By requesting and obtaining a report of the examination so ordered or by taking the deposition of the examiner, the party examined waives any privilege the party may have in that action or any other involving the same controversy, regarding the testimony of every other person who has examined or may thereafter examine him in respect of the same mental or physical condition.

(3) This subdivision applies to examinations made by agreement of the parties, unless the agreement expressly provides otherwise. This subdivision does not preclude discovery of a report of an examiner or the taking of a deposition of the examiner in accordance with the provisions of any other rule.

---

- **Request for medical examination** is the method to obtain physical and psychiatric information that is relevant to a case and involves an element of the cause of action that is contained in the pleadings of the parties. It can be used for the examination of a party and of those who are in the custody or legal control of the party. Figure 11.5 contains the North Dakota rule regarding the physical or mental examination of persons, which is substantially the same as Rule 35 of the Federal Rules of Civil Procedure.

  This form of discovery is also available for examination of children in some cases. For example, when a child's health is at issue, such as special need that may require a higher amount of child support payment than that allowed under the state's child support guidelines, this form of discovery is appropriate. It should be noted that courts are reluctant to order such an examination without a showing of not only a need, but also that it is in the child's best interest that it take place.

**request for medical examination**
Form of discovery that requests a medical examination of an opposing party in a lawsuit.

**CASE BRIEF ASSIGNMENT**

Read and brief the *In Re The Marriage of Wofford,* 2004 WL 1396271 (Iowa App.Ct. 2004) case. (See Appendix A for information on how to brief cases.)

## DISCOVERY FROM NONPARTIES

Discovery is not limited to the parties themselves, as was demonstrated in the discussion of informal discovery. Formal discovery may also involve obtaining information from third parties. A subpoena is usually required to obtain information from these parties, as well as to take third parties' depositions.

**FIGURE 11.6**
**Examples of Privileged Information**

- Attorney/client information
- Attorney work product
- Physician/patient information
- Psychiatrist/psychotherapist and patient information
- Information that would be potentially incriminating

## PROTECTIVE ORDERS

**privilege**
Reasonable expectation of privacy and confidentiality for communications in furtherance of the relationship such as attorney–client, doctor–patient, husband–wife, psychotherapist–patient, and priest–penitent.

**protective order**
Court order limiting discovery by a party.

Courts generally give parties broad discretion in what information can be obtained in the discovery process. The reason for this is that each party in an adversarial proceeding, such as a contested divorce, should be allowed every reasonable opportunity to obtain relevant information that can aid in the preparation of his or her case. This is not to say that a party has unlimited access to information. As a general rule, the information sought must be relevant to the case, reasonably calculated to obtain evidence that will be admissible at trial, and not **privileged**. Figure 11.6 provides examples of privileged information.

If parties feel that they are being asked to produce information, or answer questions, about matters that are not proper, they may seek a protective order from the court. A **protective order** is a means for courts to limit or prohibit discovery for a variety of reasons, such as it is irrelevant to the case, or it requests privileged information. It may also be used in cases where the discovery process is being abused in some way, such as when it is burdensome and unduly expensive. See *In Re The Marriage of Wofford,* set out in the earlier Case In Point, to see how one court dealt with an issue relating to a claim of statutory privilege.

## SANCTIONS

If a party fails to comply with one of the forms of discovery discussed in this chapter, a court order can be sought ordering the noncomplying party to comply with the requested discovery. If the party fails to comply with the terms of the order, the court has wide latitude to impose any sanction it deems appropriate. Examples of sanctions that can be imposed include:

- Contempt of court
- Award of fees and court costs
- Order denying the noncomplying party the ability to support/oppose the claims or defenses that were the subject of the discovery
- Order striking pleading of nonconforming party
- Order to dismiss
- Order requiring payment of reasonable expenses, including attorney fees, incurred because of the failure to comply with the discovery request.
- Order barring the noncomplying party from making a claim
- Order barring party from admitting certain evidence
- Order to stay proceedings until discovery is complied with

See the *Meier v. Meier* case in the following Case In Point for more on when a motion to compel should be granted.

## ROLE OF PARALEGAL IN DISCOVERY PROCESS

The paralegal plays a very important role in the completion of the discovery process. It is for this reason that it is essential the paralegal understand the applicable rules of court and statutes that relate to it. Examples of the duties a paralegal might be called upon to perform include:

District Court of Appeal of Florida, Third District
*Meier v. Meier*
No. 3D02-2900
Jan. 29, 2003

PER CURIAM.

Petitioner Lotti Meier seeks certiorari review of the trial court's denial of her motion to compel counsel for her former husband to produce discovery documents for an in-camera inspection. We grant the petition.

The wife filed for dissolution of marriage in 2001. Shortly after the wife filed for divorce, the husband respondent Jurg Andreas Meier moved to his native Switzerland where he now resides.

On three separate occasions, the trial court ordered the husband to produce certain documents. The husband did not comply with the discovery orders and the trial court struck his pleadings and entered a default against him. Subsequently, the wife learned that the husband had provided discovery documentation to his counsel and had also instructed him not to release the documentation to the wife, to return the documentation to him. The wife again moved to compel the production of documents and to compel the husband's counsel to produce the documentation to the trial court for an in-camera inspection. The trial court denied the motion finding that it did not have the authority to order the husband's counsel to turn over the documents against the will of his client, and thereby subject the husband's counsel to a disciplinary action. The documentation the wife seeks remains in the possession of the husband's counsel.

Rule 4-3.4(d), Rules Regulating the Florida Bar, prohibits the intentional failure to comply with a discovery request.

Rule 4-3.4 provides, in pertinent part,

A lawyer shall not:

(c) knowingly disobey an obligation under the rules of a tribunal except for an open refusal based on an assertion that no valid obligation exists.

(d) in pretrial procedure, make a frivolous discovery request or *intentionally fail to comply with a legally proper discovery request by an opposing party.*

(emphasis added).

Rule 4-3.4(a), Rules Regulating the Florida Bar, also prohibits a lawyer's unlawful obstruction of another party's access to evidence and the concealment of a document or other material that the lawyer knows or reasonably should know is relevant to a pending proceeding.

The husband in this case has failed to comply with several orders of discovery and the husband's counsel plainly has the ability to do so. The wife seeks the discoverable documentation to determine the extent of the parties' assets and she is unlikely to obtain the documents' equivalent through other means. Under these circumstances, the husband's conduct constitutes an unjustified and deliberate disregard of the court's authority. The husband's counsel's obligation to comply with the orders is thus absolute. To hold otherwise not only disregards the authority of a court, but defies the importance of promoting the truth-seeking function of the discovery rules.

We therefore quash the order under review. Counsel for the husband is to release the documentation in his possession to the trial court for an in-camera review.

Petition granted.

- Gather information from the client, including taking notes at the initial interview. This may include information that will be provided to the other party as part of the discovery process.
- Draft documents such as interrogatories, request for production, and so on.
- Maintain files associated with material obtained during the discovery process.
- Maintain calendar of important dates, including tickler system for items such as when documents must be responded to, deadlines, date and time of depositions, dates of hearings, and so on.
- Select and schedule court reporters.
- Schedule depositions.
- Assist in the preparation of witnesses for depositions.

**CASE BRIEF ASSIGNMENT**

Read and brief the *Meier v. Meier*, 835 So.2d 379 (Fla. Dist.Ct.App. 2003) case. (See Appendix A for information on how to brief cases.)

- Assist in the selection of expert witnesses such as physicians or other medical professionals to conduct examinations.
- Maintain and organize information obtained in the discovery process.

## Summary

Discovery is a very important tool available to attorneys attempting to learn as much as possible about the facts surrounding the client's case. There is an old saying that, during a trial, an attorney should never ask a witness a question that he or she does not know the answer to before it is asked. Although there may be times this is not true, it is certainly good advice, and the way to learn what the witness's answer should be is through the use of discovery.

As stated in the "Why This Chapter Is Important to the Paralegal Student" section above, Chapter 11 is not intended to provide detailed coverage of the discovery process. That is best left to the civil litigation class. Instead this chapter has given the paralegal student an idea of the process and also some of the things that are a little different in a dissolution of marriage case.

## Key Terms

Deposition

Discovery

Interrogatory

Privilege

Protective order

Request for admissions

Request for medical examination

Request for production of documents

Sanctions

## Review Questions

1. What is discovery and why is it important in the family law firm?
2. What role does the paralegal play in the discovery process?
3. What is informal discovery and how does it differ from more formal discovery methods?
4. What is the advantage(s) of informal discovery?
5. What is the difference between interrogatories and depositions?
6. What is an advantage of interrogatories? What is a disadvantage of interrogatories?
7. What are the advantages of depositions? What are the disadvantages of depositions?
8. How are requests for admissions used in the discovery process?
9. How are requests for production of documents used in the discovery process?
10. What are some of the documents that may be requested using a request for production?
11. What is a protective order and when is it used?
12. What is privileged information?
13. What sanctions can be imposed for failure to comply with a request for discovery?
14. What are standard interrogatories?
15. Is discovery limited to the parties in the case?

## Exercises

1. Locate the applicable court rules/statutes dealing with discovery in your state. Prepare a set of interrogatories to be used in the Manchester divorce case from the Client Interview. Keep in mind that your firm represents Georgia Manchester.

2. Prepare a motion for production of documents for use in the Manchester case. The motion should include any documents that you feel need to be obtained from Edwin. The motion should comply with the applicable rules and statutes of your state.

3. List and discuss what job duties you may be called upon to perform if you are the paralegal working on the Manchester divorce case.

4. Assume that the attorney for Edwin Manchester refuses to produce a financial affidavit, which Edwin recently prepared for a bank loan, in defiance of a motion for production of documents. What steps would need to be taken to require the production of the document? What sanctions might be appropriate in this situation?

5. Edwin Manchester's attorney has filed a motion for production of documents that included a request for an interoffice memorandum of law prepared by you on behalf of your firm's client, Georgia Manchester. This memorandum was intended for use by your supervising attorney to aid in preparing Georgia's case. Research the statutory and case law of your state and determine whether the memorandum is discoverable. Explain what steps could be taken to prevent the production of this document.

## REAL WORLD DISCUSSION TOPICS

Maud and Tom were married for about three years before Maud filed for divorce. They had one child who was 2 years old at the time of the filing. Maud's petition requested an equitable distribution of the parties' property and for support of herself and the couple's child.

In response to these discovery requests, Tom furnished information pertaining to two family trusts, for one of which he is the sole income beneficiary and the other that provides for an equal income distribution between Tom and his sisters. He also made reference to "other trusts in which respondent is a discretionary distributee." Copies of the text of these nine "other trusts" were attached as an exhibit to Tom's answer to Maud's request, but he did not provide details on things like the current market value of the trusts, the distribution of the trusts, or income made to the beneficiaries.

Tom maintained that the information sought about the trusts was irrelevant because his beneficial interests were created by inheritance or gift, the trusts were not subject to division upon the divorce nor to disposition by the court in connection with Maud's claims for support.

Tom sought and received a protective order to prevent discovery of this information. Was the court correct in granting the protective order? Why or why not? *See In re Marriage of Meredith,* 394 N.W.2d 336 (Ia. 1986)

## PORTFOLIO ASSIGNMENTS

1. Research the state laws and court rules of your state. Locate and identify statutes and rules that deal with the discovery process. Does your state have specific rules for discovery in dissolution of marriage actions? If so, how does it differ from the general rules of discovery in your state? If your state does not have specific rules, where are your state's general rules of discovery located? Write a summary of your findings.

2. Based on your research in Assignment 1, the material contained in this chapter, and any other research you determine to be needed, write a paper setting out the discovery methods you would use in the case of Georgia Manchester and explain why you selected them.

# Chapter 12

# Negotiations, Hearings, and Trials

## CHAPTER OBJECTIVES

**After reading this chapter and completing the assignments, you should be able to:**

- Demonstrate an understanding of the difference between jury and nonjury trials.

- Understand the difference between a hearing and a trial.

- Understand what takes place in an uncontested final hearing in a dissolution of marriage case.

- Demonstrate an understanding of the steps in a disputed dissolution of marriage case.

- Understand the role of the paralegal in hearings and trials.

- Discuss the purpose of alternative dispute resolution methods in the divorce process.

- Understand the negotiation process and its use to avoid the need for an adversarial hearing or trial.

- Describe the drafting process of a separation agreement and the paralegal's role in its drafting.

---

Chapter 12 introduces the paralegal student to the next stage of the divorce process, the steps required to obtain a final judgment. How this final judgment is obtained varies depending on whether the divorce is uncontested or contested. Judgment in an uncontested divorce is simpler and obtained in a final hearing in which a judge issues the order granting the divorce. Contested divorces are more complicated and are similar to other forms of civil litigation. Negotiation is often used to try to work out as many areas of disagreement as possible.

Courts are also increasingly requiring parties to use some form of alternative dispute resolution method prior to going to trial. One of the more popular methods is mediation, where an independent person attempts to help the parties resolve their issues without going to trial. If they are successful, the parties enter into a separation

## CLIENT INTERVIEW

Sandy and Cramer Robinson were married for 15 years. During that time they prospered financially. They owned a home, some rental property, and a sizable stock portfolio. They had one child, Travis, who is 6. Everything seemed great in their marriage until Sandy found out that Cramer was having an affair with another woman. She came to your law firm to file for divorce and her case was assigned to your supervising attorney, George Wilson. Cramer hired James Cutthroat, one of the other top family law attorneys in town, who is known for his ruthless representation of his clients in divorce cases.

Despite the early contentiousness between the parties and their attorneys, Mr. Wilson and Mr. Cutthroat were able to work out a settlement agreement that seemed to be fair to both parties.

With the final draft of the agreement in hand, Mr. Wilson reviewed its contents with Sandy. Sandy was agreeable to everything but said she wanted one more clause added to the agreement. It was to require that the husband return a swimsuit he had bought for his girlfriend with a credit card that was in the name of Sandy and Cramer Robinson.

This was the first Mr. Wilson had heard of this issue. He explained that the terms of the agreement were very difficult to reach with the other attorney and that any attempt at changing it at this point may cause her husband to decide not to sign the agreement. He also pointed out how expensive going to trial would be and that he had no idea how the judge would rule in the case if it went to trial.

Sandy said she didn't care; she wanted the swimsuit back or she would go to trial.

agreement that is ultimately included as part of the judge's final order of dissolution of marriage.

If resolution is not possible, a contested trial is held after which a judge, or in some cases a judge and jury, hear and resolve the case.

## WHY THIS CHAPTER IS IMPORTANT TO THE PARALEGAL

This chapter introduces the paralegal student to a critical stage of the divorce process, the hearings and trial that bring it to an end. Just as important, however, is that it provides the paralegal student with valuable information on the vital role he or she will play in these last steps in finalizing a divorce. The paralegal will be called upon to assist in drafting documents needed to finalize the divorce and also perform many of the tasks associated with civil litigation paralegals. It is important for paralegal students to become familiar with the law related to this stage of the divorce process and the duties they may be called upon to perform.

## ALTERNATIVE DISPUTE RESOLUTION

The court system has been increasingly overwhelmed by the sheer number of divorces that are filed each year. Certainly the advent of no fault divorces and court-provided "do-it-yourself" divorce document packets have streamlined the divorce procedures in many cases, but there is still a logjam of divorce cases clogging up the system in many states. This has caused courts to come up with alternatives intended to reduce court intervention in resolving the issues related to divorce. This is known as **alternative dispute resolution (ADR)**. A wide variety of methods are included under this broad term, including negotiation, arbitration, and mediation.

**alternative dispute resolution (ADR)**
Method of settling a dispute before trial in order to conserve the court's time.

## NEGOTIATIONS

The old saying a bird in the hand is worth two in the bush means that it is sometimes better to know what you are going to get rather than hope for getting more at a later date. This can be an important concept for clients to understand when it comes to dissolution of marriage actions. As has been mentioned previously in this book, it is usually better for the parties to negotiate a settlement of as many of the disputed items in their divorce as possible, instead of leaving it up to a decision of a judge. Knowing what a party will get, even if it is less than he or she may want, may be better than the uncertainties of what the judge may award.

In fact, many, if not most, cases are settled between the parties rather than going to trial. This is an advantage to all involved, including an overtaxed court system that is struggling to come up with ways to handle the increased caseload it is experiencing. Settlements can be reached at a variety of stages in the dissolution process. The parties may have reached an agreement on all or most of the terms prior to going to their attorneys. This makes an attorney's job much easier. He or she can then focus on examining the terms of the agreement, explaining the consequences of what has been agreed to, and advising the client of his or her rights if an agreement is not reached.

Sometimes the parties cannot reach an agreement for a wide variety of reasons. One of the most common is that they just can't calmly communicate anymore. Their emotions get in the way of seeing what may be best in the long term. The Robinsons are an example of a couple who could not work out their disagreements. They needed their attorneys to help guide them through the divorce process, ensure that their rights were protected, and reach a fair settlement agreement.

**negotiation**
Bargaining process by which parties resolve issues that exist between them.

As is true in the discovery process, the **negotiation** process can be relatively informal between the parties' attorneys or it may be more formal in nature. In any case, the information obtained during discovery is critical in the negotiation process. A settlement agreement should not be entered into until the attorney and client have enough information to make an informed decision. They need to know as much as possible about the overall situation in the case so they will know what will constitute a fair settlement agreement. This includes both favorable and unfavorable information about the parties. Too often a client tells the attorney what he or she thinks the attorney wants to hear, omitting things that may cast the client in an unfavorable light. The attorneys in the Robinson case were certainly unaware of at least one very emotional item of contention.

The starting point for understanding both the case and the client's desires is the initial client interview. Although the paralegal may be present at the initial interview, and subsequently obtain preliminary information from the client, the attorney usually conducts the interview if it looks like the case will be a contested dissolution action. The attorney can make sure that he or she understands the client's position in the case and can give some initial indication of how the case will proceed and its possible outcome. This first meeting is also an opportunity for the attorney and paralegal to evaluate the client and start to establish a rapport with him or her.

Negotiations begin once attorneys feel that they have adequate information to understand what would constitute a reasonable agreement based on the facts of the case and the law. The attorneys may decide to break down their negotiations based on subject matter. Child custody, visitation, coparenting, and so on present different issues than the negotiation of alimony or other money matters. This approach also may increase the possibility of beginning to agree on some matters and leaving more contentious matters to future negotiations. If the negotiations start with the more contentious issues, the client often reacts in an emotional way, thereby increasing the chance the negotiation process will not continue or, if it does, that the parties will be unwilling to compromise as much as they would have otherwise.

The negotiations between the attorneys may take place with or without the clients present. The attorneys may wish to discuss the case without the clients present because of the animosity that exists between the parties and the attorneys' desire to focus on the case in an unemotional way. Ultimately, however, the client will need to be fully informed of what was discussed and agree to the terms that will be incorporated in the agreement. The meeting, or meetings, may take place over the phone or in person. As the Robinson case demonstrates, even a well-negotiated agreement may fall apart for some unforeseen reason.

If the attorneys decide to take a more formal approach to the negotiations, the procedure is a little more complicated. The attorneys will need to agree to a number of items to facilitate a well-organized and productive meeting. An agenda may be used to ensure that both sides understand and agree to the sequence of the meeting. If the clients will be attending the meeting, it may be advisable to agree to ground rules to avoid any hostility or impoliteness between the attendees. It is difficult to reach an agreement, which is the purpose of the meeting, if emotions get in the way.

Ultimately the process may or may not produce an agreement that resolves all issues between the parties. If some matters can be resolved, a partial settlement agreement can be reached, leaving the court to resolve those items that could not be agreed to. In some cases, negotiators fail completely and no agreement can be reached. Keep in mind, however, that the parties can resume negotiations at any time and may desire to do so as the time for trial approaches.

## MEDIATION

**Mediation** is a means of using a third party, the mediator, to help the parties reach an agreement on as many issues as possible in a less formal and less adversarial proceeding. It is increasingly being used in dissolution cases. The **mediator** is not sitting as a judge in the proceeding; rather, he or she attempts to aid the parties in identifying the issues they have and move them toward reaching an agreement on those issues whenever possible. Like the negotiation process, mediation may take more than one meeting to produce results. Also like negotiation, the goal is for the parties to reach an informed agreement of their differences that they decide is fair.

More broadly, mediation provides a way to encourage communication between the parties by removing the hostility that exists between them. The focus is on allowing the parties to exercise joint control over the decision-making process needed to end their marriage. The mediator also encourages the parties to resolve highly sensitive issues such as child custody and visitation. Courts may require or strongly encourage mediation and provide for court-connected mediation services, or the parties themselves may agree to mediation and seek out a private mediator.

Whether mediation is a viable alternative to going to trial largely depends on the parties themselves. The possibility of a successful mediation is directly related to the willingness and ability of the parties to discuss their differences and work out a meaningful compromise. This involves making trade-offs, as is the case in all negotiations. If one or both parties are unwilling to compromise, there is little likelihood of mediation being successful.

States vary on the role of attorneys in the mediation process. In some states, mediation can take place with or without legal counsel. In others, the attorney acts more in the role of a consultant to the client to answer questions as the process proceeds. Although not having attorneys present does help create a less formal atmosphere that can be beneficial to the mediator when he or she is attempting to guide the parties to agreement, it does present the possibility of a party making an agreement without a full awareness of his or her rights and the possibility the final agreement will not be fair. Even when attorneys are present, the parties themselves are the main participants in trying to reach an agreement.

**mediation**
The process of submitting a claim to a neutral third party who then makes a determination about the ultimate liability and award in a civil case.

**mediator**
Individual who facilitates a resolution by the parties using methods designed to facilitate the parties' reaching a negotiated resolution.

## ARBITRATION

**arbitration**
Alternative dispute resolution method mediated or supervised by a neutral third party who imposes a recommendation for resolution, after hearing evidence from both parties and the parties participated in reaching, that is fully enforceable and treated in the courts the same as a judicial order.

**Arbitration** is a form of ADR in which the arbitrator hears the case in much the same way as a judge does. The arbitrator, who is often an attorney or retired judge, conducts an initial hearing on the unresolved matters in the case and hears evidence from both parties. Based on the evidence presented at the hearing, the arbitrator makes findings, referred to as an *arbitration award*. The findings can be either binding or nonbinding. In binding arbitration, the ruling of the arbitrator is filed in the case and treated by the courts the same as a judicial order, unless one party appeals the decision to the court. Paralegals must become familiar with the laws of their state governing arbitration in dissolution of marriage proceedings.

Whatever form of ADR is used, it can result in the resolution of key issues between the parties. This results in savings of time and money to all involved.

## MAGISTRATES

In yet another way to try to deal with the large caseload of divorce cases, some states are now using magistrates to hear these cases. In fact the use of magistrates, sometimes referred to as *referees* or *masters,* has become common in many jurisdictions. A magistrate is an officer of the court who is appointed to fill the role of a judge for a specific purpose or case. He or she conducts hearings in the same manner as a judge and hears evidence relating to the case. Upon completion of the hearing, the magistrate files findings of fact, conclusions of law, and recommendations with the court. The report is reviewed by the judge, who has the ultimate power to decide how the case will be resolved. The judge will have a hearing on any objections/exceptions to the magistrate's recommendation if they are raised by either party prior to the judge making a final ruling. Figure 12.1 sets out the sequence in cases in which a magistrate is used.

### RESEARCH THIS

Research the laws of your state relating to alternative dispute resolution and the use of magistrates in dissolution of marriage cases. Which ADRS are used in your state? Are any mandatory? Are magistrates used? If so, when are they used, and what procedures are followed in conducting the hearings? How are objections/exceptions made?

**FIGURE 12.1**
**Sequence of a Case Heard by a Magistrate**

A typical sequence in a case that is heard by a magistrate is as follows:
- Case is referred to magistrate by judge.
- Notice of hearing is issued and served on all parties.
- Hearing is held by magistrate. The magistrate has the power to hear evidence and examine witnesses under oath in a manner that is similar to other court hearings. The magistrate also has the power to issue subpoenas compelling attendance of witnesses and the production of documents and other physical evidence relating to the case.
- Written report is issued and sent to the judge who referred the case to the magistrate. The report is also provided to all parties in the action. It includes the magistrate's findings and recommendations.
- Magistrate's report is reviewed by the court to ensure that there was sufficient evidence to support recommendations.
- The court will hold a hearing to allow either or both parties to present arguments contesting all or parts of the magistrate's report.
- Final decree is entered by court, which includes findings of fact and law.

## HEARINGS AND TRIALS

The words *hearing* and *trial* are often used interchangeably, even among legal professionals. This is all right in everyday conversations but it is important to keep in mind that they do usually refer to different things.

Hearings are conducted to handle interim matters, such as motions for temporary child support, or after final resolution of a case, such as motions to change child custody. Hearings are held in front of the judge, who makes a ruling on the issues brought before him or her by one of the parties to the legal proceeding.

Trials are the end of the legal process initiated by a petition, such as a petition for dissolution of marriage. There are jury trials and nonjury trials, which are sometimes referred to as a **bench trial**. In a jury trial, the judge acts as the **trier of law**, resolving issues relating to things like the admissibility of evidence, and the jury acts as the **trier of fact**, deciding issues such as guilt of the defendant in a criminal case.

Now, what about divorce trials—are they jury trials or nonjury trials? As with most things discussed previously in this textbook, the answer to this question depends on the state in which the action is taking place.

Divorce actions were historically viewed as **equity** cases. As a result, there was no right to a jury trial. Instead, the judge acted as both the trier of fact and the trier of law.

Today, states vary on whether a divorce case can be a jury trial or a nonjury trial. Many states, if not most, do not allow for a person to request a jury trial in a dissolution of marriage action. Other states allow such a request and allow the jury to resolve some matters. These states may specify the right to a jury trial in their rules of court, their statutes, and/or their state constitution.

Independent of whether a trial by jury is allowed, the question of going to trial is a serious one and one that the attorneys in the case usually work diligently to avoid. Trials typically result because one party does not want to compromise on a specific point, such as Sandy Robinson in the Client Interview, or is overly confident he or she will win.

Let's use the Robinson case as an example of the problems attorneys face in divorce cases. Emotions run very high and there are often deep feelings that prevent the client from seeing the big picture of what will possibly occur or, even if the client is aware of it, as was the case with Sandy Robinson, the client might not care about the risks associated with going to trial. So what would the attorneys do in a situation like the Robinson's case? There obviously was a desire on the part of the parties and their attorneys to reach a settlement of the case and take the decision-making process out of the judge's hands. One option would be for Mr. Wilson to call Mr. Cutthroat and see whether his client would be willing to produce the trouble-causing swimsuit. Mr. Cutthroat would undoubtedly have a similar conversation with his client as Mr. Wilson had with Sandy. He would explain the extra costs involved with going to trial and the fact that one never knows what a judge may due in a particular case. Perhaps Mr. Robinson would be less concerned over the swimsuit and more concerned over the issues brought up by his attorney.

Settlements can be reached at any time before trial, including just before entering the courtroom in which the trial is scheduled to be held. In fact, settlements are sometimes reached during a break in the trial itself! Last-minute settlements are not uncommon, and paralegals may be called upon to help draft a last-minute settlement agreement. Most likely there will already be several drafts of proposed settlement agreements to use as a starting point for completing the final agreement.

The need to be careful about what is agreed to in a settlement agreement, as well as the need to seek advice from an attorney before signing one, is demonstrated in the *Galloway v. Galloway* case discussed in the following Case in Point.

**bench trial**
A case heard and decided by a judge.

**trier of law**
Judge.

**trier of fact**
Jury.

**equity**
The doctrine of fairness and justice; the process of making things balance or be equal between parties.

Court of Appeals of Virginia
*Galloway v. Galloway*
Record No. 0468-05-1
Nov. 29, 2005

The parties were married June 1, 1984, and separated on October 1, 2001. There were no children born or adopted of this marriage.

At marriage, husband worked in civil service at Fort Eustis. After leaving that position in 1988, husband started his own business, Cassenvey Heating, Air Conditioning and Refrigeration, Ltd. From its inception, husband was, and continued to be, the sole stockholder and president of this business. For the first five years, husband worked alone.

At marriage, wife was employed as a nurse's aide at Eastern State Hospital where she had worked since approximately January of 1973. She retired from Eastern State Hospital July 31, 1993, after nine years of marriage to husband. At that time, she began working at Cassenvey Heating, Air Conditioning and Refrigeration, Ltd. as a secretary. Within a few months, wife began installing heating and air conditioning in the field. Wife worked for husband continuously from 1993 until six months before the April 20, 2004, commissioner's hearing.

During their eleven years employed together, both parties worked to expand the business, with its gross receipts for 2002 reaching over $1,000,000. This figure was twice that of the gross receipts for 2001. At the time of the commissioner's hearing, husband drew $900 per week from the business.

In February of 1984 and prior to the June 1, 1984, marriage, husband purchased and titled in his own name the marital home property located on a 3.5-acre tract. As a wedding present, wife gave husband a contiguous parcel containing .9 acre. The record is silent as to the value of this property at the time of the commissioner's hearing. Husband purchased a third contiguous 2-acre parcel sometime in 1994 or 1995. After the parties separated, husband sold the 2-acre parcel for $80,000, netting $18,000.

Since the business and the marital property were located on the 3.5-acre parcel, husband had the business and real property appraised as a unit in 2003 for a total of $200,000. Husband testified that if he sold the business and the home, he would ask between $200,000 and $250,000. The appraisal included shop tools and equipment worth $60,000. Additionally, the business owned three vehicles valued at $15,000, had accounts receivable between $2,000 and $7,000, and a business checking account of approximately $1,000.

The balance due on the loan for the house and business was $87,000 at the time of the commissioner's hearing. The fair market value of the residence at the time of separation was $60,000.

In 2000, wife's father died and she inherited his debt-free residence valued at $275,000, along with $30,000 in cash.

At the end of September 2001, husband brought to wife a property settlement agreement prepared by his attorney that granted him all of the interest in the marital residence and the business. Wife would receive a 1999 GMC Chevy pickup truck, valued at the time of settlement at $11,000. Each party waived spousal support and any interest in the other party's pension accounts. Each party received some personal property but the record does not disclose any value. Husband also agreed to pay wife $400 per week as an employee of the business "for as long as the parties are husband and wife" and to pay her hospitalization while she was so employed.

Prior to having the agreement drafted, husband and wife had discussed the terms of the agreement. Husband brought the agreement to wife's apartment the night before it was executed. Husband testified, "[S]he knew the agreement was coming." After reading the agreement, and prior to signing it, wife proposed no changes. Husband told wife, "[H]ere it is, look at it, and if you want to go with it, sign it." Husband also told wife she could get a lawyer, but wife declined to do so.

Husband characterized the agreement as "what we both wanted." Husband testified wife knew the value of the business and home parcel was around $200,000.

The following day, husband drove wife to a bank to execute the agreement. The notary public at the bank testified wife did not appear to be under stress or duress, nor did she appear to be worried. The agreement was executed on September 29, 2001.

At the commissioner's hearing, wife testified she had read the entire agreement and denied being forced to sign it. She indicated she voluntarily went to the bank with husband. She further testified she could easily obtain a job as a secretary. Wife testified husband, on one occasion, told her if she did not sign the agreement, he would take her to court. Nevertheless, she explained the reason why she signed the agreement, saying, "[I]f this is what he wants, I'm going to go ahead and sign it. That's the reason I signed it. Like a fool, I should have had a lawyer."

The commissioner in chancery found the property settlement agreement was unconscionable, ruling that a "gross disparity" existed between the value of the property each party would receive. The commissioner concluded:

> The husband never discussed his retirement at Fort Eustis with the wife although it doesn't appear that the amount that the husband would receive from his retirement is significant. The husband never advised the wife as to the value of the business or of the real property including the marital residence. Apparently there were no negotiations between the parties; the wife simply signed the document prepared by the husband's attorney.
>
> The only income that the wife receives is $400.00 per week from her employment at Cassenvey Heating and Air Conditioning "for so long as the parties are husband and wife." The wife waived spousal support and will be without any apparent income upon the entry of a final decree of divorce.

The wife does appear to have some marketable skills since she has previously worked in an office and as an installer for Cassenvey Heating and Air Conditioning. Her age is certainly a factor as to what type of employment she could maintain or even obtain. To waive spousal support after 17 years of marriage without apparent means to support oneself together with the gross disparity in the value of the property received by the parties creates a set of circumstances which becomes inequitable, unfair and causes enforcement of the agreement to be unconscionable.

Husband filed exceptions to the commissioner's finding of unconscionability. The trial court sustained husband's objections, finding the property settlement agreement was not unconscionable. The trial court opined:

Even accepting the commissioner's findings of the value of assigned properties, there are no accompanying circumstances indicative of bad faith or inequity under the law. There is no evidence that Husband concealed or misrepresented his financial status or coerced Wife, nor that Wife suffered from any disability or necessity. Given the status of their marriage, there was no fiduciary relationship between the parties. Each acted at arm's length. Those factors noted in *Derby* which would support unconscionability are not present here. At worst, Wife made a bad bargain, but she read the agreement and had the opportunity, as she indicated in the agreement, to consult with an attorney about it, and chose not to. She has not shown by "clear and convincing evidence" that the terms of the agreement are unconscionable.

The Commissioner apparently concluded that Wife's waiver of spousal support constituted the inequitable circumstances, apart from gross disparity, in satisfaction of the standard in *Derby*. Assuming that Wife was entitled to support (by no means determined by the evidence), her waiver is nevertheless a factor in determining the values exchanged. It does not provide separate evidence in this case of such circumstances of inequity that would render the agreement unconscionable. In other words, her waiver may increase the disparity, but the remaining circumstances do not justify a conclusion of unconscionability, however inadvisable her decision may have been.

Accordingly, the Court will enter an order concluding that the agreement is valid and enforceable. This appeal follows.

## ANALYSIS

While appellant has offered seven assignments of error, all can be distilled into one issue of whether the trial court erred in finding the property settlement agreement was not unconscionable.

Both parties agree that *Derby v. Derby,* 8 Va. App. 19, 378 S.E.2d 74 (1989), sets forth the basis for analyzing this issue:

If inadequacy of price or inequality in value are the only indicia of unconscionability, the case must be extreme to justify equitable relief. A person may legally agree to make a partial gift of his or her property or may legally make a bad bargain. *Id.* But gross disparity in the value exchanged is a significant factor in determining whether oppressive influences affected the agreement to the extent that the process was unfair and the terms of the resultant agreement unconscionable. Other unfair and inequitable incidents in addition to the inadequacy, however, may more readily justify relief.

When the accompanying incidents are inequitable and show bad faith, such as concealments, misrepresentations, undue advantage, oppression on the part of the one who obtains the benefit, or ignorance, weakness of mind, sickness, old age, incapacity, pecuniary necessities and the like, on the part of the other, these circumstances, combined with inadequacy of price, may easily induce a court to grant relief, defensive or affirmative.

Historically, a bargain was unconscionable in an action at law if it was "such as no man in his senses and not under delusion would make on the one hand, and as no honest and fair man would accept on the other.'"

"[M]arital property settlements entered into by competent parties upon valid consideration for lawful purposes are favored in the law and such will be enforced unless their illegality is clear and certain." Therefore, in this case, wife "had the burden at trial to prove by clear and convincing evidence the grounds alleged to void or rescind the agreement." On appeal, we review the evidence in the light most favorable to the prevailing party below and determine whether that evidence established as a matter of law any of the grounds wife relied upon to vitiate the agreement.

"Any issue of unconscionability of a [marital] agreement shall be decided by the court as a matter of law. Recitations in the agreement shall create a prima facie presumption that they are factually correct." Code § 20-151(B) (applied to post-marital/separation agreements through Code § 20-155).

To determine whether an agreement is unconscionable, a court must examine the "adequacy of price" or "quality of value." "If a 'gross disparity in the value exchanged' exists then the court should consider 'whether oppressive influences affected the agreement to the extent that the process was unfair and the terms of the resulting agreement unconscionable.'"

Thus, *Derby* sets forth a two-step test. Appellant must prove both 1) a gross disparity existed in the division of assets and 2) overreaching or oppressive influences. Courts must view the apparent inequity in light of other attendant circumstances to determine whether the agreement is unconscionable and should be declared invalid.

Wife argues that "gross disparity," with nothing more, should render the agreement void as being unconscionable. As discussed above, this is not the correct legal standard. While the question of unconscionability is a matter of law, the underlying facts must be determined by the fact finder, and on appeal we determine whether there is sufficient evidence to support the factual findings. If there is credible evidence in the record supporting the factual findings made by the trier of fact, we are bound by those findings regardless of whether there is evidence that may support a contrary finding.

Granted, the agreement gave husband approximately 94% of the marital assets. Yet, as the trial court correctly found, there was no evidence of overreaching or oppressive behavior by husband. Assuming the first prong of unconscionability is present, the second prong has not been proven. As wife conceded at oral argument, a spouse can give away his/her entire portion of the marital estate as long as there is no oppressive conduct by the other spouse. "[E]very person . . . is entitled to dispose of [his] property, in such manner and upon such terms as he chooses, and whether his bargains are wise, or discreet, or profitable, or unprofitable, or otherwise, are considerations not for courts of justice, but for the party himself to deliberate upon."

Alternatively, wife claims under *Derby* that there are "oppressive influences" present that render the agreement unconscionable. Wife does not claim fraud nor any breach of fiduciary relationship, yet argues the marital relationship requires "heightened examination." In her brief, wife points to the fact that the parties were living under the same roof, that husband drove wife to the bank to execute the agreement, and that wife had no attorney.

The facts belie wife's argument of overreaching. Husband and wife had discussed the contents of the agreement prior to husband having his attorney draft the agreement. Wife knew husband was going to the attorney. Husband brought the agreement to wife the night before it was executed. Wife testified she read the agreement. Husband advised wife she could consult with an attorney but wife chose not to do so. Wife testified she was not forced to sign the agreement. The notary testified wife did not seem to be under stress or duress. She voluntarily went with husband to the bank. Wife indicated she signed the agreement because "this is what he wants." Wife characterized her action as foolish but never described it as the result of any overreaching conduct by husband. At no time did wife indicate she was under duress or that husband exercised any undue influence for her to sign the agreement. There is no evidence of oppressive behavior or coercion on husband's part.

Finally, wife argues that her waiver of spousal support "represents an additional attendant circumstance" warranting a finding of unconscionability. Again, we find no merit to wife's contention. Wife was not penniless. She had inherited $30,000 cash and a home with no debt valued at $275,000. Further, she had a pension derived from working twenty years at Eastern State Hospital. She testified she would have no difficulty becoming re-employed. Nothing in the record suggests she is incapable of enjoying financial independence. Also, husband gave wife the opportunity to consult a lawyer and/or propose any changes to the agreement. She declined these offers and elected to freely sign the agreement. For the reasons stated above, we cannot say that wife's voluntary waiver of spousal support warrants a finding of unconscionability.

While the commissioner in chancery found unconscionability, the trial court found no "accompanying circumstances indicative of bad faith or inequity under the law." Wife contends the trial court erred in overturning the commissioner's recommendation. However, a trial court is not bound by a commissioner's legal conclusions.

\* \* \*

While the commissioner found husband did not disclose the value of his Fort Eustis pension and the value of the assets, and placed particular emphasis on wife's waiver of spousal support, the ultimate determination of unconscionability is a legal issue. The trial court found, as a matter of law, that the agreement was not unconscionable. We agree with the trial court.

Nothing in the record, including wife's testimony, indicates husband acted in bad faith, coerced or misled wife. She had an opportunity to obtain counsel and declined to do so. The record thus supports the trial court's ruling that the agreement constituted a valid contract. Wife did not show unconscionability by clear and convincing evidence.

## CONCLUSION

For the foregoing reasons, we find that the trial court did not err in finding that the parties' agreement is valid and enforceable. The decision of the trial court is affirmed.

**Note:** Citations omitted and case edited for brevity.

**Source:** Retrieved from www.courts.state.va.us/opinions/opncavwp/0468051.pdf.

**CASE BRIEF ASSIGNMENT**

Read and brief the *Galloway v. Galloway,* 622 S.E.2d 267 (Va.Ct.App. 2005) case. (See Appendix A for information on how to brief cases.)

## UNCONTESTED HEARINGS

Since many divorce cases are uncontested, the hearing in which the judge grants the divorce is a relatively simple one. The hearing in which this occurs is usually referred to as the *final hearing.*

Hearings are not generally held in a courtroom, although this too varies by jurisdiction. Judges often have a small hearing room adjacent to their office, often referred to as the *judge's chambers.* See Figure 12.2 for an example of how a judge's hearing room may be laid out.

The judge's main concern in a case in which the parties have entered into a settlement agreement is that it was entered into voluntarily and that they understand the consequences of the agreement that they have signed. A judge may also review items such as child custody, child visitation, and child support to ensure that the provisions of the agreement are in the best interest of the child.

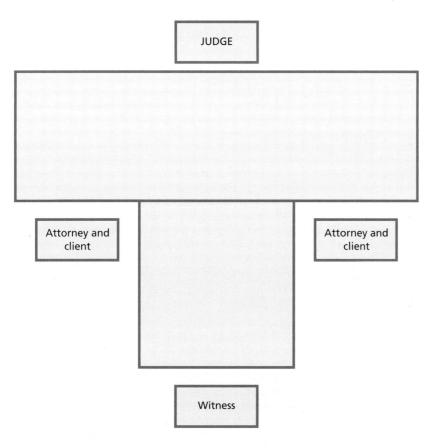

**FIGURE 12.2**
**Judge's Hearing Room**

The judge will also require some proof that establishes the court's jurisdiction to grant the divorce. This will include confirmation of service of process on the defendant spouse. A military affidavit, which is used to prove that the defendant spouse is not currently on active duty in the military, may also be required pursuant to the Soldiers and Sailors Relief Act 50 U.S.C. § 520, as updated by the Service members Civil Relief Act 2003.

In addition, proof of the jurisdictional requirements to grant the divorce itself will be needed. For example, in Florida, the filing spouse may testify that he or she has resided in the state for a period of six months immediately prior to filing the petition.

Once jurisdiction has been established, and the judge is satisfied that the settlement agreement was entered into voluntarily and the provisions relating to the children of the marriage are adequate, he or she will incorporate the settlement agreement into the final judgment of dissolution of marriage. Judges do not have unlimited discretion to reject the provisions contained in a separation agreement entered into by the spouses, as is demonstrated in the *Griffith v. Griffith* case in the next Case in Point.

**CYBER TRIP**

For an interesting tour of a courtroom, visit www.sdcourt. ca.gov/portal/ page?_pageid =53,128653&_ dad=portal& _schema=PORTAL

## TRIALS

When the parties cannot come to an understanding on the details of their divorce by entering into a settlement agreement, they lose their control over how those contested matters will be resolved. The issues pass to the judge to resolve, unless a jury trial is allowed in the jurisdiction and a party has requested one.

Pretrial conferences are required in many jurisdictions before a contested case will go to trial. The **pretrial conference** tends to be informal and, like other hearings, often takes place in the judge's chambers. It is a meeting held before the judge to handle

**pretrial conference**
The meeting between the parties and the judge to identify legal issues, stipulate to uncontested matters, and encourage settlement.

In the District Court of Appeal
First District, State of Florida
*Griffith v. Griffith*
Case No. 1d02-3229
December 9, 2003

KAHN, J.

\* \* \*

Appellee, Patricia Griffith, a successful medical doctor, earned an average salary in the three years before the dissolution of over twenty times that earned by the former husband. Over the course of their twelve-year marriage, the parties enjoyed a very comfortable lifestyle, commensurate with Dr. Griffith's professional success. Early in the marriage, the parties agreed that the husband would attend to the care and needs of the children rather than advancing his own earning ability.

Dr. Griffith filed a petition for dissolution in early 2000. During a second mediation session in January 2001, the parties reached an agreement as to alimony, child support, and custody. Again, although the exact numbers are not material, we note that the total financial obligations payable by Dr. Griffith to Mr. Griffith under the agreement are substantial. The parties agreed to joint custody of their three children, with neither designated a primary custodial parent. Dr. Griffith's attorney drafted a written document entitled "Separation and Property Settlement Agreement" to memorialize the settlement. Following execution by both parties, the lawyers filed the agreement with the court.

The matter then came on for an uncontested final hearing. At that hearing, Dr. Griffith apparently told the judge she was not sure if she could comply with the settlement agreement. The court declined to grant final judgment, prompting the husband to seek temporary support and also to file the motion to enforce the settlement agreement. When these matters came on for hearing, the trial court granted temporary support to Mr. Griffith, but again refused to enter a final judgment, concluding that an evidentiary hearing would be necessary to determine if the agreement was in the best interest of the minor children. The court then conducted a series of evidentiary hearings during the summer of 2002, after which it entered the order on appeal.

In the final judgment the trial court modified the parties' agreed-upon provisions for child support and rehabilitative alimony. The trial judge reasoned, "the court has not only the discretion and the prerogative, but a duty to scrutinize whether those provisions are in the best interest of the minor children." Based upon Dr. Griffith's testimony, the trial court determined that Dr. Griffith's previous income had resulted from her working in excess of forty hours a week and that Dr. Griffith would prefer to limit her professional week to forty hours to allow her time with the children. The court also focused upon a lawsuit pending against the wife's medical practice, acknowledging that although Dr. Griffith knew about the suit at the time she signed the agreement, she could not "knowingly perceive the outcome of the conclusion of the lawsuit." The

court then refashioned Dr. Griffith's financial obligations based upon an exhibit presented by Dr. Griffith's office manager, projecting her income for the rest of 2003, as opposed to the average earnings from the years previous to the settlement agreement, which the court characterized as "aberrations." Despite the determination that the wife's previous earnings had been an aberration, the court refused to allow the husband to present information gleaned from the wife's payroll records concerning her actual 2002 income. The court made no findings as to the wife's actual earnings as of the date of the last hearing.

On appeal, Mr. Griffith challenges several rulings of the trial court. We take, as the primary challenges, the trial court's refusal to uphold the child support and alimony provisions of the settlement agreement. Because we reverse on these issues, we do not reach the two issues raised by Mr. Griffith concerning the trial court's failure to allow evidence of Dr. Griffith's current income and the trial court's admission of certain business records purporting to project Dr. Griffith's future income. Finally, because the effect of our order will be to reinstate the settlement agreement which provided that each party would assume his or her attorney's fees and costs, we do not disturb the trial court's failure to require the wife to be responsible for the husband's attorney's fees and costs.

In analyzing the trial court's refusal to enforce the child support and alimony provisions of the agreement, we must look first to the judge's conclusion that he had an obligation to scrutinize whether those provisions were in the best interest of the minor children. Apparently, and in short, the trial judge concluded that the minor children will be better served if their mother operated under a more abbreviated work schedule. This led the trial court to come up with a projected income figure for Dr. Griffith from which he reduced her child support obligation. The court also revisited the agreed-upon payments of rehabilitative alimony to Mr. Griffith.

Appellant does not contest the general rule in Florida that settlement provisions concerning child support, custody, and visitation must be reviewed and approved by the trial court as being in the best interest of the children. *See Feliciano v. Feliciano*, 674 So. 2d 937 (Fla. 4th DCA 1996). This rule is based upon the concern that parents should not be allowed to bargain away valuable rights of minor children for reasons unrelated to the best interest of the children. Nevertheless, Florida respects the rights of parties to a dissolution to make their own agreement. As this court stated some years ago:

> Separation agreements executed by husband and wife
> prior to divorce usually provide for payment to the wife

of support or alimony; for support and custody of children; and for settlement of property rights existing between the parties. When such agreements are fairly entered into and are not tainted by fraud, overreaching or concealment, they will be respected by the courts.

*Sedell v. Sedell,* 100 So. 2d 639, 642 (Fla. 1st DCA 1958).

Unescapable here is the fact that the trial court reduced Dr. Griffith's child support obligation upon the premise that, by working less, Dr. Griffith could spend more time with the children. The record, however, contains absolutely no evidence that Dr. Griffith has neglected her children or has failed to spend appropriate time with them. The action of the court was based upon facts the parties certainly knew, or should have known, at the time of the settlement agreement, and therefore amounted to an unjustified revisiting of the parties' contract. Although we recognize the trial court's discretion to approve matters involving custody, visitation, and support, our scrutiny of the present matter does not suggest the existence of any sufficient evidence to support the trial court's order disdaining the settlement and reducing Dr. Griffith's child support obligation.

We must also disapprove the trial court's failure to enforce the provisions concerning rehabilitative alimony.

\* \* \*

One could hardly overstate the definitive quality of these acknowledgments, particularly between very well-informed persons such as these parties, and particularly in the context of a mediation settlement agreement reached under the auspices of a certified family law mediator and reduced to writing by appellant's attorney.

Florida courts do not take lightly agreements made by husband and wife concerning spousal support. "A marital settlement agreement as to alimony or property rights which is entered before the dissolution of marriage is binding upon the parties." *Dowie v. Dowie,* 668 So. 2d 290, 292 (Fla. 1st DCA 1996). The present order sets aside the alimony provisions without any indication that such provisions were involuntary or the product of fraud. Such an action is at odds with the well established policy in Florida that settlement agreements are highly favored in the law. *See Dorson v. Dorson,* 393 So. 2d 632, 633 (Fla. 4th DCA 1981). As with the child support provisions, we can find no sufficient reason to uphold the trial court's action in setting aside the alimony provisions.

As the trial judge apparently felt he had a virtually free hand to set aside the settlement agreement because the parties had minor children, we review briefly the law concerning marital settlement agreements. First, the construction of such settlement agreements is subject to the same rules of law as any other contract. *See Zern v. Zern,* 737 So. 2d 631, 633 (Fla. 1st DCA 1999). Next, a trial court should follow the stipulations entered into by the parties, which are generally binding on the parties and the court. *See Rhoden v. Rhoden,* 538 So. 2d 1274, 1275 (Fla. 1st DCA 1988). Finally, mediation and settlement of family law disputes is highly favored in Florida law. The Florida Family Law Rules of Procedure provide for mediation of all contested family matters, except as provided by law, and also provide for expedited mediation of

family issues. *See* Fla. Fam. L.R.P. 12.740(b). Moreover, once a mediation agreement is reduced to writing, as was the case here, "[a]bsent a timely written objection, the agreement is presumed to be approved by counsel. . . ." Fla. Fam. L.R.P. 12.740(f)(1). The standard for disregarding a settlement agreement between the parties is high. As the Florida Supreme Court has held:

> [T]he fact that one party to the agreement apparently made a bad bargain is not a sufficient ground, by itself, to vacate or modify a settlement agreement. The critical test in determining the validity of marital agreements is whether there was fraud or overreaching on one side, or, assuming unreasonableness, whether the challenging spouse did not have adequate knowledge of the marital property and income of the parties at the time the agreement was reached. . . . If an agreement that is unreasonable is freely entered into, it is enforceable.

*Casto v. Casto,* 508 So. 2d 330, 334 (Fla. 1987).

Of note here, the sole reason relied upon by the trial court for disregarding the settlement agreement was Dr. Griffith's claim of wanting to reduce her professional hours. Although Dr. Griffith initially brought up a lawsuit pending against her practice, by the time the dissolution was finalized, this other legal matter had been resolved favorably to Dr. Griffith. Apprised of these facts, the trial court failed to follow the law concerning enforcement of marital settlement agreements.

As we have previously observed, no valid reason related to the best interest of the children was ever raised to avoid the force and effect of the agreement. Accordingly, the court should have applied the general rule: "The inquiry on a motion to set aside an agreement reached through mediation is limited to whether there was fraud, misrepresentation in discovery, or coercion." *Crupi v. Crupi,* 784 So. 2d 611, 612 (Fla. 5th DCA 2001). No claim has ever been made in the present case that either side lacked complete and accurate information concerning the personal situation and finances of the other spouse, and the agreement recites the contrary. Once husband and wife "are involved in full fledged litigation over dissolution property and support rights, they are necessarily dealing at arm's length and without the special fiduciary relationship of unestranged marital parties. . . . [T]here can be no question of the adequacy of knowledge when an adversarial party has had the opportunity of financial discovery under the applicable rules of procedure." *Petracca v. Petracca,* 706 So. 2d 904, 911-12 (Fla. 4th DCA 1998).

No legal cause exists to support the trial court's action in disregarding the parties' settlement agreement concerning spousal and child support. Should either spouse desire relief from this agreement, that spouse would be constrained by the law regarding modification and be held to the requisite showing of substantially changed circumstances. No such showing was ever attempted here and, accordingly, we conclude the settlement agreement must be enforced by the trial court. We therefore REVERSE the order on appeal and REMAND with instructions that the trial court enforce the marital settlement agreement.

**Source:** Retrieved from http://opinions.1dca.org/opinions2003/12-09-03/02-3229.pdf.

**CASE BRIEF ASSIGNMENT**

Read and brief the *Griffith v. Griffith*, 860 So.2d 1069 (Fla. Dist.Ct.App..2003) case. (See Appendix A for information on how to brief cases.)

procedural issues relating to the trial and may include decisions on any motions that are still pending before the court. Another important purpose of the pretrial conference is that it allows the judge an opportunity to encourage the parties to settle the case. Judges' calendars are very busy and every case that can be settled before trial makes the judge's life that much less complicated. Some judges are, to say the least, very forceful in these conferences. The judge may share with the attorneys his or her inclination on how he or she will resolve the case if the case comes before him or her in an effort to encourage the parties to settle the case.

Other items that may be included in a pretrial conference include:

- Simplification of issues to be resolved at trial.

- Acquirement of admissions of fact and documents that will reduce the need for unnecessary proof of facts at trial.

- Identification of witnesses, documents, and other evidence that will be admitted at trial.

- Issuance of an order limiting the time that will be allowed for presenting evidence.

- Determination of whether a child will testify and any specific conditions that will be imposed for that testimony.

If the parties still cannot reach agreement despite the "encouragement" of the judge, the case will go to trial and follow the same basic procedure as any other civil case. Although jurisdictions vary on where the divorce trial takes place, they may be held in the judge's chambers. Figure 12.2 includes a diagram of a typical hearing room. If a jury trial is allowed by state law and requested by one of the parties, then the trial will be in a courtroom, similar to that seen on television and in the movies.

**plaintiff**
The party initiating legal action.

The **plaintiff**, in a divorce case the person who filed the initial petition for dissolution of marriage, presents his or her case first. The attorney calls witnesses, who may be cross-examined by the defense attorney, and submits evidence for the judge's consideration. Keep in mind that, unless it is a jury trial, the judge is sitting as both a trier of fact and a trier of law during a nonjury trial. Upon completion of the plaintiff's case, the **defendant** presents his or her case in a similar manner to that of the plaintiff's case. The parties' attorneys are then allowed a closing argument, also referred to as a *final argument,* summarizing the evidence presented and arguing that the judge should rule in favor of their client.

**defendant**
The party against whom a lawsuit is brought.

As the steps in this process are laid out, it should become increasingly obvious why contested divorces are so expensive. Also, this brief outline of a contested trial only scratches the surface of the costs associated with a trial. For example, attorneys will normally have a **transcript** made of the hearings and trials held in a contested divorce. These are prepared by a court reporter. Then there are expert witnesses, such as psychologists who testify on the issue of child custody, who can demand a nice fee for their services. The list of expenses goes on and on, which is a reminder to all involved of the value of reaching a settlement agreement as early as possible in the divorce process.

**transcript**
Written account of a trial court proceeding or deposition.

**appeal**
Tests the sufficiency of the verdict under the legal parameters or rules.

Ultimately, the judge will take the case under consideration and subsequently issue a final order that includes his or her rulings on all matters in dispute. This is usually the end of this phase of the litigation process, but in some cases a party who is not happy with the results of the judge's ruling may choose to **appeal**. Appealing a judge's decision is difficult for a variety of reasons. For example, appellate courts give a trial judge's decisions great deference and are reluctant to overturn the decision. In addition, the costs of appealing a case are prohibitive for many people.

# THE ROLE OF THE PARALEGAL IN HEARINGS AND TRIALS

The paralegal is a valuable member of the litigation team and is responsible for many important tasks that are critical to the trial process. Attorneys differ on how they use their paralegals in hearings and trials. Some allow the paralegal to not only prepare for the hearing/trial, but also attend to aid the attorney during the hearing/trial itself. Other attorneys do not bring the paralegal to the hearings/trials but do rely on the paralegal to aid in the pretrial preparation.

Duties often performed by paralegals include:

- Organizing information gathered during the course of handling the case.

- Locating and scheduling expert witnesses.

- Preparing **trial notebook**—this is a notebook that contains all the important information and documents that may be needed at trial. Examples of what may be included in the trial notebook include pleadings filed in the case, discovery materials obtained in preparation of trial, and relevant motions that have been made along with any pretrial orders entered by the court. Figure 12.3 contains information on what may be included in a trial notebook.

- Locating and scheduling court reporters.

- Note taking at trial.

- Keeping track of all exhibits to be used at trial.

- Ensuring all documents that the attorney may need at trial are present.

- Assisting in preparing questions for witnesses.

- Reviewing depositions to aid in examination/cross-examination of witnesses.

**trial notebook**
Started and organized prior to the pretrial conference, it contains all documentary and other tangible evidence or materials used by the attorney in trial.

**FIGURE 12.3**
**Contents of Trial Notebook**

Although the content and organization of trial notebooks vary, this is one example of how a trial notebook can be organized and what information it may include.

1. Trial schedule/calendar—Includes key information relating to the case and hearing dates, such as the name of the judge, the name of the judge's clerk, the hearing date and time, and information on the witnesses who will be appearing at trial. Sometimes a separate section is used that contains a directory with detailed contact information on the witnesses, the attorneys on the opposing side of the case, and those who are in possession of exhibits that will be used at trial.
2. Summary of facts of case.
3. Pending matters before the court and information on any temporary orders still in effect.
4. Pleadings—Includes copies of all pleadings filed by both parties in the case, such as the petition and answer.
5. Research material—Includes trial memoranda, trial briefs, and other legal research material prepared for the case.
6. Discovery materials—Includes all discovery information obtained. Key information that may be used at trail should be flagged and/or indexed to ensure quick retrieval at trial
7. Inventories/appraisals—Includes financial information relating to the valuation of marital assets.
8. Jury selection—If a jury will be hearing the case, information to aid in jury selection can be included. Examples include a jury chart and questions to be asked of prospective jurors.
9. Witness list—Includes key information on each witness and a brief summary of what the witnesses' testimony will include.
10. Examination questions/cross-examination questions of witnesses.
11. Exhibits that will be used at trial.

**CYBER TRIP**

For more information on how alternative dispute resolution is dealt with in some court systems, visit:
Connecticut
www.jud.ct.gov/external/super/altdisp.htm
Tennessee
www.tsc.state.tn.us/GENINFO/Publications/ADR/WhatIs Mediation.pdf

## ETHICS ALERT

A review of the facts of the Sandy and Cramer Robinson set out in the Client Interview will demonstrate how emotional divorce cases can be. Those facts are real; they are based on an actual case. It may seem like an extreme example of emotional issues in a divorce, but it was not extreme to Sandy. To her, the issue of the swimsuit was a deal breaker.

Mr. Wilson was faced with a potential ethical issue. He could have just thrown the proposed separation agreement out and started to bill more hours to Sandy's account as he moved forward with the contested divorce. There was, therefore, a possible financial incentive to go to trial.

What should he have done in this situation? The correct approach was to give complete information to the client relating the cost, delay, and unpredictability of not signing the settlement agreement. He might also contact Mr. Cutthroat and see whether that swimsuit was a deal breaker for Cramer. Cramer might be more willing to produce the swimsuit than go to trial and gamble on how the judge would rule.

In the end, it is the client's decision on how to proceed with the case after being fully informed of the consequences of the decision. Mr. Wilson, his paralegal, and his staff owe it to the client to act professionally and ethically in accomplishing her goals and desires.

## COPARENTING CLASSES

The children are often the innocent victims of a divorce. The impact of divorce on children is well known and a concern to not only psychologists but also the legal system. Some of the steps the legal system has taken to minimize the effect of divorce on children, such as granting liberal visitation to the noncustodial parent, have been previously discussed.

States are trying to find more ways to help the children of divorce families. One is coparenting classes. These classes provide awareness to the parents about the possible effects the divorce may have on their children and give them training in ways to minimize those effects. Parents usually attend separately but, in some states, children may also attend the classes with their parent.

The popularity of these classes seems to be growing and, as another example of the age of the Internet, classes are even offered online.

## DRAFTING SEPARATION AGREEMENTS

Settlement agreements, also referred to as *marital settlement agreements,* have been mentioned throughout this textbook. The reason is simple. They are the most common way for issues related to divorces to be settled. They can be entered into at any time, including right up to the day of trial. Attorneys like them and judges like them. But clients like Sandy Robinson might not like them or may be willing to walk away from the negotiation table if they do not like the direction that the negotiations are taking. A sample marital separation agreement is set out in Appendix C.

In the end, however, the majority of cases are settled and never go to trial. Instead the parties are able to work out their differences. The next step is to reduce the agreement to writing, which is the separation agreement. Like a premarital agreement, a separation agreement is a contract. Unlike a premarital agreement, the parties are assumed to be negotiating at arm's length, with each party objectively trying to protect his or her own best interests.

Paralegals usually play an active role in the drafting of the separation agreement, in the same manner as they may help draft the premarital agreement. Form clauses are selected whenever possible that reflect the terms agreed to by the parties. These clauses are customized as needed and, occasionally, clauses will need to be drafted specifically to meet the needs of the parties.

Although paralegals may be key players in the preparation of the separation agreement, they must remind themselves regularly that they are not the attorney handling the case. Drafts of the agreement must be reviewed by the supervising attorney to ensure that the document meets the needs of the client and the requirements of the law. Paralegals must be on guard against an attorney becoming overly reliant on the drafting skills of the paralegal, no matter how many legal documents that paralegal may have drafted before. In the end, it is the attorney, who is licensed to practice law and has the ethical duty to look out for the needs of the client, who is responsible for the contents of the final document.

An issue that sometimes arises when both parties are represented by counsel is which attorney will draft the agreement that will set out the various oral agreements reached during negotiations. The attorney who drafts the initial draft has the first crack at interpreting the agreement and putting his or her "spin" on what the terms of the agreement will be by the language and wording used. The other attorney does, of course, have the opportunity to review the agreement and request that changes be made in the draft. The attorney and paralegal working for each party must be continually vigilant in ensuring that the terms of the agreement accurately reflect the negotiated facts and that the interests of the client are protected.

Other documents may need to be prepared in conjunction with the settlement agreement. Examples include deeds for the transfer of real property and promissory notes to secure future payments under the note.

The parts of the settlement agreement are:

- Caption—taken from the initial pleading in the case.

- Heading—some descriptive phrase is used, such as Settlement Agreement.

- Body of the agreement—including information on when the document was entered into; who the parties to the agreement are; specific allegations, such as the fact the marriage is irretrievably broken; clauses setting out the agreement of the parties on issues such as alimony, child support, custody, visitation, property distribution, health insurance, statement of disclosure; and any other clause needed to reflect the agreement between the parties.

- The body of the agreement contains the key information that the parties have agreed to in the course of negotiations. Although there is no specific sequence the various clauses presenting the agreed terms should be set out in, it is always a good idea to have them flow in a logical manner. For example, placing clauses relating to one issue, such as child support, should be together rather than spread throughout the document.

- It is important that all issues agreed to have been included in the settlement agreement. Failure to include some agreed-to terms may result in future legal action or in one party being barred from attempting to get some benefit, such as alimony.

Examples of clauses that may be included in the body of the agreement include:

- Names of the parties.

- Effective date of the agreement.

- Key information on parties, for example, date of marriage, where the parties were married, name of children, the ages and birth dates of children.

- Stated purpose of the agreement.

- Clause relating to the transfer of real and personal property.

- Liability for marital debts.

- Treatment of pension plans.

- Child custody.

- Provision of health care for child(ren) of the marriage.

- Child visitation.

- Who will receive dependency tax exemption for the child(ren).
- Alimony.
- How payments of child support and/or alimony will be made.
- When alimony will cease, for example, a clause addressing the termination of alimony if the receiving spouse cohabitates and has sexual relationship with another person.
- Signature and acknowledgment.

## Summary

This chapter provides a basic explanation of how the divorce process itself is brought to a conclusion. Although some posttrial actions may be required, such as motions to enforce child support payments, and sometimes a final judgment is appealed, the reality is that for most divorces, the final judgment of dissolution of marriage is the end of the long road to ending a couple's marriage.

It is often a difficult time for all involved, including the paralegal and attorney who work on the case. Paralegals are key players in bringing both contested and uncontested divorces to a conclusion. The process requires that the paralegal not only understand the law but also the emotions that are involved in divorce case. A good example of that is the Sandy and Cramer Robinson case, which, as strange as it sounds, is based on a real case.

In the end, it is the law firm's duty to help the client through this difficult process. Any lawyer who has practiced in this area of the law for any length of time will testify to the fact that it is a thankless task at times. Those hard feelings that are brought about in the divorce are sometimes directed at the attorney and his or her staff. But the firm plays an important part in reaching as good a resolution of the issues involved as possible and, hopefully, ensures that the best interests of the innocent parties, the children of the marriage, are provided for.

## Key Terms

Alternative dispute resolution (ADR)
Appeal
Arbitration
Bench trial
Defendant
Equity
Mediation
Mediator

Negotiation
Plaintiff
Pretrial conference
Transcript
Trial notebook
Trier of fact
Trier of law

## Review Questions

1. What are the differences between a jury and a nonjury trial?
2. What are the parts of a separation agreement?
3. Why is it an advantage for the parties to reach an agreement as to the terms of their divorce and reduce that agreement to writing in a separation agreement?
4. What are the differences between arbitration and mediation?
5. Describe the role the paralegal plays in hearings and trials.
6. What are the purposes of a pretrial conference?
7. What are coparenting classes and why are they used?
8. Why is appealing a judge's decision in a dissolution of marriage case difficult?
9. What is a trial notebook and why is it used?
10. What role does the judge play in a contested dissolution of marriage trial?

11. Compare and contrast premarital agreements and separation agreements.

12. What is a bench trial?

13. What is a magistrate and what is his or her role in dissolution/divorce cases?

14. How is negotiation used in resolving issues in family law cases?

15. What are five examples of clauses that may be included in the body of a separation agreement?

1. Research the law of your state relating to alternative dispute resolution and its use. What forms of ADR are available in your state? Which might have been helpful in resolving the conflicts between Sandy and Cramer Robinson from the Client Interview?

2. José and Chloe have been married for 15 years. José is now seeking a divorce. While married, Chloe started her own company that markets cosmetics to working women via the Internet. Her company has done well and it is now worth in excess of one million dollars. José is a pharmacist and works for a major drug store chain. He has recently inherited money from his deceased aunt. They have one child, Nathan, age 12. José has retained your firm to handle the divorce. Chloe has retained an attorney to represent her. The only thing they can agree on is that the child should live with José and that there should be liberal visitation. Discuss how negotiations could be used in this case. Explain how other ADRs might be used.

3. Starting with the facts set out in Exercise 2 and creating additional facts as needed, prepare a detailed fact pattern for José and Chloe's dissolution of marriage. Assuming that the parties could not resolve their differences by using ADRs, list what would be included in the trial notebook when the case went to trial.

4. Research the laws and court rules of your state to determine if magistrates, also referred to as referees or masters, are used. If yes, describe how they are used. If no, locate the laws/rules of a neighboring state that does allow their use. Describe how they are used in that state.

5. Using the facts set out in the Client Interview and creating new facts as needed, draft a separation agreement to be used by Sandy and Cramer Robinson.

**Exercises**

## REAL WORLD DISCUSSION TOPICS

A husband and wife were the only witnesses in a bench trial. The couple had no children, and the only issue before the court was the distribution of the marital property. The assets in dispute included a brokerage firm account. The record reflected that the brokerage account was opened with funds from the wife's father and the account was held jointly between the wife and her father. When her father died, the wife became sole owner of the account. She later added the husband as a joint tenant with right of survivorship on the account and had him sign a signature card for the account. Should the judge rule that the brokerage account is the wife's separate property? See *Tate v. Tate*, 55 S.W.3d 1 (Tex.App. 2000).

## PORTFOLIO ASSIGNMENT

Research the laws of your state to determine if a party in a divorce has the right to request a jury trial. If yes, what are the requirements for making the request and are the factual matters subject to being resolved by the jury limited in any way? Write a summary of your findings.

# Chapter 13

# Postjudgment Matters

## CHAPTER OBJECTIVES

**After reading this chapter and completing the assignments, you should be able to:**

- Demonstrate an understanding of jurisdiction and how it relates to the enforcement of child custody, child visitation, child support, and alimony.

- Describe how the legal system has changed in an effort to reduce the problem of parental kidnapping and forum shopping.

- Describe what methods are available for the enforcement of alimony and child support awards.

- Understand how alimony, child support, and child custody are modified.

- Discuss the factors courts look at when determining whether a custodial parent should be allowed to move out of the state in which the custody order was issued.

Chapter 13 introduces the paralegal student to some of the issues that may arise after the entry of the final order of dissolution of marriage. Topics include jurisdiction as it relates to postjudgment matters; the factors courts look for when considering modification of child custody, child support, and alimony; and the means that are available for enforcing the payment of child support and alimony. The impact of bankruptcy on postjudgment maters will also be considered.

### CLIENT INTERVIEW

Kimberly and Jonathan Lincoln were divorced in Savannah, Georgia. They had one child, Ricky. The final divorce decree awarded primary physical custody of the child to Kimberly. Jonathan was ordered to pay Kimberly $500 a month in alimony and $900 per month in child support. Kimberly has re-mained in Savannah while Jonathan has relocated to Cleveland, Ohio. Jonathan has not made his alimony or child support payments for the last four months. Kimberly has come to your firm to see what steps she will need to take to collect the past due payments.

## WHY THIS CHAPTER IS IMPORTANT TO THE PARALEGAL

The entry of the final order of dissolution of marriage is, unfortunately, not necessarily the end of the legal proceedings involving the parties of a divorce. Sometimes this is due to the carryover of bitterness from the divorce and sometimes it is due to a change of circumstances of the parties. Whatever the reason, the family law firm is often called upon to aid in the enforcement or modification of the final order of dissolution of marriage. As with other stages of the divorce process, the paralegal plays an important role in meeting the needs of his or her client. The information contained in this chapter is a starting point for paralegal students to learn about the law associated with postjudgment matters and the procedures that are used to complete the tasks that they may be called upon to complete.

## JURISDICTION—POSTJUDGMENT MATTERS

As a general rule, a court retains jurisdiction over the enforcement of the terms of a final judgment of dissolution of marriage, including matters relating to child custody, child support, alimony, and so on. This retention of jurisdiction also includes matters contained in the separation agreement, since its terms are incorporated in the final decree. The idea is that the court that entered the initial decree will be best suited to handle matters associated with its modification or determining what enforcement actions may be appropriate if child support and/or alimony is not being paid. For example, if the judge who grants the dissolution of marriage is the same one who holds hearings on a father's failure to pay child support, that judge is better able to determine whether the father has some reason to be behind on payment of child support, such as a recent loss of job or serious illness, or whether the father is just trying to avoid meeting his financial obligations to his child by not working or by taking cash payments for work under the table.

This works very well if the spouses stay in the state in which the divorce was initially granted. Unfortunately, this is often not the case in our highly mobile society, which raises the issue of which state law should be applied when an issue of modification of a final order of dissolution of marriage is entered, especially in the area of child custody.

In the past, noncustodial parents were often tempted to take their children to other states to have the custody order modified to give them custody of the child and sometimes did so by removing the child from the custodial parent without permission. The topic and extent of parental kidnapping was brought to the public's attention in an odd way several years ago. At the time, milk containers often had pictures of missing children on them. It turned out that many of those missing children were actually victims of parental kidnapping.

The law has attempted to reduce parental kidnapping and its motivating factor, **forum shopping**. The Uniform Child Custody Jurisdiction Act (UCCJA), introduced in 1968, was an early attempt to resolve this issue. The UCCJA was ultimately enacted into law in all 50 states, although states did vary on the version they adopted. Its intent was to reduce the problem of parental kidnapping and of cases where the noncustodial parent refuses to return a child after visitation, by allowing the arrest of the noncustodial parent and return of the child. It also set out specific ways for a court to acquire jurisdiction over a child custody case. The UCCJA did help resolve many of the conflicts and parental kidnappings that had previously occurred but additional changes in the law were needed.

Another major change was the **Parental Kidnapping Prevention Act (PKPA)**, which was passed by the U.S. Congress in 1980. Like the UCCJA, this act requires states to honor the child custody decrees made in other states and limited the ability to modify the other states' custody decrees, as long as at least one of the parents still resided in the jurisdiction in which the original decree was entered.

Although the UCCJA and PKPA were valuable steps in trying to establish rules to limit forum shopping and parental kidnapping, the two acts did contain some

**CYBER TRIP**

Visit www.law. upenn.edu/bll/ archives/ulc/ fnact99/1920_69/ uccja68.htm to see the full text of the UCCJA.

**forum shopping**
Plaintiff attempts to choose a state with favorable rules in which to file suit.

**Parental Kidnapping Prevention Act (PKPA)**
An act related to jurisdictional issues in applying and enforcing child custody decrees in other states.

**CYBER TRIP**

To view the full text of the Uniform Child Jurisdiction and Enforcement Act, visit www.law.upenn. edu/bll/ulc/fnact99/ 1990s/uccjea97.htm.

inconsistencies. This resulted in the introduction of the Uniform Child Jurisdiction and Enforcement Act (UCCJEA) in 1997. Among other things, the act simplifies how an original state's order is registered in the new state, limits the new state to only being able to enforce the original order, provides the power to issue warrants to take the child into physical custody if there are concerns over his or her custody, and grants power to prosecutors to pursue civil and criminal actions that are appropriate to locate the child or punish the noncustodial parent if there was a violation of criminal law. The UCCJEA also addresses an area of increasing concern, international parental kidnapping. The act allows a court to enforce orders made under the Hague convention on the civil aspects of international child abduction as if it were a child custody determination. Figure 13.1 contains some key provisions of the UCCJEA as adopted by North Dakota, including the jurisdiction to modify orders of other states. Figure 13.2 provides information on the adoption of the UCCJEA by state/jurisdiction.

Jurisdiction is also an issue in the enforcement of child support and alimony. One problem that has occurred in the past was determining what law to apply in cases brought in states other than the original state in which the order was entered. To simplify this, the Uniform Interstate Family Support Act (UIFSA) was proposed and subsequently adopted by all 50 states. It replaced earlier attempts at resolving these issues by two earlier uniform laws, the Uniform Reciprocal Enforcement of Support Act (URESA) and the Revised Uniform Reciprocal Enforcement of Support Act (RURESA).

The UIFSA introduced the concept of continuing exclusive jurisdiction of the original court. This means that the issuing court retains jurisdiction over postjudgment matters, as long as at least one of the parents or the child remains in the state.

**FIGURE 13.1**
**North Dakota
Century Code 2005**

**14-14.1-12. (201) Initial child custody jurisdiction.**
1. Except as otherwise provided in section 14-14.1-15, a court of this state has jurisdiction to make an initial child custody determination only if:
   a. This state is the home state of the child on the date of the commencement of the proceeding, or was the home state of the child within six months before the commencement of the proceeding, and the child is absent from this state but a parent or person acting as a parent continues to live in this state;
   b. A court of another state does not have jurisdiction under subdivision a, or a court of the home state of the child has declined to exercise jurisdiction on the ground that this state is the more appropriate forum under section 14-14.1-18 or 14-14.1-19, and:
      (1) The child and the child's parents, or the child and at least one parent or a person acting as a parent, have a significant connection with this state other than mere physical presence; and
      (2) Substantial evidence is available in this state concerning the child's care, protection, training, and personal relationships;
   c. All courts having jurisdiction under subdivision a or b have declined to exercise jurisdiction on the ground that a court of this state is the more appropriate forum to determine the custody of the child under section 14-14.1-18 or 14-14.1-19; or
   d. No court of any other state would have jurisdiction under the criteria specified in subdivision a, b, or c.
2. Subsection 1 is the exclusive jurisdictional basis for making a child custody determination by a court of this state.
3. Physical presence of, or personal jurisdiction over, a party or a child is not necessary or sufficient to make a child custody determination.

**FIGURE 13.1**
*(concluded)*

**14-14.1-13. (202) Exclusive, continuing jurisdiction.**

1. Except as otherwise provided in section 14-14.1-15, a court of this state which has made a child custody determination consistent with section 14-14.1-12 or 14-14.1-14 has exclusive, continuing jurisdiction over the determination until:

   a. A court of this state determines that neither the child, nor the child and one parent, nor the child and a person acting as a parent have a significant connection with this state and that substantial evidence is no longer available in this state concerning the child's care, protection, training, and personal relationships; or

   b. A court of this state or a court of another state determines that the child, the child's parents, and any person acting as a parent do not presently reside in this state.

2. A court of this state which has made a child custody determination and does not have exclusive, continuing jurisdiction under this section may modify that determination only if it has jurisdiction to make an initial determination under section 14-14.1-12.

**14-14.1-14. (203) Jurisdiction to modify determination.** Except as otherwise provided in section 14-14.1-15, a court of this state may not modify a child custody determination made by a court of another state unless a court of this state has jurisdiction to make an initial determination under subdivision a or b of subsection 1 of section 14-14.1-12 and:

1. The court of the other state determines it no longer has exclusive, continuing jurisdiction under section 14-14.1-13 or that a court of this state would be a more convenient forum under section 14-14.1-18; or

2. A court of this state or a court of the other state determines that the child, the child's parents, and any person acting as a parent do not presently reside in the other state.

**14-14.1-15. (204) Temporary emergency jurisdiction.**

1. A court of this state has temporary emergency jurisdiction if the child is present in this state and the child has been abandoned or it is necessary in an emergency to protect the child because the child, or a sibling or parent of the child, is subjected to or threatened with mistreatment or abuse.

2. If there is no previous child custody determination that is entitled to be enforced under this chapter and a child custody proceeding has not been commenced in a court of a state having jurisdiction under sections 14-14.1-12 through 14-14.1-14, a child custody determination made under this section remains in effect until an order is obtained from a court of a state having jurisdiction under sections 14-14.1-12 through 14-14.1-14. If a child custody proceeding has not been or is not commenced in a court of a state having jurisdiction under sections 14-14.1-12 through 14-14.1-14, a child custody determination made under this section becomes a final determination, if it so provides and this state becomes the home state of the child.

3. If there is a previous child custody determination that is entitled to be enforced under this chapter, or a child custody proceeding has been commenced in a court of a state having jurisdiction under sections 14-14.1-12 through 14-14.1-14, any order issued by a court of this state under this section must specify in the order a period that the court considers adequate to allow the person seeking an order to obtain an order from the state having jurisdiction under sections 14-14.1-12 through 14-14.1-14. The order issued in this state remains in effect until an order is obtained from the other state within the period specified or the period expires.

4. A court of this state which has been asked to make a child custody determination under this section, upon being informed that a child custody proceeding has been commenced in, or a child custody determination has been made by, a court of a state having jurisdiction under sections 14-14.1-12 through 14-14.1-14, shall immediately communicate with the other court. A court of this state which is exercising jurisdiction pursuant to sections 14-14.1-12 through 14-14.1-14, upon being informed that a child custody proceeding has been commenced in, or a child custody determination has been made by, a court of another state under a statute similar to this section shall immediately communicate with the court of that state to resolve the emergency, protect the safety of the parties and the child, and determine a period for the duration of the temporary order.

**FIGURE 13.2**
**Adoption Status of the Uniform Child Custody Jurisdiction and Enforcement Act**

States/jurisdictions that have adopted the UCCJEA as of 2007:

| | |
|---|---|
| Alabama | Montana |
| Alaska | Nebraska |
| Arizona | Nevada |
| Arkansas | New Jersey |
| California | New Mexico |
| Colorado | New York |
| Connecticut | North Carolina |
| Delaware | North Dakota |
| District of Columbia | Ohio |
| Florida | Oklahoma |
| Georgia | Oregon |
| Hawaii | Pennsylvania |
| Idaho | Rhode Island |
| Illinois | South Carolina |
| Indiana | South Dakota |
| Iowa | Tennessee |
| Kansas | Texas |
| Kentucky | U.S. Virgin Islands |
| Louisiana | Utah |
| Maine | Virginia |
| Maryland | Washington |
| Michigan | West Virginia |
| Minnesota | Wisconsin |
| Mississippi | Wyoming |

States/jurisdictions that have not adopted the UCCJEA as of 2007:

Missouri (introduced in 2007 Legislature)
Massachusetts
New Hampshire
Vermont
Puerto Rico

Courts can lose the continuing exclusive jurisdiction over most aspects of the case if all parties, including the child leave the state. One exception is alimony, over which the issuing state retains jurisdiction even if all parties have left the state.

**CYBER TRIP**

To view the full text of the Uniform Interstate Family Support Act, visit www.law.upenn.edu/bll/archives/ulc/uifsa/famsuul6.htm. To view the Uniform Interstate Family Support Act forms, visit www.courts.state.va.us/forms/district/uifsa.html.

**ETHICS ALERT**

Attorneys and paralegals owe a variety of ethical duties to their clients. Perhaps one of the most basic is the duty to represent the client competently. Competent representation is a rather broad concept but an important one nonetheless. A review of the changes that have taken place with regard to jurisdiction in family law cases is an example of how important it is for legal professionals to stay abreast of changes in the law that affect working on their clients' cases.

Completing a paralegal program is not the end of the educational process. It is only the start. Paralegals also must take steps to stay up-to-date on the changes in the law. Continuing education classes are one way to accomplish this. Another skill that will allow the paralegal to be aware of changes in the law is good legal research skills. A paralegal with good legal research skills has the ability to check on changes in the law and how they may affect the firm's clients.

Whatever the means, paralegals owe an ethical duty to their clients to stay abreast of the changes in the law in order to provide competent legal services.

# ENFORCEMENT OF ALIMONY AND CHILD SUPPORT

One key tool available to a spouse who is not receiving court-ordered alimony is to seek an order of contempt. The process is fairly simple, at least on paper. The spouse seeking enforcement files a motion for contempt with the court that initially issued the order granting alimony; a copy of the motion is served on the other spouse and a hearing is held. If the spouse has not in fact paid the alimony due, then an order is issued requiring payment. Failure to pay the past due alimony may result in the nonpaying spouse being held in contempt of court and the judge will impose sanctions, which may include incarceration, intended to coerce payment. See Figure 13.3, which contains a portion of the Uniform Interstate Family Support Act, as adopted by the State of Montana, for more information on how this is done.

The civil contempt process can also be used to enforce child support, which can include incarceration of the parent who is not paying his or her alimony/child support. In addition, courts have the ability to use a number of other ways to enforce payment of child support; examples include the following:

- Wage **garnishment**.
- Intercepting federal/state income taxes.
- Liens being placed on property owned by nonpaying parent.
- **Writ of execution** on personal property, such as cars and bank accounts.
- Unemployment compensation being received by the nonpaying parent.
- Revocation of professional licenses and driver's license of the nonpaying parent.
- Denial of issuance of passport or suspension of passport.
- Criminal prosecution.
- Negative report filed with credit reporting agencies.

**garnishment**
Legal proceeding in which the court orders a party who is indebted to a debtor to deliver the debtor's property to creditor.

**writ of execution**
Court order used to enforce a judgment.

---

**40-5-601. Failure to pay support—civil contempt.**
(1) For purposes of this section, "support" means child support; spousal support; health insurance, medical, dental, and optical payments; day care expenses; and any other payments due as support under a court or administrative order. Submission of health insurance claims is a support obligation if health insurance coverage is ordered.
(2) If a person obligated to provide support fails to pay as ordered, the payee or assignee of the payee of the support order may petition a district court to find the obligated person in contempt.
(3) The petition may be filed in the district court:
 (a) that issued the support order;
 (b) of the judicial district in which the obligated person resides; or
 (c) of the judicial district in which the payee or assignee of the payee resides or has an office.
(4) Upon filing of a verified petition alleging facts constituting contempt of the support order, the district court shall issue an order requiring the obligated person to appear and show cause why the obligated person should not be held in contempt and punished under this section.
(5) The obligated person is presumed to be in contempt upon a showing that:
 (a) there is a support order issued by a court or administrative agency of this or another state, an Indian tribe, or a country with jurisdiction to enter the order;
 (b) the obligated person had actual or constructive knowledge of the order; and
 (c) the obligated person failed to pay support as ordered.
(6) Certified payment records maintained by a clerk of court or administrative agency authorized by law or by the support order to collect support are admissible in a proceeding under this section and are prima facie evidence of the amount of support paid and any arrearages under the support order.

*(cont.)*

**FIGURE 13.3**
**Montana Code Annotated 2005**

FIGURE 13.3
*(concluded)*

(7) Following a showing under subsection (5), the obligated person may move to be excused from the contempt by showing clear and convincing evidence that the obligated person:
   (a) has insufficient income to pay the arrearages;
   (b) lacks personal or real property that can be sold, mortgaged, or pledged to raise the needed sum;
   (c) has unsuccessfully attempted to borrow the sum from a financial institution;
   (d) has no other source, including relatives, from which the sum can be borrowed or secured;
   (e) does not have a valid out-of-court agreement with the payee waiving, deferring, or otherwise compromising the support obligation; or
   (f) cannot, for some other reason, reasonably comply with the order.

(8) In addition to the requirement of subsection (7), the obligated person shall also show by clear and convincing evidence that factors constituting the excuse were not occasioned or caused by the obligated person voluntarily:
   (a) remaining unemployed or underemployed when there is employment suitable to the obligated person's skills and abilities available within a reasonable distance from the obligated person's residence;
   (b) selling, transferring, or encumbering real or personal property for fictitious or inadequate consideration within 6 months prior to a failure to pay support when due;
   (c) selling or transferring real property without delivery of possession within 6 months prior to a failure to pay support when due or, if the sale or transfer includes a reservation of a trust for the use of the obligated person, purchasing real or personal property in the name of another person or entity;
   (d) continuing to engage in an unprofitable business or contract unless the obligated person cannot reasonably be removed from the unprofitable situation; or
   (e) incurring debts subsequent to entry of the support order that impair the obligated person's ability to pay support.

(9) If the obligated person is not excused under subsections (7) and (8), the district court shall find the obligated person in contempt of the support order. For each failure to pay support under the order, the district court shall order punishment as follows:
   (a) not more than 5 days incarceration in the county jail;
   (b) not more than 120 hours of community service work;
   (c) not more than a $500 fine; or
   (d) any combination of the penalties in subsections (9)(a) through (9)(c).

(10) An order under subsection (9) must include a provision allowing the obligated person to purge the contempt. The obligated person may purge the contempt by complying with an order requiring the obligated person to:
   (a) seek employment and periodically report to the district court all efforts to find employment;
   (b) meet a repayment schedule;
   (c) compensate the payee for the payee's attorney fees, costs, and expenses for a proceeding under this section;
   (d) sell or transfer real or personal property or transfer real or personal property to the payee, even if the property is exempt from execution;
   (e) borrow the arrearage amount or report to the district court all efforts to borrow the sum;
   (f) meet any combination of the conditions in subsections (10)(a) through (10)(e); or
   (g) meet any other conditions that the district court in its discretion finds reasonable.

(11) If the obligated person fails to comply with conditions for purging contempt, the district court shall immediately find the obligated person in contempt under this section and impose punishment.

(12) A proceeding under this section must be brought within 3 years of the date of the last failure to comply with the support order.

## ADMINISTRATIVE ENFORCEMENT

The federal government became more involved with the issue of enforcement of child support with the enactment of the Child Support Enforcement and Establishment of Paternity Act in 1974, and later with the passage of the Child Support Enforcement Amendments of 1984, the Family Support Act of 1988, and the Personal Responsibility and Work Opportunity Reconciliation Act of 1996. The Child Support Enforcement and Establishment of Paternity Act mandated that states create agencies to aid in the enforcement of child support order. States now have Bureaus of Support Enforcement or IV-D agencies to assist in enforcement of these orders. A list of state child support enforcement offices is contained in Figure 13.4.

There are many reasons that both the state and federal governments have become more active in trying to aid in the collection of child support. One is a growing demand by the public that something be done to stop deadbeat parents from avoiding their responsibility to support their children. Another motivating factor in causing both state and federal governments to become more active in the enforcement of child support is that many custodial parents must turn to the government for aid when the noncustodial parent does not pay child support. It is, therefore, to the advantage of the government and the taxpayers to ensure that the noncustodial parent pay his or her share of child support for the child(ren).

These agencies provide a variety of services to the public, including:

- *Locating noncustodial parents and their assets.* One problem with trying to enforce child support orders has been locating the noncustodial parent. In the past, it was relatively easy for a parent to "disappear" when he or she wanted to avoid payment of child support. This is becoming more difficult in the computer age. A list of databases and information sources that are available to help locate these parents is included in Figure 13.5.

- *Establishing paternity.* There are times when paternity must be established in order to determine who is responsible for paying child support. This can be done voluntarily, such as when the father signs a written admission/acknowledgment of paternity. It can also be done involuntarily by an administrative action in which a hearing paternity is established.

**Alabama**
Department of Human Resources, Child Support Enforcement Division
50 Ripley Street, P.O. Box 304000, Montgomery, Alabama 36130-1801
Phone: 334-242-9300(P); 334-242-0606(F)

**Alaska**
Child Support Services Division, Department of Revenue
550 West 7th Avenue, 2nd Floor, Suite 280, Anchorage, Alaska 99501-6699
Phone: 800-478-3300(P); 907-269-6813(F)

**Arizona**
Division of Child Support Enforcement, Arizona Department of Economic Security
3443 N. Central, 4th Floor, Phoenix, Arizona 85067
Phone: 602-252-4045(P); 602-274-8250(F)

**Arkansas**
Office of Child Support Enforcement, Department of Finance and Administration
P.O. Box 8133, Little Rock, Arkansas 72203-8133
Phone: 501-682-6169(P); 501-682-6002(F)

**California**
Dept. of Child Support Services
P.O. Box 419064, Mail Station-10, Rancho Cordova, California 95741-9064
Phone: 866-249-0773(P); 910-464-5211(F)

**Colorado**
Division of Child Support Enforcement, Department of Human Services
1575 Sherman St. 5th Floor, Denver, Colorado 80203-1714
Phone: 303-866-4300(P); 303-866-4360(F)

**Connecticut**
Department of Social Services, Bureau of Child Support Enforcement
25 Sigourney Street, Hartford, Connecticut 06105-5033
Phone: 860-424-4989(P); 860-951-2996(F)

**Delaware**
Division of Child Support Enforcement, Delaware Health and Social Services
P.O. Box 904, New Castle, Delaware 19720
Phone: 302-326-6200(P); 302-324-6246(F)
Cust. Svc.: 302-577-7171

**District of Columbia**
Child Support Services Division, Office of the Attorney General
Judiciary Square, 441 Fourth Street NW, 5th Floor, Washington, District of Columbia 20001
Phone: 202-724-2131(P); 202-724-3710(F)

**Florida**
Child Support Enforcement, Department of Revenue
P.O. Box 8030, Tallahassee, Florida 32399-7016
Phone: 850-488-8726(P); 850-921-0792(F)

**Georgia**
Child Support Enforcement, Department of Human Resources
2 Peachtree Street, Room 20-460, Atlanta, Georgia 30303
Phone: 404-657-3851(P); 404-657-3326(F)

**Guam**
OAG, Child Support Enforcement Division
The Justice Building, 287 West O'Brien Drive, Hagatna, Guam 96910
Office: 671-475-3324(P); 671-475-3203(F)

**Hawaii**
Child Support Enforcement Agency, Office of Attorney General
601 Kamokila Boulevard, Suite 207, Kapolei, Hawaii 96707
Phone: 808-692-7000(P); 808-692-7134(F)

**Idaho**
Bureau of Child Support Services, Department of Health and Welfare
P.O. Box 83720, Boise, Idaho 83720-0036
Phone: 800-356-9868(P); 208-334-5571(F)

**Illinois**
Division of Child Support Enforcement, Illinois Department of Public Aid
509 S. 6th St., 6th Floor, Springfield, Illinois 62701
Phone: 800-447-4278(P); 217-524-4608(F)

**Indiana**
Child Support Bureau, Department of Child Services
402 West Washington Street Room W360, Indianapolis, Indiana 46204-2739
Phone: 317-233-5437(P); 317-233-4932(F)

**Iowa**
Bureau of Collections, Department of Human Services
400 S.W. 8th Street, Suite M, Des Moines, Iowa 50319-4691
Phone: 515-281-5647(P); 515-281-8854(F)

**Kansas**
Child Support Enforcement Program, Department of Social & Rehabilitation Services
P.O. Box 497, Topeka, Kansas 66601-049
Phone: 785-296-3237(P); 785-296-5206(F)

**Kentucky**
Division of Child Support, Cabinet for Families and Children
730 Schenkel Lane, P.O. Box 2150, Frankfort, Kentucky 40602-2150
Phone: 502-564-2285(P); 502-564-5988(F)

**Louisiana**
Office of Family Support, Support Enforcement Services Division
P.O. Box 94065, Baton Rouge, Louisiana 70804
Phone: 225-342-4780(P); 225-342-7397(F)

FIGURE 13.4 **State Child Support Enforcement Offices**

**Maine**
Division of Support Enforcement & Recovery, Bureau of Family Independence, Dept. of Health and Human Services
11 State House Station, Augusta, Maine 04333-0993
Phone: 800-371-3101(P); 207-287-2886(F)

**Maryland**
Child Support Enforcement Administration, Department of Human Resources, Saratoga State Center
311 West Saratoga Street, Room 301, Baltimore, Maryland 21201-3521
Phone: 410-767-7065(P); 410-333-6264(F)

**Massachusetts**
Child Support Enforcement Division, Department of Revenue
P.O. Box 6561, Boston, Massachusetts 02114-9561
Phone: 617-626-4064(P); 617-887-7550(F)

**Michigan**
Office of Child Support, Department of Human Services
235 South Grand Avenue, P.O. Box 30037, Lansing, Michigan 48909-7978
Phone: 517-373-2035(P); 517-373-4980(F)

**Minnesota**
Office of Child Support Enforcement, Department of Human Services
444 Lafayette Road, 4th Floor, St Paul, Minnesota 55155-3846
Phone: 651-296-4085(P); 651-297-4450(F)

**Mississippi**
Division of Child Support Enforcement, Department of Human Services
750 North State Street, Jackson, Mississippi 39202
Phone: 800-434-5437(P); 601-359-4415(F)

**Missouri**
Division of Child Support Enforcement, Department of Social Services
615 Howerton Court Bldg., P.O. Box 2320, Jefferson City, Missouri 65101
Phone: 800-859-7999(P); 573-751-0507(F)

**Montana**
Child Support, Department of Public Health & Human Services
3075 N. Montana Ave., Suite 112, Helena, Montana 59620
Phone: 800-346-5437(P); 406-444-1370(F)

**Nebraska**
Office of Economic & Family Support, Department of Health and Human Services
P.O. Box 94728, Lincoln, Nebraska 68509-4728
Phone: 402-471-1400(P); 402-471-7311(F)

**Nevada**
State of Nevada Division of Welfare and Supportive Services
1470 College Parkway, Carson City, Nevada 89706-7924
Phone: 775-684-0705(P); 775-684-0702(F)

Cust. Svc.: 775-684-7200; Cust. Svc.: 702-486-1646
Toll Free: 800-992-0900

**New Hampshire**
Division of Child Support Services, Health & Human Services
129 Pleasant Street, Concord, New Hampshire 03301-8711
Phone: 800-852-3345(P); 603-271-4787(F)

**New Jersey**
Office of Child Support, Department of Human Services
P.O. Box 716, Trenton, New Jersey 08625-0716
Phone: 609-588-2915(P); 609-588-2354(F)

**New Mexico**
Child Support Enforcement Division, Department of Human Services
P.O. Box 25110, Santa Fe, New Mexico 87504
Phone: 505-476-7207(P); 505-476-7045(F)

**New York**
Division of Child Support Enforcement, Office of Temporary Assistance and Disability
40 North Pearl Street, Room 13C, Albany, New York 12243-0001
Phone: 518-474-9081(P); 518-486-3127(F)

**North Carolina**
Child Support Enforcement, Department of Human Resources
P.O. Box 20800, Raleigh, North Carolina 27619-0800
Phone: 919-255-3800(P); 919-212-3840(F)

**North Dakota**
Child Support Enforcement Agency, Department of Human Services
P.O. Box 7190, Bismarck, North Dakota 58507-7190
Phone: 701-328-3582(P); 701-328-5497(F)

**Ohio**
Office of Child Support Enforcement, Department of Human Services and Jobs and Family Services
30 East Broad Street, 31st Floor, Columbus, Ohio 43215-3414
Phone: 614-752-6561(P); 614-752-9760(F)

**Oklahoma**
Child Support Enforcement Division, Department of Human Services
P.O. Box 53552, Oklahoma City, Oklahoma 73152
Phone: 405-522-5871(P); 405-522-2753(F)

**Oregon**
Division of Child Support, Oregon Department of Justice
494 State Street, S.E., Suite 300, Salem, Oregon 97301
Phone: 503-986-6166(P); 503-986-6158(F)

**Pennsylvania**
Bureau of Child Support Enforcement, Department of Public Welfare
P.O. Box 8018, Harrisburg, Pennsylvania 17105-8018
Phone: 800-932-0211(P); 717-787-9706(F)

*(cont.)*

**FIGURE 13.4**   *(continued)*

**Puerto Rico**
Department of the Family
P.O. Box 70376, San Juan, Puerto Rico 00936-8376
Phone: 787-767-1500(P); 787-723-6187(F)

**Rhode Island**
Office of Child Support Services, Department of Human Services
77 Dorrance Street, Providence, Rhode Island 02903
Phone: 401-222-4368(P); 401-222-2887(F)

**South Carolina**
Child Support Enforcement Division, Department of Social Services
P.O. Box 1469, Columbia, South Carolina 29202-1469
Phone: 803-898-9210(P); 803-898-9201(F)
Toll Free: 1-800-768-5858

**South Dakota**
Division of Child Support, Department of Social Services
700 Governor's Drive, Pierre, South Dakota 57501-2291
Phone: 605-773-3641(P); 605-773-5246(F)

**Tennessee**
Child Support Services, Department of Human Services
400 Deadrick Street, Nashville, Tennessee 37248-7400
Phone: 615-313-4880(P); 615-532-2791(F)

**Texas**
Child Support Division, Office of the Attorney General
P.O. Box 12017, Austin, Texas 78741-2017
Phone: 800-252-8014(P); 512-460-6867(F)

**Utah**
Child Support Services, Department of Human Services, Office of Recovery Services
P.O. Box 45033, Salt Lake City, Utah 84145-0033
Phone: 801-536-8901(P); 801-536-8509(F)

**Vermont**
Office of Child Support
103 South Main Street, Waterbury, Vermont 05671-1901
Phone: 802-786-3214(P); 802-244-1483(F)

**Virgin Islands**
Child Support Enforcement, Department of Justice
Nisky Center, Suite 500, 2nd Floor, St. Thomas, Virgin Islands 00802
Phone: 340-777-3070(P); 340-775-3808(F)
Fax/St.Croix: 340-779-3800

**Virginia**
Division of Child Support Enforcement
7 N. Eighth St., 1st Floor, Richmond, Virginia 23219
Phone: 800-257-9986(P); 804-726-7476(F)

**Washington**
Divison of Child Support, Economic Services Administration
P.O. Box 9162, Olympia, Washington 98507-9162
Phone: 360-664-5000(P); 360-664-5444(F)

**West Virginia**
Bureau for Child Support Enforcement, Department of Health and Human Resources
350 Capitol Street, Room 147, Charleston, West Virginia 25301-3703
Phone: 800-249-3778(P); 304-558-2445(F)

**Wisconsin**
Bureau of Child Support, Division of Economic Support
201 E. Washington Ave. E200, P.O. Box 7935, Madison, Wisconsin 53707-7935
Phone: 608-266-9909(P); 608-267-2824(F)

**Wyoming**
Department of Family Services, Child Support Enforcement
122 W. 25th St., Herschler Building, 1301 First Floor East, Cheyenne, Wyoming 82002
Phone: 307-777-7631(P); 307-777-5588(F)

**FIGURE 13.4** (concluded)

- *Establishing child support orders.* States can establish the obligation to pay child support and, in some cases, provide or assist in payment for health insurance for the child by administrative procedure, which involves a hearing master of the court or administrative officer.

- *Enforcing child support orders.* Payroll deduction is one of the most common ways used to ensure that child support payments are made on a regular basis. This is done in much the same manner as the withholding of income tax out of each paycheck. Federal and state law now requires that withholding be used in most cases.

- *Modifying child support orders.* This is done when it is appropriate.

- *Collecting and distributing child support payments.* State disbursement offices are responsible for the receipt and prompt disbursement of child support payments that are handled by the government agencies, and they can furnish information on the status of payments.

**FIGURE 13.5**
**Federal Citizen Information Center**

*Source:* Retrieved from www.pueblo.gsa.gov/cic_text/family/childenf/location.htm on 9/3/07.

**Handbook on Child Support Enforcement**

## FINDING THE NONCUSTODIAL PARENT: LOCATION

In most cases, to establish the paternity of a child, to obtain an order for support, and to enforce that order, the Child Support Enforcement (CSE) agency must know where the other parent lives or works. When one person makes a legal claim against another, the defendant must be given notice of the legal action taken and the steps necessary to protect his or her rights. To notify the noncustodial parent in advance under the state's service of process requirements–for example, by certified mail or personal service–child support enforcement officials need a correct address. If you do not have the address, the CSE office can try to find it. The most important information that you can provide is the noncustodial parent's Social Security number and any employer that you know about.

State/tribal CSE agencies, with due process and security safeguards, have access to information from the following:

- State and local government:
  Vital statistics
  State tax files
  Real and titled personal property records
  Occupational and professional licenses and business information
  Employment security agency
  Public assistance agency
  Motor vehicle department
  Law enforcement departments
- Records of private entities like public utilities and cable television companies (such as names and addresses of individuals and their employers as they appear in customer records)
- Credit bureaus
- Information held by financial institutions, including asset and liability data.
- The *State Directory of New Hires,* to which employers must report new employees
- The *Federal Parent Locator Service (FPLS)*

  The FPLS, which includes the Federal Case Registry (FCR) and the National Directory of New Hires (NDNH), has access to information from:
  - The Internal Revenue Service (IRS), the Department of Defense, the National Personnel Records Center, including quarterly wage data for Federal employees, the Social Security Administration, and the Department of Veterans Affairs
  - *State Directories of New Hires (SDNH)*
  - *State Workforce Agencies (SWAs)*

The FCR includes all *IV-D child support* cases from the 54 states and territories and non-IV-D support orders established after October 1998. The NDNH contains new hire records, quarterly wage records for almost all employed people, and unemployment insurance claims.

If you have access to the Internet, there is information about the FPLS at: www.acf.hhs.gov/programs/cse/newhire/.

## MODIFICATION OF ALIMONY

Modification of alimony, also referred to as *spousal support and maintenance,* can be pursued in cases where the alimony is not identified as nonmodifiable in the original dissolution of marriage decree. The court that originally issued the dissolution of marriage decree, which included the award of alimony, has jurisdiction over the motion to modify alimony. Although modification may be available, it is not necessarily an easy thing to accomplish.

As mentioned in Chapter 6, the following three factors need to be present before a court will grant a change in the amount of alimony, either increasing it or decreasing it:

- There has been a substantial change in circumstances.
- The change was not contemplated at the time the divorce decree was entered.
- The change is material, involuntary, and permanent.

The manner in which a request for modification of alimony is initiated varies by state. In some states, the application for modification is treated as an independent process, whereas in others it is a supplementary proceeding. Either party is entitled to seek modification of alimony since the changes that may occur to either of them may warrant either an increase or a reduction in the amount of alimony based on a change in circumstances. Unless otherwise provided by state statute, a request for modification may be made at any time after the entry of the final judgment, although the grounds for modification need to have occurred after the entry of the final decree ordering payment of alimony.

Not all types of alimony can be modified. Although permanent periodic alimony and rehabilitative alimony are usually modifiable, lump-sum alimony is not, although some states allow a change in how the lump-sum alimony is paid. In addition, courts are generally limited to modify future alimony payments and not any payments that are past due at the time of the petition for modification.

The court's ability to modify permanent periodic alimony that is made pursuant to a marital settlement agreement depends on a number of factors. The court must determine whether the alimony is being paid as support and maintenance or whether it is being paid as part of an overall plan of property distribution. If it is the latter, the court may lack the power to modify the payments.

### RESEARCH THIS

Research how a request for modification of alimony is initiated in your state. Resources to consult in your search should include state statutes, rules of court, and case law. Write a brief summary of your findings.

A hearing is required to determine if the petition should be granted. The court will consider evidence and take testimony to aid in this determination. It should be noted that this hearing is not meant to rehash the matters covered in the original divorce hearing but instead covers the facts that support that circumstances have changed sufficiently to warrant the modification. As is the case in the initial determination of rights in a dissolution of marriage action, courts are granted broad discretion in whether modification should be allowed. Appellate courts are reluctant to overturn a trial court's decision relating to the granting of or denial of modification of alimony unless it can be shown that there was an abuse of discretion.

## MODIFICATION OF CHILD CUSTODY OR VISITATION

One of the most difficult things to modify in a dissolution of decree is the custody of the child, unless the parties agree and the court will be able to see it is in the best interest of the child.

Why is it more difficult to modify child custody than child support? A modification of child custody can be far more disruptive to the child and have a more negative long-term impact on him or her.

As mentioned in Chapter 7, courts look for a material change in circumstances that affects the well-being of the child. It is not merely another chance to argue the initial custody arraignment. In addition, courts apply more stringent standard criteria in deciding whether modification should be allowed as compared with those used to make the initial award of custody. This is due to the desire to avoid any more disruptions in the life of the child than have already occurred due to the dissolution of marriage or separation of an unmarried couple. The key determination to be made is whether the change is required for the child's welfare.

The *Jackson v. Jackson* case is an example of how a court approaches the issue of changing child custody.

The court that originally granted the divorce retains continuing jurisdiction to modify orders relating to child custody and visitation and conducts the hearing to decide whether there is sufficient cause to modify the agreement. The action is normally begun by one of the parents or a nonparent who claims a right to custody/visitation to the child pursuant to state statute. The person who brings the action has the burden to prove the state's requirements for modification are met. For example, in some states the petitioner must prove that a change in circumstances has occurred since the initial order was entered and that the change would be in the child's best interest. As was the case in the original action on custody, the parties may avail themselves of discovery to obtain the information needed to support their position in court.

## MODIFICATION OF CHILD SUPPORT

A substantial change in circumstances must have occurred since entry of the divorce decree in order to modify child support. The word *substantial* should be emphasized because it demonstrates that courts are reluctant to make changes unless it is warranted. The changes can be either changes in the situation of the parents or changes in the needs of the child.

Examples of a substantial change include the loss of one's job, becoming disabled, getting a better-paying job, or a change in the parenting plan that increases the time a child stays with a parent on an extended basis. Figure 13.6 contains a sample petition for modification of child support.

## RELOCATION OF PARENT

The relocation of the custodial parent is another issue that has to be increasingly dealt with in the family law firm and the court system. Like other postjudgment matters, the mobility of our society presents legal issues relating to a custodial parent moving. It presents a number of conflicts. The custodial parent feels that he or she has a right to move as an American. This may be true, but this right to move has to be balanced with the impact it will have on the child and the impact it will have on the ability to exercise liberal visitation of the child by the noncustodial parent.

Courts look to the reasons the custodial parent has for the move to ascertain if the move is being made in good faith, as compared to moving to prevent visitation by the noncustodial parent. The other main factor is whether the move is in the child's best interest. Courts decide what constitutes the best interest of a child on a case-by-case basis. Examples of factors that may be viewed favorably include the move's

**FIGURE 13.6**

**West Virginia Family Law Petition for Modification Form**

*Source:* Retrieved from www.state.wv.us/WVSCA/rules/FamilyCourt/FC201.pdf on 3/21/07.

---

**IN THE FAMILY COURT OF_____COUNTY, WEST VIRGINIA.**

**In Re:**

**The Marriage / Children of:**

_____,

Petitioner

_____

Address

_____

Daytime phone

**Civil Action No. _____**

and _____.

Respondent

_____

Address

_____

Daytime phone

**PETITION FOR MODIFICATION**

**1. General Information**

a. The Petitioner is: _____, who is: (Print your name.)

___ the mother / wife whose name is listed in the case style at the top of this page.

___ the father / husband whose name is listed in the case style at the top of this page.

___ other person, whose relationship to the Respondent / children is:_____.

b. The Petitioner requests that the Order entered on the date of _____ be modified with regard to:

___ Parenting Plan

___ Child support

___ Spousal support

___ Other; (Explain)

_____

**2. I want the Court to modify the Order in these ways:** (Check all that apply.)

___ Increase child support

___ Decrease child support ___ End child support

___ Change Parenting Plan with regard to: ___ Decision making;

___ Time spent with the children; ___ Other; (Explain) _____.

___ Order child support *paid to* another person, who is:_____.

___ Order child support *paid by* another person, who is:_____.

___ Increase spousal support

___ Decrease spousal support ___ End spousal support

___ Other modification request(s); (Explain.)

_____

**3. Circumstances that justify the modification I am requesting.**

(Explain all of the changes in circumstances you think justify the modifications you requested.):

_____

_____

_____

**4. Information concerning Public Assistance and Child Support Enforcement Services**

a. ___ A Public Assistance check from Health and Human Services is now being received by: ___ The Children; ___ The Petitioner; ___ The Respondent.

b. ___ A Public Assistance check from Health and Human Services was received in the past by: ___ The Children; ___ The Petitioner; ___ The Respondent.

c. ___ Services from the Bureau for Child Support Enforcement have been applied for by: ___ The Petitioner; ___ The Respondent.

d. ___ Income withholding services are currently being received from the Bureau for Child Support Enforcement.

_____          _____

Petitioner's Signature                    Date

**You must sign the Verification on the next page before a Notary Public.**

**FIGURE 13.6**
*(concluded)*

**VERIFICATION**

I, _____, after making an oath or affirmation to tell the truth, say that the facts I have stated in this Petition are true of my personal knowledge; and if I have set forth matters upon information given to me by others, I believe that information to be true.

_____        _____
Signature                                                      Date
This Verification was sworn to or affirmed before me on the _____ day of _____, 2____.

_____
Notary Public / Other official
My commission expires:_____.

**CERTIFICATE OF SERVICE**
State of West Virginia County of_____
I, _____, the Petitioner for Modification, mailed my Petition by first class United States Mail, postage paid, to:

_____
(Name and Address)
_____
(Date mailed)
And:

_____
(Name and Address)
_____
(Date mailed)

_____        _____
Petitioner's Signature                                       Date

economic benefit for the child and the willingness to work out a reasonable visitation plan if the relocation is allowed.

States do vary on the issue of what must be shown to allow relocation of the custodial parent. The items discussed are the general rules that many states apply. Others, such as Arkansas, create a presumption that the custodial parent should be allowed to move. The noncustodial parent has the burden to rebut that presumption. States that apply this standard remove from the custodial parent the duty to show that the move would be a real advantage to the parent and the child to move.

## THE IMPACT OF BANKRUPTCY ON ALIMONY AND CHILD SUPPORT

Divorce affects the lives of the couple in many ways, including financially. There are new expenses, such as the maintenance of two homes, which can put a strain on the financial resources of the formerly married couple. This strain often results in one or both of the parties filing bankruptcy. The question then becomes, what effect does filing of bankruptcy by the person who is required to pay alimony have on future payments and efforts to collect alimony payments?

Two aspects of bankruptcy can have a potential impact on the payment and collection of alimony. The first is the **automatic stay**, which stops almost all enforcement actions against the person who files bankruptcy. The second is that one goal of a person who is filing bankruptcy is the discharge, or wiping out, of his or her debts.

However, the bankruptcy code, as modified by the Bankruptcy Abuse Prevention and Consumer Protection Act, does provide exemptions from both the operation of

**automatic stay**
A stay that stops almost all collection actions against the debtor at the time of the filing for bankruptcy protection.

*Jackson v. Jackson*
August 26, 2004
No. 03-220
2004 WY 99

## ISSUES

The parties agree that the issues presented are as follows:

1. Did the trial court abuse its discretion when it found that a material change in circumstances had occurred despite the lack of significant or compelling evidence to support that finding?
2. Did the court abuse its discretion when it found that it would be in the best interests of the children to award custody to father?
3. Did the trial court abuse its discretion when it failed to consider the evidence of spousal abuse presented to it, and when it failed to make arrangements for the Children that best protected the children from further harm, as mandated by Wyoming Statute, § 20-2-201(c)?

## STRONG FACTS

Kevin and Misty Jackson were married on December 11, 1999, in Las Vegas, Nevada, and divorced on November 7, 2000, in Laramie, Wyoming. The couple has two children together, a girl born on January 2, 1998, and a boy born on June 16, 2000. The divorce decree ordered joint custody and awarded primary physical custody of the children to Ms. Jackson. The court granted Mr. Jackson reasonable visitation and ordered him to pay child support.

Despite their divorce, the Jacksons continued to live together until June 2002. However, their relationship during that time remained troubled. In August 2001, Ms. Jackson filed a petition for a restraining order against Mr. Jackson pursuant to the Family Violence Protection Act after Mr. Jackson attacked a man with whom she had been dancing in a bar. No hearing was held. However, a stipulated order was to be prepared by Father's attorney and submitted to the court. An order was never entered, but both parties testified they believed one was in effect and acted accordingly. Ultimately, the couple reunited and moved to Wendover, Nevada in October 2001 to "start over." While in Wendover, Ms. Jackson worked as a waitress and Mr. Jackson worked for a cable company. However, in June 2002, in what would be their final separation, Ms. Jackson and the children moved back to Laramie, while Mr. Jackson remained in Wendover. Ms. Jackson lived with her parents in their home, together with her brother and sister-in-law. From September to December 2002, Ms. Jackson changed jobs five times. In February 2003, after being unemployed for over two months, she enrolled in cosmetology school. She left that program, and enrolled in a different school a few months later. While Ms. Jackson was at school, the children attended daycare. Mr. Jackson remained in

Wendover and continued working for the cable company. He made significant improvements in his lifestyle including quitting drinking, smoking, and chewing and ending his association with "bad influences." He received a promotion at work and was able to provide health insurance for the children. He also developed a stable relationship with a woman whom he ultimately married less than two weeks before the hearing on his petition for modification of custody.

In January 2003, Mr. Jackson filed a petition for modification of custody and support alleging it was in the best interests of the children that he be granted primary physical custody of them. Ms. Jackson filed an answer and counterclaim requesting that the court dismiss Mr. Jackson's petition and increase his child support obligation. At a hearing on June 13, 2003, the district court heard testimony from both parties, as well as their friends and family. The district court issued its decision letter on July 1, 2003, finding "a change of circumstances sufficient to warrant modification of custody and support and that such modification is in the best interests of the minor children." Ms. Jackson timely filed this appeal.

## STRONG DISCUSSION

Ms. Jackson argues the district court abused its discretion when it found that a material change in circumstances had occurred and that it would be in the best interests of the children to award primary physical custody to Mr. Jackson. She also claims the court erred when it failed to consider evidence of spousal abuse in making its determination. This Court has prescribed the following test to be applied in such situations:

> A party who is seeking to modify the child custody provisions of a divorce decree has the burden of showing that a substantial or material change in circumstances, which affects the child's welfare, occurred subsequent to the entry of the initial decree, that the change warrants modification of the decree, and that the modification will be in the child's best interests.

*Cobb v. Cobb*, 2 P.3d 578, 579 (Wyo. 2000) (citations omitted). Wyo. Stat. Ann. § 20-2-201(a) (Lexis-Nexis) sets forth the factors the court must consider in making custody determinations. The statute states the court shall consider, but is not limited to, the following factors:

> (i) The quality of the relationship each child has with each parent;
> (ii) The ability of each parent to provide adequate care for each child throughout each period of responsibility, including arranging for each child's care by others as needed;

(iii) The relative competency and fitness of each parent;

(iv) Each parent's willingness to accept all responsibilities of parenting, including a willingness to accept care for each child at specified times and to relinquish care to the other parent at specified times;

(v) How the parents and each child can best maintain and strengthen a relationship with each other;

(vi) How the parents and each child interact and communicate with each other and how such interaction and communication may be improved;

(vii) The ability and willingness of each parent to allow the other to provide care without intrusion, respect the other parent's rights and responsibilities, including the right to privacy;

(viii) Geographic distance between the parents' residences;

(ix) The current physical and mental ability of each parent to care for each child;

(x) Any other factors the court deems necessary and relevant.

The district court found "that there has been a change of circumstances sufficient to warrant modification of custody and support and that such modification is in the best interests of the minor children of the parties." The court found there was no real change in Ms. Jackson's circumstances, citing she "continues to live with her parents, and they continue to provide for her and her children. She has been through numerous jobs, none of which have worked out . . . . there is no prospect of employment for at least another year. She continues to prowl the bars at least two nights each week, sometimes more, while her parents look after the children." On the other hand, the court found "significant" changes in Mr. Jackson's circumstances, including: regular employment for over 18 months, financial responsibility for himself and his children, and lifestyle changes which enhanced his ability to parent his children. The court found, "None of these changes have been of long-standing duration and none of them would be sufficient, standing alone, to justify a finding that there has been a significant change in circumstance." Yet, the court concluded the combined changes were significant enough to warrant custody modification.

**Change in Circumstances.** In considering requests for custody modification, the courts are usually faced with changes in circumstances that cause the custodial parent's situation to deteriorate in some way to the detriment of the children. However, in some cases neither parent deteriorates, but one parent improves substantially, while the other does not.

\*\*\*

\*\*\*Mr. Jackson progressed, while Ms. Jackson "maintained." Mr. Jackson had been regularly employed for over 18 months; however, in the course of less than five months, Ms. Jackson switched jobs five times, enrolled in beauty school, quit, and then enrolled in another beauty school, never achieving a stable source of income. Mr. Jackson provided health insurance for the children, which the divorce degree required of him in the event that Ms. Jackson could not. Mr. Jackson also stopped smoking, drinking and chewing, while Ms. Jackson "partied" at least two, sometimes four, times a week. Mr. Jackson married

his girlfriend of six months, albeit one week before the modification hearing, and established a household with her and his two children while Ms. Jackson continually relied on her parents for housing and support.

Although the district court found none of these factors alone would amount to a change in circumstances, together they constituted a material change. We have recognized that courts must consider all of the circumstances together in determining whether a material change has occurred. As one treatise states:

> The consideration and weighing of the factors in a custody dispute is essentially factual . . . . Cases with very similar facts may be decided in divergent ways by courts of different states, and even by courts within the same state. The differing results often come from the hearts and emotions of judges, rather than from the facts of the case.

Certainly, the district court was in a much better position to weigh and judge the credibility of the witnesses than we are. Our review of the record discloses a careful, thoughtful analysis by the district court and we discern no abuse of discretion in its conclusion that a material change in circumstances had occurred.

**Best Interests of the Children.** A *material change* of circumstances does not automatically equate with a change in custody, however. Custody must be arranged so as to be in the best interests of the child(ren) on an individualized basis. The core of the inquiry must reach the question of reasonableness of the choice made by the district court.

Ms. Jackson argues that the district court was unreasonable in finding it was in the children's best interests to award Mr. Jackson custody claiming it did not consider the required statutory factors. While she admits the court's decision letter lists the nine required factors set out in § 20-2-201(a), she complains that the court only specifically addressed the "stability of the parents" factor.

\*\*\*while § 20-2-201(a) does not specifically require *findings* as to the various factors, the statute does direct the court to *consider* those factors in ordering the disposition of children. "On appeal, this court can ascertain whether the factors have been appropriately weighed only if the district court's consideration is reflected in the proceeding transcripts, by opinion letter, or as findings in the written order." Thus, this Court may look beyond the district court's written decision to the hearing transcript in determining whether the court considered the required factors in compliance with § 20-2-201(a). In this case, the transcript evidences the district court fulfilled its responsibility to weigh all of the statutory factors to determine what was in the children's best interests. The court explained its role stating:

> I do want to make one thing clear. The purpose of a hearing like this today, and what the Court is charged with the responsibility of doing here, is not choosing which of you is the better parent. I don't doubt that both of you love your kids. I don't question that at all. It is the Court's responsibility, like it or not, to decide without regard to what you want (pointing) and without regard to what you want (pointing), and fortunately or unfortunately, what grandparents want doesn't count, isn't considered, to decide what is

253

best for the children in this case, and to do that based on what I've heard today, because I don't know either one of you. I don't favor either one of you.

Each case requires the district court to carefully weigh the relevant factors while looking to the unique and individual family relationships in reaching a resolution that is in the best interests of the children in that family. In this case, the district court heard testimony that Ms. Jackson, upon moving back to Laramie, moved in with her parents, and relied completely on them for support. The court also heard testimony that indicated the grandparents are the children's parents. Other testimony included accounts of Ms. Jackson's propensity to party and drive drunk with her children in the car. On the other hand, the court heard testimony about the increasing stability of Mr. Jackson's life including his job security, his avoidance of harmful substances, and his stable relationship. The district court's decision letter stated "[Mr. Jackson] has shown himself capable of providing a stable, nurturing and responsible home without the aid or interference of relatives. Ms. Jackson has not." We are persuaded the court considered the factors in § 20-2-201(a), and its reasoning is adequately reflected in the record. Therefore, the district court's decision that it would be in the children's best interests to be in their father's custody was not an abuse of discretion.

**Evidence of Spousal Abuse.** In her final argument, Ms. Jackson asserts the district court abused its discretion when it failed to consider evidence of spousal abuse, which Ms. Jackson alleged her former husband had committed against her, as contrary to the best interests of the children as required by § 20-2-201(c) which provides:

> The court *shall* consider evidence of spousal abuse or child abuse as being contrary to the best interest of the children. If the court finds that family violence has occurred, the court shall make arrangements for visitation that best protects the children and the abused spouse from further harm.

In no way does this Court minimize domestic violence and its effects on those involved. We are especially aware of the negative effects domestic violence and spousal abuse can have on children. Having said that, however, the record before us does not establish clear incidences of spousal abuse for the district court to consider. Rather, the record indicates Mr. Jackson assaulted one of Ms. Jackson's companions, and both parties perpetrated abuse on each other.

\* \* \*

While it is clear from the record that the Jacksons' relationship was volatile, we must defer to the district court to determine whether their actions constituted spousal abuse such that it should impact the court's custody evaluation. Again, the trial judge is in the best position to assess the credibility of the witnesses and weigh their testimony. It appears from the record that the district court was not convinced of any clear-cut spousal abuse by Mr. Jackson and found the attacks by both parties did not rise to a level that should impact its decision as to what was in the children's best interests. Accordingly, we hold the district court did not abuse its discretion in the manner in which it considered the conflicting testimony regarding spousal abuse.

## CONCLUSION

We affirm the district court's conclusion that a change in circumstances occurred and it was in the best interests of the children to grant primary physical custody to Mr. Jackson. His efforts to improve his life personally and professionally, juxtaposed with Ms. Jackson's instability and reliance on her parents for support of her and the two children, is determinative. As the district court stated, both could be suitable parents, however, it is in the children's best interests to be in the stable environment their father can provide them at this time. Under the circumstances of this case, we hold that the district court could have reasonably concluded as it did and, thus, did not abuse its discretion.

**Note:** Citations omitted and case edited for brevity.

**Source:** Retrieved from http://wyom.state.wy.us/applications/oscn/deliverdocument.asp?id=441099&hits=.

### CASE BRIEF ASSIGNMENT

Read and brief the *Jackson v. Jackson*, 96 P.3d 21 (Wyo. 2004) case. (See Appendix A for information on how to brief cases.)

**domestic support obligation (DSO)** Phrase used in bankruptcy code that describes support obligations.

the automatic stay and the ability to discharge domestic support obligations. Specifically, proceedings related to a divorce or dissolution of marriage (except if it is an effort to take or divide property that is part of the bankruptcy estate), child custody, child visitation, domestic violence, or paternity actions are exempt from its application of the automatic stay. This includes actions for the collection of current child support and alimony and of past due child support and alimony from property that is not part of the bankruptcy estate. Nor can a spouse discharge child support or alimony obligations by filing bankruptcy, meaning that they will be continued to be owed as if the filing spouse had never done so. The bankruptcy code now uses the term **domestic support obligation (DSO)** when discussing what debts are not dischargeable, which include child support, alimony, or other debts in the nature of alimony. This phrase is much broader than the ones that have been used in the past, which reflects the desire of Congress to reduce the use of bankruptcy to delay or avoid payments of obligations such as child support and alimony. The obligation must have been created by a separation/settlement agreement, divorce decree, court order imposing support

**11 U.S.C. 101 (14A)** The term "domestic support obligation" means a debt that accrues before, on, or after the date of the order for relief in a case under this title, including interest that accrues on that debt as provided under applicable nonbankruptcy law notwithstanding any other provision of this title, that is-
(A) owed to or recoverable by-
    (i) a spouse, former spouse, or child of the debtor or such child's parent, legal guardian, or responsible relative; or
    (ii) a governmental unit;
(B) in the nature of alimony, maintenance, or support (including assistance provided by a governmental unit) of such spouse, former spouse, or child of the debtor or such child's parent, without regard to whether such debt is expressly so designated;
(C) established or subject to establishment before, on, or after the date of the order for relief in a case under this title, by reason of applicable provisions of-
    (i) a separation agreement, divorce decree, or property settlement agreement;
    (ii) an order of a court of record; or
    (iii) a determination made in accordance with applicable nonbankruptcy law by a governmental unit; and
(D) not assigned to a nongovernmental entity, unless that obligation is assigned voluntarily by the spouse, former spouse, child of the debtor, or such child's parent, legal guardian, or responsible relative for the purpose of collecting the debt.

**FIGURE 13.7**
**Definition of Domestic Support Obligation**
*Source:* Retrieved from http://uscode.house.gov/uscode-cgi/fastweb.exe?getdoc+uscview+t09t12+3682+1++%28%29%20%20AND%20%28%2811%29%20ADJ%20USC%29%3ACITE%20AND%20%28USC%20w%2F10%20%28101%29%29%3ACITE%20%20%20%20%20%20%20%20

obligations, or a determination by a state agency that has authority to impose support obligations. See Figure 13.7 for the definition of domestic support obligation as set out in the Bankruptcy Code.

Other important changes include:

- DSOs are no longer dischargeable.
- DSOs are now first property claim, behind only the trustee's administrative expenses in **Chapter 7** bankruptcy cases.
- Property that would normally be **exempt** from the reach of creditors is now subject to being taken to pay child support or alimony.
- In **Chapter 13** bankruptcy cases the debtor is required to stay current in payments of DSO obligations or the case may be dismissed or converted to a Chapter 7 case.
- Debtor's failure to pay all DSOs, whether they occurred before the filing of bankruptcy or after, may result in a denial of **discharge.**
- Income deductions made pursuant to an income deduction order continue even after the filing of bankruptcy in both Chapter 7 and 13 cases.

**Chapter 7**
Liquidation bankruptcy.

**exempt property**
Property that cannot be taken to satisfy debts owed creditors.

**Chapter 13**
Individual reorganization bankruptcy.

**discharge**
Extinguishment of debts or obligations by legal action.

**CYBER TRIP**

To learn more about the impact bankruptcy has on enforcement of child support and alimony payments, visit www.divorcenet.com/states/nationwide/impact_of_bapcpa_on_family_practitioner.

## APPEAL

Up to this point the focus has been on matters that may ultimately be decided by a judge who handles family law cases, such as the one who hears a dissolution of marriage action and determines issues such as child custody and/or alimony. But take a moment and look at the cases that have been set out in this textbook and it will become apparent that they all have one thing in common—they are all appellate court cases. That means that a lower court judge made a ruling on a matter that one of the parties did not agree with and that party decided to appeal the decision.

Let's use the *Jackson v. Jackson* case to show the role of appeals in a family law case. In that case, the district court granted a petition to modify primary physical custody of the children because Mr. Jackson had substantially improved his life and had become more stable. Ms. Jackson was unhappy with the decision and appealed the decision. Even though she was unsuccessful in her appeal, the case does show how an appellate court is used to review a lower court's decision to see if reversible errors were made.

Although, because of its complexity, appellate practice is beyond the scope of this textbook, it is important for the paralegal student studying family law to have a basic understanding of the process.

Generally, a case can only be appealed if the order or judgment was final. For example, in the *Jackson* case the judge had entered an order making a change in custody of the child. Some states do allow the appeal of some nonfinal orders.

**de novo**
Standard appellate review where the appellate court reviews the facts and law independent of the trial court's decision.

Trial court rulings are usually left undisturbed unless a ruling is found to be contrary to the weight of the evidence. Even courts in states that use the **de novo** standard of review will usually not disturb the trial court's findings in dissolution cases unless equity was not done by judge. Appellate courts recognize that trial courts must have broad discretion in resolving family law matters, and most states provide a presumption of correctness of the trial court's decision.

### RESEARCH THIS

Research the statutory and constitutional law in your state and determine which court has jurisdiction to hear appeals of dissolution of marriage cases. What is the name of the court? How many such appellate courts does your state have? Which appellate court would hear an appeal from a trial court in the city that you live in?

Can the appellate courts in your state hear only final orders or can they hear nonfinal orders? If they can hear nonfinal orders, which ones can be reviewed by the appellate court?

## Summary

Postjudgment legal issues are often as complicated and emotional as the other matters discussed in this textbook. They include a wide range of motions and proceedings that may be needed to enforce the original divorce decree or to modify the decree to reflect the changes that have occurred since its filing. These include enforcement of child support payments and alimony, as well as issues such as the desire of the custodial parent to relocate to another state. Recent changes in the bankruptcy act have made it more difficult for people to try to avoid payment of alimony and child support by filing bankruptcy.

Those who are unhappy with the outcome of dissolution of marriage case may seek appellate review of those items in which the trial court made errors in its order. The likelihood of success on appeal, however, is not good since appellate courts usually give the trial court great discretion in resolving the issues before it in a family law case.

## Key Terms

Automatic stay
Chapter 7
Chapter 13
De novo
Discharge
Domestic support obligation

Exempt property
Forum shopping
Garnishment
Parental Kidnapping Prevention Act (PKPA)
Writ of execution

1. What was the purpose of the Parental Kidnapping Prevention Act and how does it relate to the Uniform Child Jurisdiction and Enforcement Act?
2. How does the Uniform Child Jurisdiction and Enforcement Act deal with international child abduction?
3. What is forum shopping and how does it relate to parental kidnapping?
4. What is the purpose of the Uniform Interstate Family Support Act?
5. What factors must be present in order for a spouse to have the amount of alimony awarded changed?
6. What factors must be present in order to have the amount of alimony awarded?
7. What factors do courts consider when asked to change child custody?
8. What factors do courts consider when asked to allow the custodial parent to relocate?
9. What are some of the ways that are available to collect unpaid child support?
10. List the services that are provided by IV-D agencies?
11. What is a domestic support obligation?
12. What changes have recently been made to the bankruptcy code that make it difficult to discharge a debt created by a DSO?
13. What kind of court orders are normally appealable?
14. What is an automatic stay?
15. What is exempt property?

1. Thomas, who lives in your state, has retained your firm to file a motion for a change of custody of his child, Luke. Thomas had been married to Mia until their divorce 2 years ago. Mia was awarded primary custody of their only son, Luke. Thomas refused to return Luke to his mother after his most recent visitation 2 months ago. Instead he decided to seek a change in custody. Will your state be able to hear a change of custody request by Thomas? Explain.
2. Explain why jurisdiction is important in the enforcement of alimony and child support. Include how the law has changed to resolve issues relating to cases that are brought in states other than the original state in which the order was entered. Also, discuss whether there is a difference between jurisdictional issues in child support as compared with alimony.
3. Janice is a lawyer. She recently divorced Adam, who was awarded primary physical custody of the child and child support. Adam, who was a stay-at-home husband during the marriage, continued not to work after the divorce so that the child would not have to go to day care. Janice was very bitter over having to pay so much child support, even though she had agreed to the amount in the couple's separation agreement, which was incorporated in the judge's final order of dissolution of marriage. She became so bitter that she stopped paying child support. Adam has retained your firm to assist in collecting the unpaid child support. Research the laws and court rules of your state to determine what steps will need to be taken to collect the unpaid child support. Also determine which of the methods of enforcing child support would be applicable in this case.
4. Julie, who was recently divorced, has lived in your state all of her life. She has primary physical custody of her son, Larry, age 13. She is now engaged to marry John, who lives in another state that is over 500 miles away. She has retained

your firm to find out what her legal rights are as to relocating to her fiancé's state while retaining custody of her son. Research the statutory and case law of your state. Prepare a written explanation of your findings for use by your supervising attorney when she meets with Julie.

5. Kyle is over $5,000 behind in court-ordered child support payments. He has lost his job and made no real effort to find another. He doesn't want to pay child support since his ex-wife recently became remarried to a local doctor. Kyle has come to your firm to find out what his legal options are to stop payment of child support and eliminate his past due child support. Would Kyle be able to have his dissolution of marriage decree modified to eliminate the requirement to pay child support? Modify the payment of child support? Would bankruptcy be a means to avoid payment of the past due child support? Explain.

## REAL WORLD DISCUSSION TOPICS

1. The parties' divorce decree awarded custody of the minor child of the marriage to the wife. The husband was ordered to pay child support. The amount of child support was later modified, increasing the amount from $100 to $200. The modification also added a requirement that the wife be responsible for the first $250 of the child's medical bills each calendar year plus 20 percent of the medical care over that amount. The husband was required to pay the remaining 80 percent of the excess of $250. The mother moved for a modification of the child support payments, stating in support of her motion that (a) she had the lost of use of her fingers and legs, (b) her employment would terminate at the end of the summer, (c) the child required ordinary and extraordinary medical, dental, optometric, and orthodontic care as a result of the child's advancing age and new medical developments, and (d) she had moved to the Tacoma, Washington, metropolitan area and the inflated cost of living there. Should the mother's motion be granted? See *Gross v. Gross,* 355 N.W.2d 4 (S.D.1984).

2. At the time of their marriage, Mother was a part-time actress and Father was a radiology technician. They subsequently moved to Orlando, Florida, where Mother's family is located. The couple had two children. The mother worked part-time in the entertainment industry for a time and later began working full-time as a bookkeeper and salesperson. The father's employment history was uneven. The family relocated to Pennsylvania. The mother continued doing sales work for her Orlando employer out of her Pennsylvania home for a time. The parties had a period of attempted reconciliation but made a final separation in 2004. The mother filed an emergency motion to allow her to return to Orlando, Florida. In support of the motion, she stated that the move to Orlando would provide a supportive environment from her family that lives there, a better job opportunity, and the possibility of working in the entertainment industry. The noncustodial parent objected to the move. Should the court grant the wife's motion? See *Billhime v. Billhime,* 869 A.2d 1031 (Pa.Super. 2005)

## PORTFOLIO ASSIGNMENT

1. Review the facts of the Kimberly Lincoln case from the Client Interview at the beginning of this chapter. Next, research the statutory and case law of your state to determine the proper jurisdiction for an action to collect Kimberly's ex-spouse's past due alimony and child support payments. Would your answer differ if Kimberly had also left Georgia and lived in Florida? If so, why? Write a brief paper setting out the basis for your conclusions.

2. Research the laws of your state relating to modification of alimony, child support, and child custody. Write a summary of your findings.

# Chapter 14

# Adoption, In Vitro Fertilization, and Surrogacy

## CHAPTER OBJECTIVES

**After reading this chapter and completing the assignments, you should be able to:**

- Demonstrate an understanding of jurisdiction and venue in the adoption process.

- Discuss the various types of adoption.

- Understand what constitutes a black market adoption.

- Describe the adoption process.

- Discuss the legal consequences of an adoption.

- Understand the legal issues associated with in vitro fertilization and surrogacy.

Many of the chapters of this textbook have focused on some of the more unpleasant aspects of family law, such as divorce. This chapter introduces the paralegal student to a happier procedure—adoption.

The paralegal student will learn about the legal concepts of adoption, the various types of adoptions, the adoption procedure, and the consequences of adoption.

Chapter 14 also introduces the paralegal student to in vitro fertilization and surrogacy and the impact that the scientific advancement in these areas has had on the legal system.

## CLIENT INTERVIEW

Jill Simpson wants to adopt the child of a young woman who is pregnant. They both live in your town. The soon-to-be mother is unmarried and not financially able to support the child once he or she is born. Jill is also unmarried but financially well off and has always wanted a baby. She has come to your firm because of its reputation of helping people adopt children.

## WHY THIS CHAPTER IS IMPORTANT TO THE PARALEGAL

The family law firm is often called upon to help a couple adopt a child. In fact, some family law firms specialize in adoptions and work to bring the parties together, execute the formal documents required, and handle the case as it moves through the adoption process. It is important for paralegal students to understand the basic adoption process, the forms commonly used, and the law surrounding adoption to perform the duties they may be required to complete in the family law firm.

In addition, two procedures covered in this chapter, in vitro fertilization and surrogacy, have created many challenges for the legal system. It is important that the paralegal understand how the legal system is adjusting to the rapid advancement and utilization of these medical procedures.

## WHAT IS ADOPTION?

**adoption**
The taking of a child into the family, creating a parent-child relationship where the biological relationship did not exist.

**Adoption** is something most people are familiar with, at least in general terms. It is the legal process that allows a child to be brought into a family and creates a parent-child relationship where the biological relationship did not exist. In many cases, it results in the child being removed from his or her biological family tree and being inserted into the adoptive parents' family tree.

**closed adoption**
A form of adoption in which biological parents of the child have no contact with the child or the adopting parents.

Traditionally, most people thought of **closed adoptions** when they heard the word *adoption.* Closed adoptions are ones in which the child's biological parents have no contact with the adopting parents. In addition, they generally prevent the revelation of information of the biological parents and the child.

**open adoption**
A form of adoption in which a varying degree of contact occurs among the biological parent(s) of his/ her child, the child, and the adoptive parent(s).

**Open adoptions** are much more common today. They allow a varying degree of contact between the biological parents and the adopting parents. Often they meet prior to the birth of the baby.

The adoption process is created by state statute. The goal is to provide for the child's well-being by establishing a permanent family when none exists or where circumstances prevent the biological parents from providing one for the child.

As will become apparent in the discussion contained in this chapter, the area of adoption is a complicated one. It incorporates a wide variety of adoption proceedings and situations where those proceedings are used.

## JURISDICTION AND VENUE

As noted in previous chapters, determining the court with jurisdiction over a case is critical. The names of the courts that have jurisdiction over adoptions vary by state. Some of the common names include: circuit court, district court, superior court, probate court, family court, and juvenile court. So, the first question that must be asked is what state court has jurisdiction to handle adoption matters.

The second question that must be asked, since there are numerous circuit courts, and so on, throughout the state that have jurisdiction over an adoption proceeding, is where the proper venue is for the case to be heard. Although states vary on where the proper venue for an adoption case is, they often include the county where the person seeking to adopt (petitioner) and/or the child to be adopted reside, or where the child-placing agency is located. See Figure 14.1 for the Montana statute on venue.

**14-15-04. Venue-Inconvenient forum-Caption.**

1. Proceedings for adoption must be brought in the court for the place in which, at the time of filing or granting the petition, the petitioner, or the individual to be adopted resides or is in military service or in which the agency having the care, custody, or control of the minor is located.
2. If the court finds in the interest of substantial justice that the matter should be heard in another forum, the court may transfer, stay, or dismiss the proceeding in whole or in part on any conditions that are just.
3. The caption of a petition for adoption must be styled substantially "In the Matter of the Adoption of _____". The individual to be adopted must be designated in the caption under the name by which that individual is to be known if the petition is granted. If the child is placed for adoption by an agency, any name by which the child was previously known may not be disclosed in the petition, the notice of hearing, or in the decree of adoption.

**FIGURE 14.1**
**Montana Venue Statute**

**RESEARCH THIS**

Locate the statute from your state that deals with venue in an adoption proceeding. How does it compare with the Montana statute contained in Figure 14.1?

**CYBER TRIP**

Visit the Child Welfare Information Gateway, a service of the Children's Bureau, Administration for Children and Families, U.S. Department of Health and Human Services, at www.childwelfare.gov/ to learn more about adoptions and the adoption process. Use the site to locate the laws of your state and other state-specific information.

Jurisdiction is also an issue in appellate court cases. *In the matter of: The Adoption of Brianna Marie D.* (see the following Case in Point) involved a case in which the appellate court determined that it did not have jurisdiction to consider the biological father's appeal over a trial court's determination that it would be in the child's best interest that she be adopted by her stepfather. Although the trial court had ruled on what would be in the best interest of the child, it had not issued a final order, only referred the case to the clerk for finalization. Because of this fact, the appellate court lacked jurisdiction to hear the biological father's appeal in which he contended the trial court erred in ruling that it would be in the best interest of the child to be adopted by her stepfather.

## TYPES OF ADOPTION

A number of types of adoptions may be used depending on the facts of a particular case. They include:

*Agency adoption.* An **agency adoption** is what many people think of when they hear the word *adoption.* They include public agencies, run or supported by the state, and private agencies, ones that are licensed by the state but run privately. Public agencies generally handle adoptions of children who are in the state child welfare or foster care system. Adoptive parents who are seeking to adopt infants will often have to use one of the other adoption options discussed next because of the relatively few infants in the state welfare or foster care system as compared with older children.

*Licensed agency adoptions.* Traditionally, state-licensed agencies were one of the main providers of child adoptions. The natural parents give up their parental rights to the agency and the adoptive parents deal directly with the agency when attempting to adopt a child. These agencies must meet state licensing requirements and tend to provide extensive oversight during the adoption process. They

**agency adoption**
Using an agency, either government or private, but government-regulated, to facilitate the process.

# CASE IN POINT

In the Court of Appeals of Ohio
Sixth Appellate District
Lucas County
*In the matter of: The Adoption of Brianna Marie D.*
Court of Appeals No. L-04-1139
September 29, 2004

PER CURIAM

**{¶ 1}** This case is before the court sua sponte. Appellant, the biological father of Brianna D., a minor, has appealed from an order of the trial court which finds that finalization of the adoption of Brianna by her step-father is in her best interest. The probate court did not, however, finalize the adoption, but referred the case to the clerk "for scheduling of finalization." Thus, the adoption proceeding is not yet completed and no final order of adoption pursuant to R.C. 3107.14(C) has been entered. Civ.R. 73(H) requires that the probate court use the Standard Probate Forms specified in the Sup. R. 51, specifically Standard Probate Form 18.6 or 18.7, for finalizing adoptions. There is no such entry in the record of this case. Thus, this court must raise the issue of whether it has jurisdiction to hear this appeal before the adoption is finalized.

**{¶ 2}** Courts of appeals only have jurisdiction to hear appeals from "final orders."

Section 3(B)(2), Article IV of the Ohio Constitution. R.C. 2505.02 governs what is a final order and states:

**{¶ 3}** "2505.02 Final order.

**{¶ 4}** "(A) As used in this section:

**{¶ 5}** "(1) 'Substantial right' means a right that the United States Constitution, the Ohio Constitution, a statute, the common law, or a rule of procedure entitles a person to enforce or protect.

**{¶ 6}** "(2) 'Special proceeding' means an action or proceeding that is specially created by statute and that prior to 1853 was not denoted as an action at law or a suit in equity.

**{¶ 7}** "(3) 'Provisional remedy' means a proceeding ancillary to an action, including, but not limited to, a proceeding for a preliminary injunction, attachment, discovery of privileged matter, or suppression of evidence.

**{¶ 8}** "(B) An order is a final order that may be reviewed, affirmed, modified, or reversed, with or without retrial, when it is one of the following:

**{¶ 9}** "(1) An order that affects a substantial right in an action that in effect determines the action and prevents a judgment;

**{¶ 10}** "(2) An order that affects a substantial right made in a special proceeding or upon a summary application in an action after judgment;

**{¶ 11}** "(3) An order that vacates or sets aside a judgment or grants a new trial;

**{¶ 12}** "(4) An order that grants or denies a provisional remedy and to which both of the following apply:

**{¶ 13}** "(a) The order in effect determines the action with respect to the provisional remedy and prevents a judgment in the action in favor of the appealing party with respect to the provisional remedy.

**{¶ 14}** "(b) The appealing party would not be afforded a meaningful or effective remedy by an appeal following final judgment as to all proceedings, issues, claims, and parties in the action.

**{¶ 15}** "(5) An order that determines that an action may or may not be maintained as a class action."

**{¶ 16}** If the order finding it in the best interest of Brianna that her adoption be finalized, but not actually finalizing the adoption, is a "final order" pursuant to R.C. 2505.02, it could only be so pursuant to sub-section (B)(2), the "affects a substantial right made in a special proceeding" provision of that statute. The Supreme Court of Ohio has held that adoption proceedings are "special proceedings" as defined in R.C. 2505.02(A)(2). *See In re Adoption of Greer* (1994), 70 Ohio St.3d 293, 297, where the court states:

**{¶ 17}** "Indeed, 'the provisions authorizing adoptions are purely statutory.' *Lemley v. Kaiser* (1983), 6 Ohio St.3d 258, 260, 6 OBR 324, 326-327, 452 N.E.2d 1304, 1307. As noted in *In re Adoption of Hupp, supra*, 9 Ohio App.3d at 128, 9 OBR at 193, 458 N.E.2d at 880, fn. 1: 'Adoptions are special statutory proceedings, which have no counterpart at common law. *In re Adoption of Biddle* (1958), 168 Ohio St. 209 [6 O.O.2d 4, 152 N.E.2d 105].'"

**{¶ 18}** Given that adoption proceedings are "special proceedings," we must determine whether the order finding it in the best interest of Brianna to be adopted affects a substantial right. In *Bell v. Mt. Sinai Med. Ctr.* (1993), Ohio St. 3d 60, 63, 616 N.E.2d 181, modified on other grounds in *Moskovitz v. Mt. Sinai Medical Ctr.* (1994), 69 Ohio St. 3d 638, the Supreme Court of Ohio held that even if the order was issued in a "special proceeding" and that order involves a "substantial right," it is not immediately appealable unless the order *affects* the substantial right. The court then holds that a substantial right is affected if "in the absence of immediate review of the order effective relief will be foreclosed." This rule is often articulated as follows:

**{¶ 19}** "A substantial right is not affected by an order, so as to be appealable, merely because an order has the immediate effect of restricting or limiting that right. ***. A substantial right is affected only where there is virtually no opportunity for an appellate court to provide relief on appeal after final judgment from an order that presumably prejudiced a legally protected right. * * *. An order that affects a substantial right is one that, if not immediately appealable, would foreclose appropriate relief in the future.* *." *Mazurek v. Hoover* (Feb. 28, 2001), 4th Dist. No. 00 CA 50. (Citations omitted.).

{¶ 20} We find that Brianna's biological father has a substantial right not to have his daughter adopted by her stepfather.

We further find that having to wait to appeal until after the adoption is finalized will not foreclose appellant's chance of obtaining appropriate relief from this court.

{¶ 21} We find that the order from which this appeal is taken is not final and appealable. Therefore, the court dismisses this appeal at appellant's costs. *See* App.R.

APPEAL DISMISSED.

**Source:** Retrieved from www.sconet.state.oh.us/rod/newpdf/6/2004/2004-ohio-5402.pdf.

---

often deal with infant adoptions, but the wait for getting an infant can be longer than independent adoptions or unlicensed adoptions.

*Independent adoptions.* Private agencies may be licensed by the state to assist in the adoption of children. The types of agencies that handle **independent adoptions** often include attorneys. They most commonly deal with the adoption of infants.

*Facilitated and unlicensed adoptions.* Some states allow unlicensed facilitators and unlicensed private agencies to assist a person seeking to adopt a child from an expectant mother for a fee. A **facilitated adoption** is the least supervised of all the adoption procedures discussed in this chapter. These types of adoptions also are the ones that usually make the news when things do not go according to plan.

*Black market adoptions.* As noted, some forms of adoption receive little oversight. These include independent, facilitated, and unlicensed adoptions. That does not mean that these forms of adoptions are bad or immoral. It just means that they are more likely to be abused because of the lure of money. It is appropriate for the private agency or facilitator to collect a reasonable fee for their services. The demand for infants, however, creates a degree of desperation on the part of some couples. Some unethical facilitators feed on this desperation and cross the line between charging a legal fee and actually selling the baby, sometimes to the highest bidder, in what are known as **black market adoptions**. This is a common topic of news stories on adoptions that have gone bad, as are stories where a mother has promised her child to a number of couples for adoption, each of which may have been contributing to the mother financially. The following *In the Matter of the Adoption of Marta Bruner* case includes a discussion of what fees, including attorney and paralegal fees, are reasonable.

**CASE BRIEF ASSIGNMENT**

Read and brief the *In the matter of: The Adoption of Brianna Marie D.,* WL 2260118 (OhioCt. App. 2004) case. (See Appendix A for information on how to brief cases.)

**independent adoption**
Adoptions arranged by intermediaries as compared to agency adoptions; also referred to as *private adoption.*

**facilitated adoption**
An adoption arranged by a facilitator.

**black market adoption**
Illegal adoption.

## ETHICS ALERT

Attorneys play an active role in the adoption process and many firms specialize in dealing with adoption cases. This is a valuable service and one that can bring a great amount of joy to all involved, including the attorney's staff who help in the process.

But attorneys are human and subject to making mistakes in judgment that may cause the paralegal to be concerned that the firm is crossing the line between legally providing services to facilitate adoptions and being involved in black market adoptions. This raises

more than just ethical concerns. It could result in criminal charges for those involved if it is determined that the fees and costs charged constituted a black market adoption.

Paralegals must be careful not to cross this line. They need to stay fully informed of the laws of their state relating to adoption fees. When in doubt, they should discuss their concerns with their supervising attorney. If a paralegal still has concerns over the legality of the cases being handled in the firm, he or she may have to consider seeking employment in another law firm.

State of Ohio, Mahoning County
In the Court of Appeals
Seventh District
*In the Matter of the Adoption of Marta Bruner*
CASE NO. 05 MA 68
February 2, 2006

Marta Stephanova Kokhonova was born in Belarus on March 12, 1987, to alcoholic parents from whom she was taken when she was very young. She first visited the United States and lived in the home of Dennis and Jeanne Bruner during the summer of 1995, when they hosted her as part of the Kids from Chernobyl program. In June 2001, Marta began residing permanently with the Bruners, who were granted legal custody of Marta in March 2002.

Subsequently, the Bruners sought to adopt Marta and hired Attorney Byron D. Van Iden to represent them in that adoption. Attorney Van Iden ran into difficulties due to the international nature of the adoption during the course of the adoption. The Bruners became disillusioned with his representation, terminated him, and hired Attorney Dann. They agreed that Attorney Dann's time would be billed at $175.00 per hour, that his paralegal's time would be billed at $90.00 per hour, and that his associate's time would be billed at $110.00 per hour. Attorney Dann overcame the difficulties involved in obtaining the consent of Marta's birthparents to the adoption and the probate court entered a final decree of adoption on January 31, 2005.

In July 2004, Attorney Dann moved for extraordinary fees in the amount of $3,623.50 and expenses of $977.20 for this adoption and submitted an itemized bill listing the work he, his paralegal, and his associate performed in this case. When the probate court granted the adoption on January 31st, it had not yet ruled on Attorney Dann's motion and held the matter for a later date. On March 22, 2005, it entered judgment on Attorney Dann's motion. In doing so, it disallowed all fees generated by Attorney Dann's paralegal, reasoning that these amounts should be considered part of Attorney Dann's overhead, not a fee chargeable to a client. It also concluded that $100.00 per hour was a reasonable hourly rate. Thus, the probate court awarded Attorney Dann $935.00 in fees and $977.20 in expenses.

## PROBATE COURT'S AUTHORITY TO REVIEW ATTORNEYS' FEES IN AN ADOPTION CASE

Attorney Dann raises three assignments of error on appeal, all of which challenge the manner in which the probate court determined the reasonableness of his attorneys' fees. However, before we address the merits of those assignments of error, we wish to explain the source and scope of the probate court's authority to review attorney fees in adoption cases.

A probate court is a court of limited jurisdiction and can only exercise just such powers as are conferred on it by statute and constitution. So any discussion of whether a probate court has acted properly must first begin with a review of the scope of the probate court's jurisdiction.

In Ohio, the probate court has exclusive jurisdiction over adoption proceedings. The legislature has given probate courts "control over the placement of children for adoption which is not conducted under the auspices of a statutorily recognized and authorized agency * * * [so] children could [not] be sold to the highest bidder and shuffled around like objects on an auction block." To prevent a black market in the buying and selling of children, the legislature only authorizes someone petitioning for an adoption to make certain disbursements in connection with the minor's permanent surrender, placement, or adoption. R.C. 3107.10(C); *In re Adoption of Howell* (1991), 77 Ohio App.3d 80, 87. That statutes provides:

> "(C) No petitioner, person acting on a petitioner's behalf, or agency or attorney shall make or agree to make any disbursements in connection with the minor's permanent surrender, placement, or adoption other than for the following:
>
> "(1) Physician expenses incurred on behalf of the birth mother or minor in connection with prenatal care, delivery, and confinement prior to or following the minor's birth;
>
> "(2) Hospital or other medical facility expenses incurred on behalf of the birth mother or minor in connection with the minor's birth;
>
> "(3) Expenses charged by the attorney arranging the adoption for providing legal services in connection with the placement and adoption, including expenses incurred by the attorney pursuant to sections 3107.031, 3107.081, 3107.082, 3107.09, and 3107.12 of the Revised Code;
>
> "(4) Expenses charged by the agency arranging the adoption for providing services in connection with the permanent surrender and adoption, including the agency's application fee and the expenses incurred by the agency pursuant to sections 3107.031, 3107.09, 3107.12, 5103.151, and 5103.152 of the Revised Code;
>
> "(5) Temporary costs of routine maintenance and medical care for a minor required under section 5103.16 of the Revised Code if the person seeking to adopt the minor refuses to accept placement of the minor;
>
> "(6) Guardian ad litem fees incurred on behalf of the minor in any court proceedings;

"(7) Foster care expenses incurred in connection with any temporary care and maintenance of the minor;

"(8) Court expenses incurred in connection with the minor's permanent surrender, placement, and adoption." *Id.*

Before a probate court can issue a final decree of adoption, the petitioner must file a final accounting specifying "all disbursements of anything of value the petitioner, a person on the petitioner's behalf, and the agency or attorney made and has agreed to make in connection with the minor's permanent surrender under division (B) of section 5103.15 of the Revised Code, placement under section 5103.16 of the Revised Code, and adoption under this chapter." R.C. 3107.10(B), (D). The probate court may either enjoin any "disbursement for an expense not listed in" R.C. 3107.10(C) or order that any person receiving such a disbursement return it to the person who made the distribution. R.C. 3107.10(D). Likewise, the trial court may either reduce any amount to be disbursed for an expense listed in R.C. 3107.10(C) if the amount in the accounting is unreasonable or order that a person receiving an unreasonable amount of such a disbursement refund to the person who made the disbursement an amount the court orders. *Id.*

The payment of reasonable attorney fees lies within the sound discretion of the probate court.

\*\*\*

## PARALEGAL FEES AS ATTORNEY FEES

In his third assignment of error, Attorney Dann argues:

"The Mahoning County Probate Court erred by denying reasonable separate paralegal fees as expenses agreed upon by the parties."

According to Attorney Dann, the legal fees generated by his paralegal should be awarded to him as part of the reasonable value of the services he provided to the Bruners. When requesting extraordinary attorney fees, Attorney Dann submitted an itemized bill showing the amount of work both he and his paralegal, Sarah Twyford, performed on the case. The probate court refused to compensate Attorney Dann for the time billed to Twyford, stating the following:

"As a preliminary matter, it is noted that it has long been the position of this Court that it does not allow paralegal expenses as a part of the attorney fee billing. Neither Sup.R. 71 nor DR 2-106 contemplate such billings. In this case at least twenty seven (27) hours were billed to one Sarah Twyford, a paralegal employed by Attorney Dann. These requested fees, billed at $90.00 per hour are therefore not allowed. Paralegal's services, along with secretarial support, are considered to be a part of the attorney's office overhead and are not separately billable."

The probate court's position on this issue is directly contrary to Ohio caselaw on the subject, including a case which was affirmed by the Ohio Supreme Court.

In *Jackson v. Brown* (1992), 83 Ohio App.3d 230, the Eighth District was asked to decide whether work performed by legal interns could be included as attorney fees. The court noted that legal interns were a recognized position within Ohio's legal system and that it had previously included the efforts of legal interns and paralegals in an award of attorney fees. *Id.* at 232. Given this history, the court definitively concluded "that an award for the effort of a legal intern on behalf of a client is properly compensable as part of an award of attorney fees." *Id.*

The Twelfth District relied on *Jackson* in *Ron Scheiderer & Assoc. v. London* (Aug. 5, 1996), 12th Dist. No. CA95-08-022, to reach a similar conclusion. When asked whether fees generated by a paralegal can be awarded as attorney fees, it concluded as follows:

"The supreme court has stated that one factor to consider when awarding attorney fees is the miscellaneous expenses of litigation. *Villella v. Waikem Motors, Inc.*(1989), 45 Ohio St.3d 36, 42. In determining whether to include certain expenses as part of "attorney fees,' the trial court should consider the actual billing practices of the parties' attorney. Today, modern electronic accounting methods allow attorneys to submit detailed and specialized billing for their services. Many attorneys now charge lower hourly rates and bill clients directly for paralegal time and for other legal expenses. Where expenses can be clearly and directly traced to the costs associated with a particular matter, those expenses are not properly considered part of an attorney's 'overhead.'

"Moreover, when properly employed and supervised, legal assistants may decrease litigation expenses, and their use should not be discouraged. In *Jackson v. Brown* (1992), 83 Ohio App.3d 230, the Eighth District Court of Appeals concluded that an award of "reasonable attorney's fees' under R.C. 5321.51 properly encompassed the fees for the efforts of a legal intern on behalf of a tenant." (Footnote omitted) *Id.* at 6–7.

\*\*\*

We realize that neither we nor the Ohio Supreme Court had yet directly addressed this issue, so the probate court had no binding precedent on this subject. However, in light of this caselaw, particularly the Ohio Supreme Court's affirmance of the Twelfth District's decision, we cannot agree with the probate court's position. When the expenses generated in an attorney's office can be clearly and directly traced to the costs associated with a particular matter, those expenses are not properly considered part of an attorney's overhead and can properly be charged as legal fees for that particular matter. In this case, Twyford's efforts are clearly and directly traceable to the work performed for the Bruners, so the fees she generated should not be considered part of Attorney Dann's overhead. The probate court erred when it refused to consider these fees as a part of Attorney Dann's fee award.

## HEARING TO DETERMINE REASONABLENESS OF ATTORNEYS' FEES

In his first assignment of error, Attorney Dann argues:

"The Mahoning County Probate Court erred by reducing Appellant's requested legal fees without holding a hearing on Appellant's motion for extraordinary legal fees in an adoption case."

\*\*\*

This Rule is clear; a trial court must hold a hearing before awarding attorney fees and it can only relieve itself of this obligation if it adopts a local rule providing otherwise. In this case, no local rule modifies the probate court's obligation to hold a hearing when reviewing attorney fees in an adoption proceeding.

The Mahoning County Probate Court has adopted a variety of local rules addressing how it would award fees to attorneys and other fiduciaries. *** but does not specifically authorize the probate court to award those fees without a hearing.

Loc.R. 75.4 deals with adoptions and subsection (F) of that rule establishes the manner in which the probate court will award fees in adoption cases. It provides:

"(F) Attorney's fees.

"(1) Attorney fees for services rendered on matters filed under authority of O.R.C. Chapter 3107 and 5103 shall be based upon the actual services rendered and the reasonable value of the services performed.

"(2) The Court may allow the following amounts as attorney fees for ordinary services rendered.

"(a) Petitions for placement and adoption $600.00

"(b) Petition for adoption only $350.00

"(c) Petition for issuance of foreign birth record $350.00

"(d) Petition for release of information (O.R.C. 3107.41) $100.00

"(3) Attorney fees classified as extraordinary due to services rendered, will be considered by the Court only upon the filing of a written application that is supported by an itemization of time spent and recorded at the time services were performed and by any other information deemed pertinent."

In contrast, Loc.R. 72.5 specifically states that the probate court will not have a hearing unless it determines one is necessary when awarding compensation to the executor, administrator or other fiduciary of a decedent's estate; Loc.R. 73.5 provides likewise in regard to a guardian's compensation; and Loc.R. 74.5 also states that the probate court does not need to hold a hearing when determining a trustee's compensation.

The probate court has demonstrated that it knows how to draft a local rule which clearly states that it will not hold a hearing to determine a particular person's compensation. However, none of its local rules specifically states that it does not need to hold a hearing before awarding attorney fees. Thus, the probate court is required to hold a hearing before awarding attorney fees in an adoption case.

In this case, the record does not clearly state whether the trial court held a hearing on the motion for extraordinary legal fees. Attorney Dann states that the probate court did not hold such a hearing in his appellate brief, but has failed to provide this court with proof of such a hearing through an App.R. 9 alternative. Nevertheless, no appellee has filed a brief challenging that assertion. App.R. 18(C) provides:

"If an appellee fails to file the appellee's brief within the time provided by this rule, or within the time as extended, the appellee will not be heard at oral argument except by permission of the court upon a showing of good cause submitted in writing prior to argument; and in determining the appeal, the court may accept the appellant's statement of the facts and issues as correct and reverse the judgment if appellant's brief reasonably appears to sustain such action."

In the past, this court has used this Rule to reverse a trial court's decision even though the appellant did not file a transcript or App.R. 9 alternative to support its arguments. We noted that since the trial court's judgment entries were detailed and the appellant's presentation of the facts was reasonable in light of those entries, we could determine that the facts did not support the probate court's judgment. *Id.*

In this case, the probate court provides a detailed journal entry, but does not specifically state whether it held a hearing to determine whether the fees requested were reasonable. In light of this, we conclude that we will accept Attorney Dann's statement of the facts as correct. Since those facts state that the probate court did not hold the required hearing, we must conclude that Attorney Dann's first assignment of error is meritorious.

## REASONABLENESS OF ATTORNEY DANN'S FEE

In his second assignment of error, Attorney Dann argues:

"The Mahoning County Probate Court erred by reducing Appellant's requested legal fees by arbitrarily excluding details of and failing to evaluate the reasonable value of the Appellant's extraordinary expenses in the court's judgment entry."

***Because the trial court did not hold the required hearing, there is nothing within the record which supports the reduced hourly fee the probate court awarded to Attorney Dann. Attorney Dann's second assignment of error is meritorious.

## CONCLUSION

In conclusion, we reverse the probate court's judgment regarding Attorney Dann's fees for multiple reasons. First, the probate court's policy to never include fees generated by a paralegal in an attorney fee award is an abuse of discretion. Second, the probate court erred because it did not hold a hearing on attorney fees before awarding those fees as required by Rule. Finally, nothing in the record supports the probate court's decision to reduce the hourly rate for the services requested by Attorney Dann.

Accordingly, the judgment of the probate court is reversed and this cause is remanded to the trial court with specific instructions to hold the hearing required by Sup.R. 71(C).

**Note:** Citations omitted and case edited for brevity.

**Source:** Retrieved from www.sconet.state.oh.us/rod/newpdf/7/2006/2006-ohio-497.pdf.

# INTERNATIONAL ADOPTIONS

International adoptions, also referred to as *intercountry adoptions,* are those that involve the adoption of a child from another country. These types of adoptions are historically rather rare but have increased in recent years.

The adoptive parents must disclose a wide variety of personal information. U.S. law and the laws of the child's country set out what must be disclosed and the procedures to be followed. Parents are usually required to make at least one visit to the child's country.

# SINGLE-PARENT ADOPTION

Historically, single people had little chance to adopt a child. Today, an increasing number of single-parent adoptions occur in the United States. As previously noted, adoption agencies have fewer healthy infants available to adopt. Instead, these agencies often have older children and children with disabilities. Single parents have shown an increasing interest in adopting these children and have been able to demonstrate an ability to provide them good homes. Some state statutes, such as the one contained in Figure 14.2, specifically recognize the right of a single person to adopt.

# STEPPARENT ADOPTION

**Stepparent adoptions** are ones in which a stepparent adopts the child of his or her spouse and assumes both financial and legal responsibility of the child. The stepparent adoption may release the noncustodial parent from payment of child support and other legal obligations but does not disturb the parental rights of the custodial parent. This type of adoption has become common, and many states have established simplified procedures in these cases. For example, some states eliminate the need to have a home study completed as part of the adoption process. Consent of both parents is normally required by state law in stepparent adoptions, but some states do not impose this requirement under certain circumstances, such as a parent's failure to support the child or to stay in contact with the child.

**CASE BRIEF ASSIGNMENT**

Read and brief the *In the Matter of the Adoption of Marta Bruner,* 2006 WL 278123 (Ohio Ct. App. 2006) case. (See Appendix A for information on how to brief cases.)

**CYBER TRIP**

To learn more about international adoptions visit www.childwelfare.gov/pubs/f_inter/index.cfm.

---

## RESEARCH THIS

Research the laws of your state relating to stepparent adoption. Are there special procedures used for this type of adoption? If so, how do the procedures differ from those in other forms of adoptions?

---

**stepparent adoption**
Adoption in which a stepparent adopts the child of his/her spouse and assumes both financial and legal responsibility of the child. The stepparent adoption may release the noncustodial parent from payment of child support and other legal obligations.

# NATIVE AMERICAN ADOPTIONS

The federal government has recognized the special issues relating to the adoption of Native Americans. To correct problems that have occurred in the past, Congress passed the Indian Child Welfare Act of 1978 (25 U.S.C. Chapter 21) in an attempt to limit removal of Native American children from their tribe and allow them to remain in homes that would reflect their Indian culture. The act regulates how states deal with the adoption and child custody of Native American children and grants Native American Indian nations and tribes the power to control the adoption of their members. The act also grants the Native American child the legal right to grow up

**CYBER TRIP**

To learn more about the Indian Child Welfare Act, visit www.ssw.umich.edu/tpcws/articles/legal_ICWA.pdf or http://209.85.165.104/search?q=cache:Jxp7Wyv5bRYJ:www.ssw.umich.edu/tpcws/articles/legal_ICWA.pdf+ Frank+E.+Vandervort+Michigan+Child+Welfare+Law+Resource+Center&hl=en&ct=clnk&cd=3&gl=us.

This site contains an interesting article on the act by Frank E. Vandervort of the Michigan Child Welfare Law Resource Center.

with an understanding and appreciation of his or her heritage. The act covers virtually all matters relating to custody, adoption, placement in foster homes, voluntary termination of parental rights, and involuntary termination of parental rights.

## SECOND-PARENT ADOPTIONS

**Second-parent adoptions** are those in which a parent's domestic partner adopts that parent's child. This type of adoption does not terminate the parental rights of the natural parent. A number of states now allow second-parent adoptions either by statute or case law. However, as will be discussed later, some states specifically prohibit homosexuals from adopting a child.

## WHO MAY ADOPT

As with many areas of family law, state law must be consulted to see who can adopt a child in the vast majority of cases. Factors that may be considered, depending on the state, include: residency, whether the parties are married, the age of the person seeking to adopt, sexual orientation, religion, criminal history of the person seeking adoption, economic status of the person seeking to adopt, and race. Some states require that individuals be certified before they can start adoption proceedings.

The sexual orientation of the prospective adopting parents is also an area that the states have dealt with differently. Some states specifically prohibit homosexuals from adopting children. See, for example, § 63.039 (3), Florida Statutes. However, other states do not prohibit same-sex couples who are in a committed relationship from adopting children. This difference reflects how the states view what is best for the child and also what the intent of adoption statutes should be. The states that allow same-sex couples to adopt view it as a way to facilitate the adoption of as many children as possible. Those that do not allow homosexuals to adopt children maintain, among other things, that it is in the child's best interest to be raised in a heterosexual family because it provides for a more stable home environment and gender identification.

Ultimately it is what is in the best interest of the child and his or her welfare that should be the primary factor considered in an adoption. See Figure 14.2 for Montana's statute on who may adopt.

**second-parent adoption**
Adoption in which a domestic partner of a parent of a child adopts that child. This type of adoption does not terminate the parental rights of the natural parent.

### RESEARCH THIS

Locate the statute from your state that sets out who can adopt. How does it compare with the Montana statute contained in Figure 14.2?

**FIGURE 14.2**
**North Dakota Statute on Who May Adopt**

**14-15-03. Who may adopt.** The following individuals may adopt:
1. A husband and wife together although one or both are minors.
2. An unmarried adult.
3. The unmarried father or mother of the individual to be adopted.
4. A married individual without the other spouse joining as a petitioner, if the individual to be adopted is not the adopting person's spouse, and if:
   a. The petitioner is a stepparent of the individual to be adopted and the biological or legal parent of the individual to be adopted consents;
   b. The petitioner and the other spouse are legally separated; or
   c. The failure of the other spouse to join in the petition or to consent to the adoption is excused by the court by reason of prolonged unexplained absence, unavailability, incapacity, or circumstances constituting an unreasonable withholding of consent.

## WHO CAN BE ADOPTED

As was the case with who can adopt, states vary on who can be adopted. Normally we think of infants or children being adopted, but state statutes are often worded very broadly. Some merely state that any individual may be adopted. See, for example, § 14-15-02, Montana Statutes.

If the person who is being adopted lives in another state, the Interstate Compact on the Placement of Children (ICPC) will need to be complied with. Families involved in an adoption where the child is living in another state will work with adoption workers in both their state and the child's state of residence to coordinate things like the home study and training. The ICPC offices in both states coordinate the transfer of the child. Once the requirements are met, the ICPC office in the child's state will authorize transfer of the child.

## FACTORS CONSIDERED IN ADOPTION CASES

As was the case in determining issues relating to child custody, the key factor in deciding whether someone can adopt a child is what is in the best interest and welfare of the child. Factors that may be considered by the court include whether the child was abandoned by the biological parents and the unfitness of the biological parent.

In addition to the fundamental rule that the child's best interest and welfare be considered, the court must also keep in mind that the law presumes, absent a clear showing to the contrary, that it is in the best interest of the child to be with a biological parent. This is one key reason that a voluntary, written consent be obtained from the biological parents.

Take, for example, the heartbreaking case of Baby Jessica that took place in the early 1990s. Although the case was known by the public as the Baby Jessica case, the case had many names as it moved through the court systems of two states and ultimately the United States Supreme Court. They included, *Matter of Clausen,* 501 N.W.2d 193 (Mich.Ct.App. 1993), *In Interest of B.G.C.,* 496 N.W.2d 239 (Iowa 1992), and *DeBoer by Darrow v. DeBoer,* 509 U.S. 1301, 114 S.Ct.1 (1993). Whatever the name, it touched the hearts of many people and created a tremendous debate over what standards should be applied in determining who would have custody of Baby Jessica. The case involved Jan and Roberta DeBoer, who attempted to adopt the child, and the child's natural parents, Daniel Schmidt and Cara Clausen. Cara Clausen became pregnant and put the child up for adoption without letting the natural father know. The baby was adopted with only the mother's consent to the adoption. When the natural parents reunited and the biological father found out about the child, they took legal action to regain custody of the child. The courts reversed the adoption and returned the child to the natural parents. Television showed images of the child being taken from the only parents she knew, the adoptive parents, to be returned to her natural parents.

Many argued that the Baby Jessica case, and the similar case of Baby Richard, was inconsistent with putting the best interest of the child first. Instead the courts in those cases had to deal with the difficult job of balancing the welfare of the child and the rights of the natural parents.

## TERMINATION OF PARENTAL RIGHTS

A key step in the adoption procedure is the termination of parental rights. The procedure to terminate parental rights pending adoption is set out by statute. This step is not usually required for adoptions of relatives, adults, or stepchildren.

Termination may be accomplished by a parent's voluntarily surrendering the child to the appropriate state agency for adoption and a court subsequently ruling that the parents voluntarily relinquished the child to the agency for adoption.

**CYBER TRIP**

To learn more about the case that became known as the Baby Jessica case, visit http://law.jrank.org/pages/13217/In-Re-Baby-Girl-Clausen.html.

**FIGURE 14.3**

Washington State—
Termination of Parent-
Child Relationship

**Statute RCW 26.33.120** (1) Except in the case of an Indian child and his or her parent, the parent-child relationship of a parent may be terminated upon a showing by clear, cogent, and convincing evidence that it is in the best interest of the child to terminate the relationship and that the parent has failed to perform parental duties under circumstances showing a substantial lack of regard for his or her parental obligations and is withholding consent to adoption contrary to the best interest of the child.

(2) Except in the case of an Indian child and his or her alleged father, the parent-child relationship of an alleged father who appears and claims paternity may be terminated upon a showing by clear, cogent, and convincing evidence that it is in the best interest of the child to terminate the relationship and that:
(a) The alleged father has failed to perform parental duties under circumstances showing a substantial lack of regard for his parental obligations and is withholding consent to adoption contrary to the best interest of the child; or
(b) He is not the father.

(3) The parent-child relationship of a parent or an alleged father may be terminated if the parent or alleged father fails to appear after being notified of the hearing in the manner prescribed by RCW 26.33.310.

(4) The parent-child relationship of an Indian child and his or her parent or alleged father where paternity has been claimed or established, may be terminated only pursuant to the standards set forth in 25 U.S.C. Sec. 1912(f).

Termination may also be accomplished involuntarily by the state. This process, which is sometimes called a *dependency proceeding,* is used in cases where a parent is not adequately providing for his or her child. Figure 14.3 contains a Washington State statute relating to termination of parental rights.

## ADOPTION PROCEDURE

The adoption procedure is similar to that of other civil litigation matters. The initial step is the filing of a petition that requests the court to take action on a specific matter, in this case an entry of order approving the adoption. States vary on what information needs to be included in the initial petition, but it often includes the names of those filing the petition, their marriage status and details involving the child, such as name and age. Notice must then be given to the child's natural parents. As with dissolution of marriage petitions, this is usually done by personal service of a summons. Figure 14.4 provides information on the adoption process in California. Figure 14.5 sets out some of the common steps that are part of the adoption process. Figure 14.6 provides an example of an Adoption Request from California that is used as a petition to adopt.

The natural parents' consent to the child's adoption simplifies the adoption procedure. Paralegals should check their state statute to determine specifically when and how consent can be obtained. Some states do not allow the mother to consent until after the birth of the child to be adopted. Others allow consent before the child is born but give the mother a period of time in which she can change her mind. As noted in the comments relating to Baby Jessica and Baby Richard, the importance of obtaining consent of both parents cannot be overstated. It should also be noted that the consent must be voluntary and not obtained through means such as duress or fraud.

Other steps that may be involved in the adoption procedure include the following:

*Answer.* In the event that a natural parent does not consent to the adoption, an answer will be filed responding to the allegations of the petition.

*Hearing.* Hearings on the facts of the case will be held to determine whether consent was entered into voluntarily, that the adoption appears to be in the best

**ADOPT-050**   How to Adopt a Child in California

In California, there are several kinds of adoption. Learn about stepparent/domestic partner adoptions on page 1, and independent, agency, and international adoptions on page 2.

### Stepparent/Domestic Partner Adoptions

If you want to adopt your stepchild or the child of your domestic partner, fill out and file the forms listed below. You can get them from the court clerk or from the California Courts Self-Help Web site: ***www.courtinfo.ca.gov***

**1   Fill out court forms.**

☐ ADOPT-200    Adoption Request       This tells the judge about you and the child you are adopting.

☐ ADOPT-210    Adoption Agreement    This tells the judge that you and the child, if over 12, agree to the adoption. Fill it out, but do not sign it until the judge says so.

☐ ADOPT-215    Adoption Order        The judge signs this form if your adoption is approved.

**2   Take your forms to court.**

Take the completed forms to the court clerk in the county where you live. The court will charge a filing fee. Or, if you have a lawyer or are using an agency, take the forms to them.

**3   The social worker writes a report.**

In every adoption, a social worker writes a report. This report gives important information to the judge about the adopting parents and the child. The social worker will ask you questions. You may have to fill out forms. The social worker will file the report with the court and send you a copy. When you get the report, ask the clerk for a date for your adoption hearing.

**4   Go to court on the date of your hearing.**

Bring:

☐ The child you are adopting

☐ Form ADOPT-210

☐ Form ADOPT-215

☐ A camera, if you want a photo of you and your child with the judge

☐ Friends/relatives

Judicial Council of California, *www.courtinfo.ca.gov*
Rev. January 1, 2003, Optional Form    **How to Adopt a Child in California**    **ADOPT-050**, Page 1 of 2
→
American LegalNet, Inc.
www.USCourtForms.com

**FIGURE 14.4**   **How to Adopt a Child in California**                           *(cont.)*

*Source:* Retrieved from www.courtinfo.ca.gov/forms/documents/adopt050.pdf.

## ADOPT-050   How to Adopt a Child in California

### Independent, Agency, or International Adoptions

If this is an independent, agency, or international adoption, fill out and file the forms below. You can get them from the court clerk or from the California Courts Self-Help Web site: ***www.courtinfo.ca.gov***

**1**  **Fill out and file court forms.**

☐ ADOPT-200     Adoption Request          This tells the judge about you and the child you are adopting.

☐ ADOPT-210     Adoption Agreement      This tells the judge that you and the child, if over 12, agree to the adoption. Fill it out, but do not sign it until the judge says so.

☐ ADOPT-215     Adoption Order            The judge signs this form if your adoption is approved.

☐ ADOPT-230     Adoption Expenses       This tells the judge about all your adoption expenses.

**2**  **The social worker writes a report.**

In every adoption, a social worker writes a report. This report gives important information to the judge about the adopting parents and the child. The social worker will ask you questions. You may have to fill out forms. The social worker will file the report and send you a copy. When you get the report, ask the clerk for a date for your adoption hearing.

**3**  **Go to court on the date of your hearing.**

Bring:

☐ The child you are adopting

☐ Form ADOPT-210

☐ Form ADOPT-215

☐ Form ADOPT-230

☐ A camera, if you want a photo of you and your child with the judge

☐ Friends/relatives

**4**  **Is this an "open" adoption?**

If you want your child to have contact with his or her birth family, fill out ADOPT-310, which asks for an open adoption.

**5**  **If you are adopting an Indian child…**

Also fill out and bring:

☐ Form ADOPT-220     Adoption of Indian Child

☐ Form ADOPT-225     Parent of Indian Child Agrees to End Parental Rights

**FIGURE 14.4**   *(concluded)*

FIGURE 14.5
**Adoption Procedure**

Specific procedures for adoptions vary by state and by type of adoption. The following procedure are illustrative of some of the more common steps used in the adoption process:

**Termination of Parental Rights**—A judgment for termination of parental rights must be entered prior to the filing of the initial petition for adoption. Some states require that the petition be filed within a specific period of time after the entry of the judgment for termination of parental rights has been entered.

**Parties**—The required parties in an adoption action may include: the adoptive parent(s), the child's mother, the adoption agency, and, in some cases, the father of the child.

**Filing of Petition**—The petition for adoption must be filed in the court with jurisdiction over the matter and of the proper venue. The name of the court that has jurisdiction over adoption matters varies. The case might be handled as other family law matters, or, in some states, the probate court may deal with adoption cases. Proper venue also varies by state law. Possible locations include the county the judgment for termination of parental rights was entered, the county where the petitioner resides, or where the child resides.

**Final Home Study**—A final home study may be required prior to the finalization of the adoption decree.

**Hearing**—Notice of the hearing must be provided to the required parties. Hearings may be held in closed court to ensure confidentiality.

**Judgment**—If the judge determines that it is in the best interest of the child, it may enter a judgment granting the adoption.

**Application for New Birth Certificate**—The adoptive parents may select a new name for the child. The necessary paperwork to have a new birth certificate issued reflecting the new name is normally prepared by the attorney or agency that handled the adoption. Once a new birth certificate is issued and received, the adopting family can apply for a new social security number for the adopted child.

interest of the child, and to hear any objections to the adoption, such as in the *In the matter of: The Adoption of Brianna Marie D* case. Notice of hearings need to be provided to all the parties to the case.

*Home studies.* A preliminary and final home investigation/study is required prior to placement of the child. This study is completed by a child welfare agency, which ultimately provides the results of the study to the judge.

*Final hearing/judgment of adoption.* This is the step in which the adoption is finalized. Assuming that a favorable report is filed by the child welfare agency and that all statutory and court requirements have been met, the judge will sign a final judgment of adoption.

**CYBER TRIP**

To learn more about the adoption process, visit www.childwelfare. gov/pubs/ f_basicsbulletin/.

**RESEARCH THIS**

Locate the laws and court rules of your state that relate to adoption. Based on the authority that you have located, answer the following questions: What court has jurisdiction in adoption matters? How is venue determined? Who are the necessary parties? Who must be notified of the hearing on the petition for adoption?

## THE EFFECT OF ADOPTION

Several changes take place when the court enters the final decree of adoption. In many situations, an adoption results in the child being added to the family tree of the adopting parents and removed from the family tree of the natural parents. As a result, the adopted child will inherit as if he or she were the adoptive parents' natural child. The child will

## ADOPT-200    Adoption Request

**If you are adopting more than one child, fill out an adoption request for each child.**

(1)    Your name (adopting parent):

a. _____

b. _____

Relationship to child: _____

Street address: _____

City: _____ State: _____ Zip: _____

Telephone number: (_____) _____

Lawyer (if any): (Name, address, telephone numbers, and State Bar number):

_____

_____

_____

Clerk stamps date here when form is filed.

Fill in court name and street address:

Superior Court of California, County of

Fill in case number if known:

Case Number:

(2)    Type of adoption (check one):

☐ Agency (name): _____

    ☐ Joinder has been filed.

    ☐ Joinder will be filed.

☐ Independent

☐ International (name of agency): _____

☐ Stepparent

☐ Relative

(3)    Information about the child:

a. The child's new name will be:

_____

b. ☐ Boy   ☐ Girl

c. Date of birth: _____ Age: _____

d. Child's address (if different from yours):

   Street: _____

   City: _____ State: _____ Zip: _____

e. Place of birth (if known):

   City: _____

   State: _____ Country: _____

f. If the child is 12 or older, does the child agree to the adoption? ☐ Yes ☐ No

g. Date child was placed in your physical care:

_____

(4)    Child's name before adoption: (Fill out ONLY if this is an independent, relative, or stepparent adoption.)

_____

(5)    Does the child have a legal guardian? ☐ Yes ☐ No

If yes, attach a copy of the Letters of Guardianship and fill out below:

a. Date guardianship ordered: _____

b. County: _____

c. Case number: _____

(6)    Is the child a dependent of the court? ☐ Yes ☐ No

If yes, fill out below:

Juvenile case number: _____

County: _____

(To be completed by the clerk of the superior court if a hearing date is available.)

**Hearing Date**

Hearing is set for:

Date: _____

Time: _____

Dept.: _____ Room: _____

Name and address of court if different from above:

_____

To the person served with this request: If you do not come to this hearing, the judge can order the adoption without your input.

Judicial Council of California, www.courtinfo.ca.gov
Revised January 1, 2007, Mandatory Form
Family Code, §§ 8714, 8714.5, 8802, 8912, 9000; Welfare &
Institutions Code, § 16119; Cal. Rules of Court, rule 5.730

Adoption Request

ADOPT-200, Page 1 of 3

American LegalNet, Inc.
www.FormsWorkflow.com

**FIGURE 14.6    California Request for Adoption**

*Source:* Retrieved from www.courtinfo.ca.gov/forms/documents/adopt200.pdf.

Your name: _____

Case Number:

⑦ Child may have Indian ancestry:   ☐ Yes ☐ No
If yes, attach Form ADOPT-220, Adoption of Possible Indian Child.

⑧ Names of birth parents, if known:
a. Mother: _____
b. Father: _____

⑨ If this is an agency adoption
a. I have received information about the Adoption Assistance Program Regional Center and about mental health services available through Medi-Cal or other programs.   ☐ Yes ☐ No

b. All persons with parental rights agree that the child should be placed for adoption by the California Department of Social Services or a licensed adoption agency (Fam. Code, § 8700) and have signed a relinquishment form approved by the California Department of Social Services.  ☐ Yes ☐ No   (if no, list the name and relationship to child of each person who has not signed the consent form): _____

_____

⑩ If this is an independent adoption
a. A copy of the Independent Adoptive Placement Agreement, a California Department of Social Services form, is attached. (This is required in most independent adoptions; see Fam. Code, § 8802.)

b. All persons with parental rights agree to the adoption and have signed the Independent Adoptive Placement Agreement, a California Department of Social Services form.  ☐ Yes ☐ No
(if no, list the name and relationship to child of each person who has not signed the consent form): _____

_____

c. I will file promptly with the department or delegated county adoption agency the information required by the department in the investigation of the proposed adoption.

⑪ If this is a stepparent adoption
a. The birth parent (name): _____   ☐ has signed a consent   ☐ will sign a consent

b. The birth parent (name): _____   ☐ has signed a consent   ☐ will sign a consent

c. The adopting parents were married on   or   The domestic partnership was registered on
(date): _____. (For court use only. This does not affect social worker's recommendation. There is no waiting period.)

⑫ ☐ There is no presumed or biological father because the child was conceived by artificial insemination, using semen provided to a medical doctor or a sperm bank. (Fam. Code, § 7613.)

⑬ Contact after adoption
Form ADOPT-310, Contact After Adoption Agreement,   ☐ is attached   ☐ will not be used
☐ will be filed at least 30 days before the adoption hearing   ☐ is undecided at this time

⑭ ☐ The consent of the   ☐ birth mother   ☐ presumed father   is not necessary because (specify Fam. Code, § 8606 subdivision): _____

Revised January 1, 2007 | **Adoption Request** | ADOPT-200, Page 2 of 3
→

**FIGURE 14.6**   *(continued)*

*(cont.)*

Your name: _____

Case Number: _____

(15)  A court ended the parental rights of (attach copy of order):
    Name: _____  Relationship to child: _____ on (date)_____
    Name: _____  Relationship to child: _____ on (date)_____

(16)  ☐ I will ask the court to end the parental rights of (attach copy of Petition to Terminate Parental Rights or
    Freedom From Parental Custody, if filed):
    Name: _____  Relationship to child: _____
    Name: _____  Relationship to child: _____

(17)  Each of the following persons with parental rights has not contacted his or her child in one year or more. (Fam.
    Code, § 8604(b)) (Attach copy of Application for Freedom From Parental Custody, if filed.)
    Name: _____  Relationship to child: _____
    Name: _____  Relationship to child: _____

(18)  Each of the following persons with parental rights has died:
    Name: _____  Relationship to child: _____
    Name: _____  Relationship to child: _____

(19)  Suitability for adoption
    Each adopting parent:

      a. Is at least 10 years older than the child    d. Has a suitable home for the child and
      b. Will treat the child as his or her own    e. Agrees to adopt the child
      c. Will support and care for the child

(20)  I ask the court to approve the adoption and to declare that the adopting parents and the child have the legal
    relationship of parent and child, with all the rights and duties of this relationship, including the right of
    inheritance.

(21)  If a lawyer is representing you in this case, he or she must sign here:

    Date: _____  _____  ▶ _____
                     Type or print your name       Signature of attorney for adopting parents

(22)  I declare under penalty of perjury under the laws of the State of California that the information in this form
    is true and correct to my knowledge. This means that if I lie on this form, I am guilty of a crime.

    Date: _____  _____  ▶ _____
                     Type or print your name       Signature of adopting parent

    Date: _____  _____  ▶ _____
                     Type or print your name       Signature of adopting parent

Revised January 1, 2007          **Adoption Request**          ADOPT-200, Page 3 of 3

**FIGURE 14.6**  *(concluded)*

**42-5-202. Effect of decree.** (1) After the decree of adoption is entered:
   (a) the relationship of parent and child and all the rights, duties, and other legal consequences of the relation of parent and child exist between the adoptee and the adoptive parent and the kindred of the adoptive parent;
   (b) the former parents and the kindred of the former parents of the adoptee, unless they are the adoptive parents or the spouse of an adoptive parent, are relieved of all parental responsibilities for the adoptee and have no rights over the adoptee except for a former parent's duty to pay arrearages for child support.

(2) A decree of adoption must include notice to the vital statistics bureau if it is known that either birth parent objects to release of the information on the original birth certificate upon the adoptee reaching 18 years of age.

(3) The relationship of parent and child for the purposes of intestate succession is governed by Title 72.

**FIGURE 14.7**
**Montana Statute—Effect of Adoption Decree**

not have any claim to the natural parents' estate. Adoption also releases the natural parents of any legal obligation to the child, and the adoptive parents assume this obligation. And the birth certificate is changed to show the adoptive parents as the parents of the child. Figure 14.7 contains the Montana statute on the effect of adoption.

## RESEARCH THIS

Locate the statute from your state that deals with the effect of an final adoption decree on the adopted child's family relationships. How does it compare with the Montana statute contained in Figure 14.7?

## ACCESSING ADOPTION RECORDS

There has been increasing pressure on state legislatures to allow adult adoptees to obtain some information from the adoption records, including their birth certificate, without a court order. Alabama, Alaska, Kansas, New Hampshire, and Oregon allow such access. Other states allow only limited access to records.

## EQUITABLE/VIRTUAL ADOPTION

When paralegal students hear the word *equity,* two words should come to their minds: *fairness* and *justice.* Equity is used by the courts to prevent the unfair consequences of the literal application of the law. This can occur in a case where a person agrees to adopt a child but does not follow through on the legal procedure to accomplish it. If the person acts as the child's parent, even though he or she did not take the steps needed to legally adopt the child, the courts may consider that the child was **equitably adopted**. The person who assumed the role of the parent may be estopped from denying being the child's parent.

In addition, some courts use the concept of equitable adoption to allow the child to take under the adoptive parent's estate as if he or she had been legally adopted.

## OTHER ISSUES RELATING TO TERMINATION OF PARENTAL RIGHTS

Up to this point, the discussion has been limited to adoptions where a person or a couple attempts to adopt a minor child. At times, it is in a child's best interest that he or she be taken from the custody of the biological parents. In those situations,

**equitable adoption**
Occurs when a person agrees to adopt a person, but fails to take steps to do so, and a court rules that the child was equitably adopted to prevent inequity from occurring; also known as *adoption by estoppel.*

an agency of the state may be awarded custody of the child and the parental rights of the biological parents are terminated. These children may then be the subject of a petition for adoption. In these situations, some states provide that the child may, under certain circumstances, be allowed to stay in touch with siblings and other relatives.

## IN VITRO FERTILIZATION

The impact of societal changes on family law has been discussed many times in the previous chapters of this textbook. Examples of these changes include the current debate over who can marry, the increasing number of children being born out of wedlock, and the large numbers of divorces that occur in the United States. These changes have had a dramatic influence on the legal system, and it is still playing catch-up in attempting to deal with them.

Societal changes are not alone in putting pressure on the legal system to change. Science has created its share of confusion in how the law will deal with the issues of in vitro fertilization and surrogacy. The law is struggling to resolve these issues while trying to apply legal principles that predate the technology that now allows couples who would otherwise have to look toward more conventional methods of adding children to their families, such as adoption, to have children.

Millions of couples have been unable to conceive a child due to fertility issues. Science has made great strides in helping many of them overcome this problem. One common method that has been successfully used for many years is **in vitro fertilization**.

In vitro fertilization is a method by which eggs are fertilized outside of the woman's womb. The resulting embryos may be transferred to the womb or frozen for future use. It is an example of what is now referred to as **assisted reproductive technology (ART)**. In vitro fertilization has grown in use in the past decades and brings with it new legal issues to resolve. Published accounts indicate that there may be in excess of 500,000 frozen embryos in the United States today, and thousands more are added each year.

One major issue is what can be done with the thousands of unused fertilized eggs that have not been implanted into the uterus, referred to as zygotes or pre-embryos. Many people support their use for stem cell research. Others, who maintain life starts at conception, oppose such use.

Since the cryogenically preserved embryos can be kept for a long period of time, another issue arises as to what happens to the unused pre-embryos when the couple who created them divorce. Does a judge hearing the dissolution of marriage case have the right to award them to one of the parties? If so, does the judge do so as if he or she were awarding custody of a child or as part of a property distribution between the husband and wife? Or should the pre-embryos be treated as something in between a child and property? States vary on which approach should be taken and only a few, including Florida, New Hampshire, and Louisiana, have enacted laws specifying how embryos can be disposed of.

**in vitro fertilization**
Procedure by which egg cells are fertilized outside the womb.

**assisted reproductive technology (ART)**
Procedure involving the handling of both eggs and sperm in which the eggs are surgically removed and combine with sperm in the laboratory.

## CYBER TRIP

To learn more about ARTs in the United States, visit the Centers for Disease Control and Prevention–Assisted Reproductive Technology site at www.cdc.gov/art/ and the Centers for Disease Control and Prevention–Assisted Reproductive Technology Surveillance site at www.cdc.gov/mmwr/preview/mmwrhtml/ss5209a1.htm.

## RESEARCH THIS

Research the laws of your state dealing with in vitro fertilization and answer the following questions: How would the courts of your state determine what would become of cryogenically preserved pre-embryos in the event there is a conflict between the parties in a divorce action? Are consent agreements between the parties and the in vitro fertilization lab or clinic valid and, if so, what it can contain?

One method that has been used is the consent agreement signed by the parties when starting the in vitro fertilization program. These agreements often specify that the unused frozen embryos will go to one of the parties, be used in medical/scientific research, or will be destroyed. States vary dramatically on what can be agreed to and what provisions are enforceable. This lack of uniformity requires that the legal professional be aware of the laws of his or her state with regard to these issues.

## SURROGACY

Although it is common that the zygote is returned to the womb of the woman whose egg was used to create it, there are times when this cannot be done. This brings in another party, the **surrogate mother**, who will help in making the couple's dream of having a child come true.

One manner in which a surrogate mother is used is referred to as *gestational surrogacy*. In this process, a woman agrees to have the fertilized egg embedded in her embryo with the intention that she will carry the child to term and then the child will be turned over to the parents who have a biological link to the child, the mother whose egg was used and the father whose sperm was used to fertilize the egg. In at least one state, a procedure referred to as *expedited affirmation of parental status* is used after the birth of a child by the surrogate mother when the pre-embryo is created from the egg and sperm of the couple contracting with the surrogate mother. The surrogate mother has no basis to claim custody since she has no genetic link with the child. This procedure eliminates the need for the natural parents to adopt the child.

Alternatively, the surrogate mother's egg is inseminated outside the womb with sperm from the father or a donor. In this type of surrogacy, the birth mother has a genetic link to the child. In fact, it is possible that neither the intended mother nor the father will have a genetic link to the child if the egg is provided by the surrogate mother and the sperm by a donor. A prearranged adoption is used in these cases.

Surrogate contracts are used to set out the rights and obligations between the couple and the surrogate mother. As was true in the discussion of what can be done with frozen embryos, the states vary on how these agreements can be used and what can be included in these contracts or whether they are valid.

Some states, such as Arkansas, Florida, and Nevada have adopted statutes that specifically allow for surrogate contracts. Figure 14.8 sets out the Nevada statute that allows for couples to enter into such contracts and sets out what provisions must be included in them.

Even states that have expressly dealt with surrogacy and surrogacy agreements vary on who may take advantage of them. For example, some restrict surrogacy to married couples, which is the case in Nevada. Some states also limit the application of their surrogacy statute to gestational surrogacy.

Other states have attempted to discourage surrogacy by not recognizing surrogacy agreements and by not allowing attorneys or physicians to charge for arranging surrogacy agreements. Some even allow the surrogate mother to change her mind within a specific period of time after the birth of the child. For example, in North Dakota, which is one of two states to have adopted a version the Uniform Status of Children of Assisted Conception Act, the statute provides that surrogacy agreements are unenforceable. See Figure 14.9.

Other states have remained silent on the issue of surrogacy contracts, leaving it to the courts to deal with the issue.

Whether a state has addressed the issue of surrogacy contracts by statute or not, legal issues arise when the surrogate mother changes her mind about turning over the child after birth. Cases involving gestational surrogacy are easier to resolve

**surrogate mother**
Woman who bears a child for another person.

**CYBER TRIP**

To view the text of the Uniform Status of Children of Assisted Conception Act, visit www.law. upenn.edu/ bll/ archives/ulc/ fnact99/uscaca88. htm.

**FIGURE 14.8**

**Surrogacy Agreements**

*Source:* Retrieved from www. leg.state.nv.us/nrs/NRS-126. html#NRS126Sec045.

**NRS 126.045 Contract requirements; treatment of intended parents as natural parents; unlawful acts.**

　1. Two persons whose marriage is valid under chapter 122 of NRS may enter into a contract with a surrogate for assisted conception. Any such contract must contain provisions which specify the respective rights of each party, including:

　(a) Parentage of the child;

　(b) Custody of the child in the event of a change of circumstances; and

　(c) The respective responsibilities and liabilities of the contracting parties.

　2. A person identified as an intended parent in a contract described in subsection 1 must be treated in law as a natural parent under all circumstances.

　3. It is unlawful to pay or offer to pay money or anything of value to the surrogate except for the medical and necessary living expenses related to the birth of the child as specified in the contract.

　4. As used in this section, unless the context otherwise requires:

　(a) "Assisted conception" means a pregnancy resulting when an egg and sperm from the intended parents are placed in a surrogate through the intervention of medical technology.

　(b) "Intended parents" means a man and woman, married to each other, who enter into an agreement providing that they will be the parents of a child born to a surrogate through assisted conception.

　(c) "Surrogate" means an adult woman who enters into an agreement to bear a child conceived through assisted conception for the intended parents.

　(Added to NRS by 1993, 2050; A 1995, 1075)

**FIGURE 14.9**

**North Dakota Statute on Surrogate Agreements**

*Source:* Retrieved from www.legis.nd.gov/cencode/t14c18.pdf.

**14-18-05. Surrogate agreements.** Any agreement in which a woman agrees to become a surrogate or to relinquish that woman's rights and duties as parent of a child conceived through assisted conception is void. The surrogate, however, is the mother of a resulting child and the surrogate's husband, if a party to the agreement, is the father of the child. If the surrogate's husband is not a party to the agreement or the surrogate is unmarried, paternity of the child is governed by chapter 14–20.

**CYBER TRIP**

To learn more about the Baby M case, visit http://womenshistory.about.com/od/motherhood/a/baby_m.htm.

because the surrogate mother has no genetic link to the child. Things are not as clear when the surrogate mother's egg is used to produce the child. The Baby M case, which drew a lot of media attention in the 1980s when this procedure was still relatively new, involved a surrogate mother who donated the egg to be used. The egg was fertilized with the sperm of the man who, along with his wife, entered into the contract with the surrogate mother. She changed her mind about giving up her rights to the child. Ultimately, the court granted the couple who contracted with the surrogate mother custody of the child but allowed the surrogate mother visitation.

In 2007, a Florida couple was not so lucky. They lost their battle to obtain custody of the child born of the surrogate mother. Tom and Gwyn Lamitina hired Stephanie Eckard to act as their surrogate mother. Mr. Lamitina provided the sperm to fertilize the egg provided by Ms. Eckard. A disagreement arose between the parties and the Lamitinas did not learn of the birth of the child until two weeks after Eckard and the baby left the hospital. At that point, they requested that the child be turned over to them. The court held that Mr. Lamitina was not the father under Florida law, but instead was just a sperm donor. As such, he had no claim to the child nor would he be responsible for payment of child support. An additional issue brought up by this case was that in Florida a woman has 48 hours after giving birth to change her mind about putting the child up for adoption.

**RESEARCH THIS**

Research the statutory and case law of your state regarding surrogacy. Are surrogacy agreements enforceable? Are gestational surrogacy and nongestational surrogacy treated differently as to their enforceability and the rights of the birth parents?

**Summary**

The adoption process is the means that allows a child to be brought into a family and creates a parent-child relationship where the biological relationship did not previously exist. Although there are numerous types of adoptions, the result is the same.

The specifics of the adoption process vary by state, but they are similar in many ways and share the common fact that the process is made easier if both natural parents of the child being adopted consent to the adoption. Failure to obtain consent from both natural parents can result in problems in the future.

In most cases, once the adoption decree is final, the child is treated as a member of the adopting parents' family tree. They assume the responsibility for raising and supporting the child. The child is treated by the law as the child of the adopting parents, including the rights to inheritance.

The increased use of in vitro fertilization and surrogacy, rather than the use of traditional adoption methods, has presented the legal system with numerous issues to resolve. These include the use of consent agreements as part of the in vitro fertilization process, the use of surrogacy agreements, and what rights the surrogate mother has to the child she bears. There is a tremendous lack of uniformity among the states on how to deal with these issues. For example, many states state that surrogacy agreements are void, whereas others have specific state statutes dealing with the use and content of these agreements. The legal system will be struggling for years to come to resolve the issues created by the advances in medical science in the area of reproduction.

**Key Terms**

Adoption
Agency adoption
Assisted reproductive technology (ART)
Black market adoption
Closed adoption
Equitable adoption
Facilitated adoption
Independent adoption
In vitro fertilization
Open adoption
Second-parent adoption
Stepparent adoption
Surrogate mother

**Review Questions**

1. What is adoption?
2. What is a closed adoption?
3. How is jurisdiction and venue important in the adoption process?
4. What is an agency adoption?
5. What are facilitated and unlicensed adoptions? How do they differ from agency adoptions?
6. What are black market adoptions? Why should the paralegal be concerned about black market adoptions?
7. Who can adopt?

8. What is a second-parent adoption?

9. Who can be adopted?

10. List and discuss the factors that are considered in an adoption case?

11. What is the effect of the adoption on the child, the natural parents, and the adopting parents?

12. What is an equitable adoption and how does it differ from a legal adoption?

13. What are the steps in the adoption process?

14. What law regulates the adoption and other child custody issues involving Native Americans?

15. What is an equitable adoption?

16. What is gestational surrogacy and why is it important in the law relating to surrogacy?

17. How do the states vary on the use of surrogacy agreements?

18. How are consent agreements used in the in vitro fertilization process?

19. What is an expedited affirmation of parental status and when is it used?

20. In what kind of surrogacy cases are prearranged adoptions used?

---

## Exercises

1. Margaret and Janice have been living together as a same-sex couple for almost 7 years. Margaret is an attorney and Janice teaches online college classes. They have heard that many older children are not being adopted because of their age. They have decided that they could provide a good home to one of these children and have come to your firm to learn more about the adoption process. Your supervising attorney has asked you to do some research on the matter before Margaret and Janice come in for their appointment. Based on the statutory and case law of your state, will they be able to adopt a child? Explain.

2. John and Julie have recently married. They have no children of their marriage, but Julie has a son, Don, from a previous marriage. John wants to adopt Don. Research the laws of your state relating to stepparent adoption. Under what circumstances would John be able to adopt Don? Would it matter if Don's natural father objected to the adoption? Would the fact that Don's father is behind on his child support payments matter?

3. Theresa works for a law firm that specializes in adoptions. The firm helps arrange adoptions of children from unwed mothers who are in financial difficulty. Theresa is increasingly concerned about the fees that her supervising attorney is charging to arrange and handle these adoptions. Even though the adopting parents are willing to pay anything to be able to adopt a child, she feels that the fees being charged are far in excess of the work involved in the process. Is Theresa justified in her concerns? Explain.

4. Barbara is a single woman who has never been married. She has a good job as a librarian at a local college and has a home of her own. The one thing missing in her life is a child. She has come to your firm to explore the possibility of adopting a little girl. Research the laws of your state to determine if this is a possibility for Barbara.

5. Leanne was divorced 3 years ago. She was granted primary physical custody of her daughter, Janet. Her ex-husband, Sam, has never paid the court-ordered child support and has only visited Janet once since the divorce, despite the fact he only lives a few miles away. Based on the statutory and case law of your state, would Leanne be able to have Sam's parental rights terminated?

## REAL WORLD DISCUSSION TOPICS

1. Heather and Andrew were unmarried when they had a child. Andrew was insistent that the child be placed for adoption. At times, he acted violently and used intimidation to have Heather agree to put the child up for adoption. Heather, despite her desires to keep the child, went along with Andrew's request. Heather and Andrew both signed consent forms after being advised of the legal rights relating to the action being taken. Heather later attempted to revoke her consent. Under the laws of your state, should she be allowed to do so? If yes, why? See *Petition of Anderson,* 565 N.W.2d 461 (Minn.App., 1997).

2. A father was convicted of second-degree burglary and later of rape and trespass and is serving a sentence of 37 years in prison. Prior to his incarceration, the father visited his son several times. He last visited the son about 5 years ago. Later attempts at arranging visitation were unsuccessful because the child's mother moved and changed her phone number, although she was listed in the phone directory. The father paid at most $300 in child support. The mother later remarried and the son began to call the stepfather "Dad" and he was treated the same as the stepfather's natural son. The son has no memory of his natural father. The mother filed a petition to terminate the parent-child relationship. Should the petition be granted? See *Matter of Interest of Pawling,* 101 Wash.2d 392, 679 P.2d 916 (Wash., 1984).

## PORTFOLIO ASSIGNMENT

Review the facts in the case of Jill Simpson from the Client Interview. Research the statutory and case law of your state and write a summary of what procedures will need to be followed for Jill to adopt the young woman's child once he or she is born.

# Appendix A

## GUIDE TO LOCATING LEGAL INFORMATION ON THE WEB AND BRIEFING CASES

Paralegal students must develop many skills before they begin working in a law office. One of the most important is legal research. This appendix is designed to give students a basic understanding of how to locate legal information via the Internet, understand the concept of legal reasoning, and learn how to brief cases.

## WHY WE RESEARCH

The foundation of the legal profession is the law itself: the Constitution; the constitution of each state; federal and state statutes; and case law. Judges seldom want to hear about an attorney's opinion on a matter. What they want to know is what legal authority is controlling in resolving the matter.

So, the simple answer to why we research is to find case and statutory law that provides information on an area of the law or that helps us answer a legal question.

How legal research is performed has undergone a tremendous change as the legal profession has moved into the computer age. Increasingly, legal research is done by use of the computer and the Internet. This has caused many law firms to reduce the size of their in-house law library or eliminate it all together.

## SEARCH TERMS

Key words and phrases are often used to locate legal information. These are the same words and phrases that the paralegal student studies in his or her law classes. For example, a student studying wills might use the term *competency* when trying to find information on the validity of a will. Like most skills, the best way to improve your ability to find legal information on the Internet is by repetition. Pick a few words from the vocabulary being studied in your current class and use them to perform Internet searches.

Start with using a source that everyone uses these days—Google! Visit www.google.com and perform searches for a number of key legal words and phrases. A vast number of sites with information will pop up. Take some time and explore the more interesting ones.

Although using Google is not the preferred means of finding legal information, it is a good way to practice searching the Internet using key words and phrases.

One word of caution: always analyze the reliability of the Web sites that turn up in your searches. *All Web sites are not equally reliable!* Many are maintained by people with no real background in the area. Others are maintained by people with a biased view on the topic being researched. Caution is the key when search engines such as Google are used because they do not screen out unreliable information.

What follows is information on other Internet resources that are more appropriate for legal research.

# INTERNET LEGAL RESEARCH RESOURCES

The Internet is a tremendous resource for legal information. Many of these sources are free. There are also pay sites that students may have access to in their classroom or will have access to in their future employment.

Whether free, or for a fee, the use of online law libraries and resources is increasingly the way legal research is done. Traditional law libraries, with hundreds of bound books, are slowly disappearing.

## Paid Sites

Westlaw and LexisNexis are the two main providers of paid computerized legal research. Both offer a wide variety of legal resources, such as cases for all state and federal courts, state and federal statutes, and treatises on various areas of the law and law reviews.

The advantages of both are their vast databases and great search engines to help researchers find the information they need. The disadvantage is that they are relatively expensive. They are very similar services and which one is used is largely based on personal preference rather than a substantive difference between the two. Attorneys often select the one they were more comfortable using while in law school.

### Westlaw

West is one of the oldest legal publishers in the United States. It developed the regional case reporter system that has been the mainstay of legal research for generations of researchers. The company's many publications are available through Westlaw.

To learn more about how to use Westlaw, visit:

http://paralegal.westlaw.com/

http://west.thomson.com/store/product.asp?product%5Fid=Westlaw&catalog%5Fname=wgstore

http://west.thomson.com/westlaw/training/paralegal/

### LexisNexis

LexisNexis is one of the pioneers in computer-aided legal research. The information contained in its databases is similar to that of Westlaw. To learn more about LexisNexis, visit:

www.Lexis.com

http://web.lexis.com/help/multimedia/tour.htm

Lexis.com Online Tutorials: http://web.lexis.com/help/multimedia/tour.htm

## Free Sites

**LexisONE**—LexisONE is a streamlined version of Lexis. The advantage is that the resources are free, including case law decided within the last 5 years. Registration is required. www.lexisone.com

**FindLaw**—One of the great free legal resource sites. It allows you to find cases and statutes for all 50 states and also locate other information, such as articles, to help in the research process. www.findlaw.com

**Library of Congress**—Official site of the Library of Congress. Provides links to numerous sites used in legal research, both in the United States and internationally. Guide to Law Online, www.loc.gov/law/guide/index.html

**The Federal Judiciary**—Information on the federal court system and links to sites that include opinions of the courts. www.uscourts.gov

**The 'Lectric Law Library**—Provides a good legal dictionary and also information on many legal topics. www.lectlaw.com//ref.html

**Laws Online**—Links to federal and state resources. www.lawsonline.com

**Law Guru**—This search engine allows you to search hundreds of legal resources. www.lawguru.com/search/lawsearch.html

**Internet Legal Research Group**—Access thousands of Web sites and legal documents at this resource. www.ilrg.com

**Cata Law**—This site bills itself as the "the catalog of catalogs of worldwide law on the Internet." www.catalaw.com

**Law Research**—Provides an extensive list of law directories. www.lawresearch.com

**The Legal Writer**—Includes articles on how to improve your legal writing. http://home.earthlink.net/~thelegalwriter/

**Barger on Legal Writing**—Provides information to aid in all phases of legal research and writing. www.ualr.edu/~cmbarger/WritersResources.HTM

**Stetson College of Law**—Provides links to various legal research resources. www.law.stetson.edu/law/

**Legal Research and Writing**—Kathryn Sampson, University of Arkansas School of Law. Good information on legal research and includes links to information on citation, writing, and other resources. http://comp.uark.edu/~ksampson

## LEGAL REASONING

The law approaches answering legal issues in a very systematic manner. This is referred to as *legal reasoning*. It is based on the use of authority, such as case and statutory law, to come to a well-supported conclusion. Reading and briefing cases is one of the key ways students of the law have developed their legal reasoning skills.

The I.R.A.C. method is an excellent way for students to approach legal questions that they are trying to answer. Although it is not used just for legal issues, the I.R.A.C. method is very well suited for paralegal students wanting to improve their analytical skills.

### I.R.A.C.

I = Issue—The question that is to be answered. For example, did John commit battery when he bit Carl's ear while they were playing basketball?

R = Rule—The rule is the legal authority that applies to a given fact pattern. For discussion purposes, let's assume the following statutory definition of battery: Battery is the nonconsensual touching of another in a harmful or offensive manner.

A = Analysis—Analysis is the thought process that occurs when applying the rule to the facts of the case. In the basketball case, Carl and John were playing basketball. They both consented to a certain amount of physical contact. That is an integral part of a basketball game. Biting a player's ear, however, is not something the average player would be consenting to when he took the court.

C = Conclusion—The conclusion is the result of the analysis. In the example under consideration, the conclusion would be that John did commit battery when he bit Carl's ear during a basketball game.

Law Nerds provides a very good discussion of the I.R.A.C. method in the legal reasoning section of its Web site. www.lawnerds.com

# BRIEFING CASES

A case brief is a summary of a court's opinion. Cases are briefed for a variety of reasons. Sometimes, attorneys brief cases to summarize the law of key cases they will use in helping a client. Sometimes they are briefed to submit to a court as part of a hearing on a motion or other matter before the court.

Paralegal students, like law students, brief cases to learn about the law and, more important, to learn how to think like an attorney. They read the opinions to see how the court reaches its conclusion. In so doing, they understand how the issues of the case become important and the law the court used to reach its conclusion.

A wide variety of formats are used in briefing cases and there is no "correct" form. The format to select is often related to how the brief will be used. A very basic format will be used in this discussion. Web sites providing information on other formats, along with sources that explain the case briefing process, are listed later in this appendix.

Case briefs are made up of elements, or components, that provide a structure to break down the key elements of a case in a systematic manner. These include:

*Caption:* The caption provides the reader with some very basic information, including the names of the parties and where the case can be located.

*Facts:* The facts of the case tell a story of how the parties ended up in court. What went wrong between them to cause a lawsuit to occur?

*Issue:* The issue is a legal question the court is being asked to resolve. Appellate courts do not hear arguments of fact; those were made before the trial court. Instead, the appellate court is asked to resolve issues of law, something that the lower court did improperly. Traditionally all issues began with the word *Whether.* This ensured that it would be answered with yes or no. Most people in the legal field have abandoned use of this approach but it is still desirable to phrase a question in a way that it can be answered with yes or no, if at all possible.

*Brief Answer:* The brief answer tells the reader how the court answered the question. It should be a yes/no answer followed by no more than a sentence or two of explanation.

*Reasoning:* Like the facts, the reasoning tells a story. The reasoning tells the story of how the court applied the law (precedent from previous cases or statutory law) to the facts of the case before it.

The following approach can be used in briefing a case:

1. Put down the pen and move away from the computer keyboard! The first thing that needs to be done is to read the case. Briefing should not start until what's important in the court's opinion can be established. Start reading where the name(s) of the judge or the phrase *per curium* are located. That is where the opinion actually starts.

2. Identify the issue. What is the legal question that the court was asked to answer? The issue is critical in determining what is important in the court's decision. It will help in identifying the facts and reasoning that relate.

3. Reread the case. Go through the case again, reading it carefully. Take notes of what you think is important, such as the key facts discussed by the court and the important legal principles contained in the opinion.

4. Start writing the brief.

# EXAMPLE OF HOW TO BRIEF A CASE

In the District Court of Appeal of the State of Florida
Fourth District January Term 2005
Case No. 4D04-1300
February 23, 2005
*Gavi Solorzano, Appellant v. First Union Mortgage Corporation N/K/A Wachovia Mortgage Corporation, a North Carolina Corporation, Appellee*

SILVERMAN, SCOTT J., Associate Judge.

Gavi Solorzano appeals the dismissal of her amended complaint with prejudice for failing to state a cause of action for fraudulent nondisclosure. Solorzano contends the dismissal is contrary to the Florida Supreme Court's decision in *Johnson v. Davis,* 480 So. 2d 625 (Fla. 1985). We agree.

On January 21, 2004, Solorzano filed her amended complaint seeking damages against First Union Mortgage Corporation (hereinafter referred to as "Wachovia"), for fraudulent nondisclosure. The complaint alleged, in pertinent part, that:

1. In or about April 2001, Wachovia sold Solorzano residential real property;
2. That prior to the sale, Wachovia knew that the City of Lake Worth determined there were material housing code violations on the property, and that the violations materially affected the value of the property;
3. That the housing code violations were not readily observable by Solorzano at the time she purchased the property;
4. That as a result of the material nondisclosure of the then existing housing code violations, Solorzano purchased Wachovia's real property; and
5. That the material decrease in the value of the home damaged Solorzano. Specifically, the City of Lake Worth, Florida had already levied housing code violation fines on the property in excess of $57,000.

Wachovia filed a motion to dismiss. The motion alleged, in apposite part, that Solorzano failed to state a cause of action, because Wachovia sold Solorzano the residential property "as is" and that Solorzano had "ample time and opportunity to conduct due diligence, examine title, and research the existence of any code violations before the closing." Wachovia further stated that the code violations were "open, notorious, and readily observable."

On March 16, 2004, the trial court granted Wachovia's motion to dismiss the amended complaint with prejudice. *rev. den.,* 725 So. 2d 1109 (Fla. 1998); *Smith v. Spitale,* 675 So. 2d 207 (Fla. 2d DCA 1996).

The filing of a motion to dismiss tests whether a plaintiff states a cause of action. *Bell v. Indian River Mem'l Hosp.,* 778 So. 2d 1030, 1032 (Fla. 4th DCA 2001). When reviewing a motion to dismiss, a trial court is limited to the four corners of the complaint, and it must accept all the allegations in the complaint as true. *Taylor v. City of Riviera Beach,* 801 So. 2d 259, 262 (Fla. 4th DCA 2001). Since a ruling on a motion to dismiss for failure to state a cause of action is an issue of law, our

standard of review is de novo. *Siegle v. Progressive Consumers Ins. Co.,* 819 So. 2d 732, 734 (Fla. 2002). In *Johnson v. Davis,* 480 So. 2d 625 (Fla. 1985), the Florida Supreme Court recognized for the first time a cause of action for fraudulent nondisclosure in connection with real estate transactions. *See Rayner v. Wise Realty Co. of Tallahassee,* 504 So. 2d 1361, 1363-64 (Fla. 1st DCA 1987). In *Johnson,* the court stated:

> Accordingly, we hold that where the seller of a home knows of facts materially affecting the value of the property which are not readily observable and are not known to the buyer, the seller is under a duty to disclose them to the buyer. This duty is equally applicable to all forms of real property, new and used. *Id.* at 629. *Johnson*'s application is limited to non-commercial real property transactions. *See Casey v. Cohan,* 740 So. 2d 59, 62 (Fla. 4th DCA 1999), *reh'g den.* (1999); *Green Acres, Inc. v. First Union Nat'l Bank of Fla.,* 637 So.2d 363, 364 (Fla. 4th DCA 1994).

Wachovia's reliance on the "as is" provision of the sales contract in support of its motion to dismiss is misplaced. The inclusion of an "as is" clause in a contract for the sale of residential real property does not waive the duty imposed upon a seller under *Johnson. Syvrud v. Today Real Estate, Inc.,* 858 So. 2d 1125, 1130 (Fla. 2d DCA 2003) ("An 'as is' clause in a contract for the sale of residential real property does not waive the duty imposed by Johnson v. Davis to disclose hidden defects in the property."); *Levy v. Creative Constr. Servs. of Broward, Inc.,* 566 So. 2d 347 (Fla. 3d DCA 1990) ("[W]e discern no 'as is' contractual exception to the duty imposed on the seller herein by the Johnson decision."); *Rayner,* 504 So. 2d at 1364 ("[W]e note that generally, an "as is" clause in a contract for sale of real property cannot be relied upon to bar a claim for fraudulent misrepresentation or fraudulent nondisclosure."); *see also* Frank J. Wozniak, Annotation, Construction and Effect of Provision in Contract for Sale of Realty by Which Purchaser Agrees to Take Property "As Is" or in Its Existing Condition, 8 A.L.R. 5th 312 § 2a ("[I]t has generally been held or recognized that an "as is" provision in a contract for the sale of realty does not bar a vendee's claim based on allegations of fraud, misrepresentation, or nondisclosure.").

Further, whether Solorzano readily observed the alleged housing code violations or whether she had adequate time to research the alleged violations is not properly resolvable on Wachovia's motion to dismiss. As we noted in *Atkins v. Topp Telecom, Inc.,* 873 So. 2d 397, 399 (Fla. 4th DCA 2004), a motion to dismiss is not a motion for summary judgment and a trial court is precluded from relying on depositions, affidavits, or other proofs.

Additionally, when ruling on a motion to dismiss, a trial court may not speculate whether a complaint's allegations will ultimately be provable. *Id.; see also Mancher v. Seminole Tribe of Fla., Inc.,* 708 So. 2d 327 (Fla. 4th DCA 1998).

We find that Solorzano stated a cause of action under *Johnson.* In granting Wachovia's motion to dismiss, the trial court incorrectly went beyond the four corners of the amended complaint, did not accept all the allegations as true, and mistakenly speculated on whether Solorzano will ultimately be able to prove her allegations.

Accordingly, we reverse the trial court's order dismissing the amended complaint with prejudice, and remand for further proceedings consistent with this opinion.

REVERSED AND REMANDED.

WARNER, J., concurs.

GROSS, J., concurring specially. I concur in the majority opinion. I write only to express my concern that dicta not be read to narrow the holding of *Johnson v. Davis,* 480 So. 2d 625 (Fla. 1985).

The majority writes that "whether Solorzano readily observed the alleged housing code violations or *whether she had* *adequate time to research the alleged violations* is not properly resolvable on Wachovia's motion to dismiss." (Emphasis added). My concern is with the italicized portion of the sentence.

In *Johnson,* the supreme court extended the reasoning of *Besett v. Basnett,* 389 So. 2d 995 (Fla. 1980), a case involving an "affirmative" fraudulent misrepresentation, "to the arena of nondisclosure of material facts." *M/I Schottenstein Homes, Inc. v. Azam,* 813 So. 2d 91, 93 (Fla. 2002). The supreme court described *Johnson's* holding as being "very clearly stated," that "where the seller of a home knows of facts materially affecting the value of the property which are not readily observable and are not known to the buyer, the seller is under a duty to disclose them to the buyer." *M/I Schottenstein,* 813 So. 2d at 93 (quoting *Johnson,* 480 So. 2d at 629).

A fact that is "readily observable" in a *Johnson* nondisclosure case is analogous to a misrepresentation in Besett, the falsity of which is disclosed by a cursory glance; neither the nondisclosure nor the misrepresentation is actionable. Thus, I would look to *Besett* to define a "readily observable" fact in a Johnson nondisclosure case as one that is not obvious from a "cursory examination or investigation." *M/I Schottenstein,* 813 So. 2d at 93 (quoting *Besett,* 389 So. 2d at 997).

## Sample Case Brief

*Caption: Solorzano v. First Mortgage Corporation,* 896 So. 2d 847 (Fla.Dist.Ct. App. 2005)

*Facts:* Gavi Solorzano purchased residential real property from First Union Mortgage Corporation (referred to as Wachovia). The property was sold "as is." The residential property was in violation of several material housing code violations, which Wachovia was aware of prior to the sale. Solorzano alleged that the defects were not readily observable by her at the time of the sale and materially affected the values of the property. She filed suit alleging fraudulent nondisclosure. The trial court dismissed the lawsuit with prejudice for failure to state a cause of action. Solorzano appealed.

*Issue:* Whether the trial court properly dismissed Solorzanno's lawsuit for failure to state a cause of action.

*Brief answer:* No.

*Reasoning:* The court held that Solorzano's lawsuit sufficiently stated a cause of action for fraudulent nondisclosure. The court relied on the Florida Supreme Court's case of *Johnson v. Davis,* 480 So. 2d 625 (Fla. 1985) in which the court for the first time recognized this cause of action for cases involving the sale residential property. In that case the court imposed a duty on the seller who has knowledge of defects in the property to disclose defects in the home that are not readily observable, which materially impacted the value of the home and of which the buyer was unaware. The court rejected Wachovia's argument that the inclusion of a "as is" clause within the sales contract supported the trial court's granting its motion to dismiss, stating that such a clause does not relieve the duty to disclose imposed by the *Johnson* case. The question of whether the violations were readily observable was a question of fact that could not be addressed in a motion to dismiss, in which a trial court cannot speculate whether the allegations were provable.

*Reversed and Remanded:*

*Separate Opinion:* Justice Gross concurred specifically to express concern that the holding of *Johnson v. Davis,* 480 So. 2d 625 (Fla. 1985) not be too read narrowly. He stated the definition of a "readily observable" fact in a *Johnson* nondisclosure case is one that is not obvious from a "cursory examination or investigation."

## Visit These Sites for More Information on How to Brief a Case

Professor Byron Warnken and Professor Elizabeth Samuels. The Need to Make Written Case Briefs (n.d.)
www.onlineasp.org/class/case09.htm

How to Brief Cases
Created by Christopher Pyle, 1982
Revised by Prof. Katherine Killoran, Feb. 1999
www.lib.jjay.cuny.edu/research/brief.html

Law Nerds. How to Brief Cases (n.d.)
www.lawnerds.com/guide/briefing.html#HowtoBriefaCase

University of Central Florida. Introduction to Case Briefs.
http://reach.ucf.edu/~pla3013/ponderx.html

Criminal Justice Education. Writing a Case Brief.
www.cjed.com/Write_Brief.pdf

## Visit These Sites to Learn More About How to Cite Authority

Peter W. Martin, Introduction to Basic Legal Citation (2006)
www.law.cornell.edu/citation/

Kathryn Sampson, University of Arkansas School of Law. Citation to Authorities (2001).
http://comp.uark.edu/~ksampson/citation.html

# Appendix B

## PARENTING PLAN GUIDELINES

As of August 28, 1998, section 452.310, RSMo, requires, "A party shall submit a proposed parenting plan at the time of filing of a motion to modify or a petition involving custody or visitation issues. A party shall submit a proposed parenting plan when filing the answer in such cases or within thirty days after service of a motion to modify." The requirements for the proposed parenting plan are outlined in the same statutory section.

A parenting plan is intended to assist *parents* who are not living together in developing the ideal environment for their child(ren). When making arrangements for the child(ren), parents need to consider the child(ren)'s needs and interests above all else. Since every family is unique, parents are encouraged, whenever possible, to work together to develop a plan that they both agree will meet the best interests of their child(ren). When preparing the parenting plan, it is important to remember that specific information in the following four areas must be included:

- Custody and visitation.
- Decision-making rights and responsibilities.
- Dispute resolution.
- Expenses of the child(ren).

To assist parents with providing all required information, a parenting plan form and instructions for completing the form are included with these guidelines. This form is intended for use by the child(ren)'s mother and father. Any other party, such as a grandparent, filing a motion to modify or a petition involving custody or visitation issues may wish to use this form for guidance in preparing his or her own plan to be submitted to the court.

**Note:** Instructions for completing the form are in **bold.** Statements that should be included in all parenting plans are marked with a checked box.☒

*This specific parenting plan form may be used for the proposed parenting plan, but use of this specific form is not required.*

*IN THE CIRCUIT COURT OF* _____ *COUNTY, MISSOURI*

| **Judge or Division:** | **Case Number:** | |
|---|---|---|

| Petitioner: | ☐ Proposed Parenting Plan of: <br> ☐ Petitioner ☐ Respondent ☐ Both Parties | |
|---|---|---|
| Respondent: | ☐ Court Ordered Parenting Plan: (Court Use Only) <br> ☐ Temporary Order & Judgment ☐ Final Judgment | (Date File Stamp) |

| Petitioner's Information (unless waived) <br> Home Address: <br><br><br> Home Phone Number: | Respondent's Information (unless waived) <br> Home Address: <br><br><br> Home Phone Number: |
|---|---|

## Parenting Plan

The following child(ren) were born to or adopted by the parties:

| Name | Birth Date | Name | Birth Date |
|---|---|---|---|
|  |  |  |  |
|  |  |  |  |
|  |  |  |  |
|  |  |  |  |

### A. CUSTODY AND PARENTING TIME

1. CUSTODY: Specify who shall have legal and physical custody of all child(ren). Section 452.375 RSMo, provides the following definitions: **"Custody"** means joint legal custody, sole legal custody, joint physical custody or sole physical custody or any combination thereof. **"Joint legal custody"** means that the parents share the decision-making rights, responsibilities, and authority relating to the health, education and welfare of the child(ren), and unless allocated, apportioned, or decreed, the parents shall confer with one another in the exercise of decision-making rights, responsibilities and authority. **"Joint physical custody"** means an order awarding each of the parents significant, but not necessarily equal, periods of time during which the child(ren) reside with or are under the care and supervision of each of the parents. Joint physical custody shall be shared by the parents in such a way as to assure the child(ren) of frequent, continuing and meaningful contact with both parents.

   **Indicate the legal custody and physical custody arrangements for all child(ren). Complete a, b, c or d.**

   a. ☐ Mother and Father shall have joint legal custody and joint physical custody of all children.

   b. ☐ Mother and Father shall have joint legal custody and ☐ Mother ☐ Father shall have sole physical custody of all children.

   c. ☐ Mother ☐ Father shall have sole legal custody and Mother and Father shall have joint physical custody of all children.

   d. ☐ Mother ☐ Father shall have sole legal custody and sole physical custody of all children.

   **Check box if there is a different legal custody and physical custody arrangement for any child. Complete a separate Attachment A for each child for whom there is a different legal custody or physical custody arrangement.**

   ☐ There are different legal custody and physical custody arrangements for the following child(ren) in

   Attachment A: _____, _____, _____ and _____.

2. PRIMARY RESIDENCE OF CHILD(REN): Indicate the residence of all child(ren). In situations of "joint   legal custody and joint physical custody" or "sole legal custody and joint physical custody", the residence of one of the parents shall be designated as the address of the child(ren) for mailing and educational purposes (Section 452.375 RSMo).

**Check one:**   ☐ Mother   ☐ Father

**NOTE:** Neither parent shall move his or her residence or the residence of the child(ren) without giving 60 days written notice by certified mail, return receipt requested, to any party with custody or visitation rights. (Section 452.377 RSMo)

**Check box if there is a different primary residence for any child. Complete a separate Attachment A for each child for whom there is a different primary residence.**

☐ There is a different primary residence for the following child(ren) in Attachment A:

_____, _____, _____ and _____.

3. PARENTING TIME: Children, whenever possible and appropriate, need to have frequent, continuing and meaningful contact with *both* parents. (Section 452.340.7 RSMo)

**Complete the parenting time schedule for each parent. Make sure to include the beginning and ending days and times.**

*Example: The children will spend time with Father every Tuesday from 5 p.m. to 9 p.m. and the 1ˢᵗ and 4ᵗʰ weekends of each month from 6 p.m. on Friday to 7 p.m. on Sunday.*

All children shall spend time with Mother on the following days and times: (For holidays and vacations see items 6 and 7.)

Weekends:   ☐ every   ☐ every other   ☐ other (specify)

_____

from _____ to _____.

Weekdays: specify days _____

from _____ to _____.

Other (specify) _____

_____

_____

All children shall spend time with Father on the following days and times: (For holidays and vacations see items 6 and 7.)

Weekends:   ☐ every   ☐ every other   ☐ other (specify)

_____

from _____ to _____.

Weekdays: specify days _____

From _____ to _____.

Other (specify) _____

_____

_____

**Check box if there is a different parenting time schedule for any child. Complete a separate Attachment A for each child for whom there is a different parenting time schedule.**

☐ There is a different parenting time schedule for the following child(ren) in Attachment A.

_____, _____, _____ and _____.

4. EXCHANGES: State the location where exchange of all child(ren) shall occur at both the beginning and end of all scheduled parenting times, including weekdays, weekends, holidays and vacations.

**Indicate where all child(ren) will be picked up and dropped off for both the start and end of the scheduled parenting times. Complete both "a" and "b" if there are school age child(ren). Complete <u>only</u> "b" when all child(ren) are not school age.**

a. ☐   When school is in session:
   Exchange of all child(ren) from Mother to Father shall occur at:
   ☐   Residence of Mother      ☐ Residence of Father      ☐ School
   ☐   Other Location (specify) _____

   Address

   Exchange of all child(ren) from Father to Mother shall occur at:
   ☐   Residence of Mother      ☐ Residence of Father      ☐ School
   ☐   Other Location (specify) _____

   Address

b. ☐   When school is not in session or if all child(ren) are not school age:
   Exchange of all child(ren) from Mother to Father shall occur at:
   ☐   Residence of Mother      ☐ Residence of Father
   ☐   Other Location (specify) _____

   Address

   Exchange of all child(ren) from Father to Mother shall occur at:
   ☐   Residence of Mother      ☐ Residence of Father
   ☐   Other Location (specify) _____

   Address

   ☒   If an exchange occurs at a location other than a parent's residence, the parent scheduled to have time with the child(ren) shall pick up and return the child(ren) to the specified location and the other parent shall be responsible for assuring the child(ren) are at the specified location for pick up, unless other arrangements are described:
   _____.

**Check box if there is a different exchange arrangement for any child. Complete a separate Attachment A for each child for whom there is a different exchange arrangement.**

   ☐         There are different exchange arrangements for the following child(ren) in Attachment A.

   _____, _____, _____ and _____.

5.   TRANSPORTATION: State who will be responsible for transporting all child(ren) between the parents and how any extraordinary transportation costs will be covered.

> *Example: Mother will be responsible for transportation of the children on the weekends, and Father will be responsible for transportation during the week and for all holiday and vacation times. Each parent will be responsible for his or her transportation costs.*

**Complete <u>either</u> "a" or "b."**

Transportation arrangements for all child(ren) for all scheduled parenting times, including weekdays, weekends, holidays, and vacation times, shall be as follows:
a.   ☐ Mother ☐ Father   shall be responsible for all transportation of the children, including cost.
b.   ☐ Mother and Father shall share responsibility for transportation of the child(ren), including cost, as follows: (describe) _____ .

**Complete "c" <u>only</u> if necessary. An example of an extraordinary cost might be airfare if one parent lives out-of-state.**

c.   ☐ Extraordinary Transportation Costs (bus, taxi, train, airfare) shall be the responsibility of:
☐ Mother   ☐ Father   ☐ Shared: _____% Mother   _____% Father

**Complete "d" <u>only</u> if necessary and describe other arrangements.**

> *Example: On the first Wednesday of each month, Grandmother, Mary Smith, will pick up David from the day care and take him to Father's residence. Father will be responsible for taking David back to Mother's residence at the end of the visit. Father will be responsible for all transportation costs.*

d.   ☐ Other Transportation Arrangements: (describe)

_____

_____ .

**Check box if there is a different transportation arrangement for any child. Complete a separate Attachment A for each child for whom there is a different transportation arrangement.**

☐   There are different transportation arrangements for the following child(ren) in Attachment A.

_____ , _____ , _____ and

_____ .

6. HOLIDAY SCHEDULE: The holiday schedule allows each parent to share holidays and other special days with their child(ren).
   a. **Check each box that applies.**

   ☐ Friday and Monday holidays include Saturday and Sunday.
   ☐ Holidays take precedence over regular parenting time.
   ☐ Holidays take precedence over vacations.
   ☐ If the scheduled holiday weekend causes either parent to lose his or her regular weekend time, the parent losing the regular weekend shall receive the other parent's next regular weekend. Then the original schedule will be followed so that each parent has two consecutive weekends.

   *Example: Labor Day is a Monday. It is Father's holiday and, as a result, the children will be with him for the three day weekend. If this is the scheduled weekend for the child(ren) to be with Mother, the child(ren) will now be with Mother for the following two weekends. The first weekend, which is Father's scheduled time, becomes Mother's make-up time; the second weekend is Mother's scheduled time. On the third weekend, the child(ren) will go with Father and the regular schedule will resume.*

   b. Complete chart by stating with which parent all child(ren) will spend each holiday. Be sure to include the start and end times. [See item 7, Vacation Schedule when completing Holiday Schedule]

### Example:

| Holiday | Even Years | Odd Years | Parenting Time From: To: |
|---|---|---|---|
| *Memorial Day* | *Mother* | *Father* | *8 a.m.-7 p.m.* |

| Holiday | Even Years | Odd Years | Parenting Time From: To: |
|---|---|---|---|
| New Year's Eve | | | |
| New Year's Day | | | |
| Martin Luther King Day | | | |
| Presidents' Day | | | |
| Memorial Day | | | |
| Independence Day | | | |
| Labor Day | | | |
| Thanksgiving | | | |
| Christmas Eve | | | |
| Christmas Day | | | |
| **Other Holidays (specify)** | | | |
| | | | |
| | | | |
| | | | |
| **Special Occasions (specify)** | | | |
| Halloween | | | |
| Mother's Day | | | |
| Father's Day | | | |
| Mother's Birthday | | | |
| Father's Birthday | | | |
| Child's Birthday | | | |
| | | | |
| | | | |

**Check box if there is a different holday schedule for any child. Complete a separate Attachment B for each child for whom there is a different holday schedule.**

☐ There are different holiday schedules for the following child(ren) in Attachment B:

_____, _____, _____ and _____.

7.   VACATION SCHEDULE: The vacation schedule allows each parent to share vacation time with their child(ren). Each parent may have parenting time with the child(ren) during the following vacation periods: Winter, Spring, Thanksgiving, Summer and any other specified vacation period.

☒         Each parent shall provide the other parent with a basic schedule, location and telephone numbers for emergency purposes when traveling out-of-town with the child(ren).

**Complete <u>either</u> "a" or "b".**

**Complete "a" <u>only</u> if the parents have a specific vacation schedule which does not require prior notification.**

*Examples: Summer Vacation: Mother will have six weeks of vacation time with the children each summer as follows: the first two weeks of June, the last two weeks of July, and the first two weeks of August. The vacation period will begin at 7 p.m. on Friday and end at 5 p.m. on the following Sunday.*

*Spring vacation: Mother will have the children in odd years from 3 p.m. on the last day of school before the Spring Break until 7 p.m. on the last day of the Spring Break.*

**Complete "b" <u>only</u> if the parents will make specific arrangements at a later date and prior notification is required. If you complete "b", list the amount of vacation time (days or weeks) each parent shall have with the child(ren) for each vacation period and the date by which arrangements must be made between the parents for each period. To complete "b" proceed to next page and see item b.**

*Example: Winter vacation: The children shall spend 5 days with Mother and 9 days with Father. The parents will make arrangements for specific dates and times no later than November 1st of each year.*

a.    ☐ All children shall be with Mother during vacation periods as follows: [See item 6, Holiday Schedule when completing Vacation Schedule]

Winter:         ☐ even years:   From _____ to _____ .
                                              date and time                              date and time

               ☐ odd years    From _____ to _____ .
                                              date and time                              date and time

Spring:         ☐ even years:   From _____ to _____ .
                                              date and time                              date and time

               ☐ odd years    From _____ to _____ .
                                              date and time                              date and time

Summer:         ☐ even years:   From _____ to _____ .
                                              date and time                              date and time

               ☐ odd years    From _____ to _____ .
                                              date and time                              date and time

Thanksgiving:    ☐ even years:   From _____ to _____ .
                                              date and time                              date and time

               ☐ odd years    From _____ to _____ .
                                              date and time                              date and time

Other Vacation Time (describe): _____ .

               ☐ even years:   From _____ to _____ .
                                              date and time                              date and time

               ☐ odd years    From _____ to _____ .
                                              date and time                              date and time

☐ All children shall be with Father during vacation periods as follows: [See Item 6, Holiday Schedule when completing Vacation Schedule]

Winter: ☐ even years: From _____ to _____.
   date and time                                           date and time

☐ odd years   From _____ to _____.
   date and time                                           date and time

Spring: ☐ even years: From _____ to _____.
   date and time                                           date and time

☐ odd years   From _____ to _____.
   date and time                                           date and time

Summer: ☐ even years: From _____ to _____.
   date and time                                           date and time

☐ odd years   From _____ to _____.
   date and time                                           date and time

Thanksgiving: ☐ even years: From _____ to _____.
   date and time                                           date and time

☐ odd years   From _____ to _____.
   date and time                                           date and time

Other Vacation Time (describe): _____

☐ even years: From _____ to _____.
   date and time                                           date and time

☐ odd years   From _____ to _____.
   date and time                                           date and time

**Check box if there is a different vacation schedule/arrangement for any child. Complete a separate Attachment B for each child for whom there is a different vacation schedule/arrangement.**

☐ There are different vacation schedules/arrangements for the following child(ren) in Attachment B:

_____, _____, _____ and _____.

**NOTE: If you completed "a", go to item 8, Changes. Do not complete "b."**

b. ☐ Each parent will have a specific number of days or weeks for each vacation period with all children. However, since it is not always possible for each parent to know in advance when he or she will be able to take a vacation period, the parents shall mutually schedule the arrangements and dates for these vacation periods as follows:

Winter: All child(ren) shall spend _____ (days) (weeks) with Mother and _____ (days) (weeks) with Father.
   number                                           number

The parents will make arrangements for specific dates and times no later than _____ of each year.
   date

Spring: All child(ren) shall spend _____ (days) (weeks) with Mother and _____ (days) (weeks) with Father.
   number

Thanksgiving:    All child(ren) shall spend _____ (days) (weeks) with Mother and _____ (days) (weeks) with
Father.                                number                                        number

The parents will make arrangements for specific dates and times no later than _____ of each year.
                                                                                                    date

Other (describe): _____

_____

All child(ren) shall spend _____ (days) (weeks) with Mother and _____ (days) (weeks) with Father.
                            number                                        number

The parents will make arrangements for specific dates and times no later than _____ of each year.
                                                                                                    date

☒  Any vacation periods for which the parents do not make arrangements shall be scheduled as follows: **(Complete a and b)**

a.  In even numbered years, ☐ Mother ☐ Father shall determine the length and beginning and ending times for the other
parent's specified vacation time, and shall mail written notification of the scheduled arrangements to the other parent
within _____ days of the scheduled vacation,
         number
and

b.  In odd numbered years, ☐ Mother ☐ Father shall determine the length and beginning and ending times for the other
parent's specified vacation time, and shall mail written notification of the scheduled arrangements to the other parent
within _____ days of the scheduled vacation.
         number

**Check box if there is a different vacation schedule/arrangement for any child. Complete a separate Attachment B for
each child for whom there is a different vacation schedule/arrangement.**

☐  There are different vacation schedules/arrangements for the following child(ren) in Attachment B:

_____, _____, _____ and _____.

8.  CHANGES: The parents' schedules and commitments may require occasional changes in the parenting time schedule. Parents
shall attempt to agree on any changes, but the parent receiving a request for a change shall have the final decision on
whether the change shall occur. **Complete a, b ,c, d, and e, if applicable.**

a.      The parent making the request may make such request **(check all that apply):**

☐ in person    ☐ by phone    ☐ in writing to the other parent    ☐      other (specify) _____

b.      The request for change shall be made no later than:

☐ 24 hours    ☐ one week    ☐ two weeks    ☐ other (specify) _____

prior to date of the requested change.

c.      The parent receiving the request shall respond no later than:

☐ 24 hours    ☐ one week    ☐ two weeks    ☐ other (specify) _____

after receiving the requested change.

d.      The response to the request may be made **(check all that apply):**

☐ in person    ☐ by phone    ☐ in writing to the other parent    ☐      other (specify) _____

e.      ☐ Any parent requesting a change of schedule shall be responsible for any additional child care or
transportation costs resulting from the change.

☒  Mother and Father shall cooperate to allow the children to meet their school and social commitments.

9.  TELEPHONE CONTACTS: Each parent shall have reasonable access to all child(ren) by telephone during any period in
which the child(ren) are with the other parent, unless specified below:

**Complete this section <u>only</u> if restrictions on non-emergency telephone contact are necessary.**

☐      Mother                                    ☐      Father

Day(s) and Time(s) for phone calls: _____    Day(s) and Time(s) for phone calls: _____

Restrictions _____    Restrictions: _____

_____    _____

10. SPECIAL NEEDS (If applicable): Provide this information <u>only</u> if there are special needs, such as supervised visits, supervised exchanges, or other restrictions necessary to assure the safety and well being of all child(ren).

**complete this section <u>only</u> if necessary.**

**If "a" is completed, "b" must be completed. In "a" state how often the supervised visits will be held and the length of visits, and in "b" state who will supervise the visits and where the visits will take place.**

*Example: Mother will have supervised visits twice a week. Each visit will last four hours. Aunt Mary Smith will supervise the visits in her home.*

**In "c" include who will supervise at the exchange for both the beginning and end of the visit.**

**If "a" or "c" is completed, "d" must be completed.**

**Complete "e" only if there are other restrictions related to persons the child(ren) should not have contact with or places where the child(ren) should not be taken, and state the restrictions.**

a. ☐ Mother ☐ Father shall have supervised visits with the child(ren).

How often visits will be held: (specify)

_____

Length of visits: (specify)

_____

b. Visits shall be supervised by a ☐ mutually agreed upon third party ☐ professional person/agency

Name: (specify)

_____

Location: (specify)

_____

c. ☐ Exchanges of all child(ren) shall be supervised by a mutually agreed upon third party or professional agency or person. Specify agency or person:

for beginning of visit

_____

for end of visit

_____

d. State the reasons for the restriction(s) listed in "a" or "c":

_____

_____

_____

e. ☐ Other restrictions: (describe and state reasons for restrictions)

_____

_____

_____

**B. DECISION-MAKING RIGHTS AND RESPONSIBILITIES**

Section 452.375 RSMo, provides that "…it is the public policy of this state to encourage parents to participate in decisions affecting the health, education and welfare of their children, and to resolve disputes involving their children amicably through alternative dispute resolution."

Section 452.375 RSMo, provides that "If the parent without custody has been granted restricted or supervised visitation because the court has found that the parent with custody or the child has been the victim of domestic violence, as defined in Section 455.200 RSMo, by the parent without custody, the court may order that the reports and records made available pursuant to this subsection not include the address of the parent with custody of the child."

**Check each box that applies.**

☐ All reports and records made available to ☐ Mother ☐ Father shall not include the address of the other spouse.

☐ Each parent shall make decisions regarding the day-to-day care and control of each child while the child is with that parent. Regardless of the decision-making responsibilities stated in this parenting plan, either parent may make emergency decisions affecting the health or safety of the child(ren).

☐ Each parent shall have access to medical and school records pertaining to the child(ren) and be permitted to independently consult with any and all professionals involved with the child(ren). The parents shall cooperate with each other in sharing information related to the health, education and welfare of the child(ren).

☐ Each parent shall be responsible for getting records and reports directly from school and medical care providers.

1. DECISION-MAKING: Parents should attempt to share responsibility for making all major decisions regarding each child. If not shared, explain the reason and which parent will be responsible for the decision. Include how decisions will be made and information shared on all aspects of the child(ren)'s lives, including, but not necessarily limited to, education, health care, child care and extracurricular activities.

**Major decisions regarding the child(ren) may be shared. If not shared, check the responsible party and indicate reason why.**

| Decision-Making Rights and Responsibilities | Shared | If Not Shared, Reason Why | Person Responsible Mother | Father |
|---|---|---|---|---|
| **Education** (what school the child(ren) will attend, entry into special classes) | | | | |
| **Medical** (medical procedures needed, medications to be taken, mental health treatment decisions) | | | | |
| **Dental** (procedures needed, including orthodontics) | | | | |
| **Selection of Health Care Providers** (doctor, hospital, therapist and psychiatrists) | | | | |
| **Selection of Child Care Providers**     When with Mother | | | | |
|     When with Father | | | | |
| **Extracurricular Activities** (what the child(ren) will participate in when these activities involve each person's parenting time) | | | | |
| **Religious Upbringing** | | | | |
| **Other** (specify) | | | | |

2. COMMUNICATION: Parents need to communicate information to each other concerning the child(ren)'s needs and performances in different areas, including educational and medical information, and the children)'s activities.

☒ Each parent shall inform the other parent as soon as possible of all school, sporting and other special activity notices and cooperate in the child(ren)'s consistent attendance at such events.

☒ Each parent shall always keep the other parent informed of his or her actual residence address, mailing address if different, home and work telephone numbers and any changes within _____ hours of such change occurring.
number
(Exception to this is defined in Section 452.375 RSMo)

☒ Neither parent shall say or do anything in the presence or hearing of the child(ren) that would in any way diminish the child(ren)'s love or affection for the other parent and shall not allow others to do so.

☒ All court related and financial communications between the parents shall occur at a time when the child(ren) are not present and, therefore, shall not occur at times of exchanges of the child(ren) or during telephone visits with the child(ren).

☒ Neither parent shall schedule activities for the child(ren) during the other parent's scheduled parenting time without the other parent's prior agreement, with the following exceptions: _____
(indicate if **none**).

**The method by which information is communicated should be stated here. Check acceptable methods of communication. If all apply, check all boxes.**

| Type of Information | Personal Contact | Telephone | U.S. Mail | Other |
|---|---|---|---|---|
| **School and Day Care** (knowledge of progress or problems in school and day care) | | | | |
| **Medical and Dental** (concerning the child(ren)'s medical and dental care) | | | | |
| **Extracurricular Activities** | | | | |
| **Appropriate Telephone Numbers** (persons caring for the child(ren), numbers at locations that are deemed appropriate in case the parent needs to reach the child(ren)) | | | | |
| **Other** (specify) | | | | |

**C. DISPUTE RESOLUTION**

State how the parents will resolve any matters on which they disagree or which involve interpreting the parenting plan. Parents should attempt to solve these disputes through mutual discussion. If that fails, parents can seek assistance through a neutral party, such as professional counselor or trained mediator. Parents are encouraged to use the court as a last resort.

**Complete either "1" or "2."**

1. ☐ Parents shall attempt to resolve any matters on which they disagree or which involve interpreting the parenting plan through the following alternative dispute resolution process prior to any court action:

    a. ☐ Counseling by

    _____ ; or

    ☐ Mediation by

    _____ ; or

    ☐ Other (specify)

    _____

    b. The cost of this process shall be allocated between the parties as follows:

    ☐ _____% Mother    _____% Father; or

    ☐ based on each party's proportional share of income; or

    ☐ as determined in the dispute resolution process

    c. The process shall be started by notifying the other party by:

    ☐ written request    ☐ certified mail    ☐ other (specify) _____

2. ☐ All matters on which the parents disagree or which involve interpreting the parenting plan and for which the court has authority to act shall be resolved through appropriate court action.

### D.  EXPENSES OF THE CHILD

Expenses of the child(ren) are the responsibility of both parents. The parenting plan must state who will pay child support and include the amount of child support to be paid by that parent. Section 452.340 RSMo, and Missouri Supreme Court Rule 88.01 should be referred to before determining the amount of child support. Also, if other expenses, such as child care, educational, medical, dental and other extraordinary expenses of the child(ren), are not included in the child support amount, the parenting plan must state by whom these expenses will be paid.

**Complete "a" by stating the amount and how often child support will be paid by the named parent.**

*Example: Father will pay to Mother $100 per month for support of the minor child(ren).*

a.  ☐ The amount of child support to be paid by        ☐ Mother    ☐ Father

to the other parent is as follows: (describe)

_____

_____

_____

_____

**Complete "b" only if one or more of the listed expenses is <u>not</u> included in the child support amount. Many times expenses will change in amount or the amount is unknown. It may be appropriate, therefore, to list either the dollar amount of the expense to be paid by each parent or a percentage of that expense to be paid by each parent. If it is intended that one parent will pay the entire expense, use 100% in the box to indicate that amount.**

b.  ☐ Expenses not included in the stated child support amount shall be paid as follows:

| Expense (specify) | Mother—amount or % | Father—amount or % |
|---|---|---|
| **Health Insurance Coverage** | | |
| **Medical** (including co-pays) | | |
| **Dental** (such as braces, crowns) | | |
| **Vision** (such as eyeglasses, contacts) | | |
| **Psychological** (counseling, therapy) | | |
| **Other Health Care** (list) | | |
| **Educational** (tuition, books, fees) | | |
| **Childcare** (work-related) | | |
| **Extraordinary Expenses** (music lessons, sports equipment, car insurance) | | |

**E.  ADDITIONAL ITEMS:**

_____

_____

_____

_____

_____

_____

_____

_____

_____

_____
Signature of Petitioner            date

_____
Signature of  Respondent           date

_____
Counsel for Petitioner (if applicable)      date

_____
Counsel for Respondent (if applicable)     date

_____
Guardian ad litem (if applicable)       date

"Absent exigent circumstances as determined by a court with jurisdiction, you, as a party to this action, are ordered to notify, in writing by certified mail, return receipt requested, and at least sixty days prior to the proposed relocation, each party to this action of any proposed relocation of the principal residence of the child, including the following information:

(1)  The intended new residence, including the specific address and mailing address, if known, and if not known, the city;
(2)  The home telephone number of the new residence, if known;
(3)  The date of the intended move or proposed relocation;
(4)  A brief statement of the specific reasons for the proposed relocation of the child; and
(5)  A proposal for a revised schedule of custody or visitation with the child.

Your obligation to provide this information to each party continues as long as you or any other party by virtue of this order is entitled to custody of a child covered by this order. Your failure to obey the order of this court regarding the proposed relocation may result in further litigation to enforce such order, including contempt of court. In addition, your failure to notify a party of a relocation of the child may be considered in a proceeding to modify custody or visitation with the child. Reasonable costs and attorney fees may be assessed against you if you fail to give the required notice."

**SO ORDERED**

_____
date
_____
Judge's Signature

**ATTACHMENT A**

**CHILD:** _____

**1.   CUSTODY**

Indicate the legal and physical custody arrangement for the child. Complete a, b, c or d.

a.   ☐ Mother and Father shall have joint legal custody and joint physical custody of the child.

b.   ☐ Mother and Father shall have joint legal custody and ☐ Mother ☐ Father shall have sole physical custody of the child.

c.   ☐ Mother ☐ Father shall have sole legal custody and Mother and Father shall have joint physical custody of the child.

d.   ☐ Mother ☐ Father shall have sole legal custody and sole physical custody of the child.

**2.   PRIMARY RESIDENCE OF CHILD:** Indicate the residence of the child. In situations of "joint legal custody and joint physical custody" or "sole legal custody and joint physical custody", the residence of one of the parents shall be designated as the address of the child for mailing and educational purposes (Section 452.375 RSMo)

**Check one:**     ☐ Mother     ☐ Father

**3.   PARENTING TIME**

Complete the parenting time schedule for each parent. Make sure to include the beginning and ending days and times.

***Example: The child will spend time with Father every Tuesday from 5 p.m. to 9 p.m. and the 1st and 4th weekends of each month from 6 p.m. on Friday to 7 p.m. on Sunday.***

The child shall spend time with Mother on the following days and times: (For holidays and vacations see Attachment B.)

Weekends:     ☐ every     ☐ every other     ☐ other (specify)

_____

from _____ to _____.

Weekdays: specify days _____

from _____ to _____.

Other (specify)_____

_____

_____

The child shall spend time with Father on the following days and times: (For holidays and vacations see Attachment B.)

Weekends: ☐ every     ☐ every other     ☐ other (specify)

_____

from _____ to _____.

Weekdays: specify days _____

from _____ to _____.

Other (specify)_____

_____

_____

**4.   EXCHANGES:** State the location where exchange of the child shall occur at both the beginning and end of the scheduled parenting times, including weekdays, weekends, holidays and vacations.

**Indicate where the child will be picked up and dropped off for both the start and end of the scheduled parenting times. Complete both "a" and "b" for a school age child. Complete only "b" if the child is not school age.**

a.   ☐ When school is in session:
Exchange of child from Mother to Father shall occur at:
☐ Residence of Mother     ☐ Residence of Father     ☐ School
☐ Other Location (specify) _____

Address

Exchange of child from Father to Mother shall occur at:
☐ Residence of Mother     ☐ Residence of Father     ☐ School

**ATTACHMENT A**

b.    ☐ When school is not in session, or if the child is not school age
Exchange of child from Mother to Father shall occur at:
☐ Residence of Mother   ☐ Residence of Father
☐ Other Location (specify) _____

        Address

Exchange of child from Father to Mother shall occur at:
☐ Residence of Mother   ☐ Residence of Father
☐ Other Location (specify) _____

Address

☒    If an exchange occurs at a location other than a parent's residence, the parent scheduled to have time with the child shall pick up and return the child to the specified location and the other parent shall be responsible for assuring the child is at the specified location for pickup, unless other arrangements are
described:_____

5.   **TRANSPORTATION**: State who will be responsible for transporting the child between the parents and how any extraordinary transportation costs will be covered.

*Example: Mother will be responsible for transportation of the child on the weekends, and Father will be responsible for transportation during the week and for all holiday and vacation times. Each parent will be responsible for his or her transportation costs.*

**Complete either "a" or "b".**

Transportation arrangements for the child for all scheduled parenting times, including weekdays, weekends, holidays, and vacation times, shall be as follows:
a.   ☐ Mother ☐ Father    shall be responsible for all transportation of the child, including cost.
b.   ☐ Mother and Father    shall share responsibility for transportation of the child, including cost, as follows: (describe)

_____

_____

**Complete "c" only if necessary. An example of an extraordinary cost might be airfare if one parent lives out-of-state.**

c.   ☐ Extraordinary Transportation Costs (bus, taxi, train, airfare) shall be the responsibility of:
        ☐ Mother        ☐ Father        ☐ Shared: _____ % Mother        _____ % Father

**Complete "d" only if necessary and describe other arrangements.**

*Example: On the first Wednesday of each month, Grandmother, Mary Smith, will pick up David from the day care and take him to Father's residence. Father will be responsible for taking David back to Mother's residence at the end of the visit. Father will be responsible for all transportation costs.*

d.   ☐ Other Transportation Arrangements: (describe) _____

_____.

(use additional pages as necessary)

**ATTACHMENT B**

CHILD: _____

6.  HOLIDAY SCHEDULE: The holiday schedule allows each parent to share holidays and other special days with their child.

    a.  **Check each box that applies.**
       ☐ Friday and Monday holidays include Saturday and Sunday.
       ☐ Holidays take precedence over regular parenting time.
       ☐ Holidays take precedence over vacations.
       ☐ If the scheduled holiday weekend causes either parent to lose his or her regular weekend time, the parent losing the regular weekend shall receive the other parent's next regular weekend. Then the original schedule will be followed so that each parent has two consecutive weekends.

*Example: Labor Day is on a Monday. It is Father's holiday and, as a result, the child will be with him for the three day weekend. If this is the scheduled weekend for the child to be with Mother, the child will now be with Mother for the following two weekends. The first weekend, which is Father's scheduled time, becomes Mother's make-up time; the second weekend is Mother's scheduled time. On the third weekend, the child will go with Father and the regular schedule will resume.*

    b.  Complete chart by stating with which parent the child will spend each holiday. Be sure to include the start and end times. [See item 7, Vacation Schedule when completing Holiday Schedule]

*Example:*

| Holiday | Even Years | Odd Years | Parenting Time From: To: |
|---|---|---|---|
| *Memorial Day* | *Mother* | *Father* | *8 a.m. –7 p.m.* |

| Holiday | Even Years | Odd Years | Parenting Time From: To: |
|---|---|---|---|
| New Year's Eve | | | |
| New Year's Day | | | |
| Martin Luther King Day | | | |
| Presidents' Day | | | |
| Memorial Day | | | |
| Independence Day | | | |
| Labor Day | | | |
| Thanksgiving | | | |
| Christmas Eve | | | |
| Christmas Day | | | |
| Other Holidays (specify) | | | |
| | | | |
| | | | |
| | | | |
| Special Occasions (Specify) | | | |
| Halloween | | | |
| Mother's Day | | | |
| Father's Day | | | |
| Mother's Birthday | | | |
| Father's Birthday | | | |
| Child's Birthday | | | |
| | | | |
| | | | |
| | | | |
| | | | |

**ATTACHMENT B**

7. **VACATION SCHEDULE:** The vacation schedule allows each parent to share vacation time with their child. Each parent may have parenting time with the child during the following vacation periods: Winter, Spring, Thanksgiving, Summer and any other specified vacation period.

☒ Each parent shall provide the other parent with a basic schedule, location and telephone numbers for emergency purposes when traveling out-of-town with the child.

**Complete either "a" or "b."**

**Complete "a" only if the parents have a specific vacation schedule which does not require prior notification.**

*Examples: Summer Vacation: Mother will have six weeks of vacation time with the child each summer as follows: the first two weeks of June, the last two weeks of July, and the first two weeks of August. The vacation period will begin at 7 p.m. on Friday and end at 5 p.m. on the following Sunday.*

*Spring vacation: Mother will have the child in odd years from 3 p.m. on the last day of school before the Spring Break until 7 p.m. on the last day of the Spring Break.*

**Complete "b" only if the parents will make specific arrangements at a later date and prior notification is required. If you complete "b," list the amount of vacation time (days or weeks) each parent shall have with the child for each vacation period and the date by which arrangements must be made between the parents for each period. To complete "b" proceed to next page and see item b.**

*Example: Winter vacation: The child shall spend 5 days with Mother and 9 days with Father. The parents will make arrangements for specific dates and times no later than November 1st of each year.*

a.  ☐ The child shall be with Mother during vacation periods as follows: [See item 6, Holday Schedule when completing Vacation Schedule]

Winter:  ☐ even years:  From _____ to _____ .
                                       date and time                        date and time

         ☐ odd years  From _____ to _____ .
                                     date and time                        date and time

Spring:  ☐ even years:  From _____ to _____ .
                                       date and time                        date and time

         ☐ odd years  From _____ to _____ .
                                     date and time                        date and time

Summer:  ☐ even years:  From _____ to _____ .
                                       date and time                        date and time

         ☐ odd years  From _____ to _____ .
                                     date and time                        date and time

Thanksgiving:  ☐ even years:  From _____ to _____ .
                                             date and time                        date and time

               ☐ odd years  From _____ to _____ .
                                         date and time                        date and time

Other Vacation Time (describe): _____

**ATTACHMENT B**

☐ The child shall be with Father during vacation periods as follows: [See item 6, Holiday Schedule when completing Vacation Schedule]

Winter:      ☐ even years:   From _____ to _____.
                                       date and time                    date and time

             ☐ odd years    From _____ to _____.
                                       date and time                    date and time

Spring:      ☐ even years:   From _____ to _____.
                                       date and time                    date and time

             ☐ odd years    From _____ to _____.
                                       date and time                    date and time

Summer:      ☐ even years:   From _____ to _____.
                                       date and time                    date and time

             ☐ odd years    From _____ to _____.
                                       date and time                    date and time

Thanksgiving: ☐ even years:  From _____ to _____.
                                       date and time                    date and time

             ☐ odd years    From _____ to _____.
                                       date and time                    date and time

Other Vacation Time (describe): _____

             ☐ even years:   From _____ to _____.
                                       date and time                    date and time

             ☐ odd years    From _____ to _____.
                                       date and time                    date and time

**NOTE:** If you completed "a", do not complete "b".

b.   ☐        Each parent will have a specific number of days or weeks for each vacation period with the child. However, since it is not always possible for each parent to know in advance when he or she will be able to take a vacation period, the parents shall mutually schedule the arrangements and dates for these vacation periods as follows:

Winter:   The child shall spend _____ (days) (weeks) with Mother and _____ (days) (weeks) with Father.
                              number                                    number
          The parents will make arrangements for specific dates and times no later than _____ of each year.
                                                                                              date

Spring:   The child shall spend _____ (days) (weeks) with Mother and _____ (days) (weeks) with Father.
                              number                                    number
          The parents will make arrangements for specific dates and times no later than _____ of each year.
                                                                                              date

**ATTACHMENT B**

Other (describe): _____

_____

The child shall spend _____ (days) (weeks) with Mother and _____ (days) (weeks) with Father. The parents
                              number                                                            number

will make arrangements for specific dates and times no later than _____ of each year.
                                                                                              date

☒        Any vacation periods for which the parents do not make arrangements shall be scheduled as follows: **(Complete a and b)**

    a.   In even numbered years, ☐ Mother ☐ Father shall determine the length and beginning and ending times for the other
        parent's specified vacation time, and shall mail written notification of the scheduled arrangements to the other parent
        within _____ days of the scheduled vacation,
               number
        and

    b.   In odd numbered years, ☐ Mother ☐ Father shall determine the length and beginning and ending times for the other
        parent's specified vacation time, and shall mail written notification of the scheduled arrangements to the other parent
        within _____ days of the scheduled vacation.
               number

(use additional pages as necessary)

*Source:* Retrieved from: www.courts.mo.gov/sup/index.nsf/d45a7635d4bfdb8f8625662000632638/629aab74004234eb862566e2006b5181/$FILE/Parenting%20Plan%20Guidelines. dot on 4/09/07

# Appendix C

## SAMPLE FORMS

Premarital Agreement

Client Intake Sheet

Civil Cover Sheet

Petition for Dissolution of Marriage

Marital Settlement Agreement

Final Judgment of Dissolution of Marriage

All Documents are prepared using ProDoc document assembly software. To learn more about ProDoc visit www.prodoc.com or call 1-800-759-5418.

# PREMARITAL AGREEMENT

THIS AGREEMENT is made by and between John Allen Lancaster, hereinafter referred to as "Husband," and Samantha Elizabeth Johnson, hereinafter referred to as "Wife," in contemplation and consideration of their forthcoming marriage. As used in this Agreement, Husband and Wife will sometimes be singularly referred to as "Party" and jointly referred as "Parties." The Parties acknowledge, represent and recite as follows:

A.    A marriage is contemplated between the Parties to each other. The Parties are to be married in Orange Park, Clay County, Florida, and both Parties have declared Florida as their residence and domicile, notwithstanding that from time to time in the future, each may maintain one or more residences in other states or jurisdictions.

B.    Husband has not been previously married, and has no children. Wife has not been previously married, and has no children.

C.    The Parties desire and intend to define and fix their respective rights and claims in the property of each other and to avoid the possession of such interests which, except for the operation of this Agreement, each might have acquired or might acquire in the property of the other as incidents of their marriage relationship. The Parties agree to accept the provisions of this Agreement in full discharge and satisfaction of all marital rights in the property now owned or hereafter acquired by either of them or in their estates upon the death of either of them.

D.    The Parties intend that no marital property be created during their marriage, except as specifically provided by this Agreement.

E.    It is also the desire of Wife to maintain as her Separate Property the assets accumulated and to be accumulated through her ownership interest in her non-marital business, known as Johnson Realty Corporation.

F.    The Parties are aware that there is or may be substantial disparity in their assets and incomes and that the disparity may be expected to be substantially greater in the future. Nevertheless, it is the intention of the Parties that upon their marriage, the consequences of this Agreement shall be binding on the Parties, their heirs, legal representatives, personal representatives, and assigns, for all time.

G.    The Parties have determined that the contemplated marriage will have a better chance of success if their respective rights and obligations by reason of the marriage are fixed and determined by the terms and provisions of this Agreement, and the Parties believe this Agreement will be conducive to their marital tranquility and harmony, although recognizing that there is always the possibility that their marriage may not succeed.

H.    The Parties acknowledge that each of them would not enter into the contemplated marriage except for the execution of this Agreement and the expectation that both Parties shall at all times fully and faithfully perform and be bound by all of its provisions, and the further expectation that both Parties shall at all times be absolutely and forever precluded and estopped from seeking any benefits and/or imposing any obligations on the other, other than as expressly provided in this Agreement, whether greater than or different from those expressly provided.

I.    This Agreement is therefore entered into in consideration of marriage, and its effectiveness is expressly conditioned on such marriage between the Parties actually taking place, and it shall become effective upon the date of the marriage of the Parties. If, for any reason, the marriage is not consummated, this Agreement shall become null and void and of no force or effect.

**NOW, THEREFORE,** in consideration of the promise to marry and its consummation, the Parties do hereby mutually agree and stipulate as follows:

**I. Recitals.**  Husband and Wife acknowledge that the Recitals stated above are true and correct and are incorporated herein by reference.

**II. Free and Voluntary Act: Time for Reflection.**  The Parties acknowledge and agree to the following:

2.1   This Agreement provides fair and reasonable provisions for each of the Parties.

2.2   There has been full and frank disclosure between the Parties of all property owned and each Party has a satisfactory understanding of their rights relating to such property.

2.3   Neither Party desires or requires additional information or disclosure from the other Party.

2.4   Each Party asserts that all of their questions have been satisfactorily answered regarding the character, nature, and extent of the other Party's property and financial condition. The financial disclosure attached is a good faith approximation of the values of the various assets and liabilities. Each Party acknowledges that he or she has had the right and the opportunity to request and receive further information regarding the valuation and description of each item contained in the financial disclosure of the other Party, and that he or she was free to conduct independent evaluations concerning the exact value of such items.

2.5   Each Party has given careful and mature thought to the making of this Agreement and to its specific terms.

2.6   Each Party has taken sufficient time to reflect on the seriousness of this Agreement and its terms.

2.7   Each Party enters into this Agreement intending to be bound by it.

2.8   The Parties fully acknowledge that they enter into this Agreement freely and voluntarily and for no reason other than a desire for the furtherance of their relationship in the marriage.

**III. Financial Disclosure.**  Before the execution of this Agreement, Husband and Wife have made to each other a complete disclosure of the nature, extent, and probable value of all of their Property, estate, and expectancies, and of their respective debts and liabilities. Husband's financial disclosure is attached as **Exhibit A** and Wife's financial disclosure is attached as **Exhibit B**, both being made a part hereof. Each Party acknowledges that he or she has had the right and the opportunity to request and receive further information regarding the properties and estates of the other. The Parties are each satisfied that they have sufficient information and knowledge regarding the finances of the other to enter into this Agreement, and, before the execution of this Agreement, the Parties have voluntarily and expressly waived, in writing, any right to disclosure of the property or financial obligations of the other party beyond the disclosure provided.

**IV. Husband's Separate Property.**

4.1   The separate property of Husband is listed in the financial disclosure attached as **Exhibit A**, and shall also include:

(a)   any property and beneficial interests in property which are given to or inherited by Husband;

(b)   any recovery for personal injuries and/or property losses sustained by Husband during the Parties' marriage, including any recovery for loss of earning capacity during the marriage;

(c)   any future contributions to individual retirement accounts, retirement plans, and any other employee benefit plans made by or on behalf of Husband after the date of the Parties' marriage, together with any increases in value of all such plans;

(d)   any interests in trust in which Husband has an interest, including but not limited to all corpus of those trusts, as well as all distributed and undistributed income from those trusts;

(e)   any replacements of separate property;

(f)   any property exchanged for separate property;

(g)   any property purchased with separate funds or with proceeds from the sale of separate property;

(h)   any appreciation in value of separate property; and

(i)   any income and distributions from separate property, whether designated as active or passive.

4.2   Said separate property shall remain his sole and separate property throughout the marriage. Property may be tangible, intangible or mixed. Separate property is synonymous with Non-Marital Property.

4.3   Wife shall not claim or acquire any interest in any of Husband's separate property now owned or hereafter acquired during the marriage except as otherwise specifically provided in this Agreement. Husband reserves the right to make gifts to Wife of property during the marriage, which shall be deemed her separate property, but the gifts shall not constitute an amendment or other change to this Agreement.

4.4   Wife waives and relinquishes any claims or interest she may have in and to any and all of Husband's separate property, including for any appreciation in said property and any income or distributions from said property, for any special equity, or for any contribution to or reimbursement from Husband's separate property, even if such a claim or interest for contribution or reimbursement arises from the marital estate, her separate property, or services rendered by her (unless agreed to in writing and signed by both Parties).

4.5   Husband shall be solely responsible for the costs of operating, maintaining, or improving his separate property, including any income taxes, property taxes, state taxes, and intangible taxes which may be levied on Husband's separate property and income, from his separate property and income, except as may be agreed to otherwise by the Parties, in accordance with the provisions set forth herein.

### V. Wife's Separate Property.

5.1   The separate property of Wife is listed in the financial disclosure attached as **Exhibit B**, and shall also include:

(a)   any property and beneficial interests in property which are given to or inherited by Wife;

(b)   any recovery for personal injuries and/or property losses sustained by Wife during the Parties' marriage, including any recovery for loss of earning capacity during the marriage.

(c)   any future contributions to individual retirement accounts, retirement plans, and any other employee benefit plans made by or on behalf of Wife after the date of the Parties' marriage, together with any increases in value of all such plans;

(d)   any interests in trust in which Wife has an interest, including but not limited to all corpus of those trusts, as well as all distributed and undistributed income from those trusts; and

(e)   any replacements of separate property;

(f)   any property exchanged for separate property;

(g)   any property purchased with separate funds or with proceeds from the sale of separate property;

(h)   any appreciation in value of separate property; and

(i)   any income and distributions from separate property, whether designated as active or passive.

5.2   The business interest of Wife known as Johnson Realty Corporation, along with the assets accumulated and to be accumulated through her ownership, any and all enhancement and appreciation thereof, either active or passive, and any and all income and profits therefrom shall be Wife's non-marital property. In the event that a proceeding for dissolution of the Parties' marriage (or similar proceeding) is filed, Wife shall be free from any request for an evaluation, accounting, appraisal, or discovery pertaining to said business.

5.3   Said separate property shall remain her sole and separate property throughout the marriage. Property may be tangible, intangible or mixed. Separate property is synonymous with Non-Marital Property.

5.4   Husband shall not claim or acquire any interest in any of Wife's separate property now owned or hereafter acquired during the marriage except as otherwise specifically provided in this Agreement. Wife reserves the right to make gifts to Husband of property during the marriage, which shall be deemed his separate property, but the gifts shall not constitute an amendment or other change to this Agreement.

5.5   Husband waives and relinquishes any claims or interest he may have in and to any and all of Wife's separate property, including for any appreciation in said property and any income or distributions from said property, for any special equity, or for any contribution to or reimbursement from Wife's separate property, even if such a claim or interest for contribution or reimbursement arises from the marital estate, his separate property, or services rendered by him (unless agreed to in writing and signed by both Parties).

5.6   Wife shall be solely responsible for the costs of operating, maintaining, or improving her separate property, including any income taxes, property taxes, state taxes, and intangible taxes which may be levied on Wife's separate property and income, from her separate property and income, except as may be agreed to otherwise by the Parties, in accordance with the provisions set forth herein.

**VI. Management and Control of Separate Property.**    Each Party retains the management and control of all separate property belonging to the Party, and may encumber, sell or dispose of such property without the consent of the other Party. Each Party shall be solely responsible for tax consequences for acquiring or selling separate property. Each of the Parties agrees to evidence his or her consent for the other Party to make gifts of their separate property to third Parties for whatever reason, including to obtain the benefits of any split gift provisions of the federal gift tax laws and to sign any tax return required to evidence same: it being understood and agreed that the consenting Party shall have no responsibility or liability for any federal gift tax arising out of such transfer, and that such gifts shall not require the utilization of any part of the consenting Party's unified credit or exemption equivalent allowance under the Internal Revenue Code. If either Party fails or refuses to join in or execute any instrument as required by this Paragraph, the other Party may sue for specific performance or for damages, regardless of the doctrine of spousal immunity, and the defaulting Party shall be responsible for the other Party's costs, expenses and attorney's fees. This Paragraph shall not require a Party to execute a promissory note or other evidence of indebtedness for the other Party, and if a Party shall sign a note or other evidence of indebtedness at the request of the other Party such other Party shall indemnify the accommodating Party executing the note or other evidence of debt from any claims or demands arising from the execution of the instrument, including reasonable attorney's fees, costs and suit money. Execution of an instrument shall not give the Party executing it any right or interest in the separate property of the Party requesting execution.

**VII. Retirement and Pension Benefits.** Unless named by a written instrument as a beneficiary, each Party waives all right, title, and interest, if any, that he or she may acquire by virtue of the marriage to the retirement benefits and disability benefits, whether lump sum or installment, any profit-sharing interests, and any other employee benefits arising out of the other Party's past, present, or future employment. Each Party agrees to sign a waiver, if requested to do so in writing by the other Party, of any interest in any plan subsequent to the marriage as required by ERISA, by the Internal Revenue Service Code, and/or by the Administrator of any such plan, necessary to grant each Party complete freedom to designate any beneficiary of any qualified plan proceeds or any other pension or retirement account belonging to a Party without any further consent of the other Party.

**VIII. Debts.** Neither Party shall assume or become responsible for the payment of any pre-existing debts or obligations of the other Party because of the marriage. Further, neither Party shall incur any debts or obligations during the marriage for which the other could be held responsible without the express written consent of the other. Neither Party shall do anything that would cause the debt or obligation of one of them to be a claim, demand, lien or encumbrance against the property of the other Party without the other Party's written consent. If a debt or obligation of one Party is asserted as a claim or demand against the property of the other without the written consent of the other Party, the Party who is responsible for the debt or obligation hereby indemnifies the other Party from the claim or demand, including the indemnified Party's costs, expenses and attorney's fees. Any obligation jointly entered by the Parties, either prior to or during the marriage, shall remain a joint obligation of both.

**IX. No Existing Right, Title or Interest.** Each Party acknowledges to the other that: (a) he or she does not now have and has never had any right, title, or interest in or to the property, income, assets, or estate of the other Party by reason of their pre-marital relationship, or otherwise; (b) neither Party is indebted to the other; and (c) with the exception of gifts given by one to the other, each has acquired and accumulated all of their respective separate, non-marital property, both real and personal, and income, independently of, and without the joinder, help, or assistance of, the other.

**X. Income Earned During Marriage.** Except as otherwise provided by this Agreement, income earned or received during marriage (and any property acquired during marriage that is clearly and directly traceable to such income) shall constitute marital property subject to equitable distribution upon the dissolution of marriage. However, such marital property shall NOT INCLUDE any income earned, received or derived from (a) the nonmarital business of Wife, (b) any retirement and other employee benefit plans of either Party, or any increases in value thereof, (c) any trust not expressly created for the benefit of both Parties, (d) any separate property of either Party, (e) any replacements of separate property of either Party, (f) any property exchanged for separate property, (g) any property purchased with separate funds of either Party, (h) any proceeds from the sale of separate property of either Party, (i) any appreciation in value of separate property of either Party, or (j) any distributions from separate property of either Party.

**XI. Marital Residence.** The Parties anticipate the joint acquisition of a marital home, which property shall be titled to the Parties jointly, and the Parties shall contribute in equal proportion to the purchase price, closing costs, and payment of any indebtedness associated therewith.

**XII. Maintenance of the Parties.** The Parties agree that they will establish a jointly held bank account, to which each Party shall make deposits and contributions in proportion to that Party's relative income. The purpose of said joint bank account will be for the normal marital living expenses of the Parties, and for the operation, routine maintenance, property taxes, and expenses associated with the marital residence. Said account shall be considered a marital asset of the Parties, subject to equitable distribution in a proceeding for dissolution of the Parties' marriage (or similar proceeding).

**XIII. Disposition of Jointly Held Property.**    Any property acquired by the Parties during the marriage, titled as joint tenants with rights of survivorship, as tenants by entirety, or otherwise titled jointly, shall be deemed marital property, and in the event of dissolution of the marriage, the Parties shall divide such property between themselves equally. Upon the death of a Party during the marriage, the surviving Party shall hold and acquire the sole title and incidents of ownership of such property. In the event that the Parties die simultaneously so that it is impossible to determine the order of their deaths, the Parties agree that the property shall be sold by their respective personal representatives, and the net proceeds of such sale divided equally between the Parties estates. A Party's individual one-half (1/2) interest in any property held as tenants in common shall pass under the Party's will as specified in the will.

**XIV. Gifts to the Parties and Untitled Personalty.**    Any items that were gifts from one Party to the other during the marriage shall remain the sole property of the recipient. The Parties recognize that they may receive joint gifts during the marriage from third Parties. In the event the contemplated marriage dissolves for any reason whatsoever, all such joint gifts shall be equally divided between the Parties. In the event the Parties cannot reach an amicable agreement as to the division of such joint gifts, then the item(s) shall be sold and the net proceeds divided equally. Each Party shall pay one-half (1/2) of the costs and expenses of any such sale, including any appraisal fees and any income taxes. The same process will hold for any untitled items (a) purchased with marital funds accumulated during the marriage or (b) which are not specifically identified in writing as the separate property of one or the other Party.

**XV. Disposition of Property on Death.**

15.1    Each Party acknowledges that, if the other were to die, whether testate or intestate, during marriage, then the share of the decedent's estate to which the surviving Party would be entitled or could assert a right would, except for this Agreement, be greater than provided in this Agreement. Each Party consents that the separate property of the other may be disposed of by Will or Codicil to such persons as the Party making the Will or Codicil may elect, or, in the absence of a Will, the estate of each Party may descend to the heirs of that Party as if the marriage had not taken place. In either event, the separate property shall be free of any claim or demand of inheritance, dower, curtesy, elective share, family allowance or any spousal or other claims given by law, irrespective of the marriage and any law to the contrary. The Parties acknowledge that either Party shall have the right voluntarily to transfer or convey to the other any property or interest during his or her lifetime or at the time of his or her death, and nothing in this Agreement is intended to limit or restrict the right of the Party to receive any voluntary transfer or conveyance from the other.

15.2    Husband may, in his sole discretion, provide for Wife in his will, and Wife expressly waives all rights or claims that she may have in Husband's estate. Wife states that she has full knowledge and understanding of the effect of this waiver.

15.3    Wife may, in her sole discretion, provide for Husband in her will, and Husband expressly waives all rights or claims that he may have in Wife's estate, EXCEPT as specifically provided in Paragraph 15.4 below. Husband states that he has full knowledge and understanding of the effect of this waiver.

15.4    In the event of the death of Wife, the estate of Wife shall pay an amount to Husband (based on the length of the marriage as provided below) within sixty (60) days of the appointment of a

Personal Representative for Wife's estate, if at the time of her death, neither Party has filed a petition for separation, annulment or dissolution of the marriage, AND the Parties were living together as husband and wife:

(a)   If the Parties have been married for four (4) years or less at the time of Wife's death, the estate of Wife shall pay to Husband a sum of Five Hundred Thousand and No/100 Dollars ($500,000).

(b)   If the Parties have been married for more than four (4) years but less than eight (8) years at the time of Wife's death, the estate of Wife shall pay to Husband a sum of One Million and No/100 Dollars ($1,000,000).

(c)   If the Parties have been married for more than eight (8) years but less than twelve (12) years at the time of Wife's death, the estate of Wife shall pay to Husband a sum of One Million Five Hundred Thousand and No/100 Dollars ($1,500,000).

(d)   If the Parties have been married for more than twelve (12) years at the time of Wife's death, the estate of Wife shall pay to Husband a sum of Two Million and No/100 Dollars ($2,000,000).

## XVI. Dissolution of Marriage.

16.1   This Agreement shall be construed as a settlement agreement in the event that a proceeding for dissolution of marriage (or other similar proceeding) is filed, and this Agreement shall govern all of either Party's rights, including but not limited to property, alimony (temporary, rehabilitation, lump sum, permanent or otherwise), temporary support, permanent support, equitable distribution, property settlement, costs, suit money, or attorney's fees.

16.2   The Parties understand that existing or future Florida law may prevent them from waiving the rights of either Party to temporary alimony and spousal support, and that the right to support remains for the duration of the Parties' marriage. However, the Parties wish to fix such rights in a reasonable manner in order to minimize any conflict which may arise out of a proceeding for dissolution of the Parties' marriage (or similar proceeding). Notwithstanding any existing or future Florida law, each Party wishes to waive any right to receive temporary alimony and spousal support from the other Party in the event a proceeding for dissolution of the Parties' marriage (or similar proceeding) is filed, knowing that he or she might otherwise be entitled to a significant amount, but for this Agreement.

16.3   The Parties also understand that existing or future Florida law may prevent them from waiving the rights of either Party for temporary attorney's fees and costs incurred in a proceeding for dissolution of the Parties' marriage (or similar proceeding). However, the Parties wish to fix such rights in a reasonable manner in order to preserve their separate estates and to minimize litigation between them. Notwithstanding any existing or future Florida law, each Party wishes to waive any right to receive temporary attorney's fees from the joint marital estate or from the other Party in the event that a proceeding for dissolution of the Parties' marriage (or similar proceeding) is filed.

16.4   In the event that a proceeding for dissolution of marriage (or other similar proceeding) is filed by either Party, Husband shall be entitled to lump sum alimony from Wife based upon the length of the marriage as provided below. The date for determining the length of the marriage shall be the date of the filing of petition for dissolution or annulment or similar pleading. Both Parties agree the lump sum alimony provided herein is non-modifiable both as to amount and duration. One-half (1/2) of any such sum due shall be due and payable within thirty (30) days after the date the judge signs a final judgment or decree in such proceeding, and the balance shall be payable in sixty (60) equal monthly payments beginning sixty (60) days after the date the judge signs said final judgment or decree.

(a)    If the Parties have been married for four (4) years or less at the time such a petition is filed, the sum of non-modifiable lump sum alimony shall be Five Hundred Thousand and No/100 Dollars ($500,000).

(b)    If the Parties have been married for more than four (4) years but less than eight (8) years at the time such a petition is filed, the sum of non-modifiable lump sum alimony shall be One Million and No/100 Dollars ($1,000,000).

(c)    If the Parties have been married for more than eight (8) years but less than twelve (12) years at the time such a petition is filed, the sum of non-modifiable lump sum alimony shall be One Million Five Hundred Thousand and No/100 Dollars ($1,500,000).

(d)    If the Parties have been married for more than twelve (12) years at the time such a petition is filed, the sum of non-modifiable lump sum alimony shall be Two Million and No/100 Dollars ($2,000,000).

(e)    All payments of lump sum alimony shall for federal income tax purposes be tax deductible by Wife and includable as income to Husband.

(f)    The obligation to pay lump sum alimony shall cease upon the death or remarriage of Husband, if it has not been fully paid prior to Husband's death or remarriage. The payments herein shall not cease upon the death of Wife. If Wife dies before full payment, the alimony payments shall be an obligation of her estate and shall be paid by Wife's personal representative when and as due.

16.5    In the event that a proceeding for dissolution of marriage (or other similar proceeding) is filed, the marital estate available for equitable distribution shall be limited to (a) income defined as marital property by this Agreement, (b) property acquired by the Parties during the marriage that is clearly and directly traceable to such income, and (c) any other marital property expressly provided for by this Agreement.

16.6    Except as specifically provided hereinabove, Husband hereby waives and relinquishes any and all claims or rights he might otherwise have against Wife or her assets, whether for property owned solely by Wife, alimony (rehabilitation, bridge-the-gap, lump sum, permanent or otherwise), temporary support, permanent support, equitable distribution, property settlement, costs, suit money, attorney's fees, separate maintenance, support, or otherwise, connected with the dissolution of marriage or divorce. Husband acknowledges that, in a proceeding for dissolution of the marriage (or other similar proceeding), the property, alimony (rehabilitation, bridge-the-gap, lump sum, permanent or otherwise), temporary support, permanent support, equitable distribution, property settlement, costs, suit money, or attorney's fees or any other award that he might receive, except for this Agreement, might be substantially greater.

16.7    Except as specifically provided hereinabove, Wife hereby waives and relinquishes any and all claims or rights she might otherwise have against Husband or his assets, whether for property owned solely by Husband, alimony (rehabilitation, bridge-the-gap, lump sum, permanent or otherwise), temporary support, permanent support, equitable distribution, property settlement, costs, suit money, attorney's fees, separate maintenance, support, or otherwise, connected with the dissolution of marriage or divorce. Wife acknowledges that, in a proceeding for dissolution of the marriage (or other similar proceeding), the property, alimony (rehabilitation, bridge-the-gap, lump sum, permanent or otherwise), temporary support, permanent support, equitable distribution, property settlement, costs, suit money, or attorney's fees or any other award that she might receive, except for this Agreement, might be substantially greater.

16.8    Each Party further agrees to pay his or her own attorney's fees, costs, and other expenses on final hearing of any dissolution or other similar proceeding.

16.9   If a proceeding for dissolution of marriage (or other similar proceeding) is filed by either Party, both Parties agree to present this settlement to the court for approval and incorporate this settlement into the final judgment or decree dissolving the marriage. Notwithstanding incorporation into the final judgment, this Agreement shall not be merged into said judgment but shall survive it and be binding upon the Parties for all time.

16.10   Except as provided herein, each Party agrees not to enforce or determine any rights that he or she might have as a result of the marriage of the Parties, and believes that the provisions set out herein are fair, and agrees to accept and abide by these provisions freely and voluntarily.

16.11   The Parties affirm that this Agreement is at this time and will be at all times hereafter a fair and equitable Agreement relating to, among other things, property division, equitable distribution, alimony, maintenance and support. If either Party files an action seeking a dissolution of the marriage, award of separate maintenance, annulment of the marriage, separation or similar event, the Parties agree to enter into a written stipulation carrying out the provisions of this Agreement. The Parties realize that the value of the separate property owned by each of them and the earning capacity of each of them may significantly increase or decrease in the future, and they acknowledge that any such increase or decrease shall not constitute a change of circumstances affecting the equitableness or fairness of this Agreement.

**XVII. Waiver of Modification.**   The Parties understand that waiver of alimony and/or support, whether temporary or otherwise, and attorney's fees, costs and suit money, may be unenforceable, and that Florida or any other applicable law may permit either Party at some future date to request a court of equity to modify this Agreement on the basis that it is unenforceable or no longer fair and reasonable as a result of the Parties' change in economic or social circumstances. Notwithstanding the foregoing, the Parties believe this Agreement to be fair, just and reasonable, and expressly request that no court alter or deem unenforceable the provisions of this Agreement. Both Parties waive any right that either of them now has or may have to obtain modification of this Agreement or to change any of its terms pursuant to Florida Statute Section 61.14, any amendment thereto, or under any other present or future law of Florida or any other jurisdiction. Notwithstanding the foregoing, this Agreement may be amended by a written instrument executed by both Parties with the same formalities as this Agreement.

**XVIII. Waiver of Defenses to Enforcement of Agreement.**   The Parties have executed this Agreement knowingly and voluntarily and forever waive any future right to challenge the validity or enforceability of this Agreement or any portion of it based on any of the following grounds: (a) the absence of additional financial disclosure by the other Party; (b) a claim that the Agreement is inequitable; (c) a claim that the Agreement is unconscionable; (d) a claim that the Agreement does not make a reasonable provision for one or the other of them; (e) a claim of inadequate or no legal representation; (f) a claim of failure to fully realize the extent and nature of any rights waived; (g) a claim that new statutory or decisional law overrides the enforceability of the Agreement or renders it invalid because of public policy; (h) a claim that the laws of a different jurisdiction modify the Agreement or render it unenforceable; (i) a claim that the Agreement was executed as a result or coercion undue influence or under duress; (j) a claim of invalidity relating to the execution of this Agreement shortly before a pending wedding; or (k) any other defense to the enforcement of the Agreement.

**XIX. Mutual Release.**   Except as otherwise provided in this Agreement, each Party waives, discharges, and releases any and all claims and rights, actual, inchoate, or contingent, in law or equity which he or she has acquired in the property of the other by reason of such marriage, including, but not limited to:

(a)   The rights or claims of dower, curtesy, or any statutory substitutes as provided by the statutes of the state in which the Parties or either of them domiciled or in which they or either of them may own property.

(b)    The right to exempt property or any statutory exemptions or year's support or allowance.

(c)    The right to an elective share against the WILL of the other Party.

(d)    The right to distributive share in the estate of the other Party should he or she die intestate.

(e)    The right to act as a Personal Representative or Executor of the other Party.

(f)    The right to any real property or to any estate in real property of the other Party by virtue of the homestead property provisions of the Florida Constitution or any Florida Statute concerning the descent of homestead property or any similar provision of any other state.

(g)    All right to property in which the other holds an interest, alimony (temporary, rehabilitation, lump sum, permanent or otherwise), temporary support, permanent support, equitable distribution, property settlement, costs, suit money, or attorney's fees, and separate maintenance or support, unconnected with dissolution of marriage or divorce.

(h)    Any claims or demands that either Party may acquire, except as herein provided, for special equity and equitable disposition in the other Party's sole and separate property, including but not limited to pension plans, profit sharing plans, Keogh plans, IRA's, businesses, business good will, earning capacity, partnerships, corporations, or special equity and equitable distribution in the Party's jointly owned property. This Paragraph shall include all rights now existing or that may hereafter be conferred on either Party by statute, court decision, or otherwise.

**XX. Arbitration.**    In the event a proceeding for dissolution of marriage (or other similar proceeding) is filed, and/or if a dispute arises as to the interpretation of this Agreement, the Parties agree to submit the matter to binding arbitration before an arbitrator certified by the American Academy of Matrimonial Lawyers. The Parties understand that they will be bound by the arbitrator's award and such award will not be appealable. The Parties shall equally share the costs of arbitration. In the event either Party is forced to seek a court order to enforce this Paragraph of the Agreement, the other Party shall pay all attorney's fees and costs incurred by the Party bringing the action.

**XXI. Default.**    The Parties agree that, should either Party default in or breach any of his or her respective obligations and duties as contained in this Agreement, then the defaulting or breaching Party shall be responsible for and pay to the injured Party, in addition to such other damage as may be awarded, all of his or her reasonable attorney's fees, court costs, and other related expenses, including but not limited to deposits on costs and reasonable and necessary transportation and lodging as expended or incurred by the injured Party to enforce the provisions contained herein against the defaulting Party.

**XXII. Other Instruments.**    Each Party shall execute any instruments or documents at any time requested by the other Party that are necessary or proper to effectuate this Agreement.

**XXIII. Legal Counsel.**    Each Party has sufficient funds and has had opportunity to retain another attorney of his or her own choosing to review this Agreement, obtain legal advice, and have the provisions, rights, obligations and consequences of this Agreement explained to him or her.

**XXIV. Construction and Representations.**

24.1    This Agreement shall become effective only in the event that the contemplated marriage between the Parties is hereafter solemnized.

24.2    This written Agreement contains the entire understanding and agreement of the Parties. There are no representations, warranties, promises, covenants or undertakings, oral or otherwise, other than those expressly set forth herein. This Agreement may not be changed except in writing executed by the Parties hereto.

24.3   This Agreement was the product of mutual discussions and negotiation. Both Parties acknowledge they are acting free of any coercion, duress, or undue influence. Both Parties acknowledge this instrument to be a product of their individual free will. Furthermore, both Parties acknowledge their belief that this instrument will promote a positive marital relationship by freeing the Parties from financial concerns in a proceeding for dissolution of marriage (or other similar proceeding).

24.4   Each Party has had sufficient time to consider this Agreement.

24.5   This Agreement being the result of joint negotiations and drafting, and in the event of a future ambiguity, it shall not be construed against one Party as the proponent of the Agreement.

24.6   The headings and captions contained in this Agreement shall not be considered to be a part hereof for purposes of interpreting or applying this Agreement but are for convenience only.

24.7   This Agreement may be executed in counterparts, each of which shall be deemed to be an original but all of which together shall constitute one and the same instrument.

24.8   This Agreement shall inure to the benefit of and shall be binding upon the heirs, beneficiaries, executors, administrators, personal representatives and assigns of the Parties.

24.9   All questions relating to the validity and construction of this Agreement shall be determined in accordance with the laws of the State of Florida.

24.10   If any term, provision, covenant or condition of this Agreement is held by a court of competent jurisdiction to be invalid, void or unenforceable, the remainder of the provisions shall remain in full force and effect and shall in no way be affected, impaired or invalidated.

EXECUTED by John Allen Lancaster, Husband, at _____ _____. m., on this _____ day of _____, 2007.

_____
John Allen Lancaster

**Witnesses as to John Allen Lancaster, Husband:**

_____
Signature of Witness

_____
Date

_____
Name Printed

_____
Street Address

_____
City, State, Zip

_____
Signature of Witness

_____
Date

_____
Name Printed

_____
Street Address

_____
City, State, Zip

**STATE OF FLORIDA**

**COUNTY OF CLAY**

I HEREBY CERTIFY that on this day before me, an officer duly authorized to take acknowledgments, personally appeared John Allen Lancaster. He is personally known to me or has produced a Florida driver's license as identification and executed the foregoing instrument and he acknowledged before me under oath as follows:

1. That he has carefully read and understands each and every page of this Agreement and each schedule attached or referred to, in its entirety;

2. That he has obtained adequate knowledge of Wife's financial condition;

3. That all of his questions regarding Wife's financial condition have been satisfactorily answered;

4. That, before the execution of this Agreement, he voluntarily and expressly waived, in writing, any right to disclosure of the property or financial obligations of the Wife beyond the disclosure provided;

5. That he has given careful and mature thought to the making of this Agreement;

6. That he is entering into this Agreement freely and voluntarily;

7. That he has sufficient funds and has had opportunity to retain an attorney of his own choosing to review this Agreement, obtain legal advice, and have the provisions, rights, obligations and consequences of this Agreement explained to him;

8. That he is not relying on any legal or accounting advice provided by Wife or anyone acting on her behalf; and

9. That he is executing this Agreement with intent to be bound fully by all its terms.

IN WITNESS WHEREOF, I have set my hand and seal in the County and State last aforesaid this _____ day of _____, 2007.

_____

NOTARY PUBLIC

EXECUTED by Samantha Elizabeth Johnson, Wife, at _____ ___.m., on this _____ day of _____, 2007.

_____

Samantha Elizabeth Johnson

**Witnesses as to Samantha Elizabeth Jonson, Wife:**

_____    _____
Signature of Witness                Signature of Witness

_____    _____
Date                                Date

_____    _____
Name Printed                        Name Printed

Street Address                              Street Address

_____                   _____

City, State, Zip                            City, State, Zip

**STATE OF FLORIDA**

**COUNTY OF CLAY**

I HEREBY CERTIFY that on this day before me, an officer duly authorized to take acknowledgments, personally appeared Samantha Elizabeth Johnson. She is personally known to me or has produced a Florida driver's license as identification and executed the foregoing instrument and she acknowledged before me under oath as follows:

1.  That she has carefully read and understands each and every page of this Agreement and each schedule attached or referred to, in its entirety;

2.  That she has obtained adequate knowledge of Husband's financial condition;

3.  That all of her questions regarding Husband's financial condition have been satisfactorily answered;

4.  That, before the execution of this Agreement, she voluntarily and expressly waived, in writing, any right to disclosure of the property or financial obligations of the Husband beyond the disclosure provided;

5.  That she has given careful and mature thought to the making of this Agreement;

6.  That she is entering into this Agreement freely and voluntarily;

7.  That she has sufficient funds and has had opportunity to retain an attorney of her own choosing to review this Agreement, obtain legal advice, and have the provisions, rights, obligations and consequences of this Agreement explained to her;

8.  That she is not relying on any legal or accounting advice provided by Husband or anyone acting on his behalf; and

9.  That she is executing this Agreement with intent to be bound fully by all its terms.

IN WITNESS WHEREOF, I have set my hand and seal in the County and State last aforesaid this _____ day of _____, 2007.

_____
NOTARY PUBLIC

Prepared using ProDoc Form # 11-505

## CLIENT QUESTIONNAIRE

1. Answer all questions completely. If you need more space, please use additional paper and attach it to this questionnaire.

2. If a particular question does not apply, enter "n/a".

3. **CONFIDENTIALITY:** The information you enter in this questionnaire is confidential and protected by Attorney-Client Privilege. The information will not be disclosed to anyone outside of this office, except in the course of rendering legal services on your behalf or as otherwise provided by law.

**A.   CLIENT INFORMATION:**                                                   Date: 11/15/07

Name: John Allen Lancaster      Soc. Sec. No.: 111-22-0000
Home Address: 69 Plainfield Ave.
City: Orange Park   State: Florida   Zip Code: 32073
County: Clay County   DOB: 01/30/62   State of Birth: Maryland
Home Phone: 904-555-7777   Work Phone: 904-555-9243   Fax Number: (904) 555-9244
E-mail Address: johna@www.com   Driver's License Number: FL999-000-62-111-0

Dates of residency at current address: Fifteen (15)
List any previous residences in the past five (5) years, and dates resided in each: n/a
Employer's Name (if any): Orange Park Motors
Employer's Address: 1222 Park Avenue
Job Title: Sales Manager   Nature of Job: Supervise sales representatives
Date of Employment: 1/05/1987   Occupation: n/a
Salary: $6,500.00 weekly/biweekly/twice a month/(monthly)/weekly (circle one)

Do you have a Will? Yes   If so, do you wish it to be reviewed? Yes, in contemplation of divorce
    (If so, please return a copy of the Will with this completed form.)

How did you hear about our office? Referred by James Jones, Attorney at Law

Have you retained any other attorneys on this matter prior to coming to this office? (If yes, please provide name, date retained, and reason to discontinue service.) I consulted with Mr. Jones, who has handled real estate matters for me in the past, and he referred me to your office because he does not work on divorce cases.

**B.   SPOUSE'S INFORMATION:**

Name: Samantha Elizabeth Lancaster   Soc. Sec. No.:   222-11-0000
Home Address: 69 Plainfield Ave.
City: Orange Park   State: Florida   Zip Code: 32073
County: Clay County   DOB: 7/4/61   State of Birth: Florida
Telephone Number: 904-555-8080 (cell)   Fax Number: None
E-mail Address: samanthae@www.com   Driver's License Number: FL777-000-61-888-0

Is spouse represented by counsel in this matter? <u>X</u> Yes _____ No - If yes, complete the following:
Spouse's Attorney: Sam Dickerson
Street Address: 1444 HWY 17
City: Green Cove Springs   State: FL   Zip Code: 32043
Phone Number: (904) 888-1111   Fax Number: (904) 888-1112

Employer's Name (if any): Johnson Realty Corporation
Employer's Address: 1444 Blanding Blvd. Orange Park, FL  32073
Date of Employment:  09/23/84   Occupation:  Real estate agent
Salary: $20,400 (includes all sources of income) weekly/biweekly/twice a (month)/monthly/weekly (circle one)

## C.   MARITAL INFORMATION:

Date of Marriage: 02/15/1992

Place of Marriage: Orange Park, Clay County, Florida
    (Please provide a marriage certificate)

Are you and your spouse currently living together? <u>X</u> Yes _____ No

If not, then Date of Separation: n/a

Do you have an interest in reconciliation? _____ Yes <u>X</u> No

To the best of your knowledge, does your spouse want reconciliation? _____ Yes X No

Describe the circumstances that caused your separation: While we are still living together, we have decided that it would be best for both of us to end our marriage. My wife has become increasingly involved in her business dealings and resentful of my lower income as compared to hers. This has created a very uncomfortable living situation. We have tried to work through our differences over the last two years, but now conclude that our differences are irreconcilable.

## D.   CHILDREN'S INFORMATION (from this marriage):

| Name: | SSNo.: | Place of Birth: | Date of Birth: | Living With: | Sex: |
|---|---|---|---|---|---|
| Sam Lancaster | 222-11-0000 | Orange Park, FL | 08/12/1994 | Both of us at this time | (M)/ F |
| Karen Lancaster | 555-44-0000 | Orange Park, FL | 11/02/97 | Both of us at this time | M /(F) |

Is the wife currently pregnant? <u>X</u> No _____ Yes; date child is due: _____

<u>**UCCJEA Information:**</u>

If any of the children have resided with anyone other than you and your spouse during the last five (5) years, please complete the following information:

| Name of Custodian: | Address: | Dates Resided with: |
|---|---|---|
| n/a | | |
| | | |
| | | |

Have you participated as a party, witness or any other capacity in other litigation or custody proceedings, including divorce, separate maintenance, child neglect, dependancy or guardianship, concerning custody or visitation of any child subject to this proceeding? <u>X</u> No  Yes - If Yes, please describe: _____

Do you have any information of any custody or visitation proceeding currently pending in a court of this or any other state concerning any child subject to this proceeding <u>X</u> No _____ Yes - If Yes, please describe: _____

Do you have any knowledge of any support order issued by a court of this or any other state concerning any child subject to this proceeding? X No _____ Yes - If Yes, please describe:

*Prepared using ProDoc Form # 1-010*

**I.    CASE STYLE**

IN THE CIRCUIT COURT OF THE FOURTH JUDICIAL CIRCUIT,
IN AND FOR CLAY COUNTY, FLORIDA

Case No.:  2007XXXX
Division:  Family Law

IN RE THE MARRIAGE OF:

JOHN ALLEN LANCASTER, Husband,

and

SAMANTHA ELIZABETH LANCASTER, Wife

**Judge:**   William Grant

**II.    TYPE OF CASE**  (Place an x in one box only. If the case fits more than one type of case, select the most definitive.)

| Domestic Relations | Torts | Other Civil |
| --- | --- | --- |
| ___ Simplified dissolution | ___ Professional malpractice | ___ Contracts |
| _X_ Dissolution | ___ Products liability | ___ Condominium |
| ___ Support - IV-D | ___ Auto negligence | ___ Real property/ mortgage foreclosure |
| ___ Support - Non IV-D | ___ Other negligence | ___ Eminent domain |
| ___ UIFSA - IV-D | | ___ Challenge to proposed constitutional amendment |
| ___ UIFSA - Non IV-D | | ___ Other |
| ___ Domestic violence | | |
| ___ Other domestic relations | | |

**III.   IS JURY TRIAL DEMANDED IN COMPLAINT?**

___ Yes

_X_ No

DATE: December 20, 2007

_____

SIGNATURE OF ATTORNEY FOR PARTY INITIATING ACTION

Prepared using ProDoc Form # 4-010

IN THE CIRCUIT COURT OF THE FOURTH JUDICIAL CIRCUIT,
IN AND FOR CLAY COUNTY, FLORIDA

Case No.: 2007XXXX
Division: Family Law

IN RE THE MARRIAGE OF:

JOHN ALLEN LANCASTER, Husband,

and

SAMANTHA ELIZABETH LANCASTER,
Wife

## PETITION FOR
## DISSOLUTION OF MARRIAGE AND OTHER RELIEF

Husband, JOHN ALLEN LANCASTER, by and through the undersigned attorney, files this Petition for Dissolution of Marriage and states as follows:

1. **Action for Dissolution of Marriage**.

This is an action for dissolution of the bonds of marriage between the parties in the above-styled cause, specifically Petitioner, John Allen Lancaster, hereinafter called "Husband," and Respondent, Samantha Elizabeth Lancaster, born Samantha Elizabeth Johnson, hereinafter called "Wife." Completed Notice of Social Security Number forms are attached or were previously filed with this Court.

2. **Jurisdiction and Venue**.

The parties have been residents of Florida for more than six (6) months prior to the filing of this Petition. Venue is proper in this circuit because Clay County is where the intact marriage of these parties was last evidenced by a continuing union and the intent to remain there and married to each other.

3. **Marriage Statistic**.

The parties were duly married to each other on February 15, 1992, at Orange Park, Clay County, Florida.

4. **Date of Separation**.

The parties are presently residing in the same house, but not as husband and wife. A separation is imminent.

5. **Grounds**.

The marriage of the parties is irretrievably broken.

6. **Children of the Marriage**.

The minor children common to both parties are:

**Name**: Sam Lancaster
**Place of Birth**: Orange Park, Clay County, Florida
**Birth date**: August 12, 1994
**Sex**: Male

**Name**: Karen Lancaster
**Place of Birth**: Orange Park, Clay County, Florida
**Birth date**: November 2, 1997
**Sex**: Female

7. **Uniform Child Custody Jurisdiction and Enforcement Act**

**Sam Lancaster's Residence for the past 5 years:**

| Dates (From/to) | Address (including city and state) where child lived | Name and present address of person child lived with | Relationship to child |
|---|---|---|---|
| Birth-Present | 69 Plainfield Ave. Orange Park, Florida 32073 | John Allen Lancaster 69 Plainfield Ave. Orange Park, Florida 32073 | Father |
| | | Samantha Elizabeth Lancaster 69 Plainfield Ave. Orange Park, Florida 32073 | Mother |

**Karen Lancaster's Residence for the past 5 years:**

| Dates (From/to) | Address (including city and state) where child lived | Name and present address of person child lived with | Relationship to child |
|---|---|---|---|
| Birth-Present | 69 Plainfield Ave. Orange Park, Florida 32073 | John Allen Lancaster 69 Plainfield Ave. Orange Park, Florida 32073 | Father |
| | | Samantha Elizabeth Lancaster 69 Plainfield Ave. Orange Park, Florida 32073 | Mother |

**Participation in custody proceedings:**

I HAVE NOT participated as a party, witness, or in any capacity in any other litigation or custody proceeding in this or any other state, concerning custody of a child subject to this proceeding.

**Information about custody proceedings:**

I HAVE NO INFORMATION about any custody proceeding pending in a court of this or any other state concerning a child subject to this proceeding.

**Persons not a party to this proceeding:**

I DO NOT KNOW OF ANY PERSON not a party to this proceeding who has physical custody or claims to have custody or visitation rights with respect to any child subject to this proceeding.

**Knowledge of prior child support proceedings:**

The children described in this affidavit are NOT subject to existing child support orders in this or any state or territory.

8.  **Present Parental Responsibility**.

At this time, the physical custody of the minor children is being shared by Husband and Wife.

9.  **Requested Parental Responsibility**.

Parental responsibility for the minor children of the parties should be shared by both Husband and Wife, pursuant to the applicable Florida Statutes. It would be in the best interest of the minor children of the parties if the primary residence is with the Husband.

10.  **Support of Children**.

Wife is able to contribute to the support of the minor children of the parties. Husband's resources are inadequate to provide for the needs of the minor children of the parties and therefore needs the financial assistance of Wife.

11.  **Premarital Agreement and Equitable Distribution**.

The parties have entered into a premarital agreement, dated May 12, 1992, which should govern and settle issues of equitable distribution and support between the parties herein.

12.  **Military Status**.

Both parties are over the age of eighteen (18) years and neither is, nor within a period of thirty (30) days immediately prior to this date has been, enlisted in the military service of the United States as defined by the Servicemembers Civil Relief Act of 2003.

**WHEREFORE**, Husband, JOHN ALLEN LANCASTER, respectfully requests that this Honorable Court:

A.  Award Husband the relief sought herein, and dissolve the marriage of the parties.

B.  Award parental responsibility for the minor children to both Husband and Wife, pursuant to the applicable Florida Statutes.

C.  Award primary residential responsibility for the minor children of the parties to Husband.

D.  Award Husband temporary and permanent support for said minor children, pursuant to the applicable Florida Statutes.

E.  Grant a distribution of assets and liabilities as provided by the premarital agreement of the parties.

_____

John Allen Lancaster
Husband

STATE OF FLORIDA                    )
                                    )
COUNTY OF CLAY                      )

   **SWORN TO AND SUBSCRIBED** before me, this _____ day of December, 2007, by Husband, JOHN ALLEN LANCASTER who is personally known to me or who has produced a Florida driver's license as identification.

_____

NOTARY PUBLIC


Respectfully submitted,



By: _____

John Sinclair
Florida Bar No. XXX
PO Box 9200
Orange Park, FL 32073
Tel. 904-555-1111
Fax 904-555-1112
Attorney for Husband

Prepared using ProDoc Form # 3-100

IN THE CIRCUIT COURT OF THE FOURTH JUDICIAL CIRCUIT,
IN AND FOR CLAY COUNTY, FLORIDA

Case No.: 2007XXXX
Division: Family Law

IN RE THE MARRIAGE OF:

JOHN ALLEN LANCASTER, Husband,

and

SAMANTHA ELIZABETH LANCASTER,
Wife

## MARITAL SETTLEMENT AGREEMENT

This Agreement is made in connection with an action for dissolution between John Allen Lancaster, referred to as "Husband" and as "Father" herein, and Samantha Elizabeth Lancaster, referred to as "Wife" and as "Mother" herein, who are sworn and agree as follows:

**WHEREAS**, the parties hereto were married to each other on or about February 15, 1992, in Orange Park, Clay County, Florida;

**WHEREAS**, the following children involved in this action have been born to or adopted by the parties:

| Name | Date of Birth |
|------|---------------|
| Sam Lancaster | August 12, 1994 |
| Karen Lancaster | November 2, 1997 |

**WHEREAS**, no other children were adopted, and none are expected;

**WHEREAS**, Husband has filed a petition for dissolution of marriage in the above case, and this Agreement is intended to be introduced into evidence in such action, to be incorporated in a Final Judgment entered therein;

**WHEREAS**, the parties acknowledge that irreconcilable differences exist, that the marriage is irretrievably broken, and that the parties intend to live separate and apart from each other;

**WHEREAS**, the parties wish to settle between themselves, now and forever, their respective rights, duties, and obligations regarding property, liabilities, and children;

**WHEREAS**, each party has read this Agreement and understands its terms and consequences, and each party believes that this Agreement is fair, just, and reasonable, and in the best interest of the children;

**WHEREAS**, each party has assented to this Agreement freely and voluntarily, without coercion or duress;

**NOW, THEREFORE**, in consideration of the mutual covenants, promises and undertakings set forth herein, and for other good and valuable consideration, the parties have agreed and do hereby agree as follows:

## ARTICLE I
## PARENTAL RESPONSIBILITY

1.1 Each party recognizes the deep love, devotion, and dedication of the other to the children. Each party also recognizes that the other has a right and responsibility to participate in major matters relating to the education, health, welfare, and upbringing of the children. The parties agree to use their best efforts to cooperate in such matters, and that any rights, duties or responsibilities set forth herein shall not be exercised to frustrate or control the other parent.

1.2 Father and Mother shall have shared parental responsibility and shall retain full parental rights and responsibilities with respect to the children.

1.3 The primary physical residence of the children shall be in the home of Father, and the secondary physical residence of the children shall be in the home of Mother.

1.4 Father and Mother shall consult and reasonably cooperate with each other, and share the decision-making responsibility regarding the following general areas: (a) education; (b) camp and extracurricular activities; (c) college, vocational or other post-secondary education; (d) medical, dental and surgical treatment; (e) psychological or psychiatric evaluation or treatment; (f) discipline; (g) moral and religious training; and (h) the children's estate, services and earnings.

## ARTICLE II
## PARENTING SCHEDULE

2.1 The parties agree that it is in the best interest of the children for both parties to have frequent and continuing contact with the children, and the parties shall have visitation with the children at times mutually agreed to in advance by the parties. In the absence of mutual agreement, the parties shall have visitation with the children under the Parenting Schedule attached to this Agreement as Exhibit "A," which is incorporated by reference as if set out in full. The parties understand that they are free to vary the times or days stated in the Parenting Schedule if they both agree.

## ARTICLE III
## RECOGNITION OF CHILDREN'S RIGHTS

3.1 Each child has the right to have two parents and to love each without fear of anger or hurt from the other.

3.2 Each child has the right to develop an independent and meaningful relationship with each parent and to respect the personal differences of each parent and each home.

3.3 Each child has the right to be free from being present during the parents' personal battles or being used as a spy, messenger, or bargaining chip.

3.4 Each child has the right to enjoy the mother's family and the father's family, to see each of the families as being different from each other, and not to have these differences referred to as "better" or "worse."

3.5 Each child has the right not to be questioned about the other parent's private life.

3.6 Each child has the right not to hear parents speak ill of each other, nor to have to hear about the difficulties with the other parent.

3.7    Each child has the right to see his or her parents being courteous to and respectful of each other.

3.8    Each child has the right to develop and maintain age-appropriate activities and friends without fear of losing time with a parent.

3.9    Each child has the right to his or her roots, which include grandparents, uncles, aunts, and cousins.

3.10    Each child has the right to be a child: to be free from parents' guilt and not to assume adult or parent roles.

## ARTICLE IV
## GENERAL PROVISIONS RELATING TO THE CHILDREN

4.1    <u>Relocation of Children</u>.    It is acknowledged that in the event that a Primary Residential Parent seeks to relocate the principal residence of any child subject to this order more than 50 miles away from the current residence as provided by Section 61.13001 of the Florida Statutes, such parent shall comply with the provisions of Section 61.13001 by either (a) obtaining written agreement in accordance with 61.13001(2) of the Florida Statutes from the other parent, and any other person entitled to visitation, or (b) serving a Notice of Intent to Relocate signed under oath and penalty of perjury in accordance with Section 61.13001(3) of the Florida Statutes, giving the other parent, and any other person entitled to visitation, 30 days to object to the relocation and to request a determination by the Court.

IF A PRIMARY RESIDENTIAL PARENT ATTEMPTS TO RELOCATE THE PRINCIPAL RESIDENCE OF ANY CHILD AND FAILS TO COMPLY WITH SECTION 61.13001(3) OF THE FLORIDA STATUTES REGARDING THE NOTICE OF INTENT TO RELOCATE, SUCH PARENT MAY BE SUBJECT TO CONTEMPT AND OTHER PROCEEDINGS TO COMPEL THE RETURN OF ANY CHILD, AND SUCH NON-COMPLIANCE MAY BE TAKEN INTO ACCOUNT BY THE COURT IN A SUBSEQUENT DETERMINATION OF THE RESIDENCE, CUSTODY OR VISITATION RELATING TO ANY CHILD.

4.2    <u>Notice of Parent's Relocation or Change of Residence</u>.    Either parent must give prior written notice at least thirty (30) days before the day that he or she is to relocate or change residence (regardless of whether the residence of any child will change). Such notice must be made to the other parent by certified mail, return receipt requested, and must include the new address.

4.3    <u>Removal of Child</u>.    Neither party may remove any child outside the state of Florida for a period of more than seven (7) consecutive days without the prior written permission of the other parent. Neither parent shall remove any child from the custody of the other parent or any child care provider or other person entrusted by the other parent with the care of any child without the agreement of the other party during the other party's time of parental responsibility or visitation.

4.4    <u>Notification of Medical Emergency</u>.    Each party shall inform the other party within twenty-four hours of any illness, accident, or medical condition of any child that involves surgical intervention or hospitalization. Each parent may have reasonable and immediate access to such child in such an event, regardless of custody arrangements or terms of a parenting schedule.

4.5    <u>No Disparagement of Other Parent</u>.    No parent shall make disparaging comments about the other parent to any child of the parties or while in the presence of any child of the parties, nor allow any other person to do so.

4.6    <u>Child Supervision</u>.    No parent shall leave a child under the age of fourteen (14) years unattended or alone for any period of time without adult supervision or other responsible child care.

# ARTICLE V
# CHILD SUPPORT AND HEALTH CARE COVERAGE

## Child Support

5.1   Mother shall pay to Father child support in the amount of Two Thousand and No/100 Dollars ($2,000.00) per month, to be paid in accordance with Mother's payroll cycle, and in any event at least once a month. Mother shall continue payment of child support in such manner until modified by court order, or until the date of the earliest occurrence of one of the following events:

(a)   any child reaches the age of 18 years, or if the child is between the ages of 18 and 19, a dependent in fact and still in high school performing in good faith with a reasonable expectation of graduation before the age of 19, the court may modify this order to extend support until the child graduates from high school or attains the age of 19 years, whichever comes first;

(b)   any child becomes emancipated;

(c)   any child marries;

(d)   any child dies;

(e)   any child enters military service; or

(f)   any child leaves the household or otherwise becomes self-supporting.

5.2   Thereafter, Mother shall pay to Father child support in the amount One Thousand and No/100 Dollars ($1,000.00) per month beginning in the first month immediately following the occurrence of one of the events specified above, and a like payment of $1,000.00 each month thereafter, until the next occurrence of one of the above-specified events.

## Other Provisions Regarding Child Support

5.3   <u>Manner of Payment</u>.   The parties agree that payments of child support shall be made by income deduction order and paid to the State of Florida Disbursement Unit, P.O. Box 8500, Tallahassee, Florida 32314-8500, for disbursement to Father. Mother shall be responsible for all fees charged in connection therewith.

5.4   <u>Future Disability of Child</u>.   If any child of this marriage has, receives or is diagnosed with a mental or physical disability and is not capable of providing for his or her own support, payments for the support of such child shall continue without regard to age or marital status, until the child is no longer subject to such disability.

5.5   <u>Obligation Survives Death</u>.   The provisions for child support in this decree shall be an obligation of the estate of Mother and shall not terminate on the death of Mother.

5.6   <u>Life Insurance</u>.   It is agreed that, as long as Mother is legally obligated to support any child, Mother will contract for and keep in full force and effect a life insurance policy with a face value of One Hundred Thousand and No/100 Dollars ($100,000.00), with Father, as trustee for the children, designated as irrevocable beneficiary. Within thirty (30) days after the insurance policy has been obtained, Mother will provide to Father the name and address of the insurance company, the policy number, and a copy of the insurance policy.

## Health Care Coverage

5.7   For as long as either party has a legal duty to support any child who is a subject of this agreement, or until further order of the Court, Father shall provide health care coverage for each such child through group insurance reasonably available to Father and Father shall pay the premiums for such health insurance.

5.8    For as long as either party has a legal duty to support any child who is a subject of this agreement, or until further order of the Court, Father shall provide dental care coverage for each such child through group dental insurance reasonably available to Father and Father shall pay the premiums for such dental insurance.

5.9    Each party shall cooperate with the other in the procurement of the above-described insurance and the filing of claims. The party providing an insurance policy covering any child hereunder shall (a) submit all forms required by the insurance company for payment or reimbursement of health or dental care expenses incurred by either party on behalf of the child to the insurance carrier within ten days of that party's receiving any form, receipt, bill, or statement reflecting the expenses, and (b) shall provide to the other party the following information, as applicable, no later than the thirtieth (30th) day after the date this Agreement is signed by both parties: the name and address of the employer of the party providing insurance; whether the employer is self-insured or has health or dental insurance available; proof that such insurance has been provided for that child; and the name of the insurance carrier, the number of the policy, a copy of the policy and schedule of benefits, an insurance membership card, claim forms, and any other information necessary to submit a claim or, if the employer is self-insured, a copy of the schedule of benefits, a membership card, claim forms, and any other information necessary to submit a claim. Any change in the foregoing information (including a termination or lapse in coverage) shall be provided by the party providing insurance to the other party within ten (10) days after the providing party learns of such change.

### Uncovered Health Care Expensestitle

5.10    "Uncovered Health Care Expenses" means all ordinary, reasonable and necessary expenses not covered by insurance and incurred for medical, health, dental, psychological or psychiatric care on behalf of any child who is a subject of this agreement, including but not limited to hospitalization, prescriptions, physicians, dentists, orthodontics (including braces), contact lenses and eyeglasses, examinations, and insurance copayments, and which are incurred while either party has a legal duty to support such child.

5.11    Uncovered Health Care Expenses shall be divided by the parties as follows: Father shall pay fifty percent (50%), and Mother shall pay fifty percent (50%). A party who pays for an Uncovered Heath Care Expense or receives notice of the same shall submit to the other party proof of payment or such notice within fifteen (15) days of payment or receipt of notice. Within fifteen (15) days after the other party receives such notification, the other party shall reimburse the paying party or pay the billing party directly for his or her share of the expense, as applicable.

### ARTICLE VI
### POST-SECONDARY EDUCATION

6.1    "Post-Secondary Education Expenses" means all reasonable education expenses incurred with a college or university, or a technical, vocational, or business school, including reasonable tuition, activities fees, laboratory fees, books, room and board, health insurance and related uninsured health-care expenses, college fraternity or sorority dues and expenses, and other ordinary and reasonable expenses related to such education. The amount of "reasonable tuition" should be comparable to a college or university, or a technical, vocational, or business school that is a public institution in a state where the child qualifies for resident tuition.

6.2    The parties shall equally share all of the Post-Secondary Education Expenses of each child, subject to the conditions below.

6.3    The conditions for payment of such expenses for each child are as follows:

(a)    The parties shall participate with the child in the selection of the institution and the application process.

(b)   The child must enter such an institution within one year after graduating from high school or preparatory school.

(c)   The child must be a full-time student at such institution.

(d)   The child must be progressing toward a degree or diploma at a reasonable, usual and customary pace.

(e)   The child must maintain at least a "C" or equivalent grade point average toward the completion of either a college bachelor's degree or a technical, vocational, or business school diploma.

(f)   The grades of the child must be reported to the parties within ten days after they are received.

(g)   The parties shall have the right to contact the school at any time to obtain information pertaining to the child, including but not limited to grades, academic standing and disciplinary actions.

(h)   The child is unmarried.

(i)   No payment shall be required for such expenses more than five (5) years after the child enrolls at a college or university or two (2) years after the child enrolls at a technical, vocational, or business school.

(j)   No payment shall be required for such expenses after the child turns twenty-four (24) years of age.

6.4   This obligation may be enforced by the children.

## ARTICLE VII
## REAL ESTATE

### 69 Plainfield Ave. Property

7.1   There exists certain real property in which one or both parties may claim an interest, herein referred to as the "69 Plainfield Ave. Property."

7.2   The 69 Plainfield Ave. Property shall be the property of Husband, and Wife hereby waives and releases any and all claim or interest in said property. Wife shall execute and deliver a special warranty or quitclaim deed to convey any and all such interest in said property to Husband. Wife hereby assigns to Husband any and all of her interest in any escrow accounts, homeowner's insurance policies, and/or utility deposits in connection with the 69 Plainfield Ave. Property. Husband shall pay all taxes and insurance on the 69 Plainfield Ave. Property as of January 1, 2008. Husband shall be entitled to take any itemized deductions available under the Internal Revenue Code in connection with the 69 Plainfield Ave. Property, including items such as mortgage interest and real estate taxes for the tax year in which this Agreement is executed, and every year thereafter.

7.3   There is a mortgage owing to First Mortgage, Inc. secured by said property, with a current balance of approximately $265,000.00. As of January 1, 2008, Husband shall assume said mortgage, and shall indemnify and hold Wife and her property harmless from any failure to pay the same.

### The 12 Lakeview Ct. Property

7.4   There exists certain real property in which one or both parties may claim an interest, herein referred to as the "12 Lakeview Ct. Property."

7.5   The 12 Lakeview Ct. Property shall be the property of Wife, and Husband hereby waives and releases any and all claim or interest in said property. Husband shall execute and deliver a special warranty or quitclaim deed to convey any and all such interest in said property to Wife. Husband hereby assigns to Wife any and all of his interest in any escrow accounts, insurance policies, and/or utility deposits in connection with the 12 Lakeview Ct. Property. Wife shall pay all taxes and insurance on the 12 Lakeview Ct. Property as of January 1, 2008. Wife shall be entitled to take any itemized deductions available under the Internal Revenue Code in connection with the 12 Lakeview Ct. Property, for the tax year in which this Agreement is executed and every year thereafter.

### Mortgage Secured by Other Real Estate

7.6     There is a mortgage owing to Lakes Mortgage, Inc., secured by the 12 Lakeview Ct. Property, with a current balance of approximately $110,000.00. As of January 1, 2008, Wife shall assume said mortgage, and shall indemnify and hold Husband and his property harmless from any failure to pay the same.

**ARTICLE VIII**
**RETIREMENT**

8.1     Each party shall receive any and all benefits existing by reason of his or her past, present, or future employment or military service, including but not limited to any profit-sharing plan, retirement plan, Keogh plan, pension plan, employee stock option plan, 401(k) plan, employee savings plan, military retired pay, accrued unpaid bonuses, or disability plan, whether matured or unmatured, accrued or unaccrued, vested or otherwise, together with all increases thereof, the proceeds therefrom and any other rights related thereto. The other party hereby waives and releases any and all claims or interest therein.

**ARTICLE IX**
**DIVISION OF OTHER ASSETS AND LIABILITIES**

### Division of Other Assets

9.1     The parties have already divided all other marital property in an agreeable and satisfactory manner prior to the execution of this Agreement. Each party shall have exclusive ownership in all items of property that are currently in his or her possession or control, and the other party waives and releases any and all claim or interest in such items.

### Division of Liabilities

9.2     Any obligation or liability that is not listed herein shall be the responsibility of the party that incurred the same, and the party that incurred the same shall indemnify the other party and the property of the other party harmless from liability therefor.

9.3     Neither party shall hereafter incur any obligation or liability for which the other party will be liable.

### Family Pet

9.4     The parties agree that the family dog, named Taz, will remain with the Husband.

### General Provisions

9.5     <u>Full and Complete Disclosure</u>.   Each party hereto warrants and agrees that he or she has made a full and complete disclosure to the other party of all marital and nonmarital property, income, assets and liabilities.

9.6     <u>Other Information or Instruments</u>.   Each party agrees to provide to the other party any necessary information or to execute and/or deliver any instrument or document necessary to transfer title or interest in property consistent with this Agreement.

9.7  <u>Nondischargeable in Bankruptcy.</u>  All terms of this Agreement pertaining to the division of marital property, including but not limited to any hold harmless or indemnification provisions, are specifically intended by the parties to be nondischargeable in the event of bankruptcy.

## ARTICLE X
## ALIMONY

10.1  Both parties waive any claim for alimony, whether temporary, "bridge-the gap," rehabilitative, permanent, or lump sum except as provided in the Premarital Agreement entered into by the parties on May 12, 1992. Said Premarital Agreement, attached hereto as Exhibit "B" and incorporated herein by reference for all purposes, is expressly made part of this Agreement. No other provision of this Agreement should be construed as payment of alimony by either party.

## ARTICLE XI
## TAX ISSUES

### Federal Income Taxes for Tax Year 2007

11.1  For tax year 2007, each party shall file an individual income tax return in accordance with the Internal Revenue Code.

11.2  Unless otherwise specified in this Agreement, and in addition to income attributable to each party's respective nonmarital property, each party must report as the party's income one-half of all income attributable to marital property, including earnings from personal services received on or before the date of the dissolution of the marriage. Additionally, each party may take credit for all of the reporting party's estimated tax payments and federal income tax payroll withholding deductions occurring after the date of the dissolution of the marriage, and, to the extent allowed by law, all deductions, exemptions, credits, and adjustments attributable to his or her income and expenses after the date of the dissolution of the marriage.

11.3  Each party shall timely pay his or her tax liability in connection with the tax return filed by such party. Any refund received as a result of a party's tax return shall be the sole property of the party filing such tax return.

11.4  Each party shall indemnify and hold harmless the other party for such taxes, liabilities, deficiencies, assessments, penalties, or interest due thereon or the omission of taxable income or claim of erroneous deductions of the applicable party.

### Dependency Exemption for Tax Years Subsequent to 2007

11.5  The dependency exemption for dependents for tax years subsequent to the dissolution of the marriage shall be claimed by Husband.

### Other Provisions

11.6  <u>Attorney is Not Tax Expert.</u>  The parties acknowledge that any attorney involved with this Agreement does not claim to be an expert in tax matters. Each party states that he or she has consulted or has had the opportunity to consult with a tax professional to fully evaluate the tax implications and consequences of this Agreement.

11.7  <u>Request for Information and Cooperation.</u>  It is agreed that each party shall provide any information reasonably necessary to prepare federal income tax returns, within thirty (30) days of receipt of a written request for the same. Each party shall reasonably cooperate with the other in the preparation of income tax returns as set forth hereinabove. Within five days of receipt of written notice from the other party, each party will allow the other party access to these records in order to respond to an IRS examination or request for information. Purposes for which access to such records will be granted includes, but is not limited to, the determination of acquisition dates or tax basis, and such access shall include the right to copy the records.

11.8   Preservation of Information.   Each party shall preserve for a period of seven years from the date of the filing of the applicable tax return, all financial records relating to the marital property. Each party shall preserve indefinitely, any records which determine or affect the tax basis in any marital property.

11.9   No Waiver of "Innocent Spouse".   The parties agree that nothing contained herein shall be construed as or is intended as a waiver of any rights that a party has under the "Innocent Spouse" provisions of the Internal Revenue Code.

## ARTICLE XII
## COURT COSTS AND ATTORNEY'S FEES

12.1   Any costs of court, including the filing fee for the petition for dissolution, will be borne by the party incurring the same.

12.2   Each party will be responsible for his or her own attorney's fees incurred herein.

## ARTICLE XIII
## CONFIDENTIALITY

13.1   The parties hereto agree that, due to the private nature of the personal and financial information of the parties, the contents of this Agreement and the pleadings in this case are confidential and shall not be disclosed to a third party, except to a third party with whom a party has a strict confidential relationship, such as an attorney, psychologist, accountant, or the like, or by court order.

## ARTICLE XIV
## GENERAL PROVISIONS

14.1   Exchange of Information Relating to Income.   As long as any child support is payable under this Agreement, each party shall provide to the other party a true and correct copy of federal and state income tax returns, along with all documentation filed therewith (including W-2 forms, 1099s, returns showing partnership and other income or loss, and the like), to be delivered to the other party within fifteen (15) days of filing such returns.

14.2   Mutual Release.   Each party waives, releases and relinquishes any actual or potential right, claim or cause of action against the other party, including but not limited to asserting a claim against the estate of the other party or to act as a personal representative of such estate, except as otherwise provided for in this Agreement or arising hereunder.

14.3   Resolution of Future Disputes.   In the event of any disagreement regarding an issue between the parties, the parties shall first confer and exercise reasonable efforts to resolve such a dispute. Except in an emergency, before a party files legal action regarding an issue of any such dispute or regarding modification of any terms and conditions of this Agreement, that party shall make a good faith attempt to submit the dispute or controversy to mediation.

14.4   Reconciliation.   In the event of a reconciliation or resumption of marital relations, this Agreement or its provisions shall not be abrogated in any way without further written agreement of the parties.

14.5   No Oral Agreements.   The parties agree that this Agreement constitutes the entire agreement of the parties, that this Agreement supersedes any prior understandings or agreements between them, and that there are no representations, warranties, or oral agreements other than those expressly set forth herein.

14.6    No Waiver of Breach.    The failure of a party to insist on strict performance of any provision of this Agreement shall not be construed to constitute a waiver of a breach of any other provision or of a subsequent breach of the same provision.

14.7    Severability.    This Agreement is severable, and if any term or provision is determined to be unenforceable, this shall not render the remainder of the Agreement unenforceable.

14.8    Other Acts.    Each party agrees to timely perform such other acts that are reasonably necessary or that may be reasonably requested by the other party to effectuate the provisions of this Agreement.

14.9    Survival of Agreement; No Merger.    This Agreement may be offered into evidence by either party in an action for dissolution of marriage, and may be incorporated by reference in a final judgment entered therein. Notwithstanding incorporation, this Agreement shall not be merged in such judgment but shall survive the judgment and be binding on the parties.

14.10    Remedies for Enforcement.    The terms and provisions of this Agreement are enforceable in contract, in addition to any remedies for enforcement that may also be available under any final judgment of dissolution of marriage entered between the parties.

**I, JOHN ALLEN LANCASTER, certify that I have been open and honest in entering into this Agreement. I am satisfied with this Agreement and intend to be bound by it.**

Dated: December 23, 2007

_____
JOHN ALLEN LANCASTER

**Witnesses as to JOHN ALLEN LANCASTER:**

_____
Signature of Witness

_____
Signature of Witness

_____
Date

_____
Date

_____
Name Printed

_____
Name Printed

_____
Street Address

_____
Street Address

_____
City, State, Zip

_____
City, State, Zip

STATE OF FLORIDA

COUNTY OF CLAY

Sworn to or affirmed and subscribed before me on ———————————————————by
JOHN ALLEN LANCASTER.

————————————————————————
NOTARY PUBLIC - STATE OF FLORIDA

————————————————————————
Printed Name of Notary

———— Personally known
———— Produced identification
Type of identification produced ———————————————————————

**I, SAMANTHA ELIZABETH LANCASTER, certify that I have been open and honest in entering into this Agreement. I am satisfied with this Agreement and intend to be bound by it.**

Dated: December 23, 2007

————————————————————————
SAMANTHA ELIZABETH LANCASTER

**Witnesses as to SAMANTHA ELIZABETH LANCASTER:**

————————————————————
Signature of Witness

————————————————————
Date

————————————————————
Name Printed

————————————————————
Street Address

————————————————————
City, State, Zip

————————————————————
Signature of Witness

————————————————————
Date

————————————————————
Name Printed

————————————————————
Street Address

————————————————————
City, State, Zip

STATE OF FLORIDA
COUNTY OF CLAY

Sworn to or affirmed and subscribed before me on ————————————————————
by SAMANTHA ELIZABETH LANCASTER.

————————————————————————
NOTARY PUBLIC - STATE OF FLORIDA

————————————————————————
Printed Name of Notary

———— Personally known
———— Produced identification
Type of identification produced ———————————————————————

## EXHIBIT A
## PARENTING SCHEDULE

(1)  <u>By Mutual Agreement.</u>  The parties agree that it is in the best interest of the children for both parties to have frequent and continuing contact with the children, and the parties shall have visitation with the children at times mutually agreed to in advance by the parties. However, in the absence of mutual agreement, the parents shall have visitation with the children as provided by this Parenting Schedule. The parties understand that they are free to vary the times or days stated in the Parenting Schedule if they both agree.

(2)  <u>Reference to "Visitation" Does Not Limit Residence.</u>  The children shall reside with Father at all times not specifically designated for visitation with Mother. Any reference to the right of "visitation" with respect to Father herein (and any specific times or days in this regard) shall not be construed to limit or interfere with the ordinary and usual residence of the children with Father.

(3)  <u>Definitions</u>

(a)  In this Schedule "school" means the primary or secondary school in which the child is enrolled or, if the child is not enrolled in a primary or secondary school, the public school district in which the child primarily resides.

(b)  In this Schedule "child" includes each child, whether one or more, who is a subject of this suit while that child is under the age of eighteen years and not otherwise emancipated.

(4)  <u>Parents Who Reside 100 Miles or Less Apart</u>

Except as otherwise explicitly provided in this Parenting Schedule, when Mother resides 100 miles or less from the primary residence of the children, Mother shall have the right to visitation with the children as follows:

(a)  <u>Weekends</u> - On weekends, beginning at 6:00 p.m. on the first, third, and fifth Friday of each month and ending at 6:00 p.m. on the following Sunday.

(b)  <u>Weekend Visitation Extended by a Holiday</u> - Except as otherwise explicitly provided in this Parenting Schedule, if a weekend period of visitation by Mother begins on a Friday that is a school holiday during the regular school term or a federal, state, or local holiday during the summer months when school is not in session, or if the period ends on or is immediately followed by a Monday that is such a holiday, that weekend period of visitation shall begin at 6:00 p.m. on the Thursday immediately preceding the Friday holiday or school holiday or end at 6:00 p.m. on the Monday holiday following the weekend, as applicable.

(c)  <u>Wednesdays</u> - On Wednesday of each week during the regular school term, beginning at 6:00 p.m. and ending at 8:00 p.m.

(d)  <u>Christmas Holidays in Even-Numbered Years</u> - In even-numbered years, beginning at 6:00 p.m. on the day the child is dismissed from school for the Christmas school vacation and ending at noon on December 26.

(e)  <u>Christmas Holidays in Odd-Numbered Years</u> - In odd-numbered years, beginning at noon on December 26 and ending at 6:00 p.m. on the day before school resumes after that Christmas school vacation.

(f)  <u>Thanksgiving in Odd-Numbered Years</u> - In odd-numbered years, beginning at 6:00 p.m. on the day the child is dismissed from school for the Thanksgiving holiday and ending at 6:00 p.m. on the following Sunday.

(g)  <u>Spring Break in Even-Numbered Years</u> - In even-numbered years, beginning at 6:00 p.m. on the day the child is dismissed from school for the school's spring vacation and ending at 6:00 p.m. on the day before school resumes after that vacation.

(h)    <u>Extended Summer Visitation by Mother</u>

<u>With Written Notice by April 1</u> - If Mother gives Father written notice by April 1 of a year specifying an extended period or periods of summer visitation for that year, Mother shall have visitation with the children for thirty days beginning no earlier than the day after the child's school is dismissed for the summer vacation and ending no later than seven days before school resumes at the end of the summer vacation in that year, to be exercised in no more than two separate periods of at least seven consecutive days each, as specified in the written notice. These periods of visitation shall begin and end at 6:00 p.m.

<u>Without Written Notice by April 1</u> - If Mother does not give Father written notice by April 1 of a year specifying an extended period or periods of summer visitation for that year, Mother shall have visitation with the children for thirty consecutive days in that year beginning at 6:00 p.m. on July 1 and ending at 6:00 p.m. on July 31.

(i)    <u>Child's Birthday</u> - If Mother is not otherwise entitled under this Parenting Schedule to present visitation with the child and the child's siblings on the child's birthday, Mother shall have visitation in odd-numbered years with the child and the child's siblings beginning at 6:00 p.m. and ending at 8:00 p.m. on that day, provided that Mother picks up the child from Father's residence and returns the child to that same place.

(j)    <u>Mother's Day Weekend</u> - Each year, beginning at 6:00 p.m. on the Friday preceding Mother's Day and ending at 6:00 p.m. on Mother's Day, provided that if she is not otherwise entitled under this Parenting Schedule to present visitation with the children, she shall pick up the children from Father's residence and return the children to that same place.

Notwithstanding the weekend and Wednesday periods of visitation agreed for Mother, it is explicitly agreed that Father shall have a superior right of visitation with the children as follows:

(a)    <u>Christmas Holidays in Odd-Numbered Years</u> - In odd-numbered years, beginning at 6:00 p.m. on the day the child is dismissed from school for the Christmas school vacation and ending at noon on December 26.

(b)    <u>Christmas Holidays in Even-Numbered Years</u> - In even-numbered years, beginning at noon on December 26 and ending at 6:00 p.m. on the day before school resumes after that Christmas school vacation.

(c)    <u>Thanksgiving in Even-Numbered Years</u> - In even-numbered years, beginning at 6:00 p.m. on the day the child is dismissed from school for the Thanksgiving holiday and ending at 6:00 p.m. on the following Sunday.

(d)    <u>Spring Break in Odd-Numbered Years</u> - In odd-numbered years, beginning at 6:00 p.m. on the day the child is dismissed from school for the school's spring vacation and ending at 6:00 p.m. on the day before school resumes after that vacation.

(e)    <u>Summer Weekend Visitation by Father</u> - If Father gives Mother written notice by April 15 of a year, Father shall have visitation with the children on any one weekend beginning at 6:00 p.m. on Friday and ending at 6:00 p.m. on the following Sunday during any one period of the extended summer visitation by Mother in that year, provided that Father picks up the children from Mother and returns the children to that same place.

(f)    <u>Extended Summer Visitation by Father</u> - If Father gives Mother written notice by April 15 of a year or gives Mother fourteen days' written notice on or after April 16 of a year, Father may designate one weekend beginning no earlier than the day after the child's school is dismissed for the summer vacation and ending no later than seven days before school resumes at the end of the summer vacation, during which an otherwise scheduled weekend period of visitation by

Mother shall not take place in that year, provided that the weekend so designated does not interfere with Mother's period or periods of extended summer visitation.

(g)  Child's Birthday - If Father is not otherwise entitled under this Parenting Schedule to present visitation with the child and the child's siblings on the child's birthday, Father shall have visitation in even-numbered years with the child and the child's siblings beginning at 6:00 p.m. and ending at 8:00 p.m. on that day, provided that Father picks up the child from Mother's residence and returns the child to that same place.

(h)  Father's Day Weekend - Each year, beginning at 6:00 p.m. on the Friday preceding Father's Day and ending at 6:00 p.m. on Father's Day, provided that if he is not otherwise entitled under this Parenting Schedule to present visitation with the children, he shall pick up the children from Mother's residence and return the children to that same place.

(5)  Parents Who Reside More Than 100 Miles Apart

Except as otherwise explicitly provided in this Parenting Schedule, when Mother resides more than 100 miles from the residence of the children, Mother shall have the right to visitation with the children as follows:

(a)  Weekends - Unless Mother elects the alternative period of weekend visitation described in the next paragraph, Mother shall have the right to visitation with the children on weekends, beginning at 6:00 p.m. on the first, third, and fifth Friday of each month and ending at 6:00 p.m. on the following Sunday. Except as otherwise explicitly provided in this Parenting Schedule, if such a weekend period of visitation by Mother begins on a Friday that is a school holiday during the regular school term or a federal, state, or local holiday during the summer months when school is not in session, or if the period ends on or is immediately followed by a Monday that is such a holiday, that weekend period of visitation shall begin at 6:00 p.m. on the Thursday immediately preceding the Friday holiday or school holiday or end 6:00 p.m. on the Monday holiday following the weekend, as applicable.

(b)  Alternate weekend visitation - In lieu of the weekend visitation described in the foregoing paragraph, Mother shall have the right to visitation with the children not more than one weekend per month of Mother's choice beginning at 6:00 p.m. on the day school recesses for the weekend and ending at 6:00 p.m. on the following Sunday. Except as otherwise explicitly provided in this Parenting Schedule, if such a weekend period of visitation by Mother begins on a Friday that is a school holiday during the regular school term or a federal, state, or local holiday during the summer months when school is not in session, or if the period ends on or is immediately followed by a Monday that is such a holiday, that weekend period of visitation shall begin at 6:00 p.m. on the Thursday immediately preceding the Friday holiday or school holiday or end 6:00 p.m. on the Monday holiday following the weekend, as applicable. Mother may elect an option for this alternative period of weekend visitation by giving written notice to Father within ninety days after the parties begin to reside more than 100 miles apart. If Mother makes this election, Mother shall give Father fourteen days' written or telephonic notice preceding a designated weekend. The weekends chosen shall not conflict with the provisions regarding Christmas, Thanksgiving, the child's birthday, and Father's Day Weekend below.

(c)  Christmas Holidays in Even-Numbered Years - In even-numbered years, beginning at 6:00 p.m. on the day the child is dismissed from school for the Christmas school vacation and ending at noon on December 26.

(d)  Christmas Holidays in Odd-Numbered Years - In odd-numbered years, beginning at noon on December 26 and ending at 6:00 p.m. on the day before school resumes after that Christmas school vacation.

(g)   <u>Thanksgiving in Odd-Numbered Years</u> - In odd-numbered years, beginning at 6:00 p.m. on the day the child is dismissed from school for the Thanksgiving holiday and ending at 6:00 p.m. on the following Sunday.

(h)   <u>Spring Break in All Years</u> - Every year, beginning at 6:00 p.m. on the day the child is dismissed from school for the school's spring vacation and ending at 6:00 p.m. on the day before school resumes after that vacation.

(g)   <u>Extended Summer Visitation by Mother</u> -

<u>With Written Notice by April 1</u> - If Mother gives Father written notice by April 1 of a year specifying an extended period or periods of summer visitation for that year, Mother shall have visitation with the children for forty-two days beginning no earlier than the day after the child's school is dismissed for the summer vacation and ending no later than seven days before school resumes at the end of the summer vacation in that year, to be exercised in no more than two separate periods of at least seven consecutive days each, as specified in the written notice. These periods of visitation shall begin and end at 6:00 p.m.

<u>Without Written Notice by April 1</u> - If Mother does not give Father written notice by April 1 of a year specifying an extended period or periods of summer visitation for that year, Mother shall have visitation with the children for forty-two consecutive days beginning at 6:00 p.m. on June 15 and ending at 6:00 p.m. on July 27 of that year.

(h)   <u>Child's Birthday</u> - If Mother is not otherwise entitled under this Parenting Schedule to present visitation with the child on the child's birthday, Mother shall have visitation in odd-numbered years with the child and the child's siblings beginning at 6:00 p.m. and ending at 8:00 p.m. on that day, provided that Mother picks up the child from Father's residence and returns the child to that same place.

(i)   <u>Mother's Day Weekend</u> - Each year, beginning at 6:00 p.m. on the Friday preceding Mother's Day and ending at 6:00 p.m. on Mother's Day, provided that if she is not otherwise entitled under this Parenting Schedule to present visitation with the children, she shall pick up the children from Father's residence and return the children to that same place.

Notwithstanding the weekend periods of visitation agreed for Mother, it is explicitly agreed that Father shall have a superior right of visitation with the children as follows:

(a)   <u>Christmas Holidays in Odd-Numbered Years</u> - In odd-numbered years, beginning at 6:00 p.m. on the day the child is dismissed from school for the Christmas school vacation and ending at noon on December 26.

(b)   <u>Christmas Holidays in Even-Numbered Years</u> - In even-numbered years, beginning at noon on December 26 and ending at 6:00 p.m. on the day before school resumes after that Christmas school vacation.

(c)   <u>Thanksgiving in Even-Numbered Years</u> - In even-numbered years, beginning at 6:00 p.m. on the day the child is dismissed from school for the Thanksgiving holiday and ending at 6:00 p.m. on the following Sunday.

(d)   <u>Summer Weekend Visitation by Father</u> - If Father gives Mother written notice by April 15 of a year, Father shall have visitation with the children on any one weekend beginning at 6:00 p.m. on Friday and ending at 6:00 p.m. on the following Sunday during any one period of visitation by Mother during Mother's extended summer visitation in that year, provided that if a period of visitation by Mother in that year exceeds thirty days, Father may have visitation with the children under the terms of this provision on any two nonconsecutive weekends during that period and provided that Father picks up the children from Mother and returns the children to that same place.

(e)  <u>Extended Summer Visitation by Father</u> - If Father gives Mother written notice by April 15 of a year, Father may designate twenty-one days beginning no earlier than the day after the child's school is dismissed for the summer vacation and ending no later than seven days before school resumes at the end of the summer vacation in that year, to be exercised in no more than two separate periods of at least seven consecutive days each, during which Mother shall not have visitation with the children, provided that the period or periods so designated do not interfere with Mother's period or periods of extended summer visitation.

(f)  <u>Child's Birthday</u> - If Father is not otherwise entitled under this Parenting Schedule to present visitation with the child on the child's birthday, Father shall have visitation in even-numbered years with the child and the child's siblings beginning at 6:00 p.m. and ending at 8:00 p.m. on that day, provided that Father picks up the child from Mother's residence and returns the child to that same place.

(g)  <u>Father's Day Weekend</u> - Each year, beginning at 6:00 p.m. on the Friday preceding Father's Day and ending at 6:00 p.m. on Father's Day, provided that if he is not otherwise entitled under this Parenting Schedule to present visitation with the children, he shall pick up the children from Mother's residence and return the children to that same place.

(6)  <u>General Terms and Conditions.</u>  Except as otherwise explicitly provided in this Parenting Schedule, the terms and conditions of visitation with the children that apply regardless of the distance between the residence of a parent and the children are as follows:

(a)  <u>Pickup of Child.</u>  Unless a particular period of visitation begins at the time the children's school is regularly dismissed as otherwise specified herein, the parent whose visitation is beginning shall pickup the children at the residence of the other parent.

(b)  <u>Return of Child.</u>  Unless a period of visitation ends at the time the children's school resumes as otherwise specified herein, the parent whose visitation is ending shall surrender the children at his or her residence.

(c)  <u>Personal Effects.</u>  Each parent shall return with the children the personal effects that the children brought at the beginning of the period of visitation.

(d)  <u>Designation of Competent Adult.</u>  Each parent may designate any competent adult to pick up and return the children, as applicable. A parent or a designated competent adult must be present when the children are picked up or returned.

(e)  <u>Inability to Exercise Visitation.</u>  A parent shall give advance notice to the other parent on each occasion in the event that such parent will be unable to exercise visitation for any specified period.

(f)  <u>Notice to School and Other Parent.</u>  If a parent's time of visitation with the children ends at the time school resumes and for any reason the children are not or will not be returned to school, such parent shall immediately notify the school and the other parent that the children will not be or have not been returned to school.

(g)  <u>Reasonable Telephone Contact.</u>  Any parent shall be entitled to reasonable telephone contact with the children, and the other parent will exercise reasonable efforts to make the children available for such telephone contact.

(h)  <u>Informed Whereabouts.</u>  Each parent shall keep the other parent reasonably informed regarding the whereabouts of the minor children, including with respect to overnight visits with relatives or friends.

Prepared using ProDoc Form # 3-700

IN THE CIRCUIT COURT OF THE FOURTH JUDICIAL CIRCUIT,
IN AND FOR CLAY COUNTY, FLORIDA

Case No.: 2007XXXX
Division: Family Law

IN RE THE MARRIAGE OF:

JOHN ALLEN LANCASTER,
　　　Husband,

　　　and

SAMANTHA ELIZABETH LANCASTER,
　　　Wife

## FINAL JUDGMENT OF DISSOLUTION OF MARRIAGE

**THIS CAUSE** came to be heard on December 27, 2007, upon the Petition for Dissolution of Marriage filed by Husband. After taking testimony and other evidence in open Court and reviewing the Court file, the Court FINDS as follows:

1. The Court has jurisdiction of the parties and the subject matter herein.

2. The Petitioner has been a resident of the State of Florida for at least six (6) months prior to the filing of the Petition for Dissolution of Marriage.

3. The parties were married on or about February 15, 1992, in Orange Park, Clay County, Florida.

4. The following children involved in this action have been born to or adopted by the parties:

| Name | Date of Birth |
|------|---------------|
| Sam Lancaster | August 12, 1994 |
| Karen Lancaster | November 2, 1997 |

5. No other children were adopted, and none are expected.

6. Irreconcilable differences exist and have caused the irretrievable breakdown of the marriage, and all efforts and hope of reconciliation would be impracticable and not in the best interests of the parties.

7. The parties wish to settle between themselves their respective rights, duties, and obligations regarding property, liabilities, and children, and so have entered into a written Marital Settlement Agreement. This Agreement, attached hereto as Exhibit "A," was entered into voluntarily by each party, and has been filed of record and introduced into evidence at the final hearing in this cause.

IT IS, therefore, **ORDERED** and **ADJUDGED** as follows:

1. The parties are awarded Judgment for Dissolution of Marriage, and the bonds of matrimony heretofore existing between John Allen Lancaster (hereinafter referred to as "Husband" or as "Father") and Samantha Elizabeth Lancaster (hereinafter referred to as "Wife" or as "Mother") are hereby dissolved.

2.    The Marital Settlement Agreement of the parties, attached hereto as Exhibit "A" and incorporated herein by reference for all purposes, is approved and expressly made a part of this Final Judgment for Dissolution of Marriage, and all of the terms and provisions of said Agreement are RATIFIED, CONFIRMED, and ADOPTED as Orders of this Court to the same extent and with the same force and effect as if its terms and provisions were set forth verbatim in this Final Judgment, and the parties are **ORDERED** to comply with the terms and provisions of said Agreement.

3.    The Court finds that the parties have the present ability to pay support as agreed to in the Marital Settlement Agreement as ratified, confirmed, and made part of this Final Judgment.

## Parental Responsibility

4.    Father and Mother shall have shared parental responsibility and shall retain full parental rights and responsibilities with respect to the children.

5.    The primary physical residence of the children shall be in the home of Father, and the secondary physical residence of the children shall be in the home of Mother.

## Relocation of Children

6.    In the event that a Primary Residential Parent seeks to relocate the principal residence of any child subject to this order more than 50 miles away from the current residence as provided by Section 61.13001 of the Florida Statutes, such parent shall comply with the provisions of Section 61.13001 by either (a) obtaining written agreement in accordance with 61.13001(2) of the Florida Statutes from the other parent, and any other person entitled to visitation, or (b) serving a Notice of Intent to Relocate signed under oath and penalty of perjury in accordance with Section 61.13001(3) of the Florida Statutes, giving the other parent, and any other person entitled to visitation, 30 days to object to the relocation and to request a determination by the Court.

7.    IF A PRIMARY RESIDENTIAL PARENT ATTEMPTS TO RELOCATE THE PRINCIPAL RESIDENCE OF ANY CHILD AND FAILS TO COMPLY WITH SECTION 61.13001(3) OF THE FLORIDA STATUTES REGARDING THE NOTICE OF INTENT TO RELOCATE, SUCH PARENT MAY BE SUBJECT TO CONTEMPT AND OTHER PROCEEDINGS TO COMPEL THE RETURN OF ANY CHILD, AND SUCH NON-COMPLIANCE MAY BE TAKEN INTO ACCOUNT BY THE COURT IN A SUBSEQUENT DETERMINATION OF THE RESIDENCE, CUSTODY, OR VISITATION RELATING TO ANY CHILD.

## Child Support

8.    Mother shall pay to Father child support in the amount of Two Thousand and No/100 Dollars ($2,000.00) per month, to be paid in accordance with Mother's payroll cycle, and in any event at least once a month. Mother shall continue payment of child support in such manner until modified by court order, or until the date of the earliest occurrence of one of the following events:

(a)    any child reaches the age of 18 years, or if the child is between the ages of 18 and 19, a dependent in fact and still in high school performing in good faith with a reasonable expectation of graduation before the age of 19, the court may modify this order to extend support until the child graduates from high school or attains the age of 19 years, whichever comes first;

(b)    any child becomes emancipated;

(c)    any child marries;

(d)    any child dies;

(e)    any child enters military service; or

(f)    any child leaves the household or otherwise becomes self-supporting.

9. Thereafter, Mother shall pay to Father child support in the amount of One Thousand and No/100 Dollars ($1,000.00) per month beginning in the first month immediately following the occurrence of one of the events specified above, and a like payment of $700.00 each month thereafter, until the next occurrence of one of the above-specified events.

10. Payments of child support shall be made by income deduction order and paid to the State Disbursement Unit for disbursement to Father. Mother shall be responsible for all fees charged in connection therewith.

11. If any child of this marriage has, receives or is diagnosed with a mental or physical disability and is not capable of providing for his or her own support, payments for the support of such child shall continue without regard to age or marital status, until the child is no longer subject to such disability.

12. The provisions for child support in this decree shall be an obligation of the estate of Mother and shall not terminate on the death of Mother.

13. As long as Mother is legally obligated to support any child, Mother will contract for and keep in full force and effect a life insurance policy with a face value of One Hundred Thousand and No/100 Dollars ($100,000.00), with Father, as trustee for the children, designated as irrevocable beneficiary. Within thirty (30) days after the insurance policy has been obtained, Mother will provide to Father the name and address of the insurance company, the policy number, and a copy of the insurance policy.

## Health Care Coverage

14. For as long as either party has a legal duty to support any child who is a subject of this Final Judgment, or until further order of the Court, Father shall provide health care coverage for each such child through group insurance reasonably available to Father and Father shall pay the premiums for such health insurance.

15. For as long as either party has a legal duty to support any child who is a subject of this Final Judgment, or until further order of the Court, Father shall provide dental care coverage for each such child through group dental insurance reasonably available to Father and Father shall pay the premiums for such dental insurance.

16. Each party shall cooperate with the other in the procurement of the above-described insurance and the filing of claims. The party providing an insurance policy covering any child hereunder shall (a) submit all forms required by the insurance company for payment or reimbursement of health or dental care expenses incurred by either party on behalf of the child to the insurance carrier within ten days of that party's receiving any form, receipt, bill, or statement reflecting the expenses, and (b) shall provide to the other party the following information, as applicable, no later than the thirtieth (30th) day after the date this Final Judgment has been signed: the name and address of the employer of the party providing insurance; whether the employer is self-insured or has health or dental insurance available; proof that such insurance has been provided for that child; and the name of the insurance carrier, the number of the policy, a copy of the policy and schedule of benefits, an insurance membership card, claim forms, and any other information necessary to submit a claim or, if the employer is self-insured, a copy of the schedule of benefits, a membership card, claim forms, and any other information necessary to submit a claim. Any change in the foregoing information (including a termination or lapse in coverage) shall be provided by the party providing insurance to the other party within ten (10) days after the providing party learns of such change.

## Uncovered Health Care Expenses

17. "Uncovered Health Care Expenses" means all ordinary, reasonable and necessary expenses not covered by insurance and incurred for medical, health, dental, psychological or psychiatric care

on behalf of any child who is a subject of this agreement, including but not limited to hospitalization, prescriptions, physicians, dentists, orthodontics (including braces), contact lenses and eyeglasses, examinations, and insurance copayments, and which are incurred while either party has a legal duty to support such child.

18.    Uncovered Health Care Expenses shall be divided by the parties as follows: Father shall pay fifty percent (50%), and Mother shall pay fifty percent (50%). A party who pays for an Uncovered Heath Care Expense or receives notice of the same shall submit to the other party proof of payment or such notice within fifteen (15) days of payment or receipt of notice. Within fifteen (15) days after the other party receives such notification, the other party shall reimburse the paying party or pay the billing party directly for his or her share of the expense, as applicable.

## Real Estate

19.    There exists certain real property in which one or both parties may claim an interest, herein referred to as the "69 Plainfield Ave. Property."

20.    The 69 Plainfield Ave. Property shall be the property of Husband, and Wife hereby waives and releases any and all claim or interest in said property.

21.    There is a mortgage owing to First Mortgage, Inc. secured by said property, with a current balance of approximately $265,000.00. As of January 1, 2008, Husband shall assume said mortgage, and shall indemnify and hold Wife and her property harmless from any failure to pay the same.

22.    There exists certain real property in which one or both parties may claim an interest, herein referred to as the "12 Lakeview Ct. Property."

23.    The 12 Lakeview Ct. Property shall be the property of Wife, and Husband hereby waives and releases any and all claim or interest in said property.

24.    There is a mortgage owing to Lakes Mortgage, Inc., secured by the 12 Lakeview Ct. Property, with a current balance of approximately $110,000.00. As of January 1, 2008, Wife shall assume said mortgage, and shall indemnify and hold Husband and his property harmless from any failure to pay the same.

## Retirement

25.    Each party shall receive any and all benefits existing by reason of his or her past, present, or future employment or military service, including but not limited to any profit-sharing plan, retirement plan, Keogh plan, pension plan, employee stock option plan, 401(k) plan, employee savings plan, military retired pay, accrued unpaid bonuses, disability plan, whether matured or unmatured, accrued or unaccrued, vested or otherwise, together with all increases thereof, the proceeds therefrom and any other rights related thereto. Any claim or interest therein that could be asserted by the other party is hereby released and terminated.

## Costs of Court

26.    Any costs of court, including the filing fee for the petition for dissolution, will be borne by the party incurring the same.

## Attorney's Fees

27.    Each party will be responsible for his or her own attorney's fees incurred herein.

## Confidentiality

28.    Due to the private nature of the personal and financial information of the parties, the contents of the Marital Settlement Agreement, this Final Judgment, and the pleadings in this case are confidential and shall not be disclosed to a third party, except to a third party with whom a party has a strict confidential relationship, such as an attorney, psychologist, accountant, or the like, or by court order.

**Other Orders**

    29.   As long as any child support is payable under the Marital Settlement Agreement or this Final Judgment, each party shall provide to the other party a true and correct copy of federal and state income tax returns, along with all documentation filed therewith (including W-2 forms, 1099s, returns showing partnership and other income or loss, and the like), to be delivered to the other party within fifteen (15) days of filing such returns.

    30.   Each party shall (a) provide to the other party any necessary information or to execute and/or deliver any instrument or document necessary to transfer title or interest in property consistent with this Final Judgment or the Marital Settlement Agreement, and (b) timely perform such other acts that are reasonably necessary or that may be reasonably requested by the other party to effectuate the provisions of this Final Judgment or the Marital Settlement Agreement.

    31.   Any right, claim, demand or interest of the parties in and to the property of the other, whether real, personal or mixed, of whatever kind and nature and wherever situated, including but not limited to homestead, succession and inheritance arising out of the marital relationship existing between the parties hereto, except as expressly set forth or arising out of said Marital Settlement Agreement, is forever barred and terminated.

    32.   The Court expressly retains jurisdiction of this cause for the purposes of enforcing, construing, interpreting, or modifying the terms of this Final Judgment and the terms of the Marital Settlement Agreement entered into by the parties herein.

    **DONE AND ORDERED** in Chambers at Green Cove Springs, Clay County, Florida on the _____ day of _____, 2007.

_____

CIRCUIT JUDGE

Copies to:

John Allen Lancaster
69 Plainfield Ave.
Orange Park, FL 32073

Samantha Elizabeth Lancaster
120 Red Bud Lane
Orange Park, FL 32073

John Sinclair
Attorney for Husband
PO Box 9200
Orange Park, FL 32073

Sam Dickerson
1444 HWY 17
Green Cove Springs, FL 32043

Prepared using ProDoc Form # 3-800

# Glossary

## A

**acceptance** The offeree's clear manifestation of agreement to the exact terms of the offer in the manner specified in the offer.

**adoption** The taking of a child into the family, creating a parent-child relationship where the biological relationship did not exist.

**age of majority** Age at which person attains full legal rights.

**agency adoption** Using an agency, either government or private, but government-regulated, to facilitate the process.

**alimony pendente lite (APL)** Temporary order for payments of a set amount monthly while the litigation continues.

**allegations** Facts forming the basis of a party's complaint.

**alternative dispute resolution (ADR)** Method of settling a dispute before trial in order to conserve the court's time.

**appeal** Tests the sufficiency of the verdict under the legal parameters or rules.

**arbitration** Alternative dispute resolution method mediated or supervised by a neutral third party who imposes a recommendation for resolution, after hearing evidence from both parties and the parties participated in reaching, that is fully enforceable and treated in the courts the same as a judicial order.

**assisted reproductive technology (ART)** Procedure involving the handling of both eggs and sperm in which the eggs are surgically removed and combine with sperm in the laboratory.

**automatic stay** A stay that stops almost all collection actions against the debtor at the time of the filing for bankruptcy protection.

## B

**bench trial** A case heard and decided by a judge.

**bigamy** One spouse knowingly enters a second marriage while the first remains valid.

**black market adoption** Illegal adoption.

**blended family** Family made up of one or more parents having been previously married and having children of that previous marriage. Sometimes referred to as stepfamilies.

**body** Main text of the argument section of the appellate brief.

**bridge-the-gap alimony** Alimony intended to aid the receiving spouse's move from being married to being single.

## C

**capacity** The ability to understand the nature and significance of a contract; to understand or comprehend specific acts or reasoning.

**caption** The full name of the case, together with the docket number, court, and date of the decision.

**case law** Published court opinions of federal and state appellate courts; judge-created law in deciding cases, set forth in court opinions.

**ceremonial marriages aka traditional marriage** A marriage between a man and a woman that was entered into by a civil or religious ceremony.

**Chapter 7** Liquidation bankruptcy.

**Chapter 13** Individual reorganization bankruptcy.

**checklist** Tool used in law offices to ensure that adequate information is obtained from the client to properly complete the task.

**child custody** Arrangement between the parties for residential and custodial care of the minor children.

**child support** The right of a child to financial support and the obligation of a parent to provide it.

**child support guidelines** State statutory guidelines that are used to establish how much child support should be paid.

**civil litigation** Lawsuits that do not involve criminal prosecution.

**closed adoption** A form of adoption in which biological parents of the child have no contact with the child or the adopting parents.

**coercion** Compelling someone to do an act through physical force or threat of physical force.

**cohabitation agreement** A contract setting forth the rights of two people who live together without the benefit of marriage.

**collusion** Illegally created agreement of the parties.

**common law marriage** A form of marriage that is legally recognized in certain states, if the two people have been living together for a long period of time, have represented themselves as being married, and have the intent to be married.

**community property** All property acquired during marriage in a community property state, owned in equal shares.

**condonation** Defense in divorce based on spouse's awareness of a ground for divorce but who expressly or impliedly forgives those acts.

**conflict of interest** Clash between private and professional interests or competing professional interests that makes impartiality difficult and creates an unfair advantage.

**connivance** Defense in divorce action that is based on the fact that one spouse allowed or consented to the other committing the acts that are alleged as grounds for the divorce.

**consent decree** A decree that all parties to the case agree to.

**consideration** Parol evidence is permitted to show that the subject matter of the contract as received was not as it was bargained for.

**covenant marriage** The couples make an affirmative undertaking to get counseling prior to the marriage and to seek counseling if contemplating divorce.

# D

**de novo** Standard appellate review where the appellate court reviews the facts and law independent of the trial court's decision.

**defendant** The party against whom a lawsuit is brought.

**defense** Legally sufficient reason to excuse the complained-of behavior.

**deposition** A discovery tool in a question-and-answer format in which the attorney verbally questions a party or a witness under oath.

**discharge** Extinguishment of debts or obligations by legal action.

**discovery** The pretrial investigation process authorized and governed by the rules of civil procedure; the process of investigation and collection of evidence by litigants; process in which the opposing parties obtain information about the case from each other; the process of investigation and collection of evidence by litigants.

**dissipating** Wasting the marital estate.

**divorce *a mensa et thoro*** Divorce from bed and board.

**divorce *a vinculo matrimonii*** Total divorce.

**domestic support obligation (DSO)** Phrase used in bankruptcy code that describes support obligations.

**domicile** The place where a person maintains a physical residence with the intent to permanently remain in that place; citizenship; the permanent home of the party.

**duress** Unreasonable and unscrupulous manipulation of a person to force him to agree to terms of an agreement that he would otherwise not agree to. Also, any unlawful threat or coercion used by a person to induce another to act (or to refrain from acting) in a manner that he or she otherwise would not do.

# E

**equitable adoption** Occurs when a person agrees to adopt a person, but fails to take steps to do so, and a court rules that the child was equitably adopted to prevent inequity from occurring; also known as *adoption by estoppel*.

**equitable distribution** Divides the assets acquired during the marriage between the parties.

**equity** The doctrine of fairness and justice; the process of making things balance or be equal between parties.

**ex parte** A communication between one party in a lawsuit and the judge.

**exempt property** Property that cannot be taken to satisfy debts owed creditors.

**expert witness** A witness who has special knowledge of a subject based on education or experience in the field.

# F

**facilitated adoption** An adoption arranged by a facilitator.

**family law** Area of the law that involves family-related matters such as divorce, prenuptial agreements, postnuptial agreements, adoptions, child custody, wills, and probate.

**forum shopping** Plaintiff attempts to choose a state with favorable rules in which to file suit.

**fraud** A knowing and intentional misstatement of the truth in order to induce a desired action from another person.

# G

**garnishment** Legal proceeding in which the court orders a party who is indebted to a debtor to deliver the debtor's property to creditor.

# I

**in personam jurisdiction** A court's authority over a party personally.

**in rem jurisdiction** A court's authority over claims affecting property.

**in vitro fertilization** Procedure by which egg cells are fertilized outside the womb.

**incest** Marriage/sexual relations between closely related relatives or family members.

**independent adoption** Adoptions arranged by intermediaries as compared to agency adoptions; also referred to as *private adoption*.

**injunction** A court order that requires a party to refrain from acting in a certain way to prevent harm to the requesting party.

**intangible property** Personal property that has no physical presence but is represented by a certificate or some other instrument, such as stocks or trademarks.

**interrogatory** A discovery tool in the form of a series of written questions that are answered by the party in writing, to be answered under oath.

**intestate** The state of having died without a will.

# J

**joint custodial arrangements** Detail the scope of the shared parental responsibility, whether legal, physical, or both.

**joint tenancy with right of survivorship (JTWROS)** Form of tenancy that requires four unities: (1) possession, (2) interest, (3) title, and (4) time.

# L

**legal custody** The right and obligation to make major decisions regarding the child, including, but not limited to, educational and religious issues.

**legal ethics** A code of conduct set out to regulate the proper conduct and behavior of attorneys.

**legality** Adherence to the law.

**lump sum alimony** Alimony paid in a specific amount that is not subject to modification.

# M

**marital estates (marital property)** The property accumulated by a couple during marriage, called community property in some states.

**marriage** A union between a man and a woman.

**mediation** The process of submitting a claim to a neutral third party who then makes a determination about the ultimate liability and award in a civil case.

**mediator** Individual who facilitates a resolution by the parties using methods designed to facilitate the parties' reaching a negotiated resolution.

**meeting of the minds** A legal concept requiring that both parties understand and ascribe the same meaning to the terms of the contract; a theory holding that both parties must both objectively and subjectively intend to enter into the agreement on the same terms.

**motion for award of temporary attorney fees, suit money, and costs** Motion filed by a party to obtain payment of temporary attorney fees and costs during the pendency of the dissolution action.

**motion for temporary alimony** Motion filed by a party to obtain alimony/spousal support during the pendency of the dissolution action.

**motion for temporary child custody and visitation** Motion filed by a party to provide for child custody and/or child visitation during the pendency of the dissolution action.

**motion for temporary child support** Motion filed by a party to obtain child support to provide for the care of the child during the pendency of the dissolution action.

# N

**negotiation** Bargaining process by which parties resolve issues that exist between them.

**no fault divorce** A divorce in which one spouse does not need to allege wrongdoing by the other spouse as grounds for the divorce.

# O

**offer** A promise made by the offeror to do (or not to do) something provided that the offeree, by accepting, promises or does something in exchange.

**open adoption** A form of adoption in which a varying degree of contact occurs among the biological parent(s) of his/her child, the child, and the adoptive parent(s).

# P

**palimony** A division of property between two unmarried parties after they separate or the paying of support by one party to the other.

**Parental Kidnapping Prevention Act (PKPA)** An act related to jurisdictional issues in applying and enforcing child custody decrees in other states.

**paternity action** A lawsuit to identify the father of a child born outside of marriage.

**pendente lite order** Order entered while litigation is pending

**permanent alimony** Alimony paid for an indefinite period of time.

**personal property** Movable or intangible thing not attached to real property.

**physical custody** Child living with one parent or visiting with the noncustodial parent.

**plaintiff** The party initiating legal action.

**pleadings** Formal documents filed with the court that establish the claims and defenses of the parties to the lawsuit; the complaint, answer to complaint, and reply.

**prayer for relief** A summation at the end of a pleading, which sets forth the demands by a party in the lawsuit.

**premarital preparation course** Course designed to strengthen marriages and reduce divorce.

**prenuptial agreement** An agreement made by parties before marriage that controls certain aspects of the relationship, such as management and ownership of property.

**pretrial conference** The meeting between the parties and the judge to identify legal issues, stipulate to uncontested matters, and encourage settlement.

**pretrial motions** Used to challenge the sufficiency of evidence or the suppression of allegedly tainted evidence or other matters that could impact the focus, the length, and even the need for trial.

**privilege** Reasonable expectation of privacy and confidentiality for communications in furtherance of the relationship such as attorney–client, doctor–patient, husband–wife, psychotherapist–patient, and priest–penitent.

**protective order** Court order limiting discovery by a party.

**proxy marriage** An agent for the parties arranges the marriage for the couple.

**putative marriage** The couple completes the requirements in good faith, but an unknown impediment prevents the marriage from being valid.

# Q

**qualified domestic relations order (QDRO)** Retirement account distributions' legal documentation requirement for ultimate distribution.

# R

**real property** Land and all property permanently attached to it, such as buildings.

**rebuttable presumption** In the law, an assumption that a fact is true unless proved otherwise.

**recrimination** Defense in divorce based on the fact the person seeking the divorce was, in fact, him- or herself guilty of an act that would be grounds for divorce.

**rehabilitative alimony** Alimony, usually granted to a specific time, which is intended to allow the receiving party time to gain needed education or training to enter the workforce.

**reimbursement alimony** Alimony used to reimburse the receiving spouse for working or providing financial assistance that enhanced the spouse's future.

**request for admission (request to admit)** A document that provides the drafter with the opportunity to conclusively establish selected facts prior to trial.

**request for medical examination** Form of discovery that requests a medical examination of an opposing party in a lawsuit.

**request for production of documents (request to produce)** A discovery device that requests the production of certain items, such as photographs, papers, reports, and physical evidence; must specify the document sought.

**rotating custody** A custody arrangement in which the child resides with each parent on a rotating basis.

# S

**same-sex marriage** Marriage of two people of the same sex living together as a family.

**sanctions** Penalty against a party in the form of an order to compel, a monetary fine, a contempt-of-court citation, or a court order with specific description of the individualized remedy.

**second-parent adoption** Adoption in which a domestic partner of a parent of a child adopts that child. This type of adoption does not terminate the parental rights of the natural parent.

**separate property** One spouse is the exclusive owner.

**sham marriage** Marriage in which the parties never intended to live as a married couple.

**sole custody** Only one of the divorcing spouses has both legal and physical custody, but the noncustodial parent may have visitation rights.

**solemnization** A formalization of a marriage, as in for example a marriage ceremony.

**split custody** A custody arrangement in which siblings are separated.

**Statute of Frauds** Rule that specifies which contracts must be in writing to be enforceable.

**stepparent adoption** Adoption in which a stepparent adopts the child of his/her spouse and assumes both financial and legal responsibility of the child. The stepparent adoption may release the noncustodial parent from payment of child support and other legal obligations.

**subject matter jurisdiction** A court's authority over the res, the subject of the case.

**surrogate mother** Woman who bears a child for another person.

# T

**tangible property** Personal property that can be held or touched, such as furniture or jewelry.

**temporary injunction** A court order that prohibits a party from acting in a certain way for a limited period of time.

**temporary restraining order** A court order barring a person from harassing or harming another.

**tenancy by the entirety** A form of ownership for married couples, similar to joint tenancy, where the spouse has right of survivorship.

**tenancy in common** A form of ownership between two or more people where each owner's interest upon death goes to his or her heirs.

**tender years doctrine** Legal presumption that states the mother should be awarded custody of a young child, unless she was deemed unfit.

**tickler file** System of tracking dates and reminding what is due on any given day or in any given week, month, or year.

**title** The name/designation of a pleading.

**tort** A civil wrongful act, committed against a person or property, either intentional or negligent.

**transcript** Written account of a trial court proceeding or deposition.

**trial notebook** Started and organized prior to the pretrial conference, it contains all documentary and other tangible evidence or materials used by the attorney in trial.

**trier of fact** Jury.

**trier of law** Judge.

# U

**unconscionable contract** A contract so completely unreasonable and irrational that it shocks the conscience.

**Uniform Interstate Family Support Act** State law used in cases involving the establishment and enforcement of child or spousal support obligations when the obligor lives in one state and the obligee/children live in another.

**uniform statute** Model legislation drafted by the National Conference of Commissioners on Uniform State Laws, dealing with areas of the law such as sales transactions.

**unjust enrichment** The retention by a party of unearned and undeserved benefits derived from his own wrongful actions regarding an agreement.

# V

**venue** County in which the facts are alleged to have occurred and in which the trial will take place.

**verification** Acknowledgment by a party of the truthfulness of the information contained within a document.

**vested** Having a present right to receive the benefit of the performance when it becomes due.

**void** A transaction that is impossible to be enforced because it is invalid.

**voidable** Having the possibility of avoidance of performance at the option of the incapacitated party.

# W

**writ of execution** Court order used to enforce a judgment.

# Index